THE BLOOMSBURY HANDBOOK OF INDIAN CUISINE

Also Available from Bloomsbury:

The Bloomsbury Handbook of Food and Popular Culture, Edited by Kathleen LeBesco and Peter Naccarato

The Handbook of Food and Anthropology, Edited by Jakob A. Klein and James L. Watson

The Handbook of Food Research, Edited by Anne Murcott, Warren Belasco and Peter Jackson

THE BLOOMSBURY HANDBOOK OF INDIAN CUISINE

Edited by Colleen Taylor Sen, Sourish Bhattacharyya and Helen Saberi

BLOOMSBURY
NEW DELHI • LONDON • OXFORD • NEW YORK • SYDNEY

METHUEN DRAMA
Bloomsbury Publishing India Pvt. Ltd
Second Floor, Building No. 4 , DDA Complex LSC, Pocket C – 6 & 7
Vasant Kunj, New Delhi 110070
www.bloomsbury.com

BLOOMSBURY, Methuen Drama India and the Diana
logo are trademarks of Bloomsbury Publishing Plc

First published in India 2023
First published in Great Britain 2023

A catalogue record for this book is available from the British Library.

ISBN: PB: 978-93-56403-11-6
For sale in the Indian subcontinent only

Typeset by Integra Software Services Pvt. Ltd.
Printed and bound in India by Replika Press Pvt. Ltd.

To find out more about our authors and books visit www.bloomsbury.com
and sign up for our newsletters

CONTENTS

ENTRIES

ILLUSTRATIONS

PREFACE

Editing and writing this book proved to be a challenge. How can the cuisine of a country as vast, as diverse and as ancient as India be summarized in a single volume? Every state of India, indeed every city (and perhaps even certain neighbourhoods) warrants a book of this scope and size. We see this book as the next iteration in the ever ongoing expansion of the body of knowledge of and writing on Indian food.

While we have written much of the book ourselves, we have also drawn on the expertise of India's leading food writers, whose names will be familiar to every aficionado of Indian food. These writers bring their own unique and personal perspective to their subjects. While striving for consistency in content and style, we have tried to retain the writers' own voices. And to some extent the available expertise has determined what topics are covered. There are a great many areas of Indian cuisine that still await their chroniclers.

The only works of a similar scope were written by the late K.T. Achaya more than twenty years ago. Achaya, a scholar of Sanskrit as well as a noted food chemist, focuses to a large degree on historical roots of Indian cuisine. Since then, much has changed. More states have been added to the Republic of India, including Jharkhand, Chhattisgarh and Uttarakhand, whose cuisines are different from what is mainstream. This work contains what may be the most comprehensive description yet of the ingredients that go into Indian cuisine, especially the individual spices and spice mixtures that give it its unique flavours. Furthermore, the history and usage of ingredients essential – potato, chilli, onion, garlic, paneer, pulses, ghee, etc. – and special – ajowan, *kokum*, lotus, etc. – are described. Iconic dishes such as butter chicken and dosas have their own separate entries. There are major entries on important topics such as alcohol, breads, spice mixtures and rites of passage.

The book also features profiles of individuals who have had a major impact on the development of Indian food, including agriculturalists, restaurateurs, authors and rulers (Ashoka, the Mughals). The connections between food and medicine and food and worship are explored in separate entries. New creations such as chicken 65 have become international favourites. The Indian diaspora has been the source of exciting new dishes, such as roti, the national food of Trinidad and Tobago. And recent years have seen a surge in the writing of not only collections of recipes, but also articles and, even, entire books on regional and local cuisines in both English and Indian languages – some of them written by contributors to this work. The availability of such work was a great help in putting together this work which would have been much more difficult to write ten years ago.

ACKNOWLEDGEMENTS

This book could not have been written without the contributions of the twenty-seven writers who generously shared their expertise in their areas of speciality. We owe a great debt of gratitude to Jyotirmay Nirjhar who reviewed the copy and put it into its final form; Nirjhar is a paragon among editors. Thanks to our agent Max Sinsheimer who solved some of the knotty problems that arose during the book's creation, and to Lily McMahon and Kaveya Saravanan, our editors at Bloomsbury Berg for their patience. Above all we thank our spouses – Ashish Sen, Kaveree Bamzai and the late Nasir Saberi – for their understanding and continuing support.

NOTES ON TEXT

Cross-references to other entries are indicated in the text in small caps but not for states and union territories, which have separate entries. We attempted to be as thorough as possible with the cross-referencing. Most entries are followed by suggestions for further reading. The English spelling of words in Hindi and other languages was a challenge since there is no recognized system of transcription; for example, laddu/laddoo, pakora/pakoda, etc. In these cases we have relied on common usage. We also had to make a decision about when to italicize 'foreign' words and have used the Oxford English Dictionary as a guide and, in some cases, also made our own calls about which words we thought would be 'foreign' to our non-Indian readers.

Introduction

India is an extremely diverse country, virtually almost a universe by itself. Perhaps no other nation has such a multiplicity of languages, religions, communities, ethnicities – and cuisines. The seventh-largest country by area, the second largest in population and the most populous democracy in the world, India occupies most of the land mass called the Indian Subcontinent and stretches 3,214 km from north to south and 2,933 km from east to west. Some of India's twenty-nine states (plus seven union territories, including the capital DELHI) are larger than many countries.

Indians speak eighteen official languages and more than sixteen hundred minor languages and dialects. More than 80 per cent of Indians are Hindus and 12 per cent are Muslims, making India the world's third largest Muslim country after Indonesia and Pakistan. India also has 30 million Christians belonging to different denominations; 15 million Sikhs, plus small communities of PARSIS (Zoroastrians), Jains, Buddhists, Jews and Animists. A common belief is that Indians are overwhelmingly vegetarian but only 39 per cent of Indians are vegetarian (mainly Hindus and Jains). Many Indians practise varying degrees of VEGETARIANISM: avoiding meat on certain religious holidays or during certain fasts, for example. Eating patterns are also rooted in moral and medical beliefs in Ayurveda, the ancient Indian school of medicine; Unani, the traditional Islamic medical system; and folk beliefs (see FOOD AND MEDICINE).

India is still predominantly a rural country, with 70 per cent of the population living in villages. Most rural Indians are engaged in farming, much of it on a subsistence level. As a result, even today most Indian food is produced regionally and locally and is highly seasonal. In urban areas, where incomes are higher, people have access to a wider variety of food. Eating out in restaurants is still a relative luxury but India has a vibrant STREET FOOD economy which plays an important role in meeting people's nutritional needs.

Geographers divide India into three regions. In the North, the Himalaya Mountain range extends for 2,400 km from northern Pakistan to southern Tibet in China and the northeastern tip of India. This range has served as a barrier to both cold Arctic winds and invaders. Melting snows from the mountains and seasonal rains feed the three great river systems: the Indus, the Yamuna-Ganga and the Brahmaputra. Their basins form the 2,400 km long fertile Indo-Gangetic plains. The western portion, once covered with forests, is today a barren wasteland, the Great Thar Desert. The northern states of Punjab and Haryana are the breadbasket of Indian producing wheat and other grains, while the eastern states of West Bengal and Assam produce two or even three crops of RICE a year. Thus, the basic staples are WHEAT-based BREADS in the West and rice in the East.

The third region is the Deccan Plateau, sometimes called Peninsular India, which is separated from the plains by the Vindhyas and other mountain ranges of Central India. They served historically as a barrier to communication between southern and northern

India and led to the development of distinct cultures, languages and cuisines in the southern states of Kerala, Karnataka, Tamil Nadu, Andhra Pradesh and Telangana and the union territory of Puducherry. The Western Ghats, a mountain range running down the southwest side of India, blocks the rain that blows from the Arabian Sea during the Monsoon season, giving the plateau, which lies on its leeward side, a hot dry climate. Between the Western Ghats and the Arabian Sea lies the narrow Malabar Coast, one of India's most fertile regions and now part of the state of Kerala. This was the centre of India's spice industry since Roman times and where the first Europeans arrived in the fifteenth century.

The traditional Indian calendar had six seasons:

- Vasanta (spring), mid-March to mid-May. (Many festivals are held at this time.)
- Grishma (summer), mid-May to mid-July.
- Varsha (rainy or monsoon), mid-July to mid September.
- Sharad (autumn), mid-September to mid-November.
- Hemant (winter), mid-November to mid-January.
- Shishir (cool season), mid-January to mid-March.

In Ayurveda, the traditional Indian system of medicine, the seasons determined diet, with cooling foods recommended in the hot months, drying foods in the wet seasons and so on. Today the Indian Meteorological Department designates four official seasons: winter (December to early April), summer/pre-monsoon (roughly April to June), rainy/monsoon (June to September) and post-monsoon (October to December).

The timing of the monsoons and the amount of rain they bring are critical for food supplies. Before modern methods of irrigation and the 'Green Revolution', the failure of the monsoon resulted in devastating famines. The heaviest rainfall (more than 2,000 mm a year) falls in Northeast India and along the western coastal strip. Here rice, which requires a lot of water for cultivation, is the main crop. The northern plain receives moderate rainfall, between 1,000 and 2,000 mm annually, but many crops, including wheat, can still be grown without irrigation. Wheat, a winter crop which is the dietary staple in northern India and Pakistan, is sown at the end of the rainy season and ripens in December. BARLEY also grows in northern India. Much of India has two growing seasons: winter and summer. Winter crops, called *rabi*, are sown in the winter and harvested in the summer, while summer crops, or *kharif*, are sown in the summer and harvested in the winter.

The low rainfall zone (500–1,000 mm) is home to dry-zone crops, including varieties of MILLETS which can be grown without irrigation even when there is little rainfall. CORN flourishes on the plains and in the hills and can thrive in both dry and moderately damp regions. Sugarcane is grown nearly everywhere but today most is grown in the irrigated lands of the Upper Ganges Basin and Punjab.

The first humans probably came to India from East Africa around 65,000 years ago. The earliest known inhabitants lived all over the subcontinent but were, over the millennia, pushed into the forests. The staples of these early inhabitants included rice, millet, barley, lentils (*moong*, *masoor* and *urad*, see PULSES), GOURDS, AUBERGINE (eggplant), BANANA, JACKFRUIT, CITRUS FRUITS and MANGOES – all native to the Subcontinent. Ancient spices include long pepper (see PEPPER, LONG), TURMERIC, GINGER, TAMARIND and the betel nut, while oil came from SESAME and MUSTARD seeds. Chickens (see POULTRY AND EGGS) were first bred by these early inhabitants, although probably for fighting and not for eating.

The cradle of Indian civilization rose around 3000 BCE on the alluvial plains of the Indus Valley in a vast area today located in Pakistan and Northwest India, extending from Gujarat almost to the gates of Delhi. Called the Harappan or Indus Valley Civilization, this network of five cities and 1,500 towns had well-developed agriculture, with sophisticated irrigation and water storage systems; planned cities; and extensive trade with the Middle East. Its script has never been deciphered so much about it remains a mystery. It reached its height between 2600 BCE and 1900 BCE. Around 1300 BCE it began to gradually disintegrate, perhaps for environmental reasons, and its residents scattered throughout India, merging with local populations. Their diet included wheat and barley bread baked in tandoor-like ovens, chickpeas, lentils, river and ocean FISH, baked tubers, dairy products including buffalo milk, MELONS, DATES (used for sweetening), and spices such as turmeric, black pepper (see PEPPER, BLACK), ginger and GARLIC.

Around 1500 BCE, the speakers of an Indo-Aryan language related to Sanskrit and many modern Indian and European languages began migrating in small groups from the northwest into the Subcontinent. They were in search of better pastures for their cattle and also arable land; dairy products, including GHEE, were an important part of their diet. The *Rig Veda*, an ancient text probably composed 1500–1200 BCE, alone contains seven hundred references to the cow. Their original staple was barley, which was parched and eaten whole, ground and made into cakes fried in ghee, or made into a porridge. Later they grew wheat and rice which they might have learned how to cultivate from the indigenous people. They also ate many kinds of pulses. Sugarcane, native to India, was grown and processed into jaggery and other forms of SUGAR.

The *Vedas* (1500–900 BCE), collections of hymns, incantations, chants, prayers for life and prosperity, and philosophical speculations, were composed and passed down orally at this time. Their rituals centred around animal sacrifice performed by Brahmin priests and the meat from the animals killed was consumed. Some of the concepts and rituals were the basis for the religion today called Hinduism, although that name was not used until fairly recently. One of their most intriguing foods was a hallucinogenic drink called *soma* which was offered to the gods, but today no one knows what it was.

In the Northeast, people in the so-called Seven Sister states (Arunachal Pradesh, Assam, Manipur, Meghalaya, Mizoram, Nagaland and Tripura) belong to nearly 500 ethnic groups with distinct languages, customs and cuisines. Their ancestors came from southwestern China and South East Asia and arrived in several waves of migrations after the coming of the Indo Aryans. Because of these ties, their food has distinctive features such as minimal use of spices and oil, fish and sticky rice.

In the South, farmers cultivated rice, sugarcane, black and long pepper, COCONUTS and other crops. The Sangam Age from 300 BCE to 300 CE (named after the Sangam academies of poems and scholars in Madurai) was a period of cultural and artistic refinement and culinary sophistication. Festivals, feasts and meals were abundant. The five traditional landscapes of mountains, forests, fertile plains, deserts and the coastal region each had their own food cultures.

Clans and tribes morphed into states and the period starting around 600 BCE saw the rise of kingdoms, republics and cities. Ultimately one state, Magadha, with its capital in Pataliputra, conquered or assimilated the others to become the dominant power in northern and eastern India. Its centre in modern Bihar was home to large deposits of iron, which led to the production of iron tools and implements, including the plough. ASHOKA Maurya (r. c. 268 to 232 BCE), considered one of India's greatest rulers, ruled over almost the entire Subcontinent as far as Persia. This period saw the rise of cities and the development of urban culture which was accompanied by philosophical debates, the rise of ascetic movements and the emergence of two major religions, Jainism and Buddhism. These religions emphasized personal behaviour and asceticism, rejected animal sacrifice and advocated VEGETARIANISM – ideas that were eventually adopted by the adherents of the Vedic religion.

After the fall of the Mauryas around 183 BCE, smaller empires and kingdoms arose and eventually were consolidated under the Guptas who ruled much of India from the fourth to the late sixth century CE. This is called the Golden Age of Indian civilization when art and literature flourished. India was one of the wealthiest countries in the world, exporting spices and luxury goods to Europe and China. During this period, the technique of refining SUGAR was developed and spread to China and the Middle East. By the sixth century CE Christianity was firmly established in southwestern India (see SYRIAN CHRISTIANS). Small communities of Jews were also established on the West Coast (see BENE ISRAELIS). The Medieval Period (from the decline of the Guptas to the rise of the Mughal Empire in 1526) was characterized by the emergence of several strong regional centres. During this period the first collection of recipes appeared (see COOKBOOKS, EARLY).

In the eight century CE, Arabs arrived on the West Coast, bringing Islam. Between 1200 and 1500, North India was ruled by various dynasties of Afghan and Turkic origin. They enriched native Indian dishes with dried fruits and introduced many new dishes from Central Asia and the Middle East, including SAMOSA, HALWA, *HALEEM*, BIRYANI, KULFI and *NIHARI*. In the West, Rajput rulers in present-day Rajasthan established powerful small kingdoms. Regional dynasties such as the Cholas, Cheras and Pandyas flourished in the South. South Indian food was well documented as early as the tenth century CE and mentioned precursors of such dishes as IDLIS, DOSAS, VADAS, *papadums* (see PAPAD) and many kinds of PICKLES.

By the fifteenth century Indian was fragmented politically. The power vacuum was filled by Babur, the ruler of a small kingdom in Central Asia, who invaded Punjab in 1526 and declared himself the ruler of all Hindustan. He founded what came to be called the MUGHAL dynasty. By the end of his reign in 1605, his grandson Akbar had extended the empire over all northern India as well as parts of the Deccan Plateau. Akbar's son Jahangir (1605–27) and grandson Shah Jahan (1627–58) preserved and extended the empire. The Rajput rulers were allowed to maintain their kingdoms in return for their loyalty. But by the early eighteenth century, the empire began to disintegrate. In 1738 the Persians invaded India and defeated the Mughal army. From their base in Western India, the Marathas took over major territories of the Mughal Empire.

Meanwhile, foreign powers were making inroads, starting with the Portuguese who arrived on the West Coast in search of spices. They established a fortress at Goa which became a key link in the worldwide chain of Portuguese forts around the world and the hubs of a global exchange of fruits, vegetables and other plants between the Western Hemisphere, Africa, Oceania and the Indian Subcontinent – the so-called 'Columbian Exchange'. As a result many new ingredients entered Indian cuisine, including the POTATO, TOMATO, CHILLIES, peanuts, GUAVAS and PINEAPPLES.

Other European countries set up settlements, including the Dutch, the French (see Puducherry), the Danes and the British who eventually pushed out all their rivals and gradually came to dominate most of the Subcontinent. The British East India Company (EIC), a corporation founded in 1600, set up trading posts at sites that became KOLKATA and CHENNAI. It had its own army and, in 1757, the EIC and its Indian allies defeated the Mughal army, installing puppet rulers in Bengal, Odisha and Bihar. The British government established a civil service and in 1857, following a revolt by Indian troops, it took direct control, ruling from its capital in Calcutta, which in 1911 was moved to Delhi. Around two-fifths of India was left to quasi-independent rulers who were vassals of the British.

Until the early nineteenth century, the EIC men in India lived much like the locals: speaking Indian languages, marrying Indian women and eating food prepared by local cooks. The meals eaten at British settlements were similar to those eaten by the Mughals, featuring heavily spiced PULAOS and BIRYANIS, CURRIES, KEBABS and KHICHRI. But after 1857 many of the bridges between Indian and British cultures were destroyed. British wives, the so-called 'memsahibs', had no interest in exploring Indian cuisine and culture and dishes such as legs of lamb, boiled chicken and articles imported from England became the order of the day. However, a hybrid cuisine also emerged, such as mulligatawny soup, KEDGEREE and curries made with ready-made CURRY POWDER, first produced in London in the late eighteenth century. The British also introduced TEA drinking to India after discovering tea growing in the Northeast and launching a tea industry in India.

Indian influence also spread abroad. After slavery was abolished in the British Empire in 1833, the freed African slaves were replaced by people from the Subcontinent, especially Bihar and eastern Uttar Pradesh, and later from South India. They agreed to work as indentured labour for five years after which they could stay on or return home; most stayed on. Between 1834 and 1917 when the system was abolished, nearly 1.5 million Indians migrated to Trinidad, Guyana, Jamaica and Mauritius. Later the system was extended to South Africa, Malaysia and Fiji. Members of this DIASPORA brought their own religions, cultures and cuisines which were adapted to new soils and climates. In the process, new hybrid cuisines were created.

Discontent with British rule grew and in the twentieth century, Mahatma GANDHI led a nonviolent movement for independence. Independence was achieved in 1947 when the Subcontinent was partitioned into the independent nations of India and Pakistan (which in 1971 was further divided into Pakistan and Bangladesh).

The decades since 1947 have seen many dramatic changes in the way Indians eat. The Green Revolution greatly increased Indian grain production, ending the famines that had plagued the country, while the White Revolution boosted the production of milk and dairy products. Although street food has been a part of Indian life from times immemorial (stands selling take-out food go back to the third century BCE, if not earlier), eating out in restaurants had not been a part of Indian culture. This changed dramatically in the second half of the twentieth century when fast food and restaurants serving both Western and Indian food proliferated. Television cooking shows helped spread awareness of other Indian cuisines. Hospitality and culinary institutes sprung up everywhere, and those who prepare food have been elevated from '*bawarchi*' to 'chefs'.

Discussions of Indian food sometimes emphasize its diversity and the contribution of foreign influences. However, there is a historical continuity that makes Indian food 'Indian'. The commonality of aubergine, mangoes and other ingredients native to the Subcontinent; the intensive use of spices (with a few exceptions, such as the Northeast); the importance of dairy products; a love of SWEETS; and the integration of food and medicine are threads that run through the history of Indian cuisine and make Indian food the brilliant palette of flavours it is today.

Entries

ACHAYA, K.T.

Kollegal Thammu Achaya (1923–2002) was a pioneering food historian whose *Indian Food: A Historical Companion,* published by Oxford University Press India in 1994, was the first comprehensive history of Indian food. Born in Kollegal, Tamil Nadu (now in Karnataka), Achaya came from the KODAVA community. In 1942, he graduated in Chemistry (Hons) from Madras University and spent three years at the Indian Institute of Science in Bangalore researching oil, fats and foods. His first book (with K.S. Rangappa) was *Indian Dairy Products* (1974). After receiving his PhD from the University of Liverpool, Achaya established a School of Fat Chemistry and Technology in HYDERABAD (today the Indian Institute of Chemical Technology). In 1971, he moved to MUMBAI as Executive Director of the Protein Foods and Nutrient Development Association of India.

In 1974, he wrote *Your Food and You* and in 1975, he co-authored *Cottonseed Chemistry and Technology*. In 1977, he moved to the Central Food Technological Research Institute in Mysore. In 1984, he published *Everyday Indian Processed Food.* After retiring in 1978, Achaya started writing about food from a historical standpoint. His works include *Oilseeds and Oil Milling in India: A Cultural and Historical Survey* (1990), *Ghani: The Traditional Oil Mill of India* (1997), *The Food Industries of British India* (1994), and *The Story of Our Food* (2000). In 1998, Oxford University Press published *A Historical Dictionary of Indian Food* – an alphabetical guidebook with entries on food items, regional cuisines, dishes, cooking techniques and other topics. A lifelong bachelor, Achaya was described by his editor Rukun Adavani as, 'dapper, a bit like the actor David Niven', and slim, despite his love of Indian flavours and preparations.

Colleen Sen

- Sen, Mayukh. 'Setting the Table: K.T. Achaya's Pioneering Scholarship on Indian Food'. *Caravan Magazine*, 31 May 2018.

AGRA PETHA

Petha is a candied sweet made from two main ingredients – ash GOURD (*Benincasa hispida*, Hindi *petha, kashiphal*) and refined SUGAR. The ash gourd is widely grown in the region around Agra in Uttar Pradesh, with demand supplemented with supplies from Karnataka. Sugar, too, is abundantly processed in the region and transported to Agra. Some sugar is supplemented from Maharashtra. Family-owned cottage industries dominate *petha* production in Agra. The Noori Darwaza locality in Agra is an important production site and is also the largest *petha* market in the area.

Ripe ash gourds are ideal for making *petha*. As they ripen on the vine, they get heavier and take on a thick layer of a whitish, waxy coating. Washing and scrubbing help remove the waxy coating from the harvested gourds. Care is taken to ensure the thorough removal of the thick skin, pith and seeds. The gourd is cut into smaller chunks. Workers use a wooden stamp with pinheads (*gudai*) to puncture holes in the ash gourd pieces. Pricking is a very vital step as it allows for better absorption of liquids during processing. The process starts by dissolving a paste of calcium hydroxide (*chuna*) in water. The ash gourd pieces are soaked in this water overnight. The salt tenderizes the ash gourd and helps reduce the cooking time in the next stage of processing. The pieces are thoroughly rinsed and boiled in fresh water. Some manufacturers add alum (*phitkari*) at this stage. The ash gourd pieces are cooked for about fifteen minutes or until translucent. The soaking of raw ash gourd pieces in lime, pricking and boiling in alum water help maximize the sugar solution's osmotic diffusion. The ash gourd is then boiled in a simple syrup until the solution reduces and begins to crystallize. This process may take up to an hour. The sugar syrup is sometimes flavoured with rosewater or screw pine water (*kewra*) (see FLOWER WATERS).

The pieces are then separated and allowed to dry completely before being packed and sent to various points of sale. Manufacturers prefer canning *petha* in a semi-dry state for export. *Petha* flavoured with grapes, PINEAPPLE, SAFFRON, rose, PAAN, MANGO and COCONUT have become available in recent years.

The traditional coal-fired stoves used for cooking have come under scrutiny as a significant cause of air pollution in the area. Only about 40 per cent of the ash gourd is usable as there is much wastage when the skin, pith and seeds are removed. Because of the unorganized nature of the industry, large areas of decomposing organic waste are an additional source of air pollution.

Priya Mani

AJMUD

Ajmud, (*Trachyspermum roxburghianum*), is a plant related to celery and is sometimes called wild celery. It is widely cultivated in India. Its small dried fruits, commonly referred to as seeds, look similar to those of AJOWAN, celery and caraway. In fact, they are often confused with or substituted for celery seeds which are also, confusingly, often given the name of *ajmud*.

The seeds have a strong flavour with a smell similar to parsley and taste like celery. They are used to flavour PICKLES, CHUTNEYS and preserves as well as CURRIES and kormas and are often used to alleviate digestive problems.

In West Bengal, where it is known as *radhuni*, it is commonly used in the famous Bengali dish of mixed vegetables and bitter GOURD called *shukto*. It is also, sometimes, part of the Bengali spice mixture called *panch phoron* (see SPICE BOX). The leaves, which smell of CARROTS, are sometimes used as a substitute for parsley.

Helen Saberi

- Facciola, Steve. *Cornucopia II: A Source Book of Edible Plants*. Vista, CA: Kampong Publications, 1998.

AJOWAN

Ajowan (*ajwain, ajowain*), *Trachyspermum ammi*, is an umbelliferous plant which grows in Afghanistan and Iran but chiefly in India (largely in Uttar Pradesh, Bihar, Madhya Pradesh, Punjab, Rajasthan, Bengal, Tamil Nadu and Andhra Pradesh). Its Sanskrit name is *yavani*, meaning 'the Greek spice', which suggests that it may have arrived in India via one of the Greek kingdoms of the Middle East. It is related to *AJMUD*, caraway and CUMIN, although its taste is quite different, having a close affinity to thyme. The small, tear-shaped, ochre coloured seeds, sometimes referred to as carom seeds or lovage, are aromatic and pungent.

For centuries, ajowan has been used in cooking in India to flavour vegetables, especially root vegetables such as POTATOES and RADISHES. Ajowan is also used sparingly in stews, RICE dishes, PICKLE- and CHUTNEY-making and chaat masala (see SPICE BOX), as well as to flavour BREADS, biscuits and fried snacks such as *sev* (see *SEV* AND *SEVIYAN*), PAKORAS and PAPADS.

Ajowan is mainly cultivated for its essential oil, the main ingredient of which is thymol, a germicide and antiseptic. It is also used for digestive purposes, either added to foods or made into an infusion. It alleviates flatulence, indigestion, colic and other bowel disorders. It is also used to help decongest the lungs.

Helen Saberi

- Dalby, Andrew. *Dangerous Tastes: The Story of Spices*. London: British Museum Press, 2000.
- Devi, Yamuna. *The Art of Indian Vegetarian Cooking*. London: Leopard Books, 1995.

ALCOHOL

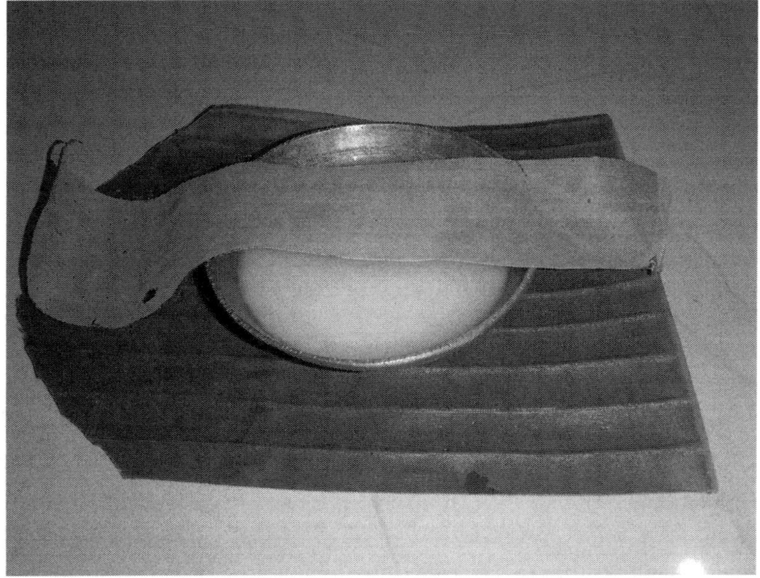

FIGURE 1 ALCOHOL. Rice beer of Assam. Chiring Chandan/Wikimedia Commons.

For a long time, India's national identity was thought of as linked to a sense of abstinence from alcohol which was 'corrupted' by the coming of the Europeans. However, recent research shows that this is an invented tradition of colonial times. From early India, Sanskrit and Pali texts and texts from medieval India, Persian and other language contain information not just about abstinence, control and prohibition but also narratives of alcohol. While the exploration of drinks and drinking culture are important, there is a third aspect which is equally intriguing – the ambivalence of attitude towards drinking which changes with the setting. As the saying goes, a drink without the right accompaniments and company might not reveal all its flavours.

Decisive evidence of liquor production in Harappan urban settlements (*c.* 3000–2200 BCE) is lacking even though starchy sources and utensils have been found in archaeological excavations. The earliest literary evidence of a drinking culture among Indians is in the ancient Vedic texts (*c.* 1500–1000 BCE) where two eponymous drinks – *soma* and *sura* – emerge as complementary and antithetical to the other. *Soma* is pure, clear and light with divine associations used for rituals while *sura* denotes the falsehood and darkness, debasing qualities of intoxicated individuals.

The *soma* plant is elusive and has not been identified conclusively. *Sura*, on the other hand, had more tangible associations. This grain-based drink was a fermented brew made from BARLEY, RICE or WHEAT flour in a semi-solid state through saccharification. Sanskrit sources mention the fermentation of different ingredients to make *sura* which shows that this was a generic term as well. Although mentioned in the ancient texts such as *Rig Veda* and *Atharva Veda* (*c.*1500–1000 BCE), James McHugh finds that the earliest recorded recipe of the brew is in the *Baudhayana Srauta Sutra* of *c.* 500 BCE. To make *sura*, the rice was divided into two parts: one was dry and was roasted while the other comprising wet rice was cooked. The cooked rice was put in a hanging pot. The dry roasted part was pounded and mixed with the cooked rice where it became a floating scum. Then four ingredients – sprouted barley, sprouted rice, popped rice and *urad* lentils – were put in a powdered form into the mixture. The brewer put a stool to the south of the cooking fire with a support on it. The jar containing the gruel was placed on the support and on this jar was placed a fermentation-drainage structure (*karotara*) made of wood, split bamboo or clay. The gruel was then spread all around the *karotara* and this arrangement was kept undisturbed for three nights for the *sura* to be ready. In later brewing processes, the four ingredients mixed in the gruel were concentrated into starter cakes called *kinva* to start the fermentation instead of malt which was key to European brews. Several variations of this brewing process occur in other early Indian texts.

Drinking culture in early India is associated with numerous myths which show an interesting ambivalence – ritual disinterest coupled with evidence of social drinking. The Brahmin priests who were considered the upholders of the ritualistic order are found to brew and consume liquor only in the Sautramani ritual. Caste associations of alcohol consumption developed during later Vedic times (*c.* 1000 BCE) onwards, as *sura* was prohibited for the Brahmins and allowed for the other three castes of Kshatriyas, Vaishyas and Shudras. A fantastic story in the epic *Mahabharata* provides a mythopoeic rationale. The Brahmin priest Sukracharya, who knew the art of reviving the dead, had to part with his secret when he mistakenly drank alcohol mixed with the remains of his disciple! Since then, according to the ancient texts, Brahmins have had to abstain from alcohol.

In early India, the strain of abstention from drinking for ritual purity coexisted with narratives of joy and prosperity linked to drinking liquor. In *Atharva Veda*, a middle-aged married couple applaud the prosperity in the kingdom of Parikshit, a famous king, by alluding to the availability of good liquor. At the palace of Parikshit's son Janmejaya, fiery liquor was served to guests and the same spirit of joy from drinking is reflected in the house of this couple when the wife asks her husband whether he should be served 'curd, stirred drink or liquor'! Except the restrictions on Brahmins, the drinking culture in the subcontinent is beyond doubt.

Increasing urbanization, the formation of guilds and states and the emergence of Buddhism and Jainism in the sixth century BCE led to a transformation in the social drinking patterns and ethical discourse. In one of the earliest origin myths of alcohol, one of the Jataka texts, which recount the previous incarnations of Buddha, says that a hunter, Sura, discovered the intoxicating effect of a brew of fruit, rice and water which fermented due to the heat of the direct sun in the mountains. Buddha warns Visakha, his female disciple, about the kingdoms which were laid waste when Sura and his friend Varuna took the drink to humans. The ambivalence of the prescriptive texts becomes apparent as the Buddhist canons use the word *surāmerayamajja* to denote a range of alcoholic drinks – beer-like beverages produced by fermentation like *surā*, wine-like drinks or spirits like *majja*, and distilled drinks produced from SUGAR or fruit like *meraya* – available to the people.

As states became larger, state controls became more intricate. The ancient Indian manual of statecraft *Arthashastra* (late third or early second century BCE) mentions a range of intoxicating grain or sugarcane-based beverages: *medaka*, *prasannā*, *āsava*, *ariṣṭa*, *maireya* and *madhu*. To control and tax the drinks, the exact measure of ingredients of *medaka*, a rice wine, had, 'one Droṇa of water, half an Āḍhaka of rice kernels, and three Prasthas of ferment'. *Prasannā* was made from specific quantities of flour in the form of a ferment or a mélange and was mixed with the bark and fruit of areca palm. WOODAPPLE, treacle and HONEY were also used for the sweet liquor, *āsava*. *Ariṣṭas*, with specific ingredients combined with the fermented liquor, were formulated by the physicians for various kinds of illnesses. *Maireya*, a fruit liquor, was an extract from a decoction of *meṣaśṛṅgī* bark infused with jaggery and combined with a mélange of long pepper (see PEPPER, LONG) and black pepper (see PEPPER, BLACK) or mixed with the three fruits which were either three varieties of myrabolan or nutmeg (see NUTMEG AND MACE), areca nut and CLOVE. This drink, based on sugars mixed with the cereal-based *surā*, became a marker of social distinction in the period up to the first millennium CE. Also, a MANGO *sura*-liquor was made out of a high proportion of juice or pulp of the fruit and it was considered a great alcoholic drink (Olivelle 2013: 155). *Kumbhi* was considered a drink fit for the king and contained a number of herbs such as *moraṭā*, *palāśa*, *pattūra* and *meṣaśṛṅgī* and also the pulp of many ingredients such as *lodhra*, *citraka* and NEEM among other things and these were added to jaggery to increase the sweetness. *Sidhu*, a liquor produced from the juice of sugarcane – a predominant produce of northern India – was one of the most prominent drinks available locally. Though no recipes exist, the texts of Sushruta (see FOOD AND MEDICINE), the epics and Kalidasa's famous poems mention that there were jaggery or sugar crystal-based *sidhu* as well as two variations of cooked and uncooked sugarcane juice.

The wine from grape juice was called *madhu* and was referred to as have been sourced from 'Kāpiṣāyana' and 'Hārahūraka' – names of the area around Kabul and the people there.

Although grapes were found in India, the influence of wine came from the northwestern region of South Asia through Greek and Roman influences from the time of Alexander's campaign. Wine was not the staple brew but was consumed in elite circles of the Kushana and Gupta dynasties. Depicted in Gandhara and Mathura art, and procured through trade networks from Persia and Rome, grape wine was the imported foreign liquor of the era. Roman amphorae found in South India, Persian wine jars in the north and west of the subcontinent, and literary evidence show that while it became popular by the beginning of the first millennium CE it was mostly imported. By the medieval era, from eleventh century CE, wines were commonly consumed in the courts of rulers and the elite circles of nobility and business. At a more popular level, locally made grain liquor *sura* fell into oblivion, giving way to arrack obtained from cane juice.

Liquor was a minor source of revenue and the superintendent also collected one-twentieth portion of liquor for the king's treasury, according to the *Arthashastra*. However, its major significance was in surveillance for the states that were rapidly expanding to assimilate diverse places and communities that needed to be controlled. By the third century BCE, the prescriptions of Kautilya ranged from warning the king about poisoned mixtures if there was a dark streak between the liquor and the water to advising officials to use undercover agents acting as thaumaturgic ascetics to get the criminals drunk to spell out their crimes and then punish them.

The *Arthashastra* states that the superintendent of liquor regulated the prices and prevented hoarding; the law breakers would be punished with a hefty fine. Clearly showing marginalization, workers or slaves could be given only spoilt liquor as, at this time, in the absence of distillation the concept of good liquor was of fresh production and consumption. In contrast, and invoking tropes of morality, the affluent could make elaborate arrangements for their drinking parties at taverns or in their homes. The tavern was a site controlled by the state where the superintendent was to make arrangements for the ambience, including rooms comfortable for all seasons with beds, seats, perfumes and garlands. Tavern-keepers were to find out the disposition of their clients through 'charming female slaves when they were resting'.

Unlike the prescriptive texts such as the *Vedas* or the *Dharmashastras* where the *sura* is a necessary evil, the medical texts of Charaka and Sushruta adopt a pragmatic tone and inform us about the ways in which medicinal alcoholic drinks (*aristas* and *asavas*) can be used to bring varying effects on different types of bodily constitutions for curing ailments which continue to be part of contemporary Ayurvedic practices. According to Charaka, the ideal drink should produce 'happiness, sexual potency and corpulence'. The text gives a list of intoxicating drinks though it does not specify the ingredients or the process of preparation. *Sura* is celebrated and the ideal drinking process is explained. Drinks should be served in gold and silver vessels with beautiful women around and along with fruits, vegetables and roasted meats, clearly alluding to drinking among the elites of the society.

The access and denial of liquor in early Indian texts are evidence that women's sexuality and work were controlled in ceremonies and drinking sessions. While the *Arthashastra* mentions that only women and children could collect the ingredients for the special white-*sura* liquor during festivities, it also states that if the wife drank liquor or left her husband while he was drunk, a fine had to be paid for these offences by the man.

For early Indians, the colour and flavour of the brew were more important than the purity of the alcohol and the cup holds special significance in the drinking culture. Distillation appeared much later and adding different flavours such as the pulp of MANGO or MELON was more desirable than the purity of alcohol. The manual for pleasure, *Kamasutra*, mentions drinking parties at houses where courtesans serve the 'man-about-town' and themselves drink wine made from honey, grapes, other fruits or sugar, with various sorts of SALT, fruits, greens, vegetables, and bitter, spicy and sour foods. During lovemaking, the man was advised to offer drinks to the woman at specific moments along with 'fruit juice, grilled foods, sour rice-broth, soups with small pieces of roasted meats, mangoes, dried meat, and CITRUS FRUITS with sugar, according to the tastes of the region'. The *Kamasutra*, too, reflected contradictory notions around drinking as the implied notion of specific instructions for drinking, especially for women in specific settings were to evoke their sexuality for the man-about-town.

An influential text, the law code of Manu (*Manusmriti*) prohibits all three higher castes – Brahmins, Kshatriyas and Vaishyas – and especially women from drinking intoxicating liquor. On the other hand, it specifies three kinds of liquor: one made from molasses, another made from ground grain and a third from honey. Kulluka, the commentator on the *Manusmriti,* tells us that there were eleven types of *madya*, and calls the twelfth, *sura*, the worst kind of intoxicant. So while the prescriptive texts give an impression of prohibition, the range of drinks seemed to have expanded by this time between the second and seventh centuries CE. Fa-Hien, the Buddhist Chinese traveller in India, mentions that in the reign of the famous Gupta dynasty ruler Vikramaditya during the fifth century CE, people were not given to killing animals, corruption or drinking intoxicating liquor. However, it is interesting to note that Kalidasa, the Sanskrit poet, alludes to the special charm exuded by women drinking wine. McHugh mentions that the twelfth-century text *MANASOLLASA* depicts luxurious drinking parties and also shows a distinctive shift from grain-based *sura* to grape wine, DATE wine and other liquors.

By the twelfth and thirteenth centuries, distillation had become common in the subcontinent. The archaeological finds of 'equipments' – John Marshall's 'Gandhara stills' (150 BC to 150 CE) which were equated by later archaeologists with distillation of alcohol – remain inconclusive due to the limitations of these devices as well as the paucity of literary evidence for distillation in early India. The historian of science Joseph Needham identified three kinds of stills – the Mongol/Chinese type, Gandharan stills and the Italian-Arab stills. Irfan Habib observes that although the Gandhara stills were known in early India, they were not used extensively. The more efficient Mediterranean (Italian-Arab) type of stills, where the distilled liquor was immediately cooled in water through a unique funnel known as the 'Moor's head', came to India in the thirteenth century and led to much wider and commercial use of distilled alcohol. After the emergence of distillation simultaneously in Italy and China during the tenth- to twelfth-century period, the Islamic law-breakers of Iran and Syria perfected the art distillation of grape wine and from there it spread and became popular in South Asia.

By the late thirteenth century during the Delhi Sultanate, the medieval writer Ziauddin Barani in *Tarikh-i-Firozshahi* writes about the wine-makers of Kol and Meerut in India bringing wine flagons filled with sweet-scented (*chakainda*) liquor from un-fermented arrack for the accession ceremony of the Delhi Sultan Kaiqubad (1286–9), ignoring Islamic law. Just a decade later, although the powerful Sultan Alauddin Khalji (1296–1316) prohibited the brewing of alcohol, people continued flouting the rules by building their own boilers to extract distilled liquor from sugarcane and sold them at high prices. The text also has the recollections of Barani as a twelve-year-old in the court of Sultan Ghiyasuddin Tughlaq where he saw that amidst courtier Amir Khusrau's ghazals in praise of 'moon-faced young boys and enchanting beauties', the *saqi*s (wine server) invited the audience to drink and that a man must be devoid of any feeling if they did not feel intoxicated in such a *majlis* (gathering). By the fifteenth century, distillation was in practice in different parts of the subcontinent. In Bengal it was used for preparing most wines including those from rice and COCONUT. In Abu'l-Fazl's *Ain-i Akbari* of the sixteenth century, we find a systematic account of the three kinds of apparatus for distilling wine from sugar mentioned earlier. The first two devices use simple but not so efficient methods as the receiver is placed in the cucurbit while in the last device, called 'Moor's head', which appears in India and the Near East earlier than Western Europe. This device had a water container set above the spoon-like alembic to quickly cool the vapours and a tube that leads the spirits to the receptacle placed outside which ensured efficient collection of the distilled alcohol.

To know about the drinking culture of medieval India, it is necessary to read the inconsistencies in the texts. Following Islamic law, the normative information gleaned is about abstention since Zaiuddin Barani (1285–1358 CE) in his political manual for the Sultan, *Fatawa i Jahandari*, says that if the king drinks wine excessively the others who had refrained from drinking will also start drinking, whereas he should be following the guidance of the spiritual leader, the Imam. In contrast, the text later mentions that for 'a successful campaign, the king apart from making his soldiers free in their minds from the anxiety about their community or family, should also arrange for wine along with other enjoyments such as dry fruits, beer and bhang as well as medicines at the army-camp and gives license to entertainment with women'.

During the fifteenth to seventeenth century, European presence increased in the subcontinent with the Portuguese in Goa, followed by the Jesuits and others in the Mughal courts. The European travel accounts mention that Danes, Venetians, French and English engaged in varied professions were allowed to brew and consume their own liquor and notes the presence of different alcoholic drinks but the local population had to follow a different set of rules. The English traveller John Ovington on his voyage to Surat in 1689 mentions that in the absence of English beer, perceived as a strong malt drink in the English factory records, the sailors often took to locally produced drinks, such as arrack, toddy or punch. Sack, a liquor from Spain or Canary Islands often consumed by European sailors during their voyages, was in use in the coastal regions of India and is mentioned frequently in English factory records during the early seventeenth century. Thomas Roe, ambassador of the English monarch at the court of the Mughal emperor Jahangir in 1615–16, preferred it to wine, as he stated in a letter written from the subcontinent to Sir Thomas Smythe in London. In the later decades of the century, sack yielded its place to drinks like arrack and punch.

Arrack (lit. perspiration), or 'distilled spirit', was one of the most popular drinks among Indian communities and Europeans. The Emperor Jahangir was known to be fond of arrack. In South India, the French traveller Tavernier (1660s) mentions how arrack or palm wine was distilled from toddy – from the juice of palms during the occasion of snake worship in villages near Golconda. In East and North India, arrack was distilled from cane-molasses or from rice. Ovington finds the Bengal arrack stronger than that of Goa (Nipa di Goa, made from nipa toddy) but mentions that both were used by Europeans to make punch as it was cheap. He mentions that another form of arrack was distilled from 'black sugar' (unrefined sugar) mixed with water, with the bark of the *babul* (*Acacia arabica*) tree. This was stronger than the other forms of arrack and as 'hot' as 'brandy' and was drunk in drams by Europeans. In the second half of the seventeenth century, Bernier finds that around Delhi arrack was still made from unrefined sugar. Thevenot (1666) mentions that in Gujarat it was also made by distilling toddy but was not as good as 'our Brandy'. Abbe Carre (1674) found this drink everywhere in the Deccan and Thomas Bowrey (1669–72) tells us that arrack was distilled from rice and jaggery mixed with other drugs. All these variants were much stronger than grape wine.

In seventeenth-century Goa, the Portuguese traded nipa, an arrack made from palm tree, with the English ships. The French traveller Abbe Carre (early 1670s) notes that 'sold at 33 pardos the pipe (cask)' this nipa would serve as ration for the crew on a voyage. In exchange for other similar articles, the English provided the Portuguese with Spanish wine and French brandy brought from Europe, which the Portuguese were 'very anxious to buy'. In addition to nipa and *feni*, the Portuguese import of port wine and other kinds of liquors created the creole culture of Goa. One of these lost family recipes, resurrected as Licor Armada by Oscar de Sequeira Nazareth, recently has gained international recognition and awards in 2013 and 2014.

By the third quarter of the seventeenth century, English factory towns in Indian coasts were producing arrack for their own consumption and improvised this into the punch, a drink emerging from Persian or Hindustani root of *panj* or Marathi *panch*, described by the *Hobson-Jobson* as a drink 'composed of five ingredients, namely, arrack, sugar, lime-juice, spice and water'. The English traveller John Fryer observed that a variety of liquor made of five ingredients in a base of arrack was served in the punch houses of the factories. Also called *bouleponges* (from *bowle* – the German name for punch and related drinks), the French traveller Bernier states that this was a staple drink of the Dutch and the English in seventeenth- century Bengal where they used nutmeg as the spice.

Wines of several kinds were imported from Europe, the Cape of Good Hope, Canary Islands and Persia. The Allicante, or Alegante, a Spanish wine, was often gifted to significant political persons in the subcontinent by Europeans. Apart from French wine (the variety is not always specified), Canary wine is mentioned as one of the better varieties found on the subcontinent and was brought by the Dutch to Surat. Shiraz wine was imported via Bandar-Abbas and reached Delhi from Surat in forty-six days. Bernier mentions that due to this the two wines were extremely expensive but preferred at the court and by the nobles. Another wine was brewed in Kabul by using hollow clay jars over two years and reserved only for the nobles, according to another European traveller Manucci.

The history of the MUGHAL Empire from the 1530s to the 1850s is replete with use and negation of alcohol among the royalty and the nobility. BABUR made public declarations of giving up the drink every time he intended to win a battle but then kept going back to his tipple. Abu'l-Fazl's *Ain i Akbari* provides details of distillation but does not mention anything about the drinking culture as it was supposed to be a manual for the ideal ruler embodied in AKBAR. Instead, we know from his contemporary Badauni that Akbar introduced rations of alcohol, allowing only those who had a prescription from a doctor to drink it – a rule which was promptly flouted by the people who sent in requisitions on fictitious names. Several nobles succumbed to *delerium tremens,* including Sultan Daniyal and Parwiz, sons of Akbar. Initially restrained by Akbar, his son Emperor Jahangir was especially fond of drinking wine and arrack in night parties and sometimes even through the day as witnessed by the Englishmen John Hawkins and Sir Thomas Roe. Emperor Shahjahan called for abstaining from alcohol while beginning his Deccan campaign but was seen to drink wine when English East India Company officers gifted him barrels from London. In the war of succession to Shahjahan, Aurangzeb used the ploy of getting his brother Murad Baksh drunk at a party to imprison him for acting against Islamic law.

Alcohol was intricately linked to the life of the lowest strata of society. Alcoholic drinks were served to the 'coolies' and palanquin bearers by villagers on the route through the treacherous mountains of Bijapur. During festivals such as snake worship or for childbirth, European travellers observed the use of alcoholic drinks in various parts of the subcontinent including the Coromandel Coast and Bengal. These drinks, often not distilled, were thought of as necessary for the sustenance of these functions.

Although the later Mughals lost their power to the Marathas, Sikhs and then the British, Bahadur Shah Zafar, renowned poet and the last Mughal emperor, patronized a stellar group of Urdu poets, including the brilliant Mirza Ghalib. Ghalib loved his tipple and preferred foreign-made liquor with references to 'French' which was an allusion to red wine, Old Tom gin and 'Castelline' (Castellino from Italy). Evoking defiance amidst the gloom in Delhi due to the decline of powers of the Mughal emperor, Ghalib's poetry is philosophical when critiquing the existing social and political order, imaged on the pleasure of the cup:

The tavern's threshold and the preacher's steps never meet
But yesterday, Ghalib, I saw the preacher entering while I left.

In 1857 both the rebels and the British troops took advantage of the chaos in Delhi to plunder stocks of liquor, while Begum Hazrat Mahal of Lucknow asserted that she had opposed the British in the Uprising because of their wish to grant freedom to 'eat pigs and drink wine' while the places of worship of the Muslims and Hindus are neglected.

During the British Raj, although wines were popular during the initial period, the other drinks such as beer and whisky were to soon make their mark. The British had been bringing their beer which was often found to get stale by the time they reached the Indian shores after a four-to-five-month journey. The Hodgson's Bow breweries found a solution by using higher alcohol content which was aged to make the colour mellow. The first batch arrived in India in 1837 to a lot of fanfare. Aged on the journey with the ship's motion contributing to it, the beer became popular as Indian pale ale (IPA). And like wine earlier, it was found that the barrels which remained in the ship and were taken back to England also tasted well due to the action of the sea which matured the beer.

While IPA became popular, the Indian breweries were opening up. Beer was transported in big barrels known as 'Hogsheads'. The first brewery and distillery, owned by General Edward Abraham Dyer, the father of the infamous Colonel Reginald Dyer of the Jallianwala Bagh massacre, opened production in Kasauli in 1830 to provide cheap beer to the British garrisons. The first beer in India was brewed here under the name 'Lion Beer' and the distillery was shifted to Solan in 1835 to take advantage of the water there which was good for the beer. M.G. Meakin bought the Solan brewery and the company was now called Dyer-Meakin & Company. By 1882, Dwyer had twelve breweries, including one in Rangoon. After the separation of Burma, the company was renamed Dyer-Meakin Breweries. In 1949, N.N. Mohan acquired all the properties and in 1967 the name changed to Mohan-Meakin breweries, which now produces the Old Monk rum.

In South India, the Scotsman Thomas Leishman brought together five older breweries in 1915 to form the United Breweries Company, headquartered in Bangalore. It was the biggest firm in post-Independence India. However, this conglomerate of several breweries in the much older British-Indian brewing tradition, including Astle Brewery and Nilgiris Breweries (1857), Bangalore Brewing Co. (1885), British Brewing Corp.

(1903) and BBB Brewery Co. Ltd. (1913), is a reminder of the existence of breweries in the region for 150 years now.

Gin, too, has a history intertwined with that of India and Britain in the global imperial context. The English learnt about it from the Dutch during their war with Holland in the 1580s and its popularity in London during the eighteenth century led to riots and regulations by the British government. When India became a colony of Britain in the 1850s, the British soldiers arriving in India needed to take quinine as protection against malaria. In order to douse the bitterness they gulped it down with gin and lime. The combination of gin and tonic in the Indian context flowed back to the English and European drinking habits and played a crucial role in British imperial ambitions.

Today India is one of the largest consumers of whisky and also a producer of molasses-based Indian whiskies which are considered rum in European countries. In England, Scotch whisky had become popular in the 1860s when phylloxera invasion led to a paucity of wines, cognac and brandy. Imported in India starting in the 1880s, by the turn of the century it became the most popular drink. Nationalists tried to argue that as hemp was indigenous, there was no need for imported whisky. However, a campaign by the British authorities to prove that whisky was less harmful and the simultaneously increasing popularity of labels like The Glenlivet, Glenfiddich and Johnnie Walker led to its spread from the British initially to a wider population. After this era, Indian brands emerged but the Indian Made Foreign Liquor (IMFL) is based on sugarcane molasses unlike the malt whiskies of Europe.

The British colonial government remained ambivalent about the consumption of liquor. Despite the lucrative revenue from *abkari* (liquor tax), there were concerns about the English soldiers' intemperance. Missionaries and Indian nationalists joined in their protest against the sale of liquor. After agricultural revenue, excise was the largest proportion of revenue income for the British government. From the times of the Abkari Act of 1878, they followed a policy of institutionalizing and providing advantages to distilleries of IMFL where the colonial state could control the revenues as well as the consumption. The indigenous fermented alcoholic drinks such as mahua liquor, rice beer of the tea plantations or arrack were marginalized and pushed out of recognition by the state and society.

Prasun Chatterjee

- Bhattacharya, Nandini. 'The Problem of Alcohol in Colonial India (*c*. 1907–1942)'. *Studies in History* 33, no. 2 (2017): 187–212.
- Chatterjee, Prasun. 'The Lives of Alcohol in Pre-Colonial India'. *The Medieval History Journal* 8, no. 1 (2005): 189–225.
- Habib, Irfan. *Economic History of Medieval India, 1200–1500*. Delhi: Pearson Education, 2010.
- Mc Hugh, James. *An Unholy Brew*. New York: OUP, 2021.
- Olivelle, Patrick. *King, Law and Governance: Kautilya's Arthashastra*. New York: OUP, 2013.
- Singh, Magandeep. *The Indian Spirit: The Untold Story of Drinking in India*. New Delhi: Penguin Random House India, 2017.

AMARANTH

Amaranthus is a genus of pot-herbs with distinct inflorescence of bristly or elongated panicles of spikes and often variegated leaves. The pinkish-red colouration in the leaves, stems or inflorescence is due to the presence of anthocyanins. They are grown for their leaves and seeds throughout India and are prized for their high protein and calcium content. Since they are a pseudo-cereal, people eat them during FASTING. Many species find mention in Sanskrit texts as *tanduliya*, *kurantaka*, *guḍamūla*, among others. Today, amaranth is famous as a gluten-free grain alternative.

Amaranth seeds may be white or dark brown and are generally called *rajgira* or *ramdana* in North India. They are parched or popped on a hot iron griddle. The seeds are mixed with POTATOES and fried into VADAS. Popped amaranth is gathered with jaggery (see SUGAR) to make *rajgira* LADDU or a brittle *chikki*. Popped amaranth seeds are milled into flour and made into puri, paratha, roti (see BREADS) and *thalipeeth* (a multi-grain flatbread popular in Maharashtra). The flour is mixed with BUTTERMILK and consumed as a drink. A roux of amaranth flour is cooked with yogurt to make *kadhi* or a porridge. It can be mixed with HONEY and eaten as a medicine or mixed with fresh grated COCONUT and jaggery and eaten as *puttu* in South India. Both popped seeds and flour can be cooked with jaggery and GHEE to make HALWA. Popped amaranth seeds have ritualistic significance in the funerals of the Badagas, a tribal group in Tamil Nadu. They offer funeral baskets filled with popped amaranth into the funeral pyre.

The leaves of many amaranth species are most commonly stir-fried or cooked with lentils (see PULSES) in regional methods that lend unique tastes. *A. hybridus* leaves are stir-fried as *choulai paan nu shaak* in Gujarat, *pungai keerai poriyal* in Tamil Nadu and *cheera thoran* in Kerala. The leaves with LOTUS stems make *nadru vost haakht,* a semi-dry CURRY in Kashmir. It is commonly called *soppu* in the Nilgiris and Karnataka and people eat it with boiled RICE. The thick, fleshy stems of *A. livisus* (Tamil *thandu keerai*) are valued as a vegetable and added to SAMBAR, sautéed to make a *poriyal* or mixed with yogurt to make a *pachadi*. In Orissa, *kosala saag*, its namesake dish, is an essential preparation in the famous temple offerings of Puri (see TEMPLE FOOD). In Andhra Pradesh, it is mixed with lentils to make *thotakura pappu*, a stew, or is fried with a lentil paste to make vadas.

Bangarapan bhairi, a rice-based fritter mixed with the pulp of *A. spinosus* (Tamil *mullu keerai*), is unique to the Sourashtrians of Tamil Nadu and is also a popular STREET FOOD in Madurai. It also finds use in traditional medicine to stimulate the blood and increase milk production, among other uses. The leaves are cooked with peanut powder to make *tandulkyachi bhaji* in Maharashtra and sautéed with other vegetables to make *note shak chorchori* in Bengal. *A. tricolor* leaves are often mixed with cooked lentils and spices and served as a dal; as *arai keerai masiyal* in Tamil Nadu or *tambdi bhaji* in Maharashtra.

A. viridis leaves make *leutiaa saaga bhaaja* in Odisha and are mixed with fermented FISH *ngari* and fried fish to make *chengkruk mana thongba* in Manipur. *Bajji saaga* is prepared from the leaves of *A. dubius*. *Celosia cristata*, a member of the same family as *Amaranthus*, is prized as a food colourant in Kashmir and is locally known as *mawal*.

Priya Mani

- Food For The Soul. 'Vost Haakh T, Nadir (Lotus Stems with Amaranth Leaves)'. 7 September 2019. Available online: https://foodforthesoul00.com/2019/09/07/vost-haakh-t-nadir-lotus-stems-with-amaranth-leaves/ (accessed 11 April 2022).

- Sauer, Jonathan D. 'The Grain Amaranths and Their Relatives: A Revised Taxonomic and Geographic Survey'. *Annals of the Missouri Botanical Garden* 54, no. 2 (1967): 103–37.

AMLA

In English known as gooseberry, myrobalan or emblic, *amla* (*Emblica officinalis*) is one of the most ancient Indian fruits. It is the fruit of a deciduous tree native to India that grows in coastal, tropical and subtropical regions, and in hilly areas. India is the world's largest producer and most of the crop is used domestically. The largest producing states are Uttar Pradesh (which accounts for over half of all the production), Tamil Nadu, Gujarat, Rajasthan, Maharashtra and Andhra Pradesh.

The small, bright green fruits are fibrous and have an astringent, bitter and sour taste. Because of its flavour profile, the berry is often soaked in SUGAR syrup or cooked into dishes. It is commonly used in CHUTNEYS, *murabbas* and PICKLES. In South India, the fruit is used in preparing dal or is added to RICE. *Amla* juice is a popular drink, it is rich in vitamin C and is believed to have many health benefits.

Amla is a common component in Ayurvedic medicine, especially the ancient compound *chyawanprash* that is mentioned in the *Charaka Samhita* (see FOOD AND MEDICINE) and is still in popular use. It is made from as many as forty-three herbal ingredients including sugarcane juice, SESAME oil, HONEY and GHEE. *Amla* is also an ingredient in another important Ayurvedic compound, *triphala churna*. *Amla*'s properties are now being intensively studied: the United States's National Institutes of Health's PubMed database lists over 2,300 papers on *amla*. Among other properties, it appears to reduce total cholesterol levels, including the fatty acids called triglycerides.

Colleen Sen

AMMAL, S. MEENAKSHI

For seventy years, S. Meenakshi Ammal's cookbooks *Samaithu Par* were essential reading for young South Indian brides. The first volume of vegetarian recipes appeared in 1951 and was followed by another recipe book and then a third volume about festivals and their food preparations. They were translated into English in 1968 under the title *Cook and See* and later into Hindi, Telugu, Kannada and Malayalam.

Mrs Ammal was born in 1906 into a traditional Tamil Brahmin family in Kottur near Madurai and learned to cook at an early age. Married to a lawyer, she was widowed after just four years of marriage, leaving her to support a young son, a brother-in-law and a mother-in-law. (It's no coincidence that all the recipes in the book are for four people.) Because her cooking was so highly valued, her relatives began asking her to send them the recipes. At the suggestion of her uncle K.V. Krishnaswami Iyer, a prominent barrister, she compiled the first volume of *Samaithu Par* and published it herself using proceeds from the sale of her jewellery.

Samaithu Par was not an instant success but the migration of Tamils to other parts of India and abroad eventually boosted sales. Mrs Ammal died in 1962 at the age of fifty-six. Her grand daughter-in-law Priya Ramkumar has maintained her legacy by running a publishing house publishing her books, releasing two volumes covering more dishes, and writing a modern version – *The Best of Samaithu Par*. She also runs a website featuring many of Mrs Ammal's recipes – http://cookandsee.in

Colleen Sen

- Venugopal, Nikhita. 'How Meenakshi Ammal Made Vegetarian Cooking Accessible to Generations of Home Cooks'. *The News Minute*, 4 March 2019. Available Online: https://www.thenewsminute.com/article/how-meenakshi-ammal-made-vegetarian-cooking-accessible-generations-homecooks-97722 (accessed 11 April 2022).

AMRITSAR

Amritsar, a city in Punjab, the prosperous agricultural state in the northwest of India, has been historically famous for being the home of the Golden Temple, the most sacred shrine of the Sikh religion, and the place where Maharishi Valmiki, the author of the *Ramayana*, one of the two most important Sanskrit epics of ancient India, had his retreat.

This historical city is the closest to Lahore in Pakistan, which was once the capital of Maharaja Ranjit Singh, the builder of the Sikh empire in the first half of the nineteenth century. Because India and Pakistan have gone to war twice, Amritsar has a substantial presence of the Indian armed and border security forces. It is also significant historically because the Jallianwala Bagh Massacre took place here on 13 April 1919 when a British general ordered the cold-blooded killing of scores of unarmed men, women and children who were peacefully protesting against the colonial Raj. The massacre is said to be the spark that lit the fire of India's freedom movement under the leadership of Mahatma GANDHI and the Indian National Congress.

For all these reasons, Amritsar has been a magnet for pilgrims and tourists from all over the world. To cater to their food needs and that of the common people, the city has a robust culinary culture. The Golden Temple, also known as Sri Harmandir Sahib, is famous for running one of the greatest feeding enterprises in the world – the daily *langar*, where 50,000 to 100,000 people, irrespective of their religious affiliation, are served a humble yet wholesome meal of rotis (unleavened whole wheat breads, see BREADS), dal (lentils), a vegetable preparation and KHEER (rice pudding) served and cooked by volunteers (see TEMPLE FOOD). The kitchen, equipped with a hundred LPG cylinders and a conveyor belt-based machine that rolls out 25,000 rotis in an hour, handles 5,000 kilos of WHEAT, 1,800 kilos of lentils (see PULSES), 1,400 kilos of RICE and 700 litres of milk every day without a break. Food, therefore, is in the DNA of Amritsar.

Visitors may not be able to locate a fine-dining restaurant in the holy city, but they will find *DHABAS* serving only vegetarian delicacies around the perimeter of the Golden Temple. Elsewhere in the city, they will be able to enjoy the famous 'Amritsari fish', the city's signature dish famously served at Makhan Fish and Chicken Corner, which has been around since 1962.

To prepare 'Amritsari fish', which must not be confused with a fish PAKORA, chunky boneless fillets of *singhara* (sole), sourced from the neighbouring Beas river, are first marinated with SALT, MUSTARD oil and a bit of ASAFOETIDA (*hing*). Minutes later, according to a recipe shared by Chef Kunal Kapur, the FISH chunks are massaged with a marinade prepared with thick curd spiked with little bits of chickpea flour (*besan*) and rice flour, carom seeds (AJOWAN) and Kashmiri red CHILLI powder, and then fried in mustard oil. This makes the preparation lighter because unlike a fish pakora, it is not quilted in a chickpea-flour batter.

Amritsar's delicacies include the flaky naan bread stuffed with either spiced POTATO mash or PANEER (cottage cheese), like the ones they serve at Kulcha Land on Ranjit Avenue; the hearty Punjabi breakfast of puris (see BREADS) fried in *desi* ghee with *chhole* (chickpeas) and a potato CURRY, rounded off with lentils-and-jaggery *pinni* (Kanha Sweets); a hearty lunch or dinner, such as what is served at the city's best-known *DHABAS*, Kesar and Bharawan, consisting of the buttery dal *makhni* (or *ma ki* dal, prepared with whole black gram simmered overnight), *aloo gobhi* (potato and cauliflower), and, in winter, *sarson da saag* (a creamy mash of mustard greens and spinach cooked with spices and red chillies in mustard oil) and *makke di* roti (cornflour bread); ghee-roasted chicken strips (Beera Chicken House) and crumb-fried mutton mince cutlets (Adarsh Meat Shop); and lassi made with whipped yogurt, generous helpings of fresh cream and SUGAR, flavoured with MANGOES when in season (Ahuja Milk Bhandar) or fortified with a *peda* (Gian Di Lassi). No visit to Amritsar is complete without JALEBIS and *gulab jamuns* deep-fried in *desi* ghee and dunked in thick sugar syrup at Gurudas Ram Jalebi Wale; and the unique *kulfa*, synonymous with A-One Kulfa, which is a KULFI served on a bed of FIRNI (slow-cooked pudding made with thickened milk, ground rice and NUTS) and topped up with *FALOODA* (vermicelli strings), rose-flavoured syrup and *RABRI* (sweetened condensed milk).

Visitors return home with shopping bags laden with the city's famous *aam* papad (sun-dried fruit leather made of mango pulp mixed with concentrated sugar solution); PAPAD (the Amritsari version which has a higher pungency quotient and is spiked with ground black peppercorns, *hing* (asafoetida) and CUMIN, CORIANDER and POMEGRANATE seeds); and *vadiyan* (sun-baked ground *urad* dal, or black gram, cakes spiced with coriander, FENNEL and cumin seeds that are added to vegetarian dishes to add variety to the taste and texture). As much of a foodie magnet as it is a holy city, Amritsar has food to offer to both the pilgrim's soul and the itinerant stomach.

Sourish Bhattacharyya

- Malhotra, Nishi. '50,000 Free Hot Meals a Day and 9 Other Amazing Facts about the Langar at the Golden Temple'. *The Better India*, 1 May 2016. Available Online: https://www.thebetterindia.com/53531/golden-kitchen-10-things-didnt-know-langar-golden-temple-amritsar/ (accessed 11 April 2022).
- Paul, Satarupa. 'Here's What to Eat in Amritsar'. *Condé Nast Traveller*, 13 November 2018.

ANDHRA PRADESH

The state of Andhra Pradesh was originally created in 1956 to encompass the Telugu-speaking parts of South India and the former princely state of Hyderabad. In 2014, it was divided into two states with the creation of Telangana; its capital HYDERABAD was transferred to this new state. India's seventh largest state in area, Andhra Pradesh borders Telangana, Karnataka, Tamil Nadu and Odisha and its food shares many features in common with that of these states. Within its borders is the former French colony Yanam, part of the union territory of Puducherry. The main religious groups are Hindus (88.5 per cent), Muslims (9.5 per cent) and Christians (1.3 per cent). The state has a sizable population of Scheduled Tribes. Although Brahmins are strict vegetarians, other Hindus eat meat and FISH, especially those living near the coast, and less than 2 per cent of the state's population is vegetarian.

Around 60 per cent of the population works in agriculture. The state has a large river system which supplements rainfall. RICE is a major crop and the main staple. Other important crops are MANGOES – Banganapalli, Suvarnarekha, Neelum and Totapuri are the famous varieties – and CHILLIES, the best known being Guntur. (The town of Guntur is home to the largest chilli market in Asia, and possibly the world.) Other crops are sorghum, MILLETS and other coarse grains, especially in the southwestern part of the state; many varieties of lentils (see PULSES); oil seeds; and sugarcane. Andhra Pradesh is a major producer of poultry and the largest producer of eggs in India (see POULTRY AND EGGS). Aquaculture, including the cultivation of fish, crustaceans, molluscs and shrimp, is a major occupation in both coastal areas and inland. The government has supported the development of aquaculture farms along rivers and canals where people once raised crops. The state accounts for 70 per cent of India's shrimp production, much of it exported.

Three ingredients are essential in Andhra cuisine: TAMARIND, red chillies and *gongura*, the leaf of the roselle plant (*Hibiscus sabdariffa*). Together they give dishes their characteristic hot and sour flavour.

Tamarind, together with TOMATOES and sour mangoes, imparts sourness to dishes. Its flowers and leaves are curried, its seeds ground into a flour, and ripe tamarind fruit is mixed with *gur* (jaggery, see SUGAR) and eaten as a SWEET. It is also mixed with sugar and SALT to make a drink. (When people in parts of Andhra Pradesh started to replace tamarind with tomatoes hundreds of years ago, entire villages began suffering from fluorosis, a disease that causes permanent damage and deformity to the bones. The drinking water proved to have high concentrations of fluorine, the effects of which are mitigated by tamarind.) Tamarind is a key ingredient in the popular rice dish *pulihora*, or tamarind rice. It is often made at temples and offered to the Gods and the people as *prasadam* (see TEMPLE FOOD). *Pulusu* is a hot tamarind based soup that can be eaten alone or used as a sauce for vegetables, chicken, mutton or fish.

According to a legend, there was once a severe famine in the area and the only plants that grew were red chillies, which then became a staple of the Andhra diet. Andhra cuisine is reputed to be the hottest in India. The hottest chilli is called *koraivikaram,* meaning 'the flaming stick' in Telugu. A dry CHUTNEY is made by pounding these chillies to a fine powder and mixing it with tamarind pulp and salt. The state's most famous dish is a green mango PICKLE called *avikkai,* which is so hot that it has sent many an unsuspecting visitor to the hospital.

Gongura is used in many ways. A classic Andhra dish is *gongura pachadi*, a pickle made from fried *gongura* leaves, spices and chillies served with white rice or chapatis (see BREADS). *Gongura* is added to lentils and shrimp and mutton CURRIES.

Standard breakfast dishes include IDLI and DOSAS served with SAMBAR, chutney and *podi,* a spicy powder (see SPICE BOX) sprinkled on rice and vegetables. Andhra dosas are spicier and crispier than those in other parts of South India. *Pesarattus* are dosas made from a batter of green mung beans, topped with ONIONS, chillies and GINGER and filled with *upma* (spiced semolina).

A formal Andhra meal includes tamarind rice, a dry savoury vegetable dish, a vegetable curry, *pulusu*, *pappadum* (see PAPAD), *pappu* (dal), *pachadi* (a pickle made of vegetables or greens and roasted chillies), *chaaru* (a thin lentil stew) and yogurt. Curd rice, a dish popular throughout the South, is made with vegetables blended with ginger, chillies and CURRY LEAVES and is tempered with CUMIN, MUSTARD seeds and *urad* dal. A standard tempering mixture, called *popu*, is made with mustard seeds, *chana* dal (split Bengal gram), cumin, curry leaves and dried red chilli. Often ASAFOETIDA is added to dals and curries. Dessert is likely to be *payasam* (see KHEER), LADDUS or *shahi tukra*. A distinctive Andhra sweet is *boorelu*, deep-fried balls filled with *chana* dal, jaggery, GHEE and CARDAMOM and coated with a rice flour batter.

Common vegetables include OKRA, bitter GOURD, bottle gourd, cauliflower, *tindora* (ivy gourd), POTATO and TARO root. They may be cooked as a curry, crispy fried, or stuffed with spices and cooked whole. *Vankaya koora* is an emblematic Andhra dish: AUBERGINES stuffed with roasted spices and served in a sauce of tamarind and mustard seed.

Andhra Pradesh has two major regions: Rayalaseema in the southwest and Coastal Andhra bordering the Bay of Bengal in the east and northeast. The cuisine of Rayalaseema, a hot dry area, is similar to that of neighbouring Tamil Nadu and south Karnataka. *Ragi* (finger millet) is a common staple. Popular dishes include fritters made with black-eyed peas; horse gram soup; brain and liver fry; balls made of *ragi* and rice; a fritter made with rice flour and jaggery; and *undalu*, a laddu made with rice flour, COCONUT, steamed sorghum and other ingredients. A dish called country chicken is cooked in a spicy and tangy tamarind-based curry.

The coastal region has a vast array of seafood preparations. Dishes are prepared with fewer chillies and more coconut than in other parts of the state. In the Godavari area, prawns are cooked with vegetables and coconut milk or plain milk. Fish fillets are fried with spices, then simmered in a sauce. Prawns are curried, with water or coconut milk; dried prawns are cooked with greens.

Colleen Sen

- Latif, Bilkees I. *The Essential Andhra Cookbook*. Delhi: Penguin Books, 1999.
- Ranjan, Abhishek. 'Andhra Pradesh Cuisine (Telugu Cuisine)'. #IHM Notes#, 1 April 2020. Available Online: http://abhishekrrajan.blogspot.com/2020/04/andhra-pradesh-cuisine-telugu-cuisine.html (accessed 11 April 2022).

ANGLO-INDIANS

The community got its official name only in 1911 from Lord Charles Hardinge, the Viceroy who also created New Delhi as the new capital of the British Raj. To the world outside, because of the prefix 'Anglo', the community appears to be homogeneous in its ancestry and consist entirely of descendants of inter-marriages between British (English, Scottish and Irish) men and Indian or mixed-race women. The history and the social complexion of the community, which has been reduced to a minuscule minority of not more than 150,000 people in a country of 1.4 billion today, mainly because of migrations to Britain and Australia, are as layered as its cuisine. But, members of the community have three unifying features as identified by the All-India Anglo-Indian Association: they are all Christian, English is their mother tongue and they all have personal historical links with both Europe and India.

The intermingling of Europeans and Indians started with the Portuguese colonization of Cochin (Kochi) in 1505 and of Goa from 1510 onwards. Then came the Dutch, the English (and the Irish and the Scots), the Armenians, the French, the Italians and the Germans, all of whom left their genealogical legacies behind. That explains why at different points of Indian history the offspring of inter-racial marriages have been variously known as *mesticos* (of mixed Portuguese and Indian descent), Indo-Britons, Eurasians and finally, after 1911, as Anglo-Indians.

Culinarily, this community is as diverse as its genetic stock. The VINDALOO of the Anglo-Indians in the original capital of the Raj, Calcutta (now called KOLKATA), is cooked in MUSTARD oil (influenced undoubtedly by their Bengali or Bihari ancestry) and tastes very different from the Goan original. The former, likewise, would be loath to eat food with COCONUT milk in it; though for those living in the old railway colonies of South India, or in the Kolar Gold Fields or in Fort Kochi, it was an everyday part of the culinary repertoire. What the Anglo-Indians in Calcutta called kofta CURRY was popular as meatball curry in the South; the devilled fries of the South are more famous as the *jhalfrezi* of Calcutta. And the yellow RICE of Calcutta was as popular in Anglo-Indian homes up East as coconut rice in the South.

To understand the marriage of cultures in the Anglo-Indian kitchen, one has to delve into how the society in British India was structured and the many cultural influences at play. Back in the 1930s, Ian Stephens, a former editor of *The Statesman* newspaper, divided British India's European community on the lines of the Indian caste system and found astonishing similarities. The 'so-called heaven-born' officers of the Indian Civil Service were the Brahmins, the commissioned officers of the British Army and the upper ranks of the Indian Army, the Kshatriyas, and the British mercantile community, dismissed as the box-wallahs in their time, the Vaishyas (British lawyers, journalists and missionaries also were a part of this class). And then, as Stephens mentioned, 'You went lower down to the menials, the so-called Eurasians ... and the unfortunate domiciled community, people of pure British race whose parents, for one reason or another, had elected to settle in India.' Within the white under-class, Domiciled Eurasians were at the top followed by the 'Tommies' (British soldiers) and a host of others – from seamen on shore leave to skilled craftsmen, entertainers and barmaids. They were followed by the Anglo-Indians (who became the backbone of the railways since the first train service from Mumbai to Thane in 1854 and of the mining industry as well). The Indian Christians, although culturally the closest to their colonial masters, figured even lower.

Going back to Stephens's description of Anglo-Indian society, the 'upper castes' dug into crossover preparations such as 'KEDGEREE' (a reinvention of the Indian KHICHRI); 'mulligatawny soup' (literally pepper water, spiked with a mélange of whole spices, tempered with TAMARIND and GHEE, and with rice and meat pieces added to it); '*pish pash*' (sloppy rice soup with pieces of meat thrown in); 'fish rissole' (FISH patty encased in a pastry or rolled in bread crumbs and deep-fried); 'ball curry' (meat mince balls cooked in a TOMATO-ONION gravy spiked with GINGER and served with coconut rice); and Major Grey's Chutney.

These dishes were celebrated in Raj cookbooks such as the classic *Culinary Jottings* (1885) by 'WYVERN' (Arthur Robert Kenney-Herbert); at Sake Dean Mahomed's Hindoostane Coffee House established in 1810 on George Street, London; and, a century later, at Veeraswamy, the posh restaurant opened on Regent Street by Edward Palmer in 1926 to cater to superannuated colonials like him. All these were instances of what Sabita Radhakrishna describes in *Annapurni: Heritage Cuisine from Tamil Nadu* (2015), which has a chapter dedicated to Anglo-Indian cuisine, as 'Victorian interpretations of Indian dishes'.

More common were the Indian appropriations of British classics such as the pot roast. Anglo-Indians adopted the British tradition of roasting, but there was a critical difference – the meat was first marinated and then slow-cooked in the Awadhi *dum* cooking style (see COOKING AND DINING). In the absence of an oven, which was a luxury in most Indian homes till the 1970s, roasts were slow-cooked in steam in a charcoal-heated ICMIC cooker, which was invented in 1910 by an Indian polymath and entrepreneur, Indumadhab Mallick. At Kolar Gold Fields (KGF) near Bangalore, Karnataka, where Bridget White-Kumar, a prolific chronicler of Anglo-Indian cuisine, grew up, roasts were *dum* cooked in an aluminium *dekshi* (or *degchi*, as it is called in the North) heated by a coal fire.

Another important difference was that the roasts were spiced up with TURMERIC, red CHILLI powder, whole red chillies and peppercorns (see PEPPER, BLACK). A pot roast involved tucking in to seasonal vegetables such as POTATOES, TURNIPS, CARROTS, beans and onions, which were cooked in the natural juices of the meat. Roasts are immensely popular in the Anglo-Indian culinary tradition, according to White-Kumar, because 'they require very little work and effort'. Writes White-Kumar: 'When properly done, there's no greater pleasure than tucking into juicy, roasted meat.'

Frank Anthony (1908–93), the foremost leader of the community and its nominated representative in the Constituent Assembly and, thereafter, in eight of the first ten Lok Sabhas (the Lower House of the Parliament), offered a taste of the Anglo-Indian table in his otherwise political tract titled *Britain's Betrayal of India: The Story of the Anglo-Indian Community* (1969). 'Breakfast was essentially an English breakfast – porridge, eggs and fruit', Anthony recounted. 'Lunch was Indian, or what was, in fact, typically Anglo-Indian. In some homes, after the soup there was the usual curry and rice, vegetables, and fruit or a sweet afterwards. Dinner was something along the English pattern: roast, stews and pudding.'

In the immortal words of E.M. Forster, writing in *A Passage to India* (1924), what the colonial masters of British India ate was the 'food of exiles, cooked by servants who did not understand it'. What the Eurasian/Anglo-Indian community did was to uplift this boring fare with what Bridget White-Kumar describes as a 'judicious use of spices'. In her words: 'We use spices to enhance the main ingredient, not to smother it. We go slow on ghee and our gravies are thin. And in the South, we also use coconut milk by grinding freshly scraped coconut on a stone, like they do in traditional families.' Anglo-Indian cuisine can be appropriately described as the Indian appropriation of the English table.

Sourish Bhattacharyya

- Caplan, Lionel. 'Creole World, Purist Rhetoric: Anglo-Indian Cultural Debates in Colonial and Contemporary Madras'. *Journal of the Royal Anthropological Institute* (N.S.) 1, no. 4 (1995): 743–62.
- Connor, Richard, Harry MacLure and Beatrix D'Souza. 'The Anglo-Indians of Madras'. *Madras Musings* 20, no. 12 (1–15 October 2010).
- Fischer-Tine, Harald. *Low and Licentious Europeans: Race, Class and 'White Subalternity' in Colonial India*. New Delhi: Orient Blackswan, 2009.
- Radhakrishna, Sabita. *Annapurni: Heritage Cuisine from Tamil Nadu*. New Delhi: Lustre Press/Roli Books, 2015.
- White-Kumar, Bridget. *Anglo-Indian Delicacies: Vintage and Contemporary Cuisine from Colonial India*. New Delhi: Partridge Publishing India, 2013.

ANISEED

Aniseed (or anise; *Pimpinella anisum*, Hindi *saunf*) is an aromatic and digestive spice with distinct small, oval, light brown or pale green seeds. The plant is native to the Levant and is botanically related to caraway, CUMIN, dill and FENNEL.

Today, the plant is grown commercially in suitably warm climates all over the world, including northern and eastern India where it is most commonly used in Bengali and Kashmiri cooking. It is used either whole or ground into a fine powder and lends a licorice flavour to CURRIES, FISH, vegetable dishes, lentils (see PULSES), soups and, sometimes, BREADS and biscuits. (The French traveller Francois Bernier in the seventeenth century mentions carrying sweet biscuits flavoured with aniseed during his travels in India.) Aniseed is a component of the Bengal spice mixture *panch phoron* (see SPICE BOX).

Aniseed is also used for flavouring drinks. Infused in TEA, it is used to alleviate the symptoms of mild colds. It is also chewed after meals to sweeten the breath and aid digestion. Aniseed is sometimes confused with fennel, this is not helped by the fact that they share the same Hindi name of *saunf*. Sometimes it is called *vilayati saunf*, meaning 'foreign fennel'.

Helen Saberi

- Achaya, K.T. *A Historical Dictionary of Indian Food*. Delhi: OUP, 1998.

APPAM

FIGURE 2 APPAM. *Neyappam* is a Kerala speciality. Samphotography/Wkimedia Commons.

Appam is a Tamil word (also *aapa, appa, appe*) thought to be derived from the Sanskrit *apupa* meaning a fried dainty. They are sometimes called hoppers, an ANGLO-INDIAN adaptation of the Indian word. *Appams* are a pancake-like speciality of both South India and Sri Lanka. They are made from a RICE and COCONUT milk batter which is fermented, traditionally with palm toddy. They are cooked in a two-handled iron pan, which resembles a Chinese wok, known as a *cheena chatti* (literally 'Chinese pan') which gives them their characteristic bowl-like shape. The thin batter is spooned into the heated pan which has been greased with GHEE, then swirled so that it reaches up to the edge of the pan forming a crisp border with a lovely lacy pattern while the centre is thick, soft, white and spongy. The outer edges are dry and crisp when hot but flop when cold, thus the local nickname in Tamil Nadu of 'floppers'.

Appams are eaten throughout southern India and are a favourite breakfast dish in Tamil Nadu. They go well with thick, sweetened coconut milk. They are also eaten at other times of the day, often to sop up savoury or sweet juices. There are many variations. In Kerala, *yele* (leaf) *appams* are a mix of rice batter, grated coconut, JACKFRUIT pulp and jaggery (see SUGAR) steamed in a BANANA leaf packet. *Kuzhal-appam* is a crisp, tube-like fried product and *nai-appam* is a dark, chewy, deep-fried sort of doughnut made with palm toddy-fermented rice and jaggery mixture. SYRIAN CHRISTIANS eat *appams* as an accompaniment to meat stew.

Appams are one of the many dishes made for the ten-day festival of Dussehra.

A similar pancake known as *idiyappam* (called string hopper in Sri Lanka) is a steamed rice noodle dish, a speciality of the Indian states of Tamil Nadu, Kerala and Karnataka. The name *idiyappam* is derived from the Malayalam word *idi*, meaning 'beat', and *appam*. *Idiyappam* is often served with hard-boiled eggs, NUTS, peas, CHILLI sauce, etc. In Tamil Nadu and Kerala the dish is eaten with sweetened coconut milk or with a vegetable korma or CURRY. In Kodagu, it is known as *noolappam* or *noolputtu* (*nool* meaning thread) and is served with a chicken or meat curry. *Idiyappam* is a popular dish for festive occasions.

Helen Saberi

- Achaya, K.T. *A Historical Dictionary of Indian Food*. Delhi: OUP, 1998.
- Kingsman, Rani. *Flavours of Madras*. Reading, Berkshire: Garnet Publishing, 1994.

APPLE

Apple (*Malus pumila*, Hindi *seb*) is a member of the Rosaceae family, closely related to the pear. The large, sweet apple of modern times is essentially a product of selection and cultivation and much changed from its wild ancestors, the tiny sour fruits called crabapples. It is believed that all apples known today are direct descendants of wild apples which evolved in Kazakhstan. Today, there are thousands of named varieties, although many are not of commercial or historical importance.

An early mention of apples in Indian history comes from *Charaka Samhita* (see FOOD AND MEDICINE) where a reference is made to *sinchitikaphala*, perhaps an apple of Chinese origin. Around 1100 CE, Dalhana, a medieval commentator on the *Sushruta Samhita,* described a '*BER* as big as a fist and very sweet' growing in the northern regions of Kashmir, which suggests that it was an apple. The Delhi Sultanate court historian and poet Amir Khusrau (1253–1325 CE) noted apples as well as many other fruits of India. It is thought that the Mughals brought apple trees from Persia in their efforts to grow temperate fruits in suitable areas of India. The British also introduced apple trees, as far back as 1865, to the Kullu valley in the Himalayan state of Himachal Pradesh.

Later, the British army officer, explorer and writer, Sir Francis Younghusband in his book *Kashmir* (1909) describes wild apple trees laden with fruit. He wrote that Kashmir apples were renowned all over India saying, 'They are large, red and attractive looking and sell well as far down as Calcutta and Bombay. But they are not of really good flavour …'

Kashmir is the largest commercial producer of apples in India. There are mainly seven apple varieties:

- **Ambri** is said to have originated in Kashmir in the Himalayan hills and had been grown long before Western introductions. It is tiny, blush red in colour and is prized for its sweet crispness and aroma.
- **Hazaratbali** is the oldest variety of apple in the Kashmir Valley. It is medium-sized, usually red in colour with a thin skin which is sweet and juicy. Despite the fact that it doesn't keep well and has a short shelf life, it is consumed in large quantities.
- **Tarehli** is small and red.
- **Maharaji** apples are a high-yielding variety. They have a bright red skin and a sour taste but are juicy.
- **American Trel** has a greenish-white skin and is sweet and juicy.
- **Red Delicious** and **Golden Delicious** are popular worldwide and in Kashmir Red Delicious is the most widely grown variety in the Sopore region. These two varieties are well known for having been introduced from America in 1916 by the American missionary Samuel STOKES. This apple has a blush red skin with a smooth texture and the greenish-white flesh is aromatic, crisp, sweet and juicy. Golden Delicious has a green skin which turns golden on ripening, hence its name. The flesh is also crisp, white and juicy.

Another colourful character in the history of apple growing in India is Frederick 'Pahari' (meaning mountain) Wilson, a young British officer who, it is said, deserted during the First Afghan War (1839–42). He went to ground in the wilds of Tehri-Garhwal, settled at Harsil, near the source of the Ganges, married two local Indian girls and in a short period of time changed the face of the region forever. He was famous for introducing apples (the Vance Delicious variety), *rajma* (kidney beans) and the timber trade to the area. About 1850, he established a flourishing farm with orchards where he grew apples, which became known as Wilson apples and were described as large, red and juicy. He became a Himalayan legend and the richest man in northern India. His orchards today continue to bear fruit and the apples are in great demand. They are still sold by locals to travellers and pilgrims on their way to the Gangotri shrine.

Despite this flourishing apple cultivation, apples were not available in many areas in the nineteenth century. American ships brought in large supplies of apples but, unfortunately, they were only good when first taken out of the ICE and soon turned mealy. However, British housewives managed to make good use of them by making fruit CHEESE, jams and CHUTNEYS. Flora Annie STEEL gave a recipe for a sweet dessert '*apples à l'Indienne*' and remarked, 'Indian apples are a delusion for the most part, but cooked this way, they will prove excellent, especially the little crabs (crab apples) common in the bazaars in the early summer.' Chopped apples were often added to British CURRIES in the nineteenth and early twentieth centuries. They were used as an alternative to other sour ingredients called for in a curry such as green MANGOES or TAMARIND which were not readily available in Britain.

Tart apples are still used to make *murabbas*, chutneys, PICKLES and relishes. In Kashmir, apples and quinces are used interchangeably in cooking and are added to some stews, and they combine apples and AUBERGINES in the dish *tsoont wangan*.

Helen Saberi

- Achaya, K.T. *Indian Food: A Historical Companion*. Delhi: OUP, 1994.
- Shawl, Ishfaqullah. 'Kashmiri Apples'. *Kashmir Paradise*. Available Online: https://ishfaqullah.weebly.com/apple.html (accessed 11 April 2022).
- TarlaDalal.com. 'Recipes Using Apple'. 4 June 2021. Available Online: https://www.tarladalal.com/recipes-using-apple-seb-54 (accessed 11 April 2022).

APRICOT

Apricot (*Prunus armeniaca*, syn. *Armeniaca vulgaris*) is a fruit belonging to the rose family and is closely related to PLUM, peach, CHERRY and almond. Apricot in India is usually known as *zardalu* or *jardalu* when fresh, and *khubani* or *khumani* when dried. Apricots are golden yellow, plum-shaped fruits. The Persian word *zardalu* means 'yellow plum'. The flesh is pulpy and creamy when ripe and tastes sweet and mellow, a bit like a peach.

For a long time the apricot was thought to have originated in Armenia, hence its scientific name. However, it is now generally accepted that its origin was in China and that it was the Chinese who first domesticated the fruit, although it is possible that there were wild populations across Asia. Historians have suggested that the apricot made its way across Asia via the Silk Road and reached the Indus Valley and Kashmir by the late Harappan period, after 2000 BCE (Spengler III 2019). In *c.* 650 CE, the Chinese monk Xuan Zang recorded that apricots from Kashmir were 'grown on every side'. In the seventeenth century, Emperor Jahangir stated that the 'sweet cherry, pear and apricot, so far imported' were now being grown in Kashmir through the efforts of his nobleman Muhammed Qulu Afshar. In 1838, George Francis White wrote in his travelogue *View in India, Chiefly among the Himalaya Mountains* that apricot trees were hardy and suited to the rough soils, poor irrigation, and the dry and cold climate of mountain slopes and desert plateaus like Ladakh. He also wrote that most villages had apricot trees and which were grown as much for the high quality of oil extracted from their kernels as for their fruit that was usually dried. Sir Francis Younghusband in his book *Kashmir* (1909) also noted that apricots were grown principally for oil.

In 2011, figures published by the FAO estimated that India was producing a mere 10,000 tons of apricots per annum, ranking thirty-eighth in the world. Turkey, on the other hand, produced 716,417 tons the same year. Like other temperate fruits, apricots only flourish in mild, cooler regions. Jammu, Kashmir and the Ladakh region grow most of India's apricots. Other states which grow the fruit on a small scale include Himachal Pradesh and Uttar Pradesh. Fresh apricots also do not keep well so once harvested many of them are dried or desiccated and are available all year-round.

Dried apricots give a slightly sweet and sour taste to dishes. In Kashmir they are an essential ingredient of *zardalu boti*, a lamb dish, which is also flavoured with jaggery (see SUGAR) and vinegar. *Murgh khubani* is a classic dish with chicken, dried apricots and aromatic spices. The PARSIS also like sweet and sour flavours and make a similar stew of chicken with apricots called *jardaloo murgh* and serve it with POTATO straws called *sali*. Stewed apricots have a rich, HONEY-like flavour and are the bases of many SWEETS in India, including the HYDERABAD dessert *qubani ka meetha*. *Khubani*, a special Kashmiri stewed apricot dessert, is prepared for *wazwans* (celebratory banquets). The apricots, which are flavoured with SAFFRON and rosewater (see FLOWER WATERS), are served with their aromatic juices on top of PANEER balls.

Apricots are classed as a 'cold' food in Ayurvedic terms (see FOOD AND MEDICINE) and are valued for their many health benefits whether fresh or dried. They have, for example, a high vitamin A content and an abundance of vitamin C and beta-carotene.

Helen Saberi

- Achaya, K.T. *A Historical Dictionary of Indian Food*. Delhi: OUP, 1998.
- Doctor, Vikram. 'Little Luxuries – Fruit Most Mellow'. *The Economic Times*, 24 August 2012.
- Reddy, Catherine. 'All about Apricots (*Prunus armeniaca*) in India'. *The Earth of India*, 23 September 2012. Available online: http://theindianvegan.blogspot.com/2012/09/all-about-apricots-in-india.htmlhttp://theindianvegan.blogspot.com/2012/09/all-about-apricots-in-india.html (accessed 11 April 2022).
- Spengler III, Robert N. *Fruit from the Sands*. Oakland, CA: University of California Press, 2019.

ARUNACHAL PRADESH

Arunachal Pradesh, known as India's very own 'Land of the Rising Sun', is an Indian state at the eastern-most edge of the country. The largest of the eight states of Northeast India, Arunachal Pradesh lies to the north of Assam and Nagaland and shares international borders with Bhutan to the west, Myanmar to the east and the People's Republic of China to the north. Home to dozens of tribes and about fifty languages and dialects, the Sino-Tibetan languages-speaking population has adopted Hindi as their lingua franca.

Known for its well-preserved biodiversity, Arunachal Pradesh's many historical monuments and archaeological remains bear testimony to the rich cultural heritage and deep connections with Hindu mythology and Buddhism, among other cultures. A local animist religion called Donyi Polo is still widely practised, as are the Arunachalis' ancient tribal customs and traditional ways of life.

Chief crops are RICE, CORN, MILLETS, WHEAT, PULSES, sugarcane, GINGER, and oilseeds. The demand for kiwi fruit and high-speciality TEAS from Arunachal has seen a tremendous growth locally, domestically and internationally in recent years. Arunachal Pradesh has close to 61,000 square km of forests, 750 species of birds and more than 200 species of mammals. The conservation of indigenous biodiversity is evident in the dietary habits of locals. For example, the Monpas, a Buddhist community concentrated in the districts of Tawang and West Kameng, generally use sustainable and natural ingredients from their environment to create dishes so high in nutritional value that some are characterized as traditional medicine. Traditional foods are mainly based on yak milk, soybean, buckwheat, AMARANTH, maize, BARLEY, CHILLI, and various indigenous fruits and vegetables. Their alcoholic beverages are made from finger millets, maize, barley and rice. Another speciality is *chhurpi*, a slightly fermented milk CHEESE which is made from the milk of the *chauri*, a cross between a cow and a yak, and can be found throughout the Northeast, Nepal and Tibet. It is prepared in a number of ways, including cooking with green vegetables or as a filling with momos. While the cuisine of the *chhurpi*-eating Monpas is more reminiscent of that of Tibet, the Arunachali tribes of Galos, Apatanis, Nyishis and Adis follow other major states of Northeast India in using fermented BAMBOO SHOOTS as the chief component in dishes. They are used with boiled vegetables, cooked meat, PICKLES and CHUTNEYS. Many still prefer the taste of food cooked over wood-fire and even continue the age-old practice of cooking their rice in hollow bamboo over some hot coal.

Arunachali food is not without its own selection of side dishes. *Lukter*, a relish taken with rice, is a spicy combination of cooked dry meat and chilli flakes from the fiery *bhut jolokia*. It is packed up in batches and preserved for future meals. *Pika pila*, an Apatani-style pickled pork fat made with bamboo shoots and *raja* chilli, also serves as an accompaniment to most of their rice meals. Tucked away beyond the reach of many people are the state's sprawling tea estates that grow a very premium orthodox repertoire of tea that is yet to be explored by the world. Meanwhile, the people of Arunachal Pradesh continue to sip their homegrown tea for vigour and strength.

Hoihnu Hauzel

- Hauzel, Hoihnu. *The Essential North-East Cookbook*. New Delhi: Penguin Books, 2003.

ASAFOETIDA

Asafoetida (Hindi *hing*), a spice with a strong pungent odour, is a dried gum resin from the rhizome of giant fennels (various species of the genus *Ferula*). They grow in dry rock soil, mainly in Afghanistan and Iran, at heights of 1,200 metres above sea level. The roots are harvested when they are around four years old. After harvesting, a deep incision is made which releases a milky resinous juice that dries on exposure to air. The resin is shipped to India where it is processed to make it suitable for cooking, often by adding flour. Kandahari (after the city of Kandahar in Afghanistan) asafoetida is considered the best. Asafoetida is mentioned as a flavouring together with black and long pepper in Sanskrit works dating back to the first millennium BCE.

In India, asafoetida is used as a substitute for ONIONS and GARLIC by almost all vegetarian communities and also by Kashmiri Brahmins who do eat meat. A small amount is a popular flavouring in CURRIES, PICKLES and other dishes. A pinch is sometimes added to PULSES since it is believed to prevent flatulence. In 2020, there was excitement at the news that asafoetida was being grown in India for the first time, in Himachal Pradesh. However, it will take several years to find out if the quality is equivalent to that of imported asafoetida.

It was grown for medicinal purposes in the Middle East as early as 750 BCE and was a luxury spice during the Roman Empire. The Portuguese physician Garcia DE ORTA wrote in the mid-sixteenth century:

> You must know that the thing used most throughout India, all parts of it, is that Ass-Fetida, which is used for medicine as well as cookery. A great quantity is used, for every Hindu who can afford it will buy it to flavour his food ... They flavour the vegetables they eat with it: first rubbing the pan with it and then using it as seasoning with everything they eat.

Colleen Sen

- Saberi, Helen. 'Rosewater, the Flavoring of Venus, Goddess of Love, and Asafoetida, Devil's Dung'. In *Spicing up the Palate: Studies of Flavourings – Ancient and Modern, Proceedings of the Oxford Symposium on Food and Cookery 1992*, edited by Harlan Walker, 220–35. Totnes, Devon: Prospect Books, 1993.

ASHOKA

Often considered India's greatest ruler, Emperor Ashoka Maurya (304–232 BCE) owes his fame not to the size of his empire, which extended from Afghanistan to the Deccan, or to his military conquests but to his desire for social harmony and the happiness of all beings in his realm. He was the first world leader to advocate kindness to animals, VEGETARIANISM, protection of the environment, religious tolerance, peaceful coexistence in a multicultural society and the renunciation of war. These were tenets of his moral philosophy, called Dhamma, which he propagated on inscriptions on rocks and pillars throughout his empire.

In some of these inscriptions, Ashoka declared that no animals are to be killed for sacrifices and proclaims his own commitment to abstaining from meat:

> Formerly in my kitchen, hundreds of thousands of animals were killed daily for meat but now ... only three animals are killed, two peacocks and one deer, and the deer not all the time. And even these three animals will not be killed in the future.

Another inscription banned the killing of a wide variety of animals, including species of wild birds, FISH, lizards, domesticated animals, females that are pregnant or nursing, young animals, etc. Ashoka set up hospitals for animals and planted medicinal herbs for their treatment. Ashoka's policies reflected the influence of the Buddhists and Jains, who advocated kindness to animals, and won him popularity among his people.

Colleen Sen

- Sen, Colleen Taylor. *Ashoka and the Maurya Dynasty*. London: Reaktion Books, 2022.

ASSAM

FIGURE 3 ASSAM. Tea smoked in bamboo tube – Shing Po tribe. Colleen Sen.

The northeastern state of Assam is a land of plains, river valleys and mountains. The name Assam is derived from the word *asama* meaning 'peerless' in the Ahom language. The state has three distinct topographic regions: the Brahmaputra River valley in the north, the Barak River valley in the south and the hilly region of Eastern Himalayas in the south-central part of the state. Climatically, the state receives one of the highest rainfalls in not only the country but the entire world, with two instances of heavy flooding every year that add fertile alluvial sediments to the river valleys. The state is covered with various types of woodlands including tropical evergreen and deciduous forests, broad-leaved hill forests, pine forests and swamp forests, as well as grasslands. All this makes the state one of the richest in terms of agro-biodiversity in the world. All these factors have played a role in distinguishing the consumption patterns of the various communities in the state, which, owing to its position in the migratory route, is a demographic cocktail of various racial, ethnic, linguistic and religious identities, of which Assamese- or Oxomiya-speaking Hindus form the largest homogenous group. The Ahom or Tai-Ahom is one of the ethnic and indigenous group of communities in the state. They are the mixed descendants of the Tai people who reached the Brahmaputra valley in 1228 and the local people who joined them over the course of time.

As with every other group in the world, natural environment, socio-cultural conditions, traditional norms, religious values and myriad other influences have shaped the food culture of the Assamese Hindus, who are mainly concentrated around the Brahmaputra valley. The food can majorly be categorized into *jolpaan* (light snacks), *pitha-laru* (SWEETS), *haak-pasoli* (leafy greens and vegetables), *maas* (FISH), *manxo* (meat), *tenga* (sour), *khar* (alkaline) and *sutney/asaar* (condiments).

The society is predominantly agrarian and paddy is the mainstay of agriculture. The state is home to many varieties of RICE (*sali*), including aromatic rice and sticky rice varieties. Needless to say, rice forms the cornerstone of the diet, especially the finer and softer *sali* rice from the winter paddy in the sun-dried (*aaroi*) and parboiled (*ukhua*) forms. Rice and rice derivatives are extremely important in the daily diet, from breakfast to dinner and from everyday food to ceremonial fare.

People generally take three meals a day. Traditional breakfast is parched rice (*sira*), popped rice (*akhoi*) or puffed rice (*muri*) with curd and jaggery (see SUGAR), or porridge made of coarse powder of parched rice (*xandoh guri*) or pounded rice powder (*pitha guri*), which is also eaten in savoury forms or added to CURRIES. A unique rice derivative is the pre-cooked, dried and husked rice that can be eaten after soaking in hot water (*kumol saul*) and is eaten as breakfast or used as traditional baby food. Varieties of rice are pounded or turned into sweet cakes (*pitha*) along with COCONUT, jaggery and/or SESAME during festivals such as Bihu. Furthermore, sweets and savouries made of rice are integral to traditional snacks (*jolpaan*). *Poita bhat*, or rice soaked overnight to ferment, is consumed in the early morning in summers in most farming families.

While the food choices of Oxomiya Hindus broadly follow the larger Hindu way of eating, in departure from what is prevalent in mainland Hinduism, Oxomiya Hindus, irrespective of caste and creed, are meat eaters. Placed between one of the largest riverine systems of the world, their diet is replete with a wide array of freshwater fish that the rivers, streams and wetlands of the state yield. Ancient Assam – Kamrupa – was one of the centres of the Shakta (cult of Mother Goddess) and Tantric belief systems, which defined much of the eating practice. The *Kamarupa Yatra*, an old Assamese treatise, recommends the meat of duck, pigeon, tortoise and wild boar for the caste Hindus. While eating tortoise and wild boars is now prohibited by law, the meat of pigeon, duck and goat remains part of the diet. In fact, the Goddess in Kamakhya temple is offered *prasad* (*praxad*) of cooked sacrificial goat meat while pigeons are still given as offerings in the Devi temples across the state. Fish and meat are processed using various methods such as baking, boiling, drying, frying and smoking and are used in different types of *anja* (CURRY), *tenga* (sour), *jola* (pungent/spicy) and *khar* (alkaline) dishes. (Assamese cuisine is one of the rare cuisines in India that still retains the six flavours of traditional Indian medicine – sweet, sour, salty, bitter, pungent and alkali – in everyday eating practice.) One of the most iconic dishes of the state is the *maas tenga*, or fish in a sour soupy gravy, which uses freshwater carp. Chicken, on the other hand, has been a very late entry and it has only been about three to four decades since it was widely accepted into the dietary fold. Pork found acceptance in the traditional kitchen even later – a decade and a half ago.

The food habits imbibed certain distinctive characters from the trans-Himalayan tribes of the state who take boiled, alkaline and sour preparations in their meals. The ashes-leach of the dried bark and root of the plantain tree has been used by the tribes for its salty and alkaline properties and is called *khar*. Dishes seasoned with that liquid are also called *khar* and have become an indispensable part of the Oxomiya Hindu food habit. This alkaline solution is used with PAPAYA, GOURDS, black gram, leafy vegetables and fish to make a *khar* that is served as the first course with rice. Today, *khar* is readily available in bottles, although urban cooks often use sodium bicarbonate.

The advent of the Vaishnava movement in fifteenth century, led by Srimanta Sankardeva (1449–1568), not only had a profound effect on the culture but also influenced the food habits in the state. It brought VEGETARIANISM and the omission of ONION, GARLIC, red lentils, etc. by some sects and especially by priests (*bhakats*) and upper-caste widows. The food habits later broadened to including fish as a part of the diet. As cooking within the Vaishnav movement was shaped by ideas of purity and pollution, raw food was the acceptable food that could be shared by the community across caste, sectarian and religious lines. This gave rise to one of the most famous *prasads* which slowly spread to all sects and festival: the *boot-mah*, a mix of soaked chickpeas, green *moong* dal, coconut pieces and GINGER.

After Assam was colonized by the British in 1826, the far-reaching effects of colonialism did not spare the Oxomiya Hindu culinary practices. As elsewhere in the subcontinent, changes came to the traditional food habits of Assam. WHEAT and wheat products, CHILLIES, TOMATOES, POTATOES and, most importantly, TEA were introduced to the diet through colonial occupation. As the British set up the first tea garden in 1837, the interaction between the British and the Oxomiya Hindu elite influenced the latter's food habits and ways of eating. *Saah* (tea), especially *laal saah* (tea without milk), slowly became the go-to drink of the state. Confectioneries such as cakes and puddings, meat roasts, stews and goulashes got added to the Oxomiya table. As the British brought in other communities such as Bengalis and Marwaris for administrative purposes and trade, an array of deep-fried items, more varieties of spices, richer curries, sweetmeats, and other dishes came into the diet.

While the Oxomiya Hindu table today carries imprints of history of the state, the biggest determinant of the diet has been the rich agro-biodiversity. The cuisine is distinct in its use of a vast range of vegetables, tubers, citrus, leaf greens and fresh herbs. Varieties of lemon and lime (see CITRUS FRUITS), TAMARIND, *thekera* (*Garcinia cowa*) and tomatoes are popular souring agents. *Teeta* is prepared with vegetables like bitter gourd, NEEM leaves (*Melia indica*), cane shoots and dried tender leaves of the jute plant (*sukuta*). Several varieties of local tubers like *kaath aloo* (*Diocorea alata*) and *moa aloo* (*Dioscorea esculende*), and different varieties of gourds like *kumora* (*Benincasa hispida*) and *bhul* (*Lufa cylindica*) are part of the diet. Seasonal leafy greens and tender fiddlehead ferns are used abundantly in the kitchens. Vegetables and greens are cooked by themselves or with fish and meat as an accompaniment to rice. Sublime mashes (*pitika*), light stir-fries, thick and wholesome lentils (*daali*), and sour gravies (*tenga*) are an unmissable part of the cuisine.

The finest Oxomiya Hindu food pivots around the festival of *Maagh Bihu* or *Bhogali Bihu*, a harvest festival celebrated in January. While festivities include laden tables filled with various preparations of fish, meat and vegetables, the finest are the traditional sweetcakes, or *pithes*. The newly harvested varieties of indigenous rice are pounded and turned into delicate and scrumptious sweets by baking, frying and steaming. Traditional *pitha* such as *sunga pitha* (sticky rice, coconut, jaggery and milk stuffed inside bamboo and baked over fire), *tekeli mukhot diya pitha* (rice flour cakes steamed over a *tekeli* (clay pot of boiling water)) and *laru* (sweet balls of coconut, SESAME and pounded rice) adorn Bihu celebrations in homes. Besides these, there is also the religious offering of *prasad* that consists mainly of *boot-mah*, BANANA, coconut, betel nut and leaves, rice, *poka mithoi* (sweet ball prepared with uncooked rice flour and jaggery) and *payaokh* (sweet rice porridge) that are offered in homes and temples during festivals and in day-to-day offerings.

It is important to understand that the Oxomiya Hindu food has soaked in multiple influences but like much of the food in the state, it maintains its distinctive character of a refined, light palate. Unlike most of the food from the Indian subcontinent, it uses spices judiciously, with restraint and without overpowering the produce that the unique climate and geography offer. That, at the end of the day, remains as the lasting impression of the food.

Islam arrived in Assam in the early thirteenth century and is the second largest religion in the state. The Muslim cuisine is a mix of traditional Assamese dishes and styles, and North Indian Muslim cuisine, popularly called 'MUGHAL cuisine', but it is much lighter than the Mughal cuisine in the rest of the country. The cooking medium is often MUSTARD oil and spicing is kept to a minimum. For example, *shami* KEBABS may be made with fresh herbs and lime juice. There are also similarities with Bangladeshi food. Chicken may be cooked with white gourd (*lauki*) and beef may be cooked with pumpkin.

Around 15 per cent of the Assamese population consists of Scheduled Tribes who live in the plains and the hills. There are around 150 tribes, the largest group being the Bodo, who speak Tibeto-Burman languages and live mainly in Upper Assam in the upper reaches of the Brahmaputra Valley. The Bodo, in turn, comprise a large number of separate tribes with different customs. Most are settled farmers, although in the past they practised shifting cultivation.

All the tribes make intensive use of local vegetables such as *sooka tenga* (a sour, leafy vegetable), *outenga* (elephant apple), BAMBOO SHOOTS, *morapaat* (jute leaves), *taso bisong* (YAM leaves) and *ortena mora* (roselle leaves). Local herbs include *mosundari* (heartleaf), *maan dhjoniya* (long coriander) and *bhedai lota* (skunk vine). Pork, duck, pigeon, goose, mutton, fish (including tiny fish that live in rice paddies during the monsoon season), snails and crabs are essential parts of the Bodo diet. Meat and fish are almost always cooked with local vegetables. For example, jute leaves are cooked with fish and pork, while a leafy vegetable is boiled with fish and a few herbs. Snails are cooked with black beans and crabs with roselle leaves.

Food is cooked in little or no mustard oil and is often steamed. Ingredients may be stuffed in a hollow bamboo or wrapped in a banana leaf before steaming or roasting. Smoking is another common method of preparation. Meat, fish and some vegetables are also sundried.

Fermentation as a method of preservation is a distinctive feature of Bodo cuisine. A popular dish is *napham*, a kind of CHUTNEY made by grinding smoked fish, certain leafy vegetables and spices and is aged in a sealed bamboo cylinder. Two famous tribal dishes are silkworm pupae and red ant eggs which are popular during the Bihu festival. Silk weaving is a cottage industry and some households set some larva aside to fry them. Steamed or boiled silkworm pupae known as *leta* are usually eaten as a snack to go with rice beer (see ALCOHOL). Some communities build nests for red ants and harvest the eggs and larvae which can be stir-fried or used to make a chutney. The use of chillies depends on what is being prepared and who is preparing it.

The staple of the tribal diet is rice which grows throughout Assam. A local speciality is the short-grained black rice called *johan*. Rice is boiled, pounded and steamed, and fermented to make beer, which has different names depending on the tribe: *upong, jou bishi, xalpani*, etc. Rice beer, which is usually made at home, plays an important role in the social and ritual life and is also used for its medicinal properties. Each tribe has its own recipe for the starter cake that begins the fermentation process. An example is a *mao* – a ground mixture of rice powder, JACKFRUIT leaves, sugar cane, PINEAPPLE, and local wild plants and herbs. Added to a mixture of rice and water, it ferments for five to six days in the summer. It may be left for several months. It typically has an alcohol content of 18 to 25 per cent.

In the mid-nineteenth century, the British discovered tea growing wild in Upper Assam, where it was consumed as both a beverage and a vegetable by the local tribes. Tea leaves are dried in bamboo tubes and smoked over a fire to make a smokey-tasting drink, while the fermented leaves are made into a salad.

After tea, probably the most famous Assamese product today is the *bhut jolokia*, or ghost pepper, which is famous for its fiery taste and is now available worldwide. In Upper Assam, it is often used in chutneys and pickles and with pork and fermented fish dishes.

Tanushree Bhowmik

- Saikia, Arani. 'Food-Habits in Pre-Colonial Assam'. *International Journal of Humanities and Social Science Invention* 2, no. 6 (2013): 1–5.

AUBERGINE

Aubergine, eggplant or brinjal (*Solanum melongena*, Hindi *baingan*), by any name is one of the most ancient and widely consumed vegetables in India. It is actually a berry, belonging to the genus *Solanum,* which includes TOMATOES, tobacco and POTATOES. The word comes from a bitter chemical called solanine.

The aubergine originated in India as a wild species that had small hard bitter spiny fruit that was cultivated to reduce its bitterness. The Sanskrit names *vartaka* and *vatin-gana* may be of pre-Aryan or Dravidian origin. It reached China in the fifth century CE and later Arab traders took it to Europe. From here it reached the New World as part of the Columbian Exchange.

India is the world's second largest producer after China, with the main producing states being West Bengal, Bihar and Maharashtra. There are dozens of varieties, ranging from small white, yellow and green fruit to large purple fruit weighing as much as a kilogram. Aubergine can be grown in all types of soil, making it suitable for both kitchen gardens and commercial production. An attempt was made to introduce genetically engineered aubergine into India to make it insect resistant but in 2010 the Environment Ministry imposed a moratorium on its use.

Aubergine is an extremely versatile ingredient. It can be grilled, baked, steamed, sautéed, stewed, deep-fried and pickled. When cooked in a liquid, it absorbs fats and sauces. Recipes for aubergine dishes feature in many old cookbooks. In the *Supashastra*, written in the early seventeenth century, they are boiled as a soup; fried with spices; baked with yogurt; steamed, filled with ground spices and simmered in a thick broth;

stuffed with green leaves; grilled, then mixed with yogurt and spices or boiled in milk; stuffed with PANEER and spices; and roasted and served as a salad.

The author of the *Kshemakutuhalam*, a Sanskrit treatise in verse written around 1555, considers aubergines to be the king of vegetables. He writes: 'Fie on the meal that has no aubergine. Fie on the aubergine that has no stalk. Fie on the aubergine that has a stalk but is not cooked in oil and fie upon the aubergine that is cooked in oil without using asafoetida!' Aubergine cooked with ONIONS, GHEE and spices is one of the thirty dishes named by Abu'l-Fazl as served at Emperor Akbar's court.

A famous Punjabi dish is *baingan ka bharta:* aubergine is roasted, skinned, mashed and mixed with onions and spices. In eastern India, the pulp of charred aubergine (*begun pora*) is mixed with onions, CHILLIES and MUSTARD oil. Slices of spiced aubergine deep-fried in mustard oil is a popular Bengali dish. An emblematic Hyderabadi dish is *baghare baigan* – fried aubergine in a sauce made with COCONUT, SESAME seeds, and TAMARIND.

Colleen Sen

- Kṣēmaśarmā. *A Work on Dietetics and Well Being* [Sans. orig. *Kṣēmakūtuhalam*]. *c*. 1555. Edited by Darshan Shankar, D.K. Ved, G.G. Gangadharan, M.A. Lakshmithathacharya and M.A. Alwar, translated by R. Shankar. Bangalore: IIAIM/Foundation for Revitalisation of Local Health Traditions, 2009.

BAEL

FIGURE 4 BAEL. Asit. K. Ghosh/Wikimedia Commons.

Bael, *Aegle marmelos*, also called *bilva*, is a tree belonging to the citrus family which grows wild in much of North India and Southeast Asia. It is sometimes called Bengal or Indian quince but it is not related to the quince. The fruits are a greyish-yellow colour and resemble oranges. Depending on the variety, some have a thin hard shell while others have a thick rind. Inside there are many seeds and the ripe pulp, which is yellow and gummy, has an aromatic, refreshing flavour. The *bael* is a favourite fruit in India although many have said that the taste for *bael* is an acquired one. Thomas Augustus Firminger, writing in the *Manual of Gardening in India* (1863), describes the taste:

> The interior of the bael contains a soft yellow substance of pease pudding-like consistency, intermingled with a limpid kind of slime, a very fragrant scent and a flavour very agreeable to those accustomed to it. The high reputation it bears for its medicinal properties make many partake of it and those who do so become remarkably fond of it.

Bael can be eaten as is or can be made into a jelly, marmalade or a refreshing fruit drink or SHERBET in summer. In Odisha, a drink (*bela pana*) made of mashed BANANA, grated COCONUT, jaggery (see SUGAR) mixed with *bael* juice and sprinkled with CARDAMOM, CLOVE, nutmeg (see NUTMEG AND MACE) and a tiny amount of CAMPHOR, is made for the festive occasion of Pana Sankranti (New Year). It is first offered to the gods and goddesses before being drunk.

As Firminger remarked, *bael* is reputed for its medicinal properties and is used in Ayurvedic medicine (see FOOD AND MEDICINE). George Watt, the botanist, said in his *Dictionary of Economic Products of India* (1890) that 'no drug has been better appreciated by the inhabitants of India than "*bael*"' and that 'the unripe fruit is cut up and sun dried and, in this form, is sold in the bazaars in whole or broken slices'. *Bael* is reputed to be a tonic for the heart and brain and for reducing inflammation. It has anti-fungal properties. It is also traditionally used to cure constipation, diarrhoea, diabetes and other conditions. The leaves, bark and seeds also have medicinal properties.

Hindus hold the *bael* tree sacred to Shiva. The leaf is used in the worship of Shiva as the three prongs are believed to symbolize Shiva's trident and is also associated with the three functions of creation, preservation and destruction. It is sacrilegious to cut down a *bael* tree, but to die under one assures immediate salvation.

Confusingly, *bael* is sometimes called WOODAPPLE, although the two fruits are different from each other.

Helen Saberi

- Dasgupta, Kaushika. 'Mangoes, Peaches, Watermelons Make the Indian Summer Bearable: A Look at How They Came to Be So Popular'. *Indian Express*, 11 June 2017.
- Davidson, Alan. *The Oxford Companion to Food*. 2nd edition. ed. Tom Jaine. Oxford: OUP, 2006.

BAMBOO SHOOTS

Bamboo shoots are the edible shoots of several varieties of bamboo, a woody perennial grass belonging to the Bambusaceae family, that grow in tropical and subtropical regions. Of the 125 species found in India, thirty have commercial value. Around two-thirds are grown in the northeastern states where high rainfall and optimum temperature favour their growth. Other bamboo-growing states include Kerala, Jharkhand, Chhattisgarh, Goa and Orissa. In the past, bamboo was cultivated in peoples' gardens or harvested wild in forests but recently plantations have been developed.

In addition to its use as a fuel and for making kitchen equipment and building material, freshly sprouting shoots (Hindi *baans ki kali*) are an important ingredient in the food of the Northeast and other regions. The young shoots must be harvested within a two-week period, otherwise they will harden and become inedible. They need to be properly processed before use as freshly harvested shoots have high amount of toxin. Bamboo shoots are rich in vitamins, cellulose and amino acids and are also a good source of fibre, carbohydrates, vegetable fat and protein. In the Northeast, bamboo species are used for medicinal purposes, such as controlling internal bleeding. In many parts of the country, nursing mothers consume bamboo soup to enhance milk production.

Bamboo shoots are prepared both fresh and fermented. In Manipur, they are used to make CHUTNEYS or cooked as a vegetable with meat and FISH. In Nagaland, young bamboo shoots are sliced and then fermented in a bamboo basket lined with BANANA leaves. The juice drips out through a hole in the bottom. The shoots, which can be stored or dried in the sun, are used in many ways, especially for cooking pork and fish dishes. Other Naga dishes include *itsuk*, a stew of river fish, fresh bamboo shoots, green CHILLIES and dried local herbs; *ponsen,* a chutney made of fermented bamboo shoots and fish roasted in a bamboo receptacle; and pork, beef or chicken boiled with fresh or dried bamboo shoots. In Arunachal Pradesh, a pickle called *luktar* is made from dried pork and bamboo shoots. *Mesu,* a fermented bamboo shoot pickle, is popular in Sikkim and Darjeeling. A dish of boiled bamboo shoots and ground chillies called *rotauia* is a popular accompaniment to a meal in Mizoram.

Bamboo shoots also play a role in the cuisine of West India. In the early seventeenth-century cookbook *Supashastra*, written in Kannada, the shoots are cut into chunks or rounds and sautéed with spices; slightly fermented and cooked in a liquid, such as BUTTERMILK; mixed with GINGER, ONION and grated COCONUT to form a paste, wrapped in betel leaf cups (see PAAN) and steamed; and ground with ginger, onion and CURRY LEAVES, steamed, then mixed with RICE, *urad* dal (see PULSES) and coconut, and sautéed.

KODAVAS have a special monsoon cuisine that includes fiddlehead ferns, MUSHROOMS and different varieties of tender bamboo shoots. Bamboo shoots are also eaten in Goa during the monsoon season. In Western Odisha and Jharkhand, they are used in traditional CURRIES, often prepared with MUSTARD oil. A dish called bamboo rice was once a famine food in Kodava. Bamboo plant seeds that look like small grains of paddy are husked and then cooked like rice or ground into a BREAD.

Colleen Sen

- Hauzel, Hoihnu. *The Essential North-East Cookbook*. New Delhi: Penguin Books, 2003.
- Nongdam, P. and Leimapokpam Tikendra. 'The Nutritional Facts of Bamboo Shoots and Their Usage as Important Traditional Foods of Northeast India'. *International Scholarly Research Notices*, (2014): 679073. doi:10.1155/2014/679073.

BANANA

The origins and history of the banana (*Musa sapientum*, now *Musa x paradisiaca*; Hindi *kela*) are complex and problematic. Bananas are native to humid tropics and subtropical areas in Southeast Asia, the East Indies, the tropical Pacific and Australia. They appear to have first been domesticated in two areas, New Guinea and the Malay Peninsula, and were likely grown and consumed in the Indus Valley by the third millennium BCE. Early visitors to India, from Alexander the Great onward, noticed the abundance of varieties. Bananas are frequently mentioned in the Tamil Sangam literature (300 BCE–300 CE).

Today, India is by far the world's largest producer of bananas. Although most are used for domestic consumption, exports are increasing. The largest producing states (in order of production) are Andhra Pradesh, Gujarat, Maharashtra, Tamil Nadu, Uttar Pradesh, Karnataka, Madhya Pradesh, Bihar, Kerala, West Bengal and Assam. More than 300 varieties have been identified worldwide, fifteen to twenty of which are grown in India. Around a quarter are of the Cavendish subgroup, which have high yields and are less susceptible to environmental damage.

In India, many people, especially in villages, grow banana plants in their gardens. As a Bengali proverb says, 'If you have banana plants in your yard, you will never go hungry.' Bananas are an important source of nutrition since they are rich in carbohydrates, fibre, potassium, vitamin B6 and vitamin C. In traditional medicine, they are used to treat gastric problems.

Although bananas are often divided into two categories – those used for cooking, popularly known as plantains, and sweeter varieties used for dessert – many varieties are used for both. Plantain is used in many regions to make CURRY, with or without meat and seafood. Bananas are especially popular in southern and eastern India. In Kerala, *APPAMS* can be made with ripe bananas, RICE flour and jaggery. Banana *sheera* (also called banana HALWA) is a sweet pudding of ripe bananas and semolina prepared as a *prasadam* during Ganesh Puja and on other auspicious occasions. Bananas dipped in a sweet batter and deep-fried make a snack called *pazham pori*. Thin slices are deep-fried to make crispy chips. Fried bread made with mashed banana, flour and SUGAR is a speciality of MANGALURU. Chopped and sautéed banana leaves can be used in a *poriyal* (a stir-fried vegetable dish). Finely chopped banana stems are sautéed to prepare *kootu*, a popular South Indian side dish. IDLIS are steamed in banana leaves, especially in south Karnataka. Juice from the banana stem is a treatment for diabetes and other ailments.

In Bengal, plantains are ground and mixed with spices to prepare a *kola* kofta curry. *Mochar ghonto* is a dry curry recipe based on chopped banana flowers. Overripe bananas are mixed with COCONUT, white flour and sugar to make *kolar bola*, a popular Bengali snack.

Banana leaves are traditionally used as plates, especially in the South. They are waterproof and puncture-proof and large enough to accommodate many courses. The tip of the leaf should always be placed on the left. Often, water is sprinkled on the leaves before use. The leaves are also easily disposable. The leaf is believed to impart a fragrance to the meal and improve the taste. Banana leaves are also used to store fruits and vegetables to preserve freshness. Banana fibre is used to make plates, bowls and fabric.

Colleen Sen

- Krishi Jagran. 'What Are the Important Varieties of Banana in India'. 1 December 2019. Available online: https://krishijagran.com/agripedia/what-are-the-important-banana-varieties-in-india/ (accessed 12 April 2022).

BARFI

Barfi (also spelled *burfi*, from the Persian/Urdu word for snow) is a sweet with a fudge-like consistency popular in North India. Typically, it is made from granulated SUGAR and *KHOYA* which are cooked together and, when cooled and thickened, spread on a greased plate. The mixture is then cut into diamonds, squares or circles. Mrs Balbir SINGH in her *Indian Cookery* (1961) recommends a sugar to *khoya* ratio of one to four.

MELON seeds, grated COCONUT, grated CARROT, chocolate and NUTS can be added; flavourings may include SAFFRON, rosewater, *kewra* water (see FLOWER WATERS), orange, vanilla and CARDAMOM powder. It is often decorated with *VARK* – thinly pounded gold or silver leaf – especially when distributed at weddings and festivals such as Diwali. *Peda*, a round flattish sweet flavoured with chopped nuts and cardamom, is a variety of barfi associated with VARANASI and Mathura.

Colleen Sen

- Singh, Mrs Balbir. *Indian Cookery*. London: Mills & Boon Ltd, 1961.

BARLEY

Barley (*Hordeum vulgare*, Hindi *jau*) is probably the world's oldest cultivated cereal and for a long time was the most important food grain in the ancient world. It originated as a grass in southwestern Asia and still grows wild in North Africa, Asia Minor and Afghanistan. Its domestication is closely linked with that of WHEAT, several legumes (see PULSES), sheep, goats, pigs and cattle. Remains of barley grains have been found in the Indus Valley dating back to the sixth and fifth centuries BCE.

Barley thrives in marginal, saline or alkaline soils and in arid regions. In India, barley is a winter crop that grows mainly in the Indo-Gangetic plain. The leading producing states are Rajasthan, Uttar Pradesh, Bihar, Madhya Pradesh and Punjab. Production is small compared to other grains. India also imports barley, mainly for the production of malt.

Barley was the main staple of the Vedic Indians, who did not have wheat, and is mentioned many times in the Vedas and other texts. It was ground into flour to make BREAD, and parched and mixed with a liquid to make a gruel. By the twelfth century CE, it had largely been replaced by wheat and RICE.

Today it is enjoying something of a revival because of its healthy properties, including high fibre content and low glycaemic index. It is used as a substitute for rice in KHICHRI, IDLIS and other dishes.

Colleen Sen

BASIL

Basil (Hindi *tulsi*) is an aromatic herb in the genus *Ocimum* of which there are several species and numerous varieties. The chief kinds of basil cultivated in India are holy basil (*O. tenuiflorum*, previously *O. sanctum*), also known as Vishnu *tulsi*; sweet basil

(*O. basilicum*) known as *biswa tulsi* (which is native to North-West India); and camphor basil (*O. kilimandscharicum*) known as *kapoor tulsi*. The Sanskrit name for holy basil is *thulasi*.

Although holy basil is grown in pots in Indian homes, as a herb it is rarely used in cooking because of its deep and sacred association with the supreme god of creation Vishnu. It is used in religious ceremonies and rituals. This religious association dates back to the Vedic period and there is widespread belief that if planted around homes and temples, it ensures happiness.

Basil leaves are sometimes made into an infusion with shredded GINGER and HONEY, called *tulsi ki* chai, which is served during the winter. Camphor (*kapoor*) basil, which is grown extensively in the lower hills of the eastern Himalayas, is called the 'secret herb' and is used by the rural and hill tribes to flavour stews made with legumes (see PULSES). It is also a popular herb in the regional cuisines of Bihar and West Bengal being used in RICE, dals and vegetables.

Sweet basil seeds, also called *tukmuria* or *sabja* seeds, resemble SESAME seeds but are black. They have a mild floral flavour and when soaked in water or milk, they swell up and become transparent and jelly-like. They are considered to have cooling properties and are often added to SHERBET drinks and *FALOODA*.

Helen Saberi

- Davidson, Alan. *The Oxford Companion to Food*. 2nd edition ed. Tom Jaine. Oxford: OUP, 2006.
- Sahni, Julie. *Classic Indian Vegetarian Cookery*. London: Grub Street, 1999.

BENE ISRAELIS

Once known as Shanivar Telis (a combination of two terms connoting the day of Sabbath and the original occupation of oil-pressing of this group), the Bene Israelis have lived in India for centuries, having fled West Asia to escape persecution. They landed in Naigaon, near Alibaug on the Konkan coast, and made it their home, merging seamlessly into the local culture. Of some 67,000 Bene Israelis at the turn of the twenty-first century, fewer than 5,000 remain in India today, the majority having immigrated to Israel.

The Bene Israelis rose to prominence in the British colonial era and made significant contributions to the Indian film industry and literature. Most families still observe Sabbath and eat only kosher food which means that dairy and meat are never cooked together. Souring agents include vinegar or lime juice but not yogurt. Pork, scaly fish and crustaceans are not eaten either.

On Rosh Hashanah, the Jewish New Year, the community offers prayers by the sea and celebrate by feasting on HALWA, a sort of thick custard made from WHEAT gluten (known as *gavhacha cheek* in Marathi). The wheat needs to soak for days in advance before it can be ground and the milk extracted. This is then mixed with COCONUT milk, sweetened with SUGAR and CARDAMOM and cooked until it thickens. After setting it is cut into diamonds. This is a dying tradition as Bene Israelis are slowly moving away from the cumbersome process of making the wheat gluten and are switching to the instant agar-agar or corn starch to make the halwa.

Purim, a celebration to mark the saving of Jews from persecution, is celebrated with great gusto. On this day, both sour and sweet dishes are made – sour dishes signify the unpleasant memories of the threat to their lives and the sweet ones celebrate victory. A fast is observed to commemorate the destruction of the Holy Temple in Jerusalem. It is broken by eating a few raw *birde* (field beans) and ends with a feast of *birde* (field beans cooked with coconut; this is also why this day is known as *Birdyaancha Roja*) and puris (deep-fried unleavened BREADS).

Saee Koranne-Khandekar

BENGALURU

India's fourth largest city and capital of the state of Karnataka, Bengaluru is perched on the Deccan Plateau of peninsular India. Widely referred to as the Silicon Valley of India since the 1990s, the archaeology of this continuously expanding city stretches back 6,000 years to Stone Age settlements. Roman coinage discovered in the region indicates an ancient ocean-based trade.

A ninth century CE inscription refers to 'Bengaluru', then an agglomeration of villages. Over the centuries, the region was ruled by powerful empires such as the Gangas, Cholas and Hoysalas; its unique geography created a confluence of dynasties and cultures that anticipated its later cosmopolitanism.

The founding of the city of Bengaluru in 1537 CE is ascribed to Kempegowda the Elder, a feudatory chieftain of the Vijayanagar Empire. During the seventeenth century, Bengaluru was conquered and ruled by the Marathas under the Sultanate of Bijapur and sold by the invading MUGHALS to Chikkadevaraya Wodeyar of Mysore. Later, it passed into the hands of the East India Company following the British victory over Tipu Sultan in 1799. Settlement, conquest, continuous migrations and exchange continued to shape its growth, creating a complex mosaic of sub-cultures reflected in the diverse and vibrant food of the city.

Lying at an elevation of 920 metres, until recent times, the city relied on an ancient system of interlinked tanks that supplied water to its agriculturally rich surroundings. The outlying farmlands of the modern city continue to grow RICE, CORN, finger MILLET, groundnuts, sugarcane, tropical fruits and a wide variety of heirloom and imported vegetables. Karnataka has a long tradition of sheep and goat rearing; fresh FISH and seafood now make their way into the city's markets from the state's 320-kilometre coastline running along the Arabian Sea.

Many of the oldest eateries, which were started by migrants who brought their rural food traditions with them, are clustered in the old city. They serve a limited number of emblematic dishes that embody changes in demographics, economics and politics over the centuries.

Udupi Sri Krishna Bhavan, established originally in 1902, serves its famous masala *dose* (fermented rice crêpes with POTATOES; see DOSA) and *sagu dose* (rice crêpes with a COCONUT-based CURRY of mixed vegetables and spices). Vidyarthi Bhavan, begun as a small canteen catering to students in 1943, has customers queuing for its masala *dose*, *khara bhat* (semolina fried in GHEE, cooked with vegetables and spices, served with coconut CHUTNEY) and the popular *kesari bhat* (semolina cooked in ghee with SUGAR, cashew nuts, CLOVES and PINEAPPLE chunks). *Chow-chow bhat* is a unique dish of semolina combining both sweet and savoury flavours. *Khāli dose* (a very light, fluffy, open-faced rice crêpe) with *alugaddé sagu* (potatoes cooked with TOMATOES, ONIONS, spices) is a speciality of Chikkanna Tiffin Room.

Established in the 1930s, Sri Rama Vilas Sweets Gundappa Hotel is known for *dum root* or *kashi* halwa (ash pumpkin, semolina and sugar cooked in ghee with edible CAMPHOR) and *badam* milk (soaked almonds ground and blended with sugar, milk and CARDAMOM). Iyengar bakeries specializing in vegetarian snacks are an institution. Srinivasa Brahmin's Bakery has several unique snacks which, according to the current owner, H.R. Ramaprasad, were created in their kitchens. Congress *khara* bun (a bun spread with butter, filled with a mixture of spiced peanuts, onions, green CHILLIES and CURRY LEAVES), *nippat* (deep-fried flat discs of rice flour, peanuts and spices), *khara* biscuits (eggless biscuits baked with green chillies, curry leaves and spices) and eggless cakes are typical snacks.

An unusual legacy of military hotels survives from the period when Bengaluru was an important military hub for the training and recruitment of soldiers: their evolution is attributed to the demand created for meat-based dishes by soldiers. Typically, these tiny eateries serve a selection of village-style dishes such as *dose* and *kāal* soup (goat or lamb trotter soup); *rāgi muddé* (large, densely textured cooked balls of finger MILLET dough) and mutton CURRY; *thalé māmsa* (goat's head curry); and *bhéja* fry (spiced goat's brain). The Shivaji Military Hotel established in 1908 is well known for its mutton 'Donne biryani', named after the areca nut palm leaf cups in which it is served.

The vibrant Muslim food of Bengaluru showcased at the Ramadan street food markets along Mosque Road and Madhavaraya Mudaliar Road bring together the multiple influences of the Deccan Sultanates, Mughals and Muslim Mysore that fed the tradition over centuries, often displaying the distinctive flavourings of the South. Chichaba's Taj Hotel, established in 1935, serves *gosht* korma (mutton braised with coconut and spices) and *kut* kofta *kulthi salan* (mutton meatballs and hard-boiled eggs in a horse gram sauce).

The city under British rule was divided into the *pété* (native city) governed by the Wodeyars of Mysore and the separately administered military cantonment, established in 1807 for the largely Christian British and ANGLO-INDIAN populations, which had a lasting influence on its cultural and culinary landscape. The Albert Bakery founded in 1902 by Muhammad Yacoob supplied buns and bread to the British. It now offers an eclectic mix of mutton brain puffs during Ramadan, *khova* naan (naan filled with reduced, sweetened milk solids, see *KHOYA*), marzipan eggs at Easter, chocolate croissants and pizzas. The Excelsior Bakery continues a tradition of ribbon cakes and festive snacks such as *kal-kals* (sweetened deep-fried rolls of dough) and rose cookies (rosette-shaped deep-fried batter of eggs, sugar, coconut milk and flour) that originated with the Christian and Anglo-Indian communities. The hybrid menu of Koshy's restaurant, established in 1940, includes roast chicken as well as stew with *APPAMS* (lacy, fermented rice crêpes) and fish BIRYANI, reflecting the owner's Kerala heritage.

Andhra cuisine established a strong presence by initially catering to students who came to study at Bengaluru's numerous educational institutions: restaurants like Nagarjuna offer traditional *gongura* mutton (mutton in roselle leaves) and *natu kodi vepudu* (country chicken fry). Mangalurean (see MANGALURU) restaurants such as Fishland began by providing fresh seafood – *kane* masala fry (spiced ladyfish) and *neer dose* (unfermented rice *dose*) with *bāngdé pulimunchi* (hot, sour curried mackerel) – to the many migrants from coastal Karnataka.

The political and administrative moves that merged parts of erstwhile Hyderabad, Madras and Bombay regions with Karnataka in 1956 brought North Karnataka's characteristic dishes such as *jolada* roti (unleavened sorghum flatbreads) eaten with *badenékai yennegai* (small AUBERGINES stuffed with peanuts, coconut and a spice paste, and cooked until tender) to the city.

STREET FOODS with a distinctively rural flavour are prominent at VV Puram *thindi beedi* (food street). Snacks range from Rajasthani chaats to *avarekalu vadé* (deep-fried hyacinth bean patties, see VADA). The annual *kadalakai parishe* (groundnut festival) offers different dishes made from groundnuts and the *avarekalu mela* celebrates the hyacinth bean through dishes such as *avarekai dose* and *hithkabele saru* (spicy curry of skinned beans).

United Breweries, founded in 1915, supplied beer to British troops. It is currently the largest beer manufacturer in the country. Bengaluru's first pub Ramada opened in 1986, offering draught beer and affordable food to young professionals; a trend which grew until it earned Bengaluru the title of 'Pub City'. Grover Zampa, India's oldest winery, was established in Doddaballapura in 1988 producing wines in collaboration with French oenologist, Michael Rolland.

The economic liberalization of the 1990s and the subsequent information technology boom brought young professionals from every part of India and expatriate communities from across the globe. International cuisines such as Japanese, Korean, Italian, Mexican, Chinese and Thai and regional Indian cuisines became fashionable in high-end five-star hotels and celebrity chef-driven stand-alone restaurants as well as in the food courts of newly opened malls and shopping centres. The definition of Bengaluru's food, however, remains rooted in its rural beginnings.

Kaveri Ponnapa

- Hasan, M. Fazlul. *Bangalore through the Centuries*. Bangalore: Historical Publications, 1970.
- Iyer, Meera. *Discovering Bengaluru*. Bengaluru: INTACH Bengaluru Chapter, 2019.
- Karanth, G.K. '"Foodscapes" in Bengaluru – Changing Patterns of Family Eating Out and Waste Generation'. *International Development Policy/Revue Internationale de Politique de Développement* 8, no. 2 (2017). Available online: https://doi.org/10.4000/poldev.2480 (accessed 14 April 2022).
- Nagendra, Harini. *Nature in the City*. New Delhi: OUP, 2019.
- Ponnapa, Kaveri. 'Beyond Bangalore'. *The Taj Magazine* 40, no. 1, 2012: 104–25.

BER

Ber (*Ziziphus mauritiana*) is a member of the jujube family and is also known as the Indian jujube, Indian plum and Indian cherry. *Ber* is an ancient fruit of India. Carbonized remains, dating back to *c.* 1600 BCE, were found in Navdatoli, a Chalcolithic-era settlement which today is a village in Madhya Pradesh. Sanskrit literature describes several varieties of *ber* fruit, differing in size and ranging from the large *badara* or *vadari*, medium-sized *kuvale* or *kharkhandu*, the *sauvira* variety, and a wild orange-coloured variety. In *c.* 1100 CE, Dalhana in Kashmir tells of a '*ber* as big as a fist, and very sweet', although some say that he could have been talking about an APPLE. In the early 1900s, *ber* was known as the 'poor man's apple'. According to Dr RIDDELL (1871), *ber* trees were often cultivated around the tombs of Muslims and the cocoon of the wild silkworm could often be found attached to the tree.

In the 1980s, many *ber* orchards were destroyed to make way for urban development but it can still be found growing wild in its native regions. Today, *ber* is mainly grown commercially in India and there are at least six varieties and numerous cultivars. *Ber* fruits grow on small bushy trees that can grow twelve metres high. The fruits are small, round to oblong shaped, with a thin glossy skin. Unripe fruits are light green or yellow which ripen to an orange-red colour. They are typically eaten raw or slightly under ripe, when the white flesh is crisp and astringent, often sprinkled with a little SALT; or eaten ripe when the flesh is more spongy with a mealy texture and a slight floral flavour. The fruits contain a rough, inedible central stone. Ripe *ber* fruits are also sun-dried like raisins. They can be boiled with RICE, made into PICKLES, CHUTNEYS and *murabba* (preserve). They are used to make jellies or can be crushed in water to make a cooling drink. They were also fermented to make ALCOHOL.

Ber fruit is important in Indian mythology. It is said that the *ber* tree is 'the tree that removes sorrow' and is sacred to Shiva. *Ber* fruit is used in Ayurvedic medicine (see FOOD AND MEDICINE) and is classified as a cooling fruit. It is a common home remedy used to treat indigestion, burning sensations, fevers and thirst, as well as lung and circulatory problems. It is also said that ailments can be healed by taking a bath under the *ber* trees in the lakes of the holy city of Amritsar.

Helen Saberi

- Achaya, K.T. *A Historical Dictionary of Indian Food*. Delhi: OUP, 1998.
- Riddell, Dr R. *Indian Domestic Economy and Receipt Book*. 7th edition, revised. Calcutta: Thacker, Spink and Co., 1871.
- Speciality Produce. 'Ber (Indian Jujube)'. *n.d.* Available online: https://specialtyproduce.com/produce/Ber_Indian_Jujube_11258.php (accessed 12 April 2022).

BERRIES

Strawberries, *Fragaria indica* now *Duchesnea indica*, known as the Indian strawberry, and *Fragaria vesca*, known as the alpine or woodland strawberry, grow wild in the Himalayas in India.

Wild strawberries are little cultivated commercially because their fruits are small and have a low yield. Strawberries were not mentioned in the *Ain-i-Akbari*, which documented in detail the fruits cultivated during the reign of Akbar (1556–1605), and were largely ignored by Indian population until the British came to India and began to cultivate them in their gardens. Different varieties were introduced and since then local farmers have developed their own varieties.

With cultivation the strawberry plant spread rapidly to hill stations where the climate and conditions were similar to those of Europe. Many British men and women escaped the heat of the plains up to the cooler hill stations, such as summer capital of the Bombay Presidency, Mahabaleshwar, and strawberry teas were held during the season at the club on Fridays.

Later it was found the strawberry could also be successfully cultivated on the plains and could even withstand the hot weather. By the late seventeenth century, strawberries were being grown in Punjab (today modern Pakistan) and Bihar. Dr R. RIDDELL in *Indian Domestic Economy and Receipt Book* (1871) gives extensive details on how to cultivate strawberries and gives a recipe for strawberry ice-cream. Colonel Kenney-Herbert (see WYVERN) was also fond of strawberries and gives two recipes in his book *Culinary Jottings* (1885) – a strawberry mould and an iced pudding with strawberries.

Today cultivated strawberries are grown in Kashmir, the Doon Valley, Himachal Pradesh, Uttar Pradesh, West Bengal, Delhi, Haryana, Punjab, Mizoram, Meghalaya and Rajasthan, and Mahabaleshwar in Maharashtra is still as famous for its strawberries as it was under the British Raj. Strawberries, as well as raspberries, mulberries and gooseberries, are produced on a large scale. The Mahabaleshwar strawberry obtained a GEOGRAPHICAL INDICATION (GI) tag in 2010. They are exported frozen to countries such as France, Belgium, Malaysia and the Middle East.

Strawberries are used to make various food products such as preserves, jams, fruit drinks, ice-cream, milkshakes and strawberry wine or often are just eaten on their own or with fresh cream.

Raspberries. Wild raspberries grow in North India and the Himalayas. They are more likely to be yellow and are known as the yellow Himalayan raspberry (*Rubus ellipticus*). They are similar in flavour to the European raspberry (*R. idaeus*) and were prized by both Indians and the British as one of the finest wild fruits of India. They were collected during May and June and could be found for sale at the bazaars of most hill stations along the Himalayas. In 1836 Dr Robert Wight, writing to the Madras Agricultural and Horticultural Society, praised them as 'not inferior in size or juiciness, and but little in sweetness and flavour to the English raspberries'. They were regularly exhibited at the Horticultural Society's shows at Shimla. They were made into jams and preserves.

Another wild raspberry found in India is the red/black Mysore (or Hill) raspberry (*R. niveus*), the small fruits of which are black when ripe and covered with a fine white bloom and are often mistaken for blackberries. Their taste is more sour than sweet.

Blackberries (*R. fruticosus*), according to ACHAYA (1998), are found in the hills of South India and in the Himalayas at heights between 1,000 and 3,500 metres. **Blueberry** farming is still very limited but there is an enormous future potential for commercial farming because of blueberries' many health benefits. Blueberries like cold climates and can be found in Jammu and Kashmir, Uttar Pradesh and Himachal Pradesh, especially around Shimla.

Helen Saberi

• Burton, David. *The Raj at Table*. London: Faber and Faber, 1991.

BIHAR

FIGURE 5 BIHAR. Bihari *thali*. Wikimedia Commons: Peeyush 964.

Bihar, a state in East India, shares a border with Uttar Pradesh to its west, Nepal to the north, the northern part of West Bengal to the east and Jharkhand to the south. Bihar is on a plain which is divided by the river Ganga (Ganges), which flows from west to east. Magadh, Mithila and Bhojpur are three important ancient cultural regions in Bihar. Magadh is important in Indian history for the birth of India's first major empire, the Maurya Empire, which unified large parts of South Asia under a central rule, and for the birth of two major religions: Buddhism and Jainism.

The Ganga divides Bihar into northern and southern regions and is the major source of water for agriculture in North Bihar. North Bihar is strategically situated between the Ganga and the foothills of the Himalayas, so it is blessed with topsoil from the Himalayas and from the river flooding. The southern region slopes towards the river so that any water accumulated here automatically drains into the river. This made it difficult to grow RICE in southern Bihar, as rice grows best in waterlogged soil; however, the rulers of ancient Bihar developed a system to retain water where it was needed. Iron from Jharkhand was used to produce advanced agricultural tools which ensured better yields. Under the Maurya Empire, there were fewer borders and conflicts, thus increasing the area on which agricultural could be practised and crops grown.

Rice is one of the most important crops of Bihar, if not the most important, and is cultivated in all the districts of Bihar. The most famous rice variety is Patna rice, a long-grained, aromatic rice considered by many to be the world's best rice. Its elongated kernel (longer than 6 mm) keeps its shape well after being cooked and has a mild earthy aroma. Biharis are extremely particular about their rice which is the essence and foundation of their cuisine and understand which rice from their state will suit which dish.

Apart from rice, WHEAT and other grains are also a part of Bihari cuisine in the form of various flatbreads (rotis, see BREADS). Wheat is eaten in the form of *phulka* (a thin roti), parathas stuffed with *sattu* (see below); and puris (flatbreads stuffed with *sattu* and deep-fried in oil). A delicious snack (also eaten as a dessert) made with wheat is the *khaja*, which is said to be 2,000 years old. The crispy dessert is made from wheat flour and SUGAR dough with a *mawa* (dried whole milk) stuffing and deep-fried in oil until crisp. After being dunked into a sugar syrup known as *paga*, it is ready to eat. Another dry sweet made with wheat flour is the *thekua* which is a traditional deep-fried snack made with wheat flour, jaggery and GHEE. It is offered to God during the *Chhath puja,* an ancient festival dedicated to the sun God and one of Biharis' biggest festivals.

Chickpeas are an essential ingredient of Bihari cuisine. The most popular chickpea (*chana*) by-product is *sattu* which is also known as the poor man's protein. The word *sattu* is derived from the Sanskrit word *saktu,* meaning the coarse flour obtained by grinding parched BARLEY or parched rice. *Sattu* now refers to the coarse flour of any parched grain, including PULSES. To make *sattu*, chickpeas are soaked in water, sun-dried, roasted in an iron pan filled with hot sand and ground in a stone mill to a fine flour. What was once looked upon as a poor man's food is now known as a global superfood.

One of the earliest meals of primitive humans, *sattu* is also served in Bihar and Jharkhand as a drink in summers as it has an immediate cooling effect on the body. Traditionally, *sattu* was (and still is) a daily meal for field workers who carry it to the fields and knead it with water and CHILLI to make a dough. This energizes them for the hard work and labour that they have to put in through the day. *Sattu* is the main ingredient in the famous Bihari dish, *litti. Litti* is a dough ball made with *atta* (wheat flour), stuffed with *sattu* and different spices with a dash of MUSTARD oil-based PICKLE and then cooked on cow dung cakes or coal. Once cooked, it is tossed in ghee. The best flavour comes from cooking over a slow fire of cow dung cakes; this cooks the *littis* evenly while the cow dung smoke gives *litti* its signature flavour. *Littis* are pocket-friendly and filling. They are served with *chokha* (see below) or a meat CURRY. *Litti* with mutton curry is a signature Bihari dish served at weddings.

Another popular chickpea by-product is *besan,* a flour which is used extensively in Bihari cuisine in dishes such as *ramsal*, noodles made with *besan* cooked in a TOMATO and mustard gravy, and *kadhi buri,* which consists of *besan* dumplings in a gravy of TURMERIC and curd. Another popular chickpea dish is the *ghugni,* a spicy and tangy snack or breakfast dish made with boiled chickpeas, ONION and spices along with *chuda* (flattened rice). In winter, it is made with *matar* (fresh green peas). Chickpea leaves are also eaten in Bihar as a PICKLE or sautéed as a vegetable. Pickles are an essential component of a Bihari meal and are made with chillies (*mirchi ka achaar*), MANGOES (*aam ka achaar*), lemon (*nimbu ka achaar*) and mustard oil.

Beaten rice flakes are eaten for breakfast, very often mixed with curd and sugar, a dish known as *dahi shakkar chuda*. For an evening snack, the same beaten rice flakes are mixed with savoury ingredients. *Chuda* are flattened rice flakes made after parboiling the paddy grains of the fresh crop and pounding them. The flakes are then dried. Another iconic Bihari dish is dal *bhaat chokha* and a close second is the *litti chokha*. In the former meal, the dal (lentils) is often replaced with *maad*, which is the starchy water drained off in the initial stages of cooking rice.

Sometimes, just a simple meal of *maad* and rice is relished, even without the *chokha*, with a piece of a pickle. *Nimki*, a sour lemon pickle, is a big favourite. Biharis are extremely fond of KHICHRI, a mildly spiced porridge of rice and lentils with ghee (Indian clarified butter), PAPAD, curd and *chokha* – a mash of vegetables roasted on coals and mixed with mustard oil, onion, CORIANDER, green chilli and SALT. The most popular *chokhas* are *aloo ka chokha* (with POTATOES) and *baingan chokha* (with AUBERGINES). Sometimes, Biharis also enjoy *janera ki khichadi* which substitutes corn for the rice.

Bihar is a very large producer of vegetables such as aubergine, YAM, cauliflower, OKRA and more. A large proportion of the population, especially in towns like Gaya, is vegetarian due to Buddhist influence. Another factor contributing to the widespread consumption of vegetables is that Bihar is one of the poorest states of India so expensive items like meat and poultry are eaten only on special occasions. Most Bihari meals feature a few vegetable-based dishes which are collectively known as *tarkari*. One dish in the *tarkari* can be a *chokha*.

One of the most important influences on Bihari cuisine has been that of the Muslims. Since the sixteenth century, Bihar was under the control of various Islamic rulers from Sher Shah Suri (1486–1545) and Akbar and to the Nawabs of Bengal, Bihar and Orissa (early seventeenth to late nineteenth century). You can see the Muslim influence in the use of garam masala (see SPICE BOX) in many Bihari recipes. The Bihari KEBAB, also known as *taas* kebab, is made by marinating thin slices of goat meat in spices and raw PAPAYA (used as a tenderizer) and then cooking them on an open fire. A sweet dish, similar to FIRNI (Indian rice pudding), is *makhuti* or dal *phirni* (lentil and rice pudding). It is made with rice and *moong* dal (split green gram) and is served at every Muslim wedding in Bihar.

Another important influence has been the cuisine of Bengal. Like Bengalis, Biharis cook vegetables in a thick gravy made with *poshto* (white POPPY SEEDS). *Panch phoron*, the iconic Bengali five spice mix and one of the trademarks of Bengali cuisine, is regularly used in Bihari cuisine (see SPICE BOX).

While most people believe all Brahmins are vegetarian, many Brahmin communities in India are actually non-vegetarian. One such community are the Maithil Brahmins of Bihar who follow the goddess Shakti. She demands the sacrifice of a goat, so they consume mutton and FISH dishes. A famous dish of the Maithil Brahmins is *chokha* made with crab meat.

Bihar is extremely fertile which is why it also grows a great variety of fruits. Mangoes are the most popular fruit in summer. Biharis make a drink called *aam panna* with them, a cooling drink made with raw mangoes, chillies, salt and CUMIN that provides relief from the blazing heat. Bihar also grows BANANAS, LYCHEES and PINEAPPLES. Bananas, COCONUT and refined flour are used to make a signature Bihari sweet called the *pua*.

Sugarcane is one of Bihar's main and most ancient crops which is why Bihar boasts of many sweet dishes. *Tilkut* is a flaky toffee made of pounded *til* (SESAME seeds) and jaggery or sugar. The best *tilkut* is said to be from Gaya. *Lai ka* LADDU is made from ground *ramdana* (AMARANTH seeds). *Anarsa* is a deep-fried sweet biscuit made from reduced milk (*KHOYA*), sesame seeds and rice flour. *Balushahi,* one of the most popular sweets, resembles a glazed doughnut but the texture is different. It is made with refined flour, clarified butter, sugar and, sometimes, CARDAMOM. One of the most unique sweets of Bihar is the *parwal ki mithai* which is made with *parwal* (pointed GOURD). The scooped-out gourd is filled with sweetened *khoya* and then cooked. Most of these sweets are not made at home but are bought from *mithaiwalas* (confectioners). At home, Biharis make less complicated sweets like KHEER (rice pudding) which is made with rice or *makhana* (fox nuts).

Between 1834 and 1917, many Biharis emigrated to the Caribbean to work on the sugar plantations, and to this day the cuisines of Trinidad and Tobago, Guyana and other countries reflect this legacy (see DIASPORA).

Megha Kohli

- Singh, Shakesh. *Bhansaghar: Home Grown Flavours from the Kitchens of Bihar.* Akkalkot, Maharashtra: Vishwa Foundation, 2017.

BIKANERI BHUJIA

These crunchy, savoury fried noodles made primarily with tepary bean (moth dal) flour, spiked with powdered red chillies and black pepper are produced exclusively in the former princely state (and now district) of Bikaner in Rajasthan. Tansukh Dass Agarwal is said to have first started producing the *bhujia* in 1869 (his descendants, though heading different companies, continue to control the US$1 billion business), but it attained its elevated status after the local ruler, Maharaja Shri Dungar Singh, adopted it as the snack of the royal court in 1877. It was, in fact, originally called the Dungarshahi *bhujia* in honour of its royal patron, who served it with great pride to courtiers and visitors.

The use of the drought-resistant moth dal, which grows in abundance in and around this arid region, separates Bikaneri *bhujia* from other similar snacks made entirely from chickpea flour (*besan*). The other ingredients, apart from red chilli and black pepper powders, include up to 20 per cent chickpea flour as well as powdered cloves, dry ginger, cardamom, cinnamon, mace and nutmeg. The *bhujia* are fried in cottonseed or peanut oil.

The organized production of the *bhujia*, which is synonymous with tea-time snacking in India, has ensured a special place for the district, once an arid area on the fringes of the Thar desert that was transformed by the Indira Gandhi Canal. It did not take very long for *bhujia* manufacture to turn into a vibrant industry, which is protected from copycats by THE GEOGRAPHICAL INDICATION (GI) tag that it earned in 2010. As the poet Ashok Vajpeyi once remarked, one-half of Bikaner is employed in producing *bhujia* and the other half is engaged in consuming it!

Just three of the mega-companies producing the *bhujia* – Haldiram's, Bikaji and Bikanervala, all owned by descendant of Tansukh Dass Agarwal – logged total sales worth $1 billion during the calendar year 2018, cornering 25 per cent of the country's packaged snacks market. Bhikharam Chandmal (named after the son and grandson of the original *bhujia* maker) and Bikano are the other well-known brands. These companies started life as *bhujiawalas* (producers and sellers of the *bhujia*) in Bikaner's pokey Bhujia Bazaar.

Haldiram's, named after Ganga Vishan Agarwal (better known as Haldiram), the great-grandson of Tansukh Dass, was one of them. The company revolutionized the production of *bhujia* by replacing manual techniques using strainers (*jharras*) with noodle-making machines, but it started out as the humble Haldiram Bhujiawala in 1937. Now a global brand, it has far outgrown its Bhujia Bazaar origins, and so have its Bikaneri peers.

Sourish Bhattacharyya

- Daftuar, Swati. 'In Search of Bikaneri Bhujia'. *The Hindu*. Available online: https://www.thehindu.com/features/metroplus/Food/in-search-of-bikaneri-bhujia/article3945487.ece (accessed 22 October 2022).

BIRYANI

Biryani (*biriani*) is a dish of long-grained RICE layered with meat, poultry, FISH, seafood or vegetables, usually cooked with GHEE and flavoured with an assortment of spices (usually ground) and aromatic flavourings such as SAFFRON, rosewater, *kewra*, or jasmine (see FLOWER WATERS). There can be two or four layers. It is cooked in a pot, the lid of which is usually sealed with a dough paste to keep in all the moisture and flavours. This cooking method is known as *dum pukht* ('cooking in steam'). Biryanis are often garnished with NUTS, MINT leaves and *VARK* (silver leaf).

FIGURE 6 BIRYANI. Kolkata biryani. Garrett Ziegler/Wikimedia Commons.

The word 'biryani' can be traced to the Persian '*birinj biryan*', meaning fried rice and many historians believe that it was brought to India from Persia by the MUGHALS. However, some claim that the dish was known in India before the first Mughal emperor BABUR came to India and was derived from the PULAO brought by Arab traders.

Biryani is very similar to pulao and the difference between the two has been hotly debated. Recipes for both in the *Ain-i-Akbari* (sixteenth century) show little distinction between the two dishes. According to Pratibha Karan (2009), there is no layering in pulaos; rather, rice and other ingredients are cooked together. Biryanis, but not pulaos, are generally made with parboiled rice, use more spices than pulaos and are wetter. A pulao is usually an accompaniment to a meal, alongside gravy-based vegetables or dals, whereas a biryani is the main dish generally served with only the simplest accompaniments, such as a yogurt relish and CHUTNEY. Pulao is a dish found in many countries of the Middle East and Central Asia but biryani has become special to India.

The modern biryani was developed by cooks at the Mughal courts and became a fusion of the Persian pulao and the native Indian spicy dishes. Biryani became more elaborate and sophisticated. For special occasions, a biryani is often garnished with *vark*. Biryanis are often served at large celebrations such as weddings and religious festivals. On these occasions it is prepared by men, out of doors, in large pots over a charcoal fire.

LUCKNOW and HYDERABAD are especially renowned for their biryanis and almost every region of India has its own version. Here are a few:

Lucknow biryani, known as '*pukki*' biryani, requires no accompaniments other than plain yogurt as it is highly spiced. The meat is first boiled then fried to a golden brown. The par-cooked rice and meat are then layered in a pot and perfumed with a little rosewater or *kewra* and finally sprinkled with an infusion of saffron. This biryani is sometimes known as Awadhi biryani.

Hyderabad biryani. It is said that Emperor Aurangzeb appointed Nizam-ul-Mulk as the new ruler of Hyderabad and his chefs created almost fifty versions of biryani, using fish, shrimp, quail, deer and even hare. One version is made by marinating the meat first in a paste made with GINGER, GARLIC and green CHILLIES, then yogurt, spices (including saffron) and mint are added. The mint gives a distinctive flavour. Everything is marinated again for several hours before being cooked until almost tender. The rice is par-boiled and then the meat and rice are layered in a pot, the lid of which is sealed on with a dough paste, then cooked for a further half an hour or so.

Kolkata biryani is said to have been created by Nawab Wahid Ali Shah who was banished by the British to Calcutta in 1856. Unable to afford meat, the local cooks replaced the meat with perfectly cooked golden brown POTATOES. Nowadays meat is usually present but the potatoes remain an important part of the dish which is also lighter on spices.

Bombay biryani has the added slightly sweet flavours of dried PLUMS and *kewra* water.

Bangalorean biryani is a dish for weddings and special occasions which uses the special *zeera (jeera) samba* rice. The name comes from the fact that the grains of this sweet smelling rice have an uncanny resemblance to *zeera* (CUMIN) and *samba* refers to the season (typically August to January) when this rice is grown.

Helen Saberi

- Karan, Pratibha. *Biryani*. Noida, Uttar Pradesh: Random House, 2009.
- Sen, Colleen Taylor. *Feasts and Fasts: A History of Food in India*. London: Reaktion Books, 2015.

- Srividya, V. 'Tracing the Trails of the Nawabi Dish'. *n.d.* Available online: https://www.academia.edu/38483629/Tracing_the_Trails_of_the_Nawabi_Dish_Biryani_pdf (accessed 7 May 2022).

BOHRAS

Bohras, also called Dawoodi Bohras, are descendants of Hindu traders in Gujarat who were converted by Yemenis to a branch of Shia Islam in the tenth century. There are around a million Bohras in India, based mainly in Mumbai and Gujarat. Their name comes from Gujarati *vohryu,* meaning to trade, and even today most of the community are merchants and businessmen. The prefix Dawoodi comes from the name of a sixteenth-century leader.

Bohra cuisine incorporates Gujarati, Yemeni and Persian influences. Traditional breakfasts were generally large: perhaps *paya* (goat foot stew), keema (*qima* – ground meat) with naan or *HALEEM* and TEA. Lunch is the main meal of the day: typically chapati (see BREADS), RICE, vegetables or lentils (see PULSES) and a meat dish. Mutton is popular, prepared as CURRIES or in KEBABS. Offal is highly valued. Dinner may be a cold soup, called *sarki*, made of dal and yogurt, with KHICHRI and perhaps a meat dish. Typical Bohra dishes include dal *dhokli*, squares of roti dough simmered in a dal, and *patrel* biryani, a combination of taro leaves (*patra*) fried in chickpea flour with mutton and rice. *Chawal palidu* is an emblematic Bohra dish made of lentils (usually pigeon peas), rice and *palidu*, a gravy made of chickpea flour. Sometimes bottle GOURD or DRUMSTICK or boiled mutton is added. This dish is made for dinner on the final day of Ramadan.

Community meals to celebrate Eid, weddings and other festive occasions are important events in the Bohra community. They are served on a large circular tray called a *thaal* placed on a wooden stand over a cloth covering the floor. A *thaal* typically seats eight people, who serve themselves from communal dishes. A dinner begins and ends with SALT, believed to aid digestion. The first course is typically a SWEET dish, called *mithaas* – a traditional Indian sweet such as HALWA or BARFI often made with NUTS, or *kalamro*, a yogurt-based rice pudding. This is followed by a savoury dish called *khaara*. It could be keema SAMOSAS, grilled chop or brain cutlets. Another sweet dish would follow and then another *khaara: dabba gosht*, pieces of mutton cooked in a yogurt gravy with pasta and vegetables; tandoori chicken; a marinated leg of lamb; or a Bohra biryani, rich in aromatic spices. Traditionally, two or more sweet and savoury courses were served but in recent years the head of the community introduced a rule to limit the menu to one sweet and one savoury course for health reasons and to eliminate waste. Bohras break their Ramadan feast with a drink called *gol pani* made with water, jaggery and *tukmuria* seeds (sweet BASIL).

In 2011, the Bohra leadership introduced *Faizul al Burhaniyah* (which means the blessings that flow from the table of Mohammed Burhanuddin, a previous community leader). Volunteers, sometimes caterers, prepare a thali (called *Mawaa'id* in Arabic) containing a cooked meal and distribute it to the every member of the local Bohra community. The meals include bread, rice, dal and vegetables and sometimes meat. The purpose is to provide adequate nutrition, with the secondary effect of freeing women to pursue other work or interests. In Mumbai, where there are many distribution centres, the meals are delivered via the *DABBAWALLAH* system. The meals are free or at a nominal cost and are often sponsored anonymously by affluent community members. Meals are also distributed to the needy from other communities.

Colleen Sen

- Saha, Somdatta. 'Bohra Cuisine: A Meal Tradition That Starts with a Pinch of Salt and Dessert'. *NDTV Food*, 17 July 2020. Available online: https://food.ndtv.com/food-drinks/bohra-cuisine-a-meal-tradition-that-starts-with-a-pinch-of-salt-and-dessert-2264495 (accessed 23 April 2022).
- The Dawoodi Bohras. 'Faiz al-Mawaid al-Burhaniyah'. *n.d.* Available online: https://www.thedawoodibohras.com/about-the-bohras/faiz-al-mawaid-al-burhaniyah/ (accessed 23 April 2022).
- 'Bohra Cuisine'. *Indpaedia*, last modified 21 June 2018. Available online: http://indpaedia.com/ind/index.php/Bohra_cuisine (accessed 23 April 2022).

BOMBAY DUCK

Bombay duck is not, as one might think, a duck but a FISH, otherwise known as the bummalow (*Harpadon nehereus*). It is a relative of the lizardfish. The fish is abundant in the Arabian Sea, especially near MUMBAI, and the Ganges Delta. Local names include *bombil*, *bombaloe* and *boomla*. Fresh, it is a gelatinous fish with a delicate flavour but mostly the fish are preserved by drying, a process which Koli fishermen have been doing for hundreds of years. The whole fish are washed clean with salt water, split, boned and pegged by their heads to dry on huge racks on the beaches of fishing villages near

FIGURE 7 BOMBAY DUCK. Fried Bombay duck. Durvankur PatilWikimedia Commons.

Mumbai. When dried, the fish become crispy and have a pungent aroma, a salty taste and a crumbly texture.

How the Bombay duck got its name is a mystery. One theory is that the name comes from the way the fish swim near the surface of the water, like a duck. Another theory is that during the British Raj, the Europeans couldn't stand the smell of the fish and it reminded them of the smell of the wooden railroad cars of the Bombay Mail train. The Hindi word for mail is '*dak*' hence Bombay-*dak* which transgressed to Bombay duck. However, this theory is unlikely as the *Oxford English Dictionary* dates 'Bombay duck' to at least 1850, two years before the first railroad in Bombay was constructed. Also, an 1829 book of poems and 'Indian reminiscences' by Sir Toby Rendrag (pseudonym) notes the 'use of a fish nick-named "Bombay Duck"'. Another explanation is that it is an Anglicism from the bazaar cry in Marathi: '*bombil tak*' – 'here is Bombil'.

Despite the pungent aroma, the British acquired a taste for the strong, salty Bombay duck, often serving it with KEDGEREE for breakfast (perhaps it reminded them of kippers), and the crispy fish crumbled over plates of CURRY and RICE was a common accompaniment. King George V, noted for his love of curries, was especially fond of Bombay duck with beef curry.

Bombay duck has always been popular in Mumbai and is a special favourite of the PARSIS and Goans who buy the fish fresh and fry it until brown and crispy. The fish is also found in West Bengal where it is called *loyte* but it isn't as popular as it is in Maharashtra. Most seafood-loving communities of India's western Konkan Coast prepare it in different ways. Some grind it into a vinegary CHUTNEY, some stuff it with tiny prawns. Some Maharashtrian communities make it into a type of *bhaji*. Some cook it with greens. Sadly, the fish is rapidly disappearing from coastal waters due to overfishing and climate change.

Helen Saberi

- Burnett, David and Helen Saberi. *The Road to Vindaloo*. Totnes, Devon: Prospect Books, 2008.
- Burton, David. *The Raj at Table*. London: Faber and Faber, 1993.
- Mirza, Meher. 'India's Brilliant Bombay Duck'. *BBC Travel*, 21 January 2020. Available online: http://www.bbc.com/travel/story/20200120-indias-brilliant-bombay-duck (accessed 12 April 2022).
- Sen, Rajyasree. 'The Making of Bombay Duck'. *The Wall Street Journal*, 5 December 2012.

BREADS

India has made a place for its varied cuisine across the world but its vast array of breads have not garnered much attention. Each region of India boasts of its own local bread with flatbreads (unleavened breads) the most common. However, leavened breads are quite popular too.

North India has a particularly spectacular range of breads, made mostly with *atta* (whole wheat flour) and refined flour as WHEAT is a staple crop of this area and is grown abundantly here. In South India, RICE reigns supreme and replaces wheat even when it comes to breads. In West India, breads were traditionally made with various kinds of MILLETS which grow in dry conditions. In these dry regions, people dunk breads in clarified butter (GHEE) to provide the skin with lubrication. In northern India, breads

FIGURE 8 BREADS. *Phulka*. Colleen Sen.

FIGURE 9 BREADS. Cooking *rumali* roti. Anil Risal Singh.

are made with CORN flour (*makki*) which provide the body with warmth and are not eaten during the hot summers.

The following list represents only a small portion of the delicious universe of Indian breads.

***Akki* roti.** This Karnataka speciality can be served as a snack or as part of a meal. (*Akki* means rice in Kannada.) Fine rice flour is mixed with chopped ONIONS, CARROT, CURRY LEAVES, grated COCONUT, CORIANDER leaves, SALT, CUMIN and green CHILLI. These ingredients are thoroughly kneaded with water and oil to make a dough. The dough is spread in a circle on a lightly oiled BANANA leaf and transferred to a *tawa* (a flat pan) where it is cooked on both sides over medium flame.

APPAM. This bread is typically consumed in Tamil Nadu and Kerala, where it is culturally linked to SYRIAN CHRISTIANS who bake *appam* on a stone. *Appam* is a bowl-shaped pancake made from a fermented batter of rice flour and coconut milk. Soft and lacy in texture, it is a good accompaniment to vegetable stew or coconut milk. According to historian K.T. ACHAYA, *appam* is mentioned in the *Perumpanuru*, an ancient Tamil poem composed in the second century CE, indicating its Tamil roots. The *appam* has also long been a staple among Jewish communities in Kochi, MUMBAI and KOLKATA, pointing to Jewish Indian origins. However, *appam* is most associated with the Cochin Jews of Kerala, who arrived in India around the first century CE. *Kalappam* is a particular style of *appam* fermented with splashes of *kallu* (fresh toddy) rather than yeast, which originated in Kerala's Jew Town.

***Baati*.** This bread is synonymous with Rajasthan. A wheat ball made of ghee, camel milk and unsalted wheat flour, it was first mentioned during the time of Bappa Rawal, the founder of the kingdom of Mewar in the eighth century CE. It is said that soldiers would break the dough into chunks and leave it buried under thin layers of sand to bake under the sun. When they returned, they would find perfectly baked roundels that were eaten with ghee. The dish later evolved to the iconic combination of dal *baati churma*. When Rani Jodha Bai married the MUGHAL Emperor Akbar, dal *baati churma* reached the Mughal court. The chefs in the Mughal royal kitchen recreated their own versions of this Rajasthani dish, adapting it to make *baafla* and *kheech*. *Baafla* is a softer version of *baati* that is boiled before being baked, while *kheech* is made from sorghum or wheat and is similar to *daliya*, a porridge.

Bakarkhani is a thick, spiced sweet flatbread eaten throughout the Indian subcontinent. It travelled from Central Asia to Bangladesh during the time of the Mughals. *Bakarkhani* is almost biscuit-like in texture with a hard crust. According to legend, a highly acclaimed general in Nawab Siraj-ud-Daulah's army, Aga Bakar, fell in love with a courtesan called Khani Begum. A rival general had feelings for this lady and eventually had her murdered. A distraught Bakar was so heartbroken that he inspired his *khansamahs* (cooks) to name his favourite baked bread as an ode to his timeless love. Thus was born the 'Bakar-Khani' which later evolved into *bakarkhani*.

Bhakri is an unleavened flatbread native to Maharashtra, although it is also found throughout Gujarat, Goa and Rajasthan. It can be made with *jowar*, *ragi*, sorghum, wheat or rice flour, all high in dietary fibres, making *bhakri* a healthy flatbread. Rice *bhakris* are usually made along coastal Maharashtra since rice grows there in abundance. *Bajra bhakris* are enjoyed in cold winters as they have heat-inducing qualities. They are sometimes flavoured with ghee, butter or cumin seeds and served with CHUTNEYS. Traditionally, *bhakri* was consumed by farmers for breakfast and lunch, providing sustenance throughout the long working days.

Chapati. See **roti** below.

Kaatre pav is a Goan leavened bread made with white flour. It is also known as butterfly bread or *kannacho pav* (bread with ears) because of its distinctive shape — round but cut on both sides, very similar to a butterfly. It gets its name from the Konkani word *kator*, denoting the tool used to give it its shape. It has a slightly hard exterior and a soft chewy texture.

Kankon pav is another popular Goan bread which gets its name from *kankan,* meaning bangle. (*Pão* means bread in Portuguese.) It is ring-shaped with a hard texture and a slightly cracked crust. It is enjoyed with butter as an accompaniment to TEA.

***Khamiri* roti** is the Indian version of sourdough bread. *Khamir* means yeast or starter in Urdu. It is soft, spongy, thick, chewy and slightly tangy in taste. It is made in a tandoor. In the old days, in summertime, people used to ferment the dough by leaving it overnight to rise. Earlier, the Indian bread industry was run by Muslim *naanbais,* a community that specialized in making fermented breads, and Bhatiyaras, traditional innkeepers. Naanbais used to supply bulk orders during festivals and other family celebrations whereas Bhatiyaras (the term originates from the *bhattis*, or kilns, that they used) supplied breads to households daily. The culture of purchasing breads from outside is Central Asian and came to India with the Mughals. The best *khamiri* roti is sold in various shops in Old DELHI run by people who claim to be the direct descendants of the cooks who worked for the Mughals and use the same recipes as their ancestors.

***Khoba* roti** is a traditional flatbread that originated in and around Jodhpur in Rajasthan. The word *khoba* means deep indentation. It is traditionally made by pinching the overall surface to create an attractive and unique design. It has a longer-shelf life and is not perishable because it is loaded with salt and ghee which preserved it for longer periods. This made the roti a feasible food item to be carried by the Rajputs when they went out to war. It could be simply eaten with onions or PICKLE. This roti is known by different names – some call it *khoba* roti, some call it *jadi* roti.

Kulcha is a round bread made from white flour, milk and butter that is often stuffed with meat or vegetables and is associated with the Mughals and the Nizams of HYDERABAD. During the time of Shah Jahan, cooks used to stuff kulchas with vegetables and it was so delicious that it became the official bread for breakfast or lunch at the court. It was the Nizams who made kulcha famous in India. While the other princely states had lions and/or elephants on their flags, it became the official symbol of the Asaf Jahi dynasty and appeared on the Hyderabad state flag until Hyderabad became a part of independent India

Made with self-rising flour, kulcha almost replicates naan in its chewiness and soft bite. It could be cooked on a *tawa* or in a brick kiln, which made it easily accessible to both the masses and royalty. There are other versions of kulcha in India. In Bihar they are biscuit-like; in AMRITSAR they are soft and chewy and stuffed with POTATOES or cottage cheese (see PANEER); kulchas in LUCKNOW are fluffy and kneaded with milk and ghee; and in Delhi, the kulchas are thin with a stretchy texture.

Ladi pav is an Indian version of the Portuguese *pão* that looks like a grid of buns stuck together into a slab. *Ladi* means line, so *ladi pav* means a group of small rolls of bread joined together so that you pull one roll from the slab and consume it. It is popular in MUMBAI and is a staple in Maharashtra. It is the bread used in *pav bhaji*, an extremely popular street food from Mumbai.

Litti is the main ingredient in the iconic Bihari dish *litti chokha*. It is a dough ball made with whole wheat flour stuffed with *sattu* and spices with a dash of MUSTARD oil-based pickle and cooked on cow dung cakes or coal. After cooking it is tossed in ghee. It is served with *chokha* (mashed vegetables) or a chicken and meat CURRY.

Luchi is a deep-fried unleavened flatbread which puffs up during deep frying. Unlike puri, it is made with refined flour and is a staple in West Bengal, Orissa and Assam. It is usually made during Durga Puja celebration.

Naan is a leavened bread made with white flour that is rolled into an oval shape, sometimes sprinkled with NIGELLA seeds, and baked on the sides of a tandoor (clay oven). One of the earliest mentions of this bread is in Amir Khusrau's poetry in the fourteenth century. However, it is almost certainly older, probably dating to the time of the arrival of yeast in India from Egypt where it has been used to brew beer and make leavened breads since the second century BCE.

Paratha is a flatbread made from whole wheat flour that is lightly fried in ghee or oil in a *tawa* (pan). While naan is generally rolled out once, paratha often gets rolled out multiple times, creating a very flaky bread. Paratha originated in Peshawar (now in Pakistan) and then spread all over northern India. It began as a wholesome meal often eaten at breakfast. Paratha can be stuffed with various fillings, such as potato, cauliflower and paneer. It can also be plain, flavoured with AJOWAN or rolled out with frequent folding over while layering with ghee, and then pan fried using ghee or oil. The Parathe Wali Gali (Paratha Lane) in Old Delhi is famous for its parathas. The food here is strictly vegetarian and has no onion or GARLIC and their most regular clientele are Jains from the neighbourhood. The paratha here is a mix of the traditional Punjabi paratha and the *bedmi* puri (deep-fried stuffed Indian bread); it is cooked not on a *tawa* but instead is deep-fried in a *kadhai* (a wok-shaped pan). The paratha is usually served with sweet TAMARIND chutney, MINT chutney, mixed vegetable pickle, paneer and potato curry, potato and FENUGREEK curry, and a sautéed mash of sweet pumpkin (see GOURDS).

Parotta usually refers to the Malabar or Kerala *parotta*, a flaky, layered bread which is a popular street and restaurant food across the state. Unlike the North Indian paratha, which is made from whole wheat flour, the Kerala *parotta* is made of refined flour. Another difference is that with most parathas, you roll and fold the dough to get the layers; for the *parotta* the dough is rolled into a ball and then into a long rope, which is coiled and then rolled out again. It is an ideal companion for Kerala beef fry.

In southern Tamil Nadu, smaller, thicker and softer *parottas* called coin *parottas* are served with a thin TOMATO and onion-based gravy called *salna*. A popular street food is *kothu parotta*, which is shredded *parotta* mixed and served with a spiced gravy that includes egg or meat. It is believed to have originated in Madurai but is now found all over Tamil Nadu.

Poee/poi is a leavened bread baked by traditional bakers called *poders* in Goa, where it is a staple food, and is similar to a pita pocket. Made from a mixture of whole wheat and white flour, it is slightly chewy in texture. It is said that when the Portuguese came to India around four hundred years ago, they brought some of their key ingredients such as chilli and potatoes. Although the Portuguese adapted to the local cuisine, they missed their bread, the *pão*, but sourcing the right kind of yeast to ferment the dough was an uphill task. As an alternative, they started using toddy (local palm liquor) for leavening their breads, which were traditionally baked in a wood-fired oven placed directly on the stone.

Puri is a deep-fried bread made from unleavened whole wheat flour. It is eaten for breakfast or as a snack or light meal. It is often served with a savoury potato curry and also eaten with sweet dishes such as HALWA. No auspicious day in the Hindu calendar can be complete without the frying of the bread in a *kadhai* full of hot ghee or oil. *Aloo* puri (puri stuffed with potato) is also a staple Indian breakfast.

Roti is the generic Indian name for most Indian breads, be they baked, grilled or roasted. It refers mainly to breads based on wheat flour, but can also be applied to bread made from other grains such as *jowar*, CORN, *bajra* and chickpea. In some areas, *phulka* is the name given to chapatis/rotis that have been puffed up over a flame.

***Rumali* roti** (or *roomali*) is a soft, thin flatbread usually made with a combination of whole wheat and white flour and cooked on the convex side of a *kadhai*. *Rumal* means 'handkerchief' and it is said that during the Mughal period, *rumali* roti was used as a cloth to wipe the hands at the end of a rich meal. It is often served with curries and tandoori dishes.

Sheermal is a flatbread made from flour, milk, SAFFRON and SUGAR that is baked in a tandoor. It originated in Persia, *shir* meaning milk and *mal* meaning 'to rub' in Farsi and Urdu. It made its way to India through the Silk Route. After being introduced to North India by the Mughal emperors, it became a delicacy in Lucknow, Hyderabad and Aurangabad. It is also an integral part of Awadhi cuisine and is enjoyed in Old Bhopal and Pakistan. An alternative story is that *sheermal* was invented in Lucknow by an ace bread maker by the name of Mahmood in the early nineteenth century. He had a restaurant at Firangi Mahal where the *NIHARI* was the showstopper. He made a new kind of paratha, *sheermal*, to go with a bowl of *nihari*. Mahmood's head chef was Ali Hussain who later set up his own stall and since then, Ali Hussain's *sheermal* has been an integral part of Lucknow cuisine. The lane where this shop is located is known as the 'Sheermal Wali Gali'!

Taftun/taftoon is a leavened flour bread made with milk, yogurt and eggs and baked in a clay oven. It is often flavoured with saffron and a little CARDAMOM powder. It uses little or no salt. *Taftun* is a Persian word derived from *tafan* meaning 'heating', 'burning' or 'kindling'. In the past, the only way of making *taftun* was by baking the dough in a tandoor, or clay oven. It was commonly eaten by merchants along the Grand Trunk Road, one of history's oldest trade routes. In Kashmir, where the bread is eaten for breakfast or with stews and KEBABS, it is sprinkled with POPPY SEEDS or saffron on top.

Tchot is a traditional Kashmiri flatbread with a slightly crisp crust and a chewy interior. *Tchot* is given a milk wash before being cooked in the tandoor to impart a brown colour. Poppy seeds are added as a topping. A richer variety is the ghee *tchot*, which incorporates ghee in the dough for a richer taste.

Thepla is a popular Gujarati thin flatbread made from whole wheat, millet and sometimes chickpea flour and fenugreek leaves and eaten with pickle. *Thepla* is easy to make and pack and lasts several days, making it ideal for travel. It is a favourite snack or breakfast dish for most Gujaratis.

Tingmo is a Tibetan steamed bun made with refined flour and comes from the Indian state of Sikkim which shares a border with Tibet. It can be found on the menus of Tibetan eateries all over India together with momos (see STREET FOOD). *Tingmo* is served with a spicy red chilli chutney. It is also eaten with curries and stews.

***Warqi* paratha** is a rich flaky paratha made with a lot of ghee. (The Urdu word *warqi* means layers.) With its roots in Lucknow, the *warqi* paratha has been a part of Awadhi cuisine for centuries. It is made with refined flour and sometimes sugar or saffron is added.

The paratha is folded multiple times to create the required layers and then flattened out before being lightly fried.

Megha Kohli

- Homegrown Staff. 'Beyond Rotis & Parathas – A Guide to the Different Breads of India'. *Homegrown*, 27 May 2019. Available online: https://homegrown.co.in/article/803670/a-guide-to-the-different-indian-breads (accessed 20 April 2022).
- Koranne-Khandekar, Saee. *Crumbs: Bread Stories and Recipes for the Indian Kitchen*. Gurugram, Haryana: Hachette, 2016.

BUTTER CHICKEN

Butter chicken, or *murgh makhani* in Hindi, is a dish created by some entrepreneurial Punjabi refugees who moved to DELHI from their native Peshawar in present-day Pakistan to escape the blood-letting triggered by the Partition of India in 1947.

Contrary to the popular notion, it is neither a 'Mughlai' preparation, nor India's defining chicken dish, despite its global popularity (even Domino's has a butter chicken pizza on offer in Australia and New Zealand!). The original consists of three principal ingredients – tandoori chicken, preferably on the bone, grilled in the traditional earthen tandoor, and, therefore, bathed in its own juices and smoky; pulverized TOMATOES and ONIONS; fresh cream and butter – and one differentiating spice: *kasoori methi*, or dried FENUGREEK leaves.

Tandoori chicken, the foundation of butter chicken, is a dish associated with the Punjabi Hindu community which initiated the tradition of grilling meats in the tandoor that was traditionally used to bake breads. The chicken pieces are marinated twice before they go into the tandoor – first, with fresh lime juice and red CHILLI powder, and then, with yogurt, GARLIC and GINGER paste, garam masala (see SPICE BOX) and black SALT.

The grilled chicken fresh off the tandoor is cooked in a gravy prepared primarily with pulverized tomatoes, roughly chopped onions, fresh cream and salted or white butter, garam masala and other spice powders (the proportions vary from one restaurant to the other). The finished dish is garnished with necklaces of cream. It goes best with naan (see BREADS).

This is how the dish has been cooked at Moti Mahal, the restaurant in the Daryaganj neighbourhood of Delhi that owes its global fame to butter chicken. (Ironically, the restaurant, which has spawned a number of independent outlets owned by the families of its original owners and investors, has never promoted the dish as something special and, in fact, traditionally called it just *murgh makhani*). Cooks in restaurants around the world have been adding HONEY to balance the tartness of the tomatoes in certain months, or using cashew and almond paste to thicken the gravy, which were absolute no-nos for Moti Mahal's creators.

Butter chicken is different from chicken tikka masala, which, according to one popular theory, is an invention of the Sylheti cooks of London's East End's 'Indian' restaurants, who tossed tandoori chicken morsels into a combination of Campbell soup, a dollop of yogurt, red chilli powder and a cocktail of spices. This chilli-hot invention, meant to be washed down with chilled beer, originally catered to the 'lager louts' returning from soccer matches but was later famously held up as a symbol of British multiculturalism by the then U.K. Foreign Secretary Robin Cook in 2001. 'Chicken tikka is an Indian dish', Cook explained. 'The masala sauce was added to satisfy the desire of British people to have their meat served in gravy.'

This theory of the provenance of chicken tikka masala was challenged by the Glaswegian restaurateur Asif Ali. Appearing on a 2013 episode of the British TV cookery programme *Hairy Bikers*, Ali said that his father Ali Ahmed Aslam, a Pakistani-born Scottish national who opened the Shish Mahal restaurant in Glasgow in 1964, invented chicken tikka masala on a cold, dark, wet night in 1971. He was responding to the request of a bus driver who had dropped in for a meal and found the tandoori chicken to be just too dry. Ali Senior, in the words of his son, 'hastily prepared a sauce using various spices soaked in a tin of Campbell's condensed tomato soup, which he had been eating while recovering from a stomach ulcer'.

Asif Ali got the then MP from Glasgow Central, Chaudhary Mohammed Sarwar, who is now the Governor of Pakistan's Punjab province, to back his demand that the 'Glasgow chicken tikka masala', in the same way as the Arbroath smokie, Cornish clotted cream and Welsh lamb, be granted the European Union's Protected Denomination of Origin (PDO) status. The campaign failed, which leaves the field clear for Moti Mahal to savour its unofficial status as the birthplace of butter chicken.

Interestingly, the restaurant was reputed in its early decades for its chicken PAKORA (a Punjabi version of Kentucky Fried Chicken, where chicken chunks are quilted in a spiced chickpea flour batter and deep-fried), mutton *burrah* (marinated mutton chops roasted and charred in the tandoor), and its much-copied creamy dal prepared with whole black grams (popular among Punjabis as *ma ki* dal), but fattened with the butter chicken ingredients, minus the chicken, of course!

Even in Shanta RAMA RAU's 1969 book, *The Cooking of India*, where Moti Mahal makes an entry with a picture of its tandoor and the naans coming out of it, or in Craig Claiborne's 1970 *New York Times* article on dining out in Delhi, the restaurant is featured for its tandoori chicken and chicken pakora, and there is not a word about butter chicken. Clearly, it had not acquired the star status is subsequently did. The dish named 'butter chicken', according to the Wikipedia entry on the subject, first appeared on the menu of the Gaylord restaurant at Manhattan, New York City.

Moti Mahal was established in 1948 and run by three refugees from Peshawar – Kundan Lal Gujral, a larger-than-life character who served as the maitre d' and, therefore, was the famous face of the restaurant; Kundan Lal Jaggi, who managed the kitchen (the back-end, to use contemporary jargon); and Thakur Dass Mago, the purchase head and store supervisor. Gujral and Jaggi had both worked in a *DHABA*, also known as Moti Mahal, run by a man named Mokha Singh Lamba in the Gora Bazar area of Peshawar. Mago's family owned a wholesale business in rice and PULSES that operated out of a shop across the road from the *dhaba*.

The three young men lost touch with each other until the maelstrom of Partition threw them together in Delhi where they met accidentally, of all places, at a liquor shop where they had gone to buy their respective favourite poisons. Gujral's and Mago's wives knew each other because they stitched quilts outside the iconic Delhi Cloth Mills to make ends meet.

Together, the three men set up a tea stall where Jaggi toasted bread and Gujral made the tea. Driven by the urge to set up a bigger business together, they pooled the then princely sum of Rs 6,000 (the money they had saved and also raised by pawning the gold jewellery of their wives) and launched Moti Mahal out of a pokey little shop in Daryaganj, primarily to serve refugee families settling down in the area. Soon, they moved over to bigger premises allotted to them by India's first Prime Minister, Jawaharlal Nehru, who had become their biggest patron.

Moti Mahal's who's who clientele included a galaxy of greats, from the father of the country's atomic energy programme, Homi Jehangir Bhaba, and Nehru's sister and the first woman to be elected President of the UN General Assembly, Vijayalakshmi Pandit, to Soviet leader Nikita Khrushchev, and the prominent Pakistani politicians – late former Prime Minister Zulfikar Ali Bhutto and former Foreign Minister Gohar Ayub Khan – who had come to the restaurant with the then External Affairs Minister of India, Sardar Swaran Singh. Another famous regular was Mohan Singh Oberoi, better known as Rai Bahadur M.S. Oberoi, who founded the Oberoi Group of hotels.

Moti Mahal's competition, the Tandoor at the nearby Hotel President – the inspiration for the more famous Bukhara restaurant – and the Khyber in the bastion of Delhi's old elite, Kashmiri Gate, may have served food that won the hearts of the city's new Punjabi settlers, but the Daryaganj restaurant was without doubt the clear winner in the department of celebrity endorsements.

For a long time, it was believed that Kundan Lal Gujral was the inventor of butter chicken, but Jaggi set the record straight towards the end of his life. (His grandson, Raghav Jaggi, has revived his legacy by launching the Daryaganj restaurant franchise with his school friend Amit Bagga, with a menu crowded with Moti Mahal specials.)

Butter chicken, unlike the old and established narrative, was not invented in Peshawar by Gujral in 1920 (when he was, at best, a young adult), but it was created in the early years of Moti Mahal on a night when, unannounced, a large number of people showed up at the restaurant. The depleted supply of tandoori chicken, according to Jaggi, needed to be pumped up that night to feed the unexpected turnout of guests. The guests loved it and the dish stayed on the menu. Most likely, butter chicken, or *murgh makhani*, as it has been called for much of its history, was created by the little-known head cook of Moti Mahal, Munshi Ram, and his assistants, Madan and Hansraj.

Sourish Bhattacharyya

- Claiborne, Craig. 'In Delhi, It's Difficult to Find Bad Native Dish'. *The New York Times*, 14 April 1970.
- Loney, Gillian. 'Glasgow's History with Tikka Masala and the Restaurant Claiming to Have Created It'. *Glasgow Live*, 15 October 2020. Available online: https://www.glasgowlive.co.uk/news/history/tikka-masala-curry-glasgow-restaurant-12015915 (accessed 13 April 2022).
- Vohra, Pankaj. 'Partition Brought Moti Mahal, a Landmark in India's Culinary History, to Central Delhi'. *The Sunday Guardian*, 6 June 2015. Available online: http://www.sunday-guardian.com/investigation/partition-brought-moti-mahal-a-landmark-in-indias-culinary-history-to-central-delhi (accessed 13 April 2022).

BUTTERMILK

Churning cultured cream separates the milk fat and the liquid left behind is referred to as buttermilk. In India, two methods are used to achieve this:

- The thick creamy skin of boiled milk is cultured and churned to separate the fat (butter) from the liquid (buttermilk).
- The textured creamy skin on homemade yogurt is collected and churned to make butter and the leftover liquid is the buttermilk.

Sometimes, yogurt diluted with water is called buttermilk, though this is not 'true' buttermilk. A butter churn is used to whisk and separate butter from buttermilk and create a desirable foam on buttermilk when served as a drink.

Buttermilk is a prized summer drink served sweet or salted. Known as *mattha* in much of North India, *chaas* in Gujarat, *sambaram* in Kerala, *majjige* in Karnataka, *neer moru* in Tamil Nadu, *ghola dahi* in Odisha, *taak* in Maharashtra and *phanna tak* in the Konkan region, the various regional variants are all unique in their flavouring. Crushed CURRY LEAVES, citrus leaves, CORIANDER, green CHILLIES, GINGER, roasted CUMIN seeds, finely diced shallots or ASAFOETIDA can be added to give the drink regional flavours.

Buttermilk, collected from cultured cream, is used in an Ayurvedic therapeutic diet. It is interesting to note that buttermilk prepared so improves with further fermentation and does not split on heating. Buttermilk is cooked to make a variety of stews. *Mor kuzhambu* in Tamil Nadu and *moru kootan* in Kerala are thick stews with added COCONUT, while *moru chaaru* and *milagu vellam* are thinner stews made with black pepper (see PEPPER, BLACK). In Kerala, buttermilk is briefly cooked in gentle heat to make *kachina moru*, while prolonged cooking yields *kurukku kalan* (lit. reduced stew).

Buttermilk (also diluted yogurt) is stabilized with *besan* (ground chickpea flour) to make *kadhi* in much of North India, with many regional variations. A slurry of RICE flour and buttermilk is cooked over slow heat to yield a thick porridge with a spreadable consistency. This dish is flavoured with SALT, asafoetida, green chillies or curry leaves to make *kicchu* in Gujarat, *moru kali* in Tamil Nadu and Kerala, and *kheruor redu* or *rehru* in Himachal.

Buttermilk, being high in acidobacillus, is used to preserve many vegetables like LOTUS stems, bitter GOURD, cluster beans and berries like *Solanum torvum* or *Solanum nigrum*. These are soaked overnight in buttermilk and sun-dried, a process that is repeated thrice. Known as *vetral* in South India, they are shelf stable and are fried before serving. In Rajasthan, a paste of buttermilk and sorghum is sun-dried to make PAPADS called *rabodi* which are later added to stews. Buttermilk is an important souring ingredient, added to semolina in *rava* dosa, and to WHEAT flour to make *godhuma* dosa.

In Ladakh, buttermilk from cultured yak's milk is slowly cooked to a thick mass called *chhurpi*.

Priya Mani

CAMPHOR

Camphor (*Cinnamomum camphora*, Hindi *kapoor*) is a crystalline, white or transparent solid that originally comes from the wood of the camphor laurel, a large evergreen tree that grows throughout Asia. It was traditionally isolated by passing steam through the pulverized wood and condensing the vapours which were then purified. Today, most camphor is produced synthetically from turpentine. The largest producer is China. In India, several species of camphor trees grow in the Western Ghats. The word is derived from the Sanskrit *karpura*, which may have come from the name of a port in Sumatra. Camphor was one of the spices originally brought by traders from the Spice Islands to India and has been used as an ingredient as far back as ancient Egypt.

Camphor has a strong, pungent, woody odour. In India, it was one of the five ingredients (together with CARDAMOM, CLOVE, NUTMEG AND MACE) in *pancha-sugandha*, a filling for PAAN enjoyed by the wealthy. It also features in several dishes in the *NI'MATNAMA* of Sultan Ghiyath Shahi. Today, camphor is still an ingredient in a few Indian sweet dishes. It is also used in Hindu ceremonies, especially in South India, where people burn camphor to make a flame used in certain rites. It has the advantage of not irritating the eyes. Both edible and nonedible forms of camphor are available in the market.

Colleen Sen

CAPSICUM

Capsicum is both the botanical name for a range of species and a specific fruit that is also known as green, sweet or bell pepper. It belongs to the family Solanaceae and is thus related to TOMATO, AUBERGINE and POTATO. *Capsicum annuum*, the ancestor of most of today's peppers, both sweet and hot (see CHILLIES), appeared in the Western Hemisphere around 7500 BCE. The first peppers to be domesticated were the spicy variants. Christopher Columbus, who was in search of pepper (see PEPPER, BLACK) and other spices, discovered people in the Caribbean using hot capsicums in their food and brought the first ones to Europe. The hot varieties caught on but the mild eating variety became popular in Europe somewhat later.

Bell peppers are round or oblong in shape and are green in colour, turning red, yellow, orange or purple upon ripening, with the red ones being the sweetest. They lack the capsaicin that gives their chilli cousins their hotness. In India, they grow at mild elevations where the temperature averages between 21°C and 25°C. In Hindi, bell peppers are called *shimla mirch*, probably because they were first cultivated by the British in Shimla and were mainly intended for a British market. Today the main producing states are Tamil Nadu, Karnataka, Himachal Pradesh and Uttar Pradesh. In Pune and Bengaluru, they are cultivated year-round in green houses. Capsicum is used raw in salads, cooked in stir-fries or other mixed dishes and CURRIES, and stuffed.

Colleen Sen

CARDAMOM

There are basically two types of cardamom: green or white ('true cardamom') and brown/black ('false cardamom').

Green or white cardamoms (the white are green cardamoms that have been bleached; Hindi *chhoti ilaichi*) are the dried fruit of a perennial herb *Elettaria cardamomum* which is indigenous to South India and Sri Lanka and belongs to the GINGER family. Green cardamom is one of the most ancient and highly valued spices. Its seeds were prized in India long before the birth of Christ and it is known as the queen of spices, second only to black pepper, the king, in economic importance (see PEPPER, BLACK). India is one of the world's major producers.

In India, the best is considered to be var. *minuscula*, the pale green 'Alleppey cardamom', which is originally a variety from Mysore but is now grown in the Cardamom Hills of Idukki district in Kerala. It is called Alleppey cardamom, not because it is grown in Alleppey, but because Alleppey was the main depot through which this cardamom was processed.

Cardamom fruits are oval-shaped green pods with each pod containing twelve to twenty dark brown or black seeds. The pods are inedible; it is the small seeds which hold all the flavour. They are slightly sticky while still inside the pod and are highly aromatic with a lemony fresh flavour, yet offer a delicate warmth at the same time. Cardamom is one of the five 'warm' spices and is an essential component of garam masala (see SPICE BOX). The seeds are usually ground and are also used to flavour a wide range of dishes such as sweetmeats, pastries, desserts and savoury dishes such as korma and pulao. Green cardamom taken in TEA (and always added to *qahwa*, Kashmiri tea) helps digestion after a rich and heavy meal. It is often chewed to freshen the breath. Garcia DE ORTA wrote in the sixteenth century: 'The Indians use it a great deal against bad breath and as a masticatory; also to open the nasal passage and to clear the head.'

Brown cardamom is not a true cardamom although it belongs to the same botanical family. It generally comes from the *Amomum* or *Afromomum* genus. The large Bengal cardamom (Hindi *badi ilaichi*, or *daruharidra* in Sanskrit), which comes from *Amomum aromaticum*, is cultivated in Bengal and Assam. The large hairy pods are coarser in texture and brown in colour. The seeds have a harsher and distinctively CAMPHOR-like taste. They are usually ground and used sparingly in meat, poultry and RICE dishes. As with green cardamom, they are also an ingredient of garam masala and are sometimes used in PICKLES.

Helen Saberi

- Achaya, K.T. *A Historical Dictionary of Indian Food*. Delhi: OUP, 1998.
- Dalby, Andrew. *Dangerous Tastes: The Story of Spices*. London: British Museum Press, 2000.
- Nabhan, Gary Paul. *Cumin, Camels, and Caravans: A Spice Odyssey*. Berkeley: University of California Press, 2014.
- Pruthi, J.S. *Spices and Condiments*. New Delhi: National Book Trust, 1976.

CAREY, WILLIAM

William Carey (1761–1834) was an English Baptist missionary, polyglot, educator, campaigner for social reform and self-taught botanist who founded the Agricultural and Horticultural Society of India in 1820. The Society, which has remained at its original location in Alipore, KOLKATA, for 200 years, was responsible for propagating new commercial crops and vegetables (apart from ornamental flowers), notably TEA (the Assam variety), COFFEE, cacao, POTATOES, cabbage, cauliflower and peas.

Son of impoverished Northamptonshire weavers who started out as a shoemaker's apprentice, Carey and two fellow English Baptists established their Mission in 1800 in Serampore, a Danish trading outpost close to British India's capital, Calcutta. They made Serampore their base to escape the attention of the East India Company, which were not very kindly disposed towards missionaries till the Charter Act of 1813 allowed them a free run.

The 'Serampore Trio' went on to establish the Serampore Mission Press (later known as the Baptist Mission Press), the newspapers *Samachar Darpan* (Bengali) and *The Friend of India* (which later became *The Statesman*), and the Serampore College (now Serampore University) in 1818 under a royal charter from Frederick VI of Denmark. Carey's most enduring contribution, however, was to change forever the diet of Bengal's (and later, India's) elite because of the work done by the Society.

FIGURE 10 CAREY, WILLIAM. William Carey with Pandit.

The first job Carey tried (unsuccessfully) to get in India was that of the superintendent of the Calcutta Botanical Gardens, so he settled for the far less glamorous post of the manager of an indigo plantation in a remote village named Mudnapatty in Bengal's Malda district where he completed the Bengali translation of the New Testament and gained valuable insights into local agricultural practices. After setting up the Mission, Carey developed a mini botanical garden, an agricultural farm and a timber plantation to ensure that the institution paid for itself.

At the time, Carey was also a respected professor of Bengali, Sanskrit and Marathi at Fort William College, the training ground of colonial officials, a position he held from 1801 to 1830. This made it easy for him to get the support of the Governor-General, Warren Hastings, and his wife. To Carey's credit, though, he ensured that the Society stay an inclusive organization, perhaps the only one, where 'native gentlemen should ... not only be eligible as members but also as officers ... in precisely the same manner as Europeans'.

Bengali Nobel laureate Rabindranath Tagore's grandfather, Dwarkanath Tagore, was one of the Society's earliest Indian members. A prominent 'native gentleman', Raja Radhakanta Deb, donated 500 acres to it.

Carey made it clear in the Society's prospectus in 1820 that its objectives were 'paying close attention to the improvement of land, introducing new and useful plants, improving of implements of husbandry along with the quality of cattle, and, most importantly, bringing of waste lands into a state of cultivation'. Moving along the path laid by its founder-president (Carey held the position till 1824), the Society introduced new and improved varieties of artichokes, asparagus, Brussels sprouts, cabbage, CARROTS, cauliflower, celery, peas and TOMATOES from Europe and the Cape of Good Hope; grapefruit from Florida; pummelo from Java; and seedless LYCHEE from China. It introduced English potatoes in 1832 – the Naini Tal and Shillong varieties today owe their origin to these imports.

The Society distributed WHEAT seeds from Australia, Egypt and Europe so that Indian wheat became more amenable to the production of fine flour. It popularized CORN and Carolina rice from the United States, cacao from the West Indies and GINGER from Jamaica (the foundation of India's success with the rhizome); experimented with coffee in Dacca (present-day Dhaka); and its farm in Saharanpur (in present-day Uttar Pradesh) proved that APPLES, APRICOTS, peaches and PLUMS could be successfully grown in India. In 1833, a year before Carey died, the Tea Committee of the Society reported that it was possible to plant the species of the tea plant discovered in Assam on a commercial scale. It was singularly responsible for the inception and growth of the tea industry in Assam and North Bengal.

For his efforts, Carey was elected a Fellow of the Linnean Society and elevated to the membership of the Asiatic Society, the Horticultural Society and the Geological Society – all fraternities of the best minds of his time. His legacy lives on in the institutions he created and in the Carey Institute of Horticulture, which the Society founded in his honour in 1962. Carey came as a Baptist preacher, but he is best remembered as a missionary of modern agriculture.

Sourish Bhattacharyya

- Doctor, Vikram. 'From Potatoes and Plums to Cauliflowers and Carrots, How AHSI Has Influenced What We Grow & Eat'. *The Economic Times*, 2 August 2020.
- Mondal, Amrita. 'Agricultural Initiatives of Serampore Missionaries (1800–1840)'. *Proceedings of the Indian History Congress* 74, (2013): 426–32.
- Smith, George. *The Life of William Carey: Shoemaker and Missionary*. London: John Murray, 1885.

CARROT

Carrot (*Daucus carota* var. *sativa*, Hindi *gajar*) is a root vegetable, nowadays typically orange in colour, although purple, black, red, white and yellow cultivars also exist. All these different coloured carrots have been domesticated from the wild carrot, *D. carota*, which has an ivory-yellow colour, a long taproot, a woody core and lacy leaves (it is also known as Queen Anne's lace). It smells like the carrot we know today although the taste is bitter.

Both written history and molecular genetic studies indicate that the wild carrot was first domesticated *c.* 900 CE in a region which is now in modern-day Afghanistan. Naturally occurring subspecies of the wild carrot were, presumably, bred selectively which produced both yellow and purple carrots. From this centre of domestication, the carrot spread east and west. The yellow carrot spread to Europe where eventually, by selection, the orange carrot (which gets its colour from carotene) was developed by the Dutch in the seventeenth century. The purple carrot (which also contains some carotene but gets its colour from anthocyanin compounds) spread to Asia.

Although the hardy greenish-white wild carrot is thought to be indigenous to India, the red carrot called *desi gajar* (*desi* meaning native) was preferred. Garcia DE ORTA wrote in 1563 of 'the good carrots of Surat and the excellent ones of the Deccan'. Later, John Fryer, an English doctor with the British East India Company, also praised the 'good carrots' of the Deccan in his book *New Accounts of East India and Persia (1672–1681)* but it is not clear which colour carrot they were talking about. India also has purple/black carrots, called *kali gajar*, which are yellowy-orange inside. They are considered to be healthier as they contain more anthocyanins, which are powerful antioxidants, but are not so widely available. The British introduced European orange carrot varieties to India in the nineteenth century. At first, cultivation failed completely in the plains until they had first been successfully grown in the mountains and acclimatized seeds were produced.

Carrots are a versatile vegetable that are used in many dishes in India, giving a slightly sweet taste and rich colour. They are often cooked with other vegetables such as cabbage, POTATOES and peas, or added to dal. They are added to PULAO and other RICE dishes such as *gajar wale chaval*, which is usually made with the preferred dark red variety. Carrots are also added to soups, kormas and CURRIES and are added to or made into spicy salads. They are also good for making PICKLES and jams. A fermented drink called *KANJI* is made with black carrot juice. Carrots are also made into puddings such as KHEER and *payasam* but perhaps the most well-known carrot dish in India is the deliciously sweet and rich *gajar ka* HALWA, scented with CARDAMOM and usually studded with dried fruits and NUTS.

Helen Saberi

- Achaya, K.T. *Indian Food: A Historical Companion*. Delhi: OUP, 1994.
- *The World Carrot Museum*. Available online: http://www.carrotmuseum.co.uk (accessed 12 April 2022).

CASSAVA

Cassava, also called yuca and manioc (*Manihot esculenta*, Hindi *kassava*) is a woody shrub native to west-central Brazil. (In India, it is sometimes called tapioca, although, strictly speaking, this is the name of its powdered form.) It is a tall perennial shrub with large leaves and edible roots that are eight to thirty cm long and one to three cm in diameter. Its roots are very rich in starch but deficient in protein, while its leaves are a good source of protein. There are two varieties: bitter and sweet, the first of which is more widely grown. However, its roots and leaves contain toxic levels of cyanide and must be properly prepared by cooking or drying before consumption.

In India, the largest producing states are Kerala, Tamil Nadu and Andhra Pradesh and today it is a staple ingredient in the South as well as in some parts of Assam. There are several explanations of how cassava reached India. According to legend, it was introduced to Kerala around 1880 by the Maharajah of Travancore during a famine as a substitute for RICE. However, there are documented cases of cassava cultivation before then. The Portuguese may have brought it to the west coast of India from Africa or via the Philippines to eastern India.

Indians consume cassava tubers in two distinct forms: as a minor staple food – mainly in Kerala as *kappa*, served boiled with FISH; and as a root vegetable elsewhere, added to CURRIES or eaten as a seasonal snack. Thin slices are deep-fried to make chips. In Assam, pieces of cassava are boiled and then fried with greens and spices. The Khasi and Garo people make *tabulchu bitchi*, a liquor from the tubers, while the Gorkhas, Bhutia and Lepchas make *simal tarul ko jaanr,* a mildly alcoholic beverage (see ALCOHOL). Cassava flour is new to the Indian market and is marketed as a gluten-free flour. Cassava leaves are steamed, broiled or ground to make CHUTNEYS and salads. In Meghalaya, the stalks are charred to make a traditional aerated beverage, *tabulcho karitchi,* from the ash.

Most of the cassava grown is processed for its starch known as tapioca. It is an essential ingredient in sun-dried crackers as it expands significantly on frying. Tapioca is widely used in the food industry as a thickener. Pearl tapioca refers to globules made from tapioca starch cake, often called *sabudana.* It is also called sago, despite being made of tapioca, as it has remained a cheaper alternative to palm sago. It can be used instead of rice to make KHICHRI and KHEER or mixed with POTATOES to make VADA (a savoury fried snack). In western India, sago is commonly cooked with potatoes and peanuts to make a warm salad and fritters eaten mainly during fasts. Many milk-based Indian desserts have evolved using sago instead of local grains.

Priya Mani and Colleen Sen

- Ratnayake, W.S. and D.S. Jackson. 'Starch: Sources and Processing'. In *Encyclopedia of Food Sciences and Nutrition,* edited by Benjamin Cabellero. 2nd edition. Cambridge, MA: Academic Press, 2003.

CASSIA

Cassia, the dried bark of a tree in the laurel family, is one of the oldest spices. It was recorded in China as early as 2500 BCE and in Egypt in 1600 BCE. It is related to CINNAMON and is often called Chinese cinnamon. However, its texture is much harder and coarser than cinnamon and its taste is less delicate and fragrant, having a more intense flavour.

There are a number of species of cassia in the genus *Cinnamomum.* In India, cassia (*Cinnamomum cassia,* formerly *C. aromaticum)* is called *jungly dalchini, dalchini* being derived from the Arab term *dar-al-chin*, meaning the wood or bark of China. Cassia grows in the eastern regions of India where it is an important spice. It is also an essential spice of MUGHAL-style cookery and the spice blend garam masala (see SPICE BOX).

C. tamala (Indian cassia, also known as *tejpat*) grows in northeastern India at the foot of the Sikkim Himalayas and the Khasi hills in the state of Meghalaya. It produces large, shiny aromatic leaves which are used extensively as a spice. They are dried and used as a flavouring, especially in Odisha and West Bengal. They are often fried briefly first, releasing a strong woody flavour, and then added to dishes such as PULAO, BIRYANI, *shukto* (bitter melon stews) and *charchari* or *chorchori* (Bengali mixed vegetable dishes).

In Kashmir, the leaves serve as a substitute for PAAN (betel leaves). In classical times, the leaves, then known as *malabathrum*, were exported to Rome. *Tejpat* is sometimes translated as 'bay leaf' but it is not the same as the bay leaf used in western cuisine (*Laurus nobilis*).

Cassia bark was sometimes used to perfume drinking water. The buds, called *nagkesar* in Hindi, are the unopened flowers of the tree. They are picked just before blooming and dried in the sun. Their unique flavour is close to that of cinnamon but more flowery. They are used whole for flavouring spicy dishes and pulao, and ground for use in masalas.

Helen Saberi

CHEESE

Cattle were brought to the subcontinent by Indo-European tribes who migrated from Central Asia starting around 2000 BCE. The literature of the Vedic period (2000 BCE–800 BCE) contains many references to cow and buffalo milk and such products as yogurt, butter and clarified butter (GHEE). It also mentions a dairy product called *dadhanvat* made with and without pores, but there is disagreement among scholars as to whether this refers to cheese or curds.

The best-known and most widely used cheese in India is *CHHANA*, used mainly in making SWEETS, and PANEER. But, there are other varieties of regional cheeses that are less well known.

Bandal (also spelled *bandel*) is an unripened salted soft cheese made from cow's milk. The curd is separated from the milk by the addition of a souring agent, salted and drained in perforated pots and then soaked for several days in whey or water. It is sold in small disks seven to ten cm in diameter and has a brownish coating. The name comes from a town twenty-five miles/forty km north of KOLKATA, one of several ports settled by the Portuguese in the seventeenth century. (The word comes from the Portuguese *bandar*, which means port). A related cheese produced by the Portuguese is Dacca cheese, a dry smoked cheese shaped in disks. The size and shape of these cheeses are like those of many modern Portuguese cheeses. Today they are available only in a few speciality shops in Kolkata and Dhaka, Bangladesh.

Kalimpong is an Indian cheese named after the hill station in West Bengal. Unripened it has a semi-smooth edible rind and a slightly acidic flavour, and a crumbly texture when ripened. Its flavour has been compared to aged Gouda. It was first made by Swiss missionaries in the nineteenth century using cows and machinery imported from Europe. Called the Swiss Dairy, the enterprise originally operated as a charitable trust but it shut down in the 1970s. Kalimpong cheese is now being produced by Dairy Makarios Bous.

Because of their cold climates, mountainous areas lend themselves well to cheese making. *Chhurpi* is a yak or cow milk-based cheese that originated in Tibet and today is made in Nepal, Sikkim and Bhutan. It has a smelly odour (*churu* means spoiled in Nepali) and is sold in two versions: a soft *chhurpi* used as a filling for momos and a hard version for stews.

Kalari, also called milk chapati, is made from cow or goat milk by the semi-nomadic Gujjar Bakarwal community in Jammu and Kashmir. It has a mozzarella like texture. In winter, thick chapati-sized disks are browned on large griddles. Served between two buns and topped with CHUTNEY, it is a popular street food called *kalari* kulcha. Another cheese made by this community is *qudam* which comes from the whey produced by making *kalari*. It has a rubbery crumbly texture and when dried and salted is a source of protein during the cold winters.

In 1955, small milk producers in the western state of Gujarat formed a cooperative that markets dairy products under the Amul brand (from Sanskrit *amulya,* meaning priceless; see DAIRY SECTOR). The most popular is a soft pale yellow cheese sold in round cans and packages. This cheese is hundred per cent vegetarian and is made with microbial rennet. Other Amul products are processed cheddar cheese, mozzarella, pizza cheese, Emmenthaler and Gouda. Kraft processed cheese products have also been popular in India.

Most Indian cheeses are vegetarian, which means that the curds are not separated from the whey with rennet, which is obtained from the stomach of calves. An exception is a traditional PARSI cheese *topli nu* paneer, a velvety soft cheese made by setting the curds in baskets called *topli*. The process may have been introduced to the community by the Dutch in Surat, and the cheese is sometimes also called *Surti* paneer.

Since 1988, cheesemakers from Italy and Holland at Auroville, an experimental community in Puducherry, have been making handmade Western-style cheeses using natural, chemical-free and non-animal products under the brand name La Ferme, including cheddar, mozzarella, feta, Gruyère and Auroblochon. The monks in the Benedictine Community in Bengaluru make and sell homemade Italian cheeses under the name Vallambrosa, the name of the order's founding monastery in Italy.

The emergence of young urban 'foodies' has led to the beginnings of a wine and cheese culture and small farms near Indian cities are producing artisanal cheeses. Cheese platters are especially in demand at Diwali, featuring cheeses with a 'masala twist' – cheese infused with CHILLI, truffle and GARLIC. The Delhi-based company, Kumaoni Blessings, now produces more than ten handmade cheeses, while at Chennai's Käse, a team of young women with disabilities hand-make over two tonnes of cheese a month using no preservatives, including goat milk cheddar and Gouda. Some makers incorporate traditional Indian flavours into their cheese. Käse offers an aged cheddar rubbed with *podi* (see SPICE BOX). Mansi Jasani of the Cheese Collective replaces the traditional Herbs de Provence in her cabecou with a dish of CORIANDER- and CUMIN-scented *pav bhaji* masala. Recently, however, Indian cheesemakers have been served legal notices by Italian and Swiss cheesemakers challenging their use of the words Parmesan, Gruyère and other protected designations, with the result that some are now calling their cheeses 'alpine style'.

Colleen Sen

- Ellis-Petersen, Hannah. 'Swapping Paneer for Pecorino: India Gets Taste for European Cheeses'. *The Guardian*, 12 November 2021.
- Govil, Bhavika. 'Types of Indian Cheese You Didn't Know About'. *Outlook Traveller*, 20 November 2019.
- Outlook Traveller Staff. '8 Cheeses Made in India That You Must Pick Up on Your Travels'. *Outlook Traveller*, 17 February 2020.

CHENNAI

India's fifth largest city and the capital of the state of Tamil Nadu, Chennai is located on the Coromandel Coast of the Bay of Bengal. The area was home to Armenian and Portuguese traders before the arrival of the British in 1639. The East Indian Company built a fort, called Fort St. George, at a trading post at a fishing village called Madraspatnam, which they shortened to Madras. The EIC gradually expanded its control and by 1801, having defeated the last of the local rulers, became masters of South India, with Madras as their administrative and commercial capital. In 1996, the name was changed to Chennai (from Chennappa Naicker, the Rajah of Chandragiri).

Over the years Chennai has evolved as a culture hub. Its pristine beaches (including the world's longest, Marina beach) and heritage sites (Mamallapuram and many ancient temples) attract many domestic and foreign tourists. It is also an education hub, the site of one of the country's top universities, the Indian Institute of Technology-Madras (est. 1955), and the world-renowned arts and cultural academy, Kalakshetra Foundation. Since the 1990s, the city has been home to leading technology companies and intellectual incubators. Young people arriving from across the country for employment have made a major contribution to the city's culinary scene.

For tourists from India and abroad, the most popular foods are the iconic Tamil Nadu foods IDLI and DOSA served with an assortment of CHUTNEYS. They are available at STREET FOOD stalls and in five-star hotels. Another popular dish is *venpongal*, a savoury breakfast dish made by cooking RICE and *moong* dal (see PULSES) with slit green CHILLIES, grated GINGER and a pinch of ASAFOETIDA, and garnished with GHEE, peppercorns (see PEPPER, BLACK), CUMIN seeds, cashews and CURRY LEAVES.

Parotta or *burotta*, a flat layered BREAD made with refined flour, is the king of street food in Chennai and Tamil Nadu. It is usually served with *salna*, a spicy aromatic gravy. The popular *kothu parotta* is made with shredded *parotta*, sliced ONION, TOMATO, green chillies, ginger-GARLIC and a spice mixture. Usually egg, or, on request, chicken or mutton may be added. *Parotta* and *kothu parotta* are dinner-time specials served on highways through the night.

Every neighbourhood in the city has a couple of street food stalls serving morning breakfast dishes such as idli, dosa, *pongal* or puri. They also offer tea time snacks such as *bajji* (vegetables dipped in batter and fried in oil; see PAKORA), *bonda* (*urad* dal soaked and ground into a paste, with added green chilli, chopped COCONUT bits and black pepper), masala *vadai* (a doughnut-shaped deep-fried fritter made with gram dal, garam masala, onion, curry leaves and MINT leaves; see VADA), and *medu vadai* (a doughnut-shaped deep-fried fritter made from *urad* dal and spiced with black pepper, ginger and curry leaves). *Vada* CURRY is a typical Chennai speciality, this aromatic and spicy dish is made using leftover masala *vadai*, and goes well with idli and dosa. In the evening, these stalls serve dosa, idli, *parotta* and *kothu parotta*. Tea stalls, called *petti kadai*, are popular places to drink freshly made TEA or COFFEE and some light snacks or biscuits. Some remain open throughout the night, making it convenient for people working on night shifts. These stalls are also community hubs where people discuss politics and read newspapers. Tender coconuts, watermelons (see MELONS) and JACKFRUITS are sold on the roadside, while fruit vendors sell freshly cut fruit. Soups stalls, normally selling piping hot BANANA stem soup and herbal soup, are located near supermarkets and are well patronized by office goers and homemakers.

As a cultural melting pot, Chennai streetside vendors and many hole-in-the-wall eateries, especially in North Chennai, also sell Burmese food. (Many Tamils left Burma in the early 1960s). A typical dish is *atho* – fiery noodles tossed with cabbage, onion and TAMARIND juice. In recent times, Mediterranean food items such as falafel and shawarma have become popular fast-foods among the younger generation. Hot fresh momos are sold at kiosks set up at the entrance of supermarkets. While in other cities the street food scenario has become highly commercialized, in Chennai the sector has not undergone much change. A sense of camaraderie and equality prevails at these stalls.

Other star attractions, especially among the tourists and visiting chefs from across the globe, are the food stalls at Marina Beach, Elliots Beach and other locations along the East Coast Road. Popular FISH varieties such as barracuda, red snapper, seer fish and trevally are on display. Well marinated with spices and chilli powder, they are fried and served to customers upon order. Squids and prawns are also crowd pleasers. In the past, all that beach-goers had to snack on was *sundal*, a traditional South *Indian* dish usually made with boiled white *chana*, or chickpeas, tossed with a garnish of MUSTARD seeds, grated coconut, raw MANGO and curry leaves.

Stalls near schools, colleges and offices sell sandwiches and instant noodles made in a hundred different ways. In the past decade, mobile *pani puri* (see STREET FOOD) carts have been stationed near educational institutions.

In Chennai, people strolling in and around the beaches and in large community parks enjoy health-promoting foods such as herbal concoctions, steamed food and traditional MILLET porridge that are served in these spots during the morning hours. There has also been a rise in mobile carts serving *puttu*, a rice-based dish. To make it, rice is processed and made into flour and then steamed and served with fresh coconut, banana and jaggery (see SUGAR). As millet-based food is popular in this part of the world, certain millet-based steamed snacks such as finger millet dosa, kodo millet dumplings and foxtail millet *pongal* are also served in these carts.

Popular drinks served at fruit juice stalls include SHERBET milk, rose milk and fruit mix. Golden yellow masala *paal* (milk simmered with SAFFRON, CARDAMOM and other aromatic spices) simmering on a low heat in a pan is a post-dinner drink for many who drink it along with a banana. Chennai residents are coffee drinkers and there are establishments on every street corner serving a sweet milky coffee made from dark roasted beans mixed with chicory, with added high-fat milk and served in a *davara* tumbler set.

Chennai also has a vibrant restaurant scene. The Woodlands Hotel and Dasaprakash chains of so-called 'Udupi hotels' serving South Indian vegetarian food were both founded here (see UDUPI RESTAURANTS). Another category of restaurants are military hotels, which sprung up in Chennai and BENGALURU during the Second World War to serve non-vegetarian food to military personnel stationed in these cities. One of the oldest in Chennai is Velu Military Hotel. Their standard meal, served on a banana leaf, includes their signature *vanjaram meen kuzhambu* (with seer fish), a mutton gravy and a chicken curry along with the regular accompaniments. Their spice mixtures are all hand-ground on traditional grinding stones. Other military hotels similar to Velu Military Hotel are Ponnusamy Hotel, Junior Kuppanna, Anjappar Chettinadu Hotel and Hotel Panidan. Upscale restaurants serving South Indian food in elegant settings include Dakshin, Southern Spice in the Taj Coromandel Hotel and Raintree in the Taj Connemarra serving Chettinad cuisine.

Chitradeepa Anantharam

- Ashraf, Yasir. 'Street Food: Think before You Eat'. *The Hindu*, 24 July 2011.
- Rajagopalan, Ashwin. 'Chennai's Disappearing Military Hotels'. *The Indian Express*, 4 April 2016.
- Sinha, Vipasha. 'Street Food in Chennai: Hot without the Haute'. *The Hindu*, 21 August 2013.

CHERRIES

Cherries (Hindi *chiri*) belong to the genus *Prunus* of the rose family and are related to PLUMS, peaches, APRICOTS and almonds. There are two kinds of cultivated cherry: sweet and sour. The sour cherry, *P. cerasus* from *P. cerasoides* (wild Himalayan cherry) in India is called *paddam* or *phaya* and is still found in the Himalayan region. They are generally not eaten raw because of their acidity and astringency but can be made into CHUTNEYS and preserves. The British found that they made a very good cherry brandy or could be made into sorbet, compote or sauces.

The sweet cherry is descended from the wild species *Prunus avium* and likely came to India during Emperor Akbar's reign (1556–1605) when Akbar's governor, Mohammad Quli Afshar, brought strains of apricots and cherries from Kabul to Kashmir. Cherry varieties were developed and were purported to be even sweeter than those of Kabul.

Cherries thrive in high altitudes and colder climates so it is not surprising that the three main states cultivating cherries commercially are Jammu and Kashmir, Uttar Pradesh and Himachal Pradesh. Several varieties are produced in colours ranging from yellowish-pink to dark red. However, India's production is low compared to many other countries and despite the often poor quality – most of India's cherries are small, hard and tart – their popularity is increasing as a dessert fruit or for making juices and SHERBETS or adding to BIRYANIS.

Helen Saberi

- Achaya, K.T. *A Historical Dictionary of Indian Food*. Delhi: OUP, 1998.
- Reddy, Catherine. 'All about Cherries in India'. The Earth of India, 28 September 2012. Available online: http://theindianvegan.blogspot.com/2012/09/all-about-cherries-in-india.html (accessed 14 April 2022).

CHHANA

Chhana (also spelled *chhena*; not to be confused with *chana*, chickpea) are the curds that are produced by separating boiling cow or buffalo milk with a souring agent, such as lemon juice, sour milk or lactic acid. They are then strained to remove the whey and kneaded to produce a product with varying degrees of smoothness. PANEER is made by the same process but is pressed to remove most of the liquid.

Chhana is mainly produced in East India and, mixed with SUGAR, is the basis of many Bengali sweets, such as *SANDESH*, RASGULLA, *pantua*, *ras malai* and others (see SWEETS). A common theory is that the Portuguese introduced the process of splitting milk in the seventeenth century. However, the early twelfth-century text *MANASOLLASA* describes a similar process used to make small balls that were fried. According to K.T. ACHAYA, an Aryan taboo on the deliberate 'breaking' of milk meant that this was not a popular food item.

Colleen Sen

- Achaya, K.T. *A Historical Dictionary of Indian Food*. New Delhi: OUP, 1998.

CHHATTISGARH

The state of Chhattisgarh was formed in 2000 by combining ten Chhattisgarhi- and six Gondi- speaking districts in southeast Madhya Pradesh. Today it is India's ninth largest state in area and the seventeenth in population. The northern and southern parts of the state are hilly while the central part is a fertile plain. Located in the heart of India, its cuisine has been influenced by the seven neighbouring states of Uttar Pradesh, Madhya Pradesh, Maharashtra, Jharkhand, Odisha, Telangana and Andhra Pradesh.

Scheduled Tribes constitute over 30 per cent of the state's population (and 10 per cent of all Scheduled Tribes in India) and are located mainly in the forests of Bastar and other districts in South Chhattisgarh. The largest tribe in the state (and in India) is the twelve million Gonds. They are subdivided into the Hill Marias, the Bison Horn Marias and the Murias, all of whom speak different Dravidian dialects. Smaller tribes are the Dhurva, the Bhattra and the Halbi, who speak an Indo-European language called Chhattisgarhi that is the official state language along with Hindi. These tribes have lived in the forests for thousands of years, protected by the rugged terrain against successive waves of invaders. Their origins are unknown. Some scholars claim they are Dravidians who fled into the forests to escape the Aryans who came from the north in the second millennium BCE. Others believe they predate the Dravidians and are related to the Australoid people of the South Pacific. Still others link them to the Mongoloid tribes of northeastern India. The state has one of the highest poverty rates in the country.

The main occupations in Chhattisgarh are agriculture and animal husbandry. Productivity is low since many farmers practise traditional cultivation methods such as slash-and-burn. Moreover, the climate is very hot and irrigation and mono-cropping are limited. The main crops are RICE, kodo and other small MILLETS, *toor/tuvar* and *kulthi* lentils (see PULSES), peanuts and sunflowers. Much of the produce is consumed locally. Traditional foods are made of rice, rice flour, yogurt and green leafy vegetables. The diet of the tribals in the most remote parts of the state is austere. Staples are a gruel of rice and millet, or a dish called *bore*, made by fermenting cooked rice overnight and often eaten for breakfast. It is supplemented by whatever the women can gather in the forest: MANGOES, BANANAS, and other fruits, BERRIES, roots, MUSHROOMS (which thrive in the monsoon season), and tubers including wild tapioca and YAMS.

Meat was much more plentiful in the days when the forests were filled with game including tigers, panthers, bear, leopards, *cheetal* (spotted deer), jackal, jungle fowl and bisons. The state animal of Chhattisgarh – the wild bison – is conspicuous by its absence: today, it is found only in wildlife sanctuaries and in the name of the Bison Horn Marias, who wear elaborate headdresses made from feathers and bison horns during their famous dance. Now, the forests are almost empty because of the wholesale slaughter of animals in the past. In a traditional hunt called *porad*, hundreds of tribals would set fire to a long strip of forest and slaughter the animals with spears or poison-tipped arrows when they fled the flames.

Wealthier households raise chickens. Another source of proteins are rats and mice, which are smoked out of the fields after the rice harvest and boiled or roasted. Grubs and insects are also eaten. Red ants and red ant eggs, CHILLI and SALT are pounded and made into a piquant CHUTNEY made famous by the British chef Gordon Ramsey during a visit to India.

The tribal people make and consume their own ALCOHOL. Sago palms are tapped to make *sulfi*, a form of toddy. Immediately after it is tapped, *sulfi* has a tangy dry taste reminiscent of champagne but as it thickens it becomes stronger. Another local alcoholic beverage, *mahua,* is brewed from the flowers and seeds of the *mahua* tree (*Madhuca indica*). The flowers are placed in a large pot, soaked in water for a couple of days and then boiled. A small pot is placed inside the large pot, so that the vapours from the large pot condense inside. The liquor is decanted through a small pipe. In the mid-nineteenth century, twenty distilleries near MUMBAI produced *mahua* spirit made from the flowers transported by train from the region. The Gonds also eat *mahua* flowers, sometimes mixed with chickpea flour or parched grains.

More than 20,000 varieties of rice grow in Chhattisgarh and scientists are studying them in order to identify strains that are tasty, high-yielding and hardy. Rice is used in many dishes prepared by both tribal and non-tribal Chhattisgarhis. *Chila* is a thin DOSA-like BREAD made with rice flour seasoned with chillies, ONIONS and GARLIC and served with chutney. *Phara* are small tubes made from rice flour dough and sautéed in MUSTARD seeds, CUMIN, chilli and other spices. *Muthia* are steamed dumplings made from rice flour. A traditional dish is *iddhar* – *urad* dal paste is spread on the leaves of a local plant which are steamed, then deep-fried and served in a spiced yogurt sauce. A popular SAMBAR is *aamat* (similar to Maharashtrian *aamti*), a tangy dal made from lentils or chickpeas, TOMATOES, TAMARIND, BAMBOO SHOOTS and other vegetables and often thickened with the water from soaked rice. *Rakhi badi* are deep-fried balls of fermented *urad* dal paste mixed with pumpkin or other vegetables and served at festivals.

Colleen Sen

- Sen, Colleen Taylor. 'The Forest Foodways of the Tribals of India's Bastar District'. In *Wild Foods: Proceedings of the Oxford Symposium on Food and Cookery 2004*, edited by Ken Albala, 285–90. Totnes, Devon: Prospect Books, 2005.
- Shrivastava, Ambika. *The Complete Chhattisgarh Cookbook: Where Indian Cuisine Begins*. E-book edition. Online: Create Space Independent Publishing Platform, 2017.

CHICKEN 65

Chicken 65 is the name given to chicken pieces on the bone deep-fried and doused with generous helpings of red CHILLI and black pepper (see PEPPER, BLACK) powders. A popular offering at the Buhari Hotel, a restaurant that opened its doors on CHENNAI'S arterial Mount Road (now known as Anna Salai) in 1951, chicken 65 made headlines in 2000, when it was the subject of a question in the first season of the blockbuster TV quiz show, *Kaun Banega Crorepati* (based on the British series, *Who Wants to Be a Millionaire?*), anchored by the Bollywood superstar Amitabh Bachchan. The quiz show declared the inventor of chicken 65 to be the restaurant's stylish owner, A.M. Buhari (1910–96), who grew up in Colombo, Sri Lanka. It was then that the dish attained iconic status.

All guidebooks recommend chicken 65 as a must-have for visitors to Chennai, but Buhari was originally famous for its BIRYANIS, notably the mutton or chicken biryani that comes with a whole boiled egg and the *idiyappam* biryani where basmati rice is replaced by vermicelli. Equally popular are its mutton SAMOSAS.

Buhari Hotel had many firsts to its credit. It is still remembered, for instance, for being the first restaurant in Madras (as Chennai was known during the British Raj and for many years thereafter) to have a jukebox for its patrons to play their favourite songs. Now its patrons go there to have chicken 65 before anything else. The restaurant now also offers chicken 78, chicken 82 and chicken 90, but chicken 65 remains the unchallenged star of its menu.

The dish owes its mystique also to the nationwide guessing game set off by its enigmatic name. Does the name originate because only 65-day-old chickens are used for it? Or, because the recipe calls for sixty-five ingredients? Or, because the item appears on page 65 of the menu card? The now-accepted story is that Buhari, according to his grandson Nawaz, added this no-fuss dish to the restaurant's menu after his friends loved it at the New Year's Eve party he had hosted on the last day of 1965. Chicken 65 owes its name, without doubt, to the year in which it was born. All other variants also carry the last two digits of the years when they were introduced into the menu. Buhari may not have realized it but 65 is his lucky number.

Sourish Bhattacharyya

- Malik, Kriti. 'A Delicious History of Chicken 65 & the Ultimate Recipe'. *NDTV Food*, 19 July 2017. Available online: https://food.ndtv.com/opinions/a-delicious-history-chicken-65-ultimate-recipe-776763# (accessed 15 April 2022).
- Rajagopalan, Ashwin, 'Once and for All: Why Is the Chicken 65 Called the Chicken 65?' *The Indian Express*, 17 May 2016.

CHICKEN MANCHURIAN

Born in 1950, Nelson Wang is best known for being the principal protagonist of what is now famous as CHINESE INDIAN CUISINE and is credited with the invention of the hugely popular local favourite known as chicken Manchurian, which has spawned equivalent dishes made with PANEER (cottage cheese) and cauliflower florets (*gobhi*).

A flamboyant restaurateur who owns and runs the China Garden restaurants, Wang is a third-generation descendant of Hakka immigrants who settled in the then British Raj metropolis of Calcutta, now KOLKATA. He arrived in MUMBAI in the early 1970s with just Rs 20 and landed a job as a lowly assistant cook in Frederick's, a popular Chinese restaurant in its heyday. Here, he acquired a following because of his cooking skills and soon was approached by the owner of a hole-in-the-wall establishment called China Town. The restaurant was an instant success. One of his regular takeaway customers was the then cricket czar and former royal, Raj Singh Dungarpur, who invited Wang to open a restaurant at the prestigious Cricket Club of India. The new place was named Chinaman In Mumbai, where a member asked Wang to create a dish different from the standard fare. Wang dipped a few chicken pieces in a thick corn flour batter, deep-fried them and served them in a hot sauce made with soy sauce, vinegar, ONIONS, CHILLIES and GARLIC.

Chicken Manchurian was born and was an instant hit that was adopted with amazing alacrity by the entire Indo-Chinese restaurant community. The name is a mystery, for Manchuria is the name of a region in China's northeast that was controlled by the Japanese from 1932 to 1945. Wang once said to the writer that when he was cooking the dish, a radio news broadcast was on and there was an item on Manchuria. The name stuck in his head and that was how it became an inextricable part of the most famous and enduring Indo-Chinese dish.

Riding on the success of Chicken Manchurian and his indefatigable stamina for work, Wang established China Garden in the tony Kemps Corner neighbourhood of South Mumbai and it soon became the go-to place for the city's showbiz elite. The restaurant has survived both in Mumbai and in India's national capital, New Delhi, and so has Wang's culinary legacy.

Sourish Bhattacharyya

- Bala, Priya and Jayanth Narayanan. *Secret Sauce: Inspiring Stories of Great Indian Restaurants*. Noida, Uttar Pradesh: Harper Business, 2018.
- Sharma, Nik. 'The Manchurian Dish You'll Mostly Find in India'. *TASTE*, 15 February 2018. Available online: https://www.tastecooking.com/manchurian-dish-youll-mostly-find-india/ (accessed 15 April 2022).

CHILLIES

FIGURE 11 CHILLIES. Chilli vendor, Mumbai. Colleen Sen.

Chillies* are the fruits of plants from the genus *Capsicum* and are a relative of green pepper. The word 'chili' comes from Nahuatl, a central Mexican language. Its Hindi names, *hari* (green) and *lal* (red) *mirch*, are adaptations of *kali mirch*, black pepper.

Chillies were brought from the New World by the Portuguese in the sixteenth century and became assimilated as a replacement for long and black pepper (see PEPPER, LONG and PEPPER, BLACK). They were first introduced to Goa and from there spread to South India. However, there is no mention of chillies in the works of Garcia DE ORTA (1563) or in the *Ain-i-Akbari* (1590). According to one account, chillies were introduced to North India by the Maratha army in the mid-eighteenth century. Their victories over the MUGHALS were attributed to their fiery warlike nature that came from their consumption of chillies. At first, chillies were used to prepare PICKLES and CHUTNEYS, adding another layer of flavour to the already pungent relishes, and later were incorporated into other preparations. Today, three-fourths of India's chillies are produced in Andhra Pradesh, Maharashtra, Karnataka and Tamil Nadu and India is the largest producer of dried red chillies in the world. Six chillies have a GEOGRAPHICAL INDICATION (GI) tag.

Chillies' hotness comes from capsaicin, an alkaloid found mainly in the membranes lining the pod. (The pungency of pepper, on the other hand, is due to the volatile oil piperine and resin, which increase the flow of saliva and gastric juices.) In small quantities, it has a gentle warmth that stimulates the appetite and helps digestion, but in larger amounts it can burn the mouth. One explanation for chillies' popularity, apart from the fact that they enliven bland food, is that the burning sensation in the mouth causes the brain to produce endomorphins which produce a pleasurable feeling and may be mildly addictive. Chillies also contain powerful antibiotic chemicals that can kill or suppress the bacteria and fungi that spoil foods. The antibiotic effects are even more potent when combined with ONIONS, GARLIC, CUMIN and other spices.

The hotness of chillies is gauged in Scoville Heat Units (SHU) which measures the number of times chilli extract dissolved in water can be diluted in SUGAR before the hotness disappears. There is a worldwide competition to see who can produce the hottest chillies. As of January 2022, the title holder was the Carolina Reaper, created by crossing a ghost pepper (*bhut jolokia,* native to Northeast India) with a habanero; it has a maximum SHU of 2,220,000.

Chillies start out green and become red and slightly sweeter as they ripen. The variety of a chilli is more important than its colour. Chillies are used either whole and fresh, whole and dried, crushed or powdered.

In India, several varieties of New World capsicum were domesticated in different regions. Today the most popular chillies include the following:

- **Bhavnagri.** Large enough to be stuffed, these mild green chillies are an ingredient in *mirch ka salan,* an accompaniment to Hyderabadi BIRYANIS.
- **Bhiwapur (GI tag).** Grown in the Nagpur district of Maharashtra, these chillies are known for their bright red colour that is used as a dye in food and cosmetics.
- **Bori.** Dark red and berry shaped, they are moderately spicy and used for tempering dals and vegetable dishes.
- **Byadagi.** Dark red and fairly mild, these chillies from Karnataka are used in *bisi bhele bhat*, SAMBAR and other dishes.
- **Edayur (GI tag).** A very mild chilli grown in Kerala that is fried and served as a side dish.

- **Guntur (GI tag).** From Andhra Pradesh's Guntur district, home to the largest chili market in India, these red chillies are very hot, lending a characteristic flavour to Andhra dishes, including the famous Avikkai pickle.
- **Harmal (GI tag).** This smooth red chilli with medium to high pungency has been grown for 200 years in Goa and is used in chicken *xacuti*, VINDALOO and other Goan dishes.
- **Iwali.** The standard green or red chilli used in many Indian households, it can be quite pungent. It is an accompaniment to snacks, used to make pickles and an ingredient in many CURRIES.
- **Kanthari.** Green and red and very hot, they are used mainly in Kerala, Tamil Nadu and Meghalaya to make chutneys and pickles.
- **Khola (GI tag).** This Goan chilli has a brilliant red colour and medium pungency.
- **Kashmiri.** Deep red in colour, it is fairly mild-tasting and adds colour to a dish.
- **Longi.** Fairly hot red chillies used in some Maharashtrian dishes and in BIKANERI *BHUJIA*, a snack made with moth beans and chickpea flour.
- **Mathania.** A bright red very pungent chilli used mainly in Rajasthan to make the famous *laal maas*.
- **Mizo (GI tag).** Also called Bird's Eye chillies, they are small, red, very hot chillies used in the Northeast to make pickles.
- **Naga/Bhut Jolokia.** Cultivated in the Northeast, these roundish bright red chilis are very hot and used mainly locally, especially in pickles.
- **Ramnad Mundu.** From Tamil Nadu's Ramnad region, these round, dark red and spicy chillies are added to sambar, chutneys and curries.
- **Sankeshwari.** Red, hot and popular in Maharashtrian cuisine, especially along the coast.

*In the United States, the singular is 'chili' and the plural 'chilies'. In the UK, the spellings are 'chilli' and 'chillies'.

Colleen Sen

- Harshad. '13+ Different Types of Chillies in India'. *Sprout Monk*, 23 September 2020. Available online: https://sproutmonk.com/types-of-chilies-in-india/ (accessed 15 April 2022).
- Paralkar, Anil. 'How Potatoes and Chillies Conquered Indian Cuisine'. *Firstpost*, March 26 2019. Available online: https://www.firstpost.com/india/how-potatoes-and-chillies-conquered-indian-cuisine-6329111.html (accessed 15 April 2022).
- PepperHead. 'Top 10 Hottest Peppers'. *n.d.* Available online: https://pepperhead.com/top-10-worlds-hottest-peppers/ (accessed 15 April 2022).

CHINESE INDIAN CUISINE

Chinese Indian cuisine, also called Chindian cuisine and sometimes jokingly labelled as Sino-Ludhianvi or 'Punjchi' (Punjabi-Chinese), is the generic name given to Chinese food as it has evolved in India, from the homes of Chinese settlers in the eighteenth and

FIGURE 12 CHINESE INDIAN CUISINE. Sing Cheung sauce factory, Kolkata. Ashish Sen.

nineteenth centuries to today's neighbourhood restaurants and roadside 'Chinese vans'. It comes doused with generous helpings of Kikkoman soy sauce and Pou Chong green chilli sauce; it uses CORN flour for batters and to thicken gravies that are pumped up with red CHILLIES, GARLIC and lots of GINGER to cater to local taste buds; and adds ingredients such as PANEER and *gobhi* (cauliflower) for the vegetarians. If five dishes were to define this hybrid, Chinese-inspired Indian-influenced cuisine, they would be Hakka noodles, manchow soup, CHICKEN MANCHURIAN, chilli chicken and chicken lollipop.

The cuisine is the second most popular dining-out option in India, thanks to flourishing Indo-Chinese restaurants, many of them decades old. They are located primarily in KOLKATA, MUMBAI and DELHI and are run mainly by people of Tibetan and Nepalese origin living in India.

India's contacts with China date back to the visits of Faxian (Fa-Hien), who travelled on foot to reach the eastern parts of the country in the early fifth century, and Xuanzang (Hiuen Tsang) in the seventh century. These were sporadic appearances till the Portuguese started kidnapping Chinese children and selling them into slavery in India in the sixteenth century. One of them, in fact, was rescued from slavery and became a prized fighter in the forces of the fourth Kunjali Marakkar, the admiral of the navy of the Samoothiri Raja (Zamorin) of Calicut (Kozhikode) who fought and defeated the Portuguese till he was betrayed and beheaded.

Officially, the history of Chinese settlement in India begins with the invitation extended by the British Governor-General, Warren Hastings, to Yang Tai Chaw (better known as Tong Achew), a trader from either Guangdong or Fujian province in China who landed at

Budge Budge on the Hooghly River near Calcutta (the present-day Kolkata), to establish a SUGAR plantation in 1778. With Tong Achew, whose grave and the temple he established still survive and attract a steady stream of visitors, the Chinese community, predominantly composed of Hakka people, started growing in and around Calcutta, especially in the Bow Bazar area. They were prized for their skills in carpentry, shoe-making and, later, dentistry. Another wave of the Chinese came into the country because their labour was required in the new TEA plantations coming up in Assam in India's northeast. In the south, meanwhile, Chinese convicts externed from the Straits Settlements were settled in the hills of the Nilgiris in the then Madras Presidency (present-day Tamil Nadu). They inter-married with Tamil Paralyan women and ran tanneries and opium dens, and produced lard.

Later, throughout the late nineteenth and early twentieth centuries, especially after the Opium Wars, the Revolution of 1911 and the Japanese invasion of Manchuria, settlers from the Chinese mainland started streaming into India, and in their wake, restaurants proliferated that were initially operated out of Chinese homes by the enterprising wives of the expatriates. Kolkata is also famous for its Chinese community, which has now dwindled to a microscopic minority, primarily because the suspicion with which it was viewed and the confinement of its members in penal camps during the 1962 India-China War triggered an inevitable reverse migration, with those who were better educated moving to Canada and Australia. And wherever they went, they took their brand of Chindian cuisine with them, even giving birth to 'Tangra cuisine', a popular term that is used to describe the food served in the restaurants of the Calcutta suburb after which it is named – a suburb that used to have all the Chinese-run tanneries till they were relocated because of environmental concerns.

Tangra, however, was never on a par with the Chinese Indian restaurants of Calcutta/Kolkata, such as Eau Chew (which is regarded as the oldest surviving Chinese Indian restaurant and is still run by the Huang family who opened it four generations ago in 1922), Chungwa and Nanking. Kolkata is equally famous for its Tiretti Bazaar neighbourhood, India's original China Town, which transforms every Sunday morning into an open-air food market, where stalls spring up to serve low-priced, home-made Hakka delicacies such as fresh steaming *sui mai* and FISH ball soup, breaded pork chops, chicken pies, COCONUT balls, and RICE and SESAME seed sweet balls. At this market was born *The Legend of Fat Mama*, the award-winning BBC World documentary on the Chinese Indian community that takes off with the story of 'Fat Mama' who was famous as the maker of the best noodles in Kolkata before her family migrated to Toronto, Canada.

Nelson Wang was the inventor of chicken Manchurian whose vegetarian version with cauliflower, *gobhi* Manchurian, is more popular outside India. Apart from chicken Manchurian, the most sought-after Chindian delicacy is the manchow soup which is prepared with assorted vegetables, scallions and chicken, thickened with broth and corn flour, flavoured with generously poured soy sauce and ginger, as well as garlic, chillies and SALT, garnished with green onions and served with crispy fried noodles. Another popular invention is the chicken lollipop, essentially a chicken winglet fattened into a ball and coated with a spicy red batter prepared with corn flour, red chilli powder and TURMERIC; deep-fried; and served on a bone to give it the appearance of a lollipop. Other must-haves include the sweet-and-savoury chilli chicken (it has a paneer equivalent as well), a version of General Tso's chicken that goes by the name of sweet and sour chicken (prawns, pork and vegetables are the alternatives), fried spring rolls, and the most sought-after dessert, *darsan* noodles or honey-glazed fried flat noodles sprinkled with sesame seeds.

Such has been the abiding popularity of Chinese (and/or Chindian) food in India that the iconic Taj Mahal Palace Hotel opened Golden Dragon, a fine-dining restaurant dedicated to the cuisine of Sichuan (popularly spelt as 'Schechwan' across India), back in 1973, at a time when five-star hotels swore by 'Continental' cuisine and consigned Indian restaurants to their basements. It made five-star hotels across India open their doors to Chinese/Chindian restaurants and the trend percolated down to standalone establishments in big cities and small towns, and across the world, from Toronto and New York City to Singapore and Sydney.

Sourish Bhattacharyya

- Khamgaonkar, Sanjiv. 'Chinese Food in India: A Fiery Fusion of Flavors'. *CNN Travel*, 12 July 2017. Available online: https://edition.cnn.com/travel/article/india-chinese-food-fusion/index.html (accessed 15 April 2022).
- Sharma, Umang. 'Open at 5AM, Tiretti Bazaar in Kolkata Is a Paradise for Every Authentic Chinese Food Lover'. *Indiatimes*, 2 July 2017. Available online: https://www.indiatimes.com/culture/food/open-at-5am-tiretti-bazaar-in-kolkata-is-a-paradise-for-every-authentic-chinese-food-lover-321337.html (accessed 15 April 2022).

CHUTNEY

Derived from the Hindi word *chatni* meaning 'to lick', chutney is a sweet-and-sour, savoury or chilli-hot condiment that is popular across India, Britain and in countries where there are large Indian DIASPORAS. Such is the popularity of this condiment in the Caribbean region that the word 'chutney' is also used to describe the blend of Bhojpuri and Calypso music that has acquired a cult following in that part of the world.

In India, unlike in Britain and the United States where it is slow-cooked, bottled and sold in supermarkets, chutney is made fresh for immediate consumption from finely chopped, sliced or pulverized fruit or vegetables, finely ground lentils (see PULSES) or fresh leaves reduced to a paste. An assortment of spices and herbs are used to make chutneys, ranging from GINGER, TAMARIND and TURMERIC to whole or ground MUSTARD and even hemp seeds, CORIANDER, MINT and green or dried red CHILLIES.

As a result, just about every dish in India comes accompanied with a particular chutney, from the fluid MINT and CORIANDER chutney served with KEBABS and tikkas in the north, the walnut and RADISH chutneys of Kashmir, to the thick multi-hued individual chutneys (COCONUT by itself or with coriander, TOMATO, peanut, moringa leaves and ridge GOURD) which come on the table with South Indian breakfast items (notably DOSA, VADA, IDLI and *uttapam*). The people of Andhra Pradesh love their peanut chutney and tomato *thokku*; the Maharashtrians spice up their meals with the chilli-kick of the green chilli *thecha*; and the Gujaratis living in the Kathiawar region don't consider a meal to be complete unless it is accompanied by their favourite GARLIC chutney.

Chutneys are integral to a number of popular dishes, such as the hot and dry vada *pav* chutney made primarily with garlic and ground peanuts; or the sweet and tangy tamarind and dried ginger (*saunth*) chutney that adds a new flavour dimension to the savoury street-side snack, chaat; or the 'gunpowder' *podi*/*pudi* prepared variously with ground lentils, peanuts and dried coconut (*kopra*), garlic and red chillies, which when mixed with GHEE and spread over an idli turns it into an umami bomb.

Such is the taste-making capacity of chutneys that one of them is remembered reverentially to this day by Mangalore's Catholic community. The chutney, whose recipe is not known, is attributed to a local nobleman, Balthazar of Belthangadi, one of 60,000 Christians from southern Karnataka who was persecuted and imprisoned between 1784 and 1799 by the fanatical Tipu Sultan of Mysore, who suspected the community of being sympathetic to the British because of their religious affiliation. The Catholics who did not convert to Islam or join Tipu's army were packed into dungeons and made to subsist on bad food. To bring some joy into their lives, Balthazar, or so the legend goes, created a chutney and served it among the prisoners to make their meals a little edible. Sadly, it remains a memory.

Some chutneys may not have historical connections but have become famous because of the exotic ingredients that go into them, such as red ants in Chhattisgarh and hemp seeds (*bhang jeera*) in Uttarakhand. Some are served at the end of festive meals, as in West Bengal, to act like a bridge between the savoury and dessert courses, notably the sweet 'plastic chutney' made with raw PAPAYA or the sweet-and-sour raw MANGO *ombol* garnished with *panch phoron* (see SPICE BOX).

The chutney, therefore, is in a class apart from PICKLES which are prepared with chunks of the main ingredient (vegetables, meats, FISH, raw mango or lime) preserved in mustard or gingelly oil spiked with spices for consumption over a long time, even up to a year. Nor must it be confused with *murabba*, the fruit preserve that 'lies in the intersection of jam and candied fruit' and is said to have originated in the Arab world. Incidentally, the term 'chutney' is often used interchangeably with 'relish' in Britain and the United States, but the latter in these two countries is generally tangy or mildly sweet, contains fewer spices, and has a more fluid, liquid consistency compared to the chunkiness of the chutneys.

Among the colonial chutneys, Major Grey's Mango Chutney – a sweet combination of mango, raisins, chillies, garlic, vinegar, SUGAR and spices – remains the most popular. The identity of Major Grey has been a mystery, though the consensus view today is that this British army officer who created the chutney with his Bengali cook was a figment of a brand marketer's fertile imagination. With tony department stores such as Fortnum and Mason stocking it, Major Grey's has remained untouched by competition from the more pungent Colonel Skinner's (named after the Anglo-Indian creator of the East India Company's army regiment, Skinner's Horse) and Bengal Club.

Major Grey's has been produced since the early 1800s by Cross & Blackwell, an English company whose history goes back to 1706. Santha RAMA RAU in her book *The Cooking of India* (1969) made it abundantly clear that 'store-bought chutneys' such as Major Grey's were 'regarded with scorn' by Indians. In the end, Rama Rau quoted the verse attributed to John F. Mackay:

> 'All things chickeney and mutt'ny
> Taste better far when served with chutney.
> This is the mystery eternal:
> Why didn't Major Grey make colo-nel?'

Major Grey may not have ever lived but he lives on in popular imagination.

Sourish Bhattacharyya

- Burton, David. *Raj at Table: A Culinary History of the British in India*. London: Faber and Faber, 1993.
- Jayashankar, Lavesh. 'Food and Migration in the Twentieth Century'. In *The Routledge History of Food*, edited by Carol Helstrosky, 313–31. New York: Routledge, 2013.
- Lowe, Caitlynn. 'What Is the Difference between Relish and Chutney?' *DelightedCooking*, 4 April 2022. Available online: https://www.delightedcooking.com/what-is-the-difference-between-relish-and-chutney.htm (accessed 15 April 2022).

CINNAMON

Cinnamon is the delicately flavoured inner bark of a tree of the laurel family, *Cinnamomum verum* (previously *C. zeylanicum*). It has been an important spice since antiquity and was one of the first spices sought in the explorations of the fifteenth and sixteenth centuries. Cinnamon is indigenous to Sri Lanka and has for long been exported to India, being considered the best, even though it is also grown in Tamil Nadu and Kerala. In 1767, Lord Brown of the British East India Company established Anjarakandy Cinnamon Estate in Cannanore district of Kerala. Spread over nearly 200 acres on the banks of the Anjarakandy River, this estate, called Cinnamon Valley, is considered to be the largest cinnamon plantation in Asia. Cinnamon is also grown in Munnar at the Cinnamon Gardens Spices Plantation.

Cinnamon is related to CASSIA and both have the same Hindi name of *dalchini*. They share many similarities except that cassia has a coarser texture and cinnamon is considered to have a more delicate taste and aroma. However, the two spices are often used interchangeably.

True cinnamon bark is fermented for twenty-four hours after being peeled. This enables the corky layer to be scraped off completely, leaving the thin bark to curl forming 'quills' (usually about 7.5 cm long) consisting of many curled strips of bark rolled together. These are the best grade and in cooking are usually kept whole, mainly for aesthetic reasons. There are three other grades:

> Quillings, the second grade, are broken or smaller pieces which are often left after the preparation of quills. They are mainly used for grinding into powder and also used for the distillation of cinnamon bark oil.
>
> Featherings, the third grade, are feather-like pieces of the inner bark consisting of shavings and small pieces of bark left over. They are used the same way as quillings.
>
> Chips are rough unpeelable bark pieces scraped off from thick branches and stems.

Cinnamon lends a sweetly fragrant and warm taste to North Indian spicy meat and RICE dishes and dals. It is one of the four spices essential for PULAOS and is also an ingredient in garam masala (see SPICE BOX).

Helen Saberi

- Achaya, K.T. *A Historical Dictionary of Indian Food*. Delhi: OUP, 1998.

- Pruthi, J.S. *Spices and Condiments*. New Delhi: National Book Trust, 1976.
- Sahni, Julie. *Classic Indian Cookery*. London: Grub Street, 1997.

CITRUS FRUITS

Citrus fruits constitute several species of the genus *Citrus* of the plant family Rutaceae and many originated in Northeast India. All types of citruses currently existing have evolved from single or sequential hybridization events between three primordial Citrus species: *C. medica* (citrons), *C. maxima* (pomelos) and *C. reticulata* (mandarins), or their offspring. The citrus industry in India is the third-largest fruit industry in the country, with mandarin (*C. reticulata*, loose-sleeved, easily peeled), sweet orange (*C. sinensis*, peel adhered firmly to flesh) and key lime (*C. aurantifolia*) being the major citrus fruits produced in the country. They are grown in every state of India, but the leading producers are Andhra Pradesh, Telangana, Maharashtra, Assam and Karnataka. *C. reticulata* grown in Nagpur is considered one of the best mandarins in the world. The fruits are sold throughout the country and consumed fresh and juiced. Orange BARFI is an iconic confection made in Nagpur.

Some varieties of lemons are eaten like a fruit. *C. pseudolimon Tanaka* or the hill lemon, known as *galgal* in Himachal Pradesh, is an important fruit endemic to the region. The fruit's thick rind is peeled and the cored fruit is mashed with MUSTARD greens, GARLIC greens, wild herbs and SALT to make *khatta* (or *chachaa*), a winter delicacy. Juice from the hill lemon is collected and boiled to a thick reduction called *chukh*, which is then used as an important souring agent. *Chukh* is used in making PICKLES like *chamba chukh* (with dried red CHILLIES). Sour lemon segments mixed with hung curds, herbs, salt, jaggery (see SUGAR) and hemp seeds make *sana hua neebu*, a winter snack in Kumaon. C. *medica* is particularly celebrated in South Indian cuisine where the fruit is sun-dried or pickled with salt. It is prized for its medicinal virtues.

A variety of lemons are popular in Indian pickles flavoured with regional pickling spice blends. They pair with sugar or jaggery to make various sweet-sour relishes and a confit called *chundo* in western India.

Throughout India, a mixture of sea salt and spices like bishops weed, CUMIN, etc., are stuffed into regional citruses to preserve them. They are entirely sun-dried to make shelf-stable pickles that can last many years. Pickles made this way do not contain oil or chillies and turn almost black. Citrus and salt may also be arranged in layers to make preserved lemons. These are considered highly therapeutic and used as convalescence food.

Citrus fruit extracts are popular in sweet-salty juices, SHERBETS and drinks like *shikhanji* that are synonymous with Indian summers. C. *limetta* (*mosambi*) is the most common citrus used to make juices in India. Bengal's *lebu* ghee *bhaat* and South India's lemon rice are steamed RICE dishes flavoured with lemon juice. The juice of C. *aurantiifolia* is used as a fresh acid to make PANEER and is also used as a preservative in various seasonal-produce pickles.

Lemon leaves are used for aroma while steaming *siddu* roti, also known as *seeda* roti *or sidku* in Garhwal in Uttarakhand. Crushed leaves of C. *medica* are mixed with chillies, salt and ASAFOETIDA to make *vepilakatti*, a dry pickle, in Tamil Nadu. Citrus leaves are crushed with salt in lassis like *sambaram* in Kerala and *ghol* in Bengal. Citric acid, *nimbu ka phool* or *nimbu sar*, is used in Indian desserts to prevent sugar from crystallizing and is a mild preservative that is sometimes used to mimic the taste of fermentation.

People use lemon peels to clean traditional brass and bronze utensils. Owing to their antiquity, lemons are deeply linked to India's religio-cultural landscape. Garlands of lemon, lamps lit in lemon rind cups or lemon halves smeared with vermillion (symbolizing animal sacrifice) are offered to Hindu goddesses. Limes are strung with chillies and hung as talismans to ward off the evil eye throughout the subcontinent. During Sair, celebrated around Himachal Pradesh to mark the end of the harvest season, leaves of *C. pseudolimon Tanaka* are integral to ceremony and worship. *C. macroptera Montrouz* is a wild orange endemic to Northeast India. Members of the Garo tribe tie lemons to their waist and dance to celebrate the Wangala festival, signifying the protection of their crops from pests. The peel is used to make the Garo pork delicacy *wal chambal phura*. In southern Bengal and Bangladesh, it is an essential ingredient in beef *hatkhora*.

Priya Mani

CLOVE

Cloves are the dried unopened flower buds of the tree *Syzygium aromaticum*, which is native to the Molucca Islands (also known as the Spice Islands) in eastern Indonesia. The tree is small and evergreen, may live for a century or more and thrives in a tropical maritime environment. It flowers twice a year and the fully grown but still closed buds are harvested then sun-dried over several days before being marketed. The English word 'clove' comes from the Latin *clavus* which means nail, which the dried flower head strongly resembles. In India, cloves are known as *laung* (Hindi), *lawang* (Bengali), *lavang* (Gujarati), *kirambu* or *lavangam* (Tamil).

Cloves are one of the most ancient, valuable and important culinary spices. They have been used in India since ancient times. The Sanskrit *lavanga* derives from the Malay term *bungalavanga* and occurs in writing in Buddhist-Jain literature, the *Ramayana* and *Charaka Samhita*, suggesting that cloves were present in India a few centuries before the start of the Common Era. In Tamil Sangam literature (*c.* 300 BCE to 300 CE) there are references to cloves. They were used for spicing meat, in PICKLES and were mixed with *bhang* (an edible preparation made from the leaves of the cannabis plant) for chewing by the wealthy. They also have stimulating properties and are one of the ingredients of PAAN. A clove was also used to fasten the betel leaf for the nobility.

The clove tree was introduced to India in 1800 by the East India Company. Cultivation is largely confined to South India, the main growing regions being the Nilgiris, Tenkasi Hills and Kanyakumari district in Tamil Nadu, and Kottayam and Quilon districts in Kerala. However, although it has been cultivated for over 150 years, not enough is produced and India is a major importer of cloves, notably from Zanzibar.

Cloves have a warm and rich aroma with a distinct and strong flavour (which comes from eugenol) so is used sparingly. Chewed on their own, cloves are bitingly sharp, hot and bitter and can numb the mouth. In Indian homes, they are used either whole or powdered in both sweet and savoury dishes. They are used extensively in PULAOS, stews (especially those that have a rich ONION-TOMATO sauce), PICKLES and spice mixtures such as garam masala (see SPICE BOX). They are also used for perfuming oil to cook vegetables.

Cloves are used to relieve flatulence and dyspepsia. Oil of clove (derived from the dried buds) is an important essential oil used extensively medicinally and in perfumes and soaps.

Helen Saberi

- Achaya, K.T. *A Historical Dictionary of Indian Food*. Delhi: OUP, 1998.
- Davidson, Alan. *The Oxford Companion to Food*. 2nd edition. Ed. Tom Jaine. Oxford: OUP, 2006.

- Norman, Jill. *The Complete Book of Spices*. London: Dorling Kindersley, 1990.
- Pruthi, J.S. *Spices and Condiments*. New Delhi: National Book Trust, 1976.

COCONUT

The coconut tree (*Cocos nucifera*, Hindi *nariyal*) is a versatile plant that plays an important role in the cuisine of many regions of India, especially along the east and west coasts. (Coconut plays such an important role in the life and food of people in Kerala that some believe that the state's name, Kerala, means the land of coconut palms, or *keram*.) Besides being commercially grown, many Kerala households grow coconut trees in their backyard. A member of the palm family, the tree likely evolved in Micronesia and Indonesia. From here, the fruit floated to other parts of the world. (Water-borne coconuts can remain viable for up to six months and sprout when drifting ashore.) The English name comes from the Portuguese *coco*, 'head', because the three dents in the shell look like a human face.

Coconut trees grow in sandy soil in tropical regions that have plenty of rainfall, especially on beaches. India is the world's third largest producer (after Indonesia and the Philippines) with Kerala, Karnataka and Tamil Nadu accounting for 84 per cent of the total production. A tree can produce coconuts up to thirteen times a year, and although it takes a year for the coconuts to mature, a fully blossomed tree can produce between 60 and 180 coconuts in a single harvest.

In Sanskrit, the coconut palm is known as *kalpa vriksha* – 'the tree which gives all that is necessary for living' – because nearly all parts of the plant can be used for food, drinks, decoration and even furniture. Coconut flesh is considered *sattvic* (see FOOD AND MEDICINE) and thus can be consumed by everyone.

Despite its name, botanically the fruit of the coconut is a drupe – a fleshy fruit with a skin (exocarp), flesh or pulp (mesocarp) and a central stone (endocarp) containing the seed. The developing seed is surrounded by the endosperm which nourishes the growing seed and contains starch, proteins and other nutrients. The endocarp is initially filled with a liquid (coconut water); as development continues, cellular layers of endosperm deposit along the walls of the endocarp and thicken to form the solid endosperm – the edible flesh, also called copra. This flesh has a high percentage of unsaturated fatty acids and is slow to become rancid, which makes the oil extracted from it an ideal cooking medium.

One of coconut's most basic products is coconut water produced by drilling a hole in the shell or splitting it open. Sold by street vendors, coconut water is a popular drink throughout India (and, more recently, has been commercialized in the West as a sports drink because it contains carbohydrates and electrolytes). Another coconut-based drink is toddy, which is made by cutting the stem of the coconut palm and collecting the sap. When freshly tapped, the drink, called *neera* in Malayalam (the language of Kerala), is sweet and nonalcoholic, but, after a while, it ferments into a sour drink that is mildly alcoholic and is sometimes called palm wine (see ALCOHOL). It is sold in toddy shops throughout South India, albeit subject to occasional bans. Often the shops serve local food specialties as well. Toddy, which contains yeast, is also used as a leavening agent to make *APPAMS* and other breads. Goans distil toddy to make a variety of *feni* called *madd*. Fresh toddy can be fermented to make coconut vinegar, which has a milder taste than cider vinegar and is rich in nutrients. Coconut vinegar is the souring ingredient in such classic Goan dishes as VINDALOO and *sorpotel*.

Coconut milk is the main gravy in many CURRY-like dishes. It is made by grating the flesh and squeezing it by hand with hot water to extract the oil, proteins and aromatic compounds. (Today a blender is used to grind the flesh before straining the mixture.) The traditional method is to scrape the flesh using a metal blade with serrated edges mounted on a low stool. The first batch of liquid is thick; when the process is repeated, the coconut milk becomes thinner. Generally, thin coconut milk is used for cooking curries and soups while the thicker version is used for desserts and rich sauces. But, sometimes, both are used in the same dish, with the thicker version added at the end. Coconut milk has a sweetish, aromatic taste and a fat content that ranges from 5 to 20 per cent.

A classic Kerala dish is *meen molee*, fish filets simmered in coconut milk and vinegar. Or fish is coated with grated coconut and sautéed in coconut oil. *Isthoo,* a dish influenced by Western stews, consists of chicken or vegetables in a coconut gravy. Vegetable dishes cooked in coconut milk include *avial* (mixed vegetables), *kalan* (green bananas) and *olan* (white pumpkin and dried beans). Grated or chopped coconut is a key ingredient in a Kerala *thoran*, a dry dish of cabbage or other finely chopped vegetables. Breakfast dishes *appam* and *idiappam* are accompanied by sweetened coconut milk or a mutton stew.

Coconut oil is made by pressing fresh coconut meat or dried coconut meat called copra. Virgin coconut oil uses fresh meat, while refined coconut oil typically uses copra. Coconut oil was the traditional cooking medium in Kerala but consumption has been declining both because of concerns over health (although the jury is still out on it) and competition from cheaper, imported palm oil. Coconut's delicate sweetness and crunchy texture lend it well to SWEETS. In Kerala, one version of *payasam* (see KHEER) is made with coconut milk from three pressings as well as dry coconut cut into small wedges. A coconut pancake called *madkausan* is made with coconut milk and grated fresh coconut.

Many Bengali dishes are made with coconut milk, although Bengalis do not use coconut oil as a cooking medium. A classic dish is *chingri mach kari* – shrimp curry in coconut milk. Many Bengali sweets are made with coconut, including *SANDESH*, LADDUS, coconut balls and squares, and *chandrapuli,* a crescent moon-shaped sweet made with *CHHANA*, *KHOYA*, scraped coconut and jaggery (see SUGAR) that is a must for Durga Puja. Dried coconut is an ingredient in sweets throughout India, including laddus and BARFI.

In Goa, coconut is used extensively in both sweet and savoury dishes. Famous Goan pastries include *baath* cake, made with coconut oil, coconut milk and grated coconut, and *bibinca*, a seven-layered Western-style cake. According to K.T. ACHAYA, the Sanskrit word *narikela* is mentioned in the Sanskrit literature only after 300 BCE and frequently appears in Tamil literature starting around 100 BCE, indicating that South Indians were familiar with the coconut from ancient times. A CHUTNEY of fresh coconut and CHILLIES is a popular accompaniment to IDLIS and DOSAS throughout South India.

Another Sanskrit word for coconut is *sriphala* or God's fruit. Coconut is considered auspicious and appears in many Hindu rituals and ceremonies, although its significance and symbolism are subject to different interpretations. Some Hindus launch a new venture by breaking a coconut in front of an idol. At a wedding, the bride sometimes sits with a coconut on her lap as a symbol of fertility. People also offer it in the sacrificial fire while performing the *homa*, also known as *havan*, a fire ritual or ceremony, on special occasions. At pujas, the coconut is broken and placed before the deity, the pieces are later distributed as *prasad*.

The coconut tree has many other uses. The leaves are used as brooms and fuel to light kitchen hearths. The husk and shells can be used for fuel and are a source of charcoal. Coir (the fibre from the husk of the coconut) is used to make ropes, mats, doormats, brushes and sacks. In India, the woven coconut leaves are used to build wedding marquees, especially in the south. Coconut trunks are used for building small bridges and huts because of their strength and salt resistance.

Colleen Sen

- George, Lathika. *The Kerala Kitchen*. New York: Hippocrene, 2009.
- Kannampilly, Vijyan. *The Essential Kerala Cookbook*. New Delhi: Penguin Books, 2003.
- TarlaDalal.com. '1249 Coconut Recipes'. *n.d.* Available online: https://www.tarladalal.com/recipes-using-coconut-nariyal-269 (accessed 15 April 2022).

COFFEE

Coffee (from the genus *Coffea*; the two most species common being *C. arabica* and *C. robusta*), Hindi *kophi*, began to be planted on a large scale in India around the same time as TEA, although it never reached the same magnitude. Today, India produces around 300,000 tonnes annually. Around 70 per cent is grown in Karnataka while most of the rest comes from Kerala and Tamil Nadu. Small amounts are also grown in Andhra Pradesh and Orissa.

Coffee was first mentioned as a drink in Arab texts of the tenth century but its cultivation likely began several centuries earlier. Various legends trace its origin to either Ethiopia or Yemen, where the beans were initially eaten as a stimulant. Roasting the beans may have begun in the thirteenth century on the Arabian Peninsula, where it was known as *qahwah*. Extensive cultivation began in Yemen in the fifteenth century and it spread throughout the Islamic world as an alternative to ALCOHOL. Coffee drinking was reported in India as early as 1630 but it was likely made from imported beans. In Mughal times, coffee was available in coffee houses, called *qahwa khanas*, in the Chandni Chowk district of DELHI and in other cities.

According to legend, the first coffee was grown in India in the early eighteenth century when a Sufi cleric, Baba Budan, returned from a pilgrimage to Mecca with seven coffee beans (sometimes recorded as seven plants). He planted them outside his cave in the Chikmagalur hills in Karnataka (today the headquarters of the Coffee Board of India). After this, cultivation was done on a small scale by Indians. Starting around 1830, there was a rapid development of coffee estates by the British in Sri Lanka and in South India, first in the Shevaroy hills and, soon after, in the Nilgiris. By 1885, there were as many as 25,000 plantations, mainly in Mysore State, the Madras Presidency and Kodagu. Today, according to the Coffee Board of India, there are nearly 400,000 small coffee growers.

Around about a quarter of the coffee grown in India is of the Arabica variety, which thrives at higher elevations and has a soft, slightly sweet taste. The rest is the Robusta variety, which grows at lower elevation, has a stronger harsher taste and has twice as much caffeine as Arabica. Arabica is harvested between November and January and Robusta from December to February. Coffee grows in the shade and is often intercropped with spices such as cardamom and cloves which impart an aroma. Much of the coffee is exported, with Italy, Germany and Russia being the main buyers. One of the most popular coffees for export is Monsoon (or Monsooned) Malabar. Harvested Arabica beans are exposed to the monsoon winds in open-sided warehouses. This ferments them slightly, reducing acidity and creating a bold flavoured coffee with earthy overtones that is a component of espresso blends in Europe.

Coffee is especially popular in South India, where it is called *kaapi* or filter coffee. This is a sweet, milky coffee made from dark roasted beans mixed with chicory. It is brewed in a special metal device consisting of two cups, the top one of which has fine holes. Ground coffee (mixed with varying amounts of chicory depending on taste) is placed in the top cup, compressed lightly and covered with boiling water. The coffee brews for ten to fifteen minutes (in some households it brews overnight) and then slowly drips into the bottom cup, creating a strong decoction. Meanwhile, milk is brought to a boil on a stove, mixed with SUGAR to taste and then added to a device called a *dabarah*, consisting of a metal saucer and a tumbler. The filtered brew is poured back and forth between the saucer and the tumbler, which has the effect of aerating it and creating foam. Because of the distance between the two while pouring, this coffee is sometimes called 'metre' coffee.

India's first Western-style coffee houses, modelled after those in London, opened in Calcutta in the late eighteenth century. The Coffee Board of India was created in 1942 to encourage exports and raise domestic consumption. To this end, it opened a chain of establishments called the India Coffee House. Some fifty establishments were opened in Indian cities. After Independence, the Board decided to close them down. However, the workers took over and formed cooperatives to run them. They opened the first branch in Bangalore in 1957 and today operate some four hundred outlets. The most famous is the College Street Coffee House in KOLKATA that became a popular meeting place for intellectuals and students. In more recent times, coffee chains such as Barista and Café Coffee Day have become popular

Colleen Sen

- Bhattacharya, Bhaswait. *Much Ado about Coffee: Indian Coffee House Then and Now*. New Delhi: Social Science Press, 2017.

COOKBOOKS, EARLY

India's first cookbook, ***Pakadarpanam***, was allegedly written by Nala, a legendary prince in the great Indian epic *Mahabharata* who was famous for his culinary skills, but no copy exists. However, because of his fame, recipes are attributed to him in later works including medical texts, which are another valuable source of culinary information (see FOOD AND MEDICINE). The *Mahabharata* describes many feasts and dishes but has no recipes as such. The first collections of rudimentary recipes began to appear around the eleventh century CE and, over the next several centuries, several cooking manuals and recipe collections were written. These were called *Supasastra*, *Sudashastra* or *Pakashastra* – all meaning manuals or treatises on cooking. Most were composed at royal courts for the purpose of entertaining and educating the king and his entourage. Cooking was one of the arts cultivated by the elite.

These works do not contain recipes in the modern sense; they mainly consist of lists of ingredients. Amounts are not indicated nor are there detailed descriptions of the processes that transform them into dishes except in generic terms. 'Recipes, the elementary forms of the culinary life, are missing in the great tradition of Hinduism', writes the scholar Arjun Appadurai. Moreover, while there was a high degree of standardization in other social and cultural forms, there was no culinary tradition common to the entire country.

The collections are mainly of regional dishes, some of which are still made centuries later. As Appadurai writes, Hindu culinary traditions 'stayed oral in their mode of transmission, domestic in their locus, and regional in their scope ... traditional Hindu cuisine was thoroughly Balkanized'.

An important source of other rudimentary recipes is the writings of the Ayurvedic physicians. *Charaka Samhita* (compiled between the second century BCE and the second century CE) contains a range of recommendations for healthy living. Of the 120 chapters, five are dedicated to dietetics and contain recipes, some quite detailed, for various ailments and health conditions.

The legendary Nala is the purported author of the ***Nala Pakadarpana***, or '*Nala's Mirror on Cooking*'. The work is in the form of imaginary dialogues between Nala and the king in which Nala (the author's persona) describes various dishes and cooking techniques with an emphasis on their medical attributes. The association with the legendary Nala gives the work prestige. The work was written in Sanskrit by an unknown author at an unidentified location sometime between the twelfth and fifteenth centuries CE. A later date is unlikely because there is no mention of TOMATOES, CHILLIES or other items from the New World. Sections are devoted to dishes made with boiled RICE (*odana*), lentils (see PULSES), clarified butter, meat combined with vegetables, *payasam* (rice pudding, see KHEER), juices, soups, vegetables, milk, yogurt and buttermilk.

The work opens with a summary of the basic tenets of Ayurveda including the six tastes and their combinations, seasonal influences on diet, and foods that are to be avoided. There are few restrictions: GARLIC, ONIONS and meat (except for beef) are common ingredients and there are several dishes for chicken, a meat not usually found in the early works. Common vegetables are AUBERGINE, GOURDS, bitter melon, plantain and different green leafy vegetables. The same method of preparation is often used for different vegetables. Some dishes are cleverly contrived and intended to show the unknown author's skill. For example, in one recipe, plantain stems are cut in three different ways to mimic a PULAO-type dish. Betel leaves (*pugapatta*, see PAAN) are used for cooking, serving and storing foods instead of the usual gold utensils because they are said to impart fragrance to the contents and also to ward off insects.

Lokopakara, whose title means '*For the Benefit of the People*', was written around 1025 by Chavundaraya II, a Jain poet scholar at the court of Jaisimha II (1015–42), one of the Western Chalukya kings. In addition to food, it has chapters on astrology, architecture, omens, water diving, perfumes, and veterinary and human medicine. It was not written in Sanskrit but in the local language, Kannada, perhaps because it was intended for a wider readership. The chapter titled 'Supa Shastra' contains fifty-seven rudimentary recipes, all vegetarian and all made without onion or garlic since it was intended for a Jain court. Many are for snacks and sweet dishes. BARLEY (which by then had nearly been replaced by rice as the staple grain) is an ingredient in only two dishes. Dal, mainly *moong*, *urad* and *chana*, was a major part of the diet. Some SWEET dishes were made by curdling hot milk to make *CHHANA* (belying the oft-expressed notion that this was introduced by the Portuguese). A mixture of finely grated COCONUT, DATES and SUGAR was stuffed into pieces of dough that were fried in GHEE – the modern Karnataka sweet *sajjappa*.

A paste of ground *urad* dal soaked in the water from drained yogurt and flavoured with ASAFOETIDA, CUMIN seeds, CORIANDER and black pepper (see PEPPER, BLACK) was used to make IDLIS. However, the recipe does not include rice nor is it fermented. One story is that fermentation was introduced by the cooks of Indonesian Hindu kings who visited South India in search of brides between the eighth and twelfth centuries. A more likely explanation was that it was a natural process, since nearly all cultures use fermentation in some form. The *Lokopakara* describes in detail methods of preserving various food items by using yogurt, SALT and jaggery and removing toxicity and bitterness from fruits, vegetables, shoots and leaves that grew in the wild – an indication of their importance in the diet of common people.

Perhaps the best known of the early cookbooks, *MANASOLLASA* is a composition in Sanskrit verse written by King Somesvara III (r. 1126–38).

Another collection from Southwest India is ***Kshemakutuhalam*** (*A Work on Dietetics and Well Being)*, a Sanskrit treatise in verse written around 1550. The author, Kshemasharma, was a poet and scholar at the court of King Vikramasena in Ujjain, now in Madhya Pradesh. The author was a Brahmin and the book is filled with charming, slightly irreverent, religious references. For example, a dessert is described as having such a divine fragrance that 'even men who hanker for liberation long greedily to taste it'. Some recipes come from the medical literature, others from the *MANASOLLASA*, while still others may be his own creation.

The rudimentary recipes reveal a rich and diverse cuisine with few restrictions, although onion and garlic are used very sparingly. Except for beef, almost every kind of meat is consumed by the king including boar, venison, lizards, game birds, peacocks and tortoises. (Being a Brahmin, the author notes that he personally hasn't tasted the meat dishes but only describes what he has learned about their preparation). SESAME oil is a common cooking medium.

The longest chapter is devoted to edible plant products – leaves, flowers, fruits, stalks, bulbs and roots. A basic method of preparation is to sauté vegetables in oil with salt, asafoetida and cumin seeds, then add TAMARIND or buttermilk. The long list of plant products includes various varieties of gourd, *BAEL*, myrobalan (see *AMLA*), green Bengal gram, figs, plantain, cow peas and many others with no English equivalent. Green leafy vegetables include goosefoot, AMARANTH, CASSIA, spinach, FENNEL, FENUGREEK, black nightshade, purslane, jute leaves, black pepper leaves and safflower leaves.

The ***Supashastra*** was composed around 1608 by Mangarasa III, the Jain ruler of Kallhalli, a state in Mysore District, Karnataka that was part of the Vijayanagara Empire. Written in an old version of Kannada, it has six chapters consisting of 450 poems. Its intended audience are probably home cooks. In the introduction, the author emphasizes its roots in Hindu tradition by thanking Bhima, Nala and Gouri (an incarnation of Durga famous for her cooking skills).

All the dishes are vegetarian but a few contain onion and garlic in violation of the usual Jain proscriptions. The flavouring is both basic – coriander, cumin, MUSTARD seeds and fenugreek – and more aromatic: CARDAMOM, CAMPHOR, nutmeg (see NUTMEG AND MACE), screwpine and even musk. Often grated coconut is added. Most of the vegetable recipes call for aubergine, gourds, plantains and plantain flowers, JACKFRUIT, ridged gourds, pumpkin, BAMBOO SHOOTS and *AMLA* (Indian gooseberry).

Another category of cookbooks followed the tradition of Persian collections of recipes that were compiled by Islamic rulers and aristocrats as a means of displaying their taste. These manuscripts, written in Persian, circulated within the elite. The recipes consisted of Persian dishes, dishes from the wider Islamic world, and local and regional dishes, especially KHICHRI which is found in all the books. The following dishes, many with Persian names, appear in most of the manuscripts:

- Rice dishes, including PULAO, *tahiris* (a mixture of rice, vegetables and spices), khichris and BIRYANI (*zerbiryan*).
- BREADS (naan).
- Meat preparations, such as *yakhni* (meat broth), *dopiyaza* (meat cooked with onions), KEBABS and *qaliya*, a CURRY with a thin-ish gravy.
- *Sambosas* (SAMOSAS).
- PICKLES (*achars*) and CHUTNEYS.
- Sweetmeats (*shirini*), such as HALWA and *FALOODA*.
- Sometimes, yogurt and PANEER.

Despite their Persian origin, the dishes often show strong Indian influences such as the heavy use of fried onions and intensive spicing. The most used spices were CINNAMON, cumin, CLOVES, cardamom, black pepper, GINGER, coriander and TURMERIC. Later, contacts with European powers introduced new ingredients such as tomatoes, POTATOES and chillies. One of the oldest and most celebrated of these Indo-Persian manuscripts is the *NI'MATNAMA* by Ghiyath Shahi (written 1495–1505). For cookbooks written during the Mughal period, see MUGHALS.

Colleen Sen

- Appadurai, Arjun. 'How to Make a National Cuisine: Cookbooks in Contemporary India'. *Comparative Studies in Sociology and History* 30, no. 1 (1988): 3–24.
- Chavundaraya II. *Lokopakara. c.* 1025, translated by Valmiki S. Ayangarya. Secunderabad, Telangana: Asian Agri-History Foundation, 2006.
- Guttierez, Andrea. 'The Curious Case of Nala's Mirror on Cooking: Innovation in Medieval Indian Cookbook Writing'. In *Food and Imagination: Proceedings of the Oxford Symposium on Food and Cookery 2021*, edited by Mark McWilliams, 201–9. Totnes, Devon: Prospect Books, 2022.
- Kṣēmaśarmā. *A Work on Dietetics and Well Being* [Sans. orig. *Kṣēmakūtuhalam*]. *c.* 1555. Edited by Darshan Shankar, D.K. Ved, G.G. Gangadharan, M.A. Lakshmithathacharya and M.A. Alwar, translated by R. Shankar. Bangalore: IIAIM/Foundation for Revitalisation of Local Health Traditions. 2009.
- Madhulika, Dr, trans. *Pakadarpana of Nala*. Edited by Jay Ram Yadav. Varanasi: Chaukhambha Orientalia, 2019.

COOKING AND DINING

Indians have used many of the same cooking methods and equipment from ancient times. Excavations have shown that the ancient Harappans used a variety of hearths in different sizes and shapes made of earthenware and/or brick and fuelled by wood, cow dung and crop residue. Vessels were placed over a hole at the top. Their kitchenware included pots and pans, bowls, dishes, narrow-mouthed vessels used to store oil and costly liquids, and storage jars of different sizes. They were made of ceramic, metal and earthenware. Other implements included mortar and pestle, querns for grinding spices,

FIGURE 13 COOKING AND DINING. Idli pan. Dharmdhyaksha/Wikimedia Commons.

FIGURE 14 COOKING AND DINING. Grinding stone. Colleen Sen.

metal knives and stone blades for trimming. Underground pits were used for the long-term storage of food. Cooking methods included boiling, frying, roasting, charring, slow cooking and steaming.

Some of these techniques and instruments are in use today, especially in villages where the common stove has been the *chulha.* This is a small U-shaped stove made from local clay with an entrance on one side or at the top and fuelled with cow dung, straw, twigs, wood shavings or a mixture. The cooking vessels were placed on top or inside on the coals. The use of cow patties is an ancient form of recycling that also provides a source of income for the people who collect, dry and sell them. They provide a gentle heat ideal for slow-cooking dishes with gravies and liquids, which are sometimes left overnight on hot coals. Today, in middle-class households, the standard cooking device is a small cooktop with two burners fuelled by bottled propane gas. Pressure cookers, invented in France in the seventeenth century, are owned by three-quarters of all urban households. A sealed lid increases the air pressure, lowering the temperature at which water boils and significantly reducing cooking times.

Until the 1950s, cooking vessels were made of copper and brass, but they required regular re-tinning (*kalai*) and have largely been replaced by aluminium or stainless-steel cookware, sometimes lined with copper. One of the most frequently used receptacles is a *karahi*, a deep pot with two handles and a flat or slightly concave bottom used for sautéing and deep frying. A *patila* or *bhatona* is a circular pot with straight sides used to make CURRY-like dishes. Live charcoal can be placed on the saucer-shaped lid to heat the top of BIRYANIS and other dishes. In the *dum pukht* style of cooking popular in LUCKNOW, dishes are cooked in a brass vessel called a *degh/deghchi* with a spherical base that tapers into a narrow opening. The vessel is sealed with dough, allowing the steam to roll back into the food. For deep frying, a *jhaara,* a slotted spoon with a long handle, is used to add and remove items. It can also be used to drain chickpea batter to make *boondi,* tiny fried globules that are eaten as a snack or added to RAITA.

Rotis (flatbreads, see BREADS) are cooked on a *tawa*, a circular and slightly concave griddle that distributes heat evenly from the centre. The rotis are held and flipped by a *chimta,* a pair of tongs with pointed or flared tips made of iron or stainless steel. To ensure that the roti dough is smooth, Indian cooks sift the flour through a *charni*, a sieve with an ultra-fine mesh set in a tall metal rim. Lined with a cheesecloth, it can also serve as a strainer for yogurt. The roti dough is rolled out with a *belan,* a rolling pin that is lighter and thinner than its Western counterparts. Traditionally, Indian kitchens did not have countertops, so the cook, sitting on the floor, rolled out the dough on a *chakla*, a round wooden board. Today, however, counters are found in many urban kitchens.

Some cooks crush spices, ONIONS, GARLIC and herbs by pressing them with a *batta*, a small stone rolling pin, on a *sil*, a stone slab – an ancient device. Dried spices can be ground in a mortar and pestle. Today, many cooks use electric spice grinders and blenders for these tasks. To make the spice mixture known as *tadka* (see below), which is added at the end of cooking a dish, cooks use *tadka* pans that are small, round and deep, requiring only a little oil.

A tandoor is a large clay oven with a small opening in the top that is either built into the ground or is free standing. In North India, it is used for baking many kinds of bread and roasting meat, especially in restaurants. Most Indian households do not have tandoors, but some villages have a communal tandoor for baking bread and roasting meat.

A common technique with no exact equivalent in Western cuisine is *bhuna*, a combination of sautéing, stir frying and stewing. The cook starts by frying spices and a paste made from garlic, onions, GINGER and, perhaps, TOMATOES in a little GHEE or oil until they soften. Then he adds pieces of meat, FISH or vegetables and sautés it until it is brown. The next step is to add small amounts of water, yogurt or other liquids a little a time while constantly stirring to keep the ingredients from sticking, which can be a labour-intensive process. The amount of liquid added and the cooking time determine whether the dish will be wet or dry. Another uniquely Indian technique, called *chhaunk, tadka* or *bagar*, is the addition of spices, sautéed in a little oil or ghee, to a curry or dal after it has been cooked, imparting a fragrant aroma.

Regional dishes may require specialized equipment, a full description of which is beyond the scope of this work. For example, in Bengal, a *boti*, a large knife mounted on a wooden board, is used to cut fish and large vegetables. In Maharashtra, many homes have a *modak paatra*, a copper or brass steamer used to steam stuffed *modaks* as well as *gund* and *gundi*, which are round vessels with a lip to boil thin liquids. A *puran yantra* resembles a French moulin and is used for mashing *puran* for *puranpoli* (a sweet flatbread stuffed with a sweet lentil filling made from husked split Bengal gram (*chana* dal) and jaggery) and to blend the SUGAR and yogurt when making *SHRIKHAND*.

In South India, the soaked RICE and lentils (see PULSES) used to make IDLIS were traditionally ground in a special device consisting of a stone base with a hole in the centre and an egg-shaped stone that fits into the stone. Today, they are being replaced by electric wet grinders. Idlis are steamed in a device that looks like a stack of perforated egg poachers that is placed over boiling water. It can be made of aluminium or stainless steel.

Kerala has many distinctive kitchen devices. An *ural/iuruli* is a traditional round vessel made from bell metal or brass and often beautifully decorated. Today, it is used mainly on ceremonial occasions. A *cheena chatti* is a heavy brass wok with handles. Its name means 'Chinese pot', indicating its possible origin. A metal pot with a bamboo tube fitted inside is used to make *puttu,* a steamed rice and COCONUT tube-shaped cake, which is a popular breakfast dish. *APPAMS*, small lacy disks made of fermented rice and coconut batter, are steamed in a heavy pan with indentations. In the Northeast, one cooking method is to put ingredients inside a bamboo tube that is buried in coals.

Dining

Traditionally, Indians ate sitting on the floor using only their right hand to eat. Bite-sized pieces of the food were served on a washed banana leaf which was disposed of after eating. Even today, serving food on banana leaves, especially in the South, is considered healthy and auspicious. The leaves are large enough to serve a multi-course meal. The order and placement of the various components on the leaves vary by region.

In North and West India, food was traditionally served on thalis. The word comes from Sanskrit *sthali,* a cooking pot used in ancient times to cook rice. Today, it refers to a round metal plate thirty to thirty-five cm in diameter with raised edges that are around two cm high. A larger version is called a *thal* and is used to display foods on special occasions. Thalis can be made of brass, bell metal, tin-coated copper and stainless steel. In the past, the very wealthy used gold and silver thalis. According to traditional medicine, the materials of the serving plates affect the nutritional and medicinal value of the food served. Copper and silver thalis are considered the best for health reasons. Dry and wet vegetables, fish and meat dishes, dals, yogurt and sometimes liquid desserts are served in small bowls called *katori* placed around the edge of the thali. Breads, PICKLES and CHUTNEYS are put directly on the tray. The staple, be it rice or roti (flatbread), occupies the centre of the thali. Temples use disposable styrofoam thalis to feed the masses. The word thali can also be used to describe a regional meal, such as a Gujarati thali, a Rajasthani thali, etc. The famous Gujarati thali can have as many as twenty-five sweet and savoury dishes, including *farsans*.

Indian meals do not normally have a sequence of courses. Everything arrives more or less at once, although certain dishes may appear at different times and remain on the table throughout the meal. An exception is Bengali cuisine where lunch always starts with a bitter dish, followed by green vegetables, lentils, other vegetables, a fish, meat or egg curry, a sweet and sour chutney, and a sweet dish, such as *mishti doi* (sweet yogurt) or a traditional SWEET.

Among Hindus, notions of ritual purity and pollution traditionally affected cooking and dining behaviour. The *Dharmashastras*, ancient treatises on conduct, laid down elaborate rules that would allow members of the higher castes to avoid pollution and gave long lists of people with whom members of the higher castes could be dinner companions and from whom food could not be accepted, for example, a physician, a drunkard, a blacksmith, a prostitute, a liquor dealer, etc. These taboos may have been partially inspired by sanitary and hygienic concerns, since some of the people mentioned (physicians, hunters) would have contact with diseased or unclean substances. The anthropologist Mary Douglas argues that restriction on eating food taken from outsiders was a means of protecting one's group from 'threats from below', especially since the higher a caste's status, the more of a minority it must be. Eating with someone from outside one's group could be the first step towards marrying him or her, a concept summed up in the Hindi phrase roti = *beti* (bread = daughter-in-law).

One of the major sources of pollution is bodily fluids, especially saliva, and this concern still dictates many practices, if only unconsciously. Food that is considered polluted by bodily fluids is called *jutha* (originally meaning 'uneaten'). To this day, most Indian women do not taste the food directly from the vessel while they are cooking it; they may rely on experience or pour a little into their hand or a cup. Some people do not sip water from a glass but pour it into their mouths, since even one's own saliva can be polluting. An orthodox Hindu takes a bath before entering the kitchen and wears freshly washed clothes. The affluent have separate kitchens where vegetarian, non-vegetarian and, sometimes, Western dishes are prepared.

Women did not eat with the rest of the family but first served them and ate when everyone else was finished. Sampling food from another diner's plate, except that of a close relative, was, and still is, unacceptable. Using one's utensil to take food from a serving bowl is also considered unacceptable, along the lines of 'double dipping' in the United States.

Although many of the prohibitions and restrictions remained in force well into the twentieth century, they are breaking down, especially in cities where a neighbour's or colleague's caste may be unknown or a matter of indifference. Culinary orthodoxy is becoming more of an ideal than a reality and is observed mainly at religious ceremonies and festivals. Westernized urban dwellers eat at a table using Western utensils.

Colleen Sen

- Bhandari, Anil. 'Heritage Cuisine Utensils and Styles of Cooking'. In *Traditional Cuisines of India*, edited by Sangya Chaudhary, 78–83. New Delhi: Indian Trust for Rural Heritage and Development, 2014.
- Rowe, Caroline. 'Endless Eating: The Indian Thali'. In *Food and Material Culture: Proceedings of the Oxford Symposium on Food and Culture 2013*, edited by Mark McWilliams, 264–71. Totnes, Devon: Prospect Books, 2014.

CORIANDER

Coriander, *Coriandrum sativum*, a plant which is related to parsley, yields both the sweet, mildly pungent, pepper-like light brown seeds which form the spice and the highly aromatic herb with flat, fan-like leaves. They are quite different in smell and taste. Coriander is native to southern Europe and the Middle East, although it is now grown worldwide. In India, coriander is cultivated in practically all the states. Both the spice and the herb are called *dhania* and used extensively in cooking.

Coriander, the spice, is one of the oldest in human use, its culinary and medicinal use has been documented for over 3,000 years. It was one of the foodstuffs found in Tutankhamen's tomb dated to 1352 BCE. Andrew Dalby, in *Dangerous Tastes* (2000), relates that it was probably introduced to India by the Persians at the time when the Old Persian Empire stretched to the Indus valley, before Alexander or ASHOKA. It is mentioned in Panini's Sanskrit *Grammar*, generally dated to the fourth century BCE. Its Sanskrit name, *Kustumburu*, seems to come from Aramaic, the lingua franca of the Persian Empire.

Coriander seeds are the primary ingredient in CURRY POWDERS and spice mixtures such as garam masala (see SPICE BOX). The seeds are usually roasted, then crushed or powdered before use and are frequently added to appetizers such as chaat (see STREET FOOD) and RAITA. The spice is also an essential ingredient of many soups, CURRIES, vegetable and legume dishes (see PULSES), PICKLES and so on.

Coriander, the herb, also known by its Spanish name cilantro in the United States, resembles Italian parsley and is sometimes called Chinese parsley. The taste and flavour of fresh coriander lend itself well to the highly seasoned regional cuisines of Maharashtra, Rajasthan, Gujarat and Punjab. The leaves and stems, usually finely chopped, lend a fresh taste to curries, dal, KOFTA and salads and they are also used in CHUTNEYS or relishes to be eaten with RICE and curry dishes. The leaves are also used as a garnish for many dishes including *dahi* vada (deep-fried fritters or dumplings served with yogurt).

Coriander is rich in vitamins C and A. It is also used medicinally and considered to be a good digestive, helping to relieve flatulence, indigestion, vomiting and intestinal disorders. The seeds are sometimes chewed to sweeten the breath.

Helen Saberi

- Dalby, Andrew. *Dangerous Tastes: The Story of Spices*. London: British Museum Press, 2000.
- Norman, Jill. *The Complete Book of Spices*. London: Dorling Kindersley, 1990.
- Pruthi, J.S. *Spices and Condiments*. New Delhi: National Book Trust, 1976.

CORN

Corn (maize, *Zea mays*, Hindi *makka*) is the third most popular grain in India after RICE and WHEAT and India is the world's third largest producer. Although most corn grown in India is used for animal feed and industrial use, such as making starch, in some regions it is an important part of the cuisine.

The generally accepted point of origin of corn is Mexico and northern Central America where it still grows wild. Christopher Columbus brought corn grain (as well as its Arawak name *maiz*) from the Greater Antilles to Spain in 1493. The Portuguese spread it throughout their empire, with its first mention in India in 1590. Corn can grow in a variety of climates, is easily cultivated and can be harvested by hand. Like MILLETS, corn can tolerate dry climates and poor soils and is easier to cultivate and harvest than wheat and rice. It became particularly important among shifting cultivators in mountainous areas where it is often grown with millets.

However, according to another theory, corn has existed in India for hundreds of years and may have been introduced by sailors who crossed the Atlantic and Pacific Oceans long before Columbus. Objects that look like ears of corn are depicted in stone carvings in twelfth- and thirteen-century temples in Karnataka. However, direct archaeological evidence has not been found and no Sanskrit word for corn has ever been identified.

The real push to grow corn in India came in the early nineteenth century when the Agri-Horticultural Societies, established by the British to develop commercial crops, started importing varieties of corn from the New World to find the ones best suited for India. Today, corn production is fairly evenly distributed among Indian states, the largest producers being Andhra Pradesh, Karnataka, Rajasthan, Maharashtra, Bihar, Uttar Pradesh, Madhya Pradesh and Himachal Pradesh.

Roasted over coals and coated with butter and spices, corn on the cob, or *bhutta,* is one of India's most popular STREET FOODS. In North India, corn is harvested at the end of the rainy season and is used to make a thick unleavened bread that is eaten with greens – the classic Punjabi winter dish *sarson ka saag aur makka ki roti*. In Rajasthan it is eaten with AMARANTH and made into porridge with BUTTERMILK and *RABRI*. The Gujarati *rotla/rotli* is sometimes made with cornmeal mixed with whole wheat flour. Corn is the staple crop of some tribes in the foothills and higher reaches of the Himalayas and parts of Gujarat and Rajasthan. In the Northeast, some ethnic groups make beer from a mixture of corn, rice and millets. Corn kernels are sometime parched or fried and ground to make *sattu*. Corn can be substituted for rice in PULAO or used as a filling for PAKORA and VADAS. Indore is known for its *bhutte ka kees*, freshly grated kernels tempered with CUMIN, MUSTARD seeds and ASAFOETIDA.

Corn soup has become a standard item in Chinese-Indian (see CHINESE INDIAN CUISINE) restaurants around the world. According to one story, it was invented by the owner of Nanking Restaurant in Mumbai during the Second World War when some British soldiers walked into the restaurant at closing time. Food had run out so they asked him to make a dish using a tin of corn they had with them and enjoyed the soup so much it was added to the menu.

Colleen Sen

- Doctor, Vikram. 'Enter the Maize: How Corn from the Old World Replaced Millet in India'. *The Economic Times*, 19 July 2020.

COUNTRY CAPTAIN

Country Captain is an ANGLO-INDIAN dish, a sort of dry chicken CURRY. It was sometimes served as a breakfast dish. How it got its name is a bit of a mystery. The name 'country captain' originated in Bengal. During the Raj, the term 'country' used to refer to anything of Indian, as opposed to British, origin. Small coastal vessels carrying freight were called 'country ships' and the native Indian skippers were called 'country captains'. Hobson-Jobson says: 'We can only conjecture that it was a favourite dish at the table of these skippers ...' Somehow it became the name of this popular Raj dish which was usually described as being made of chicken (or occasionally kid or veal), often from leftovers. However, Hobson-Jobson tells us that in Madras 'the term is applied to a spatchcock, dressed with onions and curry stuff, which is probably the original form'.

Recipes and ingredients differ greatly but at its simplest, probably original form, it consisted of little more than chicken cooked with ONIONS and GHEE and flavoured with CHILLI and TURMERIC (or CURRY POWDER) as in Henrietta Hervey's recipe for 'Cold Fowl, or "Country Captain" curry' in *Anglo-Indian Cookery at Home* (1895).

Country captain turned up midway through the nineteenth century at ports as far apart as Liverpool and the American South where it became one of the most popular curries and many believed that the dish was invented in America. According to one story, a sea-captain who sailed into Charleston harbour was so graciously entertained by local hostesses that he repaid their hospitality by teaching their cooks to make a chicken curry, which was then named after him. President Franklin D. Roosevelt, who first tasted it in Warm Springs, Georgia, became a fan as did one of his guests, General George S. Patton. In 2000, the Pentagon made it into one of its packaged M.R.E.s (Meals Ready to Eat) given to soldiers to eat in the field.

Helen Saberi

- Burnett, David and Helen Saberi. *The Road to Vindaloo*. Totnes, Devon: Prospect Books, 2008.
- Burton, David. *The Raj at Table*. London: Faber and Faber, 1993.
- Sen, Colleen Taylor. *Curry: A Global History*. London: Reaktion Books, 2009.
- Yule, Henry and A.C. Burnell. *Hobson-Jobson: A Glossary of Colloquial Anglo-Indian Words and Phrases, and of Kindred Terms, Etymological, Historical, Geographical and Discursive*. 1886. New edition edited by William Crooke. 1903. Reprint. London: Routledge & Kegan Paul, 1986.

CUCUMBER

Cucumber (*Cucumis sativa*, Hindi *khira*) is of Indian origin, with a wild ancestor *C. hardwickii* still found growing in the Himalayan foothills. In Sanskrit there are over forty words for cucumber, indicating that it may have been cultivated for shape, size and bitterness at an early stage. It was mentioned around 1500 BCE in the *Rig Veda*.

Cucumbers thrive in India's warm climate and are distributed fairly evenly across the country. Haryana accounts for 22 per cent of total production followed by Madhya Pradesh and Karnataka with 10 to 12 per cent each. While Indian cucumbers are consumed domestically, India is a leading exporter of gherkins (*Cucumis anguria*) used for pickling.

A popular variety is the snake or Armenian cucumber (*Cucumis melo* var. *flexuosus*, Hindi *kakri*). It has a slender fruit that can be as long as one metre and has a very thin, light green, smooth skin that does not need to be peeled. It has a mild flavour and is often eaten raw with SALT or chopped and added to a yogurt-based RAITA. In the hot summer vendors sell cut cucumbers coated in CHILLI powder to passers-by as a cooling snack.

Sambar cucumbers grown in the south are sour and used to make pickles. A cucumber popular in Andhra Pradesh is *dosakai*. Its round yellow fruit can be prepared as a CURRY, added to SAMBAR or dal, and used in making PICKLES and CHUTNEYS. A cucumber from the Maharashtrian city Pune, called Poona *khira*, has a light green fruit with a sweet mild and juicy flesh. It is shaped like a POTATO. It is used as decorations in festivals to honour Lord Krishna.

Colleen Sen

CUMIN

Cumin (Hindi *zeera* or *jeera* or '*safaid zeera*', *safaid* meaning white) is the small greyish-brown aromatic oval-shaped seed of *Cuminum cyminum*, an annual herb belonging to the parsley family. It is believed to be native to the Nile Valley although it has been cultivated, traded and used in cooking for so long that no one is really sure. Many scholars have established that cumin was harvested and used in the Levant during biblical times. Cultivation soon spread to North Africa and eastwards to Iran, Afghanistan and could have arrived in India in the last centuries BCE, along with other spices such as CORIANDER and SAFFRON. In *Dangerous Tastes* (2000), Dalby suggests that it is possible these spices came with the conquests of the Persians or Alexander the Great, or could be credited to the Maurya emperor ASHOKA, who, as he claimed, transplanted useful plants to, and within, India. Cumin was mentioned in Indian literature after about 300 BCE as *ajaji, karavi* and *kuchika*. Late Sanskrit has *jeeraka* (Hindi *jeera*) from the Persian *zira*.

India is now the world's largest producer of cumin, contributing about 70 per cent of the total world output. Gujarat is the largest producing state, accounting for over 60 to 70 per cent of the total production. The rest comes from Rajasthan. Other states produce negligible quantities.

Cumin seeds taste slightly bitter, sharp and warm with a long-lasting pungent flavour. In India, cumin seeds are generally dry roasted before use to bring out their flavour. The seeds are then, sometimes, ground to a powder. Both the seeds and the powder are essential in spice mixtures and masalas, such as garam masala and *panch phoron* (see SPICE BOX) and in CURRIES, lending a distinctive warm flavour. A combination of roasted and ground cumin and coriander seeds called *dhania-jirga*, which gives a pungent, lemony and aromatic flavour, is used in Gujarat and Maharashtra.

Cumin seeds are also added to appetizers, PAPADS, main dishes such as BIRYANIS, PULAOS and curries, CHUTNEYS and PICKLES, and sprinkled over chaat (see STREET FOOD) and RAITA as a garnish. Cumin is made into a popular digestive, cooling and healthy drink called *jal jeera*, literally 'cumin water'. The cumin is roasted, the other ingredients include fresh lime, coriander, fresh MINT, chaat masala (see SPICE BOX) and dry MANGO powder. Black SALT may be added or it can be slightly sweetened with SUGAR. Cumin is sometimes confused with caraway (*Carum carvi*). The seeds look quite similar but the flavour is quite different and the latter is little used in India.

Black cumin is the name of a rare variety of true cumin found as a wild plant in Kashmir, Pakistan, Afghanistan and Iran. Today, it is cultivated as a cash crop in Himachal Pradesh due to its increasing demand. It comes from the plant *Bunium persicum* and is also known as royal cumin, *shahi zeera*, *siyah zeera* or *kala jeera*. The black seeds are smaller and have a sweeter aroma than 'white' cumin. Their nutty flavour brings richness and earthiness to dishes. Black cumin is much sought after for the delicate pulaos of Kashmir and for the rich biryanis and other dishes of MUGHAL origin. The seeds are ground and used in garam masala. They are also chewed as an anti-flatulent. Black cumin should not be confused with another spice NIGELLA, which is often mistakenly called black cumin.

Helen Saberi

- Achaya, K.T. *A Historical Dictionary of Indian Food*. Delhi: OUP, 1998.
- Dalby, Andrew. *Dangerous Tastes: The Story of Spices*. London: British Museum Press, 2000.
- Nabhan, Gary Paul. *Cumin, Camels, and Caravans: A Spice Odyssey*. Berkeley: University of California Press, 2014.

CURRY

Curry is one the most controversial words in the Indian culinary lexicon. During the days of the Raj, it was commonly used to describe any Indian dish with a gravy, but this usage later fell out of favour because of its association with imperialism. Lately, however, it seems to be enjoying a resurgence and the word can be found on the menus of restaurants even in India. In 1974, food writer Madhur JAFFREY declared that the word 'was as degrading to India's great cuisine as the term "chop suey" was to China's'. But, in 2003, she called her new book *The Ultimate Curry Bible*. Similarly, noted restaurateur and writer Camellia PANJABI named her book published in 2007 *Fifty Great Curries of India*.

There are many explanations of the word's origin. Some claim that it comes from *kadhi*, a liquid dish from West India made with chickpea flour and yogurt, or from *kari*, the CURRY LEAF, although the latter is rarely an ingredient in a curry. A more fanciful explanation is that a Scotsman in Bombay named Curry liked Indian food so much that curries were named after him. The most commonly accepted and likely explanation is that it comes from Tamil *karil,* meaning a watery sauce poured over RICE. This word was first used in 1502 in a Portuguese travel account and later applied by the British to any Indian dish with a gravy. By the eighteenth century, it was in general use for *salans*, *kalias*, kormas, rogan josh, VINDALOO and other 'wet' dishes (but not dal). Dr Robert Flower RIDDELL, in his classic *Indian Domestic Economy and Receipt Book* (1841), described curries in the following way (a definition that still holds good today):

> Curries consist in the meat, fish or vegetables being first dressed (sautéed) until tender to which are added ground spices, chillies and salt to both the meat and gravy … In fact, a curry may be made of almost anything, its principal quality depending on the spices being duly proportioned as to flavour and the degree of warmth to be given by the chilies and the ginger. The meat may be fried in butter, ghee, oil or fat, to which is added gravy, tyre (yogurt), milk, coconut juice or vegetables.

An influential book published a few years later, *Culinary Jottings* (1878), was written by Colonel Arthur Robert Kenney-Herbert (1840–1916) under the penname 'WYVERN'.

An admirer and proponent of French cuisine, Kenney-Herbert believed that a curry deserved the same care and attention as a classic French *fricassee*, and his elaborate and painstaking recipe for chicken curry remains a classic. He recommends CURRY POWDER be made at home in large batches and stored in tightly sealed glass bottles but does not oppose the use of ready-made curry powder.

Curry recipes began appearing in British cookbooks as early as 1747 – in Hannah Glasse's *Art of Cookery Made Plain and Easy*. The recipe was essentially an aromatic stew flavoured with peppercorns (see PEPPER, BLACK) and CORIANDER seeds but in later editions curry powder and cayenne (CHILLI) powder were added. In the mid-nineteenth century, curry became popular among the growing middle class in Britain; widely read cookbooks by Eliza Acton, Mrs Beeton and others all contained curry recipes. Queen Victoria is said to have had a curry served every day in case one of her Indian subjects visited and her son, later King Edward VII, was a great curry fancier.

Wherever the British went they took curry with them. American, Canadian and Australian cookbooks of the nineteenth century invariably feature curry recipes, often shamelessly copied from British cookbooks. The millions of indentured Indian labourers who went to British colonies in the Caribbean, Africa and Asia to work on plantations (see DIASPORA) took their dishes with them, as did later those South Asians who went as administrators, attorneys and traders. These dishes were integrated into their national culinary repertoires as 'curries'.

The post-Second World War period saw a surge of immigrants to Britain from the subcontinent, especially from the region that became Bangladesh. They opened restaurants called 'curry houses' featuring spicy dishes that were popular among pub goers. A dish invented around this time was chicken tikka masala – pieces of roasted chicken in a TOMATO sauce that a British foreign minister once called 'Britain's national dish'. (see BUTTER CHICKEN). The next popular wave was Balti cuisine, a style of cooking that started in south Birmingham. A balti consists of pieces of marinated, sometimes precooked, meat, vegetables or seafood stir-fried and served in a sauce of ONIONS, GARLIC, tomatoes and spices topped with fresh coriander.

Curries are also an important part of the cuisines of Thailand, Indonesia, Burma and Malaysia. Thai curries, called *gang* or *kari*, are made with a variety of aromatic pastes that often include lemongrass, shrimp paste, lime leaves and various spices, and have a water or COCONUT milk base. The Indian influence is apparent in Thai curries that incorporate POTATOES, roasted coriander and CUMIN seeds, and even roasted whole spices such as CARDAMOM and nutmeg (see NUTMEG AND MACE).

A country where one would not expect to see curries is Japan, where *kare raisu* (curry and rice) is one of the most popular home-cooked meals. A Japanese curry consists of chunks of meat, CARROTS, onions and potatoes simmered in an ochre-coloured, curry powder-flavoured, slightly sweetish sauce. Curry was introduced to Japan in the mid-nineteenth century by the British navy and even today, Japan Maritime Self Defense Force ships serve curry every Friday, sometimes made with unusual ingredients such as chocolate or COFFEE. Curry later reached Korea via Japan.

Colleen Sen

- Burnett, David and Helen Saberi. *The Road to Vindaloo: Curry Cooks and Curry Books*. Totnes, Devon: Prospect Books, 2008.
- Sen, Colleen Taylor. *Curry: A Global History*. London: Reaktion Books, 2009.

CURRY LEAVES

FIGURE 15 CURRY LEAVES. Curry leaves (*Murraya koenigii*). Sonja Pauen/Wikimedia Commons.

Curry leaves are the shiny, dark green, aromatic leaves of the small tree or shrub *Murraya koenigii* which grows wild in the foothills of the Himalayas, in southern India and Sri Lanka. It is also cultivated throughout India and in many Indian gardens, not just for its aromatic leaves but also for ornamental purposes.

Names of the leaf vary but *meetha* neem and *kari patta* are widely used in India.

Curry leaves have been used in cooking since Vedic times. Sahni (1999) writes that curry leaves were the only flavouring in Vedic Indian cookery and explains that the original Vedic CURRY POWDER (which contains curry leaves), *urad* dal (black gram beans, see PULSES) and black peppercorns (see PEPPER, BLACK) 'is generally prepared fresh just before the Vedic ceremony to honour the dead (*shraddha*). Because all other blends are considered new and therefore not appropriate for the holy ceremony, it is the only one used at this Hindu ritual.' Curry leaves are also mentioned in early Tamil literature. A passage from *Perumpanuru* (*c*. third century CE) describes the food served to a wandering minstrel 'the Brahmin gave him fine rice with mango pickle and the tender fruit of the pomegranate cooked with butter and fragrant curry leaves'. A few centuries later (*c*. 1485), a royal feast was described in Kannada verse by Terekanambi Bommarasa: 'the women served an unfried brinjal *baji*, which contained coconut shreds, curry leaves and cardamom, mixed well and flavoured with citrus juice and a little camphor'.

Curry leaves today are widely used in cooking throughout India and are a favourite ingredient in South Indian cuisine. The small leaves are generally bought fresh while still attached to their stems. Indian cooks remove the whole leaves from the stem just before frying them in GHEE or oil until crisp, often with other spices. A typical South Indian *chhaunk* (or *tadka*, tempering; see COOKING AND DINING) includes tossing a sprinkle of MUSTARD seeds, six to eight curry leaves and a pinch of ASAFOETIDA into hot ghee and frying until the mustard seeds pop and turn grey. This flavouring can be incorporated into a dish before serving or drizzled over the top, imparting a distinct flavour to fried snacks, curries, a pot of dal, a dish of yogurt, CHUTNEYS and relishes.

Freshly dried and ground leaves lend a characteristic flavour to the Tamil Nadu spice blend called curry powder. They can also be added to marinades, sprinkled on vegetables or yogurt, or mixed with COCONUT and other spices to make a chutney. The leaves, bark and root (of *Murraya koenigii)* are used medicinally – as a tonic, stimulant and carminative.

Helen Saberi

- Achaya, K.T. *Indian Food: A Historical Companion*. Delhi: OUP, 1994.
- Pruthi, J. S. *Spices and Condiments*. New Delhi: National Book Trust, 1976.
- Sahni, Julie. *Classic Indian Vegetarian Cookery*. London: Grub Street, 1999.

CURRY POWDER

Curry powder is a commercial spice mixture sold in markets around the world that has many variations, ranging from quite mild to fiery hot (the latter is sometimes called Madras curry powder). The most common ingredients are TURMERIC (which imparts the characteristic ochre colour), CUMIN seeds, FENUGREEK and CORIANDER seeds. Other ingredients in order of popularity are CLOVES and fennel seeds; GINGER; GARLIC and red pepper; black pepper (see PEPPER, BLACK), CURRY LEAVES, CARDAMOM, CINNAMON and nutmeg (see NUTMEG AND MACE); and white pepper, CHILLIES, MUSTARD seeds and POPPY SEEDS. Madras curry powder is generally 'hotter' and sometimes has curry leaves but does not usually contain aromatic spices such as cardamom, cloves and nutmeg.

The first curry powders were made in England during the late eighteenth century for British officials returning from India who missed Indian food and did not have access to fresh spices or the cooks to grind them. Enterprising merchants began manufacturing commercial versions, at the same time promoting their health benefits. In 1784, Sorlie's Perfumery Warehouse advertised that curry 'renders the Stomac active in Digestion – the blood naturally free in Circulation – the mind vigorous – and contributes most of any food to an increase in the Human Race' (a hint at its alleged aphrodisiac powers). In 1844, Captain William White of the Bengal Army, manufacturer of Selim's Curry Paste (sold until the late 1930s), published a pamphlet titled 'Curries: Their Properties and Healthful and Medicinal Qualities'. By the 1860s, curry powder and pastes were sold in large stores, such as Fortnum and Mason's. Although many people scorn them, curry powders are an essential ingredient in making a classical chicken CURRY such as those in the books of Colonel Arthur Robert Kenney-Herbert (see WYVERN).

Colleen Sen

- Burnett, David and Helen Saberi. *The Road to Vindaloo: Curry Cooks and Curry Books*. Totnes, Devon: Prospect Books, 2008.

DABBAWALLAHS

FIGURE 16 DABBAWALLAHS. *Dabbawallahs* tiffin carrier. Nataraja/Wikimedia Commons.

A unique Indian institution is MUMBAI's *dabbawallahs*, or TIFFIN-box carriers. A tiffin box, also called a *dabba*, is a circular steel box with three sections that fit together to form a cylinder. It contains food freshly made by a family member or servant which, when delivered, allows the recipient to enjoy a home-cooked meal at the office.

The *dabbawallahs*, usually riding bicycles, are assigned a collection and delivery area. They pick up an average of thirty boxes from homes at around 10 am, take them to a local railway station where they are labelled using a system of colours and symbols, then go by train to other stations in Mumbai where other *dabbawallahs* pick them up and carry them to the destination by 1 pm. *Dabbawallahs* are famous for their punctuality and reliability. Later, the boxes are returned to their owner in the same way.

Before the Covid pandemic that started in early 2021, between 4,500 and 5,000 *dabbawallahs*, wearing a distinctive white coat and *topi* (hat), delivered 175,000–200,000 boxes each day. Each *dabbawallah* is an entrepreneur who is responsible for negotiating prices with his own customers following guidelines based on distance. The relationships are generally long-term. The close relationship between a *dabbawallah* and his customer is featured in the 2013 epistolary romance film *Lunchbox.*

The system was created in 1890 by Mahadeo Havaji Bacche, a young man from Pune who was hired by a PARSI banker to go to his home, collect his tiffin and bring it to his office. Mumbai was rapidly expanding and Bacche saw a business opportunity. He created a union of the workers and laid down rules. Today, all *dabbawallahs* come from a rural area around Pune, which is three hours from Mumbai by train. New workers are usually friends or relatives of existing members. A small number of women *dabbawallahs* typically perform administrative functions or special services (such as pickup or delivery at irregular times) that command a higher fee. As more women enter the workforce and are unable to prepare home-cooked meals, *dabbawallahs* have started to collaborate with small companies and canteens that provide freshly prepared meals. Unfortunately, the Covid pandemic put most of the deliverers out of work and there is concern that the institution may disappear.

Colleen Sen

- Roncaglia, Sara. *Feeding the City: Work and Food Culture of the Mumbai Dabbawalas.* Cambridge: Open Book Publishers, 2013.
- Thomke, Stefan. 'Mumbai's Models of Service Excellence'. *Harvard Business Review*, November 2012.

DAIRY SECTOR

Indians have been drinking milk and perhaps even making butter and CHEESE since the Mature Phase of the Harappan Civilization (2600 to 1900 BCE). The Harappan people had domesticated the humped Zebu cattle and water buffalo, the former being cross-bred extensively across centuries for multiple functions. India's oldest surviving book, the *Rig Veda,* and the literature that followed are replete with references to cow's milk and milk products (later, of buffaloes and goats as well). Milk is at the centre of Hindu Cosmology. It is by the process of churning the 'Ocean of Milk' (upon which rests Vishnu the Preserver on the multi-headed serpent Shesha Naga that serves as his bed) that the *devas* (gods), competing against the *asuras* (demons), can attain the elusive Amrit Kalash, the pot containing the Nectar of Immortality. This myth is repeated in the *Ramayana*, the *Mahabharata* and the *Vishnu Purana,* three core texts of Indic culture.

However, India had to wait till 1997 to become the world's largest producer of milk (apart from being home to 192.9 million cows and 110 million buffaloes, last counted in 2019), overtaking the United States after decades of being a milk importer. In 2019–20, India produced 198.4 million tons of milk, more than eleven times the 1950–1 level of 17 million tons. The dramatic turnaround, which turned India into a milk-surplus nation, is called the White Revolution. It started as an independent initiative of farmers' cooperatives in the western state of Gujarat but was transformed into a national programme evocatively named Operation Flood by Prime Minister Indira Gandhi in 1970.

During the early Vedic age (*c.* 1500–1100 BCE), northwestern India was a pastoral economy. The cream of boiled milk, a favourite of Lord Krishna according to Hindu legends, was consumed in plenty. Curd, butter, GHEE – used to fry *apupa*s, sweet cakes made with BARLEY flour and cheese or *sadhanas* (with or without pores) – were the common milk products. Milk was used to make a porridge (*odana*) with grains or a gruel with parched barley and was even mixed with *soma*, the intoxicating drink used in rituals. A combination of curd and HONEY, *madhuparka*, was offered to the gods and served to special guests as a mark of honour – a practice that continues today.

Cows signified wealth and most of the battles of that era were fought over cows. The common word to describe a battle was *gavishti*, or 'search for cows'. Another signifier of the cow's primacy was the proper noun *duhitri*, or 'milker of cows', used to describe the daughter of the family. The words *kshira* and *payas* (roots of modern-day KHEER and *payasam*) appear in Vedic literature, pointing to the multiple uses of milk. A popular dish was *krishara* (believed to be the original form of today's KHICHRI), made with milk, RICE and SESAME.

In southern India, archaeological evidence points to the rearing of cows and buffaloes as early as 2000 BCE. Sangam literature, composed from the third century BCE to the third century CE, is replete with references to *vetchi*, or cattle raids, which were the prelude to war. The Sangam word for 'cattle', *maadu*, is used interchangeably for 'wealth'. It was a common practice to donate cows, milk and ghee to temples.

During the reign of the Maurya emperor ASHOKA (r. 272–232 BCE), herdsmen gave dairy products as tribute to the owners of their cattle or the state-appointed superintendents of cows. Around the same time, the first of the three unidentified Sangam women poets who went by the collective name of Avvaiyar wrote glowingly about a meal that ended with *moramoravena pulitha morum*, or tangy, frothy BUTTERMILK. In the seventh or eighth century CE, the saint-poetess Andal's devotional poem *Thiruppavai* has a passage describing a fast kept by young girls in a RITE OF PASSAGE dedicated to Lord Krishna. The fast ends with a feast, and the girls, addressing Lord Krishna, chant: 'Eat we will rice mixed with milk, | Covering the rice fully with ghee, | And with the ghee dripping from our forehands, | We will be together and be happy.'

Travelling from China in the seventh century CE, Buddhist monk and scholar Xuan Zang observed that milk, butter and cream were the 'most usual foods' of the people he met during his peregrinations across the sub-continent. The twelfth-century *MANASOLLASA* has a number of dessert recipes, including one for fried split milk (*CHHANA*) and rice flour balls dipped in SUGAR syrup – similar to *pantua*, popular in West Bengal – and another for *payasam*.

The sixteenth-century *NI'MATNAMA* calls on readers to feed sugarcane and date sugar to cows so that their milk is sweet and has multiple recipes for 'milk rice' and firni (rice pudding). Surdas, a revered sixteenth-century Hindi poet, wrote several verses describing the eating habits of his upper-class contemporaries. Breakfast would consist of BREAD, ghee, milk and yogurt, apart from ten kinds of confections and half-a-dozen different fruits and NUTS.

Milk plays a central part in the rituals associated with the celebration of Pongal (the harvest festival of Tamil Nadu), Mahashivaratri (dedicated to Lord Shiva), Holi (the festival of colours is not complete without the consumption of sweetened milk mixed with intoxicating *bhang*), Janamashtami (honouring Lord Krishna) and Onam (celebrating the annual visitation of the mythical King Mahabali to partake of the new harvest).

The East India Company's chaplain Edward Terry, who was in India between 1616 and 1619 when the Mughals ruled India, wrote with amazement about the amount of 'milk, butter, cheese, and sweetmeats' consumed by the vegetarians. This period saw the invention of the frozen dessert named KULFI as well as other milk-based desserts including firni and the Meethi Eid (Eid-ul-Fitr) delicacy *sheer khurma*, or *seviyan* (vermicelli, see *SEV* AND *SEVIYAN*) cooked in milk and enriched with *KHOYA* (dried unsweetened condensed milk), nuts and raisins.

Around the same time, the famous RASGULLA, based on *chhana*, was invented either in Odisha or in Bengal. Some historians have pointed out that the Portuguese, settled in and around Bandel in eastern India, introduced the science of making *chhana*.

The consumption of milk rose substantially after the thrust given to TEA drinking by the British Raj and the Indian Tea Association, notably among factory workers during the First World War and railway travellers. Indians adopted the English style of drinking tea with milk and sugar, but it became more a case of drinking milk with tea since North Indian were milk drinkers. Interestingly, a multicentre study found that two-thirds of the subjects in two cities in South India were lactose intolerant – meaning they lacked the enzyme needed to digest milk – compared with 27 per cent of the people in New Delhi. The lower incidence in the North Indian subjects may perhaps be because they are descendants of the Indo-Aryans who have been dairying for long and are known to be lactose tolerant. However, most lactose-intolerant people can usually digest yogurt.

Organized milk producers, though, formed a minuscule minority. Their presence was limited to the Royal Indian Army's dairy farms, which supplied nearby cantonment towns; the first was established at Allahabad in present-day Uttar Pradesh in 1886. Three years later, the colonial government hired a Swedish dairy technologist, Edward Keventer (1854–1937), who introduced pasteurization and other modern milk production techniques. He also recognized, unlike his British employers, the importance of buffalo milk. (The British Raj, unwittingly, followed the Hindu tradition of not giving the water buffalo its place in the sun. The animal responsible for more than half of milk production in India is portrayed in Hindu mythology as the carrier of Yama, the god of death.) In 1899, Keventer opened a model dairy farm at Chherath, 130 km southeast of DELHI, where he popularized Alfa Laval's cream separators, which greatly eased and enhanced the production of butter and ghee. He expanded his milk business to Karachi, LUCKNOW, Darjeeling, Calcutta and Rangoon. King George V conferred upon him a Royal Charter in 1913 to supply milk and milk products to the government and the army and the Secretary of State for India leased a twenty-two acres plot to Keventer in what were then the outskirts of Delhi in 1925.

In 1916, the colonial government initiated the first census of cows and buffaloes in the country and it has continued since with five-year intervals, most recently conducted in 2018–19. The Imperial Institute for Animal Husbandry and Dairying, which opened in Bangalore in 1923, hosted Mahatma GANDHI for two weeks in 1927 to update his knowledge of cattle management. After Independence, it was renamed the National Dairy Research Institute (NDRI) and in 1955 moved to its present campus in the historic city of Karnal, Haryana. Dairy production, however, continued to predominantly be a household enterprise. When India attained independence in 1947, a mere 2 per cent of its milk and milk products came from the organized sector.

Keventer died in 1937; three years later, his nephew and successor, Werner, sold his uncle's successful company to the Indian industrialist, Rama Krishna Dalmia. The Swedish pioneer's legacy survived and thrived under Dalmia, who turned Keventer into a brand name. Bottled flavoured milk from the Keventer dairy became a favourite beverage in Delhi. By the 1960s, the company was supplying milk powder and condensed milk to the Indian Army, its colourful ice-cream carts were a big draw during the torrid summer months, and its butter was a middle-class staple. The Keventer saga met with an unexpected end in the 1970s when the Government of India ordered the dairy's closure because the city's Diplomatic Enclave was coming up around it. Disheartened, Dalmia withdrew from the business and the twenty-two acres on which the dairy stood was at the centre of a protracted legal dispute and is now owned by DLF, the real estate conglomerate.

Dalmia's great-grandson, Agastya Dalmia, has revived the brand and retails bottled flavoured milk under the Keventer brand name. In West Bengal, Keventer Agro Limited, launched by Mahendra Kumar Jalan after acquiring the brand in 1986, set up Metro Dairy in KOLKATA a decade later with World Bank and state government funding. Keventer's legacy has survived – and continues to thrive.

Another pre-Independence pioneer who contributed significantly to organized milk production was Pestonji Eduljee Dalal (1875–1962), a self-made Bombay (now MUMBAI) businessman who started his career by selling COFFEE to British soldiers during the Boer War in South Africa at the turn of the nineteenth century. Dalal called his chicory-blended product Polson's French Coffee because he had been asked to adopt an English-sounding name. He even changed his last name to Polson. Polson's next big product was butter, made with the rich cream he sourced from the Government Central Creamery at Anand in the Kaira (now Kheda) district of Gujarat. The butter became an instant favourite of the British Indian Army. Interestingly, the butter was salty and its British fans loved it that way. It owed its unusual taste profile to its production process. The cream used was first soured for some days before it was converted into butter. SALT was added to mask the putrid taste and smell of the sour cream. By 1930, when Polson opened his then state-of-the-art Model Dairy in Anand, the brand ruled Bombay, which was emerging as India's commercial and financial metropolis. When the Second World War broke out, Polson's products were sought after by the Indian, British and American forces.

Polson's monopolistic trade practices, especially in the post-Second World War years when its contractors denied the farmers of Anand the right prices for the milk the company supplied daily to Bombay, inadvertently turned the town into the capital of the dairy cooperative movement. It was at Anand that the death knell of Polson was sounded. To counter Polson's middlemen, the milk producers of Kaira district were organized into a cooperative by a local Gandhian leader, Tribhuvandas Kishibhai Patel (1903–94), who was guided by the nationalist icon Sardar Vallabhai Patel, independent India's first home minister. Patel envisioned the cooperative, run by democratically elected representatives of the farmers, not only as an agency to procure milk from the producers at fair prices, but also as the operator of a modern processing plant. The Kaira milk producers first united to organize a strike in 1946 that denied Bombay its milk supply for fifteen days. To negotiate an end to the strike, Bombay's milk commissioner agreed to the producers' demand that Polson's monopolistic control over the city's milk supply be ended permanently. The agreement was only the first step. Patel had to go door to door to convince farmers to come together as a cooperative society. His hard work paid off and the Kaira District Cooperative Milk Producers Union Limited was officially established on 14 December 1946 – eight months before India formally attained her independence.

Similar cooperative societies were supplying milk to the cities of Allahabad, Coimbatore, Lucknow and Madras (now CHENNAI), but Kaira was different – there, the producers had been assured their entire milk supply would be picked up, even in the winter 'flush' months, when supply was much higher than demand. In the absence of a modern pasteurization plant, though, the milk producers were still dependent on Polson. It was not until 1 June 1948, and only after Patel pulled some political strings in Bombay and Delhi, that the cooperative got its own modern milk plant.

In Bombay, meanwhile, Dara Nusserwanji Khurody (1906–83), a graduate of the Imperial Institute for Animal Husbandry and Dairying, and a former superintendent of the 2,000-acre dairy at the Tata Iron and Steel Company, was appointed the deputy milk commissioner in 1946. Khurody was seen to be favouring Polson and therefore was often at odds with the Kaira milk producers, but he made two lasting contributions to dairy development in India. As an officer of the British Indian government's Agriculture Marketing Department since its inception in 1935, Khurody earned his initial spurs as a member of the team that instituted the Agmark quality control system for agricultural products. In 1941, he authored a report on milk marketing in India and Burma. But his lasting contribution was implementing his idea of toned milk – a mix of high-fat buffalo milk, skimmed milk powder and water that was as nutritive and tasted as good as cow's milk but cost half its price – to make it possible for the Bombay government to provide free milk to schoolchildren from poor families. Under Operation Flood, toned milk ensured the availability of economically priced milk across India.

Khurody's other big contribution was the creation of the Aarey Milk Colony on 1,200 hectares of forest land in the northern suburbs of Bombay in 1949. The Colony, which was formally opened by Prime Minister Jawaharlal Nehru in 1952 and supported by UNICEF, became a mega shelter for the buffaloes producing milk in Bombay. It rid the metropolis of buffalo sheds which came with hygiene issues, guaranteed a steady income for its milk producers and continues till today to be the regular source of milk and milk products for the city.

Back in Kaira, the fledgling cooperative society found an unlikely mentor in Verghese Kurien (1921–2012) who came from a well-connected Syrian Christian family. He worked for the Anand Creamery, by then in a run-down condition, for five years to fulfil his contractual obligation to the government for the scholarship he had won to study Dairy Technology at the Michigan State University, USA. Kurien was waiting to escape the boredom of Anand, using any opportunity to take a break in Mumbai, when Tribhuvandas Patel met him and persuaded him to stay on as the manager of the Kaira cooperative. The young man, thinking the job may be better than presiding over a rickety creamery, accepted Patel's offer and the government did not raise any red flags.

Kurien joined the fledgling Kaira cooperative union in 1949 and in the decades that followed, he went on to power the White Revolution and became known all over the world as the 'Milk Man of India'. He found in Harichand Megha Dalaya (1921–2004), a Michigan State University and Harvard graduate, an able ally. Dalaya revolutionized dairy production in India by inventing the process of spray drying buffalo milk, which was considered impossible because of the milk's high-fat content. The triumvirate of Patel, Kurien and Dalaya became famous in dairying circles as the 'Father', 'Son' and 'Holy Ghost' of the milk movement.

Kurien's many achievements include:

- He expanded the footprint of the Kaira milk producers' union and laid the foundation for the immensely successful Gujarat Co-operative Milk Marketing Federation, a model replicated around the country.
- He established one of India's best-known consumer brands, Amul (derived from the Sanskrit word for invaluable, *amulya*), in 1955. Today, Amul produces just about every milk product, from flavoured milk and packaged cream to yogurt, butter, ghee, cheese and ice-cream, and is equally famous for its witty advertising campaign, conceived in 1966, featuring the ageless 'Amul Girl'.

- He created the National Dairy Development Board (NDDB) in 1965 under the leadership of the then Prime Minister, Lal Bahadur Shastri, to coordinate milk production and marketing efforts around the country. He re-energized the Delhi Milk Scheme and opened the Institute of Rural Management, Anand in 1979 to groom managers for cooperatives.
- He spearheaded Operation Flood in 1970 (continued in three phases till 1996) to end milk deficiency, established Mother Dairy – along with its fruit and vegetable marketing subsidiary Safal – to serve Delhi and the National Capital Region, and rolled out the Dhara brand of edible oils to take on the cartels dominating the business.

Under Kurien's watch, India became – and continues to be – the world's largest producer and consumer of milk and per capita milk consumption has more than doubled. His expertise was sought by the Soviet Union, China, Pakistan and Sri Lanka. His birthday (26 November) is celebrated every year as the National Milk Day. His life has even inspired an award-winning movie, *Manthan* (1976), and a comic book. Thanks to milk evangelists such as Kurien, India has well and truly become the Ocean of Milk that its mythology celebrates.

Sourish Bhattacharyya

- Chakraborty, Sumit. 'On World Milk Day, a Look at How India Became the Largest Producer and Why It Continues to Be So'. *Financial Express*, 1 June 2017.
- Heredia, Ruth. *The Amul India Story*. New Delhi: Tata McGraw-Hill, 1997.
- Prakash, Om. *Food and Drinks in Ancient India: From Earliest Times to c. 1200 A.D*. Delhi: Munshi Ram Manohar Lal, 1961.
- Shrikumar, A. 'What Ancient Tamils Ate …'. *The Hindu*, 1 June 2018.
- Tandon, Suneera. 'Keventers Has Reinvented Itself for Millenials with Milkshakes and Instagramable Bottles'. *Scroll.in*, 9 September 2017. Available online: https://scroll.in/article/849619/a-legacy-ice-cream-brand-reinvented-itself-for-millenials-with-milkshakes-and-instagramable-bottles (accessed 17 April 2022).
- Wiley, Andrea S. *Cultures of Milk: The Biology and Meaning of Dairy Products in the United States and India*. Cambridge, MA: Harvard University Press, 2014.
- World Food Prize Foundation. '1989: Kurien'. *n.d.* Available online: https://www.worldfoodprize.org/en/laureates/19871999_laureates/1989_kurien/ (accessed 17 April 2022).

DALAL, TARLA

Tarla Dalal (1936–2013) was a writer, cooking teacher, television host, entrepreneur and India's first celebrity chef. As the author of some 170 cookbooks that have sold millions of copies worldwide, she is said to be one of the world's top five best-selling cookbook authors. In 2007, she was decorated with the Padma Shri by the Indian government.

Dalal was born in Pune, Maharashtra, into a conservative Vaishnav vegetarian family and moved to Bombay after her marriage in 1960. In 1966, she began offering cooking classes at her home in MUMBAI, encouraged by her husband, an engineer, who had studied in the United States and liked collecting recipes of Western food. She once told an interviewer, 'He used to write saying he wanted to eat this and that; all complicated things I had never heard of ... I was twenty years old and could cook only DBRS.' (An old-fashioned acronym for 'dal *bhat* roti *sabzi*', lentils-RICE-BREAD-vegetables.)

The classes became a great success with long waiting lists, and her students included women from the Ambanis, the Birlas and other prominent families. Her first cookbook, *The Pleasures of Vegetarian Cooking*, appeared in 1974 (now in its twenty-second reprint) and became a best seller. The recipes, which were made with the relatively limited ingredients available in India at the time, were for both Indian and non-Indian dishes, including salads with Thousand Island dressing, Chinese fried rice, lasagne and desserts such as APPLE pie and chocolate souffle (made without eggs for vegetarians). Her classes and the book appeared at a time when fewer married couples were living in extended families which meant young brides were no longer learning how to cook from their mothers or mothers-in-law.

Although Dalal specialized in Indian vegetarian cuisine, especially that of Gujarat, she popularized dishes from other parts of India, helping to launch what became a cross-pollination of regional cuisines. Today, dishes like *chhole bhature* (spicy chickpea CURRY served with leavened, deep-fried bread) from Punjab and idli sambar (see IDLI and SAMBAR) from South India have become household favourites across India. She simplified recipes to make them accessible to the average cook. For her many books on Chinese, Italian, Mexican, Thai, French and other international cuisines she converted non-vegetarian recipes to vegetarian ones. Later on, she emphasized healthy cooking by writing books for diabetics, gluten intolerant, the weight conscious, people with high blood pressure and pregnant women.

Her cooking shows *The Tarla Dalal Show* and *Cook It Up with Tarla Dalal* were broadcast in the Gulf countries, the UK and the United States. She travelled around India and the world giving cooking demonstrations. Her business endeavours included a line of cooking equipment and Tarla Dalal Foods which produced ready-to-make mixes. In 2013, the company was sold to Corn Products Co. (India) Ltd, a subsidiary of US-based Bestfood. She once opened an upscale vegetarian restaurant in Mumbai. Her website, tarladalal.com, which is being maintained by her son Sanjay Dalal, has around 17,000 recipes.

Colleen Sen

- Krishna, Priya. 'Tarla Dalal's Cookbooks Taught My Mother – And Millions of Indians – How to Cook Everything'. *Bon Appétit*, 23 August 2018. Available online: https://www.bonappetit.com/story/tarla-dalal (accessed 23 April 2022).
- Muthalaly, Shonali. 'Tarla Dalal's Dal-Bhat-Roti-Sabzi'. 30 June 2014. Available online: https://shonalimuthalaly.com/2014/06/30/tarla-dalals-dal-bhat-roti-sabzi/ (accessed 23 April 2022).

DATES

There are two species of dates: *Phoenix sylvestris*, the wild date palm which grows throughout India and southern Pakistan, and *Phoenix dacylifera*, the true date palm which originated in Africa and Western Asia. (Wild dates are generally not eaten.)

The true date palm has been grown both wild and cultivated in West Punjab and Sindh (now in Pakistan) for centuries. According to legend, the trees originated from seeds thrown away by soldiers in the army of Alexander the Great or, alternatively, by the Arab invaders of Sind in the seventh century CE. Because domestic production of dates is insufficient to meet demand, India is the world's largest importer of dates, mainly from Pakistan and the Middle East. However, in recent years, the Indian national and state governments have been promoting the cultivation of dates, especially in Gujarat and northwestern Rajasthan. Despite having sufficient area to grow the fruits, India lacks the Middle East's high-tech harvesting techniques so production remains low. Lately, farmers have been planting the high-yielding *bahri* variety. A few biotechnology laboratories have developed high-quality plants of indigenous varieties.

Dates are sold fresh or dried. Popular varieties include *medjool*, *barhi* and *khalas*. In India, dates (Hindi *khajur*) are used mainly in SWEETS, including HALWA, BARFI and LADDU. The sap may be tapped and drunk fresh, fermented into toddy and, in West Bengal, boiled to make palm jaggery. Muslims, traditionally, break their Ramadan fasts by eating dates. The leaves can be used to make mats, bags and brooms.

Colleen Sen

• India Gardening. '8 Types of Khajur | Dates Varieties in India'. *n.d.* Available online: https://indiagardening.com/lists/types-of-khajur-dates-varieties-in-india (accessed 23 April 2022).

DE ORTA, GARCIA

The first European to write about Indian medicinal plants, herbs and fruits was the medical doctor Garcia de Orta (1501?–68), a Jew of Spanish origin who served as physician to Portuguese viceroys and governors and to local rulers. The Viceroy granted him a lifelong lease on an island that later became part of Bombay where he kept his own botanical garden and laboratory. His only known work is *Coloquos dos Simples e Drogas da India* (*Conversations on the Simples and Drugs of India*) published in Goa in 1563, which was one of the first books printed in India. Today, the municipal garden in Goa's capital Panjim is named after him.

The book consists of fifty-eight dialogues between de Orta and his friend in which de Orta describes various fruits, spices, drugs, precious stones and wood found in Western India. They include CARDAMOM, cannabis, COCONUT, cubeb, areca, CINNAMON, galangal, GINGER, MANGO, TURMERIC, MELONS, pepper (see PEPPER, BLACK), TAMARIND and betel. De Orta describes the origin and properties of each item and, when applicable, its medical properties. The information is based on his personal observations and discussions with Indian traders, ascetics and doctors. Sometimes, he compares traditional Indian cures with those recommended by Greek and Arab physicians.

The longest and most detailed discussion is on the mango which he extols as superior to all the fruits in Portugal. (He also finds Indian oranges better than their Portuguese counterparts.) He serves mangoes to a guest in two ways: alone and in an aromatic wine (a common way of preparing peaches in Portugal.) He describes other ways mangoes can be prepared: in jams with SUGAR, PICKLED in vinegar or coated with olive oil and SALT and stuffed with green ginger and GARLIC.

Colleen Sen

- De Orta, Garcia. *Collogues des Simples et Des Drogues de l'Inde*. French translation by S.M. Ramos, et al. Paris: Thesaurus, 2004.

DELHI

Delhi has been the home of India's political and administrative elite, and the scene of a succession of battles, waves of invaders and a steady stream of migrants from all over the country since 1060 when Anangpal Tomar II, a Rajput ruler, established his capital Lal Kot (or Qila Rai Pithora at the site of what is now Mehrauli in Delhi) in 1060 CE. India's capital city from 1911, when the British Raj moved its political centre away from Calcutta (KOLKATA), Delhi is a city steeped in history and diversity and its cuisine is a smorgasbord of culinary traditions, from Bania to Mughlai, from Punjabi to Northeastern. For an introduction to what is known as the Great Indian Thali – the omnibus term for the country's multiple cuisines – there cannot be a better starting point than Delhi.

The history of the city's oldest ruling elite, a collection of dynasties led by Afghan and Turkic settlers known as the Delhi Sultanate, dates back to 1192 CE. The quintessential North Indian tea-time snack, SAMOSA – then known as *sambusak* – was popular at the time. The only detailed account we have of a meal served on the table of a Delhi Sultanate ruler comes from Abu Abdullah Muhammad IBN BATTUTA (1304–68/9). Ibn Battuta mentions that one meal started with a SHERBET of 'sugared water', followed by BREAD (thin round WHEAT-flour chapatis); large slabs of sheep's meat; round dough cakes cooked in GHEE (clarified butter), 'which they stuff with sweet almond paste and honey'; meat cooked again in ghee with ONIONS and green GINGER; *sambusak* (triangular pastries made of pieces of thin bread that are folded to pack in 'hashed meat' cooked with almonds, walnuts, pistachios, onions and spices, and then fried in ghee); RICE cooked in ghee with chicken on top; and 'sweet cakes and sweetmeats' for dessert. To wash all this down, they had BARLEY water, followed by the digestive betel leaf and areca nut, which is also a mild narcotic (see PAAN).

Today Mehrauli, Delhi's gentrified rural suburb where the foundations of the Delhi Sultanate were laid, and later a retreat of the city's elite, has become a conglomeration of fashion stores and haute restaurants. Notable is the Olive Bar & Kitchen, which serves European food with typically Indian ingredients (such as *aam aada*, the MANGO-flavoured galangal, and *chow chow*, the name of the popular chayote squash in Tamil Nadu) as an expression of its support for the 'Vocal for Local' movement. A recent addition is Rooh, a progressive Indian restaurant located in an 150-year old haveli in the upscale Ambawatta One shopping center. And all this food experimentation happens in the shadow of the Qutab Minar, a 72.5-metre-tall stone minaret and architectural marvel, embellished with Quranic verses and geometric patterns built in 1220 CE. The past and present are constant companions in contemporary Delhi.

Little is known about the food culture between the fading of the Delhi Sultanate and the rise of the Timurids, popularly known as the MUGHAL dynasty founded by Babur (1483–1530). Akbar (r. 1556–1605) stayed at the Lodi capital, Agra, which remained the Mughal capital for more than eight decades. In 1648 Akbar's grandson Shah Jahan moved the Mughal court, with its complement of Persian, Afghan and Rajput noblemen and bureaucrats belonging to the Kayastha caste (who absorbed numerous elements of the Timurid culture, including fine cuisine) to Shahjahanabad on the west bank of the Yamuna River. Delhi finally evolved into an imperial city, which the itinerant French physician Francois Bernier (1620–88), who spent twelve years in India, described in detail. He wrote that in the summertime, the shops in the fruit market were laden with dry fruit from Persia, Balkh, Bukhara and Samarkand – almonds, pistachios and walnuts, raisins, prunes and APRICOTS – and with the advent of winter, grapes, MELONS, pears and APPLES were available in abundance. Bernier had two gripes: the breads were 'neither well-made, nor properly baked' and wine was hard to get, imported only by Dutch merchants, and therefore 'so dear that, as we say at home, the taste is destroyed by the cost'.

As Delhi became the magnet of the nobility, it acquired a food culture of its own. The Hyderabadi nobleman of Persian descent, Dargah Quli Khan, who was in Delhi between 1737 and 1741, refers to the *qahwa khanas* (COFFEE houses) of the city's main boulevard, Chandni Chowk, in his colourful account of the imperial capital titled *Muraqqa-e-Dehli*. Poets used to hold soirees at these places of leisure, where, presumably, a lot of coffee from Arabia got drunk. The beverage, as was observed by the English clergyman Edward Terry in the second decade of the seventeenth century, had become quite popular in India because it was considered good 'to quicken the spirits and to cleanse the blood'. Consignments of coffee used to land in the port of Surat, where it fetched a higher price for the East India Company than in Iran. A regular visitor to these coffee houses was the high-ranking imperial courtier and celebrated poet and lexicographer Anand Ram 'Mukhlis', but he used to insist on getting the coffee he drank from his own kitchen. In his writings, as the scholar Abhishek Kaicker points out, 'Mukhlis' compared the 'two or three coffee shops' in Chandni Chowk with those of Iran, which he had heard were famed for their ceremonious air (*latafat o takalluf*). In eighteenth-century Delhi, coffee clearly had become a part of the daily life of the cognoscenti, enough to merit an entire poetic ode to the beverage by the Urdu poet Shaikh Zahuruddin Hatim, better known as Shah Hatim, who made it abundantly clear that it was not drink of menials. 'It is nothing if not held by the noble, | It is always annoyed by low company', the poet declared.

In the same Delhi, the 'Anglo-Mughal' elite, notably the Skinner and the Gardner families, woke up at dawn for a gluttonous breakfast: 'brain cutlets, beef rissoles, mutton hashes, brawns of sheep's head and trotters'. Lunch, consisting of mainly roast chicken, was served at noon (around the time the Mughal nobility woke up to a light breakfast of fruits and mutton *shorba*, or broth), and as the sun set, these 'White Mughals' would have another meat-heavy dinner and retire for the day. By the time Zafar would have dinner, Delhi's Anglo-Mughal elite used to be fast asleep.

The tottering Mughal dynasty could not overcome the scars left by the invasions of Nadir Shah followed by the 1857 Rebellion, when the mutinous sepoys of the East India Company declared Zafar, much to his surprise, as their 'emperor', only to be crushed brutally by the British. But their cuisine, described by Aurangzeb to a visiting *hakim* from Turkey as a combination of the pleasures of heaven and hell, being delicious and pungent at the same time, survived the vicissitudes of history. It was lovingly preserved by their cooks, who lived in the section of Chandni Chowk known as Matia Mahal. The cuisine also survived in the Mughal-inspired culinary repertoire of the Kayasthas (which incidentally is the lineage of Madhur Bahadur, better known as Madhur JAFFREY). In Matia Mahal, a beehive of activity in the shadow of the majestic Jama Masjid, Delhi's principal mosque built by Shahjahan between 1650 and 1656, you'll find the redoubtable Karim's which has been serving Mughlai fare, notably kormas and *dopiazas*, since 1931. Its lesser-known but equally acclaimed counterpart is Al Jawahar which is famous for its *ishtoo* (mutton stew pumped up with broken whole dried red CHILLIES) and chicken *changezi*, roast chicken cooked with milk, dairy cream and a mélange of spices. The neighbourhood is also home to Aslam Chicken, where people go to savour the 'Old Delhi' version of BUTTER CHICKEN in white gravy. Kallan Sweets, which has been around at Matia Mahal since 1939, is famous for another Delhi favourite, the Habshi HALWA, which gets its politically incorrect name from the pejorative Hindustani term '*habshi*' for dark-skinned people. Made with malted wheat (*sabnak*), milk, SUGAR, ghee, refined flour and edible gum, Habshi halwa gets its dark brown colour because the milk and sugar are slow-cooked till the sugar gets caramelized.

Away from the Jama Masjid, but still inside Chandni Chowk, also known as 'Dilli-6' after its postal code, is the vibrant world of *bania* cuisine (the vegetarian food, sans ONION and GARLIC, of the trading class). It is best known for its two breakfast staples: *bedmi aloo* (puris stuffed with a tangy *urad* dal, or black gram, paste served with a POTATO curry) and halwa *nagori* (semolina halwa paired with wheat flour and semolina puris cooked in ghee). Also popular and almost iconic are the deep-fried stuffed parathas sold in the narrow bylane named, appropriately, Parathe Wali Gali.

The provenance of this non-descript lane goes back to 1650, when it was laid out under the instructions of Emperor Shah Jahan's entrepreneurial daughter, Jahanara Begum, for shops selling silverware. Around the 1870s, the paratha shops moved in. Of the twenty-odd shops active in the glory days of the Paranthe Wali Gali, only three remain – Pandit Kanhaiyalal Durgaprasad Dixit (1875), Pandit Dayanand Shiv Charan (1882) and Pandit Baburam Devidayal (1886). Their most advertised regulars have included two prime ministers, Jawaharlal Nehru and Atal Bihari Vajpayee, and other notables. As many as thirty-five varieties are known to be on offer at the Paranthe Wali Gali, the stuffings range from the common potato mash, grated cauliflower or RADISH, and PANEER to the unusual CARROTS, bitter GOURD, OKRA, FENUGREEK seeds and MINT leaves and to the exotic BANANA, dry fruit and *khurchan* (the thin, sweet and flaky sheets that milk gets reduced to as a result of extensive boiling). These parathas, unlike the ones made at home or even in restaurants (on the *tawa*, or griddle, and lightly fried), are deep-fried in ghee in heavy-bottomed flat pans. Served as accompaniments are light curries made with pumpkin, and potatoes and green peas, or the same with paneer added to the mix, as well as mint CHUTNEY and the sweet and sour *kele ki saunth* (slices of bananas in chutney made with jaggery and dried ginger).

For most people visiting Paranthe Wali Gali, a meal usually ends with a walk to have the famous Daulat ki chaat – a delicious combination of creamy milk foam, *bura*, or unprocessed sugar, *mawa*, or milk solids, NUTS and SAFFRON – in the neighbouring Dariba Kalan and Kinari Bazaar segments of Chandni Chowk, or at Bazaar Sitaram a little farther away. This is where connoisseurs converge for the amazing array of KULFIS (their flavours ranging from mango and LYCHEE to *JAMUN*, blackberry and even *gulkand*, a rose petal and sugar syrup concoction served in *meetha* paan) at Kuremal Mahavir Prasad, established in 1906. On a winter day, a pit stop is *de rigueur* at Old & Famous Jalebi Wala (founded in 1884) which serves its legions of fans soft and plump JALEBIS fried in ghee on a coal fire. A longer walk takes the discerning eater to the original Giani Di Hatti for its famous *rabri-falooda* (see *RABRI*, *FALOODA*) on a street that meanders from the boundaries of the Fatehpuri mosque, completed in 1650, to St Stephen's Church built by Anglican missionaries in 1862. A stop a Chaina Ram Sindhi Confectioners along the walls of the red sandstone mosque can yield its most sought-after preparation – the Karachi halwa, a saffron-hued chewy dessert made with cornflour, dry fruits, sugar and ghee. Chaina Ram was established in 1901 in Lahore's

Anarkali Bazaar, but the partition of India and the ensuing sectarian violence brought the owners to Delhi where they found a receptive market.

As Delhi moved beyond Chandni Chowk, especially after the new capital of the British Raj, New Delhi, moved into its new location, Raisina Hill (now called Lutyens' Delhi after Sir Edwin Lutyens, the city's architect), a new food culture started emerging. Its epicentre was Connaught Place, a showpiece of Georgian architecture and the grand central business district of New Delhi modelled after the Royal Crescent of Bath. Here a Swiss couple opened the city's first European bakery and coffee shop, named Wenger's after their family name. It had a ballroom, spacious verandahs and a menu that included cakes and pastries, Swiss chocolates and savoury chicken mince puffs. It was in Connaught Place that New Delhi's first luxury hotel, The Imperial, was opened in 1936. Not far from The Imperial, in the heart of Connaught Place, the Japanwala family built the Marina in 1934. With these two hotels, and later The Ambassador, once a mess for British officers, the centre of the city's hospitality industry moved away from the old Civil Lines, which had grand hotels like the Maidens Metropolitan Hotel, commissioned for the 1903 Durbar to celebrate the coronation of Edward VII, and the Swiss and Cecil hotels.

The area around Connaught Place acquired a global vibe with the arrival of American soldiers during the Second World War – their barracks were a brief walk away from Connaught Place, where they would gather to watch Hollywood films at Regal theatre and savour the hamburgers and ice-creams served out of a hand-cranked machine at Kwality restaurant – Delhi's oldest surviving 'multi-cuisine' restaurant. The Americans went to fight the War in Burma and the city's new and Westernized elite moved into neighbourhoods around Connaught Place. In the heady years after Independence, they patronized its restaurants, including Kwality, United Coffee House, Embassy and Standard (now no more) – which served 'Continental' menus along with fusion favourites such as *nargisi* kofta (India's answer to scotch eggs), old Calcutta club must-haves (tomato fish, for instance) and exotic ice-creams, notably tutti-frutti and the Sicilian cassata.

Connaught Place had been built for the British ruling class, the royal retainers (the maharajas) and foreign diplomats. For the Indians who were the cogs in wheels of the Raj – the clerks and other petty officials – the Bengali Market came up, named after its builder Lala Bengali Mal Lohia. It served the daily needs of the families that resided around the market, but it was after an enterprising businessman from Ambala in Haryana, Lala Bhim Sain, established his TEA shop, which grew from its humble beginnings in the 1930s into the formidable Bengali Sweet House, that this area acquired its reputation as a foodie magnet. Sain introduced the Punjabi dish *chhole bhature* (spicy white chickpeas served with *bhatura* (see BREADS), sliced onions and PICKLES) in 1952 and it became not only an instant hit but also Delhi's most celebrated vegetarian dish.

Today, Bengali Sweet House and Nathu's, its rival set up by Lala Nathu Ram Gupta on the opposite side of a narrow lane, have become the favourite haunts of Delhiites, from judges and lawyers to dance and drama students, and visitors for their quintessential offerings – *chhole bhature*, *aloo tikki* (crispy outside and soft inside), *dahi bhalla* (*dahi* VADA) and *golgappa*. Bengali Market, which had come up to serve the adjacent railway station, now has the city's cultural milieu as its neighbour, with its complement of theatres, art galleries, dance academies, the National School of Drama and the Indian Council for Historical Research, all within walking distance. It is an eclectic mix of students, scholars and professionals who now gather at Bengali Market on summer evenings and winter afternoons.

Partition transformed Delhi into a city of Punjabi refugees who brought their cuisine and gave the city its best-known restaurant, Moti Mahal, and its iconic butter chicken. Delhi is also the Promised Land for settlers from all over the country and its cuisine reflects the delectable variety its residents bring to the table: KOLKATA biryani and *moghlai parotta* of Chittaranjan Park, and the more refined Oh! Calcutta; the multiple places dishing up 'South Indian' food: ubiquitous roadside stalls and popular restaurants such as Chidambaram's New Madras Hotel, Sagar Ratna, Naivedyam, Karnataka Food Centre, Saravanah Bhawan, Carnatic Cafe and Mahabelly; and eateries dedicated to the cuisines of Bihar (Potbelly), Rajasthan and Gujarat (Suruchi), Kashmir (Mealability), the Northeast (at Humayunpur) and Tibet (at Majnu Ka Tila, where Tibetan exiles have set up a vibrant community now in its third generation). Add to this mix the '*bhawans*' (or official residences) of state governments, especially the Andhra Pradesh, Assam, Gujarat, Tamil Nadu and West Bengal *bhawans*, where people go for 'authentic food'; plus the open-air Dilli Haat and, on the other end of the price band, tony restaurants such as the celebrated Indian Accent, Bukhara, Chor Bizarre and Dakshin – and you have the Great Indian Thali laid out for you with all its temptations and titillations.

Sourish Bhattacharyya

- Dalrymple, William. *The Last Mughal: The Fall of a Dynasty: Delhi 1857*. London: Bloomsbury, 2006.
- Dehlvi, Sadia. *Jasmine and Jinns: Memories and Recipes of My Delhi*. New Delhi: HarperCollins, 2017.
- Jaffrey, Madhur. *Climbing the Mango Tree: A Memoir of a Childhood in India*. New York: Knopf Doubleday, 2007.
- Smith, R.V. 'Tales from the Mughal Kitchen Recounted by Cooks of Matia Mahal'. *The Hindu*, 13 April 2020. Available online: https://www.thehindu.com/society/history-and-culture/tales-from-the-mughal-kitchen-recounted-by-cooks-of-matia-mahal/article31330900.ece (accessed 22 May 2022).

DEVI, PRAGYASUNDARI

The niece of the humanist poet and Nobel laureate Rabindranath Tagore and wife of the Father of Modern Assamese Literature, Laxminath Bezbaroa, Pragyasundari Devi (1870–1950) was Bengal's first modern cookbook writer. She was the author of *Aamish O Niraamish Aahaar*, Non-Vegetarian and Vegetarian Food, consisting of two volumes of vegetarian recipes – the first undated, presumably 1900, and the second, 1902 – and another book on non-vegetarian food, 1907.

Hailed as the co-creator of the Icmic steam cooker (a feat ascribed to the Bengali polymath Indumadhab Mallick), Pragyasundari Devi is also remembered for having started the modern Bengali tradition of putting up menu cards at special family meals. Called *kromoni* they included cosmopolitan selections such as eggs and mulligatawny soup, *bekti* mayonnaise, roast snipe, smoked *hilsa*, *oeufs a la Neige*, and cold jelly and blancmange.

Pragyasundari was the editor of the Tagore family's creative writing journal *Punya*, which had a substantial section dedicated to recipes as well as frequent contributor to a number of contemporary magazines. One was her husband's Assamese journal,

Banhi, where she published recipes based on the notes of her father and science writer Hemendranath Tagore. For enhancing our understanding of Bengali cuisine, Pragyasundari became famous as "the Indian Mrs Beeton" (a reference to pioneering English cookbook writer, Isabella Mary Beeton), as much for her modern recipes as for her advice on domestic economy.

A practitioner of what we now call 'root-to-shoot cookery', Pragyasundari, in the tradition of Bengali home-makers, used usually discarded ingredients such as seeds and peelings to create delicious dishes. Stating her philosophy of cookery, Pragyasundari wrote, 'Spending a lot of money is no guarantee for good food.' She was so concerned about regular middle-class Bengali women not being able to follow her recipes that midway through her magnum opus she switched over from teaspoons and tablespoons as measures to the traditional *tola-chhatak-ser* system.

An accomplished communicator, Pragyasundari's stated intention was to rid Bengali food of the 'disorderliness' that, according to her, pervaded it. 'The muddle of fish and milk-based dessert in our feasts results in a hodge-podge that is as contrary to the rules of the scriptures as it is harmful for health', she wrote. 'My prime objective is to save Bengali food from this disorderliness and confer on it order and discipline.' Pragyasundari was just not another writer of recipes; she had a vision for Bengali cuisine that inspired Bengali middle-class women to infuse creativity and economy into their kitchens.

Sourish Bhattacharyya

- Deb, Chitra. (Translated from the Bengali by Smita Chowdhry and Sona Roy), *Women of the Tagore Household*. New Delhi: Penguin Books, 2010.
- Das, Rituparna. 'Reading Women through Their Recipes: The Cookbooks of Bengal'. *Sahapedia*. Available online: https://www.sahapedia.org/reading-women-through-their-recipes-cookbooks-bengal (accessed 6 November 2019).
- Roy, Devapriya. 'Cooking with Pragyasundari: A Woman of the Tagore Household Tells You How to Make *Bhapa Ilish*'. *The Indian Express*. Available online: https://indianexpress.com/article/lifestyle/books/cooking-with-pragyasundari-a-woman-of-the-tagore-household-tells-you-how-to-make-bhapa-ilish-4878079/ (accessed 8 October 2017).

DHABAS

Dhabas are unpretentious eateries that dot the highways and pilgrimage destinations across India, catering mainly to truck drivers and their assistants (which is why they've been described as truckers' pit stops), and now, increasingly, also serving an outwardly mobile middle class that goes out on 'driving holidays' to hill stations, holiday resorts and other tourist magnets.

The origins of these ubiquitous shacks, many of which have been gentrified by their owners because of their expanding metropolitan clientele, are lost in layers of obscurity. The generally accepted view is that the word '*dhaba*' has its roots in the Hindi *dabba* (the lunch box that Indians carry with them to their places of work or on road and rail journeys). And they may have had their beginnings in the *serais* (inns) along the historic 2,400 km long Grand Trunk Road, which stretches from Kabul in Afghanistan to Dhaka and Chittagong in Bangladesh via Peshawar and Lahore in Pakistan, and Amritsar, Delhi, Prayagraj (Allahabad) and Kolkata in India.

FIGURE 17 DHABAS. *Dhaba* on a highway near Delhi. Ashish Sen.

Typically, most *dhaba*s are open 24/7, play loud Bollywood music and offer no-frills vegetarian fare. The menu at the more common Punjabi *dhaba*s consists of dal *makhni* (whole black lentils simmered in a buttery sauce; see PULSES); seasonal vegetable preparations such as *aloo gobhi* (POTATOES and cauliflower), or *sarson da saag* (mashed and spiced MUSTARD greens, their bitterness balanced by spinach, *bathua* (*Chenopodium album*) and RADISH leaves) served with *makke di* roti (corn bread); parathas (flatbreads, plain or stuffed with spiced mashed potatoes and ONIONS, or cauliflower florets, or shaved radish) accompanied by a generous dollop of white butter; and spiced *chhaas* (BUTTERMILK) or sweet LASSI (popular yogurt-based drink topped up with a layer of fresh cream). The accompanying 'salad' comprises roughly sliced raw onions, radishes, CARROTS and green CHILLIES. And to take care of guests who may doze off after a long journey and a heavy meal, *charpaai*s, or charpoys (the traditional Indian rope-strung cots), are laid out for them to stretch their wearied limbs.

The offerings could vary by state. A Kathiawari *dhaba* in Gujarat and Mumbai would serve you the sweet-and-sour *sev tameta nu shaak* (TOMATOES and *sev*, or crunchy chickpea flour noodles; see *SEV* AND *SEVIYAN*) and *undhiyu* (mixed seasonal vegetable casserole). On the highway from Mumbai to Nashik (India's wine capital), *dhabas* serve Maharashtrian favourites such as *bhakri* (MILLET flatbread) with *pithla* (a spicy *besan*, or gram flour, preparation) and *thecha* (green chilli and garlic CHUTNEY, occasionally with peanuts added to it). Non-vegetarian *dhaba*s serve tandoori chicken and peppery mutton CURRIES.

Some *dhabas* have a hoary history, such as Amritsar's Kesar Da Dhaba, which was opened in present-day Pakistan in 1916 and moved with its owners after Partition. Some have cult followings, such as the National Highway 1 (NH1, old Grand Trunk Road) favourites – Amrik Sukhdev Dhaba and Gulshan Dhaba at Murthal near Delhi in the state of Haryana, famous for their stuffed parathas, and Puran Singh Da Dhaba in the military cantonment town of Ambala, where the tandoori chicken is unmissable. Cheetal Grand at Khatauli, near Muzaffarnagar in Uttar Pradesh, is a must-stop destination for Delhiites headed for cooler Dehradun, because of its chicken cutlet, PAKORAS (gram flour-coated fritters) and the ultimate comfort food, bread and omelette.

Some *dhabas* stand out because of something special. The Satara Highway Dhaba on NH4 in Maharashtra is run entirely by transgender persons; the Chilika Dhaba at Barkul on NH5 in Odisha has a committed clientele because of its chilli prawns and king crabs that are sourced fresh from the nearby brackish water lagoon, Chilika Lake; and the Ice Café, at an altitude of 14,000 feet and shaped like a Buddhist stupa carved out of ice, is the reward (complete with Tibetan-style noodles, momos and TEA) that adventurous souls get after braving a motorbike ride across the treacherous Manali-Leh highway in Himalayan India.

Some *dhabas* are landmarks in their respective cities, such as Amritsar's All India Famous Amritsari Kulcha (named after its tandoor-baked white flour breads stuffed with spicy mashed potatoes and cauliflower) and Makhan Fish and Chicken Corner (home to the famous Amritsari fish *tikka*); Chandigarh's Pal Dhaba (*bheja* fry, or fried lamb brain, *dahi* chicken cooked in yogurt and mutton rogan josh are the must-haves here); Old Rao Dhaba, which came up on the outskirts of Delhi in 1995 because its founder sensed a business opportunity in the burgeoning traffic on NH8, the busy Delhi-Jaipur highway; and Kolkata's classic Bachan's Dhaba, which has a mixed menu but never falters on its Punjabi offerings, and the Azad Hind Dhaba, which is also famous for the original painting given by its most famous patron, the artist M.F. Husain. Some establishments retain their rugged rustic charm while others have been turned around by their present owners to look more like city restaurants than highway eateries.

Sourish Bhattacharyya

- Kaushik, Karan. 'Get Off the Motorway: The Best Places to Eat on Popular Highways – Part I'. *Outlook Traveller*, 19 July 2020.
- Singh, Nidhi. '20 Highway Dhabas That You Must Stop By'. *TourMyIndia*, 24 May 2019. Available online: https://www.tourmyindia.com/blog/20-highway-dhabas-in-india-that-you-must-stop-by/ (accessed 17 April 2022).
- Singh, Rocky and Mayur Sharma. *Highway on My Plate: The Indian Guide to Roadside Eating*, 2 volumes. New Delhi: Random House India, 2010 and 2014.

DHARWAD PEDHA

Dharwad *pedha* (or *peda*) is a GEOGRAPHICAL INDICATION (GI) tagged sweetmeat unique to the twin cities of Dharwad-Hubbali in north-western Karnataka. Traditionally prepared with solidified milk (*KHOYA*) and SUGAR, the doughy spheres known as *pedhas* have been historically associated with the town of Mathura in western Uttar Pradesh, which is revered as the birthplace of the Hindu deity, Lord Krishna. These sweet treats were introduced to Dharwad, at that time a sleepy, semi-rural town in the Bombay Presidency, by a man named Ram Singh Thakur in the early nineteenth century.

Thakur had left his native town, Unnao in Uttar Pradesh (then known as the North-Western Provinces), in distress in the wake of a plague epidemic. Dislocated from his hometown, Thakur began life afresh in Dharwad as a maker of *pedhas*. His recipe wasn't that complicated. All that went into the *pedhas* were the milk of the local buffaloes and sugar, stirred together continually on a slow fire for ninety minutes till the condensed milk turned into a dark brown semi-solid mass. The colour came from the sugar that got caramelized. From this semi-solid mass, after it was allowed to cool for some time, Thakur pulled out little spheres, rolled them over powdered sugar and then left them to dry.

A novelty for the local residents, the *pedha*s became instantly popular and Thakur's grandson, Babu Singh Thakur, turned the business into Dharwad's pride. He even got a silver medal and a Certificate of Merit at a local exhibition in 1913 from the Governor of Bombay, Lord Willingdon, who later became the Viceroy of India.

The Thakurs (now into the fifth and sixth generations) continue to make the *pedha*s the way Ram Singh first made them. Their creations are famous all over as the Line Bazar *pedha*s, named after the street where Babu Singh opened his shop more than 125 years ago. And, as the GI case statement notes, the milk of local buffaloes is still the main ingredient and the *pedha*s are entirely handmade, from the stirring of the milk to the rolling of the dark brown spheres on powdered sugar. The other distinguishing characteristics of the *pedhas* are their limited production, not more than 100 kilos a day, and their extended shelf life – they stay in good shape for at least twenty days. The Dharwad *pedha* may seem to be an uncomplicated sweetmeat, but its fascinating history and specific geography make it special.

Sourish Bhattacharyya

DIASPORA

FIGURE 18 DIASPORA. Menu in Doubles Shop, Santa Cruz, Trinidad. Kalamazadkhan/ Wikimedia Commons.

Although it is sometimes believed that migration from South Asia to the rest of the world is a relatively new phenomenon, South Asia was a highly mobile society from ancient times. From the time of the Indus Valley civilization, Indian traders travelled far and wide in search of markets for spices (mainly pepper (see PEPPER, BLACK), TURMERIC and CARDAMON) as well as imported goods such as silk. And not all returned to India. Traders from the Indus Valley, called Meluhha, were housed in special quarters in Sumerian cities and there is even an indication of an Indian woman running a tavern.

Indian soldiers served in the army of the Persian Emperor Darius and these contacts may have been responsible for introducing the chicken (see POULTRY AND EGGS), first domesticated in India, to Persia and Central Asia. India and Classical Greece had extensive contacts as early as the sixth century BCE and there is evidence of colonies of Indians living in the Greek city Alexandria. Among the legacies were RICE and SUGAR, which were initially used for medicinal purposes.

As early as the third century BCE, merchants from Kalinga (modern Odisha) were engaged in trade with Southeast Asia. Indian merchants, notably those from South India, were accompanied by religious leaders who introduced Hinduism and Buddhism to the region together with Indian culture and writing systems. So-called 'Hinduized' kingdoms flourished in what are now Thailand, Vietnam, Cambodia and Indonesia until well into the eighteenth century. (Today, their last trace is on the island of Bali.) Indian merchants exported spices and introduced nutmeg (see NUTMEG AND MACE) and CLOVES to India. There was also an active trade across the Indian Ocean with Indian merchant communities residing in Cairo, Baghdad, East Africa, Sri Lanka and other consumption centres.

The first Indians arrived in Britain in the early seventeenth century as sailors on British ships, lascars, or as servants to returning employees of the East India Company (EIC). The immigrant who wrote most extensively about his life in England was Sake Dean Mahomed (1759–1851), an Indian who served in the British army and married an Irishwoman. In 1809, he opened the first Indian restaurant in England, the Hindoostanee Coffee House at 34 George Street. In 1824, the Oriental Club was founded in the West End as a meeting place for ex-Company men. Its initial fare was French food; in 1839, it started serving CURRY. Richard Terry served as chief cook for ten years and wrote *Indian Cookery* in 1861. Today, its menu still features a selection of curries.

The EIC recruited thousands of Indians to work on British ships and to serve in the army. Some settled in London near the docks and other in port cities. Many came from the Sylhet region in what is now Bangladesh, which traditionally supplied cooks to the Portuguese and later the British. In the decades that followed, they opened restaurants. Other Indians came as teachers of Indian languages or to study in British technical and medical schools. By the mid-nineteenth century, tens of thousands of Indian men and women of all social and economic classes were living in Britain.

By 1920, there were a handful of Indian restaurants in London serving mainly an Indian clientele. The UK restaurant scene exploded after the Second World War following large-scale emigration from the Indian subcontinent. Many immigrants found employment in the restaurant and catering businesses and opened hundreds of small restaurants called 'curry houses' (see CURRY). Many were owned by people from Sylhet. Another sensation was Balti cuisine, which started in south Birmingham and spread to other cities. The curry and Balti house boom reached its peak in the 1970s to the 2000s but today the industry is facing a crisis. The second and third generation of South Asians do not want to enter the restaurant business while curbs on immigration are making it difficult to bring in new chefs.

In 1833, the British declared slavery illegal in its colonies. After the African slaves regained their freedom, most refused to continue their backbreaking, poorly paid work. The economic consequences for the plantation owners, many of them politically well connected, appeared devastating, so the EIC came to their rescue by recruiting workers from the poorer parts of India, mainly Bihar and Eastern Uttar Pradesh; around 10 per cent came from South India. These 'indentured labourers' signed contracts agreeing to work on a particular sugar estate for two terms of five years each, at the end of which the owner would pay for their passage back to India, or they could stay on and buy land. Most stayed on. When the French and Dutch abolished slavery in their overseas possessions in 1846 and 1873, respectively, the EIC provided them with workers as well.

Between 1834 and 1917, when the system was abolished, an estimated 1.4 million Indians left the subcontinent, including 240,000 who went to Guyana, 144,000 to Trinidad and 37,000 to Jamaica. Another destination was the island of Mauritius in the Indian Ocean which the British acquired from the French in 1810. Some 500,000 Indians came here to work on the sugar plantations. Others went to the French colonies of Reunion, Guadeloupe and Martinique; Dutch-owned Suriname; and the Danish island of St Croix. Another group went to the sugar plantations on the island of Fiji.

In 1852, the indentured labourer system was extended to Southeast Asia to supply workers for the COFFEE, palm and rubber plantations. Approximately 2 million Indians went to Malaya (now Malaysia) and another 2.5 million to Burma, the majority from South India. (Most left Burma after the 1962 military coup.) Starting in 1860, 150,000 Indian workers went to South Africa and another 30,000 came to British East Africa (now Kenya and Uganda) to help build the railway into the interior. Later, many others went as teachers, administrators, merchants and attorneys (including Mahatma GANDHI).

These workers created hybrid cuisines that combined traditional dishes with local ingredients. In Trinidad and Tobago and Guyana, an estimated 35 to 40 per cent of the populations are of Indian origin. In both countries, curry – a spiced dish of meat, vegetables or FISH stew – is a common main course. The main spices – CUMIN, CORIANDER, FENUGREEK and TURMERIC – are those found in a rural Bihari household. Curries are accompanied by CHUTNEYS and sauces, such as mango *kuchela*, a MANGO and MUSTARD oil PICKLE. Curries are typically served with rotis, which resemble parathas (see BREADS), and bake, a fried bread. Throughout the Caribbean, TARO is called *dasheen* and its leaves are combined with vegetables and/or seafood to make the emblematic stew called *callaloo*.

In Trinidad the word 'roti' also means a popular street food that has been called the country's national dish. A large round WHEAT bread coated with ground yellow peas is wrapped around a meat, fish or vegetable curry; enclosed in wax paper or foil; and eaten on the move. Another popular street food is 'doubles', a sandwich composed of pieces of turmeric-flavoured fried roti filled with curried chickpeas and topped with spicy chutneys and CHILLI sauce that is similar to the Indian snack *chhole bhature*. *Bara* and *phulorie*, made from chickpeas, are popular snacks and eaten with hot pepper or mango sauce.

Although less than 1 per cent of Jamaicans are of Indian origin, their impact on Jamaican food has been notable, especially in two of Jamaica's best-known dishes – patties (ground spiced meat in a dough pocket) and curry goat, which is served on festive occasions. In a second wave of migration, many people from the Caribbean emigrated to North America and Britain, bringing their dishes with them.

In Malaysia and Singapore, Indian workers, mainly Tamils from South India and Sri Lanka, came to work on the rubber and palm plantations. Singapore, Kuala Lumpur and other Malaysian cities are famous for their STREET FOODS. The popular breakfast dish *laksa* is a fiery chilli-infused COCONUT milk broth containing noodles, fish paste, prawns, lemongrass, shredded chicken, coriander and hardboiled egg. Another popular street food is fish head curry which incorporates South Indian ingredients such as OKRA, AUBERGINE, mustard seeds, fenugreek and CURRY LEAVES and uses the technique of 'tempering' – adding sautéed spices to a dish at the end of cooking.

South Indian curries together with IDLIS, DOSAS, VADAS, SAMBARS and rasams are served in Singapore and Malaysia's so-called 'banana leaf' restaurants. A local equivalent of an Indian stuffed roti is *murtabak* (from the Arabic word for folded). A dough made from white flour is wrapped around spiced minced meat and beaten egg and folded into packets that are sautéed, cut into pieces and served with a curry sauce.

An estimated 1.5 million South Africans are of Indian origin, located mainly in Durban. Curries or *kerries* are popular among all sections of the population. The most famous Indo-South African dish is bunny chow, a meat curry served in a hollowed-out loaf of Western-style bread. One explanation for its name is that in Durban, Indian merchants were often called *banias*, the name of a caste of traders. They opened small restaurants which Blacks could not enter because of apartheid but could (illegally) be served at the back door. An enterprising restaurant owner got the idea of hollowing out a small loaf of bread, pouring in curry, topping it with Indian pickles and handing it over to the customer without cutlery. The dish's name comes from 'bania chow'.

In North America, the earliest South Asians arrived in America just a decade after the founding of the Jamestown Colony in 1607. Some were lascars, others were servants of wealthy EIC retirees who obtained large land holdings in America. Many intermarried with local Native Americans; however, no trace of them remains today. The actual number of people of Indian origin remained small. In 1914, Ceylon India Inn restaurant opened on Eighth Avenue in New York and was followed by several more in the city.

In addition to students and religious workers, Indian immigrants came from two groups. Between 1900 and 1910 more than 3,000 farm workers, mainly Sikhs from Punjab, came to California's Sacramento Valley where they became successful farmers. In 1917, however, the Federal government banned immigration from Asia and many married local Mexican women, who were permitted to own land (unlike South Asians). Their community, which came to a total of 400 couples, became known as 'Mexican Hindus', a category that included Muslims and Sikhs.

Their cuisine combined elements of Mexican and Punjabi food, although usually not in the same dish. Home cooks would use ready-made CURRY POWDER and TOMATO sauce and curries would be served with Spanish rice. A well-known restaurant featuring this food was El Ranchero in Yuba City which closed in 1994 after a forty-year run. Today, the community has almost disappeared because of intermarriage.

Another group of immigrants were Bengali Muslim peddlers who began coming to the United States in the 1880s to sell embroidered silks and other Indian goods to a public that had a craving for all things Indian. Their operations were centred in the New Orleans neighbourhood of Treme, where some married local African American women. Another much larger group of Bengalis were lascars, many of whom jumped ship in New York. Many stayed there, marrying Puerto Rican and African American women and opening halal butcher shops and restaurants in Harlem. These restaurants became important meeting places for the local Indian community, including people seeking independence from Britain. In the 1920s, some of these seamen moved north as part of the African American migration and found work in factories and semi-skilled jobs. Here they lived in boarding houses, usually located in African American communities. Some opened small Indian restaurants in northern cities.

The Immigration Act of 1924 favoured immigration from Northern and Western European countries and excluded immigrants from Asia so that Indian immigration came to a virtual standstill. Similar policies were in place in Canada, Australia and elsewhere. The American Civil Rights movement inspired a major reform of US immigration laws. Discriminatory national origins quotas were abolished and preference was based on professional status and family reunification. In the years that followed, an average 40,000 Indians entered the United States every year. They settled in cities and university towns where grocery stores and entire shopping districts arose to meet their needs. Many more came under the H1-B visa programme created in 1990 which allowed employers to temporarily employ foreign workers in speciality jobs, especially in the IT industry.

Today there are an estimated 4.5 million people of Indian origin in the United States (plus 526,000 Pakistani-Americans and 213,000 Bangladeshi-Americans), 1.3 million in Canada and 620,000 in Australia. There has been a dramatic rise in the number of Indian restaurants that range from street food trucks to Michelin-starred temples of cuisine in San Francisco, Chicago, New York and other cities.

Colleen Taylor Sen

- Chatterji, Joya and David Washbrook, eds. *Routledge Handbook of the South Asian Diaspora*. London and New York: Routledge, 2013.
- Sen, Colleen Taylor. *Curry: A Global History*. London: Reaktion Books, 2009.

DORABJEE & SONS

Dorabjee & Sons, an IRANI CAFE in the western Indian city of Pune, is the oldest continually running restaurant in the country. The restaurant, established in 1878, is managed today by the great great grandson of its founder, Sorabjee Dorabjee, and he still symbolically follows the decades-old tradition of male members of the family doing all the cooking in the restaurant.

The present owner, Darius Marazban Dorabjee, in a departure from the practice at the time of his great grandfather, employs cooks, but he still adds the secret masalas and finishing touches to each preparation, including the restaurant's famous keema *pav* (curried minced mutton and buttered soft bread roll) and *dhansak* (mutton cubes cooked with lentils, vegetables and a masala created especially for this dish). This has been the practice since the day Sorabjee opened his establishment to counter what was then the only restaurant in the city – an Italian eatery named El Moretos in the Pune Cantonment which was not open to Indians (it was, after all, the high noon of the British Raj).

In Sorabjee's time, the men of the family would cook and the women hand-ground the masalas. It is no longer possible in the present times, although wood-fired *chulha*s (traditional earthen stoves) continue to be used for cooking, and the Sorabjee family still has its meals at the restaurant to send out the message that the food is as safe as it would be at home. Another age-old practice – that of eating seated on the floor in the old Indian style – was abandoned in the 1950s in favour of red fibre-glass chairs and wooden tables with white laminated tops.

Little else has changed about Dorabjee & Sons. The location has remained unchanged for the past sixty-five years, there's no air-conditioning and the decor is as basic as it was when it was started, the old menu cards on the walls continue to tantalize guests with their pre-inflation prices, the host (Darius) is ever-present and as affable as ever, and the food is served in time-worn stainless steel utensils. Yet, its popularity and iconic value have stayed undiminished.

Sourish Bhattacharyya

- Adhikari, Shona. 'Dorabjee's Dhansak'. *The Economic Times*, 24 July 2003.
- Khan, Alifiya. 'Families in Food: A Taste of Old Poona'. *The Indian Express*, 11 March 2018.

DOSA

Dosas (also *dosai* and *dose*) are a kind of Indian pancake which can be made with a variety of batters, each giving a slightly different texture and colour. They are the 'breads' of South India. Light and easy to digest, they may be eaten as an accompaniment, to scoop up other food and as a teatime snack and are often eaten for breakfast together with a hot spicy SAMBAR and coconut CHUTNEY. They may also be eaten with butter and HONEY.

The twelfth-century *MANASOLLASA* mentions *dhosika* – a pancake made from a paste of ground *urad* dal, black-eyed peas or green peas flavoured with ASAFOETIDA, GINGER and SALT and cooked in a lightly oiled hot pan. Today, traditional dosas made in South India are made with a paste of wet ground *urad* dal and RICE in a ratio of 2:1 which is left to ferment overnight. The same fermented batter is also used for making IDLIS but whereas idlis are steamed, the thin batter for dosa is poured onto a hot griddle or

FIGURE 19 DOSA. Marajozkee/Wikimedia Commons.

traditional cast iron dosa *kalu* (dosa stone) greased with oil or GHEE. Dosas are generally crispy on the surface but slightly spongy inside with a faintly sour taste.

Each region in India has its own favourite version which can be noticeably different. In Tamil Nadu, they are thick and small whereas in Karnataka they are thin, large and crispy. Rolled up with a spicy POTATO or vegetable stuffing, they are called masala dosa or *poora*. Other variations include *rava* dosas, sometimes called *sooji dosas*, which are made with semolina and rice and flavoured with CUMIN, ginger, asafoetida and NUTS. *Narial* dosas include COCONUT. Jaggery dosas are made with flour, rice flour, coconut and flavoured with jaggery (see SUGAR) and CARDAMOM.

New versions are emerging. For example, in Chicago the South Indian restaurant Udupi Palace serves a 'pizza' style dosa with a thin layer of blended CHEESES, finely chopped ONION and hot green CHILLIES.

Helen Saberi

- Achaya, K.T. *A Historical Dictionary of Indian Food*. Delhi: OUP, 1998.
- Devi, Yamuna. *The Art of Indian Vegetarian Cooking*. London: Leopard Books, 1995.
- Sen, Colleen Taylor. *Feasts and Fasts: A History of Food in India*. London: Reaktion Books, 2015.

DRUMSTICK

Drumstick (Hindi *sehjana*, Tamil *murangaika*), also known as *moringa*, is a long, green pod which contains fleshy pulp and seeds. It comes from the small Indian tree *Moringa oleifera*. The tree is commonly grown in villages and kitchen gardens in West Bengal, Assam and South India. The name drumstick may have come from the British in India as, when dried, the pods resemble the sticks used to beat a drum. When young and tender, the pods are esteemed as a green vegetable. They are cut into lengths and cooked in bunches like asparagus. Indeed, their flavour is often compared with the latter. They are added to soups and curries. In Maharashtrian and Gujarati households they are sometimes added to a dal or a *kadhi* (BUTTERMILK or yogurt soup flavoured chiefly with TURMERIC).

Maharashtrians also eat drumstick *bhajis* – *shevgyachya bhaji* – as do Goans and Bengalis. In Kerala, they are cooked in *avial* (a mixed vegetable curry); they are added to SAMBAR in South India; and in Bengal, they are used in *shukto* (a bitter vegetable dish) and sometimes added to *aloo posto* (see POPPY SEEDS). They are also pickled (see PICKLES).

The seeds, when mature, can be roasted or fried and are said to resemble and taste like peanuts. The seeds are also the source of ben oil, used not only in perfumery but also in salads and cooking. The flowers and tender leaves are also edible, the leaves cooked as a green vegetable, pickled or used as a flavouring agent.

Moringa is believed to have medicinal properties and is said to be good for people suffering from aches and pains. It is also purported to help lower blood sugar, reduce inflammation and improve heart function. The use of *moringa* powder, derived from the leaves and seed pods which contain many important vitamins and minerals and are packed with anti-oxidants, has become quite popular with health conscious people. It can be made into a 'tea' infusion or added to milk shakes, yogurt and so on. Some people even add the powder to chapati dough.

Europeans in India discovered that the pungent root of the *moringa* tree could be used as a substitute for horseradish which explains why this tree is also called the horseradish tree. Colonel A.R. Kenney-Herbert (see WYVERN) wrote in 1885:

> Horseradish sauce is a good standard adjunct to our national food, 'the roast beef of old England', and beef in India cries out for help far more piteously than its rich relation far away. Horseradish grows well at Ootacamund, and I grew some with success at Bangalore, but the scraped root of the moringa, or 'drumstick tree' provides so good a substitute that we may rest contented with a sauce thus composed.

Helen Saberi

- Achaya, K.T. *A Historical Dictionary of Indian Food*. Delhi: OUP, 1998.
- Davidson, Alan. *The Oxford Companion to Food*. 2nd edition. Ed. Tom Jaine. London: OUP, 2006.
- Kenney-Herbert, A.R. *Culinary Jottings: A Treatise in Thirty Chapters on Reformed Cookery for Anglo-Indian Exiles*. 1885. Facsimile reprint. Totnes, Devon: Prospect Books, 1994.

EAST INDIANS

The East Indian Christian community follows the Roman Catholic faith and is based in Mumbai. They were from the Brahmin, Kunbi, Koli and Agri communities that adopted Catholicism during Portuguese rule in Bombay. They began calling themselves 'East Indian' after the East India Company began operations in India in order to distinguish themselves from Mangalorean and Goan Christians. Like the Protestants in Maharashtra, they retained their linguistic and culinary heritage. They were recognized as a distinct community by the British in 1887.

Since they are primarily settled along the coast, seafood is an important part of their diet. Best known for their traditional bottle masala (a complex spice mix for which each family has a unique recipe spanning anything between twenty and sixty ingredients; see SPICE BOX), the East Indian culinary repertoire includes a variety of CURRIES (known as *khudi*) using meat and several deceptively simple recipes for fried and curried FISH. An essential ingredient in everyday East Indian cookery is sugarcane vinegar which is often made at home by families for their own use.

Saee Koranne-Khandekar

- The East Indian Community. 'East Indians: The Indigenous Catholic Inhabitants of Bombay, Salsette and Bassein'. *n.d.* Available online: https://www.east-indians.com/history.pdf (accessed 19 May 2022).

EGGS KEJRIWAL

Eggs Kejriwal is the name given by Mumbai's Willingdon Sports Club to a dish of fried eggs, sunny side up, served on toasted BREAD covered with molten CHEESE and chopped green chillies sprinkled on top and TOMATO ketchup on the side. A between-meals snack,

FIGURE 20 EGGS KEJRIWAL. Maharajah Mandee/Wikimedia Commons.

it acquired an international cult following after London's Dishoom restaurant put it on the menu. The dish gets its name from Devi Prasad Kejriwal, a prominent Mumbai businessman who invented it.

Founded in 1918 by the then British Governor of Bombay, Lord Willingdon (he later became the Viceroy of India), the Club has retained its colonial name, but its menu is as Indian as it can get. (It was, in fact, one of the rare clubs that allowed Indian members before Independence.) Even 'Continental' hardy perennials have got an Indian makeover. One such dish was eggs on toast, which was turned around by Kejriwal. A 'strict' vegetarian like all his moneyed Marwari peers, Kejriwal made an exception for eggs, which he ate only outside his home. Tired of eggs on toast, Kejriwal suggested the variation, which became instantly popular with other members of the Club. Like Currimbhoy salad, a tangy Indian take on the egg mayonnaise salad believed to have been created at Mumbai's iconic Taj Mahal Hotel, eggs Kejriwal has outlived its creator and travelled beyond India's borders.

Sourish Bhattacharyya

- Berrill, Anna. 'Do It Like Dishoom: Favourite Dishes from UK Restaurants to Cook at Home'. *The Guardian*, 17 April 2020.
- Doctor, Vikram. 'How about a Kejriwal for Breakfast?' *ET Panache*, 12 October 2012. Available online: https://economictimes.indiatimes.com/blogs/onmyplate/how-about-a-kejriwal-for-breakfast/ (accessed 17 April 2022).
- Rao, Tejal. 'Eggs Kejriwal'. *NYT Cooking*, *n.d.* Available online: https://cooking.nytimes.com/recipes/1018717-eggs-kejriwal (accessed 17 April 2022).

FALOODA

Falooda is a sweet noodle ('vermicelli') dessert or drink which dates back to Zoroastrian times in Iran where it is called *paludeh*, meaning 'sieved, refined'. But the meaning has been extended and the geographical range of this dessert covers a large area ranging from Egypt, where it is known as *balouza*, to Afghanistan (*faluda*) and India.

Falooda was introduced to India by the Mughal Emperors. *Falooda* became a summertime treat of syrup, fruit juice and vermicelli covered with cream. It was often served to welcome special guests. *Falooda* was a favourite dish of the Emperor Jahangir (r. 1605–27) and was described as a jelly made from the strainings of boiled WHEAT mixed with fruit juices and cream.

In India today, it is traditionally made by mixing rose syrup, vermicelli and sweet BASIL seeds with milk. The vermicelli can be made from wheat, arrowroot, cornstarch or sago, which are made into a paste then forced through a *sev* machine into iced water (or snow, as in ancient times), forming tiny rice-like grains, or small vermicelli, that are transparent and have a jelly-like consistency. Today, the mixture is often piped into iced water which results in longer vermicelli. Falooda is still a cooling summertime treat.

There are many variations in India. The 'vermicelli' can be eaten on their own with just a spoonful of SUGAR syrup and a few drops of rosewater (see FLOWER WATERS); more elaborate versions include fruits and NUTS, but *falooda* is most popularly served with KULFI. A simple version of *falooda* was once an item served by IRANI CAFES. It consisted of soft-boiled sago granules with added cream, fruit, jam and ICE.

Helen Saberi

- Achaya, K. T. *A Historical Dictionary of Indian Food*. Delhi: OUP, 1998.
- Davidson, Alan. *The Oxford Companion to Food*. 2nd edition. Ed. Tom Jaine. Oxford: OUP, 2006.

FASTING

Fasting is a common dietary practice in India. A Pew Research Center survey in 2020 found that around three-quarters of all Indians fast, including 85 per cent of Muslims, 84 per cent of Jains, 79 per cent of Hindus and 64 per cent of Christians. Sikhs and Parsis generally do not fast.

Hinduism. Fasting is an ancient custom among followers of the Dharmic religions. The *Bhavishya Purana*, first composed in 500 BCE, prescribes nearly 140 fasts a year. The eighth and eleventh days of the first half of the lunar month were cited as fast days, while other days were sacred to various deities.

Today fasting practices vary greatly depending on region, caste, religious tradition and local customs. Hindus may undertake a fast (Hindi *upavasa* or *vrata*) for one or several reasons: as a mandatory part of a religious festival, a form of worship, gratitude for a blessing, a petition to a god for a favour, an instrument of self-discipline or a method of physical cleansing. Some devotees believe fasting strengthens the mind and helps control desires. Women generally fast more than men. During *Karva Chauth,* which is observed mainly in North India, women observe a day-long fast to pray for their husband's long life and good health. Children are not expected to fast.

Fasting usually does not connote total abstention from food but rather a restricted way of eating. The dishes are always vegetarian. At its least rigorous, it may mean cooking dishes in pure GHEE instead of oil or replacing sea SALT with rock salt. Sometimes only *kaccha* (e.g. boiled) foods are permitted. Meals might be only taken once a day in the morning or only after sunset. At the most rigorous, no food at all is eaten and only sips of water are allowed.

A common form of fasting involves a category of food called *phalahar*. Food materials are divided into two categories: *anna*, those which are harvested using equipment, such as rice, wheat, barley and lentils, and *phala*, those grown without special cultivation, such as wild grains, vegetables, fruits, certain roots and tubers, leaves and flowers. Only the latter are permitted in some fasts. BREADS and snacks may be made of dried water chestnut flour or LOTUS seed flour instead of WHEAT and other grains. Prohibited foods may include TURMERIC, GINGER, and *urad* dal (perhaps because it is black and resembles meat and spices.) Milk, ghee and water are allowed.

Some people fast on certain days of the lunar cycle when the moon changes, especially the eighth and fourteenth days of each fortnight. On Mondays, which are devoted to Shiva, some devotees fast for sixteen consecutive weeks. Pious Hindus may fast for a full month during Kartik, the eighth month in the Hindu calendar in late autumn. They abstain from FISH, meat and eggs and only eat one meal a day. Communal fasts are associated with religious holidays such as Ram Navami, Mahashivratri and Janamasthami. The Navratri festivals, dedicated to the worship of the goddess Durga, are celebrated throughout India. There are four Navratris but only those in the spring and fall are widely celebrated. Some devotees fast for nine days during them.

Jainism. Jains consider fasts essential for spiritual growth. A fast is preceded by a vow, which means that it is a religious act and done with a predefined intention. There are no hard and fast rules on when or how long one should fast or what form this fasting should take but it is never obligatory. It is not enough just to stop eating, one should also lose the desire to eat and not relish food when one does eat. Fasting is not done in isolation but with one's family or as part of a community event.

Jain texts classify fasts into many categories and lay down complex rules about what can and cannot be eaten. For example, fasting can mean giving up all food and water for one day, three days, eight days, every alternative day of the year, twice a year, etc. It can entail drinking only water or *triphala* – water used to rinse out a pot used to cook food. Fasters may eat only one meal a day at a set time, limit the number of items eaten, give up favourite foods, such as SWEETS (sometimes on a permanent basis), or eliminate salt or spices from their diet. A common form of fasting requires giving up green vegetables, milk, yogurt, oil, fruits, salt, spices and SUGAR and eating only dal and RICE.

Most Jains fast during festivals, especially Paryushan Maha Pava which lasts for eight to ten days during the rainy season (usually August–September). Some fast for the entire period, others for shorter times, but fasting on the final day is considered obligatory. In this case, fasting means complete abstinence from any sort of food or drink but some people take boiled water during the daytime. However, a Jain may fast at any time, especially if they believe they have committed a sin and need to repent. The ultimate fast, called *santara* or *sallekhna,* involves giving up all food and water and starving oneself to death. This practice is undertaken by someone who is at the final stages of a fatal illness or is very old and feels they have fulfilled their duties in this life. They must have permission from a senior Jain, which is granted only if death is imminent. The practice has been challenged in Indian courts. Jain fasting served as an inspiration for Mahatma GANDHI, who used it as a political tactic.

Buddhism. The Buddha initially practised extreme forms of fasting but realized it prevented him from attaining enlightenment and abandoned it in favour of the Middle Way, which calls for moderation in all things. Instead, he recommended practising mindfulness while eating. Today different forms of fasting are practised in the worldwide Buddhist community, including intermittent fasting, eating one meal a day and avoiding certain foods.

Islam. Fasting is one of the five pillars of Islam that are mandatory for every Muslim. During the lunar month Ramadan, all Muslims refrain from eating, drinking, smoking and sex during daylight hours. The purpose of this fast is to encourage self-restraint, empathy for those who are hungry and gratitude for having food. The fast is broken at sunset with a meal called *iftar*. Often the first foods taken to break the fast are DATES, since according to tradition, Muhammad broke his fast with three dates. The *iftar* can be quite lavish and feature special dishes. The first meal taken in the morning before sunrise is called *sahoor*. Some Muslims also fast on Ashura, a day that marks the martyrdom of Husayn ibn Ali and his family. People who are sick, nursing or travelling are exempt from fasting during Ramadan but must make it up before the next Ramadan. There are also several voluntary fasts that may be observed for atonement or to observe certain religious events.

Christianity. Some Christian denominations, including Roman Catholics and Eastern Orthodox, observe partial fasts during the forty days of Lent which commemorates Christ's vigil in the desert before his crucifixion. This can entail abstention from meat throughout the entire period or only on Ash Wednesday and Good Friday, or giving up ones favourite food. In India, both Latin-rite Catholics and SYRIAN CHRISTIANS (followers of the Syro-Malabar and Syro-Malankar rites) follow a vegetarian diet and abstain from ALCOHOL during Lent.

Judaism. Judaism has two major fast days: Yom Kippur, the Day of Atonement, and Tisha B'av, which commemorates the destruction of the Temple in Jerusalem and other disasters. The fasts begin at sundown on the previous night and end after sundown the next day. No food or drink is consumed, including bread and water. Four other shorter fasts during the year begin at dawn and end after sunset.

Colleen Sen

- Corichi, Manolo. 'Eight-in-Ten Indians Limit Meat in Their Diets, and Four-in-Ten Consider Themselves Vegetarian'. *Pew Research Center*, 8 July 2021. Available online: https://www.pewresearch.org/fact-tank/2021/07/08/eight-in-ten-indians-limit-meat-in-their-diets-and-four-in-ten-consider-themselves-vegetarian/ (accessed 4 May 2022).
- Sen, Colleen Taylor. 'Jainism: The World's Most Ethical Religion?' In *Food and Morality: Proceedings of the Oxford Symposium on Food and Cookery 2007*, edited by Susan R. Friedland, 230–40. Totnes, Devon: Prospect Books, 2008.
- Times of India Online. 'Navratri Fasting Rules and Food: What to Eat and What Not to Eat', 2 April 2022. Available online: https://timesofindia.indiatimes.com/religion/rituals-puja/navratri-fasting-rules-and-food-what-to-eat-and-what-not-to-eat/articleshow/82034695.cms (accessed 5 May 2022).

FENNEL

Fennel, known as *saunf* in India, comes from the perennial plant *Foeniculum vulgare*, a member of the parsley family and native to the Mediterranean region. Fennel yields an aromatic, liquorice-tasting bulb, but in India, where it has been cultivated since Vedic times, it is mainly cultivated for its seeds which also possess a pleasing liquorice flavour. They are greenish-yellow and resemble CUMIN seeds, except that they are fatter and larger. They also look and taste like ANISE (and, confusingly, share the same Hindi name, *saunf*).

Today, fennel is cultivated mostly as a garden crop in India, requiring a fairly mild climate. It is cultivated in Maharashtra, Gujarat and Karnataka and on a small scale in Uttar Pradesh, Punjab and Rajasthan. Fennel seeds are used extensively in Indian cooking, either whole or roasted and ground into a powder. They are a popular seasoning in Kashmiri and Punjabi dishes and one of the five essential spices in the Bengali spice mix *panch phoron* (see SPICE BOX). They are also used in other spice mixes such as chaat masala, garam masala, Chettinad masala and *xacuti* masala. The seeds flavour vegetables and dals (see PULSES) and are also used in soups, meat and FISH dishes, PULAO, PICKLES, CHUTNEYS, and some SWEET pastries and beverages.

Perhaps the most important use of fennel seeds in India is that they have for long been considered a very effective digestive and mouth freshener. The seeds are lightly toasted and candied (by coating with a thin syrup) or mixed with shredded COCONUT, toasted MELON seeds and a little SUGAR and served as a digestive after a meal in Indian homes and restaurants. For this preparation, a superior quality of fennel seeds, prized for their sweetness and aroma, is preferred, called Lakhnawi or Lucknowi *saunf*. Fennel seeds are also used in PAAN. The seeds are also made into an infusion and given to infants to relieve colic and flatulence.

Helen Saberi

- Devi, Yamuna. *The Art of Indian Vegetarian Cooking*. London: Leopard Books, 1995.
- Pruthi, J. S. *Spices and Condiments*. New Delhi: National Book Trust, 1976.

FENUGREEK

Fenugreek (*Trigonella foenum-graecum*, Hindi *methi*) is native to the Mediterranean, the Middle East and India (where it has been cultivated since pre-Vedic days) and was called *methika* in Sanskrit. Today, India is a major producer and exporter of fenugreek.

Both the seeds and the leaves are used in Indian cooking but they have different properties and impart different flavours and aromas, so they are not used interchangeably.

The yellowish-brown rectangular seeds are smooth and hard, rather like tiny pebbles, and are about three to five mm long. They are actually a leguminous bean but have long been used as a spice because of their intense aroma and bitter taste. *Methi* seeds are one of the most important spices in Indian vegetarian cooking. They are used whole as well as powdered for flavouring PICKLES and CHUTNEYS. They are used in dals (see PULSES), added to FISH dishes in Kerala and are an essential ingredient in SAMBAR. To bring out the flavour, the seeds are generally dry-roasted or fried first (but only lightly as they can become intensely bitter if overcooked). *Methi* gives some of the 'hotness' in CURRY POWDERS and in the Bengali spice mix, *panch phoron* (see SPICE BOX). Mixed with red CHILLIES, roasted lentils and other spices it is known as *milagai podi* which often accompanies IDLIS and DOSAS.

The seeds are used medicinally for an array of ailments such as colic and flatulence and are also considered anti-diabetic. There is a tradition of serving sweet dishes cooked with fenugreek to mothers of newly born babies to give them extra energy and nourishment.

Fenugreek leaves, *methi ka saag*, were first mentioned in Sutra literature. They have a very strong and distinctive taste. Rich in iron, calcium, protein, vitamins A and C, they are used in CURRIES and as a vegetable, often served with other greens such as spinach, mustard greens or beetroot greens. They are also cooked in combination with starchy root vegetables such as POTATOES and YAMS. They are added to lentil stews and flat BREADS (minced and mixed into the dough), or used as stuffing in breads such as KACHORI.

Some families grow the seeds in window boxes as a pot herb and when the leaves are young and tender and the flavour of the greens is pleasantly bitter, they are added to salads or used as a vegetable.

Sun-dried fenugreek leaves, called *kasoori methi*, are the leaves of a highly scented variety of the fenugreek plant, *Trigonella corniculata*. They are first soaked in water for about thirty minutes before being used, in moderation, for flavouring dishes.

Helen Saberi

- Davidson, Alan. *The Oxford Companion to Food*. 2nd edition. Ed. Tom Jaine. Oxford: OUP, 2006.
- Devi, Yamuna. *The Art of Indian Vegetarian Cooking*. London: Leopard Books, 1995.
- Pruthi, J. S. *Spices and Condiments*. New Delhi: National Book Trust, 1976.

FIRNI

Firni (also *phirni*) belongs to an extensive family of sweet dishes, all based on milk thickened with cornflour or rice flour, sometimes with the addition of ground almonds and usually delicately flavoured with rosewater (see FLOWER WATERS) and ground CARDAMOM. The dish is also, often, decorated elaborately with chopped or ground almonds or pistachio nuts, and for special occasions, with *VARK* (silver or gold leaf).

Firni seems to have originated in ancient Persia or the Middle East and is thought to have been introduced to India by the Mughals. Firni is a popular choice of dessert for most festive occasions. It is traditionally set and served individually in small, shallow, unglazed clay bowls called *shikoras* or *katoris* which lend a special flavour to the dish and which are thrown away after use.

Helen Saberi

FIRPO, ANGELO

Angelo Firpo (1882–1948) was an Italian whose eponymous restaurant opened in 1917 on the fashionable Chowringhee Road in Calcutta (KOLKATA). It became popular around the world as the Maxim's of the East for its food, drinks and Edwardian grandeur – 'the epitome of gracious living in a country noted for its extravagant lifestyles'.

Known for his dandy looks and dapper suits (a contemporary writer, Stan Blackford, described him as 'a charming, distinguished-looking but obsequious Italian'), Firpo was born in Alessandria, Piedmont, where his father worked for Borsalino, Italy's oldest maker of luxury hats. From his hometown he moved to London and then eventually to Calcutta, where he trained under Federico PELITI before going on to open his own restaurant after working for the Peliti family for some time.

A place where 'anybody who was anybody, in this cosmopolitan metropolis, met other class-conscious people for lunch', Firpo's acquired a formidable reputation for its *table d'hote* menus, its bon-bons exported around the world, and its celebrity cocktails, notably the 'Balloon Cosmopolitan', which was featured in the 1946 edition of the *Gentleman's Companion*. It was at Firpo's that India's elite (including the Viceroy, Lord Irwin, later Lord Halifax) were introduced to the pleasures of ice-cream sodas and steaks; its jazz evenings and cabarets were the rage of their time, and its freshly baked, machine-sliced bread became a must-have for Calcutta's growing middle class.

It was also at Firpo's that Hollywood star Merle Oberon served as a telephone operator under the name of Queenie Thomson before she met a former actor, briefly her lover, who gave her a reference to a better-known actor based out of France, and who, he said, could get her a role in Hollywood if she was prepared to go to Nice to meet him. She did – in 1929 – and the rest is history. Arati Das's story may not be as glamorous as that of Oberon's, but as the cabaret artiste, Miss Shefali, she lit up the floor of Lido's, the bar at Firpo's, in the 1960s and even landed roles in two acclaimed films of the internationally celebrated maestro, Satyajit Ray.

Firpo's was one of the early victims of the advent of Left politics in Calcutta, followed by the rise of the violent Maoist Naxalite movement that saw the restaurants and nightclubs of Calcutta lose out to violent trade unions. Despite being a memory that refuses to fade away (the reason it keeps appearing in Vikram Seth's novel, *A Suitable Boy*), the best days of Firpo's were over as it saw the swinging Sixties fade away – despite the *New York Times* seeing signs of hope in the Miss Calcutta contest returning to Firpo's in 1970. The once-grand restaurant and hotel made way for a rabbit-warren of shops, which were gutted in a mysterious fire in 2002. The place was rebuilt eventually and it's back to business at 'Firpo's Market', but its *grande dame* is only a distant memory.

Sourish Bhattacharyya

- Cowan, Clyde H. 'Tales of CBI: Firpo's Restaurant'. *Ex-CBI Roundup*, November 1961: 16–17.
- Enrico De Barbieri. 'Angelo Firpo'. *n.d.* Available online: https://www.enricodebarbieri.com/afirpo.html (accessed 17 April 2022).

FISH

There are around two thousand species of fish in India and, according to the Central Marine Fisheries Research Institute, over a thousand species are caught or raised commercially. Fishing and aquaculture in India contribute 1 per cent of India's annual GDP and are a major industry in coastal states of Andhra Pradesh, Goa, Kerala, Karnataka, West Bengal, Odisha and Gujarat. Generally, freshwater fish is preferred to ocean fish, especially on the East Coast. India is the world's second largest producer of freshwater fish, most of them raised in ponds and tanks. However, currently only 10 per cent of its aquaculture potential is realized and the Indian government and fisheries

FIGURE 21 FISH. Fishing in village pond in Bengal. Ashish Sen.

research institutes are trying to encourage fish farmers and entrepreneurs to develop these untapped resources as part of a 'Blue Revolution'.

Given the long coastline and many rivers, fish and seafood played an important role in the diet of the Harappan people. Fish are the most common symbol on Harappan seals and large quantities of seashells and fish bones have been discovered including of catfish, carp, eel, shad and marine catfish. Often the fish was dried and sold as far as 900 km from the coast. Ancient Greek and Chinese travellers to India noted the abundance of both freshwater and sea fish. The twelfth-century *MANASOLLASA* describes thirty-five kinds of marine and freshwater fish including *catla*, *rohu*, catfish and carps as well as the diets given them which were carefully tailored to each variety. Some fish were fed with vegetarian food, including cooked RICE and roasted chickpea flour, others with meat and some with a mixture of both.

A complete list of Indian fish is the subject of an entire encyclopaedia. Here is a list of some of the most popular ones.

Sea Fish

– ***Bhetki*** (*Lates calcarifer*, also known as Asian sea bass) is a mild-flavoured ocean fish that resembles a cod in size and appearance. It is popular in Bengal, where it is cooked in BANANA leaf, and in Goa, where it may be pan fried.
– BOMBAY DUCK (*Harpadon nehereus*, also known as Bummalow) is abundant in the Arabian Sea and is usually preserved by drying.

- ***Hilsa*** (*Tenualosa ilisha*, also called *ilish* and *hilsa* shad) is a sea fish that swims upriver to spawn and is plentiful during the monsoon seasons. It is especially popular in West Bengal, where it is the state fish, and Andhra Pradesh, where it is called *pulasa*. The marriage of salt- and sweet-water gives it its unique taste. It is extremely bony.
- **Indian Oil sardine** (Hindi *tarali*, *Sardinella longiceps*) is the second most commercially caught fish and mainly lives in the northern Indian Ocean.
- **Pomfret** (*Brama Brama*) lives in the Indian and Pacific Oceans. It has a single bone and is usually coated with spices and fried whole.
- ***Rawas*** (Indian salmon, *Eleutheronema tetradactylum*) is a popular fish with a pink flesh and oily meat flesh found off the shore of Gujarat and Maharashtra.
- ***Surmai*** (also called *seer* or king fish, *Scomberomorus guttatus*) is an Indian Ocean fish that belongs to the mackerel family. It is considered a delicacy for its white meat and firm texture.
- **Tuna** (genus *Thunnus*). Nine varieties can be found in the Indian Ocean. However, consumption in India is limited because Indian fishing boats do not have onboard refrigeration and tuna must be sold on ice in local markets.

Freshwater Fish

- ***Magur*** (*Clarias batrachus*) is a freshwater air breathing catfish also called 'walking catfish' for its ability to wiggle across dry land to find food or suitable environments. It lives in muddy ponds, canals, ditches and similar habitats and is considered beneficial for invalids. It is the state fish of Bihar.
- ***Mahseer*** (genus *Tor*), which lives in rivers and lakes, was once a popular game fish and a favourite quarry for British anglers living in India. It is still a favourite game fish that fetches high prices. However, several species are facing extinction.
- ***Rohu*** (*Labeo rohita*), a member of the carp family, is raised in ponds in northern and central India. Available year-round, it relatively inexpensive. A recipe for *rohu* marinated in ASAFOETIDA and SALT, dipped in TURMERIC and water, and then fried can be found in the *MANASOLLASA*.
- **Tilapia** (*Oreochromis mossambicus*) was introduced in 1952 into unoccupied ponds and reservoirs and spread rapidly due to its prolific breeding and adaptability. It is sometimes referred to as 'aquatic chicken' because of its mild taste.
- ***Topse*** (also called mango fish, genus *Polynemus*) is a small freshwater fish that is deep-fried and is a popular teatime snack in Bengal.

Some species are sundried and stored for as long as several years and are eaten by some communities, notably in West Bengal, Tamil Nadu, the Northeast and Goa. Asia's largest dry fish market is in Marigaon, Assam.

Among Hindus, fish are considered auspicious (a fish is the first of the ten incarnations of the god Vishnu) and are an important part of social, cultural and religious life in some regions. In West Bengal, fish are a marker of Bengali identity, expressed in the saying 'macche bhate bangali' or 'fish + rice = Bengali'. Even Brahmins in Bengal, elsewhere usually vegetarian, eat fish (sometimes called 'fruit of the sea'). Fish play a role in many rituals and festivities, especially those involving marriage (see RITES OF PASSAGE). An emblematic Bengali dish is *machher jhol*, a CURRY made by frying *hilsa*, *rohu* or *catla* in MUSTARD oil, then cooking it in a thin spicy gravy with POTATOES. In Kerala, fish is often cooked in a COCONUT milk gravy.

Freshwater prawn farming in India has grown rapidly since 2000, led by Andhra Pradesh, Kerala and West Bengal, and India has become the world's largest exporter of frozen shrimp. The giant tiger prawn (*Penaeus monodon*) is the main species chosen for aquaculture, followed by the Indian white prawn (*Fenneropenaeus indicus*) and Pacific white shrimp (*Litopenaeus vannamei*). Several varieties of lobster are farmed in India including rock lobster, slipper lobster and deep sea lobster. Currently, 120 species of freshwater crabs (Hindi *kak*) are found in India, especially in Kerala, Maharashtra and Assam as well as varieties that live in estuaries and mangroves.

Colleen Sen

- Day, Francis. *Fishes in India*. Delhi: Daya Publishing House, 2003.
- Roberts, Joe and Colleen Taylor Sen. 'A Carp Wearing Lipstick: The Role of Fish in Bengali Cuisine and Culture'. In *Fish: Food from the Waters, Proceedings of the Oxford Symposium on Food and Cookery 1997*, edited by Harlan Walker, 252–8. Totnes, Devon: Prospect Books, 1998.

FISH KOLIWADA

This popular dish was introduced to Mumbai by two Punjabi Sikh brothers, Bahadur Singh and Hakam Singh, who ran a *DHABA* on an old highway between Delhi and Uttar Pradesh after being uprooted by Partition, and decided to move with their coal-fired stove to the country's commercial capital in 1955. The preparation consists of boneless fillets of the local *rawas* FISH (Indian salmon) slathered with a wet masala and fried in boiling oil on a coal-fired stove.

In 1970, the Singh brothers opened Mini Punjab in Sion Koliwada, an old fishing village that became the home of Punjab refugees fleeing Partition. The neighbourhood was eventually renamed Guru Tegh Bahadur Nagar after the ninth of the ten Sikh Gurus. Fish Koliwada, therefore, has nothing to do with the Kolis, the descendants of the fisher folk who were the original inhabitants of Mumbai. It is an example of Punjab 'refugee cuisine', which is most famously represented by BUTTER CHICKEN.

Now run by the Singhs' sons and grandsons, who have added pomfret and prawns to their repertoire, Mini Punjab has grown into a popular chain of restaurants and a catering company, but its star offering remains fish Koliwada. In the days when Bollywood celebrities ate hearty meals, the restaurant, which fed on the nostalgia of Punjabis resettled in Mumbai, counted among its star patrons the late Raj Kapoor and Balraj Sahni, the brothers Dara Singh and Sardar Singh Randhawa, who were celebrated wrestlers and actors, and Dharmendra, a heartthrob of his generation and former Member of Parliament. Unsurprisingly, they were all Punjabis who had made Mumbai their home.

Sourish Bhattacharyya

- Sinha, Sayoni. 'Kings of Koliwada'. *Mumbai Mirror*, 22 May 2017. Available online: https://mumbaimirror.indiatimes.com/others/why-not-declare-that-farmers-shouldnt-enter-mantralaya-cong/articleshow/58774748.cms (accessed 17 April 2022).

FLOWER WATERS

Flower waters, or essences, produced by steeping petals in water or by steam distillation, have been used since ancient times in medicine, perfumes and cosmetics. (Nowadays steam distillation is often the preferred method but water distillation is still traditionally used in many Eastern countries.) Rosewater and *kewra* water are important flavourings in Indian cuisine. Reputedly a favourite of the Mughal emperors, the use of floral waters in foods has always been considered luxurious and is often used to celebrate special occasions or religious events. They almost magically transform food by imbuing a delicate fragrance, especially to SWEET dishes.

Many of the names used for rosewater in the East derive from the Persian *gulab, gul* meaning rose and *ab* water. The word *gulab* also means rose in India, *gulab jal* meaning rosewater, and *ruh gulab,* rose essence or oil. Rosewater can be made from any sweet-scented roses, the most famous being the ancient damask rose, *Rosa damascena.*

Folklore attributes the discovery of this fragrant flavouring to the legendary Aryan King, Jamshid Shah, said to have ruled the ancient capital of Balkh four or five thousand years ago, probably by steeping the petals in water or oil. The manufacture of rosewater is usually accredited to Avicenna, the famous tenth-century physician. This was the 'Golden Age of Islam' and an age of cultural and culinary excellence. Rosewater was used to flavour a variety of dishes.

Meanwhile, some believe that rosewater had long been known and used in India. An old Sanskrit text, *Ark Prakash*, attributes the discovery of rosewater distillation to a famous Buddhist monk, Nagarjuna, who lived in the first or second century CE. When the PARSIS (originally Zoroastrians from Persia) fled their homeland and settled in India in the eighth century CE, they brought many of their ancient and traditional dishes and customs. One was the rosewater-flavoured dessert FALOODA, known in Persia as *paluda.* Later, the invading MUGHALS brought many other Persian dishes and techniques which were absorbed into Indian cuisine, particularly the use of subtle flavourings such as almonds, almond milk and rosewater for desserts and sweets.

Rose oil (*ruh gulab*), also known as *attar* (from Persian, meaning perfume), as we know it was not produced commercially in India until the seventeenth century.

In many areas of North India, especially where the soil is rich and water abundant, such as Pushkar in Rajasthan and parts of Uttar Pradesh, *Rosa Damascena* and a variety known as Rose Edward are grown on a commercial scale, for distilling both rosewater and rose oil. The ancient city of Kannauj in Uttar Pradesh has been distilling rose oil and rosewater for more than 400 years, since the time of the Mughal Emperor Jahangir. Rosewater is an important flavouring for many dishes in India, including sweetmeats such JALEBI and SANDESH; desserts such as *payasam* and FIRNI; and drinks such as SHERBET and sweet LASSI. It is also sometimes sprinkled over rice dishes such as BIRYANI, especially for festive occasions.

Rose oil is used in perfumes, soaps and other cosmetics such as creams and lotions (it is used as a skin moisturizer). Rosewater is still used as a coolant and medicinally in eye drops. It is also used as a perfume spray on festive occasions such as weddings.

Kewra water, sometimes known as *kevda* or *kewda*, is extracted from the flowers of the screw pine (*Pandanus odorifer*). Similar to rosewater, it is often used as an alternative or mixed with it. Its soft, sweet scent is prized for use in Indian cooking, mainly for desserts and sweets such as KHEER, BARFI, jalebi and RASGULLA. Some Bengali sweets are dipped or soaked in *kewra* water to imbue a floral perfume. It is also used to flavour drinks such as sherbets, added to jams and conserves, and sometimes sprinkled over elaborate RICE dishes such as biryani prepared for festive occasions. It is also used in traditional perfumery, Ayurvedic medicines, religious worship and PAAN masala.

India is a major producer of *kewra* with 90 per cent of it grown in Odisha. Sadly, the processing units, locally known as '*kia*', are on the verge of closure in Ganjam district due to outdated technology and rising fuel costs but also due to the dependency on traders from Uttar Pradesh where the *ruh* extract is sent for making the final products. The price of one *kewra* flower has dropped dramatically and workers who pluck the flowers are giving up the profession as it is no longer lucrative. In 2019, the number of *kewra* distilleries had come down from 200 to 50.

Helen Saberi

- Panigrahy, Sisir. 'Kewra Industry Dying Slow Death in Odisha's Ganjam'. *The New Indian Express*, 20 June 2019.
- Saberi, Helen. 'Rosewater, the Flavoring of Venus, Goddess of Love, and Asafoetida, Devil's Dung'. In *Spicing up the Palate: Studies of Flavourings – Ancient and Modern, Proceedings of the Oxford Symposium on Food and Cookery 1992*, edited by Harlan Walker, 220–35. Totnes, Devon: Prospect Books, 1993.

FLURYS

FIGURE 22 FLURYS. Iconic Kolkata restaurant. Colleen Sen.

Flurys is an iconic tearoom in KOLKATA (formerly Calcutta) founded at 18 Park Street in 1927 by a Swiss couple Mr and Mrs J. Flury. It quickly became regarded as one of the finest places for dining in all Kolkata and gained popularity with the British and the affluent Indians. It became renowned for its authentic Swiss and international delicacies. Its tastefully enriched interior was originally reminiscent of the Raj era but, in 2004, Flurys was given a makeover recalling the style and décor of the 1930s. Exotic cakes, creamy pastries, rich puddings and Swiss chocolates are still on the menu as well as savouries reflecting the tastes of both the East and the West such as puffs, patties, baked beans on toast and masala egg scramble. Flurys has been a meeting place for people for all ages and of different backgrounds – young mothers, students, professors, backpackers, IT professionals and 'old-timers' – and over the years has been frequented by notable people such as the famous multi-talented filmmaker, author, lyricist, editor, illustrator and composer Satyajit Ray and award-winning film director of Bengali heritage Mrinal Sen, who directed films primarily in Bengali and Hindi.

Sadly in 2010 there was a devastating fire in the 150-year-old Stephen Court in Park Street where the iconic Flurys was housed. However, by 2016 reconstruction was completed and the heritage building rose from the ashes.

Flurys has some 40 bakery outlets in Kolkata as well as outposts in Delhi, Hyderabad and Mumbai. The current owner is the Apeejay Surendra Park Hotels group.

Helen Saberi

- Karkaria, Bachi. *Flurys of Calcutta: The Cake That Walked.* Kolkata: Flurys, 2007.

FOOD AND MEDICINE

India is home to several schools of medicine, both indigenous and imported, and a feature common to them all is that food and medicine were virtually interchangeable. All foods have properties that exert an influence on the body and the mind.

Ayurveda. Ayurveda, the Indian school of medicine, is thought to have had its origins in the magic spells and incantations of the *Vedas.* It was later codified by the physicians Sushruta and Charaka. As with other ancient Indian texts, their works are compendia of the writings of earlier authorities. The earliest content of Sushruta's compendium *Sushruta Samhita* is estimated to date back to as early as 250 BCE and that of the *Charaka Samhita* to 400 BCE.

Ayurvedic physicians made house calls and saw patients in their homes, which had storerooms filled with drugs and medical equipment. They produced their own drugs from herbs and other plants, which they collected or grew in their gardens. The pharmacopoeia was very large: Sushruta mentions over 700 medicinal herbs. The Himalayas were especially famous for their medicinal herbs.

Central to Ayurveda is the role of the three *doshas* ('humours' or 'faults') in the body. They are *vata,* a product of air and ether, sometimes translated as wind; *pitta*, a product of fire and water, or bile; and *kapha,* made from water and earth, or phlegm. Their attributes can be summed up as movement, metabolism and stability, respectively. They keep the body healthy only as long as they continuously flow throughout the body and accumulate in the right places. Many things can affect the balance and activity of the *doshas*: the season, a person's age and physical activity, emotional stress, external heat and cold, and diet. People are especially prone to diseases at the junctions of the seasons, and regular purifications and fasts help protect against this. Some of these practices have been institutionalized into holiday rituals and festivals.

One of the main ways of adjusting *doshas* is diet. As Charaka wrote: 'Without proper diet, medicines are of no use; with a proper diet, medicines are unnecessary' (Achaya 1994: 76). In the *Sushruta Samhita*, the author writes that the intelligent physician determines what food his patient should eat after considering other factors, including the attributes of the ingredients and the properties they acquire through flavouring and combinations.

There are six basic tastes (*rasas*), all of which should be in a person's diet: sweet, sour, salty, bitter, pungent and alkali. (Today, the alkali taste has all but disappeared from Indian cuisine, except in Assamese dishes such as *khar* and *tenga*.) Another classification is the division of plants, animals and people based on their natural habitats: either dry (*jangala*) or wet (*anupa*). *Jangala* animals include deer and antelope and game birds. These creatures are active and eat light food, making their meat light and easy to digest. Creatures that live in *anupa* regions or wallow in mud (e.g., pigs, water buffaloes, rhinoceroses) are heavy and hard to digest. Charaka lists four *jangala* animals that should always be kept on the premises of an Ayurvedic hospital: quail, partridge, hare and antelope.

Digestion is extremely important in Ayurveda since if one cannot digest one's food it cannot produce the proper effects. Stagnant pools of undigested food, called *ama*, breed disease. To eliminate *ama*, an Ayurvedic cure usually begins with fasting, which Sushruta calls 'the first and most important of all medicines'. Foods are characterized as light (easy to digest) or heavy (difficult to digest). A heavy food can be eaten until one's appetite is only half satisfied; an article that is light to digest may be eaten to satiety. RICE is a particularly versatile remedy. For example, rice prepared with clarified butter (GHEE), meat, sour fruits or any lentils (see PULSES) helps build new tissues and imparts strength and rotundity (a valued attribute in those days). Rice gruels are prescribed for invalids or people who have gone through a regimen of purging and emetics. *Kanjika* (modern *KANJI*) is a sour rice gruel, made by leaving boiled rice overnight until it ferments slightly. Another rice preparation is *payasa* (modern *payesh* or *payasam*, see KHEER), a pudding made from boiled rice, milk and SUGAR.

Meat was an intrinsic part of the Ayurvedic diet. As an eleventh-century physician wrote, 'The recommendations of medicine are not intended to help someone achieve virtue (*dharma*) ... they are aimed at achieving health' (Wujastyk 2001: 8). A thin meat broth is prescribed for shortness of breath, cough and consumption, weak memory, and loss of appetite and emaciation. Boiled minced meat cooked with treacle, clarified butter, black pepper (see PEPPER, BLACK), long pepper (see PEPPER, LONG) and GINGER imparts strength. A broth prepared with POMEGRANATE juice and spices is considered particularly beneficial since it subdues the action of all three deranged humours. But meat whose essence has already been removed is useless, and dried meat is especially hard to digest.

Moong dal has many benefits. Cooked with grapes and pomegranate juice, it subdues deranged *doshas*; prepared with snake GOURD or NEEM, it cures skin diseases; and boiled with horseradish, it relieves cough, catarrh, fever and diseases of the throat. Dal made from horse gram is a remedy for asthma, catarrh and diseases of the bladder and abdominal glands. Other ingredients that can be added to boiled lentils are dairy products, rice gruel, CUMIN seeds, black pepper and certain fruits. A soup made of any unhusked lentil is light and wholesome. Vegetables are sometimes to be avoided during therapy since they are considered astringent and may close the channels. In Ayurveda, ghee is considered a virtual panacea. As an eighteenth-century physician wrote, 'Ghee rejuvenates, is tasty, alleviates *pitta* and *vatta*, removes poisons, prolongs life, promotes growth and destroys sins and poverty.' It features in many Ayurvedic recipes both as a cooking medium and a flavouring. It may be prepared with various spices and herbs.

In Sushruta's view, the best restorative is water mixed with molasses, unrefined sugar and sour fruit, and scented with camphor. Drinks made with pomegranate juice are especially soothing and strengthening.

Charaka has some general recommendations for healthy eating. Do not eat a lot of items having the same taste at the same time, but at the same time do not constantly indulge in items of various tastes. For the sake of digestion, eat only one main meal a day. Avoid BREAD, which is hard to digest; if you must eat it, drink twice as much water as usual. Take only half portions of heavy foods but eat as many lighter items as you like. Avoid items that are incompatible with each other, such as milk and dairy products. Food should be 'alive' in order to give life to the eater. Raw food is more alive than cooked food. Overcooked, undercooked, burnt, bad tasting, unripe or overripe, putrefied or stale food should never be eaten. Leftovers should be heated up as soon as possible or, ideally, avoided all together. A traditional Indian belief is that the materials in which the food is served affect its properties. Silver and gold are considered the best materials since they are nonreactive and 'pure'.

Unani. The Unani system of medicine (Unani *tibbia*) is practised by Muslims and is thought to be based on the writings of the Greek physicians Hippocrates (460–377 BCE) and Galen (died *c.* 200 CE). The Arabic word '*unan*' means Greece. (An alternative theory is that the system comes from China's Yunnan province.) Unani practitioners are called *hakims*.

Unani medicine assumes the presence of four humours in the body: blood, phlegm, yellow bile and black bile. These humours are composed of the four basic elements – earth, water, air and fire. The seasons also have qualities, as does an individual's temperament which can be of four kinds: sanguine, choleric, cold or phlegmatic, and melancholic. Every person is born with a unique humoural constitution. When the balance of the humours is upset because of external or internal changes, disease results. The goal of treatment is to restore the quality and balance of humours. Diet is one of the therapies, together with surgery, medicine and massage. Many diseases can be prevented by regular digestion; conversely, poor digestion can cause illness. Foods that cause indigestion are those that putrefy quickly (milk and fresh FISH), those that take time to digest (such as beef), stale foods, spices and CHILLIES, ALCOHOL, strong TEA, COFFEE and oily food. However, any food is acceptable in moderation. Aids to digestion include decoctions and teas made from AJOWAN seeds, MINT, FENNEL and CORIANDER seeds; pomegranate juice; and other herbs and spices. As in Ayurveda, often treatment starts with a total fast, which gives the patient's system a chance to rest.

People are also advised to eat foods that have the opposite quality to their distemper. For example, a person who has too much sanguine humour, which increases heat, should eat cold food such as BARLEY water and fish and also eat cooling herbs. What is cold and hot is largely determined by local and regional beliefs and customs. Weaknesses of specific organs are corrected by eating the same organ of an animal. In both Ayurveda and Unani, bitter and astringent foods are prescribed for diabetes.

Today Ayurveda and Unani are taught in government colleges in India. In recent years, Ayurveda has gained popularity both in India and in the West because of its holistic approach to disease. Clinical trials are being conducted at universities and medical centres for testing the efficacy of Ayurvedic cures, such as bitter MELON as a cure for diabetes and TURMERIC for Alzheimer's, cancer and other diseases. Fashionable spas offer Ayurvedic treatments. However, often, they generally offer a vegetarian diet, which is counter to the recommendations of the founders of Ayurveda.

Siddha. Siddha (Sanskrit for pure) medicine was developed in South India in the seventh or eighth century and, today, is practised in the Tamil-speaking regions. The principles are similar to those of Ayurveda: the human body is considered a replica of the universe as are food and drugs. The main difference is in the extensive use of metals and minerals in treatment, especially sulphur and mercury.

Colleen Sen

- Achaya, K. T. *Indian Food: A Historical Companion*. New Delhi: OUP, 1994.
- Desai, Prakash N. *Health and Medicine in the Hindu Tradition: Continuity and Cohesion (Health/Medicine and the Faith Traditions)*. New York: Crossroad, 1989.
- Kṣēmaśarmā. *A Work on Dietetics and Well Being* [Sans. orig. *Kṣēmakūtuhalam*]. *c*. 1555, edited by Darshan Shankar, D. K. Ved, G. G. Gangadharan, M. A. Lakshmithathacharya and M. A. Alwar, translated by R. Shankar. Bangalore: IIAIM/Foundation for Revitalisation of Local Health Traditions, 2009.
- Wujastyk, Dominik. *The Roots of Ayurveda*. London: Penguin, 2001.

GANDHI, MOHANDAS

Mohandas Gandhi (1868–1948), later known as Mahatma, meaning great soul, emerged as the most prominent figure in the Indian Independence movement. The basis of his political philosophy was *satyagraha*, translated as 'insistence on truth' or 'truth force'. He also advocated a policy of nonviolence, or *ahimsa*. While his religious beliefs were rooted in Hinduism, with a strong Jain influence, Gandhi said that all religions contain both truth and error. Gandhi's beliefs about food are inseparable from his moral and political philosophy.

Gandhi was born into a Vaishnav Hindu family in Gujarat, a region with a strong Jain presence. His family was vegetarian and his pious mother often fasted. When Gandhi was a teenager, a friend persuaded him to try meat. At the time there was a popular belief that the British owed their strength and dominance to their consumption of meat. A popular poem went:

> Behold the mighty Englishman
> He rules the Indian small,
> Because being a meat-eater
> He is five cubits tall.

In his autobiography, Gandhi described his first foray into meat eating:

> We went in search of a lonely spot by the river, and there I saw, for the first time in my life, meat. There was baker's [i.e., English style] bread also. I relished neither. The goat's meat was as tough as leather. I simply could not eat it. I was sick and had to leave off eating. I had a very bad night afterwards. A horrible nightmare haunted me. Every time I dropped off to sleep it would seem as though a live goat were bleating inside me, and I would jump up full of remorse. But then I would remind myself that meat-eating was a duty, and so become more cheerful.

But Gandhi eventually overcame his reluctance and began to enjoy the meat dishes. In 1888 he left for England to study law. His mother made him swear a vow before a Jain monk that he would never touch meat, ALCOHOL or women. Initially he subsisted on a diet of boiled vegetables and bread until he discovered a vegetarian restaurant in London and became a follower of the British reformer Henry S. Salt (1851–1939), an advocate of animal rights. Salt cited moral reasons for being a vegetarian, including the inherent violence in the eating of meat and the nonviolence that could be achieved from abstaining from it – ideas that Gandhi identified with *ahimsa*. 'The choice was now made in favor of vegetarianism, the spread of which henceforward became my mission', he wrote. In 1890, Gandhi joined the London Vegetarian Society and became a member of its Executive Committee.

In a speech, 'The Moral Basis of Vegetarianism', delivered to the Society in 1931, he said that people who became vegetarians purely for health reasons usually fail because vegetarianism requires a moral basis as well as a practical one. Some vegetarians made food a fetish and thought that by becoming vegetarians they could eat as much lentils, beans and CHEESE as they liked – an approach that did not improve their health. The secret to remaining healthy is to cut down the quantity of one's food and reduce the number of meals.

In later life, when drinking goat milk helped him recover from a severe case of dysentery, he admitted the necessity of adding milk to a vegetarian diet as a source of protein. However, he called his inability to give up milk 'the tragedy of my life'. Gandhi accepted the consumption of eggs as long as they were unfertilized. He recommended that green leafy vegetables be eaten every day, preferably raw, as should fruits in season. A certain amount of fat is necessary, the best being pure GHEE, followed by freshly ground peanut oil. An ounce and a half a day is necessary to meet one's bodily needs. Using more, especially to deep fry puris (see BREADS) and LADDUS, is a 'thoughtless extravagance'. Sugar consumption should be limited to 1 to 1.5 ounces a day – and more if sweet fruits are not available. But he argued that sweetmeats in a country like India where many people do not even get a full meal is equivalent to robbery.

'Food should be taken as a matter of duty – even as a medicine – to sustain the body, never for the satisfaction of the palate', he wrote. He opposed the use of spices on the grounds that their only function is to please the palate. All condiments, even SALT, destroy the natural flavour of vegetables and cereals. TEA, COFFEE and cocoa are not beneficial and can even be harmful. Alcohol was beyond the pale because of the economic, moral, intellectual and physical harm it does. Gandhi advocated the total prohibition of the manufacture, sale and consumption of alcohol, a policy still in force in his native Gujarat and some other Indian states. Gandhi's writing makes no mention of drinking urine, which some people believe was part of his food philosophy.

While Gandhi rigorously followed his own prescriptions, he was not dogmatic about imposing them on others. Prolonged experimentation and observation convinced him that there is no fixed rule for all constitutions, and that while VEGETARIANISM, which he called 'one of the priceless gifts of Hinduism', is highly desirable, it is not an end in itself. 'Many a man eating meat and with everybody but living in the fear of God is nearer his freedom than a man religiously abstaining from meat and other things, but blaspheming God in every one of his acts', he wrote. One of Gandhi's main weapons in the fight for independence was fasting. He undertook seventeen fasts during his lifetime; the longest, to stop communal rioting in 1943, lasted twenty-one days.

Colleen Sen

- Gandhi, M.K. *Autobiography: The Story of My Experiments with Truth*, translated by Mahadev Desai. 1948. Reprint of Public Affairs Press edition. New York: Dover Publications, 1983.
- Gandhi, M.K. *Key to Health*, translated by Sushila Nayar. Ahmedabad, Gujarat: Navajivan Publishing House, 1948.

GARLIC

Garlic (*Allium sativum*, Hindi *lahsun*) is one of the more problematic ingredients in Indian cuisine. Although garlic and ONIONS were native to Central Asia and Afghanistan and were used in the Harappan Civilization (2600–1900 BCE), they are not mentioned in the Vedas, perhaps because they are associated with the despised indigenous people or perhaps because of the smell they impart to one's breath. According to a verse in the *Mahabharata*, garlic (along with onions and MUSHROOMS) is not to be eaten by respectable people. The Chinese Buddhist pilgrims Faxian in the fifth century CE and Xuanzang in the seventh century CE observed that garlic was almost unknown. Onions and garlic were also reputed to have aphrodisiac properties, which is why they were forbidden to students and widows. To this day, Jains, orthodox Brahmins and ascetics avoid onions and garlic; ASAFOETIDA is often used as a substitute. Garlic is avoided in fasts (see FASTING) and is never used in religious ceremonies.

However, garlic is a common cure in Ayurvedic medicine. According to the Bower Manuscript (a collection of Sanskrit medical texts by an unknown author discovered in Eastern Turkistan in 1890 by Lieutenant H. Bower), garlic was created when the king of demons drank the elixir of immorality and Lord Vishnu cut off his head as punishment. The drops of blood that fell to earth became garlic but because they flowed from a body, it is forbidden to Brahmins.

Garlic's curative powers include subduing all diseases, vitiating wind, pacifying choler, strengthening the digestive fire, removing paralysis, and curing leprosy and many other ailments.

Since Brahmins were not allowed to eat garlic, a cow could be given almost no grass for three days and then fed a mixture of two parts grass to one part garlic stalks. A Brahmin could then consume its milk, or yogurt, GHEE or BUTTERMILK made from it with impunity.

India is the world's second largest garlic producer after China. The top garlic producing states are Rajasthan, with over 50 per cent followed by Uttar Pradesh, Gujarat, Punjab and Assam. Garlic is used in many ways in Indian cuisine. Whole cloves impart a delicate flavour to dishes. Garlic and GINGER pastes are the basis of many vegetable and meat

CURRIES. Chopped or sliced garlic may be sautéed with onions and spices at the start of a recipe. Garlic CHUTNEY is a popular accompaniment to meals.

Colleen Sen

- Wujastyk, Dominik. *The Roots of Ayurveda: Selections from Sanskrit Medical Writings*. New Delhi: Penguin, 1998.

GEOGRAPHICAL INDICATION

A geographical indication (GI) tag is a sign used on products that have a specific geographical origin (town, region, or country) and possess qualities or a reputation that are due to that origin. Moreover, the product's qualities, characteristics or reputation should be essentially due to the place of origin. It enables those who have the right to use the indication to prevent its use by a third party whose product does not conform to the applicable standards. Geographical indications are typically used for agricultural products, foodstuffs, wine and spirit drinks, handicrafts and industrial products.

GI tags are granted by the World Intellectual Property Organization (WIPO), the global forum for intellectual property (IP) services, policy, information and cooperation that is a self-funding agency of the United Nations, with 193 member states, including India. India enacted legislation to implement the Geographical Indications of Goods Act in 2003 and today, nearly four hundred products are covered under the Act.

Colleen Sen

GHEE

Ghee (also spelled *ghi*, sometimes called *asli*, or 'original', ghee) or clarified butter is made by melting butter made from cow or water buffalo milk and simmering it long enough to boil off the water. When the milk proteins rise to the surface they are skimmed off. Some solids remain on the bottom and as they brown they create a pleasant nutty flavour. The product is then filtered to remove sediment. Vanaspati ghee is a vegetable substitute made from highly saturated oils, such as COCONUT or palm oil, that is processed to look and taste like *asli* ghee.

The original reason for making ghee was to preserve butter in a hot climate. Ghee is very ancient. In the Sanskrit texts it is called *ghrta* and was the preferred cooking medium of the Indo-Aryans. Ghee has always been regarded as the best and most prestigious cooking medium and was used extensively in both Hindu and Muslim rulers' courts.

Ghee is considered a *sattvic* food, conducive of serenity and spirituality. In North India, a distinction is made between *pukka* and *kaccha* foods. *Kaccha* foods are prepared in the family kitchen by boiling or roasting, such as RICE, dal, KHICHRI, some BREADS made without oil and vegetables. This is the basic core meal of much of India and is served to family members. *Pakka* foods are prepared by frying in or basting with ghee. However, the food must come into contact with the ghee before other items are added. This includes fried breads, such as paratha, and many sweets. These foods can be taken out of the kitchen to eat and shared with people outside the family. *Pukka* foods are served at temples and during festivals so that everyone can eat them.

Ghee has always played an important role not only in cuisine but also in rituals (see RITES OF PASSAGE) and medicine (see FOOD AND MEDICINE). In the *Shastras*, consuming ghee is a method of purification for someone who has committed various sins. In Ayurveda, ghee is a virtual panacea. As the eighteenth-century physician, Ksēmaśarmā, wrote, 'Ghee rejuvenates, is tasty, alleviates *pitta* and *vatta*, removes poisons, prolongs life, promotes growth, and destroys sins and poverty.' It features in many Ayurvedic recipes as both a cooking medium and a flavouring.

Colleen Sen

- Kṣēmaśarmā. *A Work on Dietetics and Well Being* [Sans. orig. *Kṣēmakūtuhalam*]. *c.* 1555. Edited by Darshan Shankar, D.K. Ved, G.G. Gangadharan, M.A. Lakshmithathacharya and M.A. Alwar, translated by R. Shankar. Bangalore: IIAIM/Foundation for Revitalisation of Local Health Traditions, 2009.

GINGER

Fresh ginger (*Zingiber officinale*, Hindi *adrak*), sometimes called 'green' ginger, is the pungent, aromatic rhizome of a tall, reed-like tropical plant. The rhizome, known as a 'hand', is knobbly, off-white or buff coloured, and often branched into what are called 'fingers'. The flesh inside is pale yellow. Ginger can be dried and then formed into a powder known as *sunthi* or *sonth*.

One of the oldest and most important spices, ginger is almost certainly native to southeast Asia and was widely used in ancient India and China. It was one of the first spices to reach the Mediterranean, probably traded by the Phoenicians, and was known in ancient Egypt. It was highly prized by the ancient Greeks and Romans.

The use of ginger in Indian food has been recorded throughout history. The Chinese traveller, Xuanzang, in the seventh century CE mentioned that Buddhist monks were served fresh ginger with salt to begin their meals at their monasteries. Ground meat for stuffing, called *vesavara* in the *Sushruta Samhita* (see FOOD AND MEDICINE), is flavoured with molasses, black pepper (see PEPPER, BLACK) and green ginger. The *Mahabharata* features a picnic meal in which meat dishes are simmered with ginger among other spices. Much later, the Sultanate court in Delhi relished meat dishes cooked in GHEE, with ONIONS and green ginger; and practically every recipe for meat dishes in the *Ain-i-Akbari* (1590) of Akbar's court includes green ginger.

India today produces about half the world's output of ginger, 70 per cent of it in Kerala. Ginger, fresh or dried, and often in the form of a ground garlic-ginger paste, continues to be a much-relished seasoning throughout India for meat, chicken, fish and seafood dishes and is used extensively in vegetarian dishes. Fresh and dried ginger differ noticeably in their taste and flavouring effects. Fresh ginger, which is more commonly used in Indian cookery, is usually peeled before cooking, then either finely sliced, chopped or grated. It gives a hot, pungent, lemony flavour to vegetable, meat and fish dishes. When ginger is ground into a powder, called *sonth*, the flavour of fresh ginger root is transformed to a spicy-sweet flavour with a woody scent. It is used in relishes, CHUTNEYS and in Kashmiri cooking where ginger TEA is also popular.

Ginger is also used to give a certain bite to sweet items. The *samyava* described by the Ayurvedic physician Charaka, a sweet concoction of fried wheat flour, is flavoured with CARDAMOM, pepper and ginger. A preserve of ginger in SUGAR solution made by the

Portuguese living in Bengal was noted by the French traveller François Bernier in the mid-seventeenth century. These preserves, called *murabba,* were commonly eaten by Muslims, often for medicinal purposes. Today, wedges of BANANA dipped in thick jaggery batter and deep-fried are a popular snack in Kerala and owe much of their appeal to the addition of ground ginger in the sweet coating.

Ginger features in the traditional all-vegetarian feast, Onam *sadya*, served at Onam, the Malayali harvest festival. *Puli inji* or *inji puli* is an important PICKLE served at this feast. It has a wonderfully sweet-sour sharp taste accomplished by a combination of ginger, green CHILLI, TAMARIND and jaggery.

Ginger is also used in the spicing of beverages and curd products. The *MANASOLLASA* mentions BUTTERMILK spiced with fresh ginger. A *pachadi* (a relish similar to RAITA) of ginger paste in yogurt is used in Karnataka. Ginger has always been used for medicinal purposes. It is considered good for the stomach and is widely used as a digestive aid. Fresh ginger boiled with milk and sweetened is a household remedy for colds and chills.

Camphor ginger (*Zingiber zerumbet*) is a variety that has the unique aroma of raw CAMPHOR. It grows wild in the lower hills of the Himalayas and the southern regions of India. Mango ginger (*Curcuma amada*), *amada* in Hindi, is not a ginger at all but a member of the TURMERIC family. It has the aroma of raw, unripe MANGOES and is called mango ginger because of its special ginger-like texture and flavour. It generally grows wild and can be found in markets in the summer in the southern and eastern regions of India.

Helen Saberi

- Achaya, K.T. *A Historical Dictionary of Indian Food*. Delhi: OUP, 1998.
- Dalby, Andrew. *Dangerous Tastes: The Story of Spices*. London: British Museum Press, 2000.
- Sahni, Julie. *Classic Indian Vegetarian Cookery*. London: Grub Street, 1999.

GOA

The state of Goa on India's southwest coast is the smallest by area and the fourth smallest by population but also has the highest GDP per capita of all Indian states. Tourism is the state's primary industry. Ironically, despite receiving an influx of tourists over the years, not much is known about food of Goa outside its borders. An exception is one of the most iconic dishes of India – the VINDALOO. The soil is sandy and there is little arable land, but there is plenty of FISH, seafood, fruit, cashews and COCONUT. Meat plays an important role in Goan cuisine, including pork, chicken and even beef.

In 1510, the Portuguese invaded Goa, defeating the Bijapur Sultanate, and ruled Goa until 1961 when it became part of the Republic of India. The Portuguese rule saw conversions of Hindus and Muslims to the Roman Catholic faith and there was a fairly high incidence of intermarriage between the Portuguese and the new converts. Today, around a quarter of Goa's population are Catholic. This led to the permeation of Portuguese influences across different facets of Goan culture, including food. The marriage of cooking techniques from Portugal with local taste palates led to the creation of an entirely new genre of cooking that became staple of the Catholic community of

Goa. The vindaloo is an example. Originally a Portuguese dish called *vinha de alhos*, meaning vinegar and GARLIC, it became a sweet, sour and fiery hot CURRY traditionally made with pork. Other emblematic Goan dishes are:

- *Sorpotel*, pork offal cooked in a hot, sour sauce.
- *Caldo verde*, a chicken and spinach soup flavoured with ginger and black pepper.
- Goan *chouriço*, pork sausages laced with *feni*, a potent local liquor made from cashews.
- *Ambotik*, a hot and sour curry made from fish (often shark) or prawns.
- *Balchow (balchão)*, a method of cooking fish, prawns or pork in a tangy tomato CHILLI sauce that is eaten like a PICKLE.
- *Xacuti*, a meat (often chicken) curry in a gravy that contains white POPPY seeds, sliced or grated coconut and dried red chillies.
- *Caffreal*, chicken served in a green-coloured sauce made from green chillies, coriander, spices and lime juice or vinegar that may have originated in Portugal's colonies in Africa. A dish with similar origins is chicken *peri peri* which has a red sauce.

In addition to cooking techniques, the Portuguese were the ones to have introduced POTATOES, TOMATOES and chillies, considered the holy trinity of Indian ingredients today, to Goa and India in the seventeen century, all now used liberally in Goan kitchens.

The Goan Catholic diet is characterized by the copious use of pork and beef, meats not commonly eaten in most other parts of India. Both meats make their presence felt, especially when Goan Roman Catholic families meet on celebratory occasions. For many Goans, Christmas at home is incomplete without a sumptuous meal starring pork *sorpotel* and pulao, with beef croquettes, ox tongue roast, chicken *xacuti* and prawn curry added for good measure. Most are part of the everyday repertoire of the community. A common characteristic of many of these dishes is the touch of tart that accompanies them. This could come from the use of toddy vinegar, a fruit called *KOKUM* or TAMARIND.

A dish that makes an appearance in hotel banquet buffets across the country is the 'Goan fish curry' or *xit kodi*. The most common fish are kingfish, tuna, shark, pomfret and mackerel. The love for fish curry permeates religious borders. Along with the Brahmins of Bengal, the Goud Saraswat Brahmins of Goa are one of the few Brahmin communities in India to consume fish. The fish come from the local seas and are seasonal in nature. The monsoon season, when fishing stops, is when dried salted fish and shellfish come in vogue. Given the abundance of coconut trees, it is natural that freshly grated coconut forms a key element of the curries. Recipes, levels of chilli heat and shades of colour of the gravy, all vary from kitchen to kitchen. It is said that when one Goan meets another on the way back from the market and asks what fish did you buy, the subtext is: 'What is going to be cooked at home?'

Another important aspect of Goan cuisine is its bakers or *poders*. They are another legacy of the Portuguese, who introduced the Western culture of bread baking to Goa and the rest of India. Goa has a variety of local BREADS available, of which the most famous is the *poie* (from Portuguese *pão*, meaning bread). This leavened bread is made from a mixture of whole wheat and white flour and is slightly chewy in texture. As an alternative to yeast, the Portuguese used toddy (local palm liquor) for leavening their breads which were traditionally baked in a wood-fired oven. The Portuguese tradition lives on in cakes and pastries such as sweet rolls called *pau*; *bibinca*, a cake made stacking layers of pancakes; and *boliho de coco*, little coconut cakes.

The *pav*-wallahs cycling down to the village with a basket of freshly baked *poie* is how life in the villages of Goa would start every morning. This tradition is unfortunately on the wane as many *poders* are shutting shop. The newer generation of Goans are not keen to run these labour-intensive, brick kiln oven-based bakeries and the bread industry in the state is slowly getting mechanized as the state loses an integral part of its food culture in the process.

The same phenomenon is reflected in the manufacturing of *feni*, the local liquor. Traditionally, it is made from the juice of tree-ripened cashew apples that is fermented in earthen pots called *koddem* and distilled three times. Coconut *feni*, which is mainly produced and consumed in South Goa, is a distilled liquor made from fermented toddy from the coconut palm. However, today an increasing proportion of synthetic brews are dominating the market as toddy tappers fade into the sunset. *Feni* was the first liquor in India to obtain the 'Heritage Drink' status and got its GEOGRAPHICAL INDICATION certification in 2000.

It is not easy to find Goan dishes in restaurants in Goa today. You are likely to find a plethora of dals, KEBABS and tikkas, and rotis in restaurants catering to tourists. Goa has seen a huge increase in tourists from across the rest of India in the past few years, especially from the north of India. Many are not very adventurous when it comes to food and prefer to stick to the familiar rather than try Goan delicacies. The high proportion of vegetarians makes them wary of trying Goan food which they mistakenly associate only with pork, beef and seafood. This is unfortunate given that Goans do have a wide variety of vegetarian dishes which feature seasonal and local produce, most of which are not available in restaurants. Goan culture still has a strong connection with its rural roots. Vegetarian dishes using locally grown vegetables, herbs and shrubs are in vogue across the state, as are PULSES. Some are a part of the continuum of the food typical of the Konkan coast and the Konkani community, which spreads across coastal Maharashtra, Goa and Karnataka. The absence of Goan food in the dining-out landscape of Goa is slowly changing with luxury hotels such as ITC Grand Goa and restaurants such as Cavatina and Pousada By The Bay offering traditional Goan dishes for its guests.

Kalyan Karmakar

- Indian Culture. 'Goan Cuisine: A Confluence of Cultures'. *n.d.* Available online: https://indianculture.gov.in/food-and-culture/west/goan-cuisine-confluence-cultures (accessed 17 April 2022).
- Karmakar, Kalyan. *The Travelling Belly*. New Delhi: Hachette, 2016.

GOURDS

What plant taxonomists call the gourd family (Cucurbitacea) includes nearly a thousand species. Most are vines that grow in tropical and subtropical regions and require warm sunny habitats. Many bear fruits that have a hard skin and a soft interior with a lot of seeds. They are difficult to classify botanically and there is much confusion about what is a gourd, a pumpkin or a squash, especially since their names vary in different parts of the world. Squash is an American word for fruits that are called pumpkins and gourds in India. CUCUMBER is also a member of this family.

According to K.T. ACHAYA, although most species originated in the New World as long as 10,000 years ago, some have Sanskrit names. The early Vedic literature describes gourds as growing on the banks of rivers. Achaya surmises that the dried gourds floated from continent to continent with their seeds remaining viable. Some popular varieties are:

Ash gourd (*Benincasa hispida*, Hindi *petha*), also called winter melon, is a vine native to South Asia grown for its large melon-like fruit. The fruit has a rough grey-coloured skin and a soft white interior. Its best known use is in the preparation of the sweet AGRA *PETHA*. In South India, it is cooked as a vegetable in *avial* (a mixed vegetable dish in a COCONUT and yogurt sauce with a finish of coconut oil and CURRY LEAVES) and is one of the ingredients of *kootu*, a mixture of black chickpeas or *chana* dal with vegetables (including ash gourd) with ground coconut and spices.

Bitter melon (*Momordica chantaria*, Hindi *karela*), also known as bitter gourd, is an ancient vegetable probably native to India and is mentioned in the early Jain works and Ayurvedic literature. It comes in a variety of shapes and sizes. The Chinese version is twenty to twenty-five cm long and pale green in colour, with a gently undulating, warty surface. The dark green Indian version is narrower with pointed ends and a surface covered with jagged triangular teeth and ridges. The bitterness is due to an alkaloid, morodicine, which makes it toxic to insects and animals and perhaps to infections as well.

Ayurveda values bitter melon as a cooling food that helps eliminate toxins from the system and has long been valued as a treatment for diabetes (see FOOD AND MEDICINE). In North India, bitter melon is often stuffed with meat or vegetables and sautéed in oil. Thin slices coated with TURMERIC, SALT and CHILLI powder are deep-fried to make a tasty snack. In South India, it is prepared in *thoren*, a coconut stew, stir-fried with spices or cooked with roasted coconut. A Bengali meal traditionally starts with a bitter dish, such as *shukto*, a combination of bitter melon (or sometimes NEEM leaves) with other vegetables, milk and SUGAR.

Bottle gourd (*Lagenaria siceraria*, Hindi *lauki*, also called *opo*) is a large green vegetable twenty to twenty-five cm long with a hard skin and a soft white interior. It is best used immature when the skin is still thin. Cut up, it can be prepared with a TOMATO or coconut sauce, fried as a vegetable, ground to make KOFTA or cooked with dal. The juice is considered to have medicinal benefits. Shredded bottle gourd is used to make HALWA, *KHEER* and other sweet dishes.

Pointed gourd (*Trichosanthes dioica*, Hindi *parwal*) is a small green fruit with white stripes or unstriped. It can vary in size from five to fifteen cm in length and is round to oblong in shape with pointed ends. The flesh is white and moist and filled with small seeds. Its taste is mild and bland so that it can absorb flavours. It can be combined with other vegetables to make a CURRY or stuffed and fried. Pointed gourd is an important summer vegetable in India, especially in Bengal, where it is known as *potol* and cooked in a yogurt or milk-based gravy.

Red pumpkin (*Curcubita maxima*, Hindi *kaddu*) is the national vegetable of India. It is round, with a smooth, slightly ribbed yellow to orange skin and contains many seeds. It is widely grown in the rainy and summer seasons. Red pumpkin is sometimes called the poor man's vegetable because of its year-round availability. India is the world's second largest producer after China. Sweet and sour *khatta mitha kaddu* is a popular dish during the Navratri festival. In Bengal, it is called *kumro* and is an ingredient in everyday vegetable dishes. The flowers are coated with flour and fried to make a popular snack.

Ridge or ribbed gourd (*Luffa acutangular*, Hindi *thorai*) belongs to the cucumber family and looks like a cucumber with deep ridges. It has an off-white buttery flesh and is best eaten when immature. In North India, it is cooked as a vegetable. In

Bengal, it can be fried or cooked with FISH and meat and the flowers coated with spiced chickpea batter and fried as PAKORAS. When aged and dried, it is used as a bath sponge called a loofah.

Snake gourd (*Trichosanthes cucumerina*, Hindi *chichinda*) is likely native to India. Best eaten when immature, with age it can grow to be as long as 1.5 meters in length and becomes twisted like a snake. As a vegetable, it is especially popular in Maharashtra and South India. The shoots, tendrils and leaves can be eaten as greens.

Spiny gourd (*Momordica dioica*, Hindi *kantola*) is used as a vegetable across India where it is known by different names. It is a small round bright green fruit covered with spikes and is available during the monsoon season. It is especially popular in Gujarat where it is cooked with other vegetables.

Tinda (*Praecitrullus fistulous*, also known as apple gourd or Indian squash) is a small (five to eight cm in diameter) round green vegetable that looks like an apple. It has a tender moist flesh with a mild flavour and is used for curries, stuffed with meat and vegetables, or PICKLED. The seeds can be roasted and eaten as a snack.

Colleen Sen

- Achaya, K.T. *A Historical Dictionary of Indian Food*. New Delhi: OUP, 2002.
- Verma, Rahul. 'Sweet Red Ghoul: The Virtues of Pumpkin'. *The Hindu*, 26 October 2019.
- Weber, Shannon. 'Meet Dosakai, the Mysterious Little Melon That's More Versatile than Meets the Eye'. *Feast*, 26 April 2019.

GUAVA

Guava (Hindi *amrud*) is the oval fruit of a tropical and subtropical tree (*Psidium guajava*) that belongs to the myrtle family. This prolific fruit-bearing tree can grow in almost any kind of soil. Once established, it becomes hardy in high temperatures and drought conditions. In India it is grown both commercially and in peoples' gardens. Although guava is native to the New World, today India is the world's largest producer and guavas are India's fourth largest commercial fruit crop (after MANGOES, BANANAS and CITRUS FRUITS). The leading producing states are Uttar Pradesh, Punjab, Maharashtra, Karnataka and Tamil Nadu.

Guava originated in Central and South America and was introduced by the Portuguese, perhaps as early as the sixteenth century. Early references are ambiguous: for example, Abu'l-Fazl refers to an *amrud* but it could have also been the pear, which has the same name. In 1651, the naturalist and traveller William Dampier wrote of India: 'The N.W. part is full of Guaver Tree [*sic*] of the great variety', adding that, 'when the fruit is ripe, it is yellow, soft and very pleasant. It bakes as well as a pear'.

Guavas are green when unripe, becoming yellow or red once they ripen, and can be as small as a lemon or as large as a MELON. In India, white and pink guavas are mainly used in the food processing industries. A popular table and street food, guavas are best eaten within twenty-four hours of being picked. They are also made into *murabbas*, a sweet or savoury preserve served as an accompaniment to meals. Firm guavas can be prepared as a vegetable in CURRIES. They are an excellent source of vitamin C, having ten times as much as oranges.

Colleen Sen

GUJARAT

The state of Gujarat, bordered by the Arabian Sea, Pakistan and several Indian states, was created in 1960 when Bombay State was divided on linguistic grounds into Gujarat and Maharashtra. India's ninth largest state by population, two-thirds of Gujaratis live in rural areas. A large minority are merchants and businessmen. Nearly 90 per cent of the populations are Hindu, 9 per cent are Muslim (see BOHRAS) and less than 1 per cent are Jain. Around 60 per cent of Gujaratis are vegetarian, a reflection of the historical influence of the Jain community, the heritage of Mahatma Gandhi and Vaishnava Hinduism. The variety of vegetarian dishes is so rich that Madhur JAFFREY called Gujarati cuisine 'the haute cuisine of vegetarianism'.

Gujarat was part of the Indus Valley Civilization, home to several large cities and India's first port at Lothal. Over the centuries, parts of Gujarat were under various Hindu and Muslim rulers, including the Mauryas, the Solanki dynasty, the Khatri Sultanate and the Marathas. From 1818 to 1947, most of present-day Gujarat was divided into hundreds of princely states, but several districts in central and southern Gujarat, including Ahmedabad and Surat, were governed directly by the British.

Gujarat is divided into three regions:

- Western Gujarat, also known as Saurashtra or Kathiawar, is a peninsula bordering the Arabian Sea. Rainfall is low and erratic and the main crops are cotton, sorghum and peanuts. It is also a major producer of dairy products.
- Central Gujarat, called the 'granary of Gujarat', is distinguished by its BREADS, snacks and lentil dishes. MILLETS, including sorghum (*jowar*) and pearl millet (*bajra*), were originally the main staples but have been supplemented by WHEAT.
- Southern Gujarat is a fertile well-watered region that produces plenty of green vegetables and fruit, including some of India's finest MANGOES, including varieties such Alphonso, Kesar, Langra and Neelam.

Although there are differences between the cuisines of these regions, they share many features. Gujarati meals are organized around a *thali*, an array of dishes arranged on a metal plate (see COOKING AND DINING). *Thalis* typically include breads, PAPAD, RICE, a vegetable (*shaak*), dal or *kadhi*, a variety of *farsans* and *mithais* (SWEET dishes), PICKLE and often a piece of jaggery. The number of dishes depends on the occasion: a festival can have as many as several dozen. Lunch is the main meal. Often, Gujaratis have a single-dish meal for dinner, such as KHICHRI or *handvo*. Gujarat is the largest producer of milk in India, and milk and dairy products, especially yogurt and BUTTERMILK, play an important role in the diet. Because the hot and dry climate is not conducive to growing rice, breads made from wheat and millets are a dietary staple. Although rice is a part of many *thalis*, it plays a secondary role to bread. A typical Gujarati breakfast is *thepla* served with yogurt and pickle, or with JALEBI and *sambharo*, a cabbage and CARROT salad sold at roadside stands.

Batters may be fermented to create a spongy texture that is unique to the region. Sweet and sour are common flavourings, the sourness provided by *KOKUM*, the rind of a fruit related to mangosteens *(Garcinia indica)* or TAMARIND. Cooks often add a pinch of SUGAR to dishes and a piece of jaggery or a sweet dish may be served on the side. Gujarati curries have a semi-thick consistency. The main spices include TURMERIC, CORIANDER, ASAFOETIDA,

GINGER, CUMIN, FENUGREEK and CURRY LEAVES. ONIONS and GARLIC are not used as frequently as in other Indian cuisines; a common flavouring is a green CHILLI and ginger paste.

Breads. Gujarati breads include thick *bajra rotla,* made from sorghum; deep-fried wheat puris; thin unleavened wheat *rotlis; thepla/dhebra*, a flatbread made from wheat flour, boiled rice, chickpea, yogurt and fenugreek leaves; *khakras*, crisp wafer-like breads; and *bakhris*, crisp whole wheat flour breads.

Farsans. A distinctive feature of Gujarati cuisine, these savoury snacks are served with afternoon tea, as appetizers, or as part of a Gujarati *thali*. Many have become popular street foods throughout India. Perhaps the most famous Gujarati dish is *dhokla*, a spongy cake cut into squares. It is made by steaming a batter of fermented rice and chickpeas on a flat dish, then seasoning it with hot oil and MUSTARD seeds, and garnishing with chillies and coriander. *Handvo* is a thick savoury cake made from a fermented batter of rice and lentils (see PULSES), filled with vegetables, carrots, peas and bottle gourd, and baked. *Dabeli,* which originated in Kutch, is a sandwich made by filling Western-style buns with boiled POTATOES and a special masala. It is served with tamarind, DATE, garlic and other CHUTNEYS and is garnished with POMEGRANATE and roasted peanuts. *Muthia* are small cylinders made from a chickpea flour and fenugreek (or other green leafy vegetables) dough that is steamed or deep-fried, then tempered with oil and mustard seeds. *Patra* are made by spreading a batter of chickpea flour on *arbi* leaves (TARO), rolling them into tubes, steaming and cutting into slices. *Khandvi* are rolled-up pancakes made from a batter of chickpea flour and yogurt, cut into small pieces and topped with tempered mustard and SESAME seeds. *Pattice* are boiled potato balls filled with COCONUT, cashew nuts and raisins. *Pani puri*, a street food popular across India, consists of *golgappa* (tiny puris) filled with sprouted *moong dal*, boiled potato and tamarind chutney, and filled with mint water. *Ragda* patties are mashed potato balls that are fried and topped with *ragda*, a sauce made from dried white peas. Another category is *nasto* – fried crispy snacks that are packed in air-tight tins and carried to be eaten on trips. *Ganthia* is a category of snacks made from chickpea flour, including *papri* wafers, *fafda* and *muthia*.

Vegetables. Vegetable curries, called *shaak*, are made with AUBERGINE; *valor papri*, a very long thin green bean; the leaves of the *arvi* (taro) plant; and many local varieties of GOURDS and YAM. A standard way of preparing vegetables is to sauté them with cumin seeds and asafoetida, add other spices and finally add tomatoes. Yam, CUCUMBER, potatoes and peanuts are simmered to make a delicious stew. *Kathols* are lentils served not as dals but as vegetables, especially at lunch. They are often made with *moong* dal (whole green gram) and served dry or simmered with yogurt. *Undhiyu* (it has many spelling variants) is a mixed vegetable dish that is a speciality of Surat and is now popular all over Gujarat. It is a mixture of seasonal vegetables such as green beans, potatoes, purple yam, plantains, aubergine and *muthia*, flavoured with a dry masala and grated coconut, and slowly cooked in a little vegetable oil and water. The word comes from the Gujarati *undhu*, meaning 'upside down', since the dish is traditionally cooked underground in earthen pots. A version served at weddings and called *surti undhiyu* is made with lentils and seasoned with palm sugar in a mild sauce and is served with rice.

Sweets (*mithai*). In addition to sweets common throughout India (BARFI, LADDU, jalebi, etc.), there are some distinctive Gujarati sweets including *doodhpak*, a rice pudding served with puris; *ghari* puri, cookies made of puri batter, NUTS, *mawa*, ghee and sugar; *sheera*, also known as *suji* HALWA, a pudding made with semolina, ghee and sugar; *mohanthal*, a kind of fudge made from chickpea flour, ghee and milk; and *ghoogra*, a pastry filled with coconut and sweetened semolina, traditionally made to celebrate Diwali. *Ghevar hevar* are crispy deep-fried discs soaked in sugar syrup and garnished with nuts and edible silver leaves (see VARK) to make a special treat. *Khichdo* is a hearty sweet dish made of cracked wheat, milk and lots of dried fruits. It is typically eaten in the winter.

Drinks. Summers in Gujarat can be searingly hot and drinks that have a cooling effect are popular. *Chaas* is a mixture of fresh yogurt and water flavoured with black salt, sugar, roasted cumin powder and chilli-ginger paste. Another version, *vaghareli chaas*, is topped with asafoetida, cumin seeds and curry leaves sautéed in oil. *Panha* is a drink made from strained mango pulp, sugar, CARDAMOM powder and SAFFRON mixed with water and chilled. *Kadhi* is a mixture of buttermilk and chickpea flour flavoured with ginger and chilli. It is often served with khichri.

Rice. It can be served plain, with vegetables as a PULAO, as a sweet and sour *khatta-mittha bhat* with potatoes, or as KHICHRI. Khichri has many incarnations in Gujarat, including a version that is made with sprouted *moong* dal and rice flavoured with asafoetida and turmeric; *panch dhan*, made with five varieties of lentils; and *lazizan*, made from rice, lentils, ghee, spices and nuts, which was a favourite of the MUGHAL emperor Jahangir.

Colleen Sen

- Dalal, Tarla. *The Complete Gujarati Cookbook*. Mumbai: Sanjay & Co., 2001.
- Outlook Traveller Team. 'Food in Gujarat Can Be an Explosion of Flavours. Not Just Vibrant and Distinct, but Gujarati Cuisine Is Equally Colourful'. *Outlook Traveller*, 9 April 2018. Available online: https://www.outlookindia.com/outlooktraveller/explore/story/65510/indias-culinary-heritage-gujarati-cuisine (accessed 17 April 2022).

HALEEM

Haleem is an ancient dish, a kind of porridge-like soup made with cereals and meat, which seems to have originated in the region of Iran and Afghanistan but has spread to other countries of the Middle East and to India. It is also known by the name *harissa* (meaning 'well-cooked') in certain Arab countries but should not be confused with the hot sauce of North Africa also called *harissa*.

Haleem was a popular dish at the courts of the Delhi Sultanate and the Mughals and was mentioned in the *Ain-i-Akbari*. In India today, there are many versions but it is usually made with WHEAT (and, in the past, sometimes with barley) and lamb (or goat), and, sometimes, chicken. Some versions include lentils and most versions are cooked with the addition of 'hot' spices. The wheat (or barley) grains are first soaked overnight and are then, with the other ingredients, cooked slowly in water or milk or, sometimes, a broth for several hours. They are then pounded or stirred vigorously resulting in a paste-like consistency with all the flavours blending together. The cooked *haleem* is finally garnished with such things as fried ONIONS, sliced GINGER, sliced green CHILLIES, fresh CORIANDER leaves, lemon wedges and chaat masala.

Haleem is a popular snack food sold in bazaars throughout the year and is particularly favoured by the Muslims in HYDERABAD and elsewhere. It is made as a special dish during the holy months of Ramadan and Muharram. Hyderabad is renowned for its highly spiced *haleem*, which is made with wheat, lentils and goat, pounded until it is thick, cooked slowly and served with fried onions on top. It is thought to be a variant of the Arabian *harissa* introduced by the Nizam's Arab (mainly Yemeni) palace guards in the nineteenth century. In 2015, Hyderabadi *haleem* was granted GEOGRAPHICAL INDICATION tag (GI tag), the first non-vegetarian dish in India to be so designated. To qualify as authentic, it must be made with goat meat; the ratio of meat to wheat must be 10:4; the GHEE must be laboratory certified as totally pure; and the dish must be cooked in a copper pot over firewood for twelve hours.

Helen Saberi

- Sen, Colleen Taylor. *Feasts and Fasts: A History of Food in India*. London: Reaktion Books, 2015.

HALWA

Halwa is a popular sweet throughout India. Although the word comes from Arabic, meaning 'sweetmeat', Indian halwa is very different from the Middle Eastern variety, which is usually made from tahini, a SESAME-seed paste. A popular Indian version of halwa is made from semolina cooked with jaggery (see SUGAR), GHEE and sometimes NUTS and raisins. Other versions are made from vegetables, especially CARROTS, bottle GOURD, lentils (see PULSES), chickpeas, nuts and sometimes *KHOYA*. All halwas are made with a lot of ghee and are moister and flakier than the Middle Eastern halwa. Karachi halwa is a bright orange, somewhat rubbery, translucent halwa made from cornstarch, nuts and ghee. Although halwa is associated with Muslims – Muslim sweetmakers are called *halwai* – a halwa-like dish made from semolina is mentioned in the twelfth-century work *MANASOLLASA*.

Colleen Sen

HARYANA

Haryana is a state in northern India bordering the national capital territory of Delhi and it is a bundle of opposites, where remnants of the prehistoric Harappan Civilization (2500–1800 BCE) co-exist with India's Millennium City, Gurugram, and Kurukshetra, the scene of the Battle of Mahabharata, where Lord Krishna delivered the sermon that has become the most revered text of Hinduism, and is a short drive away from one of the centres for cutting-edge dairy research. It is one of India's younger states, having been created out of Punjab in 1966, yet its roots go deep into the country's vibrant past.

A Harappan site dug up at the village of Farmana, which is a two-hour drive west of Delhi, caused much excitement back in 2015 when two archaeologists, Arunima Kashyap and Steve Weber, at the Washington State University in the United States produced the oldest surviving molecular evidence of a 'proto-curry'. Not very far from it, Gurugram – previously known as Gurgaon – is one of the country's principal IT and business process outsourcing (BPO) hubs and home to leading Fortune 500 companies operating out of India. Nicknamed 'Millennium City', Gurugram is also the place where dining destinations such as the Cyber Hub and Horizon Centre have spawned a modern restaurant culture patronized by a young and global consuming class. The state's highways, linking Delhi with the historical city of Jaipur and the agriculturally rich state of Punjab, are studded with traditional DHABAS and *ahaatas* (liquor shops that serve food); they also have restaurants catering to the taste buds of Japanese and Korean expats.

Despite the state's veneer of contemporaneity, Haryana's predominantly vegetarian population is not known to have an elaborate culinary tradition. Their food is rustic, yet wholesome and light, drawing on the ingredients of neighbouring Rajasthan (such as the common *singri ki sabzi*, where the key ingredient is *ker-sangri*, or dried desert beans, and *kachri ki* chutney made with wild cucumber) as well as Punjab (such as *rajma chawal*, or kidney beans CURRY and RICE, and *kadhi pakori*, or spiced BUTTERMILK thickened with chickpea flour, with ONION fritters mixed in).

Other staples of Haryana's table include a KHICHRI made with *bajra* (black millets) as well as *bajra* rotis stuffed with spiced mashed POTATOES; a protein-rich medley of four dals – *chana* (split chickpea lentils), *toor* (pigeon peas), *masoor* (pink lentils) and *moong* (mung beans) (see PULSES) – cooked in ghee and served with fried rice spiked with CUMIN seeds; spiced rotis whose dough is prepared with chickpea flour, WHEAT and *ghee*, and served with a vegetable dish, yogurt and PICKLES; body-warming preparations such as *hari chholia* (green chickpeas) and *methi-gajar* (CARROTS and FENUGREEK leaves) in the winter, which can be quite harsh in December–January; and *bathua* RAITA (a yogurt dish very similar to the Greek *tzatziki* with a paste of antioxidant-laden goosefoot leaves stirred in).

Haryana is India's second largest producer of milk after Punjab, yet its repertoire of milk-based desserts is rather limited, maybe because the consumption of milk, buttermilk and yogurt-based LASSI is widespread in the state. Typically, a Haryanvi dessert platter would include *meethe chawal* (a combination of basmati rice, SUGAR and ghee flavoured with CARDAMOM and SAFFRON); or the slightly more elaborate roti *ka meetha churma*, which are rotis that are roasted till they turn crisp like biscuits, crushed and roughly bound together by ghee and *bhura*; *alsi ki pinni*, or balls made with flax seeds (*alsi*), wheat flour, sugar, nuts and ghee; and *malpua*, or pancakes, whose dough is prepared with *maida* (refined flour), semolina, milk and yogurt, and are deep-fried in ghee and then plunged into thick sugar syrup.

There's only one sweet that Haryana is known for and it is a unique JALEBI that weighs 250 grams and is cooked only in ghee. A speciality of a town named Gohana in the Sonipat district, ninety km north of Delhi, the unique-sized jalebis owe their origin to an enterprising *halwai* (sweetmeat seller) named Matu Ram, who started making them in 1958. The tradition is still alive and thriving in Gohana, thanks to Matu Ram's grandson and a crop of copycat *halwais*.

Sourish Bhattacharyya

- Jhaveri, Vidhi. '17 Authentic Dishes of Haryana to Get You Drooling'. *Holidify, n.d.* Available online: https://www.holidify.com/pages/food-of-haryana-157.html (accessed 18 April 2022).
- Siwach, Sukhbir. 'Haryana Farmers Milk a Success Saga with Artificial Insemination'. *The Indian Express*, 23 June 2021.
- Sura, Ajay. 'On Campaign Trail, Gohana Jalebi Adds Bit of Sweetness to Bitter Political Rhetoric'. *The Times of India*, 31 October 2020.

HIMACHAL PRADESH

Himachal Pradesh, a picturesque state nestled in the western Himalayas, was carved out by joining together the ancient kingdoms of the hilly parts of old Punjab. It owes its significance to three historical developments:

- Its state capital, Shimla, built upon a number of interlinked hills, was the summer capital of the British Raj since 1864. It was where the high and mighty of the empire used to congregate to escape the searing heart of the plains and they left an indelible imprint on the social life and culinary culture of this 'hill station';
- It is also where the Dalai Lama, who had escaped to India during the Tibetan Uprising of 1959, established the Tibetan government in exile in May 1960 at Dharamshala, an old military base of the Gurkhas at the base of the Dhauladhar Mountains. It is next to the old colonial getaway known as McLeodganj, creating a home away from home for Tibetan exiles, an international community drawn towards the spiritual leader, and, unwittingly, a magnet for honeymooners;
- It is home to India's APPLE economy, powered by the Red Delicious variety, which was propagated by the American missionary-turned-Indian freedom fighter Samuel Evans 'Satyanand' STOKES in 1916.

The state's cuisine is therefore a medley of diverse ethnic influences – Himachali, Punjabi (on account of its long association with Punjab), Tibetan and European (traditionally nurtured by hotels such as The Cecil, which emerged out of Rudyard Kipling's cottage after the Hotz family purchased it in 1902 and is now a part of The Oberoi Group). Some of the Himachali favourites, uncomplicated yet packed with flavours, are the *madra* (chickpea or kidney bean curry cooked in GHEE with yogurt mixed with *KHOYA*, or milk solids, loaded with TURMERIC and other spices), *tudkiya bhaat* (rice cooked with lentils, POTATOES and yogurt), *chha gosht* (mutton cooked with gram flour and yogurt), *babru* (crispy fried flatbreads stuffed with black gram paste, quite similar to the KACHORIS of the plains, which pair best with *madra*), *kaale chane ka khatta* (a sour preparation made with black chickpeas) and *siddu* (steamed BREAD made with a fermented WHEAT flour dough and served with dal or a sweet-and-sour tamarind CHUTNEY).

All these elements come together at the time of fairs, festivals, weddings and rites of passage. The platter is called *dham*, the local term for a 'feast' served on an auspicious day, prepared by *botis*, or specialist cooks. They are assisted by the women of the household or the village, depending on the scale of the celebrations, and served on dried *sal* leaf plates. The food is slow-cooked on firewood in thick copper and brass vessels, which have a broad base and a narrow opening at the top to prevent the loss of flavours. The simple spread, which varies from one district to another, primarily consists of rice, *madra*, *maash* (a combination of three types of dal – *moong*, *urad* and *masoor*, or green, black and pink lentils, respectively) topped up with *khatta* (a sweet and sour sauce made with tamarind and jaggery in an iron cauldron), and *meetha bhaat* (sweet rice cooked with milk and jaggery, and laced with SAFFRON and dry fruits) or *mithdee* (another sweet preparation made with *boondi*, or little chickpea flour balls doused in thick SUGAR syrup).

This is what would be served in Kangra district, but in Mandi, the feast begins with the dessert (*boondi ka meetha*). Sour preparations made with pumpkins (*kaddu*) and horse gram (*kolth*) as well as a ghee-soaked *mah ki* dal (black lentil dal) come in between, and the meal ends with *jhol* (BUTTERMILK). The variations are influenced by local ingredients and topographies. Although *dham* is mainly vegetarian, in the remote, bitterly cold and sparsely populated districts of Lahaul-Spiti and Kinnaur, mutton is a part of the spread, and so is liquor.

For the travellers who come in thousands throughout the year, the food on offer can range from North Indian staples such as puri-HALWA and JALEBIS served for breakfast, *aloo gobhi* (the ubiquitous Punjabi dish prepared with potatoes and cauliflower) and *kadhi chawal* (RICE served with a popular dish consisting of vegetable fritters soaked in a thick gram flour-yogurt gravy), to Tibetan specialities, such as momos (dumplings), *thukpa* (noodle soup), the gravy dish *shapta* served with *tingmo* (steamed buns), *chhurpi* (yak CHEESE) and the salty yak butter TEA. At Shimla, home to fashionable restaurants such as Devicos and Café Sol at Combermere Hotel, and the more commonplace yet iconic Indian Coffee House or the Himachal Rasoi, as well as Dharamshala and Kasauli, the cantonment town, European (or 'Continental') food is commonplace. Breads and bakery items compete for the attention of travellers in need of fuel after a long day of walking, shopping and soaking in the charms of these quaint places that still retain their old-world charm.

Sourish Bhattacharyya

- Pasricha, Pallavi. 'Where to Eat in Shimla This Summer'. *Condé Nast Traveller*, 15 May 2019. Available online: https://www.cntraveller.in/story/where-to-eat-shimla-summer-best-restaurants-himachal-pradesh/ (accessed 22 May 2022).
- Tanwar, Monica, Beenu Tanwar, Rattan S. Tanwar, Vikas Kumar and Ankit Goyal. '*Himachali Dham*: Food, Culture, and Heritage'. *Journal of Ethnic Foods* 5, no. 2 (June 2018): 99–104. https://doi.org/10.1016/j.jef.2017.10.006.

HONEY

Honey (Hindi *madhu*) is the sweet viscous substance produced by honeybees and related insects from the secretions of plants (floral nectar) and stored in honeycombs for their own consumption. It can be collected from wild bee colonies or hives of domesticated bees. Its sweetness comes from fructose and glucose.

The use of honey in India goes back to ancient times. Prehistoric cave paintings at Bhimbetka in Madhya Pradesh show men taking honey from beehives on rocks. Honey was one of the methods of sweetening used in the Harappan Civilization and there are several references to it in the *Rigveda* (*c.* 1500 BCE). Honey was mixed with *soma* in Vedic rituals and with yogurt or GHEE to welcome guests. However, according to the *Sutras*, it was forbidden to students and widows because it was thought to inflame the passions. One of the earliest known sweets was the *apupa* – a round cake made of flour and honey baked in ghee over a slow fire. Liquors made from fermented honey included *madhurasa* and *madhvik* (see ALCOHOL). With the discovery of SUGAR processing in the first millennium BCE, honey was largely replaced by sugar as a sweetener.

Honey was valued for its medicinal properties. Eight varieties are mentioned in the Ayurvedic texts, the best considered that made by small bees. Honey was considered a particularly efficacious cure during the rainy season. Sushruta prescribes it as a destroyer of cough, wind and bile. Honey was also considered an effective medium for administering medicines (see FOOD AND MEDICINE).

Honey is considered a very auspicious food because it is a component of the *panchamrita* (five nectars) used in Hindu pujas and in *Abhisheka* (washing of the statues of the deities). *Panchamrita* is a mixture of honey, ghee, cow milk, yogurt and sugar (and sometimes *tulsi* (holy basil) and BANANAS). The Buddha allowed his followers to partake of honey and it plays an important role in the festival of *Madhu Purnima* commemorating the Buddha's retreat to the wilderness where a monkey brought him honey to eat. Some people mix honey with bananas to feed babies their first solid food (see RITES OF PASSAGE). However, Jains ban honey since it involves violence to bees.

In India, honey comes from many plants, the most common including *JAMUN*, eucalyptus, MUSTARD, LYCHEE, clover, sunflower, rapeseed and acacia. The taste of honey reflects the flower or flowers it is extracted from. While single flower honeys are available, most that are sold are a blend of several sources.

After Indian independence, Mahatma GANDHI included beekeeping in his rural development programmes. West Bengal, Uttar Pradesh, Punjab and Bihar contribute about 61 per cent of India's total honey production. According to one estimate, 60 per cent of Indian honey is wild, much of it collected by tribals, especially in the Nilgiris in South India and the Sundarbans in West Bengal. In 2020, the Indian government allocated 500 crore (around $78 million, £56 million) to the National Beekeeping and Honey Mission for three years to promote beekeeping as a way to generate income and employment for farmers.

Because it is expensive, honey is rarely used as the main source of sweetening. However, it is sometimes used as a replacement for sugar or sugar syrup in such dishes as *balushahi*, *shahi tukra*, *MODAKA*, *SHRIKHAND*, *gulab jamun* and *malpua* (see SWEETS).

Colleen Sen

- Sinha, Anil Kishore. *Anthropology of Sweetmeats*. New Delhi: Gyan Publishing House, 2000.

HYDERABAD

Hyderabadi cuisine is rightly considered as one of the most exotic Indian cuisines, owing its rich culinary legacy to the multi-cultural influences which have played out in the Deccan region across a little more than four centuries. Thanks to its foreign conquerors, Hyderabad has been the quintessential melting pot of various cooking styles, imbibing the best food traditions of cultures foreign (Turkish, Iranian and Arabic), MUGHAL and local (Dakhni or Deccani, with its robust and earthy Telangana and Marathwada food).

Hyderabad was established in 1591 CE by Mohammad Quli Qutb Shah, the fifth ruler of the Qutb Shahi dynasty, on the banks of the river Musi to overcome water shortages at Golconda Fort. After a glorious rule by the Qutb Shahi dynasty, Golconda was annexed by Aurangzeb in 1687, but the Mughal Empire weakened after his death in 1707. The governor of Hyderabad, Asaf Jah I (titled Nizam-ul-Mulk), declared independence in 1724 and from thereon started the era of the Nizams of Hyderabad. It was a peaceful reign during which Hyderabad saw a period of glory and riches, with the last Nizam, Mir Osman Ali Khan, featuring on the cover of *Time* magazine in 1937 as the world's richest man. After resisting accession when the country gained independence in August 1947, the Nizam finally signed the accession treaty in September 1948, after the Indian government initiated 'police action' against the state.

The Nizams of Hyderabad were patrons of arts, architecture and culture; the art of fine dining was also honed to perfection by them. The dining table at the Taj Falaknuma Palace (the erstwhile palace of the Nizam, built in 1893 and now run by the Taj group of hotels), which played host to King George V and Queen Mary among other royal guests, is testament to the sumptuous dinner banquets hosted by the Nizam. The table, which is 108 feet long, can accommodate 101 guests who sit in rosewood-carved chairs lined with green leather under ornate chandeliers and dine using crockery and cutlery made of gold and silver.

While *kacchi gosht ki* BIRYANI is, unarguably, the piece de resistance of Hyderabadi cuisine, followed by *HALEEM*, its close cousin in the pecking order, there are several other gems of Hyderabadi cuisine which merit attention but which, unfortunately, get lost in the hype around biryani and *haleem*. Ironically, Hyderabadi biryani still does not have a GI tag, despite its popularity and this only shows how the origins of this iconic dish of rice, meat and spices continue to be elusive. Many food historians argue that the word *biryani* is derived from the Persian word *birian*, which means frying, and from *birinj,* the Persian word for rice.

Origins aside, it would not be far-fetched to say that the city's identity is considered synonymous with its star dish. Biryani is available in every nook and corner of the city and it is not uncommon to find speciality restaurants offering Mediterranean and pan-Asian fare to also feature a mandatory Hyderabadi *dum* biryani on their menu. The Hyderabadi biryani is cooked à la *kacchi gosht,* which means that raw meat and semi-cooked rice are cooked together along with spices like SAFFRON, MINT leaves and fried ONIONS and a secret spice mix called *potli* masala. Its most unique component is *patthar ka phool* (a LICHEN often used in Mughlai cuisine) together with star anise, CINNAMON, CARDAMOM, *khus khus* (vetiver), betel leaf roots, caraway and a host of other aromatic herbs and spices. This mix is then tied up in a muslin cloth (*potli*) and dropped into boiling water in which the rice is to be cooked to a semi-cooked consistency so that the rice absorbs all the aromatic spices. The rice is then drained and layered with mutton marinated with yogurt, ginger-garlic paste and plenty of mint leaves, along with saffron and a lot of fried onions (*brista*), which are also used as garnish. Biryani *deghs* (heavy bottomed vessels of copper, brass or aluminium) come in humungous sizes, as it is usually cooked in huge quantities. The *degh* is then sealed on the top with a dough of *atta* (WHEAT flour) around the lid and placed on *dum* (cooked in its own steam) on a slow fire for at least an hour if not more, depending on the quantity and whether it is being cooked on the gas stove or with firewood. Hyderabadi biryani is usually served with *mirchi ka salan*, made of big green CHILLIES in a tangy gravy using a peanut-tamarind-red chillies paste and RAITA. The green chillies, peanuts and TAMARIND are the local Dakhni culinary influences on an accompaniment to a dish considered Persian in origin.

Next in the pecking order, as far as popularity of Hyderabadi cuisine goes, is *haleem*, which gets its place under the sun during the holy month of Ramadan. It is a porridge of broken wheat (barley, lentils and rice are added in some versions too) cooked and mashed with minced meat (lamb, chicken, fish, beef and vegetarian versions are popular), ghee and spices. *Haleem*, which is an Arabian dish in origin and is known as *harees* or *harissa* in Arabic cuisine, involves slow cooking of six to eight hours. The meat is first cooked for about three hours in spiced water and then broken wheat, or *daliya*, that has been soaked overnight is mixed with the cooked meat along with other spices and ghee. Haleem is traditionally cooked on a slow flame of firewood in huge copper cauldrons set in brick and clay ovens. At least two persons, armed with long wooden mashers, stir the concoction continuously accompanied by some energetic bashing and clanging in order to churn it to a gooey-paste consistency. Haleem making contests by old restaurants in the Old City area (near Hyderabad's iconic monument, Charminar) of Hyderabad are not uncommon. Come dusk, every IRANI CAFE and small, big and middling restaurant, be it standalone or of the star hotel category, serves up steaming hot *haleem*, garnished with fried onions, cashews and fried mint leaves, to multitudes of people, most of whom would have broken their fast after the evening prayers. Makeshift kiosks selling *haleem* also mushroom in the month of Ramadan, offering a good business opportunity to home chefs and caterers. Hyderabadi *haleem* does have a GI tag, though it is considered Yemeni in origin. But since the Hyderabadi version has Indian spices and a slightly altered taste and presentation, the GI tag is well-deserved.

There is the rustic and robust *patthar ka gosht* – thin slivers of marinated meat, sizzled on heated stone or granite slabs until crisp. Hyderabadi cuisine also boasts of some excellent soups and broths such as the wholesome *marag*, a thin flavourful broth made from mutton with bone and into which naan (see BREADS) is dunked. *Paaya* is another robust and spicy soup made of lamb trotters which is both wholesome and all-rounded in texture and flavour.

Other specialties are *shikampurs* (meat mince patties filled with a hung curd and onion filling), *luqmis* (stuffed pastry sheets much like SAMOSA, with minced meat filling) and *talawa gosht,* or deep-fried boneless meat, which now bears a localized flavour with red chilli powder added generously. For dals and CURRIES, Hyderabadis love their *khatti* dal (the local influence of tamarind added to *toor* dal); *dum ka murgh*, or chicken curry, slow-cooked in a heavy-bottomed vessel in a marinade of curd, cashews and POPPY SEED paste and usually served at weddings; and vegetarian fare like *baghara baingan*, baby AUBERGINES cooked in a lip-smacking peanut-coconut-sesame-poppy seed-coriander-cumin-tamarind gravy. Also popular is the Hyderabadi *naashta* (breakfast) consisting of *kheema* (mincemeat spiced with garam masala), KHICHRI and *khatta* (a delectable tamarind-sesame seed watery CHUTNEY), as well as *chaar koni* naan (square-shaped soft naan with star-shaped impressions, which originated with the fourth Nizam of Hyderabad's accountant referred to as Munshi, and, therefore, is also known as Munshi naan) with *paaya*.

Hyderabadi desserts are royal in both taste and presentation. *Khubani ka meetha,* stewed APRICOT served with fresh cream or ice-cream; *kaddu ka kheer*, a pudding made of milk and grated bottle GOURD; and double *ka meetha*, a kind of bread pudding which resembles the Awadhi *shahi tukra*, are favourites. But the priceless desserts worthy of mention, now rare and made only by a couple of elite Hyderabadi families, are *badaam ki jaali* and *ashrafi*. *Badaam ki jaali* is made like almond fudge, although sometimes cashews maybe also added; the name *jaali* is ascribed to the lace-like moulds which are used to cut the fudge into floral patterns. It is then baked in an oven and garnished with *VARK*, edible silver foil, on top. *Ashrafi,* named after a Persian gold coin imprint in Urdu on the round moulds between which the almond-sugar dough is pressed, is the non-baked softer version of *badaam ki jaali* to which saffron has been added to impart the golden yellow colour. Little wonder, then, that Hyderabadi cuisine bears the imprint of its regal legacy carried forth across generations.

Swati Sucharita

- Karan, Pratibha. *Princely Legacy: Hyderabadi Cuisine*. Gurugram, Haryana: HarperCollins, 1998.

IBN BATTUTA

Abu Abdullah Muhammad Ibn Battuta (1304–68/9) was an itinerant jurist from Tangiers, Morocco, who set a contemporary record in world travel crisscrossing forty nations and 120,000 km between 1325 and 1354, and left behind an entertaining account of the politics and everyday life of India, where he lived in different parts from 1334 to 1341. Titled *Tuḥfat an-Nuẓẓār fī Gharā'ib al-Amṣār wa 'Ajā'ib al-Asfār* (*A Masterpiece to Those Who Contemplate the Wonders of Cities and the Marvels of Travelling*), Ibn Battuta's colourful chronicles of his journey, written in Arabic and known in historical literature simply as *al-Rihla*, or *The Travels*, provides very useful information on the food culture of India.

The Moroccan was attracted to India by stories of how the eccentric and erratic Sultan Mohammad Tughlaq, then believed to be the richest ruler in the world, was generously disposed towards foreigners who show signs of learning. The Sultan, whose rule between 1325 and 1351 was riddled with rebellions, famines, political misadventures and bloodshed, made the traveller the *qazi* (chief judge) of Delhi. Later, as Ibn Battuta kept piling up debts, the Sultan bailed him out financially by assigning him the additional responsibility of looking after the Qutab Minar and the mosque and mausoleum around it.

As a favourite of the Sultan, the Moroccan was invited for meals with Muhammad Tughlaq. In his account of one meal, Ibn Battuta mentions that it started with a SHERBET of 'sugared water', followed by BREAD (thin round WHEAT-flour chapatis), large slabs of sheep's meat, round dough cakes cooked in GHEE 'which they stuff with sweet almond paste and honey', meat cooked again in ghee with ONIONS and green GINGER, '*sambusak*' (triangular pastries made of pieces of thin bread that are folded to pack in 'hashed meat' cooked with almonds, walnuts, pistachios, onions and spices, and then fried in ghee), RICE cooked in ghee with chicken on top, and 'sweet cakes and sweetmeats' for dessert (see SWEETS). To wash this down, they had BARLEY water, followed by PAAN, the digestive preparation of betel leaf and areca nut.

Ibn Battuta observed that Indians ate MILLETS most often and he enjoyed pounded millet made into a porridge cooked with buffalo's milk. For breakfast, Indians ate peas and mung beans cooked with rice and ghee. Animals were fed with barley, chickpeas and leaves as fodder and even given ghee.

In Kerala, a favourite dish of the Muslim community was *rasoi* made with rice, lamb and grated onion. While in the Deccan, he met the Marathas and wrote about their Spartan diet of rice, green vegetables and SESAME oil. He also observed that they washed their foodstuff carefully, making them stand out to the modern reader as practitioners of good hygiene.

Sourish Bhattacharyya

- Chavan, Akshay. 'Everyday India, through Ibn Battuta's Eyes'. *Live History India*, 15 June 2017. Available online: https://www.livehistoryindia.com/story/people/everyday-india-through-ibn-battutas-eyes (accessed 5 May 2022).
- Dunn, Ross E. *The Adventures of Ibn Battuta: A Muslim Traveler of the Fourteenth Century*. Oakland, CA: University of California Press, 2012.
- Lee, Rev. Samuel, trans. and ed. *The Travels of Ibn Battuta: In the Near East, Asia and Africa, 1325–1354*. 1829. Reprint. Mineola, NY: Dover Publications, 2013.

ICE

Ice – water frozen into a brittle transparent crystalline solid – was savoured by the Indian ruling elite, despite the difficulties encountered transporting it from the northern mountains to the sun-baked plains. The earliest recorded instance of the use of ice dates back to Harshavardhana, who ruled much of northern India above the Narmada River from *c.* 606 to 647 CE. His hagiographer, Banabhatta, records that the BUTTERMILK for the king's consumption was stored in pails packed with ice. Most likely, it came from the Himalayas.

Babur (1482–1530) complained bitterly (and erroneously) in his memoirs, *Baburnama*, about the absence of ice and iced water in India. His son, Humayun, having had the chilled fruit SHERBETS served by Shah Tahmasp II of Persia, whose refuge he had sought after being exiled from India, brought with him a fondness for the beverage upon his return to India. His flasks of sherbets were chilled over ice from Kashmir. To prevent the ice from melting, naturally occurring saltpetre (potassium nitrate) would be strewn on the slabs. Akbar (r. 1556 to 1605) was more inventive and was credited by his chronicler, Abu'l-Fazl, with the discovery of the cooling properties of saltpetre which had been used since the thirteenth century mainly as raw material for gunpowder and also for its medicinal properties by practitioners (see FOOD AND MEDICINE).

The technique was known in the Arab world. Abu'l-Fazl describes how it took a quarter of an hour to cool water filled into a 'goglet' made with pewter or silver or any other metal and shaken round and round in a vessel filled with a mixture of water and salpetre. A 'goglet' (or *surahi* in Hindi) is 'a long-necked water vessel, usually of porous earthenware, that is used especially in India for cooling water by evaporation'. The practice seemed to have gained popularity, for Abu'l-Fazl mentions that it had become 'a source of joy for the great and small'. It seems to have been unique to India and was noticed by contemporary foreign travellers. It continued to be employed till the early decades of the 1800s by the European residents of British India.

After Akbar moved his capital from Agra and Fatehpur Sikri to Lahore in 1585, he seems to have switched over to ice. Blocks were carried on boats, each rowed by four men, sailing across the river Chenab. Ten boats were set aside for the purpose of transporting ice, covering the distance of forty-five *kos* (one kos is equivalent to three or four km) between the source in the 'northern mountains' and the *aabdaar khana* (store for water and ice) in the imperial palace in Lahore.

Ice was also brought on carriages drawn by horses and an elephant and manually by gangs of twenty-eight men at a time. Each slab of ice was first wrapped in spotlessly clean muslin, then covered twice over with jute cloth, and finally placed in a wooden box, with wood shavings filling up the gaps. 'All ranks of men use ice in summer; the nobles use it throughout the whole year', Abu'l-Fazl reported.

Ice from the Himalayas continued to be popular when it could be transported at a reasonable price, but in more distant parts, such as Allahabad, ice pits were dug up to store water in shallow, porous earthenware pans. Exposed to the chilly winter-night air of the northern plains between December and February, the water would freeze into ice to be collected the following day and stored in ice houses. The ice thus stored would last until August. It was, however, such a labour-intensive process that it was calculated that the manufacture of twenty-five to thirty tons of ice in one night required 2,000 workers and acres of land for the pits.

The East India Company (EIC), nonetheless, opened ice houses supplied by such 'ice pits' all across its domain. In Calcutta, 'Hooghly ice' from Chinsurah, made with water from the river Hooghly, a distributary of the Ganges, was produced using the same process. But the ice was filthy and sludgy and was unfit for consumption. The British residents of Kolkata, as a result, were left with little protection against the sweltering summer. 'The weather is perfectly suffocating. None can pity us but those who know our suffering', wrote the fifth Bishop of Calcutta, David Wilson, in 1833, whose predecessor had succumbed to the unrelenting heat.

The same year, a Boston businessman named Frederic Tudor arrived in Calcutta after four months on the sea with a shipment of 180 tons of ice from Walden Pond, Massachusetts. Its most famous resident was the Transcendentalist poet-philosopher Henry David Thoreau, whose *Essay on Civil Disobedience* greatly influenced Mahatma Gandhi. In 1847, by when Tudor had attained global fame as the 'Ice King', Thoreau watched with excitement as the men employed by Tudor's associate, Nathaniel Wyeth ('the servant of the Bramin [*sic*], priest of Brahma and Vishnu, and Indra'), hacked off square two-foot slabs of ice from Walden. In his recollection of the scene, punctuated with romanticized Hindu imagery, in *Walden, or Life in the Woods* (1854), Thoreau wrote rapturously: 'Thus it appears that the sweltering inhabitants of Charleston and New Orleans, of Madras and Bombay and Calcutta, drink at my well. ... The pure Walden water is mingled with the sacred water of the Ganges.'

For Tudor, the Calcutta ice trade was a desperate gamble to pay off debts he had accumulated from his unsuccessful forays into the global coffee trade. Tudor hedged his bets by bringing along crates of Baldwin apples (in fact, a third of his ice shipment had melted en route), but these were hardly needed. For the 'sweltering' Europeans in India, he was the equivalent of Thoreau's Brahma, Vishnu and Indra. Scenting a big business opportunity, Tudor expanded his trade to other parts of the country and presided over a network of ice houses at prime locations in Calcutta (1835), Madras (1841) and Bombay (1843) – all built with subscriptions from the European residents of these 'Presidency towns'.

Very soon, artist, writer and animal rights activist Colesworthy Grant wrote in 1863, 'Like most other conveniences which habit renders familiar, the ice has almost ceased to be regarded as a luxury.' Clubs added ice to their offerings to make the drink they served to their members more agreeable. The Byculla Club in Bombay ordered forty tons to be delivered by May 1840, the beginning of summer.

The easy availability of ice also made 'a handsome item of domestic furniture' – the brass-bound, zinc-lined teak 'ice chest' – 'almost as common and indispensable as the sofa or the side-board'. Unsurprisingly, the market for alcoholic beverages boomed, and by 1851 Calcutta had twenty-five 'wine merchants'. In Bombay, on the other hand, a growing number of Britons began to substitute chilled drinking water for the conventional alcoholic beverages drunk in the evening after dinner. Wealthy Indians, too, started buying American ice. Two members of the committee appointed to regularize ice supply in Calcutta were Dwarkanath Tagore (grandfather of the Nobel Laureate Rabindranath Tagore) and Kurbullai Mahommed. The firm of Jehangir Nusserwanjee Wadia, which was already trading with America, distributed the ice when it first came to Bombay. But the most hilarious episode was that of Sir Jamsetji Jeejeebhoy, renowned philanthropist who made his fortune from cotton and opium, and his guests coming down with bad colds after savouring ice-cream served at a dinner party he hosted at his Bombay home. The influential Gujarati newspaper, *Bombay Samachar*, reporting the incident, ticked off the dinner party host and his guests and said that they had paid the price for ingesting an unknown 'foreign' substance.

A grateful East India Company (and later, the British Indian authorities) did not see it that way. It granted Tudor customs duty exemptions (and he reciprocated by not getting too greedy about the pricing of his precious commodity), making India the millionaire's (and after his death in 1864, his company's) most profitable market. At the peak of the ice trade, Calcutta received three American ships laden with 500–600 metric tons of ice. The annual quantities of Tudor ice imported into India climbed from 5,000 metric tons in the 1840s to 12,000 metric tons throughout the 1860s and 1870s. But, like all good things, it had to come to an end.

Faced with new technologies (the invention of the ice-making machine and then artificial refrigeration), the pollution of the lakes of New England by coal-fired railroads and local competition, the Tudor Ice Company abruptly ceased its Indian trade in 1882 and shut shop in 1887.

No signs remain of the Calcutta ice house. The spot where it once stood is occupied by the small causes court. The one in Bombay was sold to the industrialist Jamshetji Tata. It now houses the prestigious K.R. Cama Oriental Institute. Biligiri Iyengar, a noted advocate in the Madras High Court, bought the ice house in his city and converted it into his residence. Here Iyengar hosted the famous Hindu preacher Swami Vivekananda during his triumphant visit to Madras after his return from the 1893 Parliament of Religions in Chicago. Since 1963, the birth centenary of the swami, it stands facing the Bay of Bengal as a grand architectural showpiece housing a museum dedicated to Vivekananda. (In 2014, more than a century after Tudor's company folded, one of his descendants in Coral Gables, Florida, revived it, thereby ensuring its founder's name will not go out of business.)

Back in British India, slowly but steadily, ice factories started coming up across the country, starting with the Bengal Ice Company, an enterprise of the agency house George Henderson & Co., in 1878. Giving it competition was Crystal Ice Company of Balmer Lawrie & Co. A factory bearing the same name was set up by W.B. Keene and John Ramsay Unger at Egmore in Madras in 1886, and it was still in operation in 1946, by when it was also storing fish, meat and fruits. By 1904, thirty-nine ice plants were in operation, from Peshawar to Rangoon, to Poona and Madras; their number went up to sixty-six in 1925.

These factories continue to be in operation, equipped with modern refrigeration plants, and the ice blocks they produce are still used, most visibly by the fisheries sector and in carts selling iced water on the roadside. For the steadily growing number of middle-class urban households, and a rapidly increasing number of their rural counterparts, domestic refrigerators have become the daily source of ice. In 2020, Indians spent $3.5 billion buying 12 million refrigerators. Between 2013 and 2020, in fact, 83 million refrigerators were sold in India, making them the most popular consumer appliance in the country. What was once an elite indulgence is now a mass commodity.

Sourish Bhattacharyya

- Allami, Abu'l-Fazl. *The Ain-i-Akbari*, vol. I, translated by H. Blochmann, revised and edited by D. C. Phillott. 2nd edition. 1927. Reprint. New Delhi: Atlantic Publishers, 1989.
- Chaudhuri, Moumita. 'Boston Ice Party'. *The Telegraph*, 28 March 2013.
- Dickason, David G. 'The Nineteenth-Century Indo-American Ice Trade: An Hyperborean Epic'. *Modern Asian Studies* 25, no. 1 (1991): 53–89.

- Doctor, Vikram. 'An Interesting Tale of the Business of Ice and Its History in India'. *The Economic Times*, 25 May 2013.
- Grant, Colesworthy. *Anglo-Indian Domestic Life*. Calcutta: Thacker, Spink and Co., 1862.
- Mirza, Meher. 'The British Couldn't Take India's Heat, so They Imported Ice from New England'. *Atlas Obscura*, 12 September 2018. Available online: https://www.atlasobscura.com/articles/how-did-people-get-ice (accessed 20 April 2022).

IDLI

Idli is a savoury, steamed cake made from a fermented batter of parboiled RICE and hulled black lentils (*Vigna mungo*; see PULSES). While the origins of idli are unclear, a culturally diverse consumption has evolved with hyperlocal names and nuances all over peninsular India. The Kannada text *Vaddaradhane* mentions '*iddalige*' in 920 CE, the Sanskrit *MANASOLLASA* describes '*iddarika*' in 1130 CE and the Tamil *Maccapuranam* mentions '*ittali*' in the seventeenth century.

Parboiled rice and lentils in proportions varying from 4:1 to 1:4 are soaked for six hours and drained. The lentils are ground to a soft, airy mass and the rice is ground to a fine paste and blended with 1 per cent SALT. Traditionally, hand-grinding was done in a large granite grinding stone. The mechanized wet grinder became commercially available in 1963 in Tamil Nadu. Acidification and leavening occur during fermentation in a warm place and the batter doubles in volume, achieving a ripe smell when done. Two distinct microorganisms mark the idli's taste – *L. mesenteroides* and *E. faecalis* from the black lentils develop during soaking and multiply during fermentation.

Many traditional methods of making idlis are in use today. At its simplest, the batter is poured on a cloth, tautly stretched on a *lota*'s neck, with boiling water to make *poalae* in Andhra and *ramasseri* idli in Palakkad. In other cases, the batter may be poured into plate-like moulds with six to eight shallow wells for the batter, layered with muslin; or in small metal cups, coconut shells and bamboo baskets (*chibulu* idli). Cups fashioned from leaves of screwpine (*moode* idli), JACKFRUIT (*khoto* or *hittu* in Konkan, *kottakalu* in Andhra), BANANA (*bale ele* idli), and TURMERIC or metal saucers (*thatte* idli) contain the batter and are placed in a large vessel with a lid for steaming. Most homes use the modern idli stand made of steel, created in 1969, which can simultaneously steam many layers of idli plates inside a purpose-made idly steamer or pressure cooker without pressure build-up.

Sanna is an idli-like preparation of the Konkan area but leavened by yeast, coconut water or toddy. Idlis are also a divine offering at the Varadaraja Perumal temple in Kanchipuram and are called *kovil* idli. MAVALLI TIFFIN ROOMS in Bengaluru created *rava* idli with wheat semolina and yogurt when rice was in short supply during the Second World War.

Idli is typically served with a variety of CHUTNEYS, coconut being most common, ghee or lentil-based stews like SAMBAR and *kozhambu*. They are also served with *milagai podi*, a blended powder of roasted lentils (see SPICE BOX), CHILLIES and salt mixed with oil. This may be smeared on the idli like a coating or offered as an accompaniment. Today, with a huge revival of MILLETS among urban foodies, idli is made with a variety of millets and lentils. The process of fermentation and steaming remains exactly the same, but the replacement of rice with other pseudo cereals and millets addresses India's rising problem with diabetes.

Priya Mani

- Achaya, K. T. *Indian Food: A Historical Companion*. Delhi: OUP, 1994.
- Lakshmi, K. and Deepa H. Ramakrishnan (May 11, 2013). 'In Search of Kancheepuram Idli'. *The Hindu*, 7 June 2016. Available online: https://www.thehindu.com/features/magazine/in-search-of-kancheepuram-idli/article4698641.ece (accessed 18 April 2022).

IRANI CAFES

Irani cafes are eating houses opened by entrepreneurial Zoroastrian migrants who had fled the socio-political tumult in Iran in the late nineteenth and early twentieth centuries. They settled down in Bombay, Pune and HYDERABAD, and Karachi, now in Pakistan. The Iranis are recent migrants, compared to the PARSIS, who, too, are Zoroastrians, but their ancestors had landed on India's west coast between the eight and tenth centuries.

Once bustling centres of Mumbai's cosmopolitan experience, with names such as Britannia, Kyani, Yazdani and Bastani becoming a part of Mumbai's rich folklore, the Irani cafes have dwindled in number from about 400 at the time of India's independence to less than forty today. One of the late lamented Irani cafes was Bastani and Company at Dhobi Talao, Mumbai, whose quirky 'instructions', handwritten with chalk sticks on a blackboard, inspired the poet Nissim Ezekiel, an Indian Jew, to pen his famous 1972 poem, 'Irani Restaurant Instructions':

> Please/Do not spit/Do not sit more/Pay promptly, time is valuable/Do not write letter/without order refreshment/Do not comb,/hair is spoiling floor/Do not make mischiefs in cabin/our waiter is reporting/Come again/All are welcome whatever cast/If not satisfied tell us/otherwise tell others/GOD IS GREAT

'Caste' may have been mis-spelt as 'cast' in the instructions, but Irani cafes have stayed above caste and religious considerations, being open to all migrants arriving in Mumbai at a time when the metropolis was shaping up. Well into the late 1800s, strict caste and purity codes prevented the experience of inter-dining among the native populations of Bombay.

The city's best-regarded historian, Sharada Dwivedi, is quoted by the BBC as saying that around the time the Irani cafes were coming up, Mumbai was flooded with migrants working in textile mills and the flourishing port. 'They usually came alone and needed places to eat. This is how Irani cafes became very popular', Dwivedi explained. The cafes, quote the BBC, broke down social barriers and religious taboos to become an important part of the city's public life.

And contrary to the formidable instructions immortalized by Ezekiel, the Irani cafes stood out by being loud, colourful and eccentric, letting their patrons linger over cups of 'Irani tea' with 'bun *maska*' (bread and butter) or biscuits fresh off the bakery, enticingly displayed in large glass jars at the entrance; read the day's newspaper split among several tables; or just enjoy the film music blaring out of vintage radio sets, without which no Irani cafe was complete. The other distinguishing features were the marble-topped tables, red-and-white checkered tablecloth, bent wood polished straight-back chairs, ceramic crockery and the unmissable presence of the owner, usually ancient, yet bubbling with the wry humour characteristic of the community, keeping a close watch over every movement in his establishment.

When they first landed in MUMBAI (then known as Bombay), the Iranis were literally the poor cousins of the Parsis, who, in fact, would employ their co-religionists out of a sense of solidarity. On the side, many of the Iranis would sell TEA (now famous as the *khari* chai, or strong tea, of the Irani cafes) to their compatriots when they gathered by the sea, across the road from the Taj Mahal Hotel, a landscape that has since those formative years been dominated by the Gateway of India. Some of them, according to the popular story about the origin of Irani cafes, hit upon the idea of opening tea shops and they discovered that street-corner locations were cheaper to lease because of the old Indian mental block against owning or renting property at the corner of a block.

Soon, Bombay (and later Pune, then known as Poona, and the southern city of Hyderabad, ruled by the Nizams) saw Irani cafes coming up and some of them became institutions, such as Kyani & Co (1904), Sassanian Boulangerie, now simply known as The Sassanian (1913), Britannia & Co. (1923), Koolar & Co. (1932), Cafe Military (1933) and Yazdani Bakery (1953). As their number dwindled from more than 400 to barely in the 30s, Mumbai especially mourned the loss of well-regarded hangouts such as B. Mervan and Co. and Bastani and Co.; it mourned as well the transition of reputed Irani cafes such as Cafe Leopold, turned into a must-visit tourist spot after being featured by the Australian drug runner-turned-best-selling author Shantaram, Cafe Mondegar and Cafe Excelsior, which have turned into multi-cuisine restaurants.

Apart from the atmospherics and the rich history of the Irani cafes, what really distinguishes them is their menu, which must include, to be able to lay claim to the name, 'bun *maska*' or, better still, '*brun maska*' (hard buttered croissants), mutton SAMOSAS, *kheema pav* (mutton mince served in bread rolls), *akuri* on toast (scrambled eggs), mutton or chicken PULAO drizzled with Iranian barberries (*zereshk*), vegetable puff, *dhansak* (a spiced lentil dish with mutton and vegetables), cherry cream custard, biscuits of different types, including the flaky *nan khatai*, *mawa* cake made entirely with milk solids, and Duke's raspberry drink.

Irani cafes are abiding links with a past that is slowly becoming a hazy memory. Popular modern restaurants such as Dishoom in London and the multi-outlet Sodabottleopenerwala spread across metropolitan India may attempt to recreate the form of the Irani cafes of the yesteryear, but to imbibe the spirit, one still has to go to one of the doughty last survivors.

Sourish Bhattacharyya

- Bajoria, Jayshree. 'India's Irani Cafes Fading Out'. *BBC News*, 27 April 2005. Available online: http://news.bbc.co.uk/2/hi/south_asia/4485523.stm (accessed 20 April 2022).
- Srinivasan, Madhumita. 'Bun Maska and Irani Chai'. *The Hindu*, 8 March 2015.

JACKFRUIT

Jackfruit (*Artocarpus heterophyllus*, Hindi *kathal*) is the name of both a tree and a fruit that grows worldwide in a humid tropical or subtropical climate. It likely originated in the Western Ghats in southwestern India but today is grown everywhere in India, often in gardens or along the roadside. IBN BATTUTA and other early travellers noted its abundance. The name comes from the Portuguese *jaca,* which is derived from Malayalam *chakka.* Jackfruit is the national fruit of Bangladesh and Sri Lanka and the state fruit of Kerala and Tamil Nadu. India is the world's largest producer.

The world's largest tree-borne fruit, a single jackfruit can weigh as much as forty kilograms, although the average weight is five to eight kilograms, and can be up to one metre long. The fruit consists of hundreds of 'bulbs' of seed-containing flesh around a stringy core and enclosed by a bumpy rind. The seeds are coated in a sticky substance that needs to be removed before preparation by oiling ones hands. For this reason, jackfruit is often purchased bottled or canned. Young jackfruit has a crisp, crunchy texture whereas more mature fruit may be firm or much softer and almost custard-like, depending on the variety. Some people find the taste of the ripe jackfruit unpleasant and reminiscent of overripe fruit, but the taste of the younger fruit has been compared to BANANA and PINEAPPLE.

Ibn Battuta left behind descriptions of the jackfruit, which he must have tasted during his sojourn to modern-day Kerala. He called the jackfruit the 'loveliest of all fruits of Hindustan' and one that is 'extremely sweet and well-flavoured in taste'. Elaborating on the seeds, Ibn Battuta says that each one of them has 'a stone, something like a large bean', which when roasted 'tastes like a dried bean'. Jackfruit seeds continue to be popular because of their anti-microbial, anti-ageing benefits, and in Tamil Nadu they are roasted with spices to prepare the delicious side dish known as the *palakottai varuval.*

Jackfruit is especially popular in southwestern India where it is used in many different ways. Ripe fruits are eaten fresh. Unripe jackfruit can be used as a meat substitute and roasted, baked, cooked in a CURRY, made into cutlets, or prepared in a PULAO or BIRYANI. Fried, sautéed and salted slices make tasty chips. The seeds can be boiled or roasted and eaten as a snack or dried and ground into flour. In Kerala, a pudding is made from a jackfruit jam mixed with COCONUT milk, fresh coconut and jaggery (see SUGAR). Mashed ripe fruit is mixed with roasted RICE powder and jaggery, wrapped in a leaf and steamed to make a *prasad* (see TEMPLE FOOD) offered in some Ganesh temples. In West Bengal, young jackfruit is cooked in MUSTARD oil or in a yogurt sauce. The pulp can be used to flavour SANDESH.

Jackfruit is not universally popular throughout India since some believe it causes indigestion. In some areas, the fruit and leaves are used mainly as cattle fodder. In 2014, an international jackfruit conference was held at the University of Agricultural Sciences in Bangalore, India, to discuss ways to market the fruit and expand the industry.

Colleen Sen

- Morton, Julia F. 'Jackfruit'. In *Fruits of Warm Climates*, edited by Julia F. Morton, 58–64. Miami: Florida Flair Books, 1987.
- Ramachandran, Ammini. *Grains, Greens and Grated Coconuts: Recipes and Remembrances of a Vegetarian Legacy*. New York: I-Universe, 2007.

JAFFREY, MADHUR

More than anyone else, Madhur Jaffrey (born 1933) has been instrumental in introducing Indian cuisine to the world. The author of some thirty cookbooks and the host of popular cooking shows in the UK and the United States, she has also had a distinguished acting career.

Jaffrey was born Madhur Bahadur in New Delhi into a Kayastha Hindu family. She graduated from Miranda House and in 1951 joined the Unity Theatre founded by Saeed Jaffrey. At the age of twenty, wanting to become a professional actress, she went to London to attend the Royal Academy of Dramatic Art. Feeling homesick for Indian food and finding the local food (both British and Indian) unpalatable, she asked her mother to send her recipes for dishes she had enjoyed at home. Until that time, she later wrote, she couldn't even make tea.

In 1958 she travelled to America where she married Saeed Jaffrey. The couple had three children. She and Jaffrey (who later divorced) often entertained in their New York apartment and one of their guests was *New York Times* food critic Craig Claiborne who wrote a profile of her. This led to a contract to write her first book *An Invitation to Indian Cooking*, published by Knopf in 1973. In the introduction, Jaffrey says she wrote the book 'as a gradual maneuver in self-defense'. Americans would ask her where they could enjoy good Indian food in restaurants and because there were no places she could recommend, she would invite them home. Eventually she started writing down the recipes for her guests, adapting them to American kitchens and ingredients. These were the basis of her first book.

Most of the recipes in her first book were from the Delhi region but in later books she extended her coverage to other regions of India and the world. They include *Indian Cookery* (1982), *World of the East Vegetarian Cooking* (1981), *A Taste of India* (1985), *A Taste of the Far East* (1993), *Madhur Jaffrey's Flavors of India: Classics and New Discoveries* (1995), *The Madhur Jaffrey Cookbook: Over 650 Indian, Vegetarian and Eastern Recipes* (1996), *Madhur Jaffrey's Ultimate Curry Bible* (2003), and most recently, *Madhur Jaffrey's Instantly Indian Cookbook: Modern and Classic Recipes for the Instant Pot* (2019).

Many of her books were winners of the prestigious James Beard Foundation Award. She was made a Commander of the British Empire and in January 2022 was awarded the Padma Bhushan by the President of India for her contributions to the culinary arts.

Colleen Sen

- Claiborne, Craig. 'Indian Actress Is a Star in the Kitchen Too'. *New York Times*, 7 July 1966.
- IANS. 'At 88, First Lady of Global Indian Cuisine Finally Gets Her Due'. *Lokmat Times*, 25 January 2022.
- Jaffrey, Madhur. *Climbing the Mango Trees: A Memoir of a Childhood in India*. New York: Vintage, 2007.

JALEBI

Jalebis are a popular street food throughout India. A thin batter of chickpea, *urad* dal or white flour, sometimes mixed with a little yogurt, is slightly fermented. The batter is extruded into hot oil to form large spirals that are soaked for a few minutes in warm SUGAR syrup, sometimes flavoured with lime (see CITRUS FRUITS) or rosewater (see FLOWER WATERS). In northern India, jalebis are enjoyed for breakfast, often with puris (see BREADS) and HALWA.

The name is thought to come from the Arabic *zalabiya*/Persian *zalibiya* (often spelled *zoloobiya* or *zoolabiya*). This item comes in many different shapes, one of which resembles the Indian version. It is a favourite sweet served at Eid-al-Fitr ending the Muslim fasting month of Ramadan. A variation is *imarti* which is round and has a flower-like shape.

Colleen Sen

JAMBU

Jambu, the rose-apple (*Syzygium jambos*), is native to the Malay Peninsula and is also cultivated in India and the West Indies. The plant is a small shrub and is widely used as an ornamental plant. Known by several names, *jambu* is the most common in India. The fruit, which has a yellowish or greenish colour often tinged with pink, may grow to the size of a small apple but the taste, texture and flavour are different. Ripe fruits have a waxy but crisp skin with a sweetish fleshy layer which is juicy and has a delicate rosewater fragrance. They have a large round seed. They can be eaten out of hand, stewed, candied, preserved in syrup and used in jams. Ancient Sanskrit texts mention a wine called *jambu-asava* which was made from the ripe fruits. The flowers can also be candied.

Jambu has a number of close relatives in the *Syzygium* genus and confusion can arise from the way similar names are used interchangeably across the fruits. See JAMUN (*Syzygium cumini*), which is also sometimes called *jambu*. *S. aqueum*, known as the watery rose-apple or water apple, originated in the south of India and still grows wild there. The colour of the fruit varies from white to pink, its skin is very thin and almost translucent causing the fruit to bruise easily. The flesh is crisp with a watery, faintly scented flavour. In Bengal, where this fruit is known as *jamrul*, it is enjoyed more for its crispy texture than for its flavour which many people have described as insipid.

S. malaccense, the Malay (rose) apple, is native to the Malay Peninsula and grows on a tall, striking tree. It is cultivated in India. The fruits are roundish but slightly oblong and narrower at the stalk end. They also have waxy skins with a pale green colour ripening with a rosy hue. The flesh is juicy with a slightly sweet-scented flavour. *S. samarangense*, the Java or Semarang (rose) apple, also called wax *jambu*, originated in the region between Malaysia and the Andaman and Nicobar Islands where they grow as wild trees in the coastal forests. It has now been introduced to other Asian countries including India. The fruits are bell-shaped with a pale green or whitish skin, or sometimes pink or even red. The green ones are eaten with a little SALT, the pink ones are generally juicier but less aromatic. In Kerala, this fruit is known as *chambakka* and is used in a variety of dishes and desserts.

Helen Saberi

- Arockiaraj, D. Vincent. 'Rose Apple Is Season's Favourite in Trichy'. *The Times of India*, 11 February 2017.
- Davidson, Alan. *The Oxford Companion to Food*. 2nd edition. Ed. Tom Jaine. Oxford: OUP, 2006.

JAMMU AND KASHMIR

FIGURE 23 JAMMU AND KASHMIR. Rogan josh. Miansari66/Wikimedia Commons.

At first glance, the mountain fastness of Ladakh, bordered by China to the East and Northeast; the verdant green Kashmir Valley, chiefly famous for its natural beauty and its horticulture; and Jammu would seem to have little to bind them together. Neither geography, nor religious faith, nor even ethnicity, but being border areas and having high altitudes seemed to be the only common factors. In 2019, the erstwhile state was bifurcated into two parts: Jammu and Kashmir now form one union territory and Ladakh forms another.

LADAKH, famously compared to land on the moon because of its rows of barren hills and mountains, at its lowest altitude is 2,550 metre above sea level, and the crops – and consequently, the diet of the population – make it unique in the country. The Valley of Kashmir, by contrast, is rich in SAFFRON, APPLES, stone fruit, almonds, walnuts, RICE and a profusion of vegetables. Jammu region is bordered by Pakistan and Pakistan-occupied-Kashmir as well as the Indian states of Punjab and Himachal Pradesh. Consequently, its own cuisines undergo a perceptible shift, taking on the contours of the neighbours' cuisine. Religious faith, as always, informs the trajectory of the cuisine. Thus, largely Muslim Kashmir has mutton (sheep meat) as its favoured meat, cooked in a variety of ways as to present a single ingredient in unimaginable guises. Jammu has a vegetarian population, which neither of the other two regions do, and Ladakh, with its time-rich but resource-poor population in the villages, relies on one-pot meals where the staples have traditionally been BARLEY and WHEAT.

Kashmir. The Valley of Kashmir, divided as it is into districts, is bordered on all sides by mountains. Historically, it has been difficult for invaders or adventurers to enter the Valley, or to leave it. Hence, outside influences have, as a general rule, been minimal. With its rich alluvial soil, deposited by the vast lake said to have existed in pre-historic times, Kashmir is fertile and its plethora of lakes and rivers ensure that water is abundant. Rice is the chief crop, and is not only eaten at every meal but finds its way into proverbs and aphorisms. The word for rice in Kashmiri, *batta,* is also the word for meal, and is indicative of the position that the grain plays in the mind-space of the people. The kind of rice preferred in the Valley is dense and short-grained: a far cry from the long-grained basmati of the Doon valley. The rice grown in tracts of the Kashmir Valley is prized more than any other, with a few kinds, like *mushq budij* (fragrant blossom) with its rich, creamy fragrance being the most highly sought after. However, there is an ever-lengthening gap between the amount of cultivable land and the expanding population and much of the rice consumed in the Valley must be brought in from elsewhere.

While BREADS are eaten at breakfast and with afternoon tea, in the villages of the Valley, where agriculture is the chief occupation, pounded broken uncooked rice is lightly roasted and used to make lacy pancake-like breads that are eaten with tea, so that, although they would be classified as a 'bread', they are, in fact, made from rice. More interesting is that unlike the south of India, where IDLIS, DOSAS, *uttapams, akki roti* and *pathiri,* to name a few breads made from rice, are eaten as snacks or accompaniments, Kashmir has no culture of using rice flour to ferment and make breads. In fact, in the whole of Kashmiri cookery, there is little fermentation anywhere at all, perhaps because of the low temperature: 25°C is the maximum for a couple of months in summer.

The average meal of a Kashmiri household consists of steamed rice accompanied by mutton cooked in a gravy with the vegetable of the day. Thus, meat and POTATOES, meat with peas, meat with TOMATOES and AUBERGINES and so forth. The menu depends on family preference and season. Also, the principles of Ayurveda are unconsciously practised by every traditional family; thus, green *moong* dal is considered cooling, and so is usually cooked with a fistful of pink *masoor* dal to ramp up the warming quotient. Conversely, tomatoes are considered much too cooling to be cooked on their own, so a few CLOVES are added, because 'everyone' knows that the spice with the most heat-inducing properties is the clove.

Mutton is not only the most favoured meat, it is eaten at every meal by all who can afford it. However, it is *wazwan* that is the high point of Kashmiri Muslim cuisine. A multi-course meal always served at weddings and other functions where grandeur is the objective, it is cooked by male members of a tribe of hereditary cooks who slaughter the required number of sheep in situ and cook them in copper pots arranged on wood fires in the host's courtyard. A *wazwan* is a supremely efficient way of using up the meat of a sheep 'from nose to tail' in an array of preparations with varying textures and flavourings. What makes the seven (or more) dishes of a *wazwan* so unforgettable is the freshly slaughtered meat, the expertise of the cooks, and the cooking on wood fires rather than using any other heat source.

At the opposite end of the grandeur scale, and the other area where expertise exists, is baking bread. Every neighbourhood has a few bakeries that do nothing except fire their tandoor oven for a different variety of bread depending on the time of the day. Usually baked with yeast, bread bakers are the 'nuts and bolts' of the baking world. Items from sweet cookies and savoury puffs to shortbread and flaky pastry that are baked in wood-fired ovens display the craft of home-grown pâtissiers working in antediluvian kitchens with outdated yet trustworthy ovens in an area where electricity is often as elusive as moonshine.

Nature has dealt Kashmir a generous hand: it is one of the few places in the world where SAFFRON is cultivated; morels are found at certain altitudes in spring; and though CHILLIES grow in most parts of the sub-continent, those from Kashmir have a deep carmine colour and are not as spicy as they are flavourful. Consequently, the sobriquet 'Kashmir chilli' is used to describe a variety of chillies, no matter where in the country they have been grown. Kashmir also has a large crop of cherries and APPLES, and a smaller crop of strawberries, peaches, PLUMS and APRICOTS.

Jammu. Part of the Union Territory of Jammu and Kashmir, the Jammu region is dramatically different geographically, linguistically and ethnically in each of its districts. For one, the province contains plains with a tropical climate, low foothills with a sub-tropical climate and mountainous regions that are in the temperate zone, and has, therefore, a sharp variation in climate and soil – and thereby crops. Secondly, the ethnic mix in this part of the union territory is far greater than in the Kashmir Valley, with its overwhelming population of native Muslims with a very small migratory population of Bakkarwals. Jammu's population consists of Dogras, Punjabis, displaced Kashmiri Pandits, Hindus who had migrated from Pakistan post-Partition and Muslims including 15 to 20 per cent migratory Gujar and Bakkarwal pastoralists.

Jammu, Doda, Kathua, Ramban, Reasi, Kishtwar, Poonch, Rajouri, Udhampur and Samba districts each have a distinct identity that is in turn a function of its geography and proximity to one neighbouring state or another. Kishtwar, for instance, has a large population of people who trace their ancestry to neighbouring Kashmir and their cuisine is strongly reminiscent of the Valley, whereas Samba abuts Punjab and is influenced by the cuisine of that state. Kathua abuts Punjab and Himachal Pradesh and you'll find traces of the Himachali *madra,* or dal cooked with curd, in that district. Jammu district (the capital of Jammu region is the city called Jammu, or Jammu Tawi) has a high percentage of Dogras who are roughly analogous to the Rajputs of Rajasthan. Dogra cuisine is the defining flavour of the Jammu-Udhampur-Reasi belt: robust, pungent with a characteristic sour thread permeating several of the preparations, both meat and vegetables.

The Dogra speciality, *khatta* meat, is a spicy CURRY made with the trademark combination of CUMIN, FENNEL seeds and coriander seeds pounded together (a combination not usually seen in other parts of the country) and made sour with dried MANGO powder (*aamchur*). *Ambal,* made with TAMARIND, FENUGREEK seeds and red pumpkin, has a sweet-sour appeal. *Auria* is distinctive in that it is fermented in the sun, helped along with a spoonful of MUSTARD seeds ground to a paste and added to curd. After spending around six hours in the sun, the mustard will have aided fermentation and all it needs is a handful of potato wedges sautéed in chilli powder and TURMERIC and mixed in the curd. *Kimb* is a favourite snack during the winter months. Most adults have fond memories of playing in the winter sun on the terrace of their house, while their mother or grandmother assembled the fixings of *kimb:* sections of citron – an intensely flavourful yet sour CITRUS FRUIT, not unlike the pomelo. It has to be mixed with finely pounded coriander, seasoned with SALT and chilli powder, and then smoked with a live coal. Other popular street snacks include taro root steamed and then baked atop a contraption on a cart by the side of the road.

With the soft, smoky taro root, is served a sour CHUTNEY that could be made from MINT or coriander with lemon, tamarind water or POMEGRANATE seeds steeped in water.

Food historians opine that in bygone times, salt was difficult to come by in these regions, including Himachal Pradesh and Uttarakhand. Extremely acidic foods that naturally contained minerals were found to be both nutritionally rich and tasty. Over centuries, the palate has been cultivated for extremely sour preparations. Indeed, the area between Batote and Chainan, in the lower hills is the pomegranate-growing belt of Jammu region. Used principally for *anardana*, the spice made from dried pomegranate seeds, it lends a fruity appeal to whatever it is cooked with. Just the water in which pomegranate seeds are soaked in is used to flavour chutneys and curries. The most famous chutney is the one that accompanies *rajma* (kidney bean). This bean is grown in the temperate climes of Kishtwar (formerly Marwah) and Bhadarwah, each region's produce having its own following. Light years ahead of any other variety of *rajma* throughout the country, it is a prized ingredient and rare is the family in the Jammu Province which does not enjoy *rajma* and rice at Sunday lunch, with a tangy chutney of sliced ONIONS, chopped green chillies and coriander leaves moistened with soaked pomegranate seeds. While the Bakkarwals of Kashmir make a flatbread-like cheese called *moshe kraje*, their counterparts in Jammu fashion one that is like an idli. Far sturdier than its Kashmiri counterpart, *bun kalari* (slathered over with lashings of tangy chutney) is a popular street-side snack.

Marryam Reshii

- Reshii, Marryam H. 'Kashmiri Dishes That Are Fast Disappearing from the Valley'. *NDTV Food*, 28 September 2016. Available online: https://marryamhreshii.com/kashmiri-dishes-that-are-fast-disappearing-from-the-valley/ (accessed 20 April 2022).

JAMUN

Jamun, or *jamoon*, the Indian name for the olive-shaped purple fruit, known elsewhere as *jambolan*, Java plum or black plum, comes from a tall tree *Syzygium cumini* which grows wild in India and much of southeast Asia. *Jamun* also goes by many other names in India such as *jamli, jambul, jambus, kala jamun* or by its Sanskrit name *jambu philanda*. In Tamil, it is known as *naaval pazham* or *nagapazham*.

IBN BATTUTA mentions the *jamun* fruit when on his travels in India in the fourteenth century, writing that the trees were abundant around Delhi and that 'the *jamun* is a small fruit resembling an olive, but sweet'. It does have a sweet taste but is also astringent; it is best rubbed with salt or soaked in salty water before eating and can then be eaten raw. The flesh is pinkish-white in colour, contrasting the dark purple skin which tends to stain the tongue and lips when eaten, albeit temporarily.

The acidic juice of *jamun* was called *raga* by Charaka (see FOOD AND MEDICINE) and it was a beverage permitted for Buddhist monks. Charaka also mentions a wine called *jambu asava* which was made from the ripe fruit. It can also be used for making an attractive purple-coloured, mild-flavoured vinegar called *shirka* (from the Persian word *seerkah*).

Jamun is also good for making jam, preserves, PICKLES and jelly and the juice is good for making syrups and SHERBET. One refreshing summertime treat is *kala khatta* (*kala* means black and *khatta* means tart), a tangy sherbet made from *jamun* syrup with the addition of *kala namak* (black salt) and lemon or lime. This sherbet is generously poured over ice lollies (locally called *golas*) which are crushed ice granules closely pressed together on a wooden stick. Or the *gola* can be plunged into a glass of the *kala khatta* making an intensely flavoured ice cold drink.

In Hinduism it is called the fruit of the Gods and it is said that Lord Rama lived on *jamun* for years after his exile from Ayodhya. The tree and its fruit have a religious significance for both Buddhists and Hindus, the latter believing that the god Krishna holds the fruit in special regard.

Jamun is rich in iron, minerals, vitamins A and C and is considered to have a number of medicinal benefits. The seeds are used in Ayurvedic medicine for digestive ailments. It is said to be good for diabetics and is believed to protect against cancer.

Jamun gives its name to a Bengal sweet delicacy *gulab jamun* (see SWEETS) as it is shaped like a large *jamun* fruit, is almost purplish brown in colour and is served in sugar syrup.

Helen Saberi

- Achaya, K. T. *A Historical Dictionary of Indian Food*. Delhi: OUP, 1998.
- Davidson, Alan. *The Oxford Companion to Food*. 2nd edition. Ed. Tom Jaine. Oxford: OUP, 2006.
- Malhotra, Aanchal. 'Jamun: The Humble Fruit That Holds a Special Place in India's History and Mythology'. *Scroll.in*, 10 June 2016. Available online: https://scroll.in/article/809099/jamun-the-humble-fruit-that-holds-a-special-place-in-indias-history-and-mythology (accessed 18 April 2022).

JHARKHAND

Jharkhand, meaning 'land of shrubs', was formed in the year 2000 by carving out the southern part of the larger state of Bihar. Tribals, called *adivasis* locally and designated as Scheduled Tribes by the Government of India and Indigenous Clans by the United Nations, have formed a significant chunk of local population since pre-Independence days. The state is home to thirty Scheduled Tribes, most of whom live in villages.

Jharkhand has abundant reserves of natural resources such as coal, uranium, mica, iron ore, bauxite and even gold, which should ideally bring prosperity to the region. However, undivided Bihar, including modern-day Jharkhand, always remained economically backwards. In a further strange way though, this lack of progress meant that the native cuisine of Jharkhand remained unadulterated. Certain pockets of Jharkhand did see some massive industrialization in post-Independence India. Some of the notable projects in the public sector, also called 'temples of modern India' by the first Prime Minister, Jawaharlal Nehru, were HEC, MECON, the Bokaro Steel Plant and a few power-generating units. In the private sector, the Tata Group invested in various sectors ranging from steel to heavy vehicles and cement even before Independence. The entire city of Jamshedpur (also called Tatanagar) evolved around the industrial growth triggered and sustained by the Tata Group. This industrialization also brought people from various parts of the country to Jharkhand together with their respective cuisines.

The native food of Jharkhand may be categorized in two ways: the food consumed by the native tribals and the food consumed by the mainstream urban and rural population. The tribal food of Jharkhand remains largely unadulterated and unchanged, defying the usual trend of giving traditional food a modern touch. On the other hand, the mainstream food of Jharkhand has been heavily influenced by that of the neighbouring state of West Bengal and the mother state of Bihar. KOLKATA is the closest major trading and business hub in the eastern region of India and many people from Jharkhand took up occupation in Kolkata and the massive tea gardens beyond that. Culinary influence was therefore a natural corollary of this migration.

The Bengali influence on Jharkhand food can be seen in the use of MUSTARD oil as the preferred cooking medium, the consumption of sweet-water fish and the use of the Bengali *panch phoron*, five-spices, for tempering (see SPICE BOX). *Begun bhaja* (fried AUBERGINE slices) became *baingan bachka* here and Kolkata's favourite breakfast of *kochuri* (deep-fried puffy bread filled with spiced peas) becomes popular as KACHORI-JALEBI in Jharkhand. All Bengali sweetmeats are commonly consumed in Jharkhand too. Influences from Bihar include slow-cooking mutton (without TOMATOES) and the wide use of stone-grounded red CHILLI and TURMERIC paste in cooking.

Turning to tribal food, *usna bhaat*, a very starchy and unpolished RICE variant with thick grains, is a staple across the state. Basmati is not a popular option here. *Usna* rice is used in many forms, including a unique tribal pot-rice preparation called *hadiya*, which means a pot. While making *hadiya*, rice fermented with water using the roots of a local plant called *ranu* for a couple of days first produces a rustic intoxicating drink called *hadiya,* also colloquially referred to as ABCD (meaning Adi-Basi-Cold-Drink) or rice beer. The story of the *hadiya* doesn't end here; the fermented rice is then eaten with raw green chilli and PICKLES with great relish. Another unique dish is *paani bhaat*, which means rice and water: Leftover rice is dunked in cold water and combined with all kinds of fritters, pickles, CHUTNEYS and raw green chilli and ONIONS.

Tribals of Jharkhand are not herbivores. They eat all kinds of meat – goat, sheep, pig and even buffalo. However, the most unique thing about their meat-eating habit is that they eat all their meats with skin as this is considered healthy as well as tasty. For example, a goat is shaved of all its body hair but the meat is cooked with the whole skin left on. Living in jungle-like surroundings, open-pit roasting is a fairly common cooking method amongst the tribals. In certain developed pockets, meat with greasy gravy is fairly customary.

Tribals also eat some not-so-common meats, one being the meat found inside common land snails which they fry. They also make a chutney out of tiny red ants, the inherent acid of which gives this chutney a natural sourness. On occasion of *Tusu,* the biggest tribal festival, this chutney is devoured with a local favourite called *pittha*. *Pittha* is made with thick rice batter, minced meats and spices, spread between two separate *saal* leaves and roasted indirectly over a fire pit. The *saal* leaves do not burn or char but retain heat and cook the stuffed mixture beautifully. Very clearly, the cooking methods of the tribals are versatile: they roast, they fry, they mince, they make CURRIES and even ferment their food.

Among the mainstream populace of Jharkhand, TEA (with a 50:50 mix of water and milk) is the preferred hot drink. Usually flavoured with either bay leaves or green CARDAMOMS, it is a great accompaniment to *nimki*, deep-fried crisps made with refined flour and onion seeds. COFFEE comes a distant second. The frothy milky coffee, for some inexplicable reason, is called an 'expresso' in Jharkhand.

Most of the native evening snacks of Jharkhand are deep-fried. From ubiquitous SAMOSA and *aloo* chop or unique local fritters such as *barra, kachdi, dhooska* or multiple variants of PAKODAS, everything is deep-fried and consumed with chutney, usually made with fresh CORIANDER leaves, GARLIC and green chilli. Jharkhand also has its own version of an extremely versatile tomato salsa called *tamatar* chutney. Red tomatoes are charred over open fire, fork-mashed and mixed with finely chopped onions, garlic, green chilli, coriander leaves and a generous mustard oil emulsion. It is consumed with anything, from *chawal* dal to *KHICHRI* and even the local favourite *sattu paratha*.

Nothing compares to the versatility of puri *bhujiya* in Jharkhand. In the pre-cellular world, when people used to visit each other without any notice or invitation, folklore goes that irrespective of the time of the visit, puri *bhujiya* with mango or red chilli pickle was a must-serve for the guest. Many ladies of the house used to consider it as their saviour at odd hours. A *bhujiya* is any vegetable cooked without gravy while one cooked with gravy is called *tarkari* or *sabzi*. Another similar mass trend here is to cook *khichri* for lunch every Saturday.

Most chaats in Jharkhand, from *phuchka* to *aloo tikiya*, are also largely influenced by Bengal but *aloo* cut is perhaps unique to Jharkhand. Thinly sliced boiled potatoes, sprinkled with hand-pounded roasted red chilli and CUMIN powder, SALT, rock salt, and a fair sprinkling of TAMARIND juice is simplicity at its very best.

While *litti chokha* is perhaps the most famous culinary export from undivided Bihar, Jharkhand has its own unique version. Carnivores here have the *litti* with slow-cooked spicy mutton, simply called 'meat'. 'Meat' is also eaten with *papdi*, soft and extremely thin pancakes made with rice flour; this *papdi* can also be had with cold milk and jaggery (see SUGAR) as a dessert. While *usna* rice is a firm favourite with meat, *dhooska*, a fried savoury dumpling with loads of whole peppercorns, is also hugely popular in some pockets. In terms of preferred meats, mutton and freshwater fish have been the traditional non-vegetarian staples here. Chicken meat started gaining popularity and prominence from the mid-'80s onwards.

While potato is the eternal favourite here, a local varietal of MUSHROOM called *phutka* is a craze in certain pockets of the Chhota Nagpur region of Jharkhand. This is not soft-textured and has a good bite and mouth-feel to it. Available for a very short time at the advent of the monsoons, this sells like hot potatoes and some people rate its popularity ahead of mutton during this period. Another speciality of this region during monsoons is *baans kareel ka bachka*, a pan-seared patty made with a local variant of BAMBOO SHOOTS and rice flour that has its own loyalists. YAM mash, also called *ole ki* chutney here is another unique thing from this side of the woods. Combined with loads of garlic, green chilli, onion seeds and a generous amount of mustard oil, this mash is allowed to mature and pickle to a gentle sourness over a few days before consumption. Legend has it that if you eat it before full maturity, you may suffer from mouth-itch for a while. Another root vegetable, TARO, is fairly popular for breakfast. Called *kacchu ki sabzi*, the gravy is made with yellow mustard and tamarind juice, yellow mustard perhaps being an influence from Bengal. Another Bengali speciality, *ghughni*, also is made differently. While Bengalis uses peas for *ghughni*, Jharkhandi people use black gram.

During the summer, two drinks from Jharkhand stand out. One is *sattu ka sharbat*, which is either sweetened with sugar/jaggery or made savoury with salt, roasted cumin powder, rock salt and lime juice. It is supposed to keep the stomach 'cool' during the summer months. Another is *amjhora*, a drink made with raw mangoes charred over hot coal, pulped and then mixed with salt, hand-pounded red chilli powder, roasted cumin powder, rock salt and a dash of sugar. Served chilled, it is supposed to protect people against heat waves, a common occurrence during summer.

Amongst the festival food of the region, a few things made during *Chhath*, undoubtedly the biggest mass festival here, are very unique. These include *rasiya*, a kind of a rice porridge with generous amount of jaggery; *thekua*, a deep-fried sweet with a long shelf life; and *pedakiya*, a deep-fried dumpling stuffed with sweetened *maawa* or sugar and cardamom infused semolina.

While most Bengali desserts are favourites here, Jharkhand has a few native desserts too. Prominent is *tilkut*, made by hand-pounding a SESAME seed and sugar mix; *kheermohan*, a caramelized version of RASGULLA (but not as soft); *baalushahi*, an extremely rustic dessert made with refined flour and GHEE; *khaaja*, sweetened puff pastry; and *anarasa*, made with rice flour and sesame.

Anurag Khatiar

KACHORI

Kachori (*katchuri/kachauri/kachodi*) are deep-fried spicy, stuffed pastries often described as stuffed puri (see BREADS) and are sometimes compared to samosa. They are a popular STREET FOOD, a snack for lunch boxes and a food for travellers. They are also served for TIFFIN and in the evening can accompany the main meal. Kachoris are often made for special occasions such as weddings (see RITES OF PASSAGE) and for Indian festivals such as Holi and Diwali.

Kachoris are made with a dough usually based on wheat flour and come in different shapes and sizes such as round, crescent, etc. Fillings, which are usually savoury, also vary considerably from region to region. They are usually served with CHUTNEYS such as green chutney and sweet chutney, GARLIC, CHILLI, chaat masala, etc. Some are simply sprinkled with lemon juice.

Dal kachoris are common, with yellow *moong* dal being the most popular. The latter are known as *khasta* kachori, *khasta* meaning flaky. They are a favourite street food in MUMBAI and DELHI. *Matar* kachoris are stuffed with spicy green peas and are often served for special occasions such as weddings, holidays, etc. *Aloo* kachori, made with spiced POTATOES, are popular for picnics and travelling. *Pyaaz* kachoris are stuffed with an ONION mixture. *Makkai* kachori are made with a wheat dough mixed with chapati flour and a small amount of fine cornmeal and stuffed with spiced fresh CORN.

Rajasthan is famous for its kachoris. Kota kachoris, named after the city of Kota, are renowned for their spicy flavour with a distinct smell of *hing* (ASAFOETIDA). They are sold in small street side shops all over the city and people enjoy them for breakfast, as a midday or evening snack, and also serve them at social gatherings. *Radhaballabhi* kachoris are made with flat rounds of dough (like small thick puris) and stuffed with spicy PULSES (split *urad* dal or *toovar* dal). When fried, they puff up like a balloon but then deflate and become soft. They are popular in North India in the cold winter months. *Lilva* kachoris are also popular in the winter season. They are stuffed with *toovar* dal and *lilva* beans (a type of green bean) and spiced with GINGER and green CHILLIES. Raj kachoris are so-called because they are king-sized.

Fillings can also be sweet. *Besan* kachoris are stuffed with a sort of chickpea fudge containing finely chopped dried fruits and nuts such as APRICOTS, DATES, figs, prunes, APPLES, walnuts, cashews, almonds and pistachios. Jodhpur is famous for its slightly sweet *mawa* kachoris. *Mawa* is another name for *KHOYA* (dried unsweetened condensed milk). The kachoris are stuffed with a mix of *mawa* and dried fruits and, after being deep-fried, are dipped in SUGAR syrup. They are sometimes called '*gujjias*' and are a special sweet treat for the Holi Festival. There is even a healthy baked version of kachori. The pastry, made with wheat flour and cornflour, is stuffed with yellow *moong* dal and spices including *methi* (FENUGREEK) and baked instead of being deep-fried.

Helen Saberi

- Devi, Yamuna. *The Art of Indian Vegetarian Cooking*. London: Leopard Books, 1995.
- TarlaDalal.com. 'Famous Indian Kachoris: Full of Fun and Surprises', 31 July 2020. Available online: https://www.tarladalal.com/article-famous-indian-kachoris-11 (accessed 18 April 2022).

KANJI

Kanji is a popular preparation throughout India. *Kanjis* are mostly grain-based and can be made as a drink or served like porridge. In its simplest form, the cooking liquid of grains (typically RICE) is called *kanji*. The practice of making and consuming *kanji* deeply represents a region's cultural and agricultural diversity. Fermentation is essential in many *kanji*, while others are served warm as healing, festive or simple meals or as weaning foods. There are four different types of *kanji*:

Fermented *kanji*, is most commonly consumed in North India as a probiotic drink. A starter of MUSTARD paste, TURMERIC and SALT is blended in water and fermented for up to a week. In the winter, this drink is made with seasonal black CARROT juice. Occasionally, the vessel's walls are smoked (*dhungar*) before fermentation to give the *kanji* a complex aroma. *Kanji* is also a popular street food in North India during winter. Small fried VADAS of *moong* dal, or black lentils (see PULSES), and FENNEL seeds may be added to a *kanji* to make *kanji* vada.

Cooked grain, fermented *kanji* may sometimes be allowed to become alcoholic. While many rice beers and liquors in India use cooked and fermented rice, *sunda kanji* of Tamil Nadu is perhaps the only one still referred to as a *kanji*. Yogurt is added to it and it is served with fried FISH.

Cooked grain, fermented, served reheated *kanji* uses leftover rice, covered with water and fermented overnight and sometimes up to a few days. The starch from the cooked grain may also be drained and allowed to ferment. Such preparations are widespread throughout the southern peninsula, where rice is an important grain. Known as *pakhala* in Odiya, *pazhayadhu* in Tamil Nadu, *pazhyankanji* in Kerala, *tangalanna* in Karnataka and *sheelen sheeth* along the Konkan, they pair with shallots, salt and CHILLIES, and, sometimes, dried fish or leftovers from the previous day for a refreshing breakfast.

In Odisha, women celebrate Kanji Anla in the lunar month of Mrigashirsha, and a unique rice-based *torani kanji* made with vegetables, *AMLA* and dried fish is served as an offering to the deity and eaten as *prasad* (see TEMPLE FOOD). The sour flavour from the fermentation is essential here and maybe supplemented with sour yogurt, sour BUTTERMILK or dry MANGO (*ambila* in Odia). The drained starch from cooked rice forms the base for *torani kanji*, *patra kanji* (with greens like AMARANTH) and *pariba kanji* (with mixed vegetables); all use buttermilk for added sourness.

Cooked grain *kanji* are perhaps the most significant category and refer to warm porridge. Grain-based flours like finger millet (*ragi kanji*), rice (*arisi kanji*), flours of tubers like CASSAVA and its derivative tapioca, or a blend of many PULSES, legumes and NUTS are cooked in water or milk until the starches thicken to create a thick porridge. Whole grains like lentils and rice are also cooked together like porridge and consumed without fermentation. In Kerala and Tamil Nadu, cooked *moong* dal and rice (*payaru kanji*), broken WHEAT often cooked with milk (*godhumba kanji*), black lentils spiced with dried GINGER (*ulunthu kanji*) and semolina (*thari kanji*) are the main variations.

Hindus in Kerala celebrate the lunar month of Karkadakam with a *karakadaka oushadha kanji* with herbs like AJOWAN, black pepper (see PEPPER, BLACK), FENNEL, nutmeg (see NUTMEG AND MACE) and FENUGREEK added to cooked red *matta* rice. Some families may add Ayurvedic electuaries (*choornam*) instead to the rice *kanji*. Vishu Kani festival is marked with a *vishu kanji* made with rice and beans like *moong*, adzuki or asparagus beans cooked with coconut milk and jaggery (see SUGAR).

Kerala and Tamil Nadu Muslims also break their fast during Ramadan with *nombu kanji*, made from broken rice and seasoned with shallots, spices and herbs. In Gujarat, broken rice is cooked similarly and served as *ghesh* or *kamod ni kanki*, *kothmir marcha ni kanki* or *kanji* with a chutney of coriander and chillies. In Goa, *atwal* or *methi pez*, a *kanji* of rice and fenugreek cooked with jaggery and coconut milk, is widespread. PARSIS prepare *badam ne magaz nu kanji* with almonds and melon seed meal and milk, and *sookha singhora ni kanji* with water chestnut flour and milk. They also prepare a *raabri* or *kanji masala*, a floured blend of LOTUS root, water chestnuts, almonds and spices like black pepper, white pepper and dried ginger. This is cooked with milk and served warm as a healing food.

Priya Mani

- Sheetal. ‘Ghesh – The Gujarati Congee’. *theroute2roots*, 17 January 2020. Available online: https://www.theroute2roots.com/ghesh-the-gujarati-congee/ (accessed 19 April 2022).
- Trotter, Tarani. ‘From Pakhala to Pitha – The Saga of Odia Food’. *BBSR Pulse*, 25 August 2018. Available online: http://bbsrpulse.com/2018/07/kanji-the-odia-appetizer/ (accessed 19 April 2022).

KARNATAKA

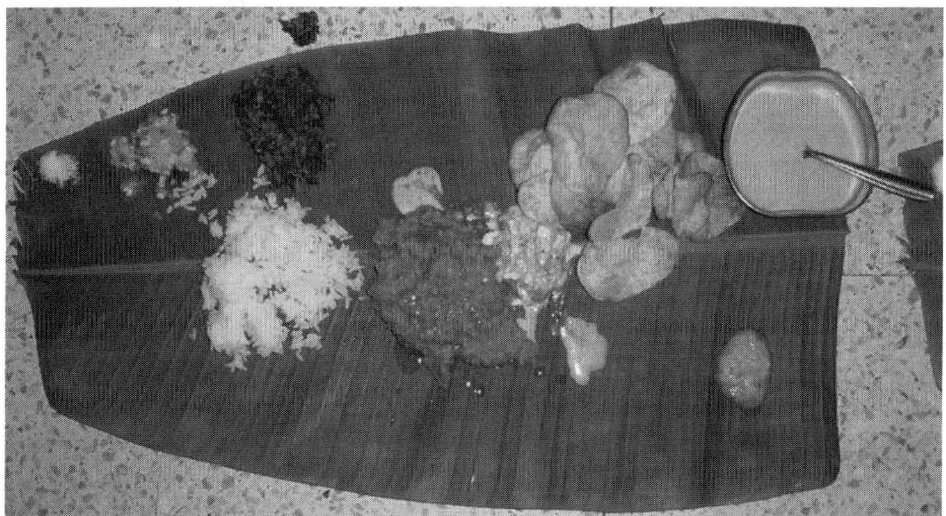

FIGURE 24 KARNATAKA. Lunch on a banana leaf. Wikimedia Commons.

Located in the western part of the Deccan Peninsula on a plateau edged by the hills of the Western Ghats, Karnataka shares borders with Maharashtra and Goa in the north and northwest, Kerala and Tamil Nadu in the south, Telangana in the northeast and Andhra Pradesh in the east. Its western borders are delineated by the Arabian Sea. With an estimated population of 6.11 crores (61.13 million), it is the sixth largest state in India with a diverse geography and climate.

Extensive excavations at Palaeolithic, Neolithic and Megalithic sites indicate a long, rich pre-history in the region distinct from what prevailed in the north of the country. *Ragi* (finger MILLET) was commonly found across pre-historic sites. In addition, paddy, *huruli* (horse gram; see PULSES), WHEAT and the remains of domesticated animals – cows, goats, sheep and dogs – have been unearthed. Early recorded history from Ashokan rock edicts (*c*.272–232 BCE) indicates a Mauryan presence and the influence of Buddhism and Jainism in northern parts of present-day Karnataka. Successive powerful dynasties in the region held extensive territory, including parts of the present-day neighbouring states, bringing in multiple cultural and culinary influences. The Deccan Sultanates introduced distinctive elements of Persian and Turkish culture. The great kingdom of Vijayanagara had thriving ports including MANGALURU, Barkur, Bhatkal and Honavar trading with Europe and Persia, enabling a rich exchange of goods and ideas. Southern Karnataka was also influenced by Jainism. This tremendous mix and movement of peoples and cultures generated rich and diverse local foodways. Mysore State, created from the erstwhile Royal State of Mysore in 1956 CE, was renamed Karnataka in 1973 CE.

The regions that comprise modern Karnataka have a strong tradition of agriculture. Literary and epigraphical sources reference rich RICE fields, COCONUT, areca nut plantations, plantains (see BANANA) and the production of *ragi* (finger millet) and *jowar* (sorghum). Domingo Paes, the Portuguese traveller who visited Vijayanagara in the first half of the sixteenth century, noted the cultivation of Indian CORN, rice and beans. The proximity of Goa meant Portuguese imports of maize, tobacco, groundnut, CHILLIES and TOMATOES were early entrants into the region.

Cereal crops – paddy, *ragi* (finger millet), *jowar* (sorghum), maize, wheat, *bajra* (pearl millet) and pulses such as *toovar* dal (pigeon peas) and Bengal gram, as well as groundnut and sunflower, important oilseed crops, are grown in the drier northern districts of modern Karnataka. *Ragi* predominates in Tumkur, Kolar, Chitradurga, Hassan and Mysore. Paddy is grown in Dakshina Kannada and Uttara Kannada as well as other southern and coastal districts. Mandya and North Karnataka grow sugarcane. Coconut, areca nut, MANGOES, grapes, sapota and CITRUS FRUITS are important fruit crops. COFFEE is a valuable crop in Kodagu and Chikmagalur. Pepper (see PEPPER, BLACK), CARDAMOM and vanilla are grown in Kodagu, Chikmagalur and the Malnad region; the popular, mildly, spiced Byadagi chillies come from the eponymous town in Haveri.

Karnataka has numerous sheep, cattle and poultry breeding farms, as well as dairy farms. Its 320 kilometres of coastline and various inland water resources provide employment to about 9.62 lakh fishermen, and the state is a major exporter and supplier of FISH, fish meal and fish oil.

Coastal Karnataka is an intricate mosaic of distinct communities and religions with an ancient history of maritime trade with the Mediterranean and the Persian Gulf. The food of the region draws on abundant local produce such as red rice; coconuts; fish, both fresh and dried; clams; mussels; JACKFRUIT; TARO leaves; *ambade* (wild hog plum); *gulla* (Udupi green AUBERGINE); *suvarnagedde* (YAM); and *tendili* (ivy GOURD). Different communities use the produce with minor variations in flavourings and methods of preparation.

Kokum (*Garcinia indica*), *bimbli* (*Averrhoa bilimbi*), TAMARIND, star fruit and raw mangoes are local souring agents. Coconut oil is a common cooking medium.

The Tulu-speaking Bunts are Hindus and an ancient farming and land-owning community; their name drawn from the Tulu word for 'warrior' indicating a military past. Bunt cuisine is extensive, and has been popularized in cities like MUMBAI by entrepreneurs who serve typical Bunt dishes in well-known restaurants. Rice is a staple, served boiled with CURRIES; as dosas (fermented rice crepes) and *neer* dosas (thin, lacy unfermented crepes made with soaked and ground rice, water and SALT); a selection of steamed rice cakes: *kotte kadubu* (steamed in jackfruit leaf cups) and *moode* (cylindrical rice cakes in palm leaf cups); and *pundi* (rice dumplings made from soaked, ground and cooked rice with coconut, steamed into round dumplings). The use of jackfruit, TURMERIC, screwpine and other leaves as wrappers adds distinctive aromas to various dishes. *Pundi* is a typical breakfast dish, served with coconut CHUTNEY, a curry or sweetened with jaggery.

Kori gassi (chicken curry) in a thick gravy, eaten with *neer* dosa or *kori rotti* (lacy rice crisps made from soaked and ground rice, spread wafer thin on a hot griddle and cooked crisp) are typical Bunt dishes. Chicken ghee roast uses ample quantities of GHEE and a marinade of curd, jaggery and *Kundapura masala* – named after the coastal town – made from toasted and ground Byadagi chillies, CUMIN seeds, CORIANDER seeds, FENUGREEK seeds, whole black peppercorns, dehydrated garlic and turmeric powder. Seafood features prominently in the cuisine, with dishes such as *yetti ajadina* (fried prawns in a coarsely ground blend of spices, coconut, tomatoes, GARLIC, chillies and ONIONS), *sunkat amtekai ambat* (prawns with hog plums) and *bangde pulimunchi* (spicy-sour curry of mackerel, flavoured with tamarind, Byadagi chillies and other spices). Local vegetables feature in dishes such as *tendli bibba upkari* (stir-fried ivy gourd and cashew nuts), *gulla huli* or *gulla bolu koddel* (lentils with local green aubergines). Sweets include *ragi manni* (an extract of soaked and ground finger millet cooked with coconut milk and palm jaggery, flavoured with cardamom and ghee, poured into a greased tray to set), *chiroti* (layered, flaky pastry semolina discs deep-fried and served with sweetened almond milk), *holige* (flatbreads filled with jaggery, lentils and coconut) and *kashi* HALWA (grated ash pumpkin cooked with ghee, sugar, raisins and cashew nuts).

Mangalorean Catholics are descended from the Konkani-speaking Christians who migrated from Goa, fleeing the Portuguese Inquisition and regional wars (*c.*1560–1762 CE) and carrying distinct elements of their cuisine, to which they added local dishes and ingredients. *Sannas* (steamed rice cakes made from parboiled rice, coconut and toddy to ferment the batter), *dukra maas* (pork cooked with whole spices and *bafat* masala), *kalleze kadi* (a curry of sheep offal, including heart, lungs and liver), *rosachi kadi* (coconut milk-based fish curry) are a few typical dishes. Chicken *indad* is a spicy, tangy dish made slightly sweet by the addition of jaggery or DATES, after the Portuguese vindaloo.

Pollu (lentils) cooked with *galmbi* (powdered dried fish) or *kambulmas* (dried tuna); *pathal bakri*, a version of *kori rotti*; and monsoons specials such as *pathrode* (taro leaves smeared with a batter of soaked and ground rice and spices and fried or steamed) are elements of local cuisine that run across cultures. Vegetable dishes include *kulta kaat* (pumpkin with horse gram) and ash pumpkin pulao. *Kuswar* refers to a range of Christmas snacks such as *neuries* (deep-fried crescent-shaped pastry cases stuffed with raisins, nuts and toasted sesame), *kidiyo* (deep-fried sweetened, pastry curls) and rose cookies (a metal mould dipped in a batter of flour, coconut milk, egg and sugar is lowered into very hot oil to make crisp fried cookies).

Gaud Saraswat Brahmins, Konkani-speaking Hindus, are thought to have migrated from the region of Gomantak, Goa during the fourteenth to sixteenth century, fleeing religious persecution. Rice, fish, coconuts, local vegetables, greens and lentils form the basis of their cuisine. Fish and seafood are regarded as 'vegetables', although meat is proscribed. Tamarind, *dharbe sol* (a variety of *Garcinia cambogia*) and star fruit are common souring agents. ASAFOETIDA and *teppal*, similar to *tirphal* (*Zanthoxylum rhetsa*), fresh and dried, are commonly used in cooking fish and vegetables. *Undi* (rice dumplings) or *polo* (rice crepes) with *tambali* (chutney) or SAMBAR (spiced lentil curry) are eaten at breakfast. *Surnali*, a soft spongy crepe made from soaked rice ground with *poha* (beaten rice), coconut and a few fenugreek seeds, fermented overnight, is a breakfast special. *Sheeth* (rice); *teeksani umman* (spicy mixed vegetable curry); *dhavi gassi* (coconut based spicy gravy), *dali toye* (thin lentil soup), *nonche* (salt pickled vegetables) and *appol* (rice or lentil crisps) make a typical lunch. Other Konkani dishes include *vali ambat* (Mangaluru spinach in lentils and coconut), *kadale ambat* (spicy curry of black chickpeas) and *nagli ambat* (ladyfish curry with coconut, spices and tamarind). *Sol kadi* (coconut milk flavoured with an extract of dried, soaked segments of *Garcinia indica*) is a popular drink along the coast.

Koshambari (soaked and seasoned green *moong* lentils), *manoli ajadina* (ivy gourd with cashew nuts), *maavinkai menaskai* (preserved mango curry), *haagalkkai kabbu saaru* (curried bitter gourd and sugarcane) and *avalakki payasa* (sweetened beaten rice cooked in milk) are typical vegetarian Havyaka Brahmin dishes. The vegetarian cuisine of Udupi, drawn from local ingredients and cooking techniques, can be found in popular restaurants across the country and the globe (see UDUPI RESTAURANTS).

The Bearys, a community engaged predominantly in trade, are believed to be some of the earliest Muslim inhabitants in India, located mainly in Dakshina Kannada. Their cuisine, heavily influenced by local foods and ingredients, is nevertheless distinctive. *Pinde* (steamed rice dumplings), similar to *pundi* in Bunt cuisine, is cooked in innovative ways, such as *erichiro pinde* (rice dumplings stuffed with meat). *Nei pattiri* (soaked and ground rice with coconut, onion and cumin cooked into a flatbread) is similar to the MAPPILA *nei pathal*. *Pulcho pole* is a lacy rice crepe made with fermented batter. The best-known dish is Beary biryani, cooked with beef or goat, subtly flavoured with FENNEL seeds, mace, star anise, nutmeg (see NUTMEG AND MACE) and SAFFRON amongst other ingredients.

Bhatkal, an important port on the West coast from the eight to the fifteenth century in Uttara Kannada, is home to the Navayaths, who are believed to be of Arab origin. *Poli* (wheat flatbreads) such as masala *poli* (spiced flatbreads), *puttus* (steamed rice cakes) and *thalla shayyo* (vermicelli) are breakfast staples. Fish and rice, as across the coastal region, are lunch staples – like *ekshiippi* (coconut-based clam curry) and *mudkuley* (rice and coconut balls cooked in a thick gravy of prawns). Chicken and meat are also popular, such as *kukdi maas* (fried chicken) and mutton *sharwo maas* (mutton curry). Other specialities include *saakuche* (mixed vegetables cooked with coconut milk), *haldipana nevari* (savoury or sweet rice crepes stuffed and steamed in turmeric leaves), *shinonya nevari* (steamed rice cakes with mussels, coconut and spices), *raithe* (chilli, tamarind and tomato-based curry with PAPAYA, breadfruit and sweet potato), *kadang* (sweet potato fritters) and sweet *payasams* such as *godan* made with jaggery, coconut milk and a variety of ingredients: *amatya godan* (with hog plums), *shayya godan* (with vermicelli) and *faua godan* (with puffed rice).

The highland regions of Malnad and Kodagu (see KODAVAS) in the Western Ghats, rising up from the coastal plains, make use of limited seasonal forest produce such as tender BAMBOO SHOOTS and MUSHROOMS in their cuisines.

The royal city of Mysore in the southern plateau region favours a predominantly vegetarian tradition. *Uppitu* (semolina roasted and cooked with vegetables), *shavige bhaat* (string hoppers, spiced vegetables), and the iconic *Mysuru* or *Mylari* masala dosa (rice crepes with spiced potato filling) are breakfast dishes. *Saarina podi* is a spice blend of slow-roasted black gram, coriander seeds, cumin seeds, black peppercorns, turmeric root and additional spices ground into a powder. A typical lunch includes rice and *huli saaru* (thick curry of lentils, vegetables and tamarind), *thilli saaru* (clear lentil soup, tomatoes and *saarina podi*), *gojju* (vegetable-based curry, flavoured with tamarind and *saarina podi*), *palya* such as *gorikkai palya* (cluster beans, Bengal gram and spices), *kosambari* (soaked and tempered green mung beans). *Chitranna* (rice flavoured with lime juice, tempered with dried red chillies, MUSTARD seeds, peanuts, CURRY LEAVES and split and skinned black gram lentils) is eaten at breakfast or lunch. MYSORE *PAK* (made from gram flour, ghee and sugar) and *bisi bele bhaat* (rice cooked with pigeon peas, spices, asafoetida, tamarind and vegetables) are believed to have originated in the Palace kitchens.

The farming community of Gowdas in the Mandya, Hassan and Maddur region draw mainly on the produce of their fields for their cuisine. *Ragi* roti (finger millet flatbreads) and *uchellu* chutney (toasted niger seed chutney); *idlis* (fermented and steamed rice and lentil cakes) with *koli saaru* (chicken curry in a thin, soupy gravy) are some breakfast dishes. Emblematic of the cuisine is *ragi mudde* (slow-cooked, dense finger millet balls) with *basaaru* (an extract of lentils cooked with fresh greens). For *basaaru*, the stock is drained (*basida*), greens tempered and served separately. Leafy greens and vegetables such as *masoppu* (mashed spiced greens) and *masekai* (mashed spiced vegetables) feature prominently. Winter beans, *avarekal*, are cooked into *hitakida bele saaru* (hyacinth beans and lentils). *Boti gojju* (lamb intestines with hyacinth beans, coconut, ginger, garlic, spices and onions), *naati koli saaru* (country chicken in a thin curry), *thale mamsa saaru* (goat's head curry) and *Bannur kuri mamsa* (mutton curry) are some well-known meat dishes. Bannur sheep from Bannur district and regions bordering Mysore is an old breed valued for its tender meat and fat. *Majjige* (spiced buttermilk) and *ragi ambli* (spiced finger millet drink) are common drinks. Gowda cuisine is very popular in tiny eateries known as 'military hotels' referring to the meat dishes that feature on limited menus.

The fourteen districts of Uttara Karnataka are part of the Deccan plateau, a predominantly drought-tolerant sorghum-growing belt with a cuisine distinct from the coastal and southern areas. *Jolada rotti* (sorghum flatbreads), *ennegai badanekayi* (aubergines stuffed with fried and ground peanuts, coconut and spices, cooked into a thick gravy), *gulagayi yenagai* (country cucumber fry), *hesarukaalu palya* (stir-fried mung beans) and *majjige saaru* (BUTTERMILK-based curry) are typical foods. A selection of protein-rich *pudis* (spiced, powdered condiments) such as *ucchelu pudi* (niger seeds), *shenga pudi* (groundnut) and *agasi pudi* (flax seed) are served with meals. Wheat is an important grain, made into flatbreads or *kuchida kadabu* (steamed dumplings). *Southe bija huggi* is a sweet that gets its name from wheat dough that is hand rolled into cucumber seed-like shapes. DHARWAD *PEDHA* (reduced milk and sugar sweet) has a GI tag. *Mandige* (crepe filled with reduced milk solids, sugar and ghee) and *antin unde* (sweet balls made with gum Arabic, jaggery, coconut, dried fruits and NUTS) are popular sweets. The influence of the twelfth-century poet and social reformer, Basavanna, is reflected in the VEGETARIANISM prevalent amongst his followers, the Lingayats.

The proximity of neighbouring states like Andhra Pradesh, however, brings in robust meat dishes such as *dalcha* (meat and lentils). Saoji cuisine, well established in nearby Maharashtra, – meat-focused and spicy, ascribed to the migrations from Malwa, Madhya Pradesh, in the twelfth century – is also present in Uttara Karnataka.

Cookbooks such as *Mangalorean Cuisine* by Saranya Hegde, *Cuisine from Karnataka* by Ranee Vijaya Kuttaiah, *Gowd Saraswat Brahmin's Cookbook* by Annapoorna R. Nayak and Maya Shenoi, and *Mangalore Ladies Club Cookery Book* document cuisines by region. Popular blogs also document community cuisines: udupi-recipes.com covers the Udupi area, justhomemade.net explores Mysore Iyengar food, kaveriponnapa.com/coorg-table.html documents Kodava foodways, ruchikrandhap.com covers Mangalorean Catholic foods and aayisrecipes.com/my-favorite-konkani-recipes-top-10/ has Konkani recipes.

Bunt cuisine has gained great popularity through successful restaurants such as Trishna and Fountain Inn in Mumbai. Karavalli, the award-winning, internationally renowned Bengaluru restaurant features multiple dishes from the West Coast, including Karnataka. Chef Sriram Aylur presents modern interpretations of South-West coastal Indian cuisine at the Michelin starred Quilon restaurant in London. Oota restaurant in Bengaluru has a wide representation of dishes from across Karnataka, particularly the lesser-known foods of the North. Bengaluru, Karnataka's capital, has seen a surge of migrations driven by the thriving IT industry, and such restaurants reflect the growing interest in local cuisines in recent years.

Kaveri Ponnapa

- Chittaranjan, H. ed. *A Handbook of Karnataka*. Bangalore: Government of Karnataka, 2005.
- Kamath, Dr. Suryanath U. *A Concise History of Karnataka*. Bangalore: MCC Publications, 2001.
- Kuttaiah, Ranee Vijaya. *Cuisine from Karnataka*. New Delhi: Sterling Publications, 2014.
- Ponnapa, Kaveri. 'The Making of an Icon'. *Sommelier India* 15, no. 1 (January–March 2019). Available online: https://www.sommelierindia.com/karavalli-a-bengaluru-restaurant-icon. (accessed 30 October 2022).
- Prajna, G. R. 'Spectrum: Aromas of the Coast'. *Deccan Herald*, 21 May 2018.

KEBAB

Cooking meat over an open flame is almost as old as the discovery of fire itself and the custom of roasting meat on a skewer seems to be very ancient. The word comes from Arabic *kabāb*, which is related to terms in Aramaic and Akkadian referring to the roasting of meat. From Arabic, it entered several other languages spoken in Islamic countries, including Turkish, Persian and Urdu.

In India roasting marinated meat on spits and basting with fat is described in Sanskrit and Tamil literature. In the ancient Indian epic *Mahabharata*, a picnic meal described 'large pieces of meat being roasted on spits'. The twelfth-century *MANASOLLASA* describes 'pieces of meat, bored, stuffed with spices and roasted on spits' and in the old Tamil literature there is mention of 'hot meats, roasted on the point of spits'. In the fourteenth century, the Moroccan traveller IBN BATTUTA recorded that chicken kebab was being served by royal houses in India.

Today, kebab usually means any food threaded on a skewer and grilled. But it can also describe any type of meat which is grilled, barbecued, cooked in the oven or fried. It can range from a whole baby lamb baked in a tandoor to ground meat formed into patties

FIGURE 25 KEBAB. *Shami* kebabs. Anil Risal Singh.

FIGURE 26 KEBAB. *Seekh* kebabs. Anil Risal Singh.

or sausage shapes. In India the kebabs' relative ease of preparation makes them ideal candidates for street food, since all that is needed is a grill and wood or charcoal. They are usually served with BREAD, such as naan or paratha, and dipping sauces or CHUTNEYS. The vendors are often Muslim, and in cities like DELHI and HYDERABAD, kebabs are sold outside mosques. The common meats are lamb, goat, chicken and beef (although the latter is avoided by most Hindus). Spicing can be intense and include garlic, ginger and aromatic spices such as CARDAMOM and CLOVES.

***Boti* kebabs** are chunks of meat marinated in yogurt, spices and herbs, threaded on a metal or wooden skewer and roasted over charcoal.

Tikka/*tikki* kebabs (tikka meaning 'bit' or 'pieces') can take several forms. Small chunks of meat or chicken which have been marinated, usually in an acidulating ingredient such as lemon juice or yogurt with some spices, are threaded onto skewers, brushed with clarified butter and cooked either in a tandoor oven or over coals. PANEER tikka are cubes of hard cheese marinated in spices and lemon juice, threaded on skewers and grilled.

***Seekh* kebabs** (*seekh* meaning skewer) are made from spiced ground lamb or goat, moulded into a sausage shape on long skewers and grilled over coals. They are sometimes called kofta kebabs.

Kakori kebabs are a Lucknow speciality coming from the small town of Kakori near Lucknow. Meat and fat are pounded for a long time until the mixture becomes paste-like. Ground spices are added and the paste pounded some more with a little water sprinkled on until it becomes almost gluey in texture. The paste is then deftly wrapped around skewers into a sausage shape and grilled quickly over hot charcoal. These kebabs are not easy to make but the end result is a kebab which has a slightly crisp outside and is meltingly soft on the inside.

***Galouti* kebab** is another speciality of Lucknow. It first originated in the kitchen of one of Lucknow's famous Nawabs, Asaf-ud-Daula, who was known for his love of kebabs. *Galouti* means 'soft' or something that melts in the mouth. Made with minced lamb which is marinated in papaya for several hours, then richly spiced and the mixture is then kneaded until it becomes like a paste. The mixture is formed into round patties before being fried in *ghee*. Another popular kebab in Lucknow is **Tunday kebab** (or Tunde *ke* kebab, also known as buffalo meat *galouti* kebab). It is the same as *galouti* kebab but made with buffalo meat and the addition of numerous spices and flavourings including SAFFRON and rosewater (see FLOWER WATERS).

***Shami* kebab** is also fried. It is a disc-shaped patty resembling a hamburger made of spiced ground meat, ONIONS, spices and cooked *chana* dal beaten (or kneaded) until it is light and airy. Another fried kebab is ***chapli* kebab** that may have originated in Peshawar. The name comes either from Pushto *chapleet*, meaning 'flat', or from *chappal*, Hindi for sandal, alluding to its shape. It is made with ground meat with onion, seasoned with CHILLIES and spices, kneaded until smooth, then formed into a large flat oval (or round) shape before being fried.

Indian workers returning from the Middle East have introduced ***shawarma***. Shaved lamb, goat or chicken are compressed on a rotating spit, grilled and sliced off as needed. The meat is placed on a flatbread and topped with chutney or ketchup.

A local Kolkata speciality popular all over India is the *kathi*/*kati* roll, invented in the 1930s at Nizam's restaurant in Calcutta. The original version was made by roasting pieces of meat on skewers, then sautéing them with onions and red chilies, and finally wrapping the meat in a paratha with various chutneys, spices and sauces. Today, *kati* rolls can contain vegetables, egg, chicken or potatoes. They are wrapped in wax paper and eaten on the go and are a favourite of students.

Colleen Sen and Helen Saberi

- Davidson, Alan. *The Oxford Companion to Food*. 2nd Edition. Ed. Tom Jaine. Oxford: OUP, 2006.
- Jaffrey, Madhur. *A Taste of India*. London: Pan Books, 1985.

KEDGEREE

Kedgeree is an old Anglo-Indian dish which evolved from KHICHRI. During the British Raj, this RICE and lentil dish was modified by the British to suit their tastes. The lentils (see PULSES) were replaced by smoked FISH and hard-boiled eggs came into the picture. Jennifer Brennan in *Curries and Bugles* (1992) gives a perfectly feasible explanation of how this may have come about:

> It is entirely possible that the *sahibs*, with their predilection for smoked fish at breakfast, and particularly their beloved kippers – brought out on slow ships from England at great expense – insisted that the cooks incorporate it into the *khichri*. Whatever the moment or method of birth, we are the benefactors, for a kedgeree, tumbled with chunks of smoked or fresh fish, gilded with crumbled or sliced egg yolks and blessed with a benediction of crisp-fried onions and pungent parsley, has to be one of the nicest ways to break a fast.

Kedgeree became a favourite breakfast dish not just for the British serving in India but also became a staple of English country house breakfasts during Victorian and Edwardian times. Today, while there are many variations, it is usually spiced with TURMERIC and cream is sometimes added for extra richness.

Colleen Sen and *Helen Saberi*

- Brennan, Jennifer. *Curries and Bugles: A Cookbook of the British Raj*. London: Penguin, 1992.
- Saberi, Helen and Colleen Taylor Sen. *Turmeric: The Wonder Spice*. E-book edition. Chicago: Agate Publishing, 2014.

KERALA

Located in the southwest corner of India, the origin of the state of Kerala came in 1949 when the Travancore and Kochi kingdoms were merged to form the state of Travancore-Cochin. In 1956, it was merged with some parts of Madras to form the predominantly Malayalam-speaking state of Kerala. It is a small state, constituting only about 1 per cent of the total area of the country and has one of the highest population densities, but it also has the highest literacy rate in India because of its advanced educational system and, especially, the widespread education of women.

Today, more than half of Malayalis are Hindus, another fourth are Muslims, and around a fifth are Christians. The latter belong to different denominations, including, Roman Catholic and various Protestant denominations. The Jewish community has almost disappeared because of immigration to Israel although a few synagogues remain. For the food habits of different communities, see MAPPILAS, NAIRS, PALGHAT AYERS, AND SYRIAN CHRISTIANS. Kerala has one of the lowest rates of vegetarianism, less than 1 per cent.

The state extends for some 580 km (360 miles) along the Arabian Sea and thus has been exposed to many foreign influences. The region supplied pepper (see PEPPER, BLACK) and other spices to the Greeks and Romans in Classical times and these contacts may have led to the introduction of Western religions. According to local tradition, in the first century CE Jews arrived, St. Thomas the Apostle visited Kerala in the same century. Arab traders introduced Islam starting in the eighth century. They were followed by the Dutch and then the Portuguese who brought the Catholic religion (and the Inquisition) to India.

The state is famous for its beautiful scenery, earning it the sobriquet 'God's Own Country'. The coast is lined with COCONUT palms while the Western Ghats and riverine areas are covered with rainforests. The upland is covered by rolling grassland. Agriculture is the state's main economic activity. Cash crops include COFFEE, TEA, betel nut, CARDAMOM, cashews, coconut, GINGER and pepper. The main food crops are rice, lentils (see PULSES), sorghum and CASSAVA. Life in Kerala is shaped by its vast numbers of rivers and lakes, and nearly 600 km of Arabian Sea coastline, ensuring an abundance of freshwater fish and seafood. The water conditions are ideal for irrigating rice paddy fields and the temperate climate allows for three growing seasons and a plethora of vegetables, YAMS, GOURDS, fruits and spices – hence its moniker, India's Spice Coast. However, the ingredient that most defines the region's flavourful cuisine is the coconut.

Colleen Sen

KHEER

Kheer (Hindi), *payesh* (Bengali) and *payasam* (Tamil) are the names of sweet dishes made with milk which can be buffalo milk or cow milk. They first find mention in Buddhist-Jain literature *c*. 400 BCE. These dishes are traditionally served at weddings and other special functions or celebrations. In South India (Andhra Pradesh, Tamil Nadu and Kerala) they use the word *payasam*, in Karnataka a version is called *payesa* and in Bengal, *payesh*. In North India it may be called kheer (or *sheer*). The Hindi word *kheer* is derived from the Sanskrit *ksheer* for milk and *kshirika* for a dish prepared with milk.

There are numerous variations and the dish can be made with RICE, *seviyan* (vermicelli, see *SEV* AND *SEVIYAN*), PULSES, semolina or other starchy ingredients sweetened and cooked in milk. Other possible ingredients and flavourings are legion: raisins; NUTS such as cashew, almond and pistachio; CARDAMOM; CINNAMON; SAFFRON; and *kewra* or rosewater (see FLOWER WATERS). It can be served hot or cold. For special occasions the chilled dish may be decorated with edible silver or even gold leaf (see *VARK*). The consistency can also vary from thick to creamy like soup. Many versions use a local variety of rice or some other grain. In Bengal, *payesh* is prepared from a variety of short-grain rice called *atap chal* (sundried rice) and is the first morsel of solid food given to a child during *annaprashana*, the rice-feeding ceremony (see RITES OF PASSAGE). It has also been eaten on the first day of the Bangla New Year for hundreds of years.

Chirupayaru payasam is made with lentils which are cooked with unrefined brown SUGAR (jaggery) then simmered with coconut milk, cardamom and ghee.

This ancient dish has, in recent times, been subject to some experimentation with cooks adding new ingredients such as JACKFRUIT, MANGO, PINEAPPLE and sometimes vegetables such as CARROTS, red pumpkin and bottle GOURD to give the pudding a new twist.

Payasam is an important part of South Indian meals and is also integral to traditional thali meals (see COOKING AND DINING) in restaurants that specialize in South Indian vegetarian meals. *Payasam* is also offered in temples and Hindu rituals.

A version made with rice and cooked with milk, sugar and aromatic spices is prepared for the beginning of the festival of Dussehra, a ten-day festival celebrated all over India to commemorate the victory of the good Prince Rama over the army of the demon Ravana.

Helen Saberi

- Dey, Ishita. 'Payasam'. In *The Oxford Companion to Sugar and Sweets*, edited by Darra Goldstein, 516–17. Oxford: OUP, 2015.

KHICHRI

Khichri (*khichari, khichdi*) is an ancient and popular Indian dish made with rice and lentils (dal, see PULSES) cooked together in water and GHEE (or butter or oil) and flavoured with spices. Sometimes NUTS such as cashews are added. It has many incarnations and every region has its own variations. Various types of lentils can be used and some recipes call for more than one type. Some khichris are made with MILLET. In some parts of India, it is given to invalids to speed their recovery.

The first written reference to this dish was by the fourteenth-century Arab explorer IBN BATTUTA: 'The mung (*moong* dal) is boiled with rice and then buttered. This is what they call Kishri, and on this they breakfast everyday.' Khichri was a popular dish with the MUGHAL emperors. Akbar led an austere existence, ate only once a day, cared little for meat and frequently fasted but khichri was one of his favourite dishes. A recipe given by Abu'l-Fazl, Akbar's prime minister, who was also a great gourmet and kept meticulous records of food eaten at the court, called for equal parts of rice, lentils and ghee, which is not what many would consider an 'austere' dish. The cooks at the court were constantly trying to outdo each other to improve the dish by adding spices, butter, cream, nuts, other flavourings and even meat. Khichri was prepared in vast quantities for the Mughal armies on the move.

A version of khichri from Gujarat called *lazizan*, containing spices and nuts, was Emperor Jahangir's favourite food on his days of abstinence from meat. In LUCKNOW, very elaborate and fanciful versions were made. Almonds were cut to resemble grains of rice and pistachios shaped to look like lentils. The British adopted and adapted khichri as a breakfast dish which became known as KEDGEREE.

Helen Saberi and Colleen Taylor Sen

- Achaya, K. T. *A Historical Dictionary of Indian Food*. Delhi: OUP, 1998.
- Sen, Colleen Taylor. *Food Culture in India*. Westport, CT, and London: Greenwood Press, 2004.

KHOYA

Khoya (*khoa*, also called *mawa*) is the name for the milk solids made by simmering full-fat milk for several hours while stirring until the water evaporates. It is white or pale yellow in colour and used mainly in making sweets, especially in North India. There are several types, depending on the moisture content such as *batti*, or rock *khoya*, which has 20 per cent moisture; *pindi*, which is drier and used in making BARFI and *peda*; and the even drier *dhap* used to make *gulab jamun* and *pantua* (see SWEETS). Buffalo milk with a higher fat content (7 to 8 per cent) yields a softer smoother *khoya* than cow milk (4 to 5 per cent fat). *Khoya* is also used to stuff parathas (see BREADS).

Colleen Sen

KHUS KHUS

Khus khus is a large bushy grass found in tropical India. Its name should not be confused with *khas khas* (POPPY SEEDS). Khus khus has been used for centuries in India as an incense or perfume and also for medicinal purposes. The roots provide an essential oil which is thought to have a cooling effect on the body and is made into a stimulating tonic drink or added to fruit drinks or SHERBET, such as s*attu ka sharbat* of Jharkhand.

Helen Saberi

KODAVAS

Kodagu, a densely forested hill region of great natural beauty, is located in the Western Ghats of Karnataka. The name is ancient, drawn from '*kodimalenad*', meaning forested, highland country. It was ruled by clan-bound, militaristic local chieftains until the mid-seventeenth century, when it came under the rule of a branch of the Hindu Lingayat kings

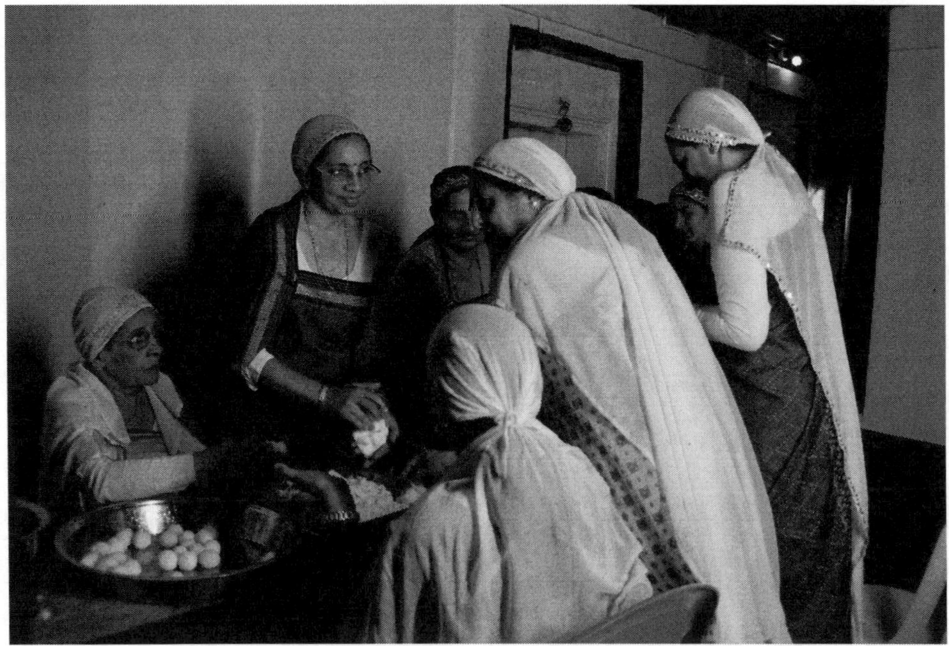

FIGURE 27 KODAVAS. Women rolling *kadambuttus*, steamed rice dumplings. Kaveri Ponnapa.

of northern Karnataka. The kingdom was annexed by the British in 1834 and remained a separate state until 1956.

Culturally distinctive, Kodavas, who are believed to have migrated to the region, had their own dress, customs, laws and religion. Skilled hunters and rice farmers, a unique cuisine developed around RICE, the staple. Rice is considered sacred and used symbolically in social and religious customs. It is cultivated in wide sweeps of fertile valleys in the south, as well as in narrow, terraced fields in the north. A range of vegetables such as GOURDS, field beans, squashes, tubers and AUBERGINES are grown in these fields between harvests. COFFEE is an important crop, introduced by the British in the nineteenth century.

Traditionally, the greater proportion of food was procured from the richly forested surroundings abundant in wild game, FISH and natural produce, leaving a lasting imprint on how Kodavas ate. Hunting was a sacred activity bound by strict rules: wild boar, bison, deer, game birds and freshwater FISH were all hunted and eaten; there were few prohibited foods and meat was an important part of the diet. Forest produce such as wild MANGOES and CITRUS FRUITS, endemic to the region, were prized.

All meals centre around rice in different forms, eaten with a CURRY (often meat or fish), a stir-fried vegetable and a PICKLE or CHUTNEY. *Akki rotis* (unleavened rice flatbreads), made from boiled rice kneaded into rice flour and cooked on a hot griddle, are usually eaten at breakfast with *elle pajji* (SESAME chutney), or *kumbala* curry (curried squash), simmered with ground COCONUT and mild spices. A range of *puttus* (steamed rice cakes and noodles) are made from *tari* (pounded, broken rice). *Noolputtu* (CARDAMOM flavoured rice noodles), made from cooked and steamed broken rice pressed out into thin strands, is eaten at lunch with *koli* curry (chicken curry). *Paputtus* (flat rice cakes), steamed with milk, coconut and cardamom, are paired with *erachi* curry (mutton curry). *Kadambuttus* (steamed rice dumplings) are eaten with *pandi* curry (curried pork). *Pandi* curry, the most famous Kodava dish, is cooked with dark-roasted CUMIN, CORIANDER, FENUGREEK and MUSTARD seeds, and spiced with black peppercorns (see PEPPER, BLACK). *Kachampuli* – a souring agent and marinade made from the fermented and boiled down juices of the ripe fruits of *panapuli* (*Garcinia gummi gutta*) – is a key ingredient in this dark spicy curry, and in most Kodava cooking. An aromatic mutton pulao is paired with *mange mor pajji* (wild mangoes in seasoned curd).

Pickles of citrus fruits, wild hog-plums, tender BAMBOO SHOOTS, *koilemeen* (tiny minnow-like fish from flooded fields) and meats are very popular. Sweets are few, made mainly with forms of rice combined with mashed or pureed fruit. *Koovale puttu* is a puree of ripe JACKFRUIT mixed with broken rice wrapped into a parcel in special leaves and steamed. *Chikkle unde* is a deep-fried sweet made from popped rice, jaggery (see SUGAR) and POPPY SEEDS. An alcoholic drink, *kachina kall,* not unlike sake, is distilled from germinated paddy.

Kodavas have a special monsoon cuisine that includes fiddlehead ferns, MUSHROOMS and different varieties of tender bamboo shoots. Mud-crabs and dried smoked meats are included in the category of 'warming' foods. A valued monsoon food comes from the boiled extract of the leaves of *Justicia wynaadensis*. An attractive shade of indigo, it is used to cook a sweetened *payasa* (rice porridge; see KHEER) or a *puttu* (steamed rice cake) with pleasing, herbal flavours. Modern scientific research has established the anti-inflammatory, anti-carcinogenic and anti-diabetic properties of the extract.

Steaming, stir-frying, stewing, deep-frying, pit-roasting and barbequing are all familiar cooking techniques. Dried and smoked meats are relished and many modern Kodava homes have a second, outdoor kitchen, where a wood-fired stove is used. A large, domed copper or brass steamer (*sakala*); a heavy, brass noodle press (*noolputtu wara*); and terracotta curry pots are important pieces of kitchen equipment (see COOKING AND DINING).

Tourism and growing interest have brought many traditional dishes to pop-ups and food festivals across the country. Dishes such as *koli barthad* (fried chicken) appear on the menu of the Bengaluru restaurant, Karavalli.

Kaveri Ponnapa

- Achaya, K. T. *Indian Food: A Historical Companion*. New Delhi: OUP, 1994.
- Ponappa, Kaveri. 'Eat Like a Local'. *BBC Good Food Magazine* 3, no. 10 (2014): 142–6.
- Ponappa, Kaveri. 'Flavours of Coorg'. *The Taj Magazine* 40, no. 2 (2013): 196–213.
- Ponnapa, Kaveri. *The Vanishing Kodavas*. Mumbai: Eminence Designs, 2013.

KOFTA

Kofta refers to a range of dishes such as rissoles, meatballs, croquettes and dumplings found all the way from India through Central Asia to the Middle East, the Balkans and North Africa.

Recipes for kofta can be found in the *NI'MATNAMA* (1495–1505) and today Indian cuisine has a stunning variety. Many kofta are made with ground meat, often mixed with spices, grains or vegetables and well kneaded until it becomes a smooth paste which is formed into balls, patties or sausage shapes. They can be cooked in numerous ways: grilled, barbecued, fried, steamed, poached, or simmered in a rich, spicy sauce. They are sometimes made with fish (as in Puducherry) and there are many vegetarian versions. One is the delicious *malai* kofta (*malai* means cream), popular in North India, made with POTATO and PANEER, then deep-fried and served in a rich creamy, sometimes slightly sweet, sauce. Other vegetarian versions include the Bengali JACKFRUIT kofta and the *kachkola* kofta *dalna* which is made with green BANANAS, mashed potatoes and spices, and fried and served with a spicy COCONUT sauce. Koftas are sometimes stuffed, typically with NUTS or CHEESE.

The word kofta comes from the Persian *koofteh* meaning pounded meat. From Persia, kofta migrated to India and became part of MUGHAL cuisine, including what is possibly the most popular kofta version, *nargisi* kofta (*nargis* means narcissus in Persian). These sumptuous kofta are made with a mixture of spiced ground meat which is wrapped round hard-boiled eggs before being simmered in a rich sauce, flavoured with *kewra* (see FLOWER WATERS) and SAFFRON. When serving, the kofta are carefully cut open to reveal their yellow and white centres, reminding people of the lovely narcissus flowers.

Helen Saberi

- Davidson, Alan. *The Oxford Companion to Food*. 2nd edition. Ed. Tom Jaine. Oxford: OUP, 2006.
- Mathur, Aanchal. '7 Best Kofta Recipes | Easy Kofta Recipes to Prepare at Home'. *NDTV Food*, 28 March 2022. Available online: https://food.ndtv.com/lists/7-best-kofta-recipes-2062220 (accessed 19 April 2022).

KOHINOOR, BOMAN

Boman Kohinoor (1923–2019) was one of Mumbai's most venerated restaurateurs. His death at the age of ninety-seven inspired obituaries by the *BBC*, *Financial Times* and *Condé Nast Traveler*, apart from every major Indian newspaper, an honour rarely accorded to the owner of an eatery.

What made Kohinoor special was that till his last days he would attend to all tables personally and amuse his guests with his banter at Britannia & Co., an IRANI CAFE, which he inherited from his father Rashid when he was in his teens and turned into the go-to address for fans of its iconic dishes: berry PULAO (SAFFRON fragrant RICE, chunks of chicken quilted with a TOMATO sauce, fried cashew and wisps of caramelized ONION, and *zereshk* barberries imported from Iran) and caramel custard. Described by *Time* magazine as being 'endearingly eccentric', Kohinoor was also famous for his much-publicized admiration for Queen Elizabeth II.

On her diamond jubilee, the Queen sent him a letter of appreciation with her full-length official portrait (it hangs at the restaurant next to images of Zarathustra – the founder of the Zoroastrian religion, which Kohinoor followed – and of Mahatma GANDHI, and the flags of India, the UK and Iran). His unscheduled meeting with Prince William and the Duchess of Cambridge during their official visit to India in 2016 was widely reported.

Kohinoor's grandfather had fled famine and persecution from Yazd, Iran and arrived in MUMBAI in the nineteenth century like hundreds of other Irani Zoroastrians. (They are related to yet different from the PARSIS whose forefathers had landed in the western state of Gujarat more than a millennium ago). It is this community that established the now-dying IRANI CAFE culture in India's western metropolis. Kohinoor's father, Rashid, started life selling the favourite Irani refreshment bun *maska* (soft, freshly baked buns smeared with cream and butter) and piping-hot sweet milky TEA on the pavement to other Iranis. With the money he had saved, Rashid opened Britannia & Co. in 1923 in a building designed by the Scotsman who also conceptualized the Gateway of India. Located in the upscale Ballard Estate neighbourhood of South Mumbai, the restaurant initially sold 'continental' dishes catering to Europeans. During the Second World War, the British commandeered the building that housed the restaurant for war efforts.

When the War was over and the family got back the premises, and the sun set on the British Raj, Kohinoor, who had taken over the business after his father's accidental death in 1939, started adding, as the sign at the restaurant says, 'Exotic Parsi and Iranian Cuisine' to the menu. The berry pulao came much later and was introduced by Kohinoor's wife, Bachan, after she discovered the dish on a visit to Iran in 1979. The original 'bland' Iranian recipe did not sit well on the local palate so Bachan Kohinoor tweaked it with her own masala. No one has yet identified the ingredients that go into the secret masala. As Kohinoor loved to recall to guests, when an American ambassador asked him for the berry pulao recipe, he replied, 'I will share it when you get me Coca-Cola's.'

Sourish Bhattacharyya

- Divan, Avanti G. 'Boman Kohinoor – The Kohinoor in Mumbai's Crown'. *The Indian Express*, 27 September 2019.

- Ray, Rajarshi. 'Boman Kohinoor of Britannia Restaurant: In Conversation'. *Parsi Khabar*, 29 March 2014. Available online: https://parsikhabar.net/food/boman-kohinoor-of-britannia-restaurant-in-conversation/7428/ (accessed 23 April 2022).
- Thakrar, Shamil, Kavi Thakrar and Naved Nasir. *Dishoom: From Bombay with Love*. London: Bloomsbury, 2019.

KOKUM

Garcinia indica is a perennial, fruit-bearing tall tree in the Clusiaceae family endemic to the Konkan region. The ripe fruits are edible with a pleasant flavour and sour taste and easy to pry open, though they are hardly consumed this way. Three distinct products – *kokum amrut*, *kokum agal* and *amsul* – are traditionally prepared from the pericarp (rind) and aril of the fruit while the seeds yield oil.

Garcia DE ORTA noted the use of the fruit of *G. indica* in 1563 among the Portuguese of Goa. It is commonly known as *kokum*, also the name of its most well-known product. It is a condiment, dark purple to black, sticky, with curled edges, used as an acidulant in this region's cuisine. It is prepared by sun-drying the rind of the ripe fruits after repeated soaking in the fermented juice of the pulp. This saturated, dried rind is also known as *amsul*. The fruits may also be halved, salted and sun-dried to make salted *kokum*.

Kokum amrut is an oleo saccharum (*kokum* peels muddled with sugar) used to make SHERBET. *Kokum agal* is a blended fresh juice of the pulp and rind concentrated with salt with therapeutic qualities. It is mixed with coconut milk to make *sol kadi*. *Kokum* wine is a fruit wine made by fermenting the fruit juice. Pre-packaged *kokum*-based juice and carbonated drinks are now readily available in the region. The sun-dried rind is ground to make *kokum* powder used in traditional medicine but which is now finding use in *masalas* and blends for sherbets. It is a very rich source of anthocyanin and a concentrated food colourant.

The seeds contain 23 to 26 per cent edible oil, which solidifies like butter at room temperature. Traditionally, *kokum* butter is shaped as a convo-convex bar and used as an emollient to treat sore or cracked skin. *Kokum* butter has gained economic importance as a cocoa butter extender in the chocolate industry today.

Priya Mani

KOLKATA

Formerly known as Calcutta, Kolkata is the capital of the state of West Bengal and the heart of the global Bengali community. Located at the site of various old villages on the banks of the Hooghly river (a distributary of the Ganga), it traces its history as an urban centre to the early British rule in India in the late seventeenth century. Bengal Subah, as it was then known, was a rich province with both agricultural abundance and highly developed industries, particularly textiles and ship building. Its position at the head of the Bay of Bengal gave it a prime role in the trade networks to Southeast Asia. The presence of the delta of two great rivers of the Subcontinent, the Ganga and the Brahmaputra, ensured connections to the hinterlands of India. It is this prime location with good access in all directions that made the British choose Kolkata as their headquarters and the same advantage also led to its development into a cosmopolitan metropolis with influences coming in from all over. A spirit of innovation was fostered both by the intermingling of various peoples and the cultures they carried and by the masses that, in search of their destiny and fortune, experimented with the traditional and the familiar. It led to the food of Kolkata being a local take on well-established cuisine and also being the syncretic mixing of disparate origins into novel creations. This is as true today as it was 200 years ago.

The base of Kolkatan cuisine is Bengali (see West Bengal). It revolves around RICE and FISH. Fried fish is a popular starter and various forms of fish CURRIES are common. Equally integral to any meal are vegetables that are cooked in various ways – from deep-fried *bhaja* to dry and wet CURRIES, to CHUTNEYS, PICKLES and other accompaniments. *Shorshe* (MUSTARD) is the principal vessel for flavour – mustard oil is the main medium of cooking and is also used raw as a seasoning in dishes like *aloo shedho* (boiled and mashed POTATOES) and *moonger* dal (mung beans, see PULSES); mustard seeds are used in tempering and are an integral part of the spice mix *panch phoron* (see SPICE BOX), but are most commonly ground into *shorshe bata*, a pungent paste of COCONUT, POPPY SEEDS, CHILLIES, SALT and mustard seeds that is used as a marinade, stuffing and as a base for curries.

The soul of Bengali cuisine, however, lies in its *mishti* (SWEETS). The most popular and common ingredient is *CHHANA* (separated milk solids) that is prepared in myriad ways. SANDESH is the favourite of Bengalis while RASGULLA is considered by non-Bengalis to be emblematic of Bengali sweet making. Legendary sweet shops such as KC Das, Balaram Mullick and Radharaman Mullick, Ganguram and Sons among others have not only produced exquisite examples of sweets but have also come up with their own unique inventions such as PAAN sandesh, *puchka* rasgulla, black currant rasgulla, chocolate sandesh and ice-cream sandesh. Bhim Chandra Nag in Bara Bazaar is famous for having concocted the *LEDIKENI*. Sweets are also made with rice flour, DATE palm jaggery (*nolen gur*) and reduced milk.

The cuisines of the MUGHALS and of LUCKNOW (Awadhi) have also influenced Bengali culinary practices as seen in the introduction of WHEAT-based BREADS, non-*channa* sweets such as *shahi tukra* and HALWAS among others, *dum* cooking (see COOKING AND DINING), BIRYANIS, KEBABS, and meat curries such as KOFTAS, kormas, *NIHARI*, etc. Kolkata food partakes of the same influence. When the last Nawab of Lucknow, Wajid Ali Shah, was exiled to Kolkata in 1858, he brought his cooks with him who adapted the Lucknow biryani by adding potatoes and cooking the dish in mustard oil, thus inventing the Kolkata biryani.

Kolkata is renowned for its STREET FOOD. The places offering street food range from small hand-portable kiosks, carts and shacks to well-established shops, cafes and restaurants. Furthermore, every neighbourhood will have its *parar dokans* (neighbourhood shops) indicating that street food is also a regular part of the everyday life of households and is not just restricted to workers, students, tourists or shoppers at marketplaces. The most popular items are *puchkas*, *jhal muri*, *ghugni*, *kathi* rolls, *hing kichuri* (see KACHORI), momos, Mughlai parathas, cutlets and chops.

Puchka, known by various names throughout the country, is essentially a deep-fried hollow ball made of semolina or wheat flour that is filled with spicy, flavoured water. Regional variations involve stuffing with potatoes, *chana* (Bengal gram) or yellow peas, as well as adding various chutneys. It is served in Kolkata, as in eastern Uttar Pradesh and Bihar, filled with a spicy mash of potatoes and the water is flavoured with TAMARIND, MINT and spices. However, unique to the Kolkatan version is the addition of the *gondhoraj* lime.

A street food dish that was invented in Kolkata and has spread all over the country is the *kathi* roll (kebabs rolled inside parathas). The word *kathi* refers to the bamboo sticks used as skewers to cook the kebabs. The creators were immigrants from North

India who had set up a stall selling kebabs and parathas (a common North Indian combination dish) near New Market in the early twentieth century. The Europeans liked this food tremendously and suggested that the kebabs be wrapped or rolled inside the parathas so that their fingers would not get greasy while eating. This roll brought great success to its creators and they opened a restaurant called Nizam's which, today, is considered to be the home of *kathi* rolls. Elsewhere in the country, this dish is eponymous with the city. Scores of modern variations on this basic roll exist made with all kinds of ingredients – eggs, fish, cooked cabbage and CARROTS, PANEER, soya *chaap* (Indian version of mock meat, usually made with the gluten from wheat flour), and even noodles.

While street food is found in every corner, certain locations have become synonymous with it such as Vivekananda Park, Dacres Lane and Gariahaat. Another iconic location is College Street where food has been influenced by the student crowd from the nearby University of Calcutta, Calcutta Medical College, Presidency College and other educational institutions. Dishes popular here include *radhaballabi* (fried flatbread stuffed with dal) served with spicy potato CURRY, *chholar* dal (split and hulled Bengal gram cooked with coconut and raisins), a variety of *telebhaja* (ingredients such as AUBERGINE, potato, fish, pumpkin, chicken, BANANA flower or eggs that are battered and deep-fried; see PAKORA) served with pungent *kasundi* (fermented sauce of ground mustard seeds and spices and, sometimes, raw MANGOES), cold COFFEE and hot TEA. One popular shop is Paramount, which was opened over 100 years ago and still remains a firm favourite for SHERBET including ones made with rose, tender coconut, green mango and SAFFRON. Indian Coffee House is another iconic institution where old-time favourites include cold coffee with cream, mutton Afghani cutlet, chicken *kabiraji*, omelette with hot buttered toast and boiled chicken sandwiches.

In the eighteenth century, the East India Company made Kolkata its India headquarters. It subsequently became the capital of the British Raj and remained so till 1911. The British residents employed Indian *khansamahs* (cooks). Some enterprising British and Indian people also set up establishments catering to the British. These exchanges between British and Bengali culinary practices led to the creation of dishes such as *deemer* devil, which is similar to Scotch eggs but is fried in mustard oil, thus absorbing its pungent flavour; *pish-pash*, which is a dish of overcooked rice, potatoes, chicken and whole spices; and *kabiraji* (spicy meat or fish cutlet covered with a lace of egg whites). They also introduced current essentials of Kolkata cuisine such as egg-based puddings, chops and cutlets, tea and coffee, and breakfast foods such as eggs and toasts.

The pubs, restaurants and cafes of Park Street are where Kolkata's colonial charm can still be witnessed. Aside from the club sandwiches, cups of Earl Grey tea and iced pastries at FLURYS, one can also find devilled crabs and chicken Kyiv at Mocambo, chicken steak sizzler at Peter Cat, lamb chops at Marco Polo, shrimp cocktails at Trincas and roasted duck at Moulin Rouge. During Christmas, the Calcutta Club hosts a lavish lunch complete with lobster bisque, roast turkey, Yorkshire pudding and meat pies.

Cabins were restaurants called so for their divided compartments (cabins) and were promoted by the British as a place for urban dining in relative privacy. Cabins later played a role in the freedom struggle as the privacy of the cabins allowed people to meet and converse. Today, the actual cabin divisions have gone but the places remain popular for their food such as Mughlai parathas, meat and seafood cutlets, and *kosha mangsho*. Some popular heritage cabins are Anadi Cabin, Niranjan Agar, Allen's Kitchens and Dilkhusha Cabin.

ANGLO-INDIANS, who are the mixed descendants of British and Indians, have also shaped the cuisine of the city. While they are a pan-Indian community with their cuisine having universally common elements, it displays regional variations. In Kolkata, Bengali ingredients, especially mustard oil, are often used in popular dishes which are still consumed today such as *dak* bungalow chicken curry, railway mutton curry, Calcutta fish KEDGEREE and Bengal shrimp curry. Anglo-Indian influence can also be found in the unlikeliest of places, such as the canteen at Frank Anthony Public School which serves *panthras*, a crumb-fried pancake roll stuffed with minced beef or chicken. Bow Street, popularly known as Bow Barracks, was built for soldiers during the Second World War. Anglo-Indian families still reside here and during Christmas one can find dishes such as fruit cake, rose cookies, *kulkuls* (sweet, deep-fried cookies), salted beef and homemade wine.

The British Empire and the position of Kolkata within it attracted immigrants from other parts of the world to the city. Foremost of them were the Chinese, the first of whom came to the city in the late eighteenth century and were followed by numerous waves of further immigrants. Many of them sold street food and opened small eating houses for their fellow Chinese. Eventually, in 1922, Eau Chew, the first (and oldest-running) restaurant serving CHINESE INDIAN CUISINE, opened in Kolkata. Like the British and the other immigrants, the Chinese in Kolkata also adopted and adapted to local flavours and tastes. Schezwan (Indian spelling of Sichuan) sauce is one such example – cooked with dried chillies instead of the traditional Sichuan peppercorns. It is used in varieties of noodles, fried rice, chicken and paneer dishes, and is, now, also being used innovatively to flavour naans, popcorns and French fries. Within Kolkata, Tirettti Bazaar and Tangra are the main neighbourhoods associated with the Chinese Indians and their food. While Chinese Indian cuisine has a pan-Indian presence, there are dishes unique to these areas such as *singhara* chow (steamed wontons, known locally as *singhara*, served with noodles and meat), Josephine noodles (vegetables, meat and noodles with a light sauce on top), dragon chicken (batter fried chicken in a spicy sauce, similar to chilli chicken) and chimney soup (lightly seasoned broth with eggs, meat and vegetables served in a brass pot with a tube through which emerges the smoke from a charcoal fire lit underneath the pot). Today, Chinese-Indian cuisine is an integral part of Indian cuisine, with a dish such as chowmein now found even in small villages.

Baghdadi Jews once had a thriving population in the city, of whom about twenty descendants remain today. A popular Jewish-Kolkatan dish is *aloo makallah* (made by pricking whole potatoes with a fork and deep frying them with salt and TURMERIC, a technique similar to that used by Bengalis for frying fish). Jewish bakers Nahoum and Sons have been making fruitcake, pastries, patties and cheesecakes in the city for over 120 years. During Easter, the bakery is especially popular for its hollow marzipan Easter eggs which come filled with sweets.

The British rule saw an influx of various Indian communities too – Marwaris, Punjabis, Biharis, Odiyas, Gujaratis, South Indians and others. For the most part, culinary boundaries remained intact and the influence between these and Bengali cuisine was minimal, limited only to one or two sweets or snacks. However, these communities continue to have a presence in the city including in the form of restaurants and cafes that offer their food.

Kolkata continues to welcome new communities and cuisines. Recently, Tibetan and Nepali food from the Darjeeling district of West Bengal has become popular with dishes such as momos and *thukpa*. Restaurants offering food from other parts of India such as the Northeast are becoming popular and global cuisine is making inroads. At the same time, there is also a thriving Bengali restaurant scene that started in Kolkata and is spreading to other Indian cities. One of the first such restaurants was Aaheli at the Peerless Hotel which serves a daily thali with seasonal fish dishes. Oh! Calcutta, which has branches all over India, is an upscale restaurant that serves traditional dishes. 6 Ballygunge Place serves uniquely Bengali dishes, as well as some fusion creations such as *nolen gurer* ice-cream (ice-cream flavoured with season-fresh date jaggery) and baked *pantua* (balls of semolina, *chhana*, milk, GHEE and SUGAR syrup that are normally fried); the *aam pora shorbot* (smoked raw mango sherbet) and *gondhoraj ghol* (LASSI with Bengal lime) are available seasonally here.

Despite the upheaval in its status, the foodways of this city are still a vibrant mix of the local, the regional, the national and the global, as they were historically.

Jyotirmay Nirjhar

• Kanjilal, Mohona. *A Taste of Time: A Food History of Calcutta*. New Delhi: Speaking Tiger, 2021.

KULFI

Kulfi (*qulfi*), sometimes called Indian ice-cream, is a popular sweet made by freezing flavoured *KHOYA* in conical metal cones. Traditional flavourings include pistachio, rose, MANGO and SAFFRON; newer versions are made with APPLE, orange or even avocado. Unlike ice-cream, it is not whipped or aerated and has a somewhat creamier texture. *Kulfi* can be garnished with ground CARDAMOM, almonds or pistachios. Sometimes it is topped with *FALOODA*.

Kulfi may have originated in Central Asia or Afghanistan and been brought to India by the MUGHALS in the sixteenth century who used ICE brought from the Himalayas or ice mixed with saltpetre to prepare it. Kulfi is a popular street food sold by *kulfiwallahs*.

Colleen Sen

LADAKH

Ladakh is a union territory that was carved out of the state of JAMMU AND KASHMIR in 2019. The name means 'Land of the Passes', which tells you about its geography. For the most part, flat, arable land is a rare commodity throughout the Leh and Kargil districts and one could generalize that BARLEY, the hardy staple crop of Tibet, used to be the mainstay of Ladakhi cuisine.

In the last three to four decades, the inexorable progress of modernization has crept into Ladakh as well. From the 1970s onwards, the Central Government provided jobs to a high percentage of the local population, chief among them being the armed forces, Indo Tibetan Border Police, and as teachers in government schools and colleges. On the plus side, employment was high; on the minus side, those who had been tending their family fields to grow barley and vegetables like TURNIPS, CARROTS, leafy greens, POTATOES and RADISH no longer had the time to do so. At about the same time, the government began sending RICE to all parts of Ladakh, and in a few years the people whose staple grain had been barley made the seemingly effortless switch to rice. Today, rice occupies a unique position in Ladakh. Rice is eaten by almost all townspeople and many village dwellers but it cannot be called the staple crop because it does not grow here. Instead, what is eaten as accompaniments to rice includes dal (also a new entrant to the diet) and vegetables. Vegetables are made into a sort of stew which, depending on the family in question, could be a mix of meat (usually lamb) and vegetables, or a medley of vegetables grown in the garden or procured from the market, supplied from elsewhere in the country. The stew, which is an interpretation of CURRY found in the rest of the country, typically has far less spice than usual, and could well have a whiff of pure GHEE from the family's own cow. Most families in Ladakh keep at least one cow for milk and ghee. It is usual to grow MUSTARD in the family's fields and harvest the crop to turn it into oil, which is the medium of cooking for the rest of the year.

Gyathuk is a hearty soup meal in a bowl, *gya* meaning 'Chinese'. *Gyathuk* always contains noodles in addition to vegetables and meat. That Ladakh, Uzbekistan, Tibet, Mongolia, Bhutan and Nepal form a contiguous chain of independent polities unified by religious faith and culture is proven by the fact that they share remarkable commonalities in their cuisines: hand-made noodles, BREADS that are baked in ash that last a long time and can be carried on journeys, and food that requires painstaking preparation of ingredients but short cooking times (a function of limited fuel). Industriousness is a highly prized virtue all over Ladakh. Even among the most elite families of Leh, the capital and the largest city, it is not a practice to leave the family's fields lying idle. Hard work and the ingrained principle of producing at least some portion of one's own food are so intrinsic to the culture that no field is left fallow.

The most famous crop of Ladakh is the APRICOT, of which there are two types: the common black variety (which is not black at all to the untrained eye), and the rarer and more prized, white variety, which is sweet, juicy and far more flavourful than its poor country cousin. Sold all over the country with their provenance mentioned, in Ladakh, the black variety is dried and pounded into a coarse meal called *sattu*. Highly nutritive, it is eaten with breakfast as apricot jam would be in the Western world. Another popular breakfast preparation is *khambiri* roti made with yeast by householders and eaten with curried potatoes. Barley in the form of *tsampa* (powdered meal) is consumed in the onomatopoeically named *gurgur* chai: salted TEA that used to have a layer of yak butter in it, but now makes use of ghee from the family's cow.

The only spice that grows in Ladakh is *konyot,* an aniseed-like flavouring that grows wild on the margins of the fields of barley. It is getting increasingly scarce now that barley as a crop is rapidly diminishing. Even though the sparse Ladakhi diet may not have the variety of ingredients and preparations as their counterparts in the plains, the traditional Ladakhi kitchen is the most lavishly decorated room in a traditional house. It is large, with floor to ceiling shelves adorned with the family's treasure trove of traditional cookware found nowhere else in India. The kitchen doubles up as a space to entertain close friends and to eat the meals, a cross between a TV room and a dining space.

Marryam Reshii

- Indian Culture. 'Ladakhi Cuisine: High Foods for the Home and Heart', *n.d.* Available online: https://indianculture.gov.in/food-and-culture/north/ladakhi-cuisine-high-foods-home-and-heart (accessed 20 April 2022).
- Reshi, Maryyam H. 'Ladakh', 22 January 2017. Available online: https://marryamhreshii.com/ladakh/ (accessed 20 April 2022).

LADDU

FIGURE 28 LADDU. *Besan* laddus. Divya Kudua/Wikimedia Commons.

Perhaps the most universal and ancient of Indian sweets, laddus are round balls made from various ingredients, held together by SUGAR syrup or jaggery and deep-fried. Every region has its own version. They are part of all happy occasions and many festivals, especially those associated with the deity Ganesh. Because of their relatively long shelf life, in the past laddus were taken by travellers on journeys.

The Sanskrit word *ladduka* is mentioned in the *Sushruta Samhita* to describe small edible balls made of SESAME seeds, jaggery and peanuts coated with HONEY. They were used as an antiseptic (honey has antibacterial properties) and as a mode of delivering medicines. With the advent of sugar processing, honey was replaced with sugar syrup.

Today the most common version is *besan* laddu, made with chickpea flour (*besan*), sugar, GHEE and CARDAMOM powder. The mixture is fried in ghee, sugar and cardamom are added, and the cooled mixture is formed into round balls four cm in diameter. Another popular variety is the *motichur* ('crushed pearls') laddu which is made with *boondi* – tiny globules of chickpea batter that are fried, soaked in sugar syrup and formed into balls. Regional variants include laddus made from WHEAT flour (Rajasthan), sesame seeds (Maharashtra), RICE flour (Kerala) or rice flakes (Andhra Pradesh). Sometimes grated COCONUT, roasted chickpeas, NUTS and raisins are added.

The city of Kanpur in Uttar Pradesh is famous for its *thaggu ke* laddu ('cheat's laddu') made from *KHOYA* and *suji* (semolina). It was created by Mattha Pandey, a follower of Mahatma GANDHI. He heard Gandhi call the white sugar popularized by the British 'white poison' and a cause of diseases. Since sugar was an essential ingredient in his laddus, he decided to let people know the truth by giving it this name.

Laddus are mentioned in the *Lokapakara* written around 1025 in Western India. They were made by mixing *savige* – vermicelli made from a dough of rice flour, yogurt and ghee – with ghee and a sugar syrup, forming it into balls and frying in ghee. TAMARIND or jujube juice was added for flavour. The fifteenth-century *NI'MATNAMA* of the Sultans of Mandu contains several recipes for opulent laddus made with white flour and dried fruits and flavoured with rosewater (see FLOWER WATERS), CAMPHOR and musk. The modern *shahi* laddu (*shahi* meaning royal) is made by grinding *peda* (a semi-soft round light-coloured sweet with different flavourings) and BARFI into a paste, then mixing it with cardamom, dried fruits and nuts and decorating it with *VARK*.

Some Hindu temples offer their own version of laddus to worshipers as *prasad* (see TEMPLE FOOD). Those at the Maa Tarini temple in Ghatagaon, Orissa, are made from coconut and *khoya*. The signature laddu at the Thiruchendur Murgan temple in Tamil Nadu is made from foxtail MILLET. The most famous temple laddu is the Tirupati laddu served at the Sri Venkateswara temple in Tirupati, Andhra Pradesh.

Colleen Sen

- Banerjee, Satarupa. *Book of Indian Sweets*. New Delhi: Rupa Publications, 1994.
- Dash, Madhulika. 'Food Story: The Journey of Laddoo from a Medicine to the Much-Loved Indian Sweet'. *Indian Express*, 16 October 2014.

LAL, PREMILA

Premila Lal was the nom de cuisine of Kiki Watsa, a best-selling cookery book writer who acquired quite a following because of her recipe columns in the now-defunct women's magazine, *Eve's Weekly*. She also wrote *Indian Recipes* (1968; Faber), which was lavishly illustrated by India's foremost caricaturist, the late Mario Miranda.

Born and brought up in Tanzania, where her father had relocated to engage in farming, dairying and ship chandling, Watsa returned to India, presumably in the late 1950s, for her college education and ventured into writing. While still a university student, as one of the rare articles about her reports, Watsa was asked to take on, without payment, the writing of a food and recipe column for a magazine called *Flair*. 'At the time I had only eight recipes given to me by my mother', Watsa recalled in a conversation with Fred Ferreti in Travel Classics. 'I began with these. It was enough for the magazine. And they also gave me my name. "Your name is Premila Lal," they said. I became the first cook to be a public figure in India', added Watsa, described as being 'not at all self-effacing when talking about her talents'.

Sourish Bhattacharyya

LANDOUR COMMUNITY CENTRE COOK BOOK

Revised in the 1960s as *The Landour Book of International Recipes*, this is the title of a collection of recipes and household tips put together by the wives of American missionaries and school masters living (or spending their summers) in the Lower Western Himalayan 'hill station' after which it is named.

Landour (elevation: more than 7,000 feet) is a quaint multi-cultural 'cantonment' (military) town situated close to Mussoorie in the northern Uttarakhand state. Its history goes back to the early 1800s, when it served as a sanatorium for ailing British troops stationed in India. Later, it became a military station and saw the opening of the famous Woodstock School by British Anglican and American Presbyterian missionaries in 1854. By the 1920s and '30s, a vibrant international, multi-denominational community grew around Woodstock and the language school for American missionaries sent to India. Irene Parker, wife of Woodstock's long-serving Principal Alan Parker (he was principal between 1922 and 1939) teamed up with the local pastor's wife to establish the Reading Club and it got a permanent home at the Community Centre, which was opened in 1928.

In 1930, the *Cook Book's* first edition, edited by a Mrs R.C. Newton, was published by the Reading Club. It was reprinted in 1938 by The Mussoorie Book Society. The Club members shared recipes and discussed, among other matters, challenges such as cooking and baking at an altitude of 7,000 feet and more, dealing with household pests, finding substitutes of ingredients not available locally and managing without refrigerators (the Landour residents used screened food cupboards, or 'doolies', instead).

The *Cook Book* was revised in 1946 by Mrs Ruth E. Merian Beckdahl and contained 614 recipes. In 1964, the daughters and daughters-in-law of the original contributors brought out a thoroughly revised edition titled *The Landour Book of International Recipes*. It was edited by Katharine 'Kittu' Parker Riddle, daughter of Irene and Alan Parker. This edition was revised again in 1969 by Cleone Warner, a member of the Reading Club, and then re-issued in 1978 (by two different publishers), 1985, 1993, 1996 and 2000 – none of whom, as Parker Riddle alleges in a web article, acknowledged the Reading Club or the women who painstakingly compiled the recipes and penned the text.

The *Cook Book* has acquired a life of its own. The heroine of Indo-Anglian novelist Anita Desai's Booker Prize-shortlisted book *Fasting, Feasting* (1999) relies on it to prepare the tea-time snacks she serves. This was an instance of literature imitating art. Writing in 2008 in *The New York Times*, the novelist's daughter Kiran Desai remembers how she "became a disciple" of the Cook Book as she navigated recipes of goodies such as the Wacky Crazy Cake, feeding the insecurity of their cook, Saratbhai.

At the turn of the new millennium, public interest in the recipes was rekindled by the publication of *The Landour Cookbook: Over Hundred Years of Hillside Cooking* (2001: Roli Books, New Delhi) by the town's best-known resident, the writer Ruskin Bond, and his friend and associate, the photographer Ganesh Saili. The ninety-plus-year-old recipes also live on in the cakes and mud pie served at the Landour Bakehouse. The legacy of the Reading Club ladies has far outlived them.

Sourish Bhattacharyya

- Desai, Kiran. 'Sacred Chow'. *The New York Times Magazine*. Available online: https://www.nytimes.com/2008/02/10/magazine/10food-t.html (accessed 10 October 2022).
- Bond, Ruskin and Ganesh Saili. *The Landour Cookbook: Over Hundred Years of Hillside Cooking*. New Delhi: Roli Books, 2005.

LASSI

FIGURE 29 LASSI. Kolkata lassi shop. Ashish Sen.

Lassi is a soothing nutritious drink enjoyed throughout India. It is made in homes as well as being a popular street food where it is traditionally sold in clay pots. It is drunk with meals and as a snack. It can be made from BUTTERMILK but more usually with yogurt which is diluted with water and then whisked until frothy. It is usually served with crushed ICE or ice cubes.

There are two versions, salty (*namkeen* lassi) and sweet (*meethi* lassi). In North India, the salted version often contains spices such as ground toasted CUMIN seeds and black pepper (see PEPPER, BLACK). Finely chopped MINT or dried mint is sometimes added. In South India, they like a spicy paste of ground green CHILLIES, GINGER, CORIANDER leaves and GARLIC to be added.

The sweet version often only contains sugar but can be flavoured with a little ground CARDAMOM or rosewater (see FLOWER WATERS) and sprinkled with chopped NUTS. In South India it is called *majjika*. In Bengal, a splash of *gondo lebu* (scented lime) may be added.

Morru, also from South India, is buttermilk or yogurt mixed with water and spiced with cumin, ASAFOETIDA, a little TURMERIC and fresh coriander or NEEM leaves. Mango is another popular flavouring.

Helen Saberi

LEDIKENI

Ledikeni (or Lady Kenny) is a sweet created in the mid-nineteenth century by Bhim Chandra Nag, a prominent confectioner (*moira*) of Bengal. He created it in honour of Countess Charlotte Canning, popularly referred to as Lady Canning, wife of the last Governor-General of India and subsequently the first Viceroy. The name Lady Canning transmuted into Lady Kenny, then *ledikeni*.

Ledikeni, which is similar to *pantua*, is made with *CHHANA* and flour formed into small balls which are stuffed with CARDAMOM-scented SUGAR balls called *nakul-dana*. The balls are deep-fried until golden and finally soaked in rose-scented sugar syrup which makes a crispy exterior with a meltingly juicy and fragrant interior.

Some say Bhim Nag created it to celebrate Lady Canning's arrival at Calcutta (Kolkata) in 1856. Others say it was to commemorate her birthday. Lady Canning sadly died of malaria five years after arriving in India. It is not known if she ever tasted this sweet but her name lives on and so does *ledikeni* which continues to occupy a prominent place in the sweetshops of Bengal.

Helen Saberi

- Dey, Ishita. 'Ledikeni'. In *The Oxford Companion to Sugar and Sweets*, edited by Darra Goldstein, 398–99. New York: OUP, 2015.
- Krondl, Michael. *Sweet Invention: A History of Dessert*. Chicago: Chicago Review Press, 2011.

LICHENS

Lichens are any of numerous complex plantlike organisms made up of an alga and a fungus growing in symbiotic association on a solid surface, such as on a rock or tree bark. In Indian bazaars, lichens are sold by the name *charrila* which consists of a mixture of two or more species of the genera *Usnea, Parmelia, Ramalina* or *Heterodermia* and are used as spices. These lichens provide a special fragrance to meat, PULSES and other vegetables. They are relatively expensive. The Himalayan ranges contribute to the bulk of lichen gathering activities in India, followed by the hills of the Western Ghats. Lichens are gathered largely by tribals who then sell them in the local markets. They are then purchased by traders who consolidate the supply and send them to larger factories across North India. Here, the lichens are classified based on their type and commercial value. They are chiefly sold to the perfume industry, spice blend makers and herbal medicines industry.

One of the most important lichens of commercial value is stone flower (*Parmotrema perlatum*). Other vernacular names include *shaileyam* (Sanskrit), *kalpasi* (Tamil), *dagad phool* (Hindi) and *shaiba* leaves (Arabic), all roughly meaning the same: stone flower, or rather, flowers that grow on stone. It is a dark, purplish, black lichen with broad, curled foliage typical of lichens with a lobed, leaflike shape. On its own, it has no taste or at best, a woody fragrance. But when added to spice blends, its aroma is activated and it imparts a deep, earthy flavour to CURRIES. It is typically roasted and then ground along with a medley of spices or is occasionally added to hot oil to infuse its flavour.

It is *the* decisive ingredient in many regional spice blends (see SPICE BOX), including the *kala* masala and *goda* masala of the Western coast (the latter is part of Maharashtrian Brahmin cooking), the Anglo Indian bottle masala, *bhojwar* masala from the HYDERABAD region, *potli* masala in LUCKNOW, and the spices that go into the making of a great Chettinad chicken curry in Tamil Nadu. Today, the stone flower has moved from its use as a hyper-local spice to a 'secret spice' used in standard garam masalas.

Priya Mani

- Mani, Priya. 'Stone Curry: Parmotrema perlatum as a Secret Spice in Indian Food'. In *Herbs and Spices: Proceedings of the Oxford Symposium on Food and Cookery 2020*, edited by Mark McWilliams, 239–49. Totnes, Devon: Prospect Books, 2021.

LOTUS

The Indian sacred lotus is an Asian aquatic plant in the Nelumbonaceae family with deep symbolism and significance in India's culinary, art, culture and religious practices. It is adapted to propagate by rhizome and seeds in still lakes or calm, slow-moving rivers. All parts of the lotus plant – the starch-rich underground rhizome, stalks, flowers, stamens, fruits and seeds are edible, while the leaves are used for wrapping.

The rhizomes are extracted from the lakes with the help of a long wooden stick with a metal hook on one end and sold in bundles as *nadru* to Kashmiris, *beeh* to Sindhis or *kamal kakdi* elsewhere in North India. It can be used fresh or preserved by sun-drying and rehydrated as a vegetable for CURRIES. It is sun-dried or batter-fried into crisps and pickled. In Manipur, fresh rhizomes are sliced thinly and used in the region's famous salad *singju*, or candied to make *thambou heingan*.

Chopped pieces of the delicate stem are coated with SALT and TURMERIC, steamed, sun-dried and stored. They are deep-fried on demand and served as *tamara vethal* in Tamil Nadu and Kerala and *beeh jyun kachryun* among SINDHIS. Deep frying thin slices of the fresh stem make *kamal kakdi* chips.

In India, the flowers are primarily used whole as an article of worship. The stamens, called *kamal kesar*, are picked, dried and used in many Ayurvedic preparations. They are a common adulterant for real SAFFRON. Yarn spun from the fibres of the stalks is used as a wick in Hindu rituals.

The lotus fruits are conical pods with seeds contained in holes in the pod. The green pods are snapped open; the tender green kernels peeled; and the soft, sweet white seed is eaten as a fresh seasonal snack or stored dried. Brown seeds are harvested from the mature fruits, dried whole and strung as a rosary or ground to a flour, *kamal gatta,* used to make HALWA or a herbal electuary. The seeds are popped and known as *phool makhana*, a very nutritious and popular snack. Lotus leaves may be used fresh or saved dried to serve food, especially in Hindu rituals, and to wrap foodstuffs.

Growing demand for lotus flowers and seeds has initiated large-scale commercial farming. Festivals celebrating Hindu Goddesses like Durga Puja in Bengal create a huge seasonal demand for the lotus. The Kang Rath Yatra in Manipur is a celebration that highlights the region's lotus harvest, where participants behold foods made from different parts of the lotus plant.

Priya Mani

LUCKNOW

Lucknow, the capital of Uttar Pradesh, is a city in what was once the MUGHAL province of Awadh, which in the eighteenth century became semi-independent under the Mughals' regents, the Nawabs of Awadh. The first Nawab was of Persian origin and this left its mark on the Nawabs' courtly culture and cuisine. The history of Lucknow's classical cuisine, also called Awadhi, can be traced to the last years of Nawab Shuja-ud-Daula (r. 1754–75). He appointed Mirza Hasnu, a culinary expert from a noble family, as head of the royal kitchen. After the Nawab's son, Asaf-ud-Daula (r. 1775–97), moved the capital of Awadh from Faizabad to Lucknow in 1775, he elevated the preparation and consumption of daily meals into an art. Lucknow came to rival Delhi as the cultural and culinary capital of North India and reached 'a level of splendor and sophistication scarcely paralleled in any other Indo-Islamic society' (Sharar [1925] 1989: 19).

FIGURE 30 LUCKNOW. Shop making *nihari*. Anil Risal Singh.

Asaf-ud-Daula encouraged hospitality and the sharing of food. Large *deghs* made of copper were in demand to simmer RICE in clarified butter and aromatic spices. Korma and *salan* CURRIES were browned and left to stew in large round pots made of iron and copper. *Maahitava*, a gigantic iron plate, was used to fry different types of melt-in-the-mouth KEBABS from the *shami* to the *galauti*. A deep round iron cast pot was turned upside down on the hearth to prepare the handkerchief thin wheat BREAD called the *roomali* roti. In an entire neighbourhood called the Bawarchi Tola, which still exists, the sale of special utensils used by fastidious chefs or *bawarchis* became big business.

In his book, *Lucknow: Last Phase of an Oriental Culture*, Sharar describes a vibrant syncretic culture that combined elements of North Indian Hindu and Muslim music, dance, clothing, painting and, especially, cuisine. Gourmetship was prized not only by the Nawabs and aristocrats but even by the middle class and the common people. The affluent vied with each other to see who could create the most refined dishes; chefs, called *rakabdars*, enjoyed a high status and salary. They were concerned with presentation, adorning dishes with dried fruits cut into the shape of flowers, or edible *VARK*. The traditional style of dining is to sit on the floor on a carpet for a meal. The centre is covered in a *chandani* or a white sheet often embroidered with Persian and Urdu couplets welcoming guests and expressing gratitude for breaking bread with the host.

In 1856, the monarchy was abolished and the last Nawab, Wajid Ali Shah, went to live in Calcutta (now KOLKATA). Awadh was brought under the British jurisdiction. The traditional city was dotted with European style bars, clubs and restaurants serving dishes more tantalizing than eateries in London and Paris.

To this day, mouthwatering recipes enjoyed by the royalty linger in Lucknow. BIRYANI is one of the most popular meals. The rice and meat are cooked separately, then layered and cooked for several hours in a sealed vessel over low heat. KEBABS, spiced minced meat in different shapes and flavours cooked over a fire, are a Lucknow speciality. The most popular ones are *galauti, kakori, boti* and *seekh*. They continue to be relished in homes as well as eateries such as Nawabeen, Nausheen and Dastarkhwan. They are traditionally eaten with breads and, although their variety has been greatly reduced, *roomali* roti, *sheermal* and kulcha continue to be a part of modern-day meals. A favourite bread from the above list is chosen and torn into pieces that are dipped in a plate of the traditional korma – braised pieces of meat slow cooked in an aromatic gravy. There are many sweet dishes made from milk, cream, SUGAR and dry fruits. A favourite is *shahi tukra:* slices of deep-fried baked bread wedged and divided into two triangles, soaked in heavy cream and covered in silver that has been pounded into a paper-thin sheet.

A characteristic feature of Lucknow cuisine is the spice blend, which is more subtle and nuanced than in so-called Mughal food. Another feature is the use of the *dum pukht* technique, which involves cooking dishes in a vessel with the lid sealed with dough and cooked slowly over a low fire so that the food absorbs its own aroma. Meat or vegetables can be stuffed with NUTS and spices, wrapped in a BANANA leaf, covered with clay and buried in the earth – a technique called *gile hikmat*. Another method is *dhungar* – smoking a dish with the fumes of charcoal. (See COOKING AND DINING.)

After Independence in 1947, refugees from West Punjab settled in Lucknow bringing the tandoor, BUTTER CHICKEN and PANEER. Immigrants from eastern Uttar Pradesh and Bihar have introduced *chokha bati* to the STREET FOOD sold here. Chinese noodles, fried rice and countless stalls selling momos from Tibet along with bakeries and restaurants specializing in Italian delicacies have also become part of meals enjoyed in Lucknow today. The favourite street food remains chaat – *golgappas*, mashed potato *tikkis* and ground lentil cakes soaked in yogurt. Lucknow is also the home of Pankaj Bhadouria, country's first Master Chef and founder of a culinary academy.

Mehru Jaffer

- Hasnain, Nadeem. *The Other Lucknow: An Ethnographic Portrait of a City of Undying Memories and Nostalgia*. Delhi: Vani Prakashan, 2016.
- Hussain, Mirza Jafar. *The Classic Cuisine of Lucknow: A Food Memoir*. 1980, translated by Sufia Kidwai. Lucknow: Sanatkada, 2016.
- Indian Culture. 'The Delicate Flavours of Awadh', *n.d.* Available online: https://indianculture.gov.in/food-and-culture/distinctive-cuisines/delicate-flavours-awadh (accessed 24 April 2022).
- Sharar, Abdul Halim. *Lucknow: The Last Phase of an Oriental Culture*. 1925, translated and edited by E. S. Harcourt and Fakhir Hussain. Delhi: OUP, 1989.

LYCHEE

Lychee (*Litchi chinensis*, Hindi *lichi*) is the fruit of an evergreen tree that originated in China in the first century BCE and was probably introduced by the Portuguese into Bengal in the eighteenth century. It adapted well to the climate of eastern India and today Bihar accounts for three-fourths of India's total production, followed by West Bengal. It is also grown in COFFEE plantations in parts of South India. Indian production is growing rapidly and today India is the world's fourth largest producer. Most lychee orchards are located on the banks of rivers.

Over thirty varieties are grown in India, which vary by fruit size, shape, colour and taste. A substantial amount of lychee produced in the country is consumed locally. The round fruit is around three cm in diameter with a bumpy skin that is red when ripe and turns brown after harvest. Inside is a juicy sweet pulp with a delicate, slightly floral flavour surrounding a seed. Lychees are usually eaten fresh, but can be juiced, sun-dried or oven-dried. The pulp is rich in vitamin C.

Colleen Sen

MADHYA PRADESH

Not a lot has been written about the cuisines of Madhya Pradesh (which means 'Central State'). As a political and administrative entity, the state is not organized on the basis of any language, ethnicity or cultural background, unlike many other states of the Indian union. Its cuisine has been greatly influenced by the cuisines of the neighbouring states of Rajasthan, Gujarat, Maharashtra and Uttar Pradesh, with strong Mughlai and Awadhi influences.

The second largest Indian state by area and the fifth largest by population, Madhya Pradesh is geographically very diverse with different climatic conditions. The state has an agrarian economy, the main crops being WHEAT, soybean, gram, sugarcane, RICE, CORN, cotton, rapeseed, MUSTARD and *arhar* dal (see PULSES). This diversity has provided cooks with a kaleidoscope of opportunities to experiment and create new flavours.

Madhya Pradesh is a part of Gondwanaland from which the Indian subcontinent got separated to join with the rest of Asia. It has one of the world's oldest mountain ranges, the Vindhyachal, which has rich mineral deposits and supports diverse flora and fauna, making certain regions abundant in food choices. This region has been inhabited since the prehistoric era. The cave paintings of Bhimbetka on the outskirts of Bhopal are listed in UNESCO's World Heritage Sites. The recorded history of the state may be traced back to the Maurya Empire (fourth to third century BCE) and it was later known as Malwa. While Hinduism remained the dominant religion for a long time, Buddhism and Jainism also flourished. The region was later ruled by many dynasties, including the Shungas, the Satavahanas or the Andhras, the Shakas and the Nagas. All of Madhya Pradesh lying north of the Narmada River formed part of the Gupta Empire (fourth to fifth century CE). The Guptas were followed by the Parmars, the Chandelas, the South Indian Chalukyas and many small Gond kingdoms before the region came under the Delhi Sultanate in the twelfth and thirteenth centuries. After the decline of the Delhi Sultanate, the Tomars, a Rajput dynasty, ruled Gwalior and the surrounding region in central India from the fourteenth to the sixteenth century. After the battle of Panipat in 1556, most of Madhya Pradesh came under MUGHAL rule and after the death of Aurangzeb in 1707, it came under the Marathas. In 1819 they lost to the British. The British controlled the region through the princes who became symbolic feudal lords accepting the British as the paramount power.

To do justice to the food of Madhya Pradesh, it needs to be classified into five distinct regions. Starting from the region of Bhagelkhand in the northeast, the city of Rewa and its erstwhile royal family occupy a special place because of the rich heritage of the rule by Rajput clans. It boasts of rustic preparations of game, chicken and mutton. *Khad* is a marinated mutton dish cooked in the ground with hot coals, which shows the link of the royal family with Rajasthan. An unusual preparation is made from lentil cakes cooked in a *kadhi* and is called *indrahar*, which means the food of Indra, the king of the Gods. This preparation uses five kinds of lentils – *malka masoor* (shelled lentils), *urad* (black gram), *chana* (Bengal gram), *arhar* (pigeon pea) and *moong* (mung beans) in equal quantities. They are soaked, ground with seasoning on a grinding stone into a thick paste, then sautéed with spices, spread on a tray like a cake batter and steamed. The steamed cake is cut into rectangles that are fried and, finally, added to a spicy *kadhi* made from yogurt and chickpea flour. This preparation occupies place of pride in banquets in the region, where it is served with rice, chapati or puris. *Aam ka bagja* or *launji* is another iconic and seasonal dish that is made by cooking semi-ripe MANGOES with SUGAR and water, then tossing it with CUMIN seeds and black SALT. It is thickened with a chickpea flour batter flavoured with cumin seed and AJOWAN. This relish is best enjoyed with dal stuffed puris or with *thedula* – a spiced puri made with a mixture of wheat flour and black gram powder.

The region of Bundelkhand in the north boasts of equally rustic food. The central place belongs to assortment of preparations like HALWA, KHEER (a pudding made by condensing milk with the fresh flowers of *mahua*), and a drink made from the dried flowers of the *mahua* tree (*Madhuca longifolia*). The tree also produces a fleshy and fruity fruit which is made into a delicious dry vegetable enjoyed with BREAD made from pearl millet flour. Travelling to Bundelkhand in the summer, it is a delight to see a green mahua tree standing tall and providing shade to weary travellers. This region has been ruled by fiery Bundel Rajputs whose food includes a lot of game meat as well as meat from domesticated animals and birds.

In the areas of Orchha and Datia, one finds many unique preparations, such as the *rasedaar guinya* made from TARO. In other parts of India, it is always cooked dry to avoid the slimy form the vegetable assumes after coming in contact with water, but here the cooks first fry the vegetable to a near dehydrated state before putting it in a yogurt-based sauce which absorbs the flavours, puzzling the uninitiated diners about what they are eating. *Besan ke aloo* (literally chickpea flour potatoes) is a misnomer, since it is made not with POTATOES, but with dehydrated *AMLA* cooked and mashed with chickpea flour and spices. The region also prepares very rustic desserts such as *ras* kheer, rice cooked with freshly squeezed sugarcane juice. Another preparation is *anarse,* which is made by cooking freshly pounded soaked rice in a thick sugar syrup cooked to a soft ball stage. The mixture is then cooled, made into cakes and deep-fried in GHEE.

Travelling westwards, the Chambal region is said to have the highest concentration of vegetarians in India (see VEGETARIANISM). The climate in this region is very harsh, with extreme heat in the summer and biting cold in the winter. A lot of leafy vegetables, unheard of in other parts of the country, are consumed as a regular feature, such as tender NEEM and DRUMSTICK leaves in the summer and *kulfa* (*Portulaca oleracea*), purslane and chickpea leaves in the winter. The latter are cooked with potatoes to make an unusual vegetable with an enticing acidity from the leaves. This region is also one of the major milk-producing regions in India and the use of milk is very popular. It does not have a great PANEER making tradition but yogurt, BUTTERMILK, ghee and dehydrated milk are used in many forms. The most notable dish is *mawabatti,* a deep-fried patty of condensed milk bound with a little refined flour, flavoured with CARDAMOM and then soaked in sugar syrup. *Motichur* laddu (see LADDU) is an unforgettable delicacy in Gwalior, where not only does the sweetmeat disintegrate on touch but even the individual pearls melt in the mouth, each exploding with the flavour of pure ghee, cooked sugar and SAFFRON. *Mathe wale aloo* made by stewing sautéed potatoes with buttermilk and light spices is a treat enjoyed in most feasts. This region also grows *arhar* dal, which makes a wonderful yellow dal with a hint of cumin seeds, green CHILLIES, GINGER and CORIANDER leaves that goes well with *phulka* (a thin puffed chapatti) or plain rice.

This region is also famous for the *gajjak*, a confection made by incorporating ground SESAME seeds into hot pulled sugar. Making *gajjak* is a cottage industry which comes alive every year with the onset of winter. The city of Gwalior also has a strong Mughal influence, so that BIRYANI, *shammi* KEBABS and *seekh* kebabs rolled in *roomali* roti, a paper-thin chapati made with whole wheat flour, are also very popular here.

Southwest of Gwalior is the Malwa region. Ujjain, the gateway city, is the city of Lord Mahakal, Lord Shiva in his destroyer form. It is also the city where Singhast, a congregation of devout Hindus, is held every twelve years in what is known as the Ujjain Kumbh Mela. Ujjain has strong Hindu traditions. The *prasad* of *peda*, a dehydrated milk cake, is a must-carry item from Ujjain's temples (see TEMPLE FOOD). Such is its popularity that it is made available by the temple authorities and may even be ordered online. *Poha* and JALEBI are emblematic breakfast foods sampled by millions of people during the Singhast and have become a breakfast staple all over Madhya Pradesh. *Poha* is made of rice flakes that are soaked in water and then tossed in a tempering of red and green chillies, peanuts and mustard seeds to acquire a light biting texture. It is served topped with freshly chopped ONIONS, green chillies, *sev* (spiced fried vermicelli; see *SEV* AND *SEVIYAN*) and a squeeze of lime.

Indore, the twin city of Ujjain, is the largest city in Madhya Pradesh and the industrial hub. This city has evolved as the go-to city for STREET FOOD. This is because of the innovative out-of-the-box problem-solving ability of the city's jewellers, who devised a solution to mitigate the risk of shop-breaking by inviting street food vendors to set up carts outside their shops after they had lowered their shutters for the evening. Hundreds of street vendors came and attracted thousands of foodies every night to savour their delectable fare until the wee hours of the morning. The most famous dishes are the *bhutte ki khees* – fresh corn kernels cooked with spices and milk to make a mouth-watering porridge-like preparation which makes it hard to decide whether you are having a snack, a mild dessert or a delectable meal in itself. The icing on the cake is the fanfare with which it is served to you by tossing *donnas* (small bowls made of *tendu, Diospyros melanoxylon*, leaves) full of *khees*. *Garadu* is another unusual snack found only in Indore – cubes of fried elephant YAM served with a powdered spice mixture. This competes with French fries of the West but has the added bonus of health benefits associated with having this exotic tuber in the winter season.

On the periphery of Indore lies the town of Jhabua which has a sizable tribal population known for rearing a special breed of chicken called *kadaknath*, or *kali masi*, in the local parlance (see POULTRY AND EGGS). This chicken is reared free range and its diet consists of foraged food from the forest. Its flesh is dark grey and is believed to be packed with a super dose of nutrients. The meat is so tough that the only way to cook it is by stewing, but the stew is so flavourful that it tastes as if the stock made from a dozen chickens has been concentrated into it. This region is also known for preparing a steamed bread, called *bafla,* which is served fried with dal. This food is enjoyed on special occasions or on weekends in the winter months. The Malwa region also uses a lot of corn to make bread or porridge as well as a vegetable preparation called *bhutte ki sabzi.* Small pieces of corn on the cob are stewed in a gravy made with TOMATO and grated corn kernels. It is served with rice or puris on special occasions.

Travelling eastwards from Indore takes us to the capital city of Bhopal, which was established in the eleventh century by the legendary King Bhoj as Bhojpal. It is also called the city of lakes as a number of water bodies are spread around the city. The recent history of Bhopal is marked by the legendary rule of women *nawabs*, called *begums*, who ruled the city and the region around. While the inspiration of food may be from the Mughal era or from the Awadh region, the patronage of women rulers inspired the royal *khansamahs* (chefs) to modify the food with *nazakat*, meaning elegance or delicate treatment, which is comparable with that of LUCKNOW. An example is in the preparation of biryani, called *biryan* in Bhopal, which is lighter, making it more like a meat pulao than a biryani by the standards of DELHI, Lucknow or HYDERABAD. *Murg rezala*, with its origin in Awadh, has adopted a new incarnation in Bhopal where it is a delicate preparation of chicken with abundant use of coriander leaves and green chillies. This makes it different from the *rezala* of Lucknow or KOLKATA, two other cities famous for their *rezalas*. Bhopal's version of rogan josh is a lighter version of the lamb dish from Kashmir. Bhopal is also famous for a strong TEA culture, where the tea made with a little salt added to it and is taken after dinner in the popular tea stalls in the old town area where people congregate and unwind until the wee hours of the morning.

Dr Kamal K. Pant

- TimesofIndia.com. 'Mouth-Watering Dishes from Madhya Pradesh That You Must Not Miss'. 14 July 2020. Available online: https://timesofindia.indiatimes.com/life-style/food-news/mouth-watering-dishes-from-madhya-pradesh-that-you-must-not-miss/photostory/76959621.cms (accessed 19 May 2022).

MAHARASHTRA

FIGURE 31 MAHARASHTRA. Vada *pav*. Srishti Gurung/Wikimedia Commons.

Translated as 'the mighty land', Maharashtra is the third largest state in India by area and the second largest in population. It was formed in 1960 by dividing the bilingual Bombay State into majority Marathi-speaking Maharashtra and Gujarati-speaking Gujarat. The vastness of Maharashtra suggests that there are many differences in topography, and therefore in products and styles of food. Maharashtra can be divided into several regions:

Konkan. Raigad, Ratnagiri, Sindhudurg, Thane and MUMBAI are the districts along the coastal belt of Maharashtra, called Konkan. Lined by the Arabian Sea from north to south, the produce of the Konkan is similar throughout, but the variety of cuisines available in this region is impressive. The different communities use the primary crops available to them – COCONUT, RICE, FISH, *KOKUM* and plantains – in different ways to create distinct flavours. The many varieties of GOURDS and CUCUMBERS available along the coast are used not only in CURRIES but also as *bhareet* (a sort of cold, mashed salad) and are also made into desserts. An example is *bhoplyaache ghaarge*, a sweetened unleavened fried bread made from pumpkin and jaggery.

Saltwater fish and crustaceans are made in a variety of ways using fresh or dried coconut as a base or without any coconut at all. Community-specific spice mixes (see SPICE BOX) define the flavours of a dish, and curries are usually eaten with local varieties of short-grain rice or *bhakri*, flatbreads made from rice or sorghum. In the Malvan and adjacent regions, chicken and mutton curries are relished with deep-fried multigrain BREADS called *vade*. MANGO, JACKFRUIT, BANANA and other fruits are abundant and are used both raw and ripe. Raw mangoes are used as souring agents for *amti* (lentil curries) and fish curries or in salads; raw jackfruit is stir-fried or curried to make a side dish; and raw bananas are milled to make flour to make *thalipeeth* (skillet flatbreads) which are part of fasts. Ripe fruits are also used in cooking, proving that the region really loves its *ambat-goad* or sweet and sour flavour profile as much as it loves its hot and spicy one.

Desh (Western Maharashtra) covers the plateau region and includes Pune, Satara, Karad, Kolhapur and other cities. It was the centre of the Maratha Empire and is now a major education and IT hub. Peanuts are a very important crop, used in cooking and pressed for oil. *Toor* dal (split pigeon pea) is more commonly eaten than other legumes (see PULSES), and sorghum and pearl millet (see MILLETS) are essential carbohydrates. Figs, GUAVA and other fruits grow in plenty. Sugarcane is another important crop; jaggery and its by-product, *kaakvi* or sugarcane molasses, are preferred to refined SUGAR.

Kolhapur and Pune preserve remnants of their regal pasts. Kolhapuri cuisine is characterized by a sophisticated use of spices and was once known for its game meat. Pune was once the home of the Peshwas, who were Brahmins, and many commercial Pune eateries also serve the vegetarian fare of the community.

Nashik and Khandesh. This is the region to the north, comprising Ahmednagar, Jalgaon, Dhule and other cities. The city of Nashik is nearby. Over the years, this region has received many immigrants from Rajasthan, Gujarat, and the Deccan and Malwa regions. Thus, the food and culture show the influences of the MUGHAL, Yadav and Chalukya cultures. For example, *choorma* LADDU (sweet balls made of crumbled wheat flour dumplings), *gulgule* (sweet fritters) and *daal batti* (wheat flour dumplings served with lentils) are made in some Marathi homes. The use of *shev* (fried gram flour noodles; see *SEV*) in savoury as well as sweet preparations like laddus reflects the influence of Gujarati and Rajasthani culture.

The Khandesh region often faces drought, so crops are limited. Sorghum is a major source of carbohydrates and is eaten in several forms from the standard *bhakri* to gruels and as popped kernels. Pearl millet is eaten in the winter. Another kind of *bhakri* called *kalnyachi bhakri*, a blend of millets and *urad* dal, is unique to this region. Green-and-white striped AUBERGINES are a Khandesh speciality and are prized for their fleshy, almost seedless interiors, which make the silkiest mash. *Khandeshi maande* is a silken sweet bread in which a soft dough is filled with the *chana* dal-jaggery filling and patted to a flatbread. It is enlarged gradually by twirling it in rhythmic patterns over one's elbows. It is then thrown over a large, inverted iron or clay *kadhai* and cooked slowly to a silky texture. The *maande* from southwest Maharashtra are, by contrast, stuffed with powdered sugar and GHEE, and are cooked to a crisp. When cooked, they are brittle and have a long shelf life.

Marathwada. Beed, Nanded, Latur, Aurangabad, Jalna and the surrounding areas form the hot and arid Marathwada region. Grains and pulses grow well here and there is a steady supply of WHEAT, sorghum, pearl millet, pigeon peas and some other legumes. Because the supply of fresh vegetables and fruits is very limited, sun-drying is a common method of ensuring that greens are available year-round. Leafy greens such as FENUGREEK and the leaves of the fresh chickpea plant are dried in the shade to preserve their colour, flavour and nutrient content. Tender vegetables such as cluster beans and OKRA are also sundried in season and cooked in the harsh summers. Local jujubes known as *bor*, pronounced 'bo-ruh', are also sun-dried and later added to vegetable preparations for a sweet-sour dimension and for their nutritive benefits.

A wide range of dry CHUTNEYS are made here, another example of the ingenuity with which limited resources are used to serve a balanced meal.

Vidarbha. This region, made up of Nagpur, Chandrapur, Bhandara, Amravati, Akola and the surrounding areas, is north of the Deccan plateau and shares boundaries with the neighbouring states of Madhya Pradesh, Chhattisgarh and Telangana. People from Vidarbha are known to love sweet, spicy and fried foods in equal measure. In addition to sorghum, pearl millet and rice, the region is known for its cash crops, oranges and cotton. SESAME and pigeon pea are other important crops, and sesame oil is the preferred cooking medium. Sun-drying vegetables are common. In the winter, bright orange pumpkins are a popular ingredient and the traditional *baakar bhaaji* (pumpkins cooked with dried coconut and an aromatic spice mix) is made on every special occasion. Grains and legumes are also used for desserts and probiotic porridges (*ambil*) for breakfast. The popular *gola bhaat* and *vada bhaat* (celebratory rice dishes with lentil dumplings) are made using local short-grain rice.

There are many communities in Maharashtra which have their own distinctive cuisines.

Brahmins. Brahmins in Maharashtra can be divided into three groups based on their geographical location and ethnographic study. These are the Koknastha Brahmins (also known as the Chitpavan Brahmins from the Konkan belt), the Deshastha Brahmins (from the plateau regions) and the Karhade Brahmins. Another smaller group, called the Devrukhe Brahmins, hails primarily from the Raigad region. Despite major similarities, VEGETARIANISM being a key one, each of these groups has unique culinary traditions.

Other Groups. Although the Pathare Prabhus are not the indigenous people of Maharashtra, they were amongst the first settlers of Mumbai and are said to have come there from Nepal via Gujarat. The influence of Gujarati cuisine and culture is evident in their use of spices and techniques. An example is the Pathare Prabhu *ghada*, a cousin of the Gujarati *undhiyu*, a melange of root vegetables flavoured with seasonal green GARLIC – except that the Pathare Prabhu version has vegetables and meat and/or seafood. Seafood and goat meat occupy a special place in the Pathare Prabhu repertoire. The choicest, most expensive fish and crustaceans find their way to the Pathare Prabhu table.

Chandraseniya Kayastha Prabhus (CKPs). This group originally came from Ayodhya, settling in parts of Malwa in Madhya Pradesh and Gujarat, and finally settled in northwestern Maharashtra. They have some similarities with the Pathare Prabhus in terms of food preferences and cooking styles, but the cuisine retains a distinct personality. Using a variety of fresh fish and crustaceans, CKPs make an array of *kaalvans* (curries) ranging from a silky green one with fresh CORIANDER, CHILLIES and coconut to a fiery red one with a slick of oil floating on top. Apart from their deep love for meat and fish, the CKPs are also very fond of monsoon vegetables, and are perhaps one of the few communities in the state that consume foraged seasonal greens. *Phodshi*, *taakla* and *sheval* are seasonal foraged greens that grow freely in the hills adjoining Thane and Palghar areas. They are CKP delicacies and are usually cooked in simple stir-fries or paired with seafood. The CKP love for elaborate sweets is also legendary. The *ninaav* is a sort of cake made using roasted wheat (coarsely ground) and split Bengal gram in combination with coconut milk, jaggery and sweet spices.

Panchaal. This is a collective term used for the five craftspeople – goldsmiths, carpenters, ironsmiths, masons and glass makers – but some theorists also include other craftspeople such as potters and weavers in their study of the community. Their cuisine is laced with the *paach* masala, a community hallmark, used to flavour meats and vegetables alike. The masala also contains split Bengal gram and rice or wheat, so it also provides body to the dish.

Kolis. The indigenous people of Mumbai, Kolis are primarily fisherfolk. They know how to respect every part of the catch. *Kaata pisara*, the skeleton of large, fleshy fish such as *ghol*, is a delicacy for festive occasions. In the monsoons, when the fish breed, Koli fishermen do not venture into the sea. This period is declared over on Narali Purnima when they offer coconuts to the sea god and resume fishing. In the meantime, dried fish are both eaten and sold. If you happen to pass by a *koliwada*, a Koli neighbourhood, in the summers, you will see curtains and curtains of *bombil*, the slimy BOMBAY DUCK fish hung out to dry in rows. These are refreshed in warm water and eaten when fresh fish is unavailable.

Marathas. The Marathas claim to be the descendants of the Aryans, a group of which moved to Maharashtra several hundreds of years ago and are said to have ninety-six clans. They differ slightly depending on the region they come from but a common thread is a general fondness for spices and sweets. Rice is reserved for special occasions but millet *bhakri* (which is being replaced by the easier wheat *poli* or chapati these days) is the main carbohydrate. An elaborate masala comprising flame-roasted ONION and dried coconut is used in most of their meat and vegetarian gravies. Salads – CARROTS, spring onions, RADISHES and a crunchy green chilli for a spice kick – are common. The green chilli is otherwise rare in Maratha cooking; dried red chillies and chilli powder are the primary sources of heat, especially for Marathas hailing from Kolhapur. *Puran poli* (silken flatbread stuffed with chickpeas and jaggery) is the sweetmeat of choice.

Christians. The Christian community in Maharashtra is made up of EAST INDIANS, ANGLO-INDIANS and Marathi Protestant Christians, although a large community of Goan Catholics have also settled in Maharashtra. Marathi Protestant Christians are local inhabitants who converted to Protestantism about 200 years ago, but retained all their other customs and traditions including food. They continue to consume *rakti* (animal blood), which was left to coagulate and then used in cooking. Their everyday foods also bear close resemblance to the Hindu food preferences of the region. Rice, lentils, *bhakri* and traditional sweets on special occasions are commonly made in both communities. Alongside Christmas cake, you will also find the table laden with delicacies such as *karanji* (pastry crescents stuffed with coconut fudge) and *chakli* (spiced, spiral-fried cookies).

Konkani Muslims. They can trace their geographical origins from Thane in the north of Mumbai to Sindhudurg on the southern coast of the Konkan. Natives of Maharashtra, this community married into travelling Arab and African trader communities that came to trade on the coast. Their cuisine is a fascinating mix of both styles of cooking. *Saandan*, an IDLI-like steamed rice and coconut milk cake, is made in both Konkani Hindu and Muslim homes, but the Konkani Muslim community eats them plain with meat curries while the Hindu community usually adds a pulp of jackfruit/mango/cucumber to the batter to eat as a breakfast or teatime treat. Rice is a staple. Meat is a significant part of the Konkani Muslim diet and were traditionally used for making curries (*saalan*) and soups (*akhni*), to be served with local varieties of short-grained rice cooked in coconut milk. Biryanis came much later. Floral essences such as rose and jasmine (see FLOWER WATERS) and a liberal use of NUTS and dried fruit are also common. Other religious communities are BENE ISRAELIS and East Indians.

Tribals. The tribal communities of Maharashtra are the true keepers of traditional food wisdom, whether it is foraging for seasonal greens, lesser-known tubers, or even indigenous varieties of millets and rice. Some of these tribes include Bhil, Banjara, Warli,

Lamaan and Thakur. Each of these has a distinct culinary signature, but they all respect the produce of the land and make the most of it with a sense of gratitude towards the earth.

Bhakri made from local millets form the basis of their everyday diet. These tribes preserve the seeds of their harvest and use them to plant the next harvest, treating hybrid seeds with caution. Rice varieties are mainly short-grain, starchy and aromatic and are usually pounded by hand to remove the husks. Rice preparations are not elaborate; a few fistfuls of rice are boiled in salted water until soft. The water is then drained out (reserved to drink) and the rice is covered again until the steam settles. It is eaten with whatever legumes or vegetables are available. Cultivated vegetables were not consumed until a few decades ago, but some tribes now grow okra, cluster beans, field beans and non-hybrid TOMATOES. Gourds grow freely in the hilly regions. The Adivasis also consume the tender shoots and flowers of various trees as well as grasses and MUSHROOMS. These are simply stir-fried in a little oil and some garlic and chillies. ALCOHOL is commonly consumed by most Adivasi tribes and liquor made of *mahua* flowers is a favourite, especially among the tribes of the Satpura region. *Saloi*, a curry made from goat head and blood, is another delicacy.

Cooking methods. Vegetables are usually stir-fried or cooked slowly under condensation while meats are stewed. Frying fish usually implies shallow frying in a minimal amount of oil on a solid iron skillet. Often, a dish begins with a *phodni* (Hindi *tarka*, tempered spices). Oil or ghee is heated in a pan, the spices are added and once they pop, the vegetables or lentils are added. Another kind of *phodni* is added at the end of the cooking process.

In Marathi cuisine, each category of dish requires a specific *phodni*. Dairy-based dishes have a ghee-based *phodni* because ghee gives the dish a more rounded flavour, although people use oil because they think it is healthier. *Phodni* for FASTING foods is always done in ghee or peanut oil and must never contain MUSTARD seeds, ASAFOETIDA or TURMERIC. Vegetables with a strong aroma, like roselle, cabbage or fenugreek, or dishes such as *kaande pohe* (beaten rice cooked with onions) demand more robust flavours with crushed garlic or extra turmeric powder or onions thrown in. Another kind of *phodni* that is now facing extinction is the *khaapraachi phodni*, which is made on a piece of clay. When clay pots were commonly used for cooking over a wood fire, bits of broken clay were heated to the point of being red hot and used to make the *phodni* in. They were then dunked whole into the dish.

In addition to common techniques such as steaming or baking, stir frying and deep frying, a method of slow cooking is also used. Utensils in which vegetable or meat dishes are being cooked are covered with a deep thali, or plate with walled sides, and water is poured on it. Droplets of water form on the underside, providing moisture without letting the flavours escape the pan or letting the contents of the pan stick to the bottom. The water in the plate also heats up slowly and this can be added in small quantities to the contents of the pan, if required, thereby retaining the natural colour and flavour of the vegetables and making meats particularly succulent.

Saee Koranne-Khandekar

- Koranne-Khandekar, Saee. *Pangat, a Feast: Food and Lore from Marathi Kitchens*. Gurugram, Haryana: Hachette India, 2019.
- Ujgare, Anupama N. *Maharashtracha Khadya Sanskruti Kosh*. Mumbai: Maharashtra State Board for Literature and Culture, 2015.

MANASOLLASA

A valuable source of historical information about food is the *Manasollasa,* a composition in Sanskrit verse written by King Somesvara III (r. 1126–38). He was the eighth king of the Western Chalukya dynasty that controlled much of southwest India from the late tenth to the thirteenth century. The land was rich and fertile, producing rice, lentils, black pepper, cardamom, betel nuts and leaves, coconuts and sugar.

Rulers of the time displayed their learning by writing on various topics. *Manasollasa,* which means 'delight' or 'refresher of the mind', covers medicine, magic, veterinary science, precious stones, painting, music, dance, literature, women, fish, plants and other topics. Food is covered in the section called *Annabhoga*, or 'enjoyment of food'. It describes nearly a hundred dishes, many of which can be found today, especially in southern and western India. Others are rarely encountered: blood-filled sausages, goat's head in sour gruel, grilled stomach membrane and barbecued river rats, the last considered a great delicacy.

The most common spice is ASAFOETIDA, often dissolved in water – a practice still common in Western India. Other flavourings are ginger, turmeric, black pepper, rock salt, mustard seeds, coriander, cumin, and occasionally camphor and cardamom. Just a few recipes call for ONIONS and GARLIC. Spices are added both during the cooking and afterward, just as they are today. Citrus fruit, AMLA, TAMARIND, POMEGRANATE, or yogurt added sourness. The six basic flavours (sweet, sour, salty, bitter, pungent and astringent) are combined both in individual dishes and in meals. Dishes were deep-fried, sautéed or cooked in a liquid and sometimes more than one technique was used. For sautéing and deep frying, the cooking medium was sesame oil or ghee. Grilling over hot coals was common, especially for meat threaded on metal skewers.

The dietary staple was rice, of which Somesvara identifies eight varieties. Boiled lentils were flavoured with asafoetida, water, salt and turmeric powder and topped with slices of fresh ginger. Pieces of eggplant, goat meat or animal marrow could be added, with black pepper or dried ginger powder sprinkled on top.

Savouries were popular, many with modern counterparts. Disks of white flour 'thin as white cloth' were sautéed to make a bread called *mandaka*, similar to modern parathas, and *polikas*, a word related to the modern *puranpoli*, a sweet paratha stuffed with lentils and sugar. Balls of white flour were baked in hot coals and slightly charred — a dish similar to Rajasthani baatis. A dough of lentil or chickpea flour mixed with spices and water was shaped into little disks, and deep-fried to make *purika,* a forerunner of modern *papdi* (the round crispy wafers used in the popular street food *papdi chaat*). A fermented paste of ground *urad* dal and black pepper was shaped into balls and deep-fried to make *vadika*, which were soaked in milk or yogurt. A modern incarnation is the popular Indian street food dahi vada, (see STREET FOOD).

Dhosika was a crepe made from a paste of ground *urad* dal, black-eyed peas or green peas flavoured with asafoetida, cumin, salt and ginger, and cooked on a thinly oiled hot pan. Its modern descendant is DOSA, which is made from a batter of lentils and rice. According to K.T. ACHAYA, rice was probably added as an ingredient in the thirteenth century.

Because Somesvara, like most Indian rulers, was a Kshatriya, he hunted and enjoyed meat, especially game such as wild boar and venison. Some of the dishes described are complex and highly aromatic, belying the notion that elaborate meat dishes appeared only with the arrival of the Muslims. Pieces of meat marinated in custard apple and ginger were threaded on skewers, grilled over red-hot coals and flavoured with powdered black pepper and a sour juice. Fruits, leaves, stems and flowers were served raw or cooked and with or without meat. Leafy vegetables (twenty-five varieties are named) were mixed with yogurt or citrus fruits (forty are listed, most with no English equivalent); roots and BAMBOO SHOOTS and leaves were salted or mixed with powdered black mustard seed, sesame oil and salt. A salad of raw mango, plantain, bitter gourd and jackfruit in a sesame and black mustard seed dressing.

Sikharini (drained spiced yogurt) is a precursor of modern SHRIKHAND. Some sweet dishes were made with KHOYA and others with CHHANA that was mixed with sugar and made into small balls that are fried and eaten. This seems to refute the claim that Hindus did not split milk and that making chhana originated with the Portuguese although the Portuguese may have been the inspiration for modern Bengali sweets. Alcoholic drinks include *gaudi*, a rum like drink made from sugar or molasses, and *madhvi*, made from the flowers of the mahua tree.

Colleen Sen

- Arundhhati, Dr (Mrs) P. *Royal Life in Manasollasa*. New Delhi: Sundeep Prakashan, 1993.

MANGALURU

Located approximately 360 km from BENGALURU, Mangaluru (formerly called Mangalore) is a quaint little cosmopolitan city that has the Arabian Sea on one side and the majestic Western Ghats just ninety km away from the city centre on the other. Mangaluru gets its name from Mangaladevi, the main deity in the Mangaladevi Temple located in Bolar. Mangaluru is mentioned in the work of IBN BATTUTA who enjoyed hospitality at eight southern ports including Mangaluru (then called Manjurur).

The food is a wonderful mix reflecting the many communities that make up the city's population. The Hindu population includes the Konkani-speaking Goud Saraswat Brahmin (GSB) community and the Tulu-speaking communities of the Bunts, the Mogaveeras and Billavas, among others. The Catholics have their culinary roots in Goa. The Christian community also includes Protestants. The Muslim community are the Bearys. Jains are also a part of Mangaluru's people.

Across the communities there is a commonality of some ingredients and masalas. As a coastal city, FISH is commonly eaten. It is usually fried or made into a COCONUT-based gravy across communities. *Bangude* (mackerel), *pamplet* (pomfret), *yetti* (prawns), *marwai* (shellfish) and *anjal* (seer fish), all names in the Tulu language, are usually fried in a masala paste made of ground red dried CHILLIES, TAMARIND and SALT. Each community has their version of this masala paste, usually ground just before use but the *meet mirsang* (unique to the Catholic community) is ground, bottled and refrigerated for use. *Pathrade*, or *patrode*, is a steamed savoury dish made with TARO leaves. The Catholics use a spiced rice paste and shredded taro leaf mix while the GSB community use a spiced gram flour paste applied onto the leaves which are then rolled, steamed, sliced and a tempering of MUSTARD seeds and chillies is added to it.

Dal (usually made of pigeon pea lentils; see PULSES) is also common across communities. Catholics make a *daaliso saar* (thin dal gravy) with *bimblis* (*Averrhoa bilimbi*) and the GSBs make *dali thove*, which is a simple dish of boiled lentils with sliced onions and green chillies with a tempering of mustard seeds. There is also the *padengi gassi* made with green mung lentils. All communities love their *ganji oota* (rice gruel meal), usually had with some PICKLE or a piece of fish and some vegetables. Mangalureans use several souring agents in their everyday cooking. TAMARIND, *KOKUM* (Garcinia indica), *bimbli*, star fruit and *ambade* (hogplums) are regularly used. Fresh toddy, when available, is used to ferment batters, especially for IDLIS and *sannas* (steamed rice cakes).

Mangalore buns are soft, fluffy buns made with a fermented batter and mashed BANANAS. *Goli bajes* are ball-shaped fritters made with a fermented batter spiced with slivers of GINGER, pepper (see PEPPER, BLACK), green chillies and CURRY LEAVES. The indulgent GHEE roast is made by dry roasting the spices, then cooking the masala in copious amounts of clarified butter for at least an hour before adding meat or fish. The *pulimunchi* (*puli* – sourness from tamarind and *munchi* – spiciness from a melange of spices) is cooked with meat and fish.

There is a wide range of steamed accompaniments such as *sannas, shevyo* or *shevay* (stringhoppers) and *kadubu* (rice cake steamed in JACKFRUIT leaves) that are made too. The Catholic community observes Lent, although the FASTING here is more an abstinence from meat and ALCOHOL. A major festival for the Catholics is the Monthi Saibinichi Fest or the Feast of Mount Mary/Nativity, also celebrated as the harvest festival. Parallels can be drawn with the celebration of the Hindu festival of Ganesh Chaturthi, going back to the time of the Inquisition.

Ramadan is observed by the Muslims and *iftar* has several delicious offerings such as beef BIRYANI, watermelon and rose syrup juice, keema *aloo* SAMOSAS (minced meat and POTATO samosas), mutton cutlets, *pindi* (steamed rice and coconut balls) with a range of meat gravies, and more.

Clay vessels are the traditional cookware. Leaves such as banana, screwpine and jackfruit are used to wrap food – from batter to fish, while steaming. These impart unique aromas and flavours to the dish.

Shireen Sequeira, a Mangalurean based in Dubai, has documented the Catholic community's food, besides the food of other communities of the region, in her blog *Ruchik Randhap* (Delicious Cooking). Jane Dsouza's *Cookbook* is a popular and simple recipe book with recipes from Mangaluru. Kuraisha Rasheed helms a YouTube channel, Beary's Kitchen, which showcases the food of the Beary community. Well-known chef Shriya Shetty moved from MUMBAI to Mangaluru to go back to her roots and document Mangalurean food. Internationally, celebrity chef Hari Nayak has put Mangalurean food on the global map with interesting renditions at his restaurant, Sona, in New York.

Ruth Dsouza Prabhu

- Prabhu, Ruth Dsouza. 'Meet Mirsang: The Heart of the Mangalorean Catholic Kitchen'. *The Goya Journal*, 23 July 2021. Available online: https://www.goya.in/blog/meet-mirsang-the-heart-of-the-mangalorean-catholic-kitchen (accessed 25 April 2022).
- Prabhu, Ruth Dsouza. 'Monti Saibinichi Fest, Celebrating the Lady of the Mount in Mangalore'. *The Goya Journal*, 31 August 2021. Available online: https://www.goya.in/blog/monti-saibinichi-fest-celebrating-the-lady-of-the-mount-in-mangalore (accessed 25 April 2022).

MANGO

Often called the 'king of fruits', the mango (*Mangifera indica*, Hindi *aam*) is the national fruit of India and the national tree of Bangladesh. It is the fruit of an evergreen tree which originated in the Northeastern India-Myanmar region where wild varieties still grow. Mango trees thrive in places where good rainfall is followed by a dry season. It may have been cultivated as early as 2000 BCE. The English word comes via Portuguese from the Malayalam *manga* and Tamil *mangai*.

Today India is the world's largest producer of mangoes, followed by China where it was introduced by Buddhist monks in the mid-eighth century CE. The more than five hundred varieties grown in India fall into two categories: firm-fleshed mangoes for eating and juicy mangoes for sucking. In appearance mangoes may be round, oval or kidney shaped, ranging from five to twenty-five cm in length and from less than hundred grams to more than two kg in weight. Some are round, others long and narrow but all usually have a slight ridge on one side that gives mangoes their distinctive appearance. The skin colour varies from yellow to deep orange, sometimes with patches of red, yellow or green. The best varieties are almost free of fibre and extremely aromatic, with a slight resinous quality.

Each region of India has its own varieties, which local residents always consider far superior to those produced elsewhere. Famous varieties include Himsagar and *fazli* in West Bengal and Orissa; Dussehri, *langra, chausa* and *ratnal* in Uttar Pradesh; *badami* and *raspuri* in Karnataka; *neelam, imam pasand* and Banganapalli in Andhra Pradesh; *benishan* and Mulgoba in Tamil Nadu; and *kesar, pairi, vanraj, mankurad* and Alphonso in West India. Some varieties such as *safeda, mallika* and *amrapali* are today grown all over India.

The mango is mentioned for the first time in the Vedic literature around 700 BCE and in Buddhist texts since it was a permitted food for Buddhist monks. The *Ramayana* has several references to mango plantations. The Maurya emperor ASHOKA planted mango trees along the roads of his empire for shade and fruit. The Khilji emperor Ala-ud-Dīn (1266–1316) is said to have held a feast featuring only mangoes which were considered an aphrodisiac. The Persian poet Amir Khusrao (1253–1325) called mangoes 'the fairest fruit of Hindustan' and wrote this famous riddle:

> He visits my town once a year.
> He fills my mouth with kisses and nectar.
> I spend all my money on him.
> Who, girl, your lover?
> No, a mango.

The world traveller IBN BATTUTA, who spent time in the port towns of Calicut (Kozhikode) and Kollam, observed people having their meals with pickled raw mango. Of the mango, he wrote,

> The fruit is about the size of a damask prune (i.e. damson plum), which, when green and not so ripe, of those which happen to fall, they salt and thus preserve them just as lemon is preserved by us. In the same manner they preserve ginger when it is green, as also pods of pepper, and this they eat with their meals.

A great deal of mango lore is associated with the MUGHALS. Babur, who preferred the melons of his native Ferghana Valley in Central Asia, found the fruit generally overrated, although he conceded that when they were good, they were excellent. His descendants had a more favourable opinion. Akbar's Prime Minister Abu'l-Fazl wrote of mangoes, 'This fruit is unrivalled in colour, smell and taste; and some of the gourmands of Turan and Iran place it above muskmelons and grapes.' Akbar planted the Lakh Bagh garden near Dehra Dun which had 100,000 trees and was one of the earliest examples of grafting. His son, Jahangir, wrote: 'Despite the sweetness of the fruits from Kabul, not one of them, to my taste, has the flavour of the mango.' Shah Jahan built a road between Delhi and the West coast so that he could have mangoes at the very beginning of spring. His son, Dara Shikoh, commissioned the Persian manuscript *Nuskha Dar Fanni-Falahat* (*The Art of Agriculture*) which described grafting and other techniques in detail.

The Mughals' gardeners developed grafting techniques to produce hundreds of varieties. (Grafting is the joining of a woody shoot from a mature tree with a seedling.) Even today, some varieties of mangoes have names such as Jahangir and Humayun-ud-Din. The rulers also gave tax incentives to noblemen who planted orchards and employed experts who indicated the precise moment at which each mango should be picked and eaten. The Nizams of Hyderabad and other rulers followed their example. The Portuguese continued grafting to produce such varieties as the *fernandin*, *pasiri* and the famous Alphonso, named after a Portuguese nobleman. Colonial powers took the mango to West Africa, Brazil, the West Indies, Mexico, the Philippines, Australia and the United States.

The Mughals rewarded their cooks for creating creations, such as *aam panna* and *aam ka meetha* pulao, a delicate dessert. To celebrate the arrival of the newly harvested fruit, parties were organized where connoisseurs discuss their merits. Today, *aam panna* is a refreshing summer drink (called *panaka* in ancient times) made from fresh mango juice. The popular North Indian drink LASSI is sometimes made from mango pulp mixed with yogurt and SALT or SUGAR. In Gujarat and Maharashtra, a popular sweet dish is *aam raas*, lightly spiced mango pulp served with puris (see BREADS). Everywhere green mangoes are used to make PICKLES, CHUTNEYS and *murabbas*. Tart green mangoes are cooked in CURRIES and dals (see PULSES). Dried unripe fruits are ground into a sour-tasting powder called *amchur*, a common flavouring in chaat masala (see SPICE BOX). All parts of the mango are used in folk and Ayurvedic medicine to cure various ailments (see FOOD AND MEDICINE).

The mango has an important place in Indian art and culture. The distinctive curved shape is a popular motif in Hindu art and textiles and was the origin of the paisley design that became popular in the West in the eighteenth century following the importation of Kashmiri shawls. There are many depictions of mangoes in the sculpture of the Great Stupas of Sanchi and the Bahrut stupa. Mango flowers are used in the worship of the goddess Saraswati and the leaves have traditionally decorated the doorways of Indian houses on festive occasions.

Colleen Sen

- Buduwar, K. *Romance of the Mango: The Complete Book of the King of Fruits*. New Delhi: Penguin, 2002.
- Desh, Madhulika. 'A Complete History of the Mango: From the Times of Mauryas to Mughals'. *Swarajya*, 19 June 2016. Available

online: https://swarajyamag.com/culture/from-chausa-to-dusseri-the-not-so-aam-story-of-mango-2 (accessed 26 April 2022).

- The Heritage Lab. 'Mango: The National Fruit of India'. 23 May 2018. Available online: https://www.theheritagelab.in/mango-national-fruit-history/ (accessed 26 April 2022).

MANIPUR

Manipur is a former princely state in the Northeast that borders Nagaland to the north, Mizoram to the south, Assam to the west and Myanmar to the east and south. It has a very diverse population. The Meitei ethnic group account for around 53 per cent of the population, various Naga tribes for 24 per cent and different Kuk-Chin tribes 16 percent. They practise a number of religions, Hinduism being the major one, followed closely by Christianity.

The state can be divided into two regions: a central valley and surrounding hills and mountains. The region has very heavy rainfall, which accounts for the cultivation of many varieties of RICE in the valley and an abundance of FISH. Vegetables are grown in kitchen gardens or bought from local markets so Manipuri cuisine is mainly seasonal and organic. Vegetables grown in the region include various beans, GOURDS, AUBERGINES and pumpkins; those introduced by the British – POTATOES, cabbage, CARROTS, etc.; and vegetables unique to the region, such as *yendem* (a kind of TARO), *kolamni* (water spinach), *yongchak* (bitter beans) and *sougri* (roselle leaves).

Rice is the staple of Manipuri cuisine. Both fresh and fermented dried fish, called *ngari*, are ingredients in many dishes. A typical Manipuri meal consists of steamed rice, *kangsoi* (a vegetable stew made with *ngari*), *ooti* (a thick CURRY made of peas, chives and beans), a fish curry, stir-fried vegetables and *singju* (a salad made from thinly sliced seasonal greens such as cabbage mixed with CHILLIES, roasted and ground black SESAME seeds and fermented fish). A meal may end with a pudding made of black rice called *chakhao*. Most dishes are boiled or steamed; oil is used sparingly, although there are a few fried items such as various kinds of *boras* (a vegetable fritter fried a chickpea flour batter). Manipur cooks use many aromatic herbs and roots, including various species of wild MUSHROOMS. A major spice is the *umorok* chilli.

The addition of fermented fish, soybeans or BAMBOO SHOOTS in cooking is a common practice in most homes. No two tribes have the same style of cooking, although this population of pork curry enthusiasts flavour their meat with a few common ingredients, such as hand-shredded MUSTARD leaves and passion fruit leaves. Sun-dried meat remains an age-old way of preservation and imparts a unique smoked aftertaste to dishes. Fermentation ensures that certain products are available year-round and also has medicinal value. The quintessential CHUTNEYS of Manipur cuisine, which go by different regional names such as *morok metpa* or *malta meh*, are made by grinding together roasted TOMATOES, GARLIC, chillies and fermented fish, along with some boiled greens, round off any meal in any part of Manipur.

Poky *pokphoms* (tiny shacks) serving local favourites of the fried variety dot the towns and line the highways of Manipur. Popular tea-time snacks served in these make-shift shacks include *bora* or PAKORAS (battered fried tempura-like in gram flour), *aloo saaak* (fried *aloo*), *kanghou* (fried chickpea with thyme and chillies) and *singju*.

The contrasting religious and cultural backgrounds of the people dictate much of their individual cuisines. The Meitei communities, for instance, who are largely followers of

Hinduism and Vaishnavism, have a more rigid outlook on culinary rules. Food is like art to them. They are particular about how they chop the vegetables and how they cook. They follow a ritual of bathing before they enter their kitchens, showing respect for the food they are about to cook. Of course, modern Meiteis may not follow this rigidly now.

Manipur is the only state that has professional cooks or people specially designated in society to cook. These are the *bamons* (Manipuri Brahmins). They are gifted with magic hands and can turn even a dull vegetable-like pumpkin into a delicacy. Usually, *bamons* are hired to cook for any special occasion. They come with their own pots and pans and although they carry no secret spices, their food is so flavourful that people often wonder if they have secret ingredients. They make do with locally available spices like *jeera* (CUMIN), *hing* (ASAFOETIDA), chilli powder, ONION, GINGER and garlic.

The kitchen in a Meitei home is regarded as sacred, which then demands several rituals to be observed while cooking and serving. For instance, one must bath before stepping into the kitchen. However, those traditional hardcore beliefs do not really hold true for the modern-day people except when it comes to the question of hygiene. Meiteis are largely considered to be vegetarians whose diet heavily centres on local greens; however, it is not uncommon for them to consume fish and chicken. This especially rings true because fermented fish, known as *ngari*, remains a pantry essential in all Manipuri homes.

Hoihnu Hauzel

- Hauzel, Hoihnu. *The Essential North-East Cookbook*. New Delhi: Penguin Books, 2003.
- Indian Culture. 'Manipuri Cuisine: A Unique Experience in Earthy Flavours'. *n.d.* Available online: https://indianculture.gov.in/food-and-culture/north-east/manipuri-cuisine-unique-experience-earthy-flavours (accessed 26 April 2021).

MAPPILAS

The Mappilas are inhabitants of Kerala's north Malabar coast, extending from Kasargod down to Quilon. From the thirteenth century onwards, the region was ruled by the Samoothiri, or Zamorin, the local monarchs who promoted trade with the Arabs, the primary spice traders at the time. The Arabs had monopoly over the sea routes to Kodangallur (port of Muziris) and Kozhikode from as early as the first century CE, long before the Europeans took control of the trade. It was through this route that Islam first arrived in Kerala in the seventh century CE. The intermarriage between the Arabs and the indigenous people led to the formation of the Mappila community.

The name 'Mappila' is a transliteration of a Malayalam word and has taken different forms including Moplah and Māppilla. The origin of the word has several interpretations but common understanding is that it was an honorific applied to foreigners or immigrants. Even today, the term Puthiya Mappila, or 'New Mappila', is used by families to refer to newly married sons-in-law or husbands-to-be. The usage continues for years after marriage and reflects the role of sons-in-law as honoured guests and partial outsiders in the erstwhile *tarawad* house tradition.

While the Mappilas share a common Malayali identity, several Arab influences can be seen in their customs, language and food. The *alisa*, a WHEAT and meat porridge, rich in GHEE and taste, has a lot in common with the Arabian *hareesa*. The Mappila biryani masala lends itself to the flavours of MINT, CORIANDER and yogurt, similar to meat preparations from the Yemen region. The biryani from this region is different from those prepared in other parts of the country, in the usage of a variety of a short-grained RICE called *jeeraka chemba* which is nuttier and more aromatic than the traditionally used basmati. The *mutta maala*, egg yolk poured into boiling SUGAR syrup using a COCONUT shell ladle with a tiny dripping hole, resembles thin strands of a gold necklace. This dish seems to have been influenced by the Portuguese *fios de ovus*. This is not surprising given that the Portuguese controlled trade in Kerala for over a century starting in 1502. The *mutta maala* is a complex dish to prepare and is a speciality served during weddings along with *pinhanathappam* (made from the egg white leftover from the *mutta maala*).

Mappila cuisine exudes some special flavours, although the food consumed daily has a lot in common with that elsewhere in Kerala. The dominant flavours come from ANISEED, shallots and GARLIC. Rice, the staple in this state, is consumed in various forms, as are coconut and coconut oil. Rice flour-based BREAD, such as *adukku* roti, literally meaning bread made in layers, and *nei pathiri*, a puri made from a dough of ground boiled rice, coconut and aniseed, are prepared during almost any occasion worthy of celebration. Wafer-thin *pathiris*, or rice chapatis, and *KANJI*, or rice gruel, are part of dinner meals. *Puttu*, steamed rice cakes, accompanied with fish CURRY and *appam*, or rice hoppers, and *ottipoli*, whole wheat crepes along with egg masala, make for a hearty Mappila breakfast. FISH, in some form or the other, is ubiquitous during afternoon meals. Sometimes marinated and fried, at other times, fish is cooked in a tangy TOMATO or TAMARIND gravy in the traditional *mann chatti* (clay pots). Seafood including squid and crustaceans such as mussels (a speciality being *arikudukka*, mussels stuffed with steamed rice mixture) and prawns are eaten with relish. Commonly cooked meats include beef and chicken and these are prepared as curries and eaten with *pathiris* or *gothamba pathil*, whole wheat parathas.

Vegetarian dishes are an integral part of the Mappila lunch. Curries with lentils, bitter GOURD and raw MANGOES in roasted coconut gravies and sautéed raw BANANAS are commonplace in Mappila homes. Most households in this region have *moringa* (DRUMSTICK) trees growing in their backyard and the leaves and pods are part of several preparations including the *muringayila charu*. A simple dish like the *vendakka mulagittathu* (a spicy OKRA based gravy) along with *neichoru*, or ghee rice, is served on the night of Mylanchi, the eve of the wedding when decorative *henna* is applied to the hands and feet of the bride.

During the month of Ramadan, a typical Mappila kitchen is busy in the hours preceding sunset. To the Mappilas, the size and diversity of the spread on a table are a measure of *thakkaram*, or hospitality, and this inherent tendency extends to the holy month of FASTING. Perhaps this is the reason why the tea time culinary culture is rich, with a variety of pies and pastries, both baked (*athishaya pathiri*, *irachi pathiri*) and deep-fried (*kozhiada*, *chukappam*). Banana-based sweet snacks include the popular *unnakayi*, a cotton pod-shaped fritter, *bariyittathu*, or rice flour-based JALEBIS, and the steamed *ada*, or parcels made of rice, banana and jaggery.

Over the last decade, there has been an increased awareness about the Mappila cuisine. Connoisseurs experiment beyond the traditional biryani and venture into more complex preparations such as *pathiri* and *kozhi nirachathu*, or whole stuffed chicken. Food tourism, fuelled by social media posts and stories, is at a pleasurable high. Today, the streets of Kozhikode and Kasargod once again see a surge of travellers, but this time to indulge in the culinary delights of the region.

Ummi Abdulla and *Nazaneen Jalaludheen*

- Abdulla, Ummi. *Malabar Muslim Cookery*. Hyderabad: Orient Blackswan, 1993.
- Miller, Roland E. *Mappila Muslims of Kerala: A Study in Islamic Trends*. 2nd edition. Hyderabad: Orient Blackswan, 1976.

MATHEW, MRS KM

Annamma Mathew (1922–2003) was a cookbook author, columnist and magazine editor in the South Indian state of Kerala. For decades she published a cooking column in a state newspaper which featured a wide array of recipes primarily from Kerala.

Born in the Godavari district of Andhra Pradesh, at the age of twenty Annamma Mathew married KM Mathew and moved to Kottayam, Kerala, after which she started cooking and experimenting in the kitchen. At the encouragement of her father-in-law KC Mammen Mappillai, who was the editor-in-chief of *Malayala Manorama*, a widely read newspaper in Kerala, she began writing her cooking column called 'Pachaka Vidhi'. Her first column appeared in 1953 and featured recipes for Goan prawn CURRY and doughnuts. In 1975, she became the founding editor-in-chief of *Vanitha*, a Malayalam women's magazine that continues its circulation today. She championed women's independence and sought to motivate her readers to forge their own path. Throughout her life, she organized cooking classes and vocational courses.

Mathew, who came to be known as Mrs KM Mathew for most of her life, wrote more than twenty cookbooks, many of which focused on the cuisine of Kerala. She travelled throughout the state to find and research her recipes and she meticulously tested each one in her kitchen before they were published in her column or books: JACKFRUIT and meat cutlets; FISH from coastal regions, such as sardines simmered in thick COCONUT milk; and stewed beef CURRY, a dish that centres on a meat so often pushed out of the narrative of Indian cuisine in favour of a vegetarian norm. A majority of the books were published in Malayalam (the local language of Kerala) while a smaller number were published in English. Her last book, *Flavours of the Spice Coast*, was published in 2002. She also published books on beauty and hair care. She won a number of awards, including the Vigjanadeepam Puraskar in 1994 and the Nirmithi Kendra Award in 1996. In 1992, she was given the Rachel Thomas Award for her contributions to social and cultural causes.

Nikhita Venugopal

- Mathew, Mrs K.M. *Annamma, Mrs. K.M. Mathew: A Book of Memories*. Delhi: Penguin, 2005.
- Mathew, Mrs K.M. *Flavours of the Spice Coast*. Delhi: Penguin India, 2002.
- Mathew, Mrs K.M. *Modern Kerala Dishes*. Kottayam, Kerala: Current Books, 1997.

MAVALLI TIFFIN ROOMS

The BENGALURU culinary legend, Mavalli Tiffin Rooms, is now present in ten locations across India and four overseas. The Brahmin Coffee Club opened in 1924 by Parameshwara Maiya ran successfully for three decades before it was re-named Mavalli Tiffin Rooms.

Managed by three brothers from rural Udupi, South Kanara – Parameshwara, Ganappayya and Yagnanarayan Maiya – MTR, as it is referred to by its aficionados, remains very much a family business currently headed by three siblings, Hemamalini, Vikram and Arvind Maiya. Hemamalini Maiya, the current Senior Partner, is the first, and, so far, the only woman in the family to be actively involved in the business, since 1991.

MTR set itself apart by balancing originality and innovation with tradition in the food business. The shortage of rice during the Second World War produced one of their iconic dishes: the *rava* idli (made from roasted semolina, cashew nuts, MUSTARD seeds, CORIANDER and yogurt) where yogurt took the place of the traditional fermentation process. *Chandrahara* (deep-fried pastry topped with a sweetened sauce of milk solids named after a popular Kannada film) was inspired by layered French pastry. *Bisi bale bhat* (cooked RICE, lentils, spices and vegetables) is a generic Mysore dish refined into a rich and spicy version at MTR.

The highly successful ready-to-eat foods business pioneered in the 1970s (sold to the Norwegian group, Orkla, in 2007) introduced instant mixes of traditional foods, spice blends and ready-to-eat foods, establishing MTR as a household name with the Indian DIASPORA across the globe. Hemamalini Maiya sees MTR's growth as organic, largely relationship driven rather than business driven: 'We look for roots, and try to bring history to the table.' On Sundays, the number of DOSAS served soars to 1,000 along with 800 plates of *rava* idlis and 200 litres of SAMBAR. The kitchens at the flagship restaurant open at 3 am every morning to cater to the first batch of customers who begin queuing by 6 am, ahead of the 2,500 walk-in customers expected over the day.

Kaveri Ponnapa

MEGASTHENES

One of the most valuable sources of information about ancient India is the writings of Megasthenes (*c.* 350–290 BCE), who was the ambassador of the Greek Seleucid king, Seleucus I Nicator, to the court of Chandragupta Maurya between 302 and 298 BCE. Megasthenes recorded his observations of the court and India in a work called *Indika*. The work was lost but passages were cited by later Greek and Latin writers that have come down to us today. Megasthenes' observations were not all firsthand; some were fantastic tales he heard from others, such as stories about people who do not eat but subsist by inhaling the odour of wild APPLES, or only eat wild meat.

Megasthenes was impressed by the wealth and abundance he encountered in India. 'The soil produces two crops every year both of fruits and grains, and because there is never a season without rain, the soil is always productive', he writes, 'much fruit is produced by trees: and the roots of plants, particularly of tall reeds, are sweet both by nature and by concoction [processing]' – an early reference to sugar cane and SUGAR manufacture.

During the summer season, MILLET, SESAME, RICE and an unknown grain called *bosmorum* were sown; in the winter, WHEAT, BARLEY, lentils and other edible fruits not known to the Greeks.

Thanks to this abundance,

> The inhabitants, in like manner, having abundant means of subsistence, exceed in consequence the ordinary stature, and are-distinguished by their proud bearing. They are also found to be well skilled in the arts, as might be expected of men who inhale a pure air and drink the very finest water.

Indians lived frugally. 'They never drink wine except at sacrifices. Their beverage is a liquor composed from rice instead of barley, and their food is principally a rice-pottage [perhaps some form of dal or CURRY or KHICHRI].' But Megasthenes is disapproving of their dining habits: 'They always eat alone and have no fixed hours when meals are to be taken by all in common, but each one eats when he feels inclined. The contrary customs would be better for the ends of social and civil life.' Megasthenes was fascinated by the austere ways of the various sects he encountered, probably Jains or other renunciants. One group, the Hyloboi, lived in the woods and subsisted on leaves, acorns and wild fruits. Another group, the physicians, ate only rice and barley meal and cured people by regulating their diets.

Colleen Sen

- McCrindle, John Watson, ed. *Ancient India as Described by Megasthenes and Arrian*. Calcutta: Thacker, Spink & Co., 1877.

MEGHALAYA

Years ago, the British imperial authorities reached Meghalaya, and owing to its lush, scenic landscapes, dubbed it the 'Scotland of the East'. Meghalaya was previously part of Assam but in 1972, the districts of Khasi, Garo and Jaintia Hills became the new state of Meghalaya. It is bounded by the Indian state of Assam to the north and northeast and by Bangladesh to the south and southwest. The state capital is the tourist-friendly hill town, Shillong. An extremely diverse society, the main tribes are Garo, Khasi and Jaintia. These are also the major languages spoken in addition to English, the state's official language.

Home to some of the wettest places on earth, Cherrapunji and Mawsynram, Meghalaya's waterfalls and crystal-clear waters are celebrated. Here, matrilineal societies operate where the lineage and inheritance are traced through women; the youngest daughter inherits all the wealth and also takes care of her parents. They are also an agrarian society, known particularly for their organically grown crops and herbs, especially Lokodia TURMERIC, which has a high percentage of curcumin.

Thanks to the state's climate and soil, turmeric, GINGER, black pepper (see PEPPER, BLACK) and CARDAMOM grow well here. Other important crops are POTATOES, RICE, CORN, BANANAS and PINEAPPLES. Rice is the dietary staple. Since meat is an expensive luxury, most people eat vegetarian dishes most days of the week, especially greens. Members of the Khasi tribe, for instance, will invariably include a soup called *syrwa*, made from a mix of vegetables with sometimes a chunk of meat added for flavour. The Garos enjoy *wak pura* (pork CURRY with MUSTARD leaves). The Jaintias, too, love their pork but, again, not without a touch of greens or SESAME seeds, another liberally used ingredient in the local cuisines. *Doh neiiong*, a rich, mouth-watering delight derives its name from *doh* meaning meat and *neiiong* meaning sesame seeds. Sesame, which lends this dish a pleasant nutty flavour, is slow roasted and ground to a paste then added to the meat, lending to the dish its almost velvet, dark green colour.

The bustling *bara* bazaars, wholesale markets for local produce, are a feast for the senses. Here, one can find the highly coveted banana flowers, considered a delicacy by locals, and tree tomatoes that grow seven feet above the ground. They are generally prepared on skewers roasted over a fire to attain a smokey flavour and garnished with chopped CORIANDER leaves and a sprinkle of SALT. Cherry TOMATOES are also sold as well as baby green tomatoes which are usually used as souring agents during cooking. Shillong is also home to a Chinese community whose food forms an important part of the larger menu. Chinese restaurants in every nook and corner of Shillong serve noodles flavoured with chunks of pork. Home-made noodles from Shillong are particularly famous.

Hoihnu Hauzel

- Hauzel, Hoihnu. *The Essential North-East Cookbook*. New Delhi: Penguin Books, 2003.

MELONS

Like squashes, to which they are related, melons (*Curcumis melo*, Hindi *kharbuja*) are described in *The Oxford Companion to Food* as 'a fruit whose history, varieties and nomenclature perplex even experts'. One reason is that all forms of the species readily hybridize each other. The wild ancestors of melons were probably native to the region extending from Egypt to Iran and Northwest India. Melon seeds have been discovered in a pot in Harappa. There is a belief that the best melons come from Iran and Afghanistan – as confirmed by Babur's famous complaint about the lack of good melons in Hindustan. Central Asian melons were transplanted in India with limited success but over time they improved. The Mughal emperor Akbar brought in experts to cultivate grapes and melons and his son Jahangir wrote that in Kashmir the melons were 'very sweet … and varieties of the best kind can be obtained'.

India is the world's fourth largest producer of melons. The main producing state is Uttar Pradesh, with 44 per cent of the total, followed by Andhra Pradesh, Madhya Pradesh, Punjab, Haryana and Karnataka. Melons are a warm-season fruit and grow best under hot and dry conditions and in any kind of soil. They grow especially well on riverbeds, as they have done from ancient times. Melons can range in size from 300 gm to as large as two kg, depending on the variety. The taste can vary from moderately sweet to very sweet.

In India, as in the West, melons are eaten for breakfast or made into a drink or smoothie. Mixed with SALT, CHILLI powder, SUGAR and lime juice, they make a refreshing salad. Slightly unripe melons are sautéed and spiced and served as a vegetable. Melon seeds (Hindi *magaz*) are added to HALWAS and BARFI while a paste of melon seeds can be used to thicken the consistency of gravies. *Panjiri* is a hearty dish of NUTS and seeds given to new mothers for six weeks after childbirth (see RITES OF PASSAGE).

Watermelon (*Citrullus lanatus*, Hindi *tarbooz*) originated in Africa and reached India in prehistoric times. (The origin of its Hindi name is uncertain.) The Ayurvedic physician Sushruta called it *kalinda* or *kalinga* and noted that it was grown along the banks of the Indus River. Today, around twenty-five commercial varieties of watermelon are grown in India. Some are named after the towns near which they are grown, such as Faizabadi, Jaunpuri, etc., all lying along the banks of the Ganges and the Yamuna rivers. Watermelon chunks are a popular STREET FOOD during the summer months.

Colleen Sen

- Indian Gardening. '7 Muskmelon Types in India | Best Muskmelon Varieties'. *n.d.* Available online: https://indiagardening.com/lists/muskmelon-types-in-india-best-varieties/ (accessed 26 April 2022).
- Joshi, Shirish. 'The Voyage of Watermelon'. *The Tribune*, 6 May 2002.

MILLETS

One of the first grains cultivated by humans, millet is not the name of a single grain but rather is used to refer to a large group of small-seeded grasses, about fifty of which have been cultivated worldwide for their seeds, mainly in Africa, India, China and other parts of Asia. They once were a staple of human diets in many parts of the world but have gradually lost ground to higher yielding crops such as RICE, WHEAT and CORN. Millets are also widely used as animal fodder.

India leads the world in millet production with an estimated 20 million tonnes in 2021–22. The most common Indian varieties are the following: barnyard millet (*Echinochloa esculenta*, Hindi *sanwa*), finger millet (*Eleusine coracana*, *ragi*), foxtail millet (*Setaria italica*, *kangni*), kodo millet (*Paspalum scrobiculatum*, *kodon*), little millet (*Panicum sumatrense*, *moraiyo*, *kutki*), proso or broomcorn millet (*Panicum miliaceum*, *cheena*), pearl millet (*Pennisetum glaucum*, *bajra*) and sorghum (genus *Sorghum*, *jowar*). The first six are often categorized as 'small millets'. Sometimes buckwheat, Job's tears and even AMARANTH are termed 'millets'.

Indian millets have different origins. Broomcorn millet, buckwheat and probably foxtail millet originated in northern China in the eighth millennium BCE. After domestication, they were taken by nomadic pastoralists to Central Asia, Europe and to India via Southeast Asia. Little millet and kodo millet are native to South India. Finger millet, sorghum and pearl millet originated in Africa, perhaps Mauritania or Ethiopia, and were domesticated there. Along with cow pea and hyacinth bean, they had reached northwest India by the second millennium BCE along one of trading routes of the Harappan Civilization. By the middle of the second millennium they were an important crop in India.

Millets are grown in every state. The largest producers are Rajasthan (mainly pearl millet), Maharashtra (mainly sorghum) and Karnataka (sorghum and finger millet). Millets have long been cultivated and consumed by tribals. Millets and BARLEY are staples of the subsistence economy of the Himalayan region. IBN BATTUTA observed that Indians ate millets most often and he especially enjoyed pounded millet made into a porridge cooked with buffalo's milk. For breakfast, he wrote, Indians ate peas and mung beans cooked with rice and ghee. Animals were fed with barley, chickpeas and leaves as fodder and even given ghee.

Since the autumn of 2007, the Government of India has promoted the cultivation and consumption of millets as part of its National Food Security Mission; some states have their own millet programmes. The Indian Institute of Millet Research, headquartered in HYDERABAD, sponsors programmes to improve productivity and consumption. Their focus has been on *ragi* and *jowar* since their seed is readily available and people are accustomed to their taste. The year 2023 will be observed as the International Year of Millets because of India's proposal to the Food and Agricultural Organization.

In India domestic production and consumption fell 50–60 per cent following the Green Revolution of the 1970s because of a preference for wheat, which is softer, easier to use and is considered more modern. Rice and wheat became more available and affordable, especially with government subsidies. But recently there has been a resurgence of interest in millets for environmental and health reasons. Most millets are *kharif* crops; that is, they are sown in the summer and watered by the monsoon rains. They require much less water than other grains, especially rice, and can grow in semi-arid regions with as little as 350–400 mm of rainfall a year. Some varieties can survive in temperatures up to 46°C. They can grow in shallow soils with low fertility and higher salinity and acidity. Most millets mature sixty to ninety days after sowing which means that they can provide quick nutrition during years of scarcity. They are environmentally friendly since they take more carbon dioxide from the atmosphere and convert it to oxygen. A disadvantage is that, except for ragi and jowar, millets have tough seed coats and require a lot more processing.

Millets used to be called 'coarse cereals' but today because of their nutritional richness they are now considered 'nutricereals' or 'smart foods'. The protein content of all the millets averages 10–11 per cent, comparable to that of wheat, with proso millet having the highest. Finger and proso millets are rich in essential amino acids. Millets, especially little and kodo millets, are a very rich source of both crude and dietary fibre, which can be as high as 38 per cent – eight times higher than rice and wheat. This lowers their glycaemic index, making them a good choice for diabetics. Millets are also rich in micronutrients. Their mineral content is several times higher than wheat and rice, while the calcium content of finger millet is eight times higher than that of wheat. Barnyard, pearl and foxtail millets are good sources of iron.

Another use of millets is to make alcoholic beverages. In the Himalayan region, the Gurkha, Lepcha and other ethnic groups prepare mild alcoholic beverages by fermenting finger millet mash. It has a sweet and slightly acidic taste and is served in a bamboo container.

Because of their health and environmental benefits, today top restaurants feature millet dishes, such as puffed *bajra* and red bean chaat, and *ragi te khubani da* halwa (Punjab Grill); sourdough millet roti, and barley and jowar salad (Bombay Canteen); and sorghum millet congee (Vivanta by Taj, Bengaluru).

Sorghum (Hindi *jowar*). It is the fourth most widely consumed cereal in the world (after wheat, rice and corn/maize). India is the world's second largest producer, with half grown in Karnataka and Maharashtra. It is highly drought-resistant and can remain dormant during dry periods. In Karnataka, up to three crops can be grown each year. Sorghum can be mixed with other crops, including various legumes, pearl millet, and even AUBERGINE, cucumber and other vegetables. The threshed grain is ground into a wholemeal flour which can be made into a porridge, a paste or a dough by boiling in water. If the seed coat is removed (which reduces the protein content by 10–20 per cent), the grain can be cooked like rice or ground into flour. Because it lacks gluten, it needs to be mixed with wheat or some other cereal flour to make parathas and other BREADS. Popular dishes include *upma* (a porridge) and rotis. Sorghum has a high nutrient profile. Around one hundred grams provide ten grams of protein, six grams of fibre and high levels of some B vitamins, magnesium and other minerals.

Pearl Millet. India is the world's largest producer of pearl millet, with Rajasthan, Maharashtra, Gujarat, Uttar Pradesh and Tamil Nadu accounting for most of India's annual production of around 5 million tons. It can grow on drier areas unsuitable for finger millet. One of the best-known dishes is *bajra ki* roti, a traditional Rajasthani dish that is becoming popular all over India because of its nutritional advantages. It is also used as a substitute for rice in KHICHRI, IDLI, DOSA and other dishes.

Finger Millet. The most widely grown small millet in India and Africa, finger millet is a staple food in central Karnataka where it is often planted with other crops, such as MUSTARD, cowpea and other millets. It is also grown in the Central Himalayan Region. Like other grains, it is preserved in earthenware or metal vessels. Traditionally in villages, especially in the Deccan, it was stored in large underground pits 2–2.5 m deep that can hold two tonnes of grain, reportedly for as long as fifty years if kept dry. Two popular Karnataka dishes are *ambali,* a summertime dish made by soaking flour in water or BUTTERMILK and cooking it to make a drink or thick gruel, and *hirihiitu*, made from popped *ragi* flour mixed with jaggery and milk.

Other Millets. Barnyard millet is an important crop in the state of Uttarakhand where the dehusked grain is cooked, like rice, with milk and jaggery (see SUGAR) on festive occasions. Foxtail millet is mainly grown in the lower Deccan Plateau and to a lesser extent in the Central Himalaya region. It is often sown with other winter crops, such as barnyard millet. The grain is eaten like rice or made into sweet puddings and porridges. Kodo millet was domesticated in India 3,000 years ago and is the coarsest cereal under cultivation. The largest producer is Madhya Pradesh. Several varieties are grown, some sweet and others more bitter. It can be grown on poor marginal soils. It has a storage life of up to a hundred years and has been used as a standby food during times of famine. Proso millet is grown in Andhra Pradesh, Maharashtra, Tamil Nadu, Uttar Pradesh and Bihar. The dehusked grain is cooked like rice or ground into flour to make snacks and bread. It has the highest protein content of any millet. Little millet grows wild in North India and is cultivated mainly in tribal areas and on marginal lands, especially in the Eastern Ghats. In Tamil Nadu, it is roasted with black gram or SESAME. Job's tears (*kauch-gurgur*) can grow at high altitudes and is an important food of the hill tribes in Assam, where it is ground into flour to make bread, eaten whole as a snack or fermented to make a beer.

Colleen Sen

- Navdanya India. *Bhoole Bisre Anaj: Forgotten Foods*. E-Book edition. New Delhi, 2010.
- Sauer, Jonathan. *Historical Geography of Crop Plants: A Select Roster*. Boca Raton, FL: CRC Press, 1992.

MINT

Mint (Hindi *pudina*) is a perennial herb from the *Mentha* genus. Mint is extremely mutable so there are many species, mostly native to the Mediterranean and western Asia. The great number of species and varieties leads to confusion though fortunately there are several whose flavour doesn't differ widely and can be used interchangeably. According to J.S. Pruthi (1976), eight species grow or are cultivated in India.

The main ones are:

- *Mentha arvensis*, known as field or wild mint, is native to hilly northwest India.
- *M. arvensis* var. *piperascens*, called Japanese mint, was obtained from Japan in 1952 and is now cultivated on a large scale in Jammu and Kashmir and Uttar Pradesh. This variety is more robust than *M. arvensis* and, because of this, can be cultivated all over India. Japanese mint is the most widely grown as a commercial crop (used in peppermint oil).
- *M. spicata*, known as spearmint, grows in many gardens and is sold in markets. This popular mint is used extensively in cooking.

Dried mint is not popular in India because of its dry taste and lack of flavour. Fresh mint leaves with their appealing cool taste and aroma are used either as whole leaves or freshly chopped for flavouring. Mint is added to yogurt dishes such as RAITA and cold appetizers. It is one of the ingredients of chaat (see STREET FOOD). Mint is also a flavouring in soups, stews, dal, vegetable dishes, KEBABS such as *shami* kebab, and KOFTA. FISH are often stuffed with a combination of fresh mint, CORIANDER and other seasonings before being baked or steamed. Mint is sometimes added to BIRYANIS and PULAOS (such as the renowned mint pulao (*pudina pillau*), a speciality of Hyderabad). Mint is sometimes used to stuff BREADS or incorporated into the dough before baking. Piquant mint CHUTNEYS are much loved and are often served as a dip to be eaten with parathas or fried snacks such as SAMOSAS and PAKORAS. Mint chutneys also mix well with yogurt.

Mint is added to beverages, hot or cold, such as TEA (*pudina* chai), LASSI, SHERBET and *jal jeera* (see CUMIN). It is sometimes added to *nimbu pani* (literally 'lime water'), also called *shikanji*, a refreshing drink consisting of lime (or lemon) juice, SUGAR (or sometimes SALT) and spices mixed with ice or water. The *shikanji* masala consists of powdered spices such as black salt, rock salt, roasted cumin, black pepper (see PEPPER, BLACK), chaat masala and dried mint. Whole mint leaves are added as a garnish to many dishes.

Helen Saberi

- Pruthi, J.S. *Spices and Condiments*. New Delhi: National Book Trust, 1976.
- Sahni, Julie. *Classic Indian Cookery*. London: Grub Street, 1997.

MIZORAM

Within India's northeast, Mizoram is the southernmost state, a landlocked region that shares an international border with Bangladesh and Myanmar. About 95 per cent of the population is of diverse tribal origins and settled here from parts of Southeast Asia. Waves of migration can be traced back to as far as the sixteenth century, but mainly occurred during the eighteenth century. Over 87 per cent of Mizoram residents are Christians and this has an important influence on their food habits. They have little restriction in their intake of meat or non-vegetarian food, although ALCOHOL has taken a backseat under the Church's influence.

Mizoram is a highly literate agrarian economy that has been invested in replacing traditional jhum (slash-and-burn) farming practices with a significant horticulture and bamboo products industry. The state horticulture department has conducted pilot projects for cultivating exotic fruits like dragon fruits and avocado that were previously unknown here. However, on Mizoram soil, the avocado tree bears fruit after four to six years, then suddenly becomes lifeless and dies.

Mizos are RICE-eaters. They start their very first rice-based meal around nine o'clock in the morning. At this morning meal, known as *tukthuan*, the entire family gathers around a low-level dining table, and seated on *moorah* (low stools made of rattan) say their grace before going about their daily routines. The meal consists of rice as the centrepiece, accompanied by boiled vegetables or fried POTATOES, and CHUTNEY made of green or red CHILLIES ground with dried shredded meat. At midday, they gather around the table for *chafe*, the midday meal, which could consist of leftovers from the *tukthuan*. *Zanriah*, or supper, is served before sunset when all the members have returned home. Once again, grace is said as the entire family is seated around the table – this practice combines their modern faith and the traditional values of unity and solidarity that are the bedrock of every Mizo family.

Traditional Mizo food is characterized by the minimal use of oil. A popular stew-like dish called *bai* is made by boiling leaves with *sa-um*, fermented pork fat. The vegetarian version calls for the addition of a dash of *bekang*, fermented soya beans. While boiled leaves form the base of many Mizo dishes, most of their meals feature generous portions of beef, pork, chicken and FISH. *Sawhchiar*, another popular Mizo dish, is a rice-based porridge-like dish cooked with beef, pork or chicken and strands of *anthur* (rosella).

Hoihnu Hauzel

- Hauzel, Hoihnu. *The Essential North-East Cookbook*. New Delhi: Penguin Books, 2003.

MODAKA

An ancient sweet, *modaka* is a stuffed dumpling that is especially popular in western and southern India. A RICE or WHEAT flour dough is shaped into little packages that can be filled with grated COCONUT, jaggery (see SUGAR), NUTS or sometimes *KHOYA*, and flavoured with CARDAMOM powder. Modern versions are filled with chocolates, DATES, TOMATOES and other ingredients. *Modaka* can be steamed and served with GHEE or deep-fried.

Modaka is often served at temples and is the favourite food of the deity Ganesh, who is depicted holding a *modaka* in one of his four hands. (His nickname, *modakapriya*, means 'one who loves *modakas*'.) During the festival Ganesh Chathurti, a puja honouring Ganesh ends with the offering of twenty-one *modakas* to the image of the deity.

Colleen Sen

FIGURE 32 MODAKA. Mahesh Mutta/Wikimedia Commons.

MUGHALS

FIGURE 33 MUGHALS. Babur and a banquet of roast goose.

At its peak under Emperor Aurangzeb (1618–1707), the Mughal (also spelled Moghul) dynasty ruled almost the entire subcontinent. The Empire was founded in 1526 when Babur conquered much of Hindustan and ended in 1858 when the British deposed and exiled the last emperor and assumed the reins of government. During this period, India had increasing contacts with the outside world as European powers established trading posts and introduced new ingredients into the cuisine.

The founder of the Mughal dynasty, Zahīr ud-Dīn Muhammad Babur (1483–1530) was a descendant of the Turco-Mongol conqueror Timur (1336–1405); hence the dynasty was originally known as Timurid. In 1526 he defeated the previous ruler of Delhi, Ibrahim Lodi. Besides being a great warrior, Babur was a poet, a sensitive memoirist and a devotee and planter of gardens. He was born in the lush green Ferghana Valley in Central Asia, a region famous for its grapes and MELONS, which, fresh or stored, were a staple food of the region. His first encounter with Hindustan was a disappointment. In a famous passage he wrote, 'Hindustan is a country of few charms ... there are no good horses, no good dogs, no grapes, muskmelons or first-rate fruits, no ice or cold water, no good bread or cooked food in the bazaars.'

The only Indian fruit he liked were MANGOES, although even then he found only a few to be first rate. Babur planted gardens wherever he went and brought in seeds, plants and gardeners from Central Asia and Persia to plant melons, peaches, APRICOTS, pistachios, walnuts and almonds. The only food mentioned in his memoirs are lamb KEBABS and *chikhi*, a porridge made from WHEAT flour paste, meat, GHEE and spices. A painting shows him enjoying a roasted goose.

At parties, guests drank *chaghir*, a cider-like alcoholic beverage that was imported from Kabul and Shiraz in Persia. However, on the eve of an important battle Babur gave up drinking alcohol. After defeating Ibrahim Lodi, Babur set up his court in Delhi. Wanting to try Hindustani dishes, he hired some of the Lodi's cooks. Ibrahim Lodi's mother tried to murder him by enlisting one of the cooks to sprinkle poison on his meal of BREAD, hare, fried CARROTS and dried meat. He died of natural causes in Agra in 1530 but in keeping with his wishes, he was buried in Kabul, a place he loved. Babur's son Humayun (1508–56) spent years in exile at the Persian court where he enjoyed the lavish banquets of his royal hosts.

The greatest of the Mughal Emperors, Jalal-ud-Din Muhammad Akbar (1542–1605), is famous for the lavish food of his court, as chronicled by his prime minister and court historian Abu'l-Fazl ibn Mubarak (1551–1602) and present in the accounts of early European travellers. According to Abu'l-Fazl, 'Every day such dishes are prepared as the notables can scarcely command at their feasts.' The grandeur of his table was a symbol of his power and prestige. The royal kitchen's staff included a head cook, treasurer, storekeeper, clerks, tasters and more than 400 cooks from all over India, Central Asia and Persia. There was no fixed time for eating so the kitchen staff had to be on constant alert and within an hour could produce 100 dishes. The food was served in gold, silver, stone and earthenware dishes; tied up in cloths, inspected and approved by the head cook; and tasted several times before being served. ICE was brought daily from the snow-capped mountains of the Himalayas by an elaborate system of couriers for cooling drinks (see SHERBET) and making frozen desserts.

Ingredients came from all over the vast empire: regional and seasonal varieties of RICE, butter from a certain town, ducks and waterfowls from Kashmir (see POULTRY AND EGGS). The palace chickens were hand-fed with pellets flavoured with SAFFRON and rosewater (see FLOWER WATERS) and massaged daily with musk oil and sandalwood. A kitchen garden provided a continual supply of fresh vegetables and, especially, fruit since, like his ancestor Babur, Akbar was a lover of fruit. He took a great interest in horticulture and this may have been a factor in the rapid adoption of PINEAPPLE, GUAVA and other fruits and vegetables from the Western Hemisphere throughout his empire.

The names of the dishes mentioned by Abu'l-Fazl indicate that they come from different culinary traditions: the Middle East – *HALEEM*, *harisa*, HALWA, *malghuba, sanbusa, qutab, qaliya*; Persia – *kashk*, PULAO, *zard birinj, shir birinj, dampukht, bandanjan, yakhni, shorba*; and Turkic/Central Asian – *bughra, shulla, qabuli, thuli*, and *yulma*. Many recipes call for ONION and GINGER but very few have GARLIC. Spicing was more lavish than in Central Asia or Persia. The main cooking medium was enormous quantities of ghee. While some of these dishes can be found in today's culinary repertoire, others have disappeared. In a list of vegetables and spices sold in markets, some are conspicuous by their absence – TOMATOES, POTATOES and CHILLIES which made their appearance at a later date

However, Akbar himself led an austere, even ascetic, life, which indicated his spirituality and dedication to ruling. It may also have been a way of connecting to his many vegetarian subjects. Abu'l-Fazl wrote of him:

> If His Majesty did not possess so lofty a mind, so comprehensive an understanding, so universal a kindness, he would have chosen the path of solitude and given up sleep and food altogether; and even now ... the question 'What dinner has been prepared today?' never passes over his tongue. In the course of twenty-four hours, His Majesty eats but once and leaves off before he is fully satisfied.

Elsewhere, Abu'l-Fazl wrote:

> His Majesty cares very little for meat and often expresses himself to that effect. It is indeed from ignorance and cruelty that, although various kinds of foods are obtainable, men are bent upon injuring living creatures and lending a ready hand in killing and eating them; none seems to have an eye for the beauty inherent in the prevention of cruelty but makes himself a tomb for animals. If His Majesty had not the burden of the world on his shoulders, he would, at once, totally abstain from meat; and now, it is his intention to quit it by degrees, conforming, however, a little to the spirit of the age.

Akbar fasted regularly and gradually increased the number of days on which he did so. But he did not impose his abstinence on his subjects, although it was his wish that people should refrain from eating meat during the month he came to the throne.

Akbar's son and heir Jahangir (1569–1627) ruled over a relatively peaceful empire and spent much of his time in Punjab and Kashmir where he built palaces, mosques and gardens. Like his father, he loved fruits, especially mangoes, and planted many orchards. Like his great grandfather Babur, he was fascinated by the natural world and left behind descriptions and paintings of plants and wildlife. Jahangir took pride in being a connoisseur of cuisine. In his memoirs he often comments on the food he samples during his travels. During a hunt, for example, he would order an animal to be cooked in a particular style to sample its taste. He gave detailed descriptions of different varieties of APPLES and mangoes based on different characteristics.

In an account of his visit to Jahangir's court, Edward Terry, the chaplain of Sir Thomas Roe, English ambassador to the Mughals, was surprised that instead of eating large joints of meat, as the English did, the Mughals cut it into small pieces and stewed it with 'onions, herbs, roots and ginger and other spices with some butter'. At one royal banquet, he was served fifty dishes; he particularly liked a dish of spiced venison with onions (*dopiaza*) and rice coloured in fantastic shades, including green and purple.

But Jahangir also honoured and emulated Akbar by ordering that no animals should be killed on Thursdays, the date of his own accession, and on Sunday, Akbar's birthday; and also observed many more days of abstaining from meat. One of Jahangir's favourite dishes was KHICHRI, especially a version he encountered in Western India. In his memoirs he writes:

> Of the food which is particular to the people of Gujarat, there is the bajra khichri, a mixture of split peas and millet boiled together. It is a kind of split grain which does

> not grow in any other country but Hindustan. It is cheaper than most vegetables. As I had never eaten it, I ordered them to make some and bring it to me. It is not devoid of flavour, and it suited me well. I ordered that on days of abstinence, when I partake of dishes not made of flesh, they should frequently bring me this khichri.

Jahangir's memoirs describe his battle with alcohol. When he fell ill from overindulgence, he was advised to cut back his drinking or he would die. He began diluting the arrack with wine and gradually diminished the quantity he imbibed for the rest of his life

Jahangir's grandson Aurangzeb (r. 1658–1707) was a frugal yet discerning eater. In a letter to his second son (and successor), Muhammad Muazzam (Bahadur Shah I), Aurangzeb praises the mangoes sent to him as a gift and names the varieties '*sudha-ras*' and '*rasna-vilas*' (in Sanskrit). In another letter, the emperor gushes about the khichri – a favourite dish of his father, Shahjahan, as well – and BIRYANI that had been served to him in the winter by his son, but he's also quick to add that the *qabooli* (a Hyderabadi favourite prepared with rice, split chickpeas, or *chana* dal, and a variety of dry fruit) cooked by Islam Khan (presumably a family retainer) tasted even better. Aurangzeb then goes on to mention how he had wanted the cook responsible for the biryani, Saliman, but his son refused to part with him. He therefore requests his son to send a pupil of Saliman, 'skillful in the art of cookery', to work in his kitchen. He ends the letter with a couplet that says, 'The desire for good food has not left me, though the blackness of my hair has departed.' Clearly, many of the dishes that are commonplace across India were savoured by the ruling class.

Between the seventeenth and mid-nineteenth centuries, several Indo-Persian cookbook manuscripts were produced by unknown authors and copied many times for the libraries of Mughal notables. One is the *Nuskha-i-Shahjahani*, which purports to be a record of the dishes served in the Emperor Shah Jahan's (r. 1627–58) kitchen. The book has sections on breads, soups, *qaliyas* and *dopiyazas, bharta* (mashes), *zerbiryans* (a layered rice based dish, i.e. biryani), pulao, kebabs, *harisas*, *shishranga* (six-coloured dish of apples, pineapples, carrots and other vegetables), omelettes, khichri, *murabbas*, PICKLES, halwa, *shirini* (SWEETS) and yogurt. Another collection is the *Bayaz-i-Khwushbu* (*Notebook of Favourite Savouries*), which reproduces recipes from the *A'in-i-Akbari* and other sources. But did these books reflect what the Mughals and their court ate? In her dissertation on Mughal cuisine, Divya Narayanan concludes:

> While it may be somewhat anachronistic and sociologically problematic to speak of a singular 'Mughal cuisine,' something approaching this concept did probably exist, at least within the corpus of Indo-Persian cookbooks. This was a well developed and consciously articulated haute cuisine, which drew on ingredients and techniques from various parts of the world, and yet was also driven by local influence and context.

The last Mughal, Bahadur Shah Zafar (r. 1837–57), despite his advanced age, had a hearty appetite. His favourite dishes were 'quail stew, venison, lamb kidneys on a sweet naan called *sheermal*, *yakhni*, fish kebabs, and meat stewed with oranges', though the royal kitchens could also produce a Mughlai feast of twenty-five types of bread, twenty-five pulaos and biryanis, thirty-five CURRIES and fifty different puddings. Zafar's fondness for venison dated back to his younger days when he was an avid hunter, but he also shared his forefathers' love for dals, particularly *moong* dal, which came to be known as Badshah Pasand during his reign, which was put to an end (along with the dynasty) by the East India Company in the wake of the Rebellion of 1857.

As the empire declined, its cuisine continued to evolve in the courts of the rulers of HYDERABAD, LUCKNOW, RAMPUR, Rajasthan, Kashmir and Murshidabad.

Today one of the most frequently used terms in the narrative about Indian cuisine is Mughal or Mughlai food – a catchall phrase loosely applied to rich, often meat-based North Indian dishes such as biryani, pulao and kebabs, often with fanciful names such as chicken Shah Jahan or pulao Nur Mahal. However, based on Google's NGram viewer (a mapping of the number of citations in books, magazines and newspapers between 1800 and the present), it appears that the term was probably first used by some enterprising restaurateur or restaurateurs starting sometime after the Second World War. Many of the dishes served under this rubric bear little resemblance to what the Mughals actually ate.

Sourish Bhattacharyya and Colleen Sen

- Allami, Abu'l-Fazl. *The Ain-i-Akbari*, vol. I, translated by H. Blochmann, revised and edited by D.C. Phillott. 2nd edition. 1927. Reprint. New Delhi: Atlantic Publishers, 1989.
- Babur. *Babur-Nama (Memoirs of Babur)*, vol. 1. *n.d*, translated by Annette Susannah Beveridge. New Delhi: Saeed International, 1989.
- Husain, Salma. *The Emperor's Table: The Art of Mughal Cuisine*. New Delhi: Roli Books, 2011.
- Narayanan, Divya. 'Cultures of Food and Gastronomy in Mughal and Post-Mughal India'. PhD Dissertation. Ruprecht-Karls-Universitat Heidelberg, Heidelberg, Germany, 2015.
- Westrip, Joyce. *Moghul Cooking: India's Courtly Cuisine*. London: Serif, 1997.

MUKHOPADHYAY, BIPRADAS

Bipradas Mukhopadhyay (1842–1914) was a best-selling Bengali cookbook writer and publisher-editor of a monthly dedicated to cooking and recipes named *Pak Pranali*, perhaps the first journal of its kind in India. A writer of instructional manuals on family life, Mukhopadhyay launched *Pak Pranali* in 1883 'to teach "modern" women [collectively known as the "*nobina*"] the culinary skills allegedly lost through education and refinement, as well as to help them keep up with changing tastes in food and save money by preparing food at home themselves' (Sengupta 2010). Women (the *bhadramahila*, or gentlewoman), in Mukhopadhyay's worldview, needed the help of men to regain their natural knack of cooking – an act that contemporary authors had lifted to the status of a holy ritual.

The journal's expanding readership encouraged contemporary Bengali women's magazines and domestic manuals, notably *Bamabodhini Patrika*, *Mahila*, *Punya* and *Antahpur* to start recipe columns, mainly with contributions from women. These columns gave the women who wrote them an identity that put them on par with their male counterparts. Mukhopadhyay, meanwhile, brought out the first Bengali cookbook – *Shoukin Khadya-Pak* (*Cooking for the Leisured Class*, 1889) – targeted at the growing *bhadralok* middle class. He acquainted his readers with 'English' vegetables – he went into a detailed discussion on cabbage, for instance – and shared 'fusion' recipes.

Utsa Ray gives Mukhopadhyay credit for the creation of the 'new' Bengali cuisine. His cookbook, later expanded into two volumes and brought out as *Pak Pranali* (1906–7), also had a number of English, Irish, Italian and Jewish recipes to which he gave imaginative Bengali titles; and some from other parts of India, such as one for a 'Hindustani' (the standard Bengali term for Hindi-speaking North Indians) yellow dal, whose ingredients included ASAFOETIDA, which was not quite popular in contemporary Bengal. Another popular recipe was for the Kashmiri sweet (*modur*) PULAO – the *zarda* of Kashmiri Muslims.

On CURRY, too, Mukhopadhyay had his own take. He said the Europeans learnt how to make curry from the Jewish people, who, in turn, picked up the art from Muslims. Ironically, he lived at a time when India's colonial masters believed they had invented curry, as some writers still claim. Undeterred, Mukhopadhyay divided his curries into the 'Muslim' and 'English' categories, and even created his own CURRY POWDER, composed of POPPY SEEDS, red CHILLI and TURMERIC powders, ground CUMIN and SALT. In an emerging field crowded with enlightened middle-class women, who saw in recipe writing an escape, albeit momentary, from the patriarchy of their time, Mukhopadhyay stood out as a gentleman gastronome who worked ceaselessly to give Bengali cuisine a global character.

Sourish Bhattacharyya

- Ray, Utsa 'Eating "Modernity": Changing Dietary Practices in Colonial Bengal'. *Modern Asian Studies* 46, no. 3 (2012): 703–29.
- Sengupta, Jayanta. 'Nation on a Platter: The Culture and Politics of Food and Cuisine in Colonial Bengal'. *Modern Asian Studies* 44, no. 1 (2010): 81–98.

MULBERRY

Mulberry, *Morus alba*, the white mulberry, and *M. nigra*, the black or Persian mulberry (*shah toot* in Hindi), grow in India. Both are fruits of Asian origin. The white mulberry is native to China and its leaves are used for rearing silkworms – they will eat nothing else. It is thought that the black mulberry originated in Persia and is usually grown for its fruits.

Mulberry trees have been grown in India for a long time. Charaka (see FOOD AND MEDICINE) refers to the mulberry as '*tuda*'. In Mughal times, figs were grafted onto mulberry trees. Willian Finch, an English merchant of the East India Company who travelled in India in the early 1600s, observed that 'from Agra to Lahore the way is set on both sides with mulberry-trees'. A few years later, François Bernier, the French physician who travelled around India for twelve years, noted that in Bengal there were 'small mulberry trees, two or three feet in height, for the food of silk worms'.

Black mulberries, which resemble blackberries, have more flavour. Some are very sweet and others quite tart. Black mulberries grow on the upper slopes of the Himalayas and are sold by street vendors in Kashmir outside MUGHAL gardens and palaces during the summer months. These berries are often eaten just on their own, perhaps sprinkled with a little black SALT. Sometimes they are mixed with other ingredients to make a chaat (see STREET FOOD).

A variety, *M. alba* var. *indica,* is called the Indian mulberry and is dark red in colour. In Bombay it is sold in the bazaars and is used for making compotes and tarts. Its edible leaves are used to wrap FISH being cooked; the unripe fruit buds are added to CURRIES and sambals and the ripe fruit can be eaten raw with salt or used to make infusions and

TEAS. (This variety should not be confused with *Morinda citrifolia*, also called the Indian mulberry.)

Helen Saberi

- Achaya, K.T. *A Historical Dictionary of Indian Food*. Delhi: OUP, 1999.
- Sahni, Julie. *Classic Indian Vegetarian Food*. London: Grub Street, 1999.

MUMBAI

Mumbai, India's answer to New York and Hollywood, bustling on the shores of the Arabian Sea, is a cosmopolitan city – 'a mecca', in Gillian Tindall's words, 'for incoming people, seeking work, seeking money, seeking life itself' – whose contemporary culinary culture mirrors its crowded history and diverse population.

The city's roots go back to what is known as the South Asian Stone Age, but the historical remains scattered across the teeming metropolis, starting with the Kanheri Caves dating back to the first century CE, indicating that it was once a part of the Maurya Empire (322–185 BCE) and was an important centre of Buddhism. The ancient Greek geographer, Ptolemy, knew it as Heptanesia, or 'cluster of seven islands', which accurately described this city that remained an archipelago till it was combined together by its English rulers in 1784.

Over the centuries, it has been ruled by a number of minor kingdoms that crowd the pages of early Indian history till it became a part of the Gujarat Sultanate, an association that resulted in the creation of one of the city's abiding landmarks, Worli's Haji Ali Dargah. It was Sultan Bahadur Shah of Gujarat who, in 1535, ceded the islands and the neighbouring strategic town of Bassein to the Portuguese, who had established themselves in Goa and farther south from the early sixteenth century. The fortifications and churches built by them, together with ancient caves (notably Elephanta) and temples (Walkeshwar), have left their permanent imprint on the topography of Mumbai.

For the Portuguese, it was a strategic acquisition because Bombay (as Mumbai was known then) turned out to be the perfect natural harbour and difficult for an army to attack. It was exactly why they got embroiled in several conflicts with the English, who had set themselves up in neighbouring Surat, till England's Charles II settled the matter by marrying the Portuguese king John IV's daughter, Catherine of Braganza, in 1661 and getting Bombay as dowry. In 1668, the King of England leased these islands, which were then mainly malarial swamps, to the East India Company for £10 per annum.

The East India Company moved its base from Surat to Bombay in 1687 and eventually joined the seven islands together in 1784 by building a causeway called the Hornby Vellard. The port, meanwhile, got busier, and its importance grew with the opening of the Suez Canal in 1869. Earlier, the disruption of cotton supplies because of the American Civil War (1861–5) propelled Bombay as the world's principal cotton market and the city eventually became a conglomeration of cotton mills, the seat of India's principal stock exchange and central bank, and the centre of its thriving film industry, which attracted entrepreneurial and talented people from across India.

Mumbai's eventful history ensured that it emerged as a melting pot of cultures, which found a culinary expression in the city's wholesome table, which is today a smorgasbord of influences that can be traced back to the city's original inhabitants, the Koli fisherfolk; followed by the Pathare Prabhus, who moved from Rajasthan; the old Catholic community known as the EAST INDIANS; and then the Portuguese, the English, the PARSIS, the Konkani-speaking Goan Christians, Maharashtrians, Gujaratis, Tamilians, Malayalis and Punjabis (after the Partition of India in 1947). Add to this rainbow coalition the populations that fled persecution in their original homelands and found a welcoming embrace in Bombay – the BOHRA Muslims, Baghdadi Jews and Iranis – and communities such as the Mangalorean Catholics, Malvanis (the original millhands) and the Chandraseniya Kayastha Prabhus (CKPs), and you have a vibrant food tradition that draws on the best of different worlds.

Nothing can be more symbolic of the city's syncretic food culture than its most popular street snack, vada *pav*, which is essentially a spiced potato croquette (or *batata* vada, a Maharashtrian preparation) stuffed inside a *pav* (bun), a Portuguese gift (they called it *pão*) made available to local communities by bakeries run by Goans or Iranis. The inside of the *pav* is slathered with garlic CHUTNEY and the combination is considered complete only if a whole green CHILLI is added.

The *pav* makes an appearance also in the *pav bhaji*, which originated as the lunchtime favourite of mill hands, with the bun being served along with a TOMATO-rich POTATO CURRY, chopped ONIONS and CORIANDER leaves sprinkled on top and crowned by a dollop of butter. It shows up again in the *misal pav*, which is synonymous with Mumbai's Aaswad restaurant, and was voted the world's best vegetarian dish in the 2015 Foodie Hub Global Awards. The bun in this snack item is served with *misal*, a spicy curry made with sprouted moth beans, sprinkled with fresh lemon juice, chopped coriander leaves and *sev* (broken fried chickpea flour noodles; see *SEV* AND *SEVIYAN*).

The Pathare Prabhu community also has its version of leavened bread, a sourdough in fact, called *parbhi pav*, which is soft and fluffy with a muffin-like texture. It is made only in the hot and humid months of April and May and served with MANGO nectar (*aamras*). The starter culture, according to Mumbai-based food blogger Kalyan Karmakar, is made with *chana* dal (split chickpeas), potato peels, milk and water fermented overnight. The foam that forms on top, along with the fermented liquid, is used to leaven the bread batter prepared with *maida* (white flour), butter or GHEE, HONEY and SALT.

Being a city of migrants, and a magnet for global wealth and talent, Mumbai has a vibrant public eating culture which is preserved in its fashionable and 'family' restaurants, its many *khau galis* (foodie streets), and its beaches, most famously in Chowpatty and Juhu. The beaches, in fact, have become synonymous with *bhelpuri*, a popular snack that essentially is a spicy mix of puffed rice (*murmura*, or *muri* in West Bengal), *sev*, chopped boiled potatoes, tomatoes and onions doused with two kinds of chutneys – one with DATES and TAMARIND (*mithi*) and the other being a paste of coriander and MINT leaves and green chillies. Another version of it is the *ragda pattice*, which is a combination of *ragda* (spiced boiled chickpeas) and *pattice* (fried mashed potato patties) tossed with finely chopped onions and coriander leaves, as well as the two flavour enhancers that go into the *bhelpuri* – *mithi* and the fiery green chutney.

Mumbai has some of India's finest restaurants – from the Harbour Bar and Wasabi by Morimoto in the iconic Taj Mahal Palace and Hotel to Olive Bar & Kitchen, The Table, The Bombay Canteen and Bastian, to the humble Bademiya and Madras Cafe. It also has some of India's oldest surviving eateries – notably Cafe Leopold (1871), Britannia & Co. (1923), Cafe Mondegar (1932), Shree Thaker Bhojanalaya (1945) and Gaylord (1956). Its roster of iconic dishes beyond the vada *pav* is as impressive, including such must-haves as the berry pulao that Britannia & Co. still serves; FISH KOLIWADA of Sion, Mumbai's 'Mini Punjab'; EGGS KEJRIWAL, the conversation starter at The Willingdon Sports Club; CHICKEN MANCHURIAN at China Garden; mutton dhansak of the Ripon Club (established in 1884); *baida* roti, either at Bademiya or the humbler stalls at Bohri Mohalla; and the creamy Parsi Dairy KULFI. One cannot talk about Mumbai without acknowledging the formidable fan following of the mass food products the city has put on the world map – from Parle-G 'glucose biscuits' to Lijjat PAPAD.

But it is in the city's *khau gali*s that the heart of its food culture beats the loudest. The food streets are open till late at night and serve food that is both light on the wallet (priced right for college students and office-goers) and inventive. One can taste the creativity that goes into making the amazing variety of unconventional DOSAS – from Thousand Island to cheese burst dosas, and even an ice-cream dosa – at Ghatkopar East; the KEBABS, tikkas and *shawarmas* at Mohammed Ali Road alongside the Minara Masjid; Indianized dim sum (or momos) that come in a variety of forms (there's even a momo chaat) at Kharghar in Navi Mumbai; the *papdi* chaat extravaganza at the city's jewellers' hub, Zhaveri Bazaar; the *Jalebi*, *RABRI* and ice-cream chaat of Princess Street; the much sought-after *khichda*, *baida* roti, *HALEEM* and kulfi *FALOODA* scooped up in the shadow of the Mahim Dargah; and the Punjabi and Sindhi delicacies of Chembur.

These are the birthplaces of uniquely Mumbai treats, such as the Bombay sandwich (buttered white bread packed with thin slices of tomatoes, cucumbers and beetroot, plus onion rings, boiled potatoes and mint chutney, and sprinkled with *sev*), the frankie (an egg-coated naan wrap stuffed with spiced mutton or chicken), the iced falooda, which comes in many flavours and colours, the chicken mayo roll (a bread roll loaded with boiled chicken drenched in a sweet mayo) and, of course, the unmistakably Irani bun *maska* (bread rolls liberally rubbed with butter). Mumbai's *khau gali*s have all the answers to the heartfelt prayers of growling stomachs and restless taste buds.

In the best traditions of the Hindi film industry, or Bollywood as the world calls it, the food of Mumbai has a bit of everything on offer – history, romance, action, colour, charisma, robust Indian flavours and global aspirations – and that is what makes it so titillating to the imagination and the palate.

Sourish Bhattacharyya

- Conlon, Frank F. 'Dining Out in Bombay'. In *Consuming Modernity: Public Culture in Contemporary India*, edited by Carol A. Breckenridge, 90–130. Delhi: OUP, 1996.
- Holidfy. 'Khau Gallis for a Gastronomic Food Tour'. *n.d.* Available online: https://www.holidify.com/pages/khau-gallis-of-mumbai-3771.html (accessed 26 April 2022).
- Khamgaonkar, Sanjiv. 'Spirit of India: 40 Mumbai Foods We Can't Live Without'. *CNN Travel*, 12 July 2017. Available online: https://edition.cnn.com/travel/article/mumbai-food-dishes/index.html (accessed 26 April 2022).
- Sharma, Vibha. 'Top 10 Iconic Restaurants in Mumbai to Take You Back in Time'. *Travenix*, 14 January 2019. Available online: https://www.travenix.com/iconic-restaurants-mumbai/ (accessed 26 April 2022).

MUSHROOMS

Fungus (Hindi *kukurmutta*) is a group of simple plants that includes mushrooms, yeasts, moulds and LICHENS (which are a symbiotic partnership of a fungus and an alga). Unlike plants, they lack chlorophyll and can only grow on dead or living plants or in a symbiotic relationship with the roots of trees. The most common fungi are mushrooms, which, strictly speaking, denote the fruiting body of certain kinds of fungus, although the term is used more loosely. They are usually consumed fresh. Mushrooms have a high nutritional value, almost twice that of any vegetable or fruit, and are rich in iron, zinc, vitamin C, potassium, some essential amino acids and fibre and are low in fat.

Fungi grow in very specific micro-habitats in forests, in hollow barks, on termite hills and even in deserts. The specific trees and soils impart a distinct flavour to the fungi. In India, tribal communities have collected and prepared wild edible fungi for centuries and consume nearly 300 of the 2,000 species found worldwide. Many varieties grow in the Northeast, where the monsoons and high humidity create ideal conditions. They form an important part of people's diet during the monsoon season and are usually prepared fresh. In Nagaland, for instance, local fungi are prepared with dry FISH and smoked green CHILLIES as a CHUTNEY. Manipuris start their traditional New Year's festival with a dish of AUBERGINES and *yuen*, a shitake-like mushroom.

Traditionally mushrooms have been foraged but deforestation, increasing demand and overharvesting have led to a depletion of some varieties. In 1993, India cultivated its first species of wild fungi that is now being commercially produced. Efforts are underway to bring more varieties under cultivation. Oyster mushrooms, paddy straw mushrooms and button mushrooms that are not native to India are grown commercially.

India's most famous wild mushrooms are morels (genus *Morchella*, Hindi *gucchi*), which have a distinctive earthy flavour much prized by chefs. When fresh, they are spongy and have a pleated honeycomb-like texture. Morels grow in the foothills of the Himalayas and in Jammu and Kashmir after the snowfall and are collected by villagers between March and the end of May. Because they may not grow in the same spot every season, locating them can be a long and arduous process. The morels are strung on a garland and hung over a fire to dry before selling. A kilogram of morels can cost between 20,000 and 40,000 rupees. In Kashmir morels are prized as a gift and served only on special occasions, such as a lavish wedding. Morels are often added to a pulao. The water extracted from soaking morels is used to cook rice.

According to the *Dharmashastras,* mushrooms are forbidden to the twice-born people; Jains also avoid them. Among the reasons for this ban are that they grow in unhygienic environments and may harbour other life forms.

Colleen Sen

- Behrawala, Krutika. 'Finding Fungi: A Look at India's Wild Edible Mushrooms and Why They Need to Be Conserved'. *Medium*, 12 July 2020.
- Choudhary, Madhu, Ritu Devi, Ashim Datta, Arvind Kumar and Hanuman S. Jat. 'Diversity of Wild Edible Mushrooms in Indian Subcontinent and Its Neighboring Countries'. *Recent Advances in Biology and Medicine* 1 (2015): 69–76.
- Sadhu, Prateek. 'Chasing Wild Mushrooms That Cost Rs 40,000 Per kg'. *Forbes*, 19 October 2018.

MUSTARD

Mustard (*Brassica juncea,* Hindi *sarson* or *rai*) has long had many uses in Indian cuisine. Charred seeds have been found in the Harappan Civilization. Today mustard seeds are used as a spice, especially in South India where they are sautéed with FENUGREEK seeds and CHILLIES and are added to dals and vegetable dishes. They are also a component of the Bengali spice mixture, *panch phoron* (see SPICE BOX). From ancient times, both black (*rai*) and yellow mustard seeds (*sarson*) have been crushed to make an oil which, today, is used as a cooking medium, mainly in eastern India. Mustard oil is a common medium for preserving PICKLES.

In Bengal, raw seeds are ground with water, TURMERIC and sometimes chilies, other spices and mangoes and are fermented to make a pungent paste called *kasundi.* It is used as a dipping sauce for cutlets, chops and other Bengal savouries, although traditionally it was an accompaniment to fried greens. There are many rituals associated with its production. In North India mustard leaves are used to make the famous winter dish *sarson ka sag*. Mustard leaves, together with spinach or some other leaves, are cooked with ONIONS, GARLIC, GINGER and chillies, then pureed, topped with butter and eaten with *makki ki* roti (CORN bread).

Colleen Sen

MYSORE PAK

Mysore *pak* is a famous SWEET that originated in the city of Mysore (now Mysuru), Karnataka. A mixture of GHEE, SUGAR and roasted chickpea flour, sometimes flavoured with CARDAMOM, rosewater (see FLOWER WATERS) or HONEY, is heated and cut into squares, cubes or rectangles. It is yellow to light brown in colour. There are two varieties: a soft, dense version made with more ghee and a harder porous variety made with less ghee.

According to one explanation of its origin, the sweet was invented around 1935 at the Amba Vilas Palace in Mysore. Kakasura Madappa, the chief chef of King Krishna Raja Wodeyar IV, wanted to prepare a special sweet for lunch. The king liked it and when asked its name, the chef replied 'Mysore *pak*'. (One meaning of *pak* in Sanskrit is sugar syrup). Another version says the king asked his cook to create a special dish that would reflect the glory of Mysore. The original version is still available at the Guru Sweets stores run by the great-grandson of Chef Madappa. Mysore *pak* is a must at Dussehra and other festivals. In 2019 it received a GEOGRAPHICAL INDICATION tag.

Colleen Sen

- Iyer, Radhika. 'How the Famous Mysore Pak Was Invented'. *NDTV*, 3 October 2014. Available online: https://www.ndtv.com/south/how-the-famous-mysore-pak-was-invented-674512 (accessed 26 April 2022).
- Mujumdar, Neha. 'In Search of Mysore Pak'. *The Hindu*, 25 November 2012. Available online: https://www.thehindu.com/features/metroplus/Food/In-search-of-Mysore-Pak/article15616920.ece (accessed 26 April 2022).

NAGALAND

One of India's smallest states, Nagaland is bordered by Arunachal Pradesh to the north, Assam to the west, Manipur to the south and Myanmar to the east. Nearly 90 per cent of the population is Christian and English is the official state language. Eighty per cent of the population is engaged in agriculture so that most festivals are harvest-related. Christmas is the most important festival.

The land of the Nagas is intriguing, given that the Nagas were once headhunters. In the nineteenth century, the coming of Protestant Christian missionaries from America in the region resulted in the Nagas embracing Christianity and that led to the dropping of many customs and traditions, including headhunting rituals. Present-day Nagaland continues to, nevertheless, draw many travellers and visitors for its vibrant culture and food. It is home to over sixteen different tribes each of whom is distinct yet shares many things in common when it comes to their food habits. However, each tribe has a delicacy that is different from the others. Nagas have a restrained style of cooking that is dedicated to bringing out the natural flavours in the ingredients. Perhaps for this reason, Nagas are not fans of oil and masala (spice mixtures, see SPICE BOX), compensating for the lack or absence with the healthier alternatives of herbs and CHILLIES from their surroundings. A quintessential Naga meal calls for BAMBOO SHOOTS called *bastenga*, ghost chilli (*bhut jolokia*), a very fiery chilli known locally as raja *mirch*, and fermented soya beans called *akhuni*, which are common ingredients that cut across all communities. Like many other tribal communities, Nagaland has retained a lot of its old charm and many homes continue to rear animals that serve as the main menu for Christmas and harvest-related festivals. Meat, mainly pork and beef (but not mutton), is smoked by hanging over a fire or on the wall of a kitchen.

Interestingly, the food culture of Nagaland remains relatively untouched by influences from neighbouring Myanmar. Boiled or steamed RICE is the staple, often paired with meat dishes, CHUTNEYS, dal and a humble bowl of boiled seasonal vegetables. The Ao Nagas take their pork dishes up a notch with the addition of *anishi* (TARO leaves), whereas the Sema tribe has been credited for marrying pork with *akhuni* (also spelled *axone*), or fermented soybeans. The Angamis cook a chunky meat dish with raja chillies and a GINGER-GARLIC paste while the Ao tribe celebrates their festivals with bamboo shoot and *amerso* (a chicken dish) served with rice and side dishes together with a boiled vegetables dish called *sungoleo*. Mind numbingly hot chutneys can build up more personality from *akuni* and dried fish.

Nagas are famous for their local rice beer, called *zu* or *zutho,* which contains around 5 per cent ethanol and is standard at every festival.

Hoihnu Hauzel

- Hauzel, Hoihnu. *The Essential North-East Cookbook*. New Delhi: Penguin Books, 2003.

NAIRS

The Nairs are a large group of Hindu castes and subcastes unique to Kerala. Many of their traditions have become synonymous with Malayali (Kerala) culture. The community had a rare matrilineal system (phased out since the 1950s), whereby property was passed through the female line and married couples resided at the maternal home. Its legacy is still felt is this socially progressive state.

The Nairs historically lived with multiple generations under one roof in a spacious building known as a *tharavad* in Malayalam, the local language. Its design reflects the centrality of RICE in Keralan society, as the structure was built around a sizable courtyard where the family de-husked and processed their rice crops. RICE was – and still is – eaten three to four times a day in the form of boiled grains, pancakes, dumplings, SWEETS and snacks. Tropical temperatures facilitate fermentation, so rice-based sourdough batters for IDLI and DOSA are mainstays of the diet. While Nair cooks excel at vegetable preparations, they also embrace dairy, various meats and FISH.

The ingredient that most defines the region's flavourful cuisine is the COCONUT. Nair cooking makes ample use of all its forms: the rich milk and scraped flesh thickens CURRIES, while the oil with its high smoke-point is ideal for frying. If Nair cuisine has a trademark technique, it is heating coconut oil to sizzle brown MUSTARD seeds, fresh CURRY LEAVES and dried red CHILLIES, known as *thaalippu*. This is the first step of many 'dry' curries and a last step when drizzled over finished 'wet' curries. The aroma is an alluring mix of nutty, citrusy and smoky notes. Sourness and chilli-heat are other key flavours in Nair food. For fish curry, cooks use the dried tart fruit *kudampuli* (*Garcinia gummi-gutta*), or Malabar tamarind or gamboge, which imparts a TAMARIND-like tang and rusty hue. Another souring agent for fish is unripe green MANGO (*amchoor* in its dried form), used when the flesh is still firm and white.

Fresh green CHILLIES are always available and deployed regularly as the primary source of heat. GINGER chimes in with a gentler warmth, while locally grown Malabar and Tellicherry black peppercorns (see PEPPER, BLACK) are crushed and added to meat and prawns to deliver a precise bite. Kerala has its own version of garam masala (see SPICE BOX), which includes the sweet liquorish notes of FENNEL and star anise alongside the usual suspects, CUMIN, CINNAMON, CLOVE and CARDAMOM, rounding out the otherwise tangy-hot flavour profile. CORIANDER, TURMERIC and mild red chilli powder are also essentials in the Nair cook's spice box. Breakfast in a Nair home resembles typical South Indian fare: idli or dosa accompanied by coconut CHUTNEY and SAMBAR. A regional speciality, *puttu*, is a mix of ground rice and grated coconut steamed in a bamboo tube, served with an earthy dish of black chickpeas, coconut milk and fennel, called *kadala*. South Indian COFFEE blended with chicory is the beverage of choice.

The midday 'rice meal' is the largest of the day and the most complex. It features a generous mound of Kerala red rice, or *matta*, topped with a teaspoon of GHEE and a ladleful of yellow dal. A *papadum* (*urad* wafer, see PAPAD) is crunched up and mixed with the rice and dal *(toor* or *moong)* to provide the binder so that each bite may be shaped into a tidy ball. There is a fish, meat or egg dish in a coconut gravy; a 'dry' finely chopped vegetable dish with grated coconut, mustard seeds, and curry leaves, called *thoren*; and a 'wet' vegetable dish such as *pachadi*, a lightly cooked vegetable with curds and mustard seeds. The meal concludes with a final serving of rice and curds as a palate cleanser.

Late afternoon is the time for visiting, snacking and TEA. A typical teatime nibble is *ethakkappam*: long slices of BANANA dipped in rice-flour batter and fried until golden. An honoured guest or relative is served a bowl of *payasam* (see KHEER), the thickened milk pudding with vermicelli, cashews and raisins. Meanwhile, the tea is strong, sweet, milky and refilled often. Lastly, around 8 pm, a light meal is served of rice pancakes or durum wheat chapati with a simple vegetable curry such as POTATO and ONION, or a 'stew' of vegetables in coconut milk. ALCOHOL is not generally consumed at family meals, but instead one might drink *jeeraka vellum*, water boiled with cumin seeds and considered a digestive aid in Ayurveda (see FOOD AND MEDICINE).

For celebration meals such as weddings or for Onam (the Malayali harvest festival), the Nairs prepare an all-vegetarian feast called *sadya*, or 'banquet', in Malayalam. Served on a large banana leaf, a *sadya* is essentially a tasting menu of classic curries, lentils and sweets, featuring seasonal vegetables, fruits, YAMS, GOURDS and PULSES, seasoned with mustard seeds, curry leaves, coconut, cumin, turmeric, green chilli, ginger and more. And while there is much overlap of ingredients from dish to dish, each *thoren, pachadi, kichadi, olan, kalan, aviyal, erissery* and *kootu* curry has its own distinct personality owing to the range of ways the cook manipulates each spice and ingredient. These dishes are accompanied by *matta* rice with a sequence of 'pouring gravies' or *ozhichu,* including *parippu* (pigeon peas), sambar, *pulissery* (spiced BUTTERMILK), rasam (tamarind lentil broth) and, lastly, curds. PICKLES, *papadum,* salty and sweet banana chips, and *payasam* are also a part of the *sadya* spread. And because the meal contains all six tastes recognized in Ayurveda (sweet, sour, salty, bitter, pungent and astringent), it is designed to bring balance and a sense of well-being.

Auspicious Hindu events are honoured with vegetarian food, which allows all to partake in the feasts, especially Namboodiris, the Brahmin caste, who observe strict VEGETARIANISM. Yet, in their daily lives, Nairs take pleasure and pride in their chicken curries with Kerala garam masala, egg 'roast' curry, spicy fried fish and mutton with potatoes and coriander. Millennia of peaceful coexistence between Hindus, Christians and Muslims in Kerala has brought about a mutual appreciation of each other's cultures and foods and allowed the Nair culinary *oeuvre* to include the bounty of vegetarian and non-vegetarian ingredients at their fingertips.

Maya Kaimal

- Kaimal, Maya. *Savoring the Spice Coast of India: Fresh Flavors from Kerala.* New York: HarperCollins, 2000.
- Ramachandran, Ammini. *Grains, Greens, and Grated Coconuts: Recipes and Remembrances of a Vegetarian Legacy*. New York: I-Universe, 2007.

NEEM

Neem (*Azadirachta indica*, Hindi *nim*) is a tree belonging to the mahogany family that is native to the Indian subcontinent. It can grow in many soils and regions and is fairly drought-resistant. Products used from neem leaves and bark have been used in traditional medicine, although clinical evidence for its efficacy is lacking and it is contraindicated for pregnant women and small children. Ground neem seeds are soaked in water and sprayed on crops as an effective alternative to synthetic pesticides. Neem twigs are used as a toothbrush.

A Bengali meal starts with a bitter dish to stimulate the appetite. Because of their bitter taste, neem leaves can be sautéed with AUBERGINE, cooked with DRUMSTICKS in a light gravy, or mixed with other vegetables to make the emblematic Bengali dish *shukto*. It can also be added to dal. In Andhra Pradesh (where neem is the official state tree), Telangana and parts of Karnataka, neem flowers are an ingredient in *ugadi pachadi*, a New Year's drink that contains all six basic flavours representing the joys and sorrows of life: MANGOES for pungency, jaggery for sweetness, neem flowers for bitterness, TAMARIND for sourness, pepper for hotness, and SALT.

Colleen Sen

- National Research Council. *Neem: A Tree for Solving Global Problems.* Washington, DC: National Academy Press, 1992.

NIGELLA

Nigella seeds come from the plant *Nigella sativa* which is native to the Levant but grows wild in northern India and is also cultivated there. The seeds, which are small, black and tear-shaped, are known by many misleading and inaccurate names in India. The name most used is *kalonji* but they are also known as *kala jeera* or 'black cumin' (see CUMIN). Despite this, nigella seeds do not resemble cumin in taste, nor are they botanically related. *Kalonji* are also often called black ONION seeds although they have nothing in common with onion plants but they do, however, resemble an actual onion seed. The seeds are also, sometimes, mistakenly called black caraway and black SESAME.

The seeds are commonly used as a flavouring. Nigella's pungent aroma is not strong but the taste is nutty, a little acrid and a bit like a cross between POPPY SEEDS and pepper (see PEPPER, BLACK). They are usually dry roasted to bring out their flavour before being sprinkled on BREADS. They are used to spice vegetables and PULSES and to flavour PICKLES. In Bengal they are also used in FISH dishes and are one of the components in the Bengali five-spice mixture *panch phoron* (see SPICE BOX).

Nigella seeds are used medicinally as a carminative, stimulant, diuretic, antibacterial, etc.

Helen Saberi

- Arndt, Alice. *Seasoning Savvy*. New York: The Haworth Herbal Press, 1999.
- Norman, Jill. *The Complete Book of Spices*. London: Dorling Kindersley, 1990.

NIHARI

Nihari is a spicy meat stew associated with Muslim cuisine and is usually purchased from street vendors or restaurants. It is made by cooking meat – typically beef or mutton shanks – overnight over low heat in large pots sealed with dough. It is flavoured with many aromatic spices including CLOVES, garam masala, CARDAMOM and CUMIN as well as CHILLIES. As the meat disintegrates it blends with the gravy. The dish is usually topped with julienned GINGER, CORIANDER leaves, green chillies and GHEE.

Its history is controversial. Some claim it originated in DELHI in the late eighteenth century, others that it originated in the kitchens of Awadh (see LUCKNOW). The Persian word *nahar* means day or daybreak and *nihari* is typically eaten for breakfast by Muslims after the morning prayer, especially in the winter. However, some establishments, like Delhi's famous Kallu Mian, serve it in the late afternoon. Cities famous for *nihari* include Delhi, Lucknow and HYDERABAD, as well as places in Bangladesh and Pakistan.

Standard accompaniments are *khameeri* roti, a soft lightly leavened bread made from whole WHEAT flour, SUGAR and milk, or naan (see BREADS). The addition of bone marrow creates a more gelatinous texture. Another version, *maghaz nihari,* is made with brains. *Nihari* is a popular remedy for colds and fever.

Colleen Sen

NI'MATNAMA

A valuable source of information about food in the fifteenth century is the *Ni'matnama*, or *Book of Delights*, by Ghiyath Shahi (r. 1469–1500). He was the

Sultan of Malwa, a small kingdom in west-central India in what is now western Madhya Pradesh and southeastern Rajasthan. After ascending the throne in 1469, he left the ruling of the kingdom to his son Nasir Shah in order to devote his life to the pursuit of pleasure, especially the pleasures of the table. His capital, Mandu, became known as Shadiyabad, City of Joy.

The Sultan hired hundreds of Indian and Persian cooks and artists and put together a collection of recipes and paintings called *Ni'matnama*. Composed from 1495 to 1505, it contains several hundred rudimentary recipes written in a mixture of Urdu and Persian and illustrated by fifty paintings. The paintings depict the preparation of dishes with Giyath Shah himself watching and supervising the operations and enjoying his meals.

The recipes are for the Sultan's favourite dishes, often accompanied by comments such as 'this is delicious' or 'this is a favorite of Ghiyath Shahi'. They are not arranged in any special order and there is a lot of repetition. The recipes are basically lists of ingredients with no information about amounts or cooking methods.

Ni'matnama may owe its inspiration to the recipe collections of the Persian court. Many dishes have Persian names: *shorba* (soup), *paliv* (broth), *qima* (minced meat), *dugh* (a yogurt drink), naan (baked bread), *yakhni* (meat stew), KEBAB or *seekh* (skewered meat), *burani* (a vegetable dish, often AUBERGINE, with yogurt), HALWA (a generic word for sweetmeats), *harisya* (grains, usually WHEAT and BARLEY, with meat; see *HALEEM*), KOFTA (meat balls), *sambusa* (SAMOSA), *biryan* (a general term for baked dishes), *paluda* (water thickened with flour and HONEY; also a noodle – see *FALOODA*), *tatmaj/tutjam* (a flat noodle), *thuli* (spiced cracked wheat), *kaliya* (a stew) and SHERBET (a cold drink made from different ingredients).

A Persian touch is the flavouring of stews with sour fruits, fruit juices and green herbs, including BASIL, orange and lime leaves (see CITRUS FRUITS), and MINT. The lavishness of the Shah's cuisine is apparent in the extensive use of three flavourings: CAMPHOR, ambergris and musk, valued both for their powerful, complex scents and because they were rare and expensive. Some dishes are prepared with as many as fifty spices and flavourings which were added at different stages of the cooking process.

Other dishes are of local origin, probably made by local cooks, and many are vegetarian: for example, *bara/bari* (also spelled vada/*vadi*), deep-fried balls made from ground grain or lentils, *bhat* (plain boiled RICE), *bhuji* (fried vegetables), dal, puri, KHICHRI, *karhi* or *kadi* (a yogurt and lentil stew), and RAITA. A few dishes are called *ganvari* or *gharib*, which means rustic or a poor man's food. These are very simple dishes, such as green vegetables boiled in water, or dal spiced with ASAFOETIDA, GINGER, ONIONS and black pepper (see PEPPER, BLACK) and served with MILLET bread. Millets feature in a dozen recipes.

Techniques include sautéing in ghee or oil, deep frying, steaming, boiling, grilling, roasting on hot stones, baking on or in hot coals, and roasting in a pit. Many recipes call for venison, partridge and other game. Sometimes meat is marinated before cooking. Like other Indian culinary collections, *Ni'matnama* contains recipes/prescriptions for many ailments and conditions, including impotence – a major concern of rulers.

Colleen Sen

- *The Ni'matnama Manuscript of the Sultans of Mandu. c.* 1500, translated by Norah M. Titley. London and New York: Routledge, 2005.

NUTMEG AND MACE

Nutmeg (*jaiphal* in Hindi) and mace (Hindi *javriti*), two distinct spices, are both part of the same fleshy fruit of the nutmeg tree *Myristica fragrans*. The spreading, evergreen tree is native to the Banda Islands in the Moluccas (Spice Islands) in Indonesia. The pale yellow fruit resembles a peach in appearance but not in texture, as its flesh is fibrous and husky. When ripe, the fruit splits and exposes the hard, brown kernel (nutmeg) which is covered with a lace-like red aril or membrane (mace). The mace is carefully peeled off the kernel, pressed flat and dried until it turns translucent yellowish-brown in colour, and, when brittle, is cut into strips (called mace blades) for sale. The grey-brown wrinkled kernel is also dried until the nutmeg rattles around inside its shell. The shell is then broken and discarded, leaving a light brown, woody nutmeg which can vary in shape from a long oval to round.

Nutmeg and mace were traded along the caravan trade route to Alexandria in Egypt in the sixth century. At about the same time, China was using nutmeg as a medicine for digestive disorders. Indians and Arabs also valued the spice for its medicinal and aphrodisiac properties.

Mace and nutmeg both have a rich aroma and warm aroma and taste. Nutmeg has a sweetish taste whereas that of mace is stronger and slightly bitter. Myristicin is one of the substances responsible for the 'warm' taste and special flavour of nutmeg. It has a narcotic effect but is safe in the quantities called for in cooking. Nutmeg is still valued for its medicinal properties and is used for bronchial disorders, rheumatism and flatulence. However, larger amounts should not be consumed as this can lead to disorientation and hallucinations and can even be fatal.

The nutmeg tree was originally brought to India from Indonesia in the late eighteenth century. It is now grown on a small scale in Tamil Nadu, Kerala, Assam and some other states but production is not enough to meet the country's requirements, even though both nutmeg and mace are used sparingly in cooking. Although ground nutmeg is available, it is preferable to purchase whole nutmegs and grate directly into the dish as the chemistry of nutmeg is such that the aroma and flavour disappear quite quickly once grated or ground.

Nutmeg is primarily used in North Indian and Kashmiri cooking. Ground or grated, it is used to spice RICE, meat and vegetable dishes. It has a particular affinity for spinach and is also good with winter squash, YAMS or sweet potatoes. Nutmeg is also added to relishes as well as jams and PICKLES. In Bengal and Gujarat, nutmeg is occasionally used to flavour milk-based SWEETS and yogurt desserts, often in combination with CARDAMOM. It is also one of the ingredients of a number of spice mixtures such as Chettinad masala, garam masala and *xacuti* (see SPICE BOX). Mace is usually used in powder form and, like nutmeg, is used in MUGHAL and Kashmiri dishes, and certain sweet pickles and relishes.

Helen Saberi

- Devi, Yamuna. *The Art of Vegetarian Cooking*. London: Leopard Books, 1995.
- Norman, Jill. *The Complete Book of Spices*. London: Dorling Kindersley, 1990.

NUTS

Nuts – fruits consisting of a hard or tough shell around an edible kernel – are widely used in Indian cuisine. For vegetarians, they provide a source of protein and add richness to North Indian meat-based dishes. Nuts, often salted, are a popular snack and part of gift

FIGURE 34 NUTS. Nutseller, Delhi. Ashish Sen.

boxes presented to friends and family on Diwali and other festive occasions. They are a component of many SWEETS. But most nuts are processed to make cooking oil. Two nuts are indigenous – charoli and pine nuts – while others arrived to the subcontinent both in prehistoric times and with the arrival of the Europeans.

Almonds (*Prunus amygdalus*, Hindi *badam*) are the delicately flavoured nut of the almond tree that is native to the Mediterranean basin and southwestern Asia where it was domesticated as early as 3000 BCE. They came to India via Persia and by the sixteenth century were in fairly common use. Almonds are produced in Jammu and Kashmir and Himachal Pradesh, but most of India's almonds consumption is imported, mainly from the United States.

Almonds are extensively used in Indian haute cuisine, including rich CURRIES such as korma and *pasanda* style curries, both as decoration and, when finely ground, as a thickener for gravies. Ground almonds are used in many desserts including *badam* HALWA, *sohan* BARFI and *badam* KHEER. They are also used to make summer drinks such as almond SHERBET.

Cashews (*Anacardium occidentale*, Hindi *kaju*) are native to Brazil. The name comes via Portuguese from the Tupian word *acaju*. The Portuguese brought cashews to India in the 1560s, more as a source for making ALCOHOLIC beverages than as a food ingredient. By the mid-1570s and 1580s, cashew trees were reported growing in gardens in Cochin and Goa. From India, cashew plants were taken to Southeast Asia and Africa. Today, India is the world's second largest producer of cashews after Vietnam.

Cashews have a slightly sweet and delicate flavour. The pulp of the fruit surrounding the nut, called an apple, can be processed into a sweet, astringent fruit drink. After mashing the pulp, the juice can be fermented for a few days and then distilled to make the famous Goan beverage, *feni*, which is about 40 per cent alcohol. In cuisine, the nuts are used whole for garnishing sweets or curries, or ground into a paste that forms a base for gravies for curries.

Charoli (*Buchanania lanzan*, Hindi *chironji*) are native to the subcontinent and grow mainly in western India where they are gathered by tribal peoples. When the shell is removed, they look like small lentils. They have a sweet nutty taste that becomes slightly bitter when heated. Their most common use is as a topping for sweets. In Maharashtra, charoli is ground into a powder as a thickener for soups and sauces. Elsewhere in India, the seeds are sometimes used to flavour KEBABS and BIRYANIS.

Groundnuts/peanuts (see PULSES).

Pine nuts (*Pinus gerardiana*, Hindi *chilgoza*) are the small edible seeds of many species of pine trees around the world. In India, they come from the pine tree native to the northeastern Himalayas, where they are harvested by local tribal people. Pine nuts are very expensive and are often prepared with spinach.

Pistachios (*Pistacia vera*, Hindi *pista*), a member of the cashew family, originated in Central Asia and the Mediterranean region. The only Indian production is in Jammu and Kashmir. Most are imported, mainly from Iran and Afghanistan. Pistachios are mentioned in the ancient medical texts while Akbar's chronicler Abu'l-Fazl writes that they were once scarce but are now 'found everywhere'. They are distinguished by their green colour, which comes from chlorophyll, and are often used whole, sliced or ground to garnish RICE puddings and other sweets.

Walnuts (*Juglans regia*, Hindi *akrot*) are native to a vast region of Eurasia, including Iran, the Himalayan region and western China, and can tolerate extremes of heat and cold. Indian consumption is small but growing because of their perceived health benefits and improved methods of preservation. Domestic production is limited to Jammu and Kashmir, Himachal Pradesh and Uttarakhand. India is both an exporter and importer of walnuts, with most imports coming from the United States. In Indian cuisine they are used mainly in sweets.

Colleen Sen

- Sauer, Jonathan D. *Historical Geography of Crop Plants: A Select Roster*. Boca Raton, FL: CRC Press, 1992.

ODISHA

Odisha, called Kalinga, Oddra and Utkala in ancient times, is located on the southeastern coast of India, bounded by the Bay of Bengal on its east, with a coastline spanning a length of around 480 km. It has a diverse topography with fertile coastal plains on the east, plateaus bounded by Chhattisgarh on the west, borders with Andhra Pradesh on the south, and West Bengal on its north. The emerald-hued Chilika, Asia's largest inland

FIGURE 35 ODISHA. *Chenna poda*, a popular dessert. Subransuphotography/Wikimedia Commons.

salt-water lagoon on the eastern coast, plays host to several migratory birds in winter. Odisha is also geographically prone to cyclones, because of its proximity to the Bay of Bengal, a hotbed of cyclonic activity.

Odisha has a rich cultural legacy of art and architecture. It is home to several ancient Hindu temples, including the exquisitely stone-sculpted Konark Sun Temple, and the Jagannath Temple in Puri, considered as one of the holy Chaar Dhams (four pilgrimage sites) for Hindus. It is also considered to be an important centre of Buddhism, owing to the fact that Buddhism was patronized by ASHOKA, the mighty Maurya ruler who won the War of Kalinga in 261 BC but went on to repent the war excesses and began propagating a policy of nonviolence (Dhamma).

The state was constituted as a separate province based on language by the British on 1 April 1936 which is celebrated as Utkala Divas. This eastern Indian state also boasts of an ancient history of maritime trade with Southeast Asian countries, such as Ceylon (now Sri Lanka), Myanmar (Burma) and Indonesia. An annual trade fair called Bali Jatra is held on Karthik Purnima, or full moon night, to commemorate the sea voyage undertaken by traders sailing from the ancient port city of Cuttack to Bali in Indonesia.

While Odia cuisine is healthy, light and flavourful, using minimal spices and quite like its more popular Bengali counterpart, it is still little-known or patronized outside the state. There are hardly any restaurant chains or outlets in metros offering Odia food to the rest of India, except for a couple of state-run outlets, like the Odisha Bhawan/Niwas in DELHI.

In 1928, Sarojini Chaudhury had penned *Gruhini Sarbaswa*, which, while one of the earliest known cuisine-related books in Odia, went beyond Odia cuisine to feature recipes from across the globe such as crab soup. She also delineated the science of running a hygienic and well-stocked kitchen, including storage of grains and cleanliness as well as cooking methods. Even then, Chaudhury, the daughter of eminent Odia litterateur and social reformer Fakir Mohan Senapati, had written that there was hardly any documentation of Odia cuisine. Not much has changed, only a few books have been written about Odia cuisine and most are recipe books.

Ironically, it is this understated, offbeat cuisine which won the jury's hearts at the *MasterChef India Season* 6 in March 2020. Young Odia techie, Abinas Nayak, won the MasterChef India title with his skilfully crafted dishes, which retained the organic elements of his native cuisine while being plated with global appeal. Nayak feels that his domicile cuisine has not been popularized because of the lack of both documentation and any sense of initiative or pride by the Odia community.

With plans of starting his own Odia restaurant chain, this self-taught chef is upbeat that Odia food will get its rightful place under the sun with better presentation. His dessert creation named Shuddhata (Purity) which won hearts of jury, food critics and viewers alike, was a work of art. It consisted of *chhenapoda* (an Odia cheesecake baked traditionally on *sal* leaves, placed on a wood fire and baked to a slightly burnt crust consistency), topped with tempered white chocolate, garnished with popped AMARANTH seeds and paired with *arna rasabali,* a rice-based pudding.

Food in Odisha, like most coastal states, is centred around rice and fish, with regional variations in cuisine across the state. A typical Odia meal will consist of *bhaata* (rice, a coarser unpolished variety called *usuna* is eaten in rural areas while the polished *arua* is for city-breds), *daali* (lentils, usually pigeon pea or *moong* dal), paired with a couple of *bhaajas* (sautéed or fried vegetables/FISH), greens (called *saagaw*) like spinach or AMARANTH or even *moringa* (see DRUMSTICK) leaves fried with GARLIC and red CHILLIES, vegetable/fish curries (*tarkari*), and a few tangy-sweet CHUTNEYS and *khattas* (made with TAMARIND or curd).

Odia cuisine can be broadly divided into four regions: South, North, Coastal and West Odisha. In South Odisha districts such as Ganjam and Koraput, which continued being part of the Madras Presidency in British India, food is tangy and spicy, remarkably like Andhra cuisine. South Indian staples such as IDLI, DOSA, COCONUT and TOMATO chutneys are popular, and so is the use of tamarind and gingelly oil. In North Odisha, including Balasore and Mayurbhanj districts, the impact of Bengali cuisine is evident in the addition of SUGAR to both vegetable and fish dishes. West Odisha has a sizeable tribal population and therefore food is organic and relates to plants and roots, such as BAMBOO SHOOTS or *karadi.* The fruits and flowers of the *mahua* tree are used in making delectable desserts such as BARFI, while the fermented sap is used for locally consumed ALCOHOL.

One of the more popular Odia staples across regions is *daalma*, which has dal, usually pigeon peas or split *moong* beans, cooked with different vegetables, usually POTATO, pumpkin, RADISH, AUBERGINE, raw BANANA, drumstick, pointed GOURD, TARO and the like, and then tempered with a seasoning of GHEE, CUMIN, ASAFOETIDA and dried red chillies.

Another popular staple, especially in summers, is *pakhala*, rice soaked in water to which curd and SALT are added. Sometimes garnishes of one's choice are added too, like chopped GINGER, green chillies, CORIANDER leaves or CURRY LEAVES. It is accompanied by a bevy of sides like *aloo* (potato), *baigana* (aubergine), *potola* (pointed gourd), *sagaw* (greens), *macchaw* (fish), *bhaja* (fried stuff), and also with *aloo bharta*, or potato mash, to which is added a dash of MUSTARD oil, green chillies and chopped onions. With excellent probiotic properties, *pakhala* can also be fermented overnight for a more delightful experience and is the perfect antidote to hot summer afternoons.

Another staple with regional variants is *KANJI* or *ambil*, a soup-like dish made of rice water/gruel to which seasonal vegetables like radish, OKRA, green PAPAYA and sometimes, even, bamboo shoots (in the West Odisha version) are added, and either chickpea flour or rice flour is used to thicken the broth.

Odia food is mostly steamed or sautéed lightly with minimal use of spices. A unique mix of five spices called *phutana* (see SPICE BOX), consisting of cumin, NIGELLA, mustard, FENUGREEK and FENNEL, is an oft-used seasoning in daily cooking and is typical to Odia and Bengali cuisine (known as *panch phoron* in the latter). Mustard oil is the preferred cooking medium for most dishes and so is the use of mustard paste called *besara*, made of both yellow and black mustard seeds.

Most of the Odia population is non-vegetarian and, as in other coastal states, fish, crab, prawns and lobster are preferred, though mutton and chicken are also becoming popular. River fish like *rohu* and *catla* (both are of the carp family) are commonly eaten, though hilsa fish from both the river and sea are considered most premium. The Chilika lagoon's blue and mud crabs and lobsters are sold at Balugaon, a fishing village near the lake. Most crabs are exported to Asian countries, including the bulk to Japan (see FISH).

No Odia meal is complete without SWEETS or *mitha,* especially those made of *chhena* (see *CHHANA*) or cottage cheese. Of these, the most well known is *rasagolla* (also spelled RASGULLA and *rosogolla* in different regions of India).

The Odia *rassagolla* (pronounced 'raw-saw-gola'), decidedly different in texture and taste, continues to be embroiled in an ownership debate with West Bengal over which version came first – the softer, brown Odia ones or the spongy, chewy and white Bengali ones. While both versions received a GEOGRAPHICAL INDICATION tag, the question is still out: Did Odia *rassagollas* precede the Bengali *rosogolla*?

Another delightful Odia sweet, which deserves special mention, is *chhenapoda*, or burnt *chenna*. A big mound of *chhena*, to which sugar, semolina and CARDAMOM powder are added, is wrapped in *sal* leaves and placed on a low wooden fire for long hours until the upper crust gets a burnt, blackish texture. *Chhena jilaapi* and *rasabali* (flattened and golden-fried discs made of cottage cheese, semolina, sugar and cardamom powder simmered in a watery milk concoction) are other popular sweets.

Pitha-panna is the name of the special delicacies cooked during religious ceremonies, festivals and special occasions. *Panna* is a liquid concoction made of several ingredients like fruits, *chhena*, spices, curd, milk, sugar, herbs, etc. *Panna* not only helps beat the heat of the sultry summers but also keeps the digestive system healthy because of its probiotic values. *Bellaw panna*, which is made of WOODAPPLE pulp mixed with water and crushed pepper (see PEPPER, BLACK), is highly recommended for gut health.

Pithas are either sweet or savoury and are made of rice flour, semolina, all-purpose flour, green lentils and black lentils. Jaggery or sugar and coconut are caramelized and used as filling, and as the occasion demands, *chhena* and dried fruits like raisins and cashews are also used, along with spices like green cardamom, CAMPHOR, nutmeg (see NUTMEG AND MACE), etc. *Pithas* are mostly steamed, though they can be fried too. The more popular *pithas* are *monda pitha,* steamed rice flour cakes filled with a caramelized coconut-jaggery mix, somewhat like the Maharashtrian *MODAKAS*; *enduri* or *haldi patra* (TURMERIC leaf) *pitha,* long cylindrical ones steam-wrapped in turmeric leaves; and *poda pitha*, with rice paste, coconut and jaggery, and today baked in modern ovens, though traditionally they were made on a charcoal fire and wrapped in banana leaf.

According to the scriptures on the Chaar Dhaams (four holy pilgrimage sites), Lord Vishnu bathes at Rameswaram, meditates at Badrinath, dines at Puri and retires at

Dwaraka. The culinary significance of Odisha in Hindu religion as well as on the palates of those who have sampled its cuisine cannot be overemphasized.

Swati Sucharita

- Chaudhury, Sarojini. *Gruhini Sarbaswa*. Cuttack, Orissa: Dutta Press, 1928.
- Tripathy, Usha Rani. *A Taste of Odisha*. Bhubaneswar, Odisha: Amadeus Press, 2011.

OKRA

Okra, also called lady fingers (*Abelmoschus esculentus*, Hindi *bhindi*), probably originated in East Africa, although some authors claim it was native to India and tropical Asia. Today India is by far the world's largest producer, accounting for nearly three-quarters of total production. The major growing states are Andhra Pradesh, Bihar, West Bengal, Odisha and Gujarat.

Okra is an annual herbaceous plant that grows in a wide range of soils in tropical and subtropical regions. It is mainly grown for its fruits – small green tapered pods containing many small seeds. They have a slightly fuzzy exterior and a thick gooey interior that becomes slimy when cooked. Okra is a good source of vitamins A and B and especially iodine. The skin and fibres are used to manufacture paper. Charaka mentions a plant called *bhandika* but whether this was okra is problematic. There is no sign of it in the Harappan Civilization so it may have been introduced later by Arab or African traders.

In India, okra is used mainly in vegetarian dishes, although it is sometimes cooked in a meat curry. Because of its slimy texture, a common method of preparation is to fry thin slices with spices in a little oil to make a dry dish (*bhindi* masala). In Gujarat, thick slices are first fried in GHEE and then simmered in spiced BUTTERMILK thickened with chickpea flour (*bhindi kadhi*). In Goa, okra is cooked in a spicy blend of ONIONS, GARLIC and toddy vinegar. In West Bengal, slices may be stir-fried and then cooked in a MUSTARD and POPPY SEED mixture (*shorshe dharosh*). Okra can also be stuffed with almonds, cashews, onions and/or a spice mixture (see SPICE BOX).

Colleen Sen

- Iyer, Raghavan. *660 Curries*. New York: Workman Publishing, 2008.

ONION

The onion (*Allium cepa*, Hindi *pyaaz*) likely originated in Afghanistan or Central Asia and was widely used in Ancient Egypt and the Middle East seven thousand years ago. Today, India is the second largest producer of onions in the world after China. The major producing states include Maharashtra, with nearly 30 per cent of the total, Karnataka, Madhya Pradesh and Gujarat.

Onions are mainly a cool weather crop. In India, most onions are planted in December to January and harvested from March to May. Because onions play such an important role in the Indian diet, poor weather can lead to shortages and high prices, sometimes causing social and political unrest. Conversely, a bumper crop can result in lower prices and economic hardship for the farmers.

Indians have had an ambivalent relationship to onions. Although traces of onion have not yet been found in the Indus Valley, it is possible they were used there (as was GARLIC). The Ayurvedic physician Charaka praised the onion as a vegetable that could help heal joints, aid digestion and boost energy.

However, the writers of the *Shastras* and other Brahmanical texts condemned onions (and garlic) as unclean and conducive to stimulating the passions. They were forbidden to students, widows, people who were fasting, *vaishnavas* (followers of Vishnu) and people seeking spiritual enlightenment. Jains avoid onions and garlic. The seventh century CE Chinese traveller Xuan Zang observed that few people ate onions and that those who did were expelled from towns. Nonetheless, several recipes in the *MANASOLLASA*, a collection of recipes compiled by a king in the early twelfth century are made with onions, despite a warning that kings should abstain from eating chicken, RADISH, garlic and onions. A few of the recipes in the *Supashastra* (1505), a collection written for a Jain king, call for onion and garlic.

Onions became an important part in Indian cuisine with the Islamic dynasties of the Delhi Sultanate (1300–1550). The traveller IBN BATTUTA (1304–69) wrote that 'the emperor's meal included meat cooked with GHEE, onions and green GINGER and SAMOSAS stuffed with onions, NUTS and spices'. Many of the recipes for KEBABS, kormas and qima dishes in the *NI'MATNAMA* (1495–1505) call for copious amounts of onion, as do dishes in Akbar's court as described in the *Ain-i-Akbari.*

Today, onions are a standard ingredient in North Indian cuisine, often ground with garlic and ginger to make a paste used in curry-like dishes. *Dopiaza* (literally 'two onions') is a meat-based CURRY in which onions are added in two stages. Chopped raw onions, onion CHUTNEY or an onion-TOMATO salad are standard accompaniments to kebabs and tandoori dishes. A popular teatime snack is *PAKORAS* made with chopped onions deep-fried in a chickpea batter. Chopped onions are often a topping to chaat and other STREET FOODS.

India produces around thirty varieties of onion of different sizes, colours and flavours. North Indians generally prefer small red onions, which Punjabi restaurants dip in vinegar as an appetite stimulant (*sirkewali pyaaz*). In Tamil Nadu, small pink onions with a mild flavour are added to SAMBAR and other dishes. Hindu Bengalis traditionally do not use much onion in their cuisine.

Colleen Sen

- Das Gupta, Kaushik. 'The Story of the Humble Bulb'. *The Indian Express.* 12 December 2019.
- Sirur, Simrin. 'Know Your Onions: Peeling Complex Layers of a Humble, Pricey Vegetable Mughals Popularized'. *The Print*, 4 December 2019. Available online: https://theprint.in/india/know-your-onions-peeling-complex-layers-of-a-humble-pricey-vegetable-mughals-popularised/329870/ (accessed 28 April 2022).

PAAN

Paan, sometimes translated as quid (related to the word 'cud'), is a preparation of several ingredients wrapped in a betel leaf and chewed. The filling always contains grated or sliced areca nut (betel nut), lime (calcium hydroxide) and various flavourings. The lime can be made from limestone or by burning and crushing sea shells, then

FIGURE 36 PAAN. Paan in Varanasi. Scott Dexter/Wikimedia Commons.

mixing the powder with water to make a paste. Another common ingredient is *kattha*, a sticky paste made from the astringent dark brown extract of the core of the areca tree. The pastes are spread on the leaf, the spices added and the leaf folded into an elegant little triangle sometimes held together with a clove. The eater carefully places it in his mouth and chews until it disappears or spits out what is left. There are two types of paan: *sada*, plain (without sugar syrup and spices), and *mitha*, sweet. *Mitha* paan may contain CARDAMOM, CLOVES, GINGER, ambergris, SAFFRON, black pepper (see PEPPER, BLACK), nutmeg (see NUTMEG AND MACE), grated COCONUT and SUGAR syrup. Tobacco is sometimes added too.

Although betel nuts and leaves originated in Southeast Asia, the two were combined in India some time before 500 BCE. Paan consumption became widespread among the rich and the poor alike. Later, aristocrats and rich people added ground pearls and shells to the lime paste and commissioned elaborate bowls called *bargdan* – boxes and trays made of silver and gold and inset with precious stones to hold the ingredients. Paan became a symbol of hospitality and the focal point of elaborate rituals. How one served and ate paan was a marker of sophistication and affluence.

Paan serves many purposes. At the end of a meal, it stimulates saliva and gastric flow and freshens the mouth. Paan has a mild stimulant effect, so it is used to stay awake. In some parts, the exchange of paan is sometimes regarded as equivalent to a contract and done to seal a marriage engagement. However, the World Health Organization and other agencies have found that chewing paan has carcinogenic effects, mainly because of areca nut.

Colleen Sen

PAKORA

FIGURE 37 PAKORA. Ashish Sen.

Pakora (or *pakodas*, *bhaji*, *pholourie*) is the generic name for fritters, which are popular as STREET FOOD, tea-time snacks and meal accompaniments across the Indian sub-continent and among the DIASPORA. They are made by slicing vegetables, dipping them in chickpea (*besan*) batter and deep frying them. They are served with ketchup, or a CORIANDER-CHILLI or sweet-and-sour tamarind CHUTNEY. The word pakora is derived from the Sanskrit *pakvavata*, a compound of *pakva* ('cooked') and *vata* ('a small lump') or its derivative *vataka* (a round cake made of PULSES fried in oil or GHEE).

The principal ingredients could be as varied as the people making pakoras – POTATOES, cauliflower or spinach; slivers of AUBERGINE and pumpkin (popular in West Bengal and Bangladesh, where pakoras are known as *phuluri*); fat green chillies (sometimes stuffed, sometimes not; with seeds, or deseeded); ONIONS (Maharashtra's *kanda bhaji*, which got transported to Britain as simply 'bhaji'); PANEER; and, in some restaurants, broccoli, too. Equally popular are FISH (AMRITSAR's fish pakoras, known simply as 'Amritsari fish'), chicken (as in the chicken pakoras popularized by the iconic Moti Mahal restaurant) and halves of boiled eggs.

Pakoras, arguably, influenced the invention of the Japanese tempura (the knowledge of cooking batter-fried sliced vegetables was taken by the Portuguese to Nagasaki, the only port then open to foreigners), but they definitely inspired the invention of 'golden fried prawns' which are deep-fried in corn flour batter and are very popular in CHINESE INDIAN CUISINE.

Related to pakoras are the *pholourie*, which are fried dough balls made with flour, ground split peas (*matar ki* dal in Hindi) and spices, similar to the *pakoris* that go into the yogurt-based *karhi*, served with TAMARIND and MANGO chutneys on the streets of Guyana, Trinidad and Tobago, and Suriname. Today, these savoury snacks are associated with the spring festival of Phagwan celebrated in those global outposts of Hindu culture.

A popular northern Indian variant is the bread pakora, which is made by halving a slice of bread, putting mashed spiced potatoes or slices of paneer in between, dipping the sandwich in thick *besan* batter, and deep-frying it. Another variant, though not technically a pakora, but hugely popular in the north, is the *aloo tikki*, or fried flattened potato croquettes stuffed with a spicy mix of lentils and peas, deep-fried in cooking oil, and served with chilled yogurt, coriander-mint chutney and *saunth* (a paste made with dried ginger and tamarind).

Sourish Bhattacharyya

- Sanghvi, Vir. 'Take Pride in the Bonda or Pakora. It Is Our Gift to the World'. *HT Brunch*, 18 April 2015.

PALGHAT IYERS

Many generations of Iyers from different parts of Tamil Nadu have migrated to Palghat in Kerala over the last 500 years, assimilating new traditions and creating a unique blend of the vegetarian cuisine cultures of the two regions. Although they still share many culinary similarities with the Tamil Iyers as a reminder of their origins, there are many preparations unique to the Palghat Iyers. Today a significant number of Palghat Iyers have migrated to other parts of India, most notably MUMBAI. Elaborate home cooking, traditional feasts and ritualistic cooking are still practised in the community and its diaspora at large, keeping culinary practices and oral traditions alive. Many families from the region have been prominent culinary entrepreneurs and caterers and, thus, important actors in the taste-making of the region.

RICE forms the main starch and is central to a meal. Palghat, rich in black soil, is a central rice-growing region of Kerala and red *matta,* roundish with a pink epicarp, is a unique variety grown and consumed here. Lentils and beans are the primary protein sources in their diet, in addition to milk and milk products. Traditionalists avoid MUSHROOMS, alliums (GARLIC) and bottle GOURD.

Meals centre around four main types of vegetable stews: *mulakooshyam* (only lentil based), *molagootal* (lentils with COCONUT spice paste), *kootan* (coconut paste and yogurt cooked without lentils) and SAMBAR (lentils with TAMARIND and coconut). The vegetables and greens added lend their names as in *kaiyum chenaiyum mulakooshyam* (plantain and YAM), *elavan molagootal* (ash gourd), *keerai molagootal* (spinach), *mambazha kootan* (MANGOES) or *murungakkai sambar* (DRUMSTICK). *Avial* is perhaps the most well-known *kootan,* traditionally using thirteen native vegetables – AUBERGINE, elephant foot yam, yellow cucumber, ash gourd, pumpkin, green mango, plantain, TARO roots, coconut, flat beans, snake gourd, drumstick and CURRY LEAVES.

A variety of sambars, reminiscent of their Tamil heritage, are still made, albeit with coconut. *Pitlai*, with bitter gourd or aubergine, is a variation with no CORIANDER seeds, and *puthucode navaratri* sambar is a festive variation of vegetables cut into large chunks and flavoured with ground green CHILLIES and CUMIN.

The sautéing of lentils (instead of spices) in fats like GHEE or coconut oil to impart aroma is also notable. A combination of black MUSTARD, FENUGREEK seeds, black lentils, Bengal gram with ASAFOETIDA sautéed at the start of preparation, as a finishing note, or both is typical. Curry leaves and virgin coconut oil are signature elements of flavouring.

A side dish, or *erandamadhu*, is an essential part of a meal with stir-fried vegetables, PICKLES, condiments or fried crisps being common. Most vegetables are gently stir-fried in coconut oil, steaming them mostly in their moisture. Adding grated coconut to finish the dish makes *thoran,* and prolonged roasting of starchy tubers and plantain in oil gives *mezhukkupuratti.* A variety of relishes, sauces and pickles complement the dominant coconut flavours in a meal with tangy, umami notes. A reduction of tamarind pulp is cooked with yam in *chettimasiyal,* with GINGER in *inji puli* and OKRA in *vendakkai puli.* Yogurt-based *pachadi* is familiar to most Tamil kitchens, but *arachu kalakki* is a unique variation with raw yam, gooseberries (see AMLA), ginger and coconut.

Pickling and preserving are significant activities carried out in the home kitchen and as small cottage industries. *Oorugai* (lit. soaking) are pickles of seasonal fruits produced mainly – by brining as in *kanni manga* with wild tender mangoes, *manga inji* with *Curcuma amada Roxburgh* and *kurumolagu* with green pepper; by preserving in a mustard paste with wild tender mangoes as *vadu manga* or with *Hemidesmus indicus* as *mahali*; or by salting and sun-drying acid limes, lemons and citrons.

Sun-dried medicinal berries and plants are preserved by repeatedly soaking in yogurt and sun drying until saturated to make *vethal.* These can be fried or added to stews. *Solanum nigrum* (*manathakali-vethal*), *Solanum torvum* (*sundakkai-vethal*), LOTUS stems and green chillies (*mor milagai*) are very popular. A variety of rice-based crisps called *karuvadams* and lentil-based *poppadoms* (see PAPAD) are sun-dried and later fried in oil.

Ghee is an essential fat and flavouring and is eaten with rice at the meal's start. A typical weekday meal would consist of rice eaten across two-three courses. Traditionally, *toor* dal cooked with TURMERIC and eaten with a bit of ghee and rice marks the start of a meal, followed by a stew and sides. The meal always ends with rice eaten with yogurt and pickles.

Of particular interest are the diverse ways of using coconuts. The coconut meat is grated with a saw tooth scraping device to yield soft, coconut-meat flakes that are toasted on low heat for an intense nutty aroma, ground to a fine paste to thicken stews, or cut into small tooth-sized bits and used like NUTS in desserts.

Breakfasts, mid-afternoon snacks and, often, dinners are simple meals called *tiffin* varieties. Most preparations are like those in the larger Tamil Iyer community. Some unique preparations include *pidi kozhukattai* (steamed rice semolina cakes), *elai adai* (rice paste stuffed with fruit jams and cooked in a BANANA wrap), or *pazham poriyal* (batter-fried ripe plantain).

Sweet porridges are popular desserts. *Paal payasam* (see KHEER), with rice cooked in milk and SUGAR; *paruppu payasam* with lentils cooked in jaggery and thin coconut milk; and *pradhaman* with thick coconut milk and jaggery are essential varieties. The addition of fruit jams to this makes *chakka pradhaman* (JACKFRUIT) and *nendra pazham pradhaman* (plantain); cooked rice pasta makes *pal ada pradhaman* and WHEAT makes *godhumai pradhaman. Chadha chadhayam*, with rice cooked in thick coconut milk and ripe bananas added to the finish is a festive delicacy. *Nei payasam* is the most revered of desserts, prepared mainly for rituals. A portion of rice is cooked in ten times its volume of jaggery and twice its volume of ghee for many hours and topped with coconut pieces and cumin seeds fried in ghee. While most confectionaries are similar to those in the Tamil community, *porivalangai*, a dense multigrain *laddu*, is unique to the Palghat Iyers.

Priya Mani

(This article is based, in part, on oral interviews conducted by the author with Ms Bagyalakshmi Subramanian and Mr Murali Raman.)

- Lakshiminarayan, K. N. *From Cauvery to Neela: A History of the Tamil Agraharams of Palakkad*. Chennai: Notion Press, 2020.
- Mookambal, Visalam, Saradha Mookambal and Shyam Srinivasan Mookambal. Adukkulai. Available online: https://adukkulai.wordpress.com/ (accessed 29 October 2022).

PALMER, EDWARD

Edward Palmer (*c*.1860–*c*.1940) was a Eurasian trader of Indian condiments who opened The Veeraswamy, Britain's oldest surviving upper-end Indian restaurant, exuding imperial opulence and thriving on the English nostalgia for the imperialist past, on Regent Street, London, in 1926. He was also the author of what is believed to be the first Indian cookbook to be published for an international audience, *Indian Cookery: For Use in All Countries* (1936), which he wrote under the name of E.P. Veerasawmy (the last name reportedly being the family name of his paternal grandfather's Indian wife).

A printer's devil was responsible for the 'a' and 'w' being transposed in the restaurant's name on its menu card in 1934, since when it became known as The Veeraswamy, till 'The' was dropped by its present owners, Namita Panjabi and Ranjit Mathrani, in 2001. Veeraswamy got its first Michelin star in the 2017 Guide and has retained it ever since.

Edward Palmer was the great-grandson of General William Palmer, one of the original 'White Mughals' (his second wife, Faiz-un-nissa Begum, was from Awadh), who rose from being the ADC to Warren Hastings (Governor General of India from 1773 to 1785) to becoming the commander of the 4th Native Infantry till his death in 1816. General Palmer, then a Major, and his family appear in an unfinished oil painting by the Dutch artist Johann Zoffany, now in the possession of the British Library.

Edward Palmer's grandfather, William Palmer, after leading the army of the second Nizam of Hyderabad in several successful military campaigns and retiring as Brigadier General of the Nizam's Bodyguard, launched a successful bank to which the Nizam was substantially indebted. The Palmer fairytale came to an abrupt end in 1824, when it went bankrupt after incurring the wrath of Charles Metcalfe, the East India Company's Resident (or political agent) in Hyderabad.

Not much is known about Edward Palmer's father, James Edward, but the Palmer family saga resumes after the arrival of the future restaurateur in England to study Medicine in 1880. Medicine, however, wasn't to be Edward Palmer's calling.

By 1896 he had already set up Veeraswamy & Co. in Hornsey, London, to promote Indian food products, 'so that they could be used under Western conditions and yet produce Eastern results'. Under the trademark 'Nizam' these items, notably spices, pickles and chutneys such as Major Grey's Mango CHUTNEY, were sold in grocery stores across Britain. Edward Palmer was later invited to serve as the adviser to the Indian restaurant named Mughal Palace at the British Empire Exhibition in Wembley from April 1924 to October 1925. The popularity of the restaurant at the Exhibition, especially its duck VINDALOO and Madras curry, was noted by the Government of India's official report on the event.

'The Indian Restaurant with its curries drew large crowds, and at lunch and tea time on most days long queues formed up at the entrance', said the report authored by its Commissioner for India, Sir T. Vijayaraghavacharya, who went on to note that 'the success of the Indian cafe was largely due to [Palmer]'. The restaurant's stellar show – it served an average of 500 curries a day – ensured a successful take-off for Palmer's iconic restaurant. It was also at the Exhibition that Prince Axel of Denmark discovered curries. He later became a regular at Veeraswamy, where he first showed up with a barrel of Carlsberg and introduced the now-popular English tradition of washing down their curries with beer.

In 1934, the restaurant passed into the hands of Sir William Steward, a Conservative who served as an MP from 1950 to 1959, and his wife, a popular crooner of her time, Greta Gaye, who together ran the restaurant till 1967. It was under their stewardship that Veeraswamy introduced the first curry in a can in the early 1950s. Very little is known meanwhile about the career of Edward Palmer after Veeraswamy changed hands.

Sourish Bhattarcharya

- Collingham, Lizzie. *Curry: A Tale of Cooks and Conquerors*. New York: Oxford University Press, 2006.
- Leonard, Karen. *Hyderabad and Hyderabadis*. Delhi: Manohar Books, 2014.

PANEER

Paneer (sometimes written *panir*) is a soft or semi-soft cheese made from cow or buffalo milk that is a common ingredient in North India and Pakistan, but is not widely used elsewhere in the Indian subcontinent. Paneer is made by the coagulation of cow or buffalo milk using fruit- or vegetable-derived acid.

Paneer was probably introduced into northern India by Persian and Afghan invaders in the thirteenth and fourteenth centuries. In India, it is produced both domestically and commercially. At home, milk is brought to a boil, separated with vinegar, lemon juice, yogurt or BUTTERMILK, stirred, and strained in a muslin cloth. For firmer paneer, the curds are pressed under a weight or between two plates. Commercially, paneer is processed into blocks in large hoops, cut into rectangles and immersed in chilled water for several hours to make it firm. It is sold fresh, frozen and in cans.

Typical cow milk paneer contains 52 to 54 per cent moisture, 24 to 26 per cent milk fat, 16 to 18 per cent protein, and 2 per cent lactose. Buffalo milk paneer is slightly higher in milk fat and lower in protein. Paneer is used as a substitute for meat in vegetarian dishes. Fried cubes can be added to RICE, mixed with spinach, FENUGREEK or peas and cooked in a rich gravy, or placed on skewers and roasted.

Colleen Sen

- Bladholm, Linda. *The Indian Grocery Store Demystified*. Los Angeles: Renaissance Books, 2000.

PANJABI, CAMELLIA

Camellia Panjabi is best known around the world for her slim yet encyclopaedic *The Great Curries of India*, which has sold more than a million copies in seven languages since it was first published in the UK in 1994. In the hospitality industry, however, she is regarded as the pioneering promoter of Indian regional cuisines, creator of iconic restaurants, including The Bombay Brasseries in London in 1982, and now co-owner of the restaurant group that operates Veeraswamy, Britain's oldest continually running Indian restaurant established in 1926, besides Chutney Mary, Amaya and the Masala Zone franchise in the UK.

After reading Economics at Cambridge University, Panjabi joined the edible oils division of the Indian industrial conglomerate, Tata Sons, till she was moved to the Taj Hotels to develop new locations. Later, she headed the group's marketing operations both in India and overseas.

But Panjabi left an enduring culinary legacy in the form of India's first 'South Indian' eatery in a five-star hotel, Tanjore at Mumbai's Taj Mahal, which was the first in its genre when it was opened in 1973, and Karavalli, the go-to restaurant for coastal cuisine in Bengaluru, as well as such ground-breaking food destinations as Golden Dragon, the country's first Sichuan restaurant in Mumbai, and Orient Express in New Delhi, where the finest European cuisine is served in a space that recreates the dining car of the famous train,

While establishing these restaurants, and travelling around India to open new Taj hotels, Panjabi deep-dived into regional Indian cuisines, looking everywhere for well-known dishes, from a 'lowly eating house off a bazaar' to an 'aristocrat's home in Madras', to the 'table of Bombay's top society hostess' or that of a 'gourmet family in Hyderabad', to a 'third-generation wedding cook in Lucknow'. Sometimes it meant 'piecing together different little secrets from different sources', and so 'a collection of recipes began to build up, extending from one file to several'.

The Great Curries of India is the result of this painstaking work. In her reflections on the evolution of the word 'CURRY', for instance, Panjabi points out how the Tamil root word *kaari* (which is a part of the longer word *kaikaari*) for upper-caste Brahmins in Tamil Nadu means a vegetable dish cooked with spices and a dash of COCONUT, but for the non-vegetarian communities in the state, because of a slight change in the way the word is pronounced (*kaaree*, as opposed to *kaari*), it means a meat dish with gravy (*kaaree kolambu*). The book is studded with such nuggets, and, as a result, over the nearly two decades it has been in circulation, it is valued both as a gift to newly weds and as a reference book for the serious student of Indian gastronomy.

Sourish Bhattacharyya

- Panjabi, Camellia. *The Great Curries of India*. New York: Simon & Schuster, 1995.

PAPAD

Papad, also known as *appalam* in the southern state of Tamil Nadu and corrupted to 'poppadum' in overseas Indian restaurants, is a versatile snack, starter or meal accompaniment that is served all over South Asia.

The recipe for this thin, round, sun-dried flatbread varies from one part of India to the other, but essentially the varieties are made with lentil, chickpea, RICE, tapioca, (see CASSAVA), MILLET, JACKFRUIT or POTATO flour, plain or spiced with black pepper and red CHILLI powder, and come in different shapes and sizes. Papad is either fried in vegetable oil or dry heated on an open flame till it turns crunchy.

Served year-round, papad is served as a starter in restaurants, usually with pearl ONIONS dipped in red vinegar (*sirkewali pyaaz*) in Delhi restaurants, to rev up the appetite of guests; as a cocktail snack ('masala papad', topped up with chopped onions, TOMATOES and CORIANDER, drizzled with fresh lime juice and red chilli powder); and as an accompaniment to dal as well as *KHICHRI*, whose four friends (*chaar yaar*), according to a folk ditty, are GHEE, papad, tangy mutton mince (keema) and *achaar* (PICKLES).

Three holy cities are synonymous with the production and export of papad: AMRITSAR, for its papad that is seasoned liberally with SALT, black pepper (see PEPPER, BLACK), *hing* (ASAFOETIDA), CUMIN, CORIANDER, POMEGRANATE seeds, and, sometimes, even GARLIC; VARANASI, for its potato flour papad; and Madurai, for its plain, uniformly shaped papad discs, the *appalam*, made with *urad* (hulled split back gram) and *moong* (mung) dal flour, which are served fried in gingelly oil at every UDUPI RESTAURANT around the world.

India's papad story is associated inextricably with the Shri Mahila Griha Udyog Lijjat Papad, an eminently successful institution, which has become a symbol of women's empowerment since it was established by Jaswantiben Jamnadas Popat and six other housewives in a crowded tenement in Girgaum, Mumbai, in 1959 with Rs 80 borrowed from their families. They were first supported by a local visionary named Purushottamdas Damodar Dattani, who found Lijjat papad's first buyer – a neighbourhood grocery store named Anandji Premji and Company. The 'seven sisters', as the founders are known, were mentored by a renowned social worker, Chhaganlal Karamsi Parekh, popularly known as Chhagan Bappa. Under his guidance, the organization grew steadily, winning awards, being featured by the BBC and National Geographic, finding takers in global markets, and diversifying into other products, namely WHEAT flour, masalas, heat-and-serve chapatis, and even detergents and washing soaps. Popat, one of the seven co-founders, was honoured with the Padma Shri by the President of India on 26 January 1951.

What Amul is to milk (see DAIRY SECTOR), Lijjat is to papad. The women-run cooperative, headed by Swati Ravindra Paradkar, the daughter of one of the early 'Lijjat sisters', today employs 45,000 women in sixteen states, making 4.8 billion pieces of papad and *appalam* a year and exporting to fifteen countries around the world. In 2019, the cooperative's turnover was reported to be Rs 16 billion, with exports topping Rs 800 million.

Sourish Bhattacharyya

- AFP. 'Lijjat Papad: How 7 Women Wrote a Success Story with Only ₹80 for Seed Capital'. *Mint*, 15 April 2021.

PAPAYA

Although today India is by far the world's leading producer, papaya (*Carica papaya*, Hindi *papita*) reached India sometime in the mid-sixteenth century. Native to Central America, the fruit was spread by the Spanish and Portuguese throughout their vast territories. How it reached India is open to dispute: Some claim it came from the Philippines, others that it arrived from Brazil via Malaysia.

Papaya is a tropical plant that thrives in many types of soil and can be cultivated year-round. Almost all of India's production is consumed domestically. Andhra Pradesh is the leading producer, followed by Gujarat, Karnataka, Maharashtra and West Bengal. There are hundreds of varieties of papayas, ranging in size from a small apple to up to nine kilograms in weight. When ripe, the flesh is sweet with a delicate aroma, second only to the mango in its fragrance. Taken with a little lime, it is a popular breakfast fruit. Unripe papayas, especially the larger ones, are cooked as a vegetable or made into PICKLES. The fruits and leaves contain an enzyme, papain, which is used as a meat tenderizer. Papaya is rich in vitamins A and C and antioxidants.

Every region has its own way of preparing papaya. Chunks of raw papaya can be cooked as a CURRY with a TOMATO or COCONUT-based gravy. Bengalis combine unripe papaya with bitter, hot and sweet spices to make a *jhol,* a liquid curry. Pureed papaya can be mixed with dough to make a North Indian *phulka* or Gujarati *thepla* (see BREADS). Ripe papaya can be mixed with yogurt to make a LASSI or a smoothie.

Colleen Sen

PARSIS

Parsi cuisine is the umbrella expression used to describe the unique food culture of the Parsis, India's most influential micro-minority and followers of the Zoroastrian religion who fled from persecution in the Greater Khorasan region of ancient Persia (Iran) to arrive at the present-day western Indian state of Gujarat between the eighth and tenth centuries. After this first wave of migration, which saw the Parsis settle down to practise farming, trade and ship-building in Gujarat, the community attained social and economic prominence from the late seventeenth century onwards when it started facilitating the mercantile activities of the East India Company. Their proximity dates back to the time when the Company established its first 'factory' in the port city of Surat in 1668. After the Company moved its headquarters to the future metropolis of Bombay, then a zig-zag of miasmic marshlands, in 1687, the Parsis followed. It was in Bombay (renamed MUMBAI) that the Parsis acquired their wealth, culture and intellectual refinement, and created institutions dedicated to the advancement of the arts, science and education. The Tata, Godrej and Shapoorji Pallonji families – all Parsis – continue to preside over the fortunes of the city, and of India's, to a significant extent. It is this cosmopolitan, world-travelled community that has also produced a procession of accomplished people such as the father of India's atomic energy programme, Homi Bhabha; rock icon Freddie Mercury (Farrokh Bulsara); the famous conductor Zubin Mehta; pioneering woman photojournalist Homai Vyarawalla; and Indo-Canadian writer of literary fiction, Rohinton Mistry.

The celebrated novelist Amitav Ghose writes that the Parsis 'essentially created modern India'. Their influence is highly disproportionate to their numbers, which have been declining by 12 per cent every Census decade since 1941. The population of Parsis, when last officially counted in 2011, was a little over 57,000 (down from 115,000 in 1941) in a country of 1.3 billion. Another 40,000 Parsis are believed to be scattered around the world.

As the Parsis turned Bombay into a modern metropolis, the city, along with Karachi (now in Pakistan), Pune and HYDERABAD, attracted a second wave of immigrants from Iran, both Zoroastrians and Muslims, in steady trickles from 1870 to 1872. The first of these immigrants were escaping a famine that had struck the cities of Yazd and Kerman, famous for their tradition of baking and confectionary. And later they kept coming for better opportunities. These were the entrepreneurial Iranis, whose mother tongue is Dari or Farsi, not the Gujarati of the Parsis. They created the institution of the IRANI CAFES, bequeathing landmark restaurants such as Britannia & Co. (see KOHINOOR, BOMAN) and DORABJEE & SONS, and the Yazdani and Kayani bakeries, the latter being famous for Pune's SHREWSBURY BISCUITS.

The early Parsis settled down in the Gujarati port town of Sanjan, according to the *Qissa-i-Sanjan* (*Story of Sanjan*), an epic poem composed in Persian and completed in 1599 CE, which is the earliest surviving account of the arrival of the itinerant refugees who had escaped the Arab conquest of Iran. Sanjan today is a small town near the city of Valsad in Gujarat, which is on the southern tip of the state's neckline, washed up by the Gulf of Cambay (Khambat) and stretching into the neighbouring state of Maharashtra. Jadi Rana, the local ruler, according to the *Qissa*, agreed to provide refuge to the settlers if they promised to adopt the local language; wear the sari, the common dress of Indian women; refrain from eating or cooking beef; and not convert the local citizens.

The Parsis had to leave Sanjan after the town was sacked by Gujarat's Sultan Mahmud Begada in 1465 and move to Navsari, the birthplace of the pioneering industrialist Jamshetji Tata, and Udvada, home to their most sacred fire temple. Their long association with Gujarat significantly influenced the cuisine and culture of the Parsis. The best-known Parsi dish, *dhansak*, famously served on Wednesdays at the Parsis-only Ripon Club (established in 1884), is emblematic of this cross-fertilization of culinary influences.

Dhansak consists of mutton, or goat meat (what the Parsis call *gosh*), cooked with three or four different kinds of lentils (see PULSES), mainly split pigeon peas (*toovar* dal), and POTATOES, AUBERGINE, red pumpkin, spinach, TOMATOES and FENUGREEK leaves. Requiring elaborate preparation, the dish is served on Sundays, and also on the fourth day after the death of a loved one (on the first three days the Parsis abstain from non-vegetarian food). Traditionally, *dhansak* is served with brown RICE cooked with whole spices and caramelized ONIONS, *kavab*s (mutton mince cutlets) and *kachumber* (a salad of fresh chopped tomatoes, CUCUMBERS, onions and green CHILLIES drizzled with lemon juice). Its association with funerary rituals however rules it out for auspicious occasions such as festivals and marriages.

Scholars believe that the word *dhansak* is a compound of the Gujarati words *dhaan* (grains or millets) and *shaak* (vegetables). Food historian K.T. ACHAYA notes the mention of a cereal dish called *dhan* in the old Gujarati story about a valorous king named Raval Kanhadade written by the fifteenth-century poet Padmanabha (*Kanhadade Prabandha*). The Parsis, it is surmised, brought with them the tradition of cooking meat with lentils. Bhicoo Manekshaw, an authority on Parsi cooking, speculates that the dish probably evolved from the Iranian *khoresht esfenaj*, which is cooked with meat, lentils and spinach.

The Iranian original got modified in Gujarat with the addition of local vegetables and the spice mix called *dhansak* masala (see SPICE BOX), or the less elaborate *dhana jeeru* (literally translated from the Gujarati original as 'CORIANDER and CUMIN'). The *dhansak* masala is a combination of thirteen to fifteen (depending on the recipe you use) roasted and ground whole spices, including coriander (*dhania*), cumin (*jeera*), POPPY SEEDS, dry red chillies, black peppercorns (see pepper, BLACK) and MUSTARD seeds, apart from CINNAMON sticks, CLOVES, CARDAMOM, star anise, nutmeg (see NUTMEG AND MACE) and bay leaf. To these essential ingredients, as Niloufer Ichaporia King notes, are sometimes added the exotic *dugar ka phool* (a LICHEN) and *nag kesar* (a whole peppercorn with a tail). The masala today is also used to cook dal (lentils) and the Gujarati dish, *ringan ravaiya* (stuffed aubergine).

Over the centuries, the Parsis introduced freshly extracted TAMARIND pulp, jaggery (see SUGAR) and COCONUT milk into their cuisine (coconuts, incidentally, are as ritually significant in the Zoroastrian religion as in Hinduism). They started cooking in GHEE (clarified butter). They also developed their own garam masala (cardamom, cinnamon sticks, black cumin seeds, whole cloves, black peppercorns and nutmeg – all ground together) and the more elaborate *sambhar* masala (the *sambhar* in this case must not be confused with the South Indian lentil soup). The latter consists of red chilli powder, SALT, ground TURMERIC, crushed ASAFOETIDA resin (the only known instance, according to Ichaporia King, of the use of asafoetida, or *hing*, in Parsi cuisine), fenugreek and mustard seeds, black peppercorns, broken-up star anise pods, whole cloves, cinnamon sticks and untoasted SESAME (*til*) oil, also known as gingelly oil.

The Parsis started cooking mutton with vegetables as varied as potatoes and peas, OKRA, flat beans (*papdi* in Gujarati and *sem* in Hindi) and sweet potatoes, and even with sweet APRICOTS (*jardaloo*). Sweet and sour preparations, in fact, are an important part of the Parsi repertoire, a characteristic it shares with Gujarati food. Living on the coast, the Parsis developed a taste for sea FISH, notably pomfret and *surmai* (king mackerel), prawns and BOMBAY DUCK (the lizardfish, locally known as *bombil*, or *boomla* as the Parsis call it), the central ingredient of the sweet and sour Tarapori *patio* (also called *sooka boomla nu patio*). They also adopted the Gujarati *rotli*s (thin chapatis, or unleavened BREADS) and love for puffy puris, served with the potato CURRY called *papeta nu saakh* (the equivalent of the North Indian breakfast staple of puri-*bhaji*).

Tomatoes, which, like potatoes, became popular in India only in the nineteenth century, appear regularly in Parsi dishes. Colonial influences are also evident in the use of Worcestershire sauce and the rebirth of the caramel custard as the cardamom-scented *lagan nu* custard, a wedding delicacy spiked with nutmeg, charoli (wild almonds, see NUTS) and fat raisins. Béchamel sauce gets reinvented with a touch of fresh green chillies and whole cumin seeds, and the introduction of an egg-sugar-vinegar emulsion at the end of the preparation in *saas ni machchi* (where *saas* is not a reference to a mother-in-law but the colloquialization of the word 'sauce'). It is a 'real magpie cuisine', to quote the words of Ichaporia King, which has thrived on 'gleeful borrowing'. It is an 'allegory' for the community's infinite ability to adapt and survive.

Another inheritance of the Parsis – this time from the Dutch bakers of Surat, who left the port city in the late 1700s – was the invention of a unique class of biscuits, notably Faramji Pestonji Dotivala's *batasa*, made with flour, water, palm toddy (replaced by an ALCOHOL-free fermenting agent because of Prohibition in Gujarat) and ghee, and sprinkled with CARAWAY seeds, which has been selling since 1861.

The *nankhatai* – cookies made with semolina, gram flour, all-purpose WHEAT flour, sugar, butter and nuts (almonds and pistachio) – was the other tea-time snack that Dotivala popularized. When the Iranis came, they introduced *brun maska* (hard buttered croissants), the softer sweeter bun *maska* (*maska* being the combination of butter and sweet cream daubed at the centre of the bun), *khari* biscuits (savoury puff pastries) and the cardamom-flavoured *mawa* cake (made with *KHOYA*, or evaporated milk solids, butter, all-purpose flour and eggs) to serve with Irani chai (the slow-brewed, creamy tea most popular in Hyderabad).

It must also have been the Dutch who introduced the Parsis of Surat to the art of cheese-making, which resulted in the creation of the *topli* paneer (balls of cottage cheese suspended in salty whey and served in palm-sized baskets, or *toplis*), which

Meher Mirza, a chronicler of Parsi cuisine, describes as 'trembling, velvet-soft, salty, tangy, like blancmange crossed with mozzarella'. A nine-page recipe for this paneer is provided in *Vivid Vani*, the venerable Parsi cookbook by Meherbai Jamshedji Nusserwanji Wadia, first published in 1867, which describes how dried chicken gizzards were soaked in vinegar (an alternative to rennet) to produce the coagulant needed to make the cheese.

A Gujarati snack item that the Parsis have happily adopted is the *patrel*, the collective name given to fried TARO leaf rolls filled with a sweet, sour and hot paste made with rice, wheat and chickpea flours and an array of spices and condiments. The Parsis, though, stand out from their Gujarati Hindu neighbours in three respects. The first is their fondness for offal – lamb brain, or *bhejoo*, and chicken liver, or *kaleji*, which when combined with marinated gizzard leads to the lip-smacking *aleti paleti*. The second is the use of vinegar (*sarko*) – made for 135 years with barrel-fermented sugarcane juice by E.P. Kolah & Sons of Navsari – which lifts the flavours of the delicate and incomparable *patra ni machchi* (pomfret or *surmai* smeared and stuffed with a green CHUTNEY, which is prepared with grated coconut, raw MANGO, MINT and coriander leaves, GARLIC cloves and cumin seeds, wrapped in BANANA leaf, and steam cooked).

The third point of departure is the Parsi obsession with eggs, symbolized by none other than Russi Mody, the late former chairman and managing director of Tata Steel, who lived up to be 96. The multi-faceted Mr Mody was famous for having an omelette prepared with sixteen eggs for breakfast daily. It is not known whether he used to gorge only on *poro*, the Parsi masala omelette which sometimes comes with a filling of goat brain, because the community has an impressive repertoire of egg preparations to dig into. Eggs, along with fish, are permitted even during the holy month of Bahman, which coincides with the days in January–February assigned to the zodiac sign Aquarius.

Ichaporia King mentions a version of devilled eggs, mysteriously named as 'Italian' eggs (hard-boiled eggs on a bed of spiced tomato puree), described in a Parsi cookbook written in Gujarati in the 1940s. A Parsi egg classic is the community's (and the stiff upper-lipped Willingdon Sports Club's) all-time favourite called *akuri*, or scrambled eggs spiced up with fried onions, ginger-garlic paste (or *adu-lasan*, a recurring ingredient in Parsi preparations), chopped coriander leaves, green chillies and ground pepper.

Another popular preparation is *papeta par eeda* (better-known outside India as Parsi egg), or fried eggs, sunny side up, resting on top of a hash of potato cubes, tomatoes and onion slices. If the potato cubes are replaced with *saali*, or deep-fried potato straws (another favourite of the Parsis), it becomes *saali par eeda*; if we substitute the base with any other vegetable – okra or aubergine – or spinach or fenugreek leaves, it is called *bhaji par eeda*. Mirza, basing her count on Manekshaw's *Parsi Food and Customs* and a vintage Gujarati-Parsi cookbook called *Varied and Delicious Dishes*, lists eighteen similar dishes with fried eggs on top.

What sets apart Parsi cuisine is its distinctive spectrum of flavours. With the revival of the cuisine (and its Irani sibling) in acclaimed younger restaurants such as Dishoom in London, Parsi Dhaba on the Mumbai-Pune highway, Rustom's at Delhi's iconic Parsi Anjuman, and the multi-city Sodabottleopenerwala and a legion of gifted chefs and caterers, from the late Katy Dalal to Tehtman and Shernaz Dumasia, to Tanaz Godivala and Kainaz Contractor, it promises to have a long and eventful second life outside the community. Like the Parsis, the fan following of their cuisine far exceeds their miniscule numbers.

Sourish Bhattacharyya

- Dalal, Katy. *Jamva Chaloji: Parsi Delicacies for All Occasions*, 2 volumes. Mumbai: Vakil, Feffer, and Simmons, 1997.
- Manekshaw, Bhicoo. *Parsi Food and Customs*. New Delhi: Penguin, 2000.
- Mehta, Jeroo. *100 Parsi Recipes*. 1973. Reprinted. Mumbai: Popular Prakashan, 2008.
- Mirza, Meher. 'The Essential Parsi Spice Blends'. *Saveur*, 19 March 2019. Available online: https://www.saveur.com/story/recipes/parsi-spice-mixes/ (accessed 28 April 2022).
- Mishan, Ligaya. 'A Bid to Maintain One of the World's Oldest Culinary Traditions'. *T: The New York Times Style Magazine*, 8 May 2019. Available online: https://www.nytimes.com/2019/05/08/t-magazine/parsi-food.html (accessed 28 April 2022).

PELITI, FEDERICO

Federico Peliti (1844–1914) was an Italian sculptor, photographer, confectioner, pastry chef, hotelier and vermouth maker from the town of Carignano, near Turin, who was hired after a public competition by India's British Viceroy, Richard Southwell Bourke, 6th Earl of Mayo, to be his pastry chef in 1869.

After Lord Mayo was assassinated by a convicted prisoner in 1872, Peliti stayed on to open, after a couple of smaller ventures, a fashionable confectionery shop and restaurant named after him on Esplanade East (now known as the Government Place East) in Calcutta (see KOLKATA), across the road from the governor's residence (today's Raj Bhawan). 'How tongues wag and teaspoons rattle at Peliti's in Calcutta', exclaimed a contemporary observer admiringly. Peliti's became famous for its three-course Friday lunch priced at the then princely sum of Rs 1.50 per person.

In 1919 the Italian launched Peliti's Cafe next to Combermere bridge in Shimla, British India's summer capital. The cafe, which had a terrace veranda overlooking the valley and was very popular with the ruling class, finds a mention in Rudyard Kipling's 1885 poem 'Divided Destinies' and appears in his short story *The Phantom Reekshaw* (1888).

In the 1880s, Peliti went on to construct a villa in Mashobra, neighbouring Shimla, which he named Carignano after his home town and opened Peliti's Grand Hotel on the grounds where the castle of Lord William Bentinck (Governor-General from 1828 to 1835) once stood in Shimla. The hotel, which had an ice manufacturing machine, was gutted in 1922 and was never rebuilt, but not before it was immortalized in *Punch* in a poem dedicated to it on 25 June 1919.

Peliti's many achievements included the creation of a twelve-foot replica of the Eiffel Tower made entirely with SUGAR for the Calcutta International Exhibition (1883–4), which won a medal in the confectionery section. He won another medal at the Universal Exhibition of Paris (1889), which earned him a decoration from the French government in 1895. In Turin, his photographs of people from different walks of life in India were recognized and today are in the possession of the Calcografia Nazionale in Rome.

The Italian polymath's talent for making vermouth, which was being shipped to the Prince of Wales since his state visit to India in 1891 and became a favourite of

Queen Victoria, was re-discovered some years back by his grand-daughter much after it had ceased production in 1940. Of the forty recipes prepared by Peliti, only two are produced today under the Peliti's Vermut label – a classic red and a white flavoured with CARDAMOM. Peliti returned to Carignano in 1902 after handing over his Calcutta business to his sons Edoardo and Federico and his Bombay operations to an acolyte named Felice Cornaglia.

Sourish Bhattacharyya

- Hobbs, Major Harry. *Talketalkewallah and Others*. Calcutta: H. Hobbs & Co., 1938.
- Peliti, Luca. 'Federico Peliti'. *Luca Peliti, n.d.* Available online: https://www.peliti.org/Federico/ (accessed 28 April 2022).

PEPPER, BLACK

Black or round pepper (*Piper nigrum*, Hindi *mirch*) is a perennial climbing vine that originated on India's Malabar Coast. One of its Sanskrit names, *maricha*, testifies to its antiquity while archaeological evidence indicates it was used in the Harappan Civilization. Signs of a very ancient pepper trade from India to Egypt have been found, including peppercorns that had been stuffed into the nostrils of the mummy of Ramses the Great in the second millennium BCE.

Pepper vines grow best in hilly terrain with well-drained soil, high temperatures and ample rainfall, such as the Western Ghats. On farms they are usually grown with betel, palm, MANGO and other trees which provide support. The peppercorns come from the plant's green unripe drupes (a fleshy fruit surrounding a hard seed), usually referred to as berries. Black peppercorns are made by removing the outer skin, cooking them briefly in hot water, leaving them a few days to ferment, and then drying them either mechanically or in the sun. White peppercorns are berries with the outer skin removed. Green peppercorns are ripe berries that are treated in various ways to retain their green colour. Black pepper is more aromatic and pungent than white pepper and is distinct from long pepper (see PEPPER, LONG).

Today, India is the world's fifth largest producer of black pepper after Ethiopia, Vietnam, Indonesia and Brazil. While Kerala used to be the country's major producer, today it has been surpassed by Karnataka (especially Kodagu), which accounts for 45 per cent of India's total production of 66,000 tonnes in 2019.

Of all the spices, black pepper has been historically the most important both as an item of trade and as a medium of exchange. Plato (429–347 BCE) described the tiny shrivelled berries as 'small in quantity, great in virtue'. The use of pepper expanded rapidly in the Roman Empire. The Romans paid for spices mainly in gold and silver coins. The first-century Roman historian Pliny blamed the Romans' exorbitant demand for pepper and other spices as one of the causes of the Empire's decline.

The twelfth-century world traveller IBN BATTUTA was astonished to find Malabari merchants counting peppercorns one by one like pearls, which had the same value. In the Middle Ages, pepper was highly valued in Europe where the rich used it as a seasoning and a status symbol (although not, as some claim, to disguise the taste of rotten meat since people who ate it would get sick or die). Pepper, like other spices, was also valued as medicine. It reached Europe via an overland route to the Mediterranean where Venetian merchants controlled its distribution. After the discovery of a sea route to India by Vasco da Gama, who landed near Calicut (now Kozhikode) on the Malabar Coast in 1498, the Portuguese maintained a monopoly of spices for several decades until they were challenged by other European powers. Hindu traders carried black pepper to Java around 100 BCE and from here it may have reached China.

Black pepper largely replaced long pepper in culinary uses, in part because it was less expensive. Black pepper itself has, to a large extent, been replaced by CHILLIES, which can grow almost everywhere and are much cheaper. But black pepper remains an important component in many Indian cuisines, especially in the South. It is an essential ingredient in the lentil dish rasam, the basis of the famous ANGLO-INDIAN soup mulligatawny (from the Tamil words *milagu tannir*, pepper water). In Kerala, and the Kodagu region of Karnataka, it is used in many dishes. The most famous Kodava dish, *pandi* curry, uses significant amounts of black pepper, while the dish *koli nalla mallu barthad* is a dry fried chicken in which the main spice is crushed black pepper.

Pongal, a dish made to celebrate the South Indian New Year, is made with jaggery, COCONUT water, TAMARIND, RICE and black pepper. Pepper is a key ingredient in classic dishes such as *milagu kozhi*, a chicken curry that can be searingly hot, while a mixture of finely ground black pepper and CUMIN seed is added to meat dishes. Black pepper is used in many Andhra masalas and *podi* (see SPICE BOX).

Black pepper has been an important item in medicine, especially as a treatment for coughs and colds. The active ingredient responsible for its biting taste is an alkaloid, piperine. Together with long pepper and GINGER, it is one of the three components of *trikatu*, a popular remedy for disorders of the *doshas* (see FOOD AND MEDICINE). TURMERIC should always be sautéed with black pepper to enhance the absorption of curcumin.

Colleen Sen

PEPPER, LONG

Long pepper (*Piper longum*, *pipli* in Hindi) is a close relative of black pepper (*P. nigrum*, see PEPPER, BLACK). The name comes from its elongated (about 1.5 cm) fruit (the pepper itself) and resembles a small grey-black catkin-like spike made up of numerous tiny seeds, all tightly clustered round a central core.

Native to northeastern India, long pepper has been known in India since prehistoric times and is mentioned very early in Sanskrit literature, in the *Yajurveda* and *Atharvaveda*, collections of ritual and magical poetry thought to be from between 1000 and 500 BCE. In Sanskrit it is called *pippali* from which our word 'pepper' is derived.

Long pepper spread throughout southern Asia before black pepper and was probably the first variety of pepper to reach the Mediterranean. It was much sought after in ancient Greece and Rome. The Greek philosopher Theophrastus described both long and black pepper and in the first century CE, the Roman historian Pliny wrote:

> Long pepper sells at 15 d. the pound, white 7 d., black 4 d. Why do we like it so much? Some foods attract by sweetness, some by their appearance, but neither the pod nor the berry of pepper has anything to be said for it. We only want it for its bite – and we will go to India to get it! Who was the first to try it with food? Who was so anxious to develop an appetite that hunger would not do the trick? Pepper and ginger both grow wild in their native countries, and yet we value them in terms of gold and silver.'
>
> (Dalby 2000: 89)

Long pepper was widely exported to Europe until the sixteenth century but it seems that when the new 'hot' CHILLI peppers came from the Americas, their use declined. Although the two spices are nothing like each other, the use of long pepper faded almost entirely in Europe, and to some extent in India. The chilli pepper was cheaper and propagated more easily outside its native home; also, long pepper didn't travel well and was subject to mould if it wasn't dried properly before shipping. Today, long pepper is a spice which has almost been forgotten.

However, long pepper in India still grows wild (mainly for local use) and, even though black pepper yields a better return, is cultivated in West Bengal, Uttar Pradesh, Madhya Pradesh, Maharashtra, Kerala, Karnataka and Tamil Nadu. The tightly clustered peppercorns are gathered when green and unripe then dried in the sun or in special ovens. They are usually used whole but can be crushed with a mortar and pestle or ground in a spice grinder. Long pepper resembles black pepper in taste but is more complex with slightly less pungency or 'hotness' and with a hint of sweetness. Although rarely found in stores, long pepper is still used in rasam (sometimes called 'pepper water'), the hot and spicy thin soup served of southern India, the mutton stew *NIHARI*, lentil CURRIES and in PICKLES and preserves.

Long pepper is still valued for its medicinal properties and is a common ingredient in many medicines of Ayurveda (see FOOD AND MEDICINE). It is prescribed for a number of ailments including indigestion, respiratory infections, anaemia and constipation.

Helen Saberi

- Dalby, Andrew. *Dangerous Tastes: The Story of Spices*. London: British Museum Press, 2000.
- Hyman, Philip and Mary Hyman. 'Long Pepper: A Short History'. *Petits Propos Culinaires* 6 (1980): 50–2.

PICKLES

Pickles (Hindi *achaar*) are condiments either served with a meal as taste enhancers or mixed with preparations such as curd RICE (*thayir sadam* in Tamil) and KHICHRI. According to the popular doggerel, khichri is incomplete without its *chaar yaar* (four friends) – *dahi* (yogurt), PAPAD (poppadum), GHEE and *achaar*.

Indian pickles are prepared by assembling fresh ingredients – raw MANGO (the most common), Bengal currants (*karaonda*) and BAMBOO SHOOTS, lime and lemons (see CITRUS FRUITS), even mutton and shrimp; dressing them with SALT and TURMERIC; mixing them in heated MUSTARD or SESAME oil with a spice mixture; and letting the combination mature in a ceramic *martaban* jar or covered glass bowl, preferably in the sun, for three to four days. It is the last step – known in food chemistry as anaerobic fermentation – that ensures the long life of pickles and their ability to travel well. In the warmth of the sun, bacteria digest the sucrose, producing acids that preserve the food and prevent the growth of more harmful bacteria.

A pickle's main ingredient could be raw (unripe mango, for instance), blanched (as in the sweet-and-tangy cauliflower, CARROT and TURNIP pickle popular during the winter months in the north) or fried till tender (in the case of meats, FISH and shrimp). Each pickle stands out because of its distinctive spice mix, which varies by region. Mustard, FENUGREEK, FENNEL and NIGELLA seeds (either powdered or lightly fried in the pickling oil);

ground dried Mathania or Byadagi red CHILLIES; GINGER and GARLIC; and *hing* (ASAFOETIDA) are employed in varying combinations in the individual spice mixes.

Pickle-makers have enjoyed the liberty to dip into a dazzling diversity of flavours and aromas, from *panch phoron* (see SPICE BOX) to Naga king chilli. Each family has its favourite pickle, and an elderly custodian of the 'secret recipe', so the proportions of the ingredients can change as the pickles traverse the entire spectrum of individual flavour preferences – salty, sour, chilli, astringent, sweet or bitter.

Traditionally pickles were made at home, but with big brands such as Mother's Recipe, Nilon's and Panchranga taking over the market, packaged pickles are simply bought off stores or from e-commerce sites. The spice mixtures, which now come in powdered form, are also employed to cook a variety of *achaari* dishes in North India – the *achaari* chicken being the best-known.

Madhur JAFFREY evocatively describes this splendid diversity. 'Pickles in India', she writes, 'are a world in themselves. A whole book can be written about them. Pickles preserve, and in a land of warm climate and little refrigeration, almost everything gets pickled in order to extend its life.' Millions more Indians now have access to refrigerators than in 1973 (see ICE) when Jaffrey wrote *An Invitation to Indian Cooking*, but they still love their pickles – and have taken them wherever they have travelled, creating markets for international brands such as Patak's. As India's 'pickle queen', Chennai-based former lawyer Usha Prabakaran, proved with her encyclopaedic *Usha's Pickle Digest*, privately published in 1998, it is possible to rustle up 1,000 recipes fit enough for a big fat book.

Pickling is an ancient tradition in India, which explains the mind-boggling diversity, and it keeps appearing in historical texts. In 1563, the Portuguese physician Garcia DE ORTA mentioned a Goan conserve of cashews in salt, which 'they call achar'. It was, according to de Orta, 'sold in the market just as olives are with us'. The Dutch trader and historian Jan Huygen van Linschoten, who lived and worked in Goa, also mentioned the word in his *Itinerario*. Around the same time, as K.T. ACHAYA points out, Gurulinga Desika's *Lingapurana*, a Kannada work dated 1594, described 'no less than fifty kinds of pickles'. Later, in the seventeenth century, the King of Keladi, Basavaraja, in his encyclopaedia of Sanskrit verse, *Shiva Tattva Ratnakara*, identified pickles prepared without the use of fire (i.e. matured in the sun) as one of the five types of relishes (*uppadamsha*).

The authors of *Hobson-Jobson*, the timeless dictionary of ANGLO-INDIAN words, speculate that the word *achar* was brought by the Portuguese from the Malay archipelago. The English explorer and naturalist, William Dampier noted in his *New Voyages Round the World* (1697): 'They make in the East Indies, especially at Siam and Pegu, several sorts of Achar, as of the young tops of Bamboes, &c. Bambo Achar and Mango Achar are most used.' Another possible root of the word, according to *Hobson-Jobson*, is the Latin *acetaria*, which the 'Western Asiatics' got along with them to India.

Whatever the world's origin, *achaar* was a common-enough component of the daily diet of Indians for Alexander Hamilton, Scottish sea captain and privateer, to write in *A New Account of the East Indies* (1727): 'And the Soldiery, Fishers, Peasants, and Handicrafts (of Goa) feed on a little Rice boiled in Water, with a little bit of Salt Fish, or Atchaar, which is pickled Fruits or Roots.' Four decades later, the Dutch naval captain Johan Splinter Stavorinus made a similar observation in his *Voyages to the East Indies* (1768–71): 'When green it (the mango) is made into attjar, for which the kernel is taken out, and the space filled in with ginger, pimento and other spicy ingredients, which it is pickled in vinegar.'

Contemporary cookbooks, like their modern successors, invariably had a section dedicated to pickles, as in the *Nuskha-i-Shahjahani* (or the *Nan u Namak*), written during the reign of MUGHAL emperor Shah Jahan (1627–58). So did the *Khulasat-i-Makulat u Mashrubat* dating back probably to the reign of Aurangzeb (1656–1707) or somewhat later. Pickles had by then established their place on the Indian table, performing, in the words of Jaffrey, the important task of 'prodding sluggish bodies into perking up and eating', especially when appetites 'wilt and turn apathetic' during the 'blazing summer months'.

Sourish Bhattacharyya

- Achaya, K.T. *A Historical Dictionary of Indian Food*. Delhi: OUP, 1998.
- Jaffrey, Madhur. *An Invitation to Indian Cooking*. New York: Alfred A. Knopf, 1973.
- Kshitija, P. 'A Brief History of the Humble Indian Pickle'. *Culture Trip*, 28 November 2016. Available online: https://theculturetrip.com/asia/india/articles/a-brief-history-of-the-humble-indian-pickle/ (accessed 29 April 2022).
- Narayanan, Divya. 'What Was Mughal Cuisine? Defining and Analysing a Culinary Culture'. *Interdisziplinäre Zeitschrift für Südasienforschung* (IZSAF), or the *Interdisciplinary Journal of Research on South Asia* 1 (2016): 11.
- Rao, Tejal. 'India's "Pickle Queen" Preserves Everything, Including the Past'. *The New York Times*, 29 July 2020.
- Yule, Henry and A. C. Burnell. *Hobson-Jobson: A Glossary of Colloquial Anglo-Indian Words and Phrases, and of Kindred Terms, Etymological, Historical, Geographical and Discursive*. 1886. Reprint of the new edition, edited by William Crooke. 1903. London: Routledge & Kegan Paul, 1986.

PINEAPPLE

The wild ancestors of the pineapple (*Ananas comosus*, Hindi *ananas*) can be traced to the Paraguay basin and Brazil, where the fruit, called *nanas,* was first domesticated. Cultivated varieties, especially the seedless ones, were carried north to the Caribbean, Central America and southern Mexico. Christopher Columbus encountered pineapples in 1493, first on the island of Guadeloupe, later in Panama. The Dutch and Portuguese then spread them throughout their empires. According to the *Ain-i-Akbari*, by 1590 pineapples were sold in North Indian markets where they cost as much as ten mangoes. Jahangir called pineapple a fruit of the 'European ports' and noted that thousands were grown in gardens in Agra.

One reason for the rapid adoption of this and other fruits and vegetables throughout India may have been the personal interest of the Mughal emperors in horticulture. The pineapple was originally called *kathal i safari* (traveller's JACKFRUIT), perhaps because the young plants were transported in pots so that they could grow en route. Later they became known by their Portuguese name, *ananas*.

An alternative theory is that the pineapple existed in India for centuries. A pineapple-like fruit is depicted on the fifth century CE Udaygiri cave temples in Madhya Pradesh and at a thousand-year-old Jain temple in Palitana, Gujarat. As with CORN, there is a theory that the Atlantic and Pacific Oceans were navigated long before the Europeans did.

Pineapples grow as a small shrub; the individual flowers of the unpollinated plant fuse to form a multiple fruit. The pineapple grows in tropical regions and can flourish in conditions of low rainfall and poor soil. India is the world's sixth largest producer of pineapples, the leading producing states being (in order) Assam, Kerala, Meghalaya, West Bengal, Arunachal Pradesh and Manipur.

Pineapple is often an ingredient in the STREET FOOD fruit chaat and in RAITA. *Pachadi* is a South Indian variation of raita made from cooked pineapple, COCONUT and yogurt. In West Bengal pineapples are often used in a sweet and sour CHUTNEY. A popular dish in Karnataka is pineapple *sheera/kesari*, a sweet dish made from semolina, GHEE, ripe pineapple and NUTS. South Indians make a thick pineapple curry called *menaskai* or *gojju* that is eaten with RICE or with IDLIS and DOSAS. Pineapple is also added to rasam (a spicy South Indian soup), especially at weddings. Assamese sometimes add pineapple to a fish CURRY. Bengalis have been adding pineapple to *hilsa* FISH dishes as both are harvested as the same time. HALWA and SANDESH can be made with pineapple.

Colleen Sen

- Mazumdar, Sucheta. 'The Impact of New World Food Crops on the Diet and Economy of China and India, 1100–1900'. In *Food in Global History*, edited by Raymond Grew, 58–78. New York: Routledge, 2000.

PLUMS

Plums (Hindi *aloo bukhara*) are related to CHERRIES, peaches, APRICOTS and almonds, all members of the *Prunus* genus in the rose family. There are so many closely related species that it is hard to tell where a plum fruit ends and a cherry begins, and today there are many hybrids, varieties and cultivars.

Plums have a long history and it is generally believed that the Chinese were the first to cultivate plums around 470 BCE. The species native to China, *Prunus salicina,* is commonly known as the Japanese or Chinese plum but should not be confused with *P. mume*, a related species grown in China, Japan, Korea and Vietnam. The plum (*P. salicina*) is generally believed to have arrived in India from China, probably via Kashmir. The seventh century CE Chinese pilgrim Xuan Zang noted that wild plums brought from Kashmir were found 'growing on every side'.

Plums are not a very common fruit in India but the primary producing states are Punjab, Himachal Pradesh, Uttar Pradesh and Jammu and Kashmir. Plums also grow on a limited scale in the Nilgiri hills in the south. Most plum varieties belong to *P. salicina* as they are considered to have the best taste and are suitable as a fresh fruit although they are also dried. The twelve cultivated varieties include *aloo Bokhara* which is yellow in colour, sometimes with a tint of red. They are juicy and sweet. Kala Amritsari is a popular variety grown in Punjab. It is round and dark brown in colour when ripe. The flesh is yellow, juicy and considered good for making jam. Fresh or dried plums are also made into CHUTNEYS, PICKLES or preserves. They can be stewed and are sometimes used to stuff KOFTA.

These plums should not be confused with another fruit called the Indian plum, BER, which is not related. *Ber*, however, is more popular in India than the fruit bearing the same name.

Helen Saberi

- Reddy, Catherine. 'All about Plum in India'. *The Earth of India*, 6 February 2013. Available online: http://theindianvegan.blogspot.com/2013/02/all-about-plum-in-india.html (accessed 29 April 2022).

POMEGRANATE

Pomegranate (*Punica granatum*, Hindi *anaar*) is the fruit of an ancient tree which probably originated in Persia but whose cultivation quickly spread west to the Mediterranean and throughout the Middle East and east to India and China. The trees, although small, are long living and beautiful, especially with their deep orangey-red blossoms. The fruits, which can vary considerably in size, are globe-shaped with a hard red skin. When fully ripe and cut open, the inside is a pinkish red honeycomb structure full of pink-red seeds which glisten like ruby gems bursting with juice which are noted for their tangy but sweet flavour. Because of their abundance of seeds, the pomegranate became a symbol of fertility and prosperity in many cultures, including Indian, and its very antiquity has ensured that it figures in countless myths and legends.

The pomegranate may have come to India from Persia as early as the Harappan Civilization (*c.* 2000 BCE). The *Mahabharata* (c. 400 BCE) describes a picnic meal in which 'animal food' was garnished with pomegranate seeds. The seventh-century Chinese traveller Xuan Zang noted that pomegranates and sweet oranges were grown everywhere. Later, Amir Khusrau (1300 CE) remarked on the excellent flavour of pomegranates in Jodhpur. They were relished at the Mughal courts. Pomegranates are associated with Bhumidevi (earth goddess) and Ganesha. Bhumidevi is usually depicted with four arms, respectively holding a pomegranate, a water vessel, a bowl containing healing herbs and another bowl containing vegetables. Ganesha also holds a pomegranate (known as *beejapoori* in Sanskrit literature) in his hand as a symbol of both material and spiritual wealth. Pomegranate leaves and flowers are still used in the worship of Ganesha.

Maharashtra is the largest pomegranate-growing state but it is also commercially cultivated in Karnataka, Gujarat, Andhra Pradesh, Telangana, Madhya Pradesh, Tamil Nadu and Rajasthan.

Pomegranate seeds are scattered over desserts and made into a refreshing juice or SHERBET. To make pomegranate juice or sherbet, the pomegranate is cut in half, split open and the seeds are separated from the bitter white inner casing. The juicy seeds are then pressed to extract the juice. The seeds are also dried and ground to make a spice known as *anardana* that is used as a seasoning or souring agent to impart tartness. Seeds of the wild pomegranate variety found in the Himalayas, known as *daru*, are highly esteemed for making *anardana*.

The pomegranate is an ingredient in Ayurvedic medicine where it is considered soothing and strengthening.

Helen Saberi

- Achaya, K. T. *A Historical Dictionary of Indian Food*. Delhi: OUP, 1998.
- Stone, Damien. *Pomegranate: A Global History*. London: Reaktion Books, 2017.

POPPY SEEDS

Poppy seeds (Hindi *khas khas*) are a common and important spice in Indian kitchens. They are the ripe seeds of the poppy plant, *Papaver somniferum*, which translates as 'sleep-inducing poppy' and is also known as the opium poppy. This refers to the plant's narcotic properties, as opium oozes out in the form of a gummy latex when the unripe seed pods are cut. However, if the seeds are allowed to ripen in the pod, they are not narcotic and both the seeds and the oil, which can be expressed from them, are used for culinary purposes.

The poppy plant is native to the eastern Mediterranean and has been cultivated for opium and its seeds from the earliest times. Cultivation spread eastwards to Persia, India and China. In India, during the reign of the MUGHAL Emperor Akbar, poppy seeds started to be used in cooking, especially as a texture enhancer and to thicken sauces.

In the mid-eighteenth century, the British needed to balance the trade with China. The British needed silk, porcelain and tea but China didn't want any European goods except silver, and not much of that. However, they did want opium despite the fact that it was an illegal drug. The opium poppy grew abundantly in India and huge areas of land in the Bengal Presidency and later in Bihar and Orissa were cultivating poppies. Once the opium had been extracted for export to China, enormous amounts of dried out poppy seeds were left over. The Bengali farmers and their wives found that the seeds when ground to a paste exude a nutty flavour and, mixed with MUSTARD oil and other ingredients, enriched their simple diet, eventually becoming Bengal's favourite comfort food.

Today India is the world's largest consumer of poppy seeds and much of the poppy seeds, in recent times, are imported, mainly from Turkey.

There are many varieties and cultivars of the opium poppy which produce different types of poppy seeds of various colours – white, black, blue, red, grey and yellow. Poppy seeds commonly used in Europe are blue-grey in colour but in India they come from *P. somniferum* var. *album*, are smaller and have an ivory colour. Both types have a subtle but pleasantly nutty and slightly sweet taste when cooked.

In India, poppy seeds are usually roasted to intensify their flavour, then added to spice mixtures (such as *xacuti* and Chettinad, see SPICE BOX) or ground with other spices. They are often mixed with 'wet' seasonings such as GINGER and GARLIC, then used to thicken and enrich sauces for meat, FISH and shellfish. Poppy seeds are considered to be highly nutritious and are used in many vegetarian dishes.

In Bengal, the seeds (*posto* in Bengali) are traditionally soaked in water before being ground with a stone slab and pestle to produce a creamy, grainy paste called *posto bata*. A favourite Bengali dish is *aloo posto*, POTATOES cooked with the paste and flavoured with NIGELLA seeds. Poppy seeds are added to another favourite dish, *shukto*, a mix of vegetables, including bitter NEEM leaves or *karela* (bitter GOURD). *Posto* is used in a variety of vegetarian dishes such as fritters, *peyanj posto* made with ONIONS, and *roshun diye posto* with garlic. *Kancha posto* is a sort of relish or CHUTNEY, a mix of *posto* with mustard oil, chopped green CHILLIES and some fresh CORIANDER leaves.

Some sweets such as SANDESH and kheer *kadam* (*ras kadam*) are rolled in roasted poppy seeds giving a crunchy coating. They are also added to or used as a garnish on cakes, BREADS, pastries, pancakes, dumplings and HALWA.

Khas khas should not to be confused with *KHUS KHUS*.

Helen Saberi

- Banerjee, Tania. 'How Posto Became Bengal's Comfort Food'. *The Juggernaut,* 9 April 2021.
- Devi, Yamuna. *The Art of Indian Vegetarian Cooking*. London: Leopard Books, 1995.
- Sen, Pritha. 'How British Greed Spurred the Creation of One of Bengal's Most Loved Dishes'. *The Indian Express*, 31 March 2016.

POTATO

Today one of the most widely eaten vegetables in India, the potato (*Solanum tuberosum*, Hindi *aloo*) is a relatively recent addition to the Indian diet. A starchy tuber, it is native to the Americas and was first domesticated in southern Peru and northwestern Bolivia 7,000–10,000 years ago.

Potatoes are cool weather crops that grow well at higher altitudes. In India, varieties suited to the country's climate of hot summers and short winters are grown mainly on the Indo-Gangetic plain during the short winter days from October to March. The main producing states are Uttar Pradesh, West Bengal, Bihar and Gujarat. Some year-round production also takes place in relatively high-altitude areas in the south. India is the world's second largest producer of potatoes (after China) with 48.5 million tonnes in 2018.

The Portuguese introduced potatoes India in the early seventeenth century and by 1675 it was a well-established garden crop in Surat and Karnataka. (In Marathi the word for potato is the Portuguese *batata,* which also means 'sweet potato'.) However, large-scale production did not begin until the late eighteenth century when the East India Company gave seeds and cash payments to farmers in Bengal to encourage them to produce and eat potatoes. In the south, a Scottish missionary Dr Benjamin Heyne promoted the growing of potatoes to prevent famine. Soon societies were formed throughout India promoting potatoes and other crops. This reflected a belief of the time that the potato was a good source of nutrition for labourers and would encourage happiness – thereby increasing Britain's wealth and justifying Imperialism.

However, in India (unlike in the West), the potato did not become a staple but rather became a substitute for indigenous YAMS and GOURDS. (In Sanskrit, *aloo* means an edible root.) Despite its origins, which make foreign ingredients taboo for Orthodox Hindus, it was readily adapted by most sects except for Jains. Potatoes are a major ingredient in STREET FOOD, such as *aloo* chaat – crispy fried potato cubes mixed with spicy and sweet CHUTNEYS, ground spice powders and lemon juice – and a filling for SAMOSAS. The iconic Maharashtrian street food vada *pav* consists of fried potatoes in a sliced bun topped with chutneys. In North India, *aloo dum,* a boiled potato curry, and *aloo* paratha, parathas stuffed with mashed spiced potatoes, are favourites. *Aloo tikki* is a spiced cutlet made of boiled potatoes and peas. *Aloo gosht*, a meat and potato curry, is popular throughout the region. In South India, mashed potatoes are used as a filling for DOSAS and for puris (see BREADS). Bengalis enjoy *aloo posto*, a CURRY with potatoes and POPPY SEEDS. The distinctive Calcutta biryani, which descended from the LUCKNOW-style biryani that came to Calcutta (see KOLKATA) with the exiled Nawab of Awadh in the mid-nineteenth century, is a lightly spiced dish of mutton, RICE and potatoes.

Colleen Sen

- Fine, Julia. 'In India, the British Hyped Potatoes to Justify Colonialism'. *Atlas Obscura*, 9 April 2019.
- Kohli, Diva. 'How the Potato Came to India and Conquered Our Lives'. *Conde Nast Traveller,* 22 June 2020.

POULTRY AND EGGS

A major development in the Indian food scene over the past two decades has been the rapid growth in the production and consumption of poultry meat and eggs. Production of poultry meat increased from 93,220 tonnes in 1970 to 4.23 million tonnes in 2019 for an average annual growth rate of over 8 per cent. Annual consumption is now around eighty-one eggs and 3.1 kg of poultry meat per person, although this is still below the Indian Council Medical Research's recommendation of 180 eggs and 10.5 kg of poultry meat. Poultry meat, mainly chicken, now accounts for around 45 per cent of all meat consumed. Demand has been driven by rising incomes that come with sustained economic growth, especially in urban areas, and a relaxation of religious restrictions on meat and egg consumption.

In the process, the poultry industry has been transformed from a backyard activity to a major industry. More than 80 per cent of India's egg and poultry meat production now comes from commercial farms that can have as many as 50,000 birds. (In dairying, by contrast, just a quarter of the milk is handled by cooperatives and private corporate players.) By state, the leading poultry producers are Tamil Nadu, Andhra Pradesh, Telangana, West Bengal, Maharashtra and Karnataka.

India is home to many breeds of native chicken, including Assel, Kadak Nath, Tellicherry and Nicobari, which are still popular in rural and tribal areas for backyard and free-range farming. For commercial farming, high-yielding crosses are being used that yield both broilers, bred for their fat meat, and layers, bred for their eggs. One of the most expensive native breeds, a fowl with black flesh called the Kadaknath, is considered a premium breed and its meat is priced three times more than that of broiler chicken.

Charles Darwin believed the wild progenitor of the domestic chicken was the red jungle fowl, *Gallus gallus*, that was native to India and was probably first domesticated for fighting. Scientists have used DNA analysis to identify three other species that might have interbred with the red jungle fowl, including the grey jungle fowl of southern India. Chicken bones have been discovered at Lothal, a city in the Harappan Civilization, and in Mesopotamia in 2000 BCE where tablets refer to 'the bird of Meluhha', the local name for the Indus Valley.

Chicken meat has traditionally been taboo for vegetarians in India. The *Dharmashastras* forbade the eating of village cocks, which were classified among birds that feed by scratching with their feet, in other words, scavengers. Chicken meat was associated with *mlecchas* – tribal people, outcasts and foreigners. Even Kashmir Pandits and Bengali

Brahmins, who were not vegetarians, would generally avoid chicken. There are no recipes for chicken in the *MANASOLLASA* although other gamebirds are mentioned. Chicken KEBAB, *murgh musallam* (chicken stuffed with minced meat and eggs) and roasted fowl were among the dishes served at the court of the Delhi sultans and the *NI'MATNAMA* lists several recipes for chicken dishes. Under the MUGHALS, palace chickens were hand-fed with pellets flavoured with SAFFRON and rosewater (see FLOWER WATERS) and massaged daily with musk oil and sandalwood.

During the days of the Raj, a simple chicken CURRY, sometimes called 'COUNTRY CAPTAIN chicken', and omelettes were standard dishes at the dak bungalows for travelling officials, since they were readily available. Chicken pulao was in the repertoire of North Indian Muslim cooks who served the British. The most famous Indian chicken dish is tandoori chicken and its offshoots butter chicken and chicken tikka masala (see BUTTER CHICKEN), standard items on Indian restaurant menus around the world today.

Ducks. Ducks supply around 10 per cent of the country's poultry production and 6 to 7 per cent of its eggs. India is the world's second largest duck producer after Indonesia. Most are raised in southern and eastern India, where farmers breed indigenous varieties. Some are raised in paddy fields where they eat insects and snails and leave behind manure. ANGLO-INDIANS and SYRIAN CHRISTIANS enjoy roast ducks as part of their Christmas dinners. *Tharavu mappas* is a traditional duck curry from the Kuttanad region of Kerala, prepared by cooking pieces of duck in an fragrant sauce of COCONUT milk and aromatic spices. Assamese make a duck curry with POTATOES or bottle GOURD. Today, chefs in high-end restaurants are introducing duck and turkey into their menus in such dishes as duck biryani and turkey keema curry.

Turkey. The turkey (genus *Meleagri*) is a large bird native to North America and Mexico. Ironically, in many European languages – for example, Polish *Indyk*, French *dinde* and Turkish *hindi* – the name of the bird suggests that it is native to India. This is because the Spanish and Portuguese explorers who brought it from the New World at first thought they had come to India. Turkeys arrived in Hindustan in the early seventeenth century. In 1612 a courtier presented a turkey from Goa to the Mughal emperor Jahangir, who wrote a description of how the bird's wattles inflate and change colour and commissioned his court painter Mansur to paint a brilliant painting of the bird. The British later brought turkeys from North America and began raising them in North India. Flora Annie STEEL recommended feeding them yogurt and chopped greens. However, the turkeys were overfed, laden with fat and very expensive so often peacocks replaced them as the centrepiece of a Christmas meal. Peacock meat was once recommended by Ayurvedic physicians for certain disorders but today, peacock (India's national bird) is a protected species.

Turkey farming in India is still in its infancy and turkeys represent only around 2 per cent of the total poultry population. Kerala, Tamil Nadu and Assam are the leading producing states. Today, some clubs dating back to the time of the Raj serve roast turkey for Christmas made to standard British recipes.

Eggs. With a production of 114 billion eggs in FY 2020, up from 16 billion in 1986, India has become the world's third largest producer after China and the United States. Half of India's egg production comes from Tamil Nadu, Andhra Pradesh and Telangana. Most are chicken eggs, with duck eggs accounting for 7 to 8 per cent.

Although many vegetarians avoid eggs, no less a strict vegetarian as Mahatma Gandhi wrote: 'Eggs are regarded by the layman as flesh food. In reality, they are not … a sterile egg never develops into a chick. Therefore, he who can take milk should have no objection to taking sterile eggs.' In some parts of India, Kerala and the Northeast, duck eggs are considered more acceptable than chicken eggs. Duck eggs are larger than those from poultry and have a higher protein content.

A masala omelette – omelette cooked with ONIONS, CHILLIES, TOMATOES and CORIANDER leaves – is a popular breakfast dish in urban areas. PARSI cuisine has an impressive array of egg dishes including *poro*, an omelette sometimes filled with goat brain; *akuri*, scrambled eggs topped with onions, GINGER-GARLIC paste; and EGGS KEJRIWAL. HYDERABAD is famous for its *nargisi* kofta – boiled eggs coated with a layer of minced meat and fried (see KOFTA). Bengalis enjoy *dimer dalna* – boiled eggs lightly coated in SALT and TURMERIC are friend in oil (often MUSTARD oil) until they are golden. Turkey, goose and quail eggs are available in speciality stores.

Colleen Sen

- Burton, David. *The Raj at Table.* London: Faber & Faber, 1993.
- Doctor, Vikram. 'Northeast's Love for Turkeys and the Challenges Faced by Those Raising Them'. *The Economic Times,* 20 December 2019.
- Shridhar, Tarun. 'Poultry Industry: Sunday or Monday, They Won't Come Home to Roost'. *The Indian Express*, 10 October 2019.
- Siripurapu, Kanna K. and Sabyasachi Das. 'Chicken for Every Occasion: Exploring the Cultural Significance of India's Native Poultry Breeds'. *Langscape Magazine* 7, no. 2 (Winter 2018): 58–61.

PUDUCHERRY

Puducherry is a union territory of India formed from four coastal territories (*comptoirs*, or trading posts) of former French India: Pondichéry, Karikal (Karaikal), Mahe and Yanaon (Yanam). Its name comes from the largest territory, historically known as Pondicherry, a name changed to Puducherry (its original Tamil name) in 2006. The first two territories are located in Tamil Nadu, Yanaon in Andhra Pradesh and Mahe in Kerala.

In the seventeenth century, the French vied with the British and Dutch for control of the Indian spice trade and established trading posts along both coasts and on the Hooghly River. In 1763, the French lost all their possessions in India to Britain except the four trading posts and Chandanagar in West Bengal. They remained part of France until 1954 when their residents voted to join independent India. Their residents (except those of Chandanagar which, in 1954, became part of West Bengal) were allowed to opt for French citizenship and today there are around 60,000 French citizens of Indian origin in France.

With a population of 1.4 million, Puducherry is by far the largest of the four territories. The French legacy is evident in the five boulevards named after French generals that run parallel to the sea and are lined with imposing mansions in the neoclassical style. Older residents still speak French but it is disappearing. Puducherry has a tradition of cafes serving COFFEE, croissants and baguettes dating back to the eighteenth century when they were gathering places for local French and Indian merchants. A few restaurants, bakeries and cafes cater to tourists, especially the French visitors who come here out of nostalgia. Le Café, opened in the 1950s, serves French quiche, galette stuffed with TOMATOES and eggs as well as chaat and masala omelette. An example of 'Creole food' is the baguette served in cold COCONUT milk and topped with NUTS. Café Des Arts, located in a French mansion dating back to the 1880s and decorated with vintage furniture, has baguette, croissants, muesli and a variety of hot grilled or toasted sandwiches.

French onion soup is a popular restaurant item. Several restaurants serve Vietnamese food, reflecting the cross-pollination between these two former French colonies.

Many of the recipes in Lourdes Tirouvanziam-Louis' book *The Pondicherry Kitchen*, which covers the entire union territory, are for local dishes such as *sadam*, rasam, *pongal*, *kootu*, and *poriyal*. Coconut milk is a common thickener. The Kerala dish APPAM is a breakfast favourite. A distinctive Puducherry spice mixture is *vadouvan* (also spelled *vadavam*) which combines Indian spices with French herbs (see SPICE BOX). There are many recipes for CHUTNEYS and PICKLES, some made with dried FISH, meat and prawns, which people could carry with them to other French colonies. White vinegar, rarely used in Indian cuisine, is a common souring agent.

Many of the recipes call for lamb but since this is not generally available in India goat is substituted. (The use of the word lamb is significant since lamb was a marker of French identity throughout its colonies). This meat can be grilled, served with green peas, made into a ragout or roasted – but, always, the spicing is Indian. For example, a dish called gigot daube (a daube is a classic French stew braised in wine and herbs) is made with CLOVES, CINNAMON, ANISE, bay leaf, black pepper (see PEPPER, BLACK), white vinegar and a lot of GARLIC. It is served with peas and CARROTS sautéed in GHEE, cloves, cinnamon, ONION and garlic.

Seafood plays an important role in Puducherry cuisine. Fish and prawns are made into KOFTA, cooked in a soup, ground into patties and made into curries. A hot and sour prawn *vindail* reflects a Goan influence. The Puducherry version of a French bouillabaisse (a traditional fish and seafood soup from the South of France), here called *meen puyabaisse*, includes TURNIPS, cabbage leaves, AUBERGINES, POTATOES and carrots. Pastries reflect a European influence. Pondicherry cake is a rich Christmas cake made with nuts, fruits and rum. Cakes are also baked with BANANA and tapioca (see CASSAVA).

Colleen Sen

- Nandy, Priyadarshini. 'The Foodie Extravagance: Ten Restaurants in Pondicherry You Must Visit'. *NDTV Food*, 16 March 2018. Available online: https://food.ndtv.com/lists/the-foodie-extravagance-10-restaurants-in-pondicherry-you-must-visit-1201033 (accessed 29 April 2022).
- Tirouvanziam-Louis, Lourdes. *The Pondicherry Kitchen*. Chennai: Westland Ltd., 2012.

PULAO

Pulao is a dish with many connotations made with rice, meat (including whole game birds) or vegetables, and spices which may have originated in Persia (where it is known as pollo) and spread to other parts of the Middle East, evolving into Turkish pilaf, Afghan pilau, Central Asian plov and in India pulao. Chicken pulao was served at the Sultanate court in Delhi in the thirteenth century. The earliest reference to pulao in English is in the writings of Edward Terry, the chaplain to Sir Thomas Roe, the English ambassador to the MUGHAL court in 1616: 'Sometimes they boil pieces of flesh or hens, or other fowl, cut in pieces in their rice, which they call pillaw.'

Pulaos are strongly associated with the lavish cuisine of the MUGHAL courts where they became spicier and more elaborate than those of Persia and were given exotic Persian names such as *hazar pasand* (a thousand delights), *gulazar* (garden) and *moti* (pearl). Chefs vied with each other to transform pulaos into works of art, colouring the grains of rice to represent sparkling gems such as rubies. The multi-coloured *navratan* pulao with SAFFRON, sultanas, PANEER and NUTS was designed to honour the nine intellectual gems of Akbar's court.

There are innumerable regional and local variations. LUCKNOW became famous for its pulaos and great pains were taken, as with the Persian pollo, that every grain of rice remained separate, light and fluffy. At special occasions and banquets, as many as seventy kinds of pulao could be served. Pulaos are often garnished with nuts and fruits, and, for special occasions, with *VARK*. There are sweet versions called *zarda* pulao (*zard* means yellow or gold) which are coloured and flavoured with saffron. See also BIRYANI.

Helen Saberi

- Sen, Colleen Taylor. *Feasts and Fasts: A History of Food in India*. London: Reaktion Books, 2015.

PULSES

The consumption of pulses which include beans, lentils and peas is one of the most emblematic features of Indian cuisine. From ancient times, pulses have played a central role in the Indian diet, especially among vegetarians. Nutritionally, they are an inexpensive source of protein (20 to 25 per cent by weight) and fibre. They also contain potassium, folate, and polyphenols, which have antioxidant activity.

Pulses are one of the most difficult plant groups to define. They are part of an enormous family called legumes (*Fabaceae*) which covers tens of thousands of genera and species, and includes leaves, stems and pods. Legumes include peas (*Pisum*), lentils (*Lens*), chickpeas (*Cicer*), soybeans (*Glycine*), New World beans (*Phaseolus*) and peanuts/groundnuts (*Arachis*). A pulse is the edible seed from a legume plant. For example, a peapod is a legume, but the pea inside the pod is the pulse. The word pulse is more commonly used in Britain than North America, although it is gradually being replaced by the word lentil and the two are often used synonymously.

Lentils. In common usage, lentil refers to the seeds of the plant *Lens culinaris,* but the word is often applied to other species, especially in India. In Hindi, the word dal (from a Sanskrit word meaning 'to split') refers to the seeds from pulses whose outer pod has been removed and split as well as to the cooked dish made from these seeds. To confuse matters still further, Indians sometimes use the term gram to refer to pulses that are whole rather than split. The word comes from the Portuguese *grâo*, meaning grain, but is not applied to cereal grains. When used by itself without an adjective, gram means chickpeas (in North America called garbanzo beans). In South India, chickpeas are called Bengal gram. *Urad* dal is sometimes called black gram, *moong* dal green gram, and pigeon peas red gram.

India is the world's second largest producer of lentils (after Canada) and the world's largest consumer. The average Indian gets nearly four times as much nutrition from pulses as the Americans or Chinese. The main producing states are Madhya Pradesh (nearly half of 1.6 billion tonnes), Uttar Pradesh, West Bengal, Bihar and Jharkhand. It is mainly grown during the winter season (October–March) following the monsoons. Most lentil growers are small farmers. Lentils are often planted together with other crops including RICE, CORN, MUSTARD and MILLETS for efficiency and increased productivity

The lentil plant is a bushy annual grown for its seeds that are typically lens-shaped, hence its name. The seeds develop in pods, usually two seeds per pod. There are two varieties of lentils: macrosperma that have large seeds and little pigmentation and microsperma with small seeds and some pigmentation. Depending on their variety and breed, lentils can range in colour from red-orange to yellow, green, brown or black. Lentils can survive in challenging environments and can grow in semi-arid regions without irrigation. When planted in rotation with cereal crops, they reduce erosion, help control weeds and reduce the demand for nitrogen fertilizers.

Chana dal (yellow split Bengal gram), *masoor/masur* dal (red lentils), green peas and grass peas came to the Indus Valley from West Asia in the fourth millennium BCE, at the same time as WHEAT and BARLEY since they are found together in most archaeological sites. All are winter crops that were adopted in North India as part of a two-season cropping system. *Urad*, *toor*, (pigeon pea, also called *arhar*) and *moong* dal (mung bean) were cultivated in the grasslands of South India starting in the early to mid-third millennium BCE.

Vedic texts indicate that *masoor*, *moong* and *arhar* dal, kidney beans and horse gram were consumed as early as 1200 BCE. One of the most common methods of preparation was in a dish called *supa,* probably some sort of thin gruel. *Kulmasa* (horse gram) was eaten mainly by the poor and ascetics. *Chana* (*Cicer arietinum*), the chickpea, originated in the Middle East and Egypt.

Some lentils such as *urad*, *rajma* (kidney bean) and *chana* dal that are more than six months old need to be soaked overnight. The usual ratio of cooking lentils is three to four parts of water to one part of lentils. After cooking, ONIONS, GINGER, GARLIC and various spices can be sautéed in oil or GHEE, then added when the dal is cooked (a process called variously *baghar* or *tadka*, English tempering or blooming). While dal is a staple of vegetarian diets, it can also be made with meat, as in the dish dal *gosht.*

Red lentils (*Lens culinaris*, which means 'cooking lentils'; Hindi *masoor* dal) were one of the first crops to be cultivated by humans. Seeds from wild lentils (*Lens orientalis*) dating back to the seventh millennium BCE have been found in Turkey and the Middle East. From the Bronze Age onward, red lentils were grown wherever wheat and barley were cultivated. Domestication in India began in the Harappan Civilization before 2500 BCE. These small pink discs are one of the most widely eaten in India because they cook very quickly, in fifteen or twenty minutes. They are commonly used in Bengali cuisine.

Chickpeas (*Cicer arietinum*, Hindi *chana*). India is by far the world's largest producer, importer and consumer of chickpeas, which play an important role in the Indian diet, especially in North India. Despite their name, chickpeas are not a pea but a bean. Like lentils, they originated in Turkey and the Middle East around 10,000 years ago and were grown in the Indus Valley. *Chanaka* is mentioned in Sanskrit texts dating back to 1000 BCE. Chickpea has a deep tap root which enhances its capacity to withstand drought and it grows best in cooler climates with low rainfall. The main producing states are Madhya Pradesh, with 40 per cent of the production, Uttar Pradesh, Rajasthan, Maharashtra and Andhra Pradesh.

In India two varieties are grown: Bengal gram, also called *desi* dal, is small, wrinkled and dark brown in colour with a thicker seed coat. When hulled and split it is sold as *chana* dal, which is boiled as dal (the dish) and is also ground to make the flour (*besan*) that is used in PAKORAS and other snacks. Another variety, probably introduced into India in the eighteenth century, is the larger, smooth and light coloured one called Kabuli *chana* because it was thought to have originated in Afghanistan. One of the most popular STREET

FOOD dishes is *chana* masala (also called *chholey* masala, made from onion, TOMATOES, garlic, CHILLIES and spices) and eaten with puri (puffed BREAD).

Pigeon peas (*Cajanus cajan*, Hindi *toor* or *arhar* dal). These beans likely originated in southern India and still grow wild in the Western Ghats. From India, they spread to Africa and to the Caribbean and other tropical regions. They can grow on marginal land, are drought-resistant and require little fertilizer. India is the world's largest producer. Maharashtra, Karnataka and Madhya Pradesh are the largest producing states. They are the most commonly eaten dal in South India, used to make rasam (a South Indian spicy soup) and SAMBAR. Normally they are coated with oil, which needs to be washed off before use. In regions where it grows, the fresh young pods are eaten as a vegetable

Mung (*Vigna radiate*, Hindi *moong* dal, also called green gram) is native to India. Carbonized beans have been found in the ruins of the Harappan Civilization and in Karnataka dating back more than four thousand years. In the Sanskrit literature they are called *mudga* and a dish called *mudgaudana* made with rice, GHEE, yogurt and meat is described. By the sixth century BCE, the most common way of preparing mung was as *supa*, probably similar to today's dal. The Buddha described mung beans as a food that was 'full of soul qualities' and 'devoid of faults'. Mung beans were cooked with rice, ghee and spices to make *KHICHRI*, which the fourteenth-century traveller IBN BATTUTA said was the everyday breakfast dish of Indians. The plant can grow on a wide variety of well-drained soils and is fairly drought-resistant. The major growing states are Madhya Pradesh, Gujarat and Rajasthan. It is eaten both whole and split.

Black gram (*Vigna mungo*, Hindi *urad* dal) shares a common wild ancestor with *moong* dal. Wild plants have been found growing in Orissa, northern Andhra Pradesh and Chhattisgarh. These black, ovoid lentils are available whole or split with one side black and the other beige, or with both sides beige (white lentils). It is used mainly in South India, especially ground, mixed with ground rice and fermented to make the batter for IDLI and DOSA. *Urad* flour is also used to make *LADDU*, HALWA and other sweets.

Horse gram (*Macrotyloma uniflorum*, Hindi *kulthi*) originated in South India and was domesticated as early as 2500 BCE. It grows in tropical and semi-tropical climates and is fairly drought-resistant. While it grows everywhere in India, the main producing states are Karnataka, Orissa and Chhattisgarh. It is extremely nutritious. In the West, it was used as a feed for race horses, hence its name. In India it is used as a feed for cattle and is also consumed as dal, especially in South India.

Kidney bean (Hindi *rajma*) is a variety of *Phaseolus vulgaris*, named for its resemblance in shape and colour to the human kidney. It originated in Mexico and was brought to India by the Portuguese. Maharashtra, Kerala and Karnataka are the main producers. It requires adequate moisture and is very frost-sensitive. *Rajma*-based dishes are a staple in many Indian homes. *Makhani rajma* is a popular North Indian dish made by simmering kidney beans in a gravy of onions, tomatoes and cream.

Peas (*Pisum sativum*, Hindi *matar*) were domesticated as early as 8000 BCE in Western Asia. An early ancestor, a small marbled field pea, has been found at Harappan sites. Today peas are usually dried, de-husked and split and cooked as dal. Around half of peas are produced in Uttar Pradesh; other producing states are Madhya Pradesh, Bihar and Maharashtra. Peas are a winter crop that require a cool growing season without frost. The consumption of green peas fresh from the garden began in Europe in the seventeenth century and was probably introduced by the British.

Black eyed peas/cowpeas (*Vigna unguiculata*, Hindi *lobiya*) probably originated in Africa but were consumed in India from ancient times. These tiny beans can be coloured black, brown, red or green. In Punjab they are made into a rich tomato and onion based dal eaten with bread and are an essential ingredient in *olan*, a Kerala dish made with pumpkin.

Moth beans (*Vigna acontifolia*, Hindi *matki* dal). These legumes are native to the hot, dry regions of northern and western India and are one of the most drought-resistant crops. The main producing states are Rajasthan and Gujarat. Whole or split moth bean seeds can be boiled or fried and are used to make the popular street food *misal pav* (bread topped with spiced moth beans) and *dalmoth*, a dried snack. In Maharashtra they are sprouted and cooked in a stew called *matki usal*.

Groundnuts/peanuts (*Arachis hypogaea*, Hindi *mungphali*). Groundnuts are not true nuts but belong to the legume family. Native to the Andes in South America, they were probably introduced to India by Portuguese Jesuit priests in the first half of the sixteenth century, although it has also been argued that they came via China or Africa. In his 1807 account of his travels in South India, the Scottish physician James Buchanan noted that peanuts were cultivated together with TURMERIC in Mysore. Cultivation grew rapidly, especially in the Madras Presidency. A disease killed much of the crop but a disease-resistant variety called Coromandel was introduced and today is the dominant variety in India. India is the world's second largest producer (after China). Peanuts are grown mainly in Andhra Pradesh, Gujarat Tamil Nadu, Karnataka and Maharashtra. Their main use is in the production of peanut oil for cooking. Salted, roasted and spiced peanuts are eaten as a light snack or cooked with jaggery (see SUGAR) to make *chikki*, a kind of peanut brittle. In Maharashtra peanuts are used whole in rice preparations and vegetable dishes and roasted and crushed to thicken CURRIES and to add texture to salads and dessert.

Colleen Sen

- Albala, Ken. *Beans: A History*. Oxford: Berg, 2007.
- Fuller, Dorian Q. and Emma L. Harvey. 'The Archaeobotany of Indian Pulses: Identification, Processing and Evidence for Cultivation'. *Environmental Archaeology* 11, no. 2 (2006): 220.
- Yadava, Shyam S., David L. McNeil and Philip C. Stevenson. *Lentil: An Ancient Crop for Modern Times*. Dordrecht, The Netherlands: Springer, 2007.

PUNJAB

The food of Punjab is a reflection of the history, culture and lifestyle of a robust and fecund land that has its agrarian legacy rooted in Harappan times. The culinary traditions of this once vast region, defined by its many rivers, are simple, healthy and connected to the land. It was the fourteenth-century Moroccan traveller IBN BATTUTA who put a number to the watercourses he forded to reach the court of the then ruler at Delhi. *Panj* (five) *aab* (rivers). This 'Land of Five Rivers' has for centuries sat, most invitingly, in the path of invaders, cultural influences, ideas, trade and techniques. It comes as no surprise then that this region is home to a wholesome cuisine, made fragrant with generously spooned servings of syncretism alongside the desi GHEE.

'Khaada peeta lahe da, baqi Ahmed Shahe da' (What we eat and drink is ours, the rest is Ahmad Shah's) goes an eighteenth-century axiom coined when Ahmad Shah Abdali, the Afghan marauder, made his many pillaging visits to India. Food-loving Punjabis,

with their extraordinary zeal for la dolce vita, are perhaps the best personification as a community of what joie de vivre truly means.

It was around the flood plains of the Indus and undivided Punjab's five eponymous rivers (Jhelum, Chenab, Ravi, Beas and Satluj) that the Indus Valley Civilization (IVC) thrived. Excavations in the two cities of Harappa and Mohenjo-Daro (now in Pakistan) revealed the IVC to be an urban society engaged in farming and trade. The main crops grown were WHEAT, BARLEY, MILLETS, chickpeas and lentils. Buffalo milk, meat, FISH, TURMERIC and GINGER were dietary staples. Even today, Punjab is the heartland of Indian agriculture. Its fondness for all things dairy is legendary, as is for grain and seasonal vegetables. Contrary to popular belief about their carnivorous ways, over half of Punjabis subscribe to a vegetarian diet (see VEGETARIANISM). It is possibly this proclivity for greens that has resulted in Punjab's most defining food pairing – *sarson da saag* and *makki di* roti (slow-cooked MUSTARD greens and griddle-made CORN flatbreads) with dollops of freshly churned butter.

Many of the invading armies successively marched across the Khyber Pass: Mahmud of Ghazni in the tenth century, Timur following from Mongolia in the fourteenth century and Ahmad Shah in the early eighteenth century. Each of these conquests left an indelible imprint on the culinary heritage of the geography. In addition, a busy network of trade routes interlinked with the Silk Road led to an influx of ingredients, plants, dishes and cooking techniques, including the simple slow cooked fare of the tribal North Western Frontier Province. The tradition of roasted fish and meats, like the succulent mutton *barra*, came from Peshawar. The use of dried fruits and exotic NUTS – pistachios, pine nuts, almonds, APRICOTS – are a crunchy bequest of Central Asian rule. Ranjit Singh (1780–1839), maharaja of the vast Sikh Empire – it straddled Peshawar, Multan, Kashmir and Ladakh during his rule – also added some fine flourishes to Punjabi cuisine. Following the Maharaja's death, the empire fell to the British but, although they ruled the region for a century, the Punjabi palate never quite took to or imbibed colonial food habits. Except for the odd ANGLO-INDIAN dish patronized by cosmopolitan homes, the cutlets, chops, au gratins, a la kievs, caramel custards and tutti-fruttis largely found themselves relegated to laminated menu cards in a handful of clubs and restaurants.

In 1947, a land thus enriched was partitioned to coincide with India's independence from British rule. The exodus that followed introduced a whole new culinary culture. The tandoor was one of a handful of possessions that families fleeing their homes in Pakistan managed to carry along. These clay ovens would eventually help many people build their lives anew and from scratch. Several *DHABAS* (highway eateries) and food legends in Punjab such as Jaggi Sweets (Patiala), Sindhi's Liberty House (Ludhiana), Lucky Vaishno Dhaba (Jalandhar) and Bittu Meatwala (AMRITSAR), to name few, and some Punjabi-helmed ones in DELHI are an ironical yet gratifying result of a people displaced. Most notable of the latter is Moti Mahal in Daryaganj, a restaurant as old as independent India and also home to the kitchen where the now ubiquitous BUTTER CHICKEN was conceived.

Punjab's culinary traditions are fashioned as much by its geography and climate as its history. Hemmed-in by Pakistan on the west, it shares borders with Jammu and Kashmir to the north, Himachal Pradesh in the northeast, Rajasthan in the southwest, and Haryana in the south and the east. The northeastern border is marked by the woodland-rich Shivalik Ranges, while the semi-arid southwest merges with the Thar Desert. Expansive and alluvial farmlands sprawled across its three regions – Majha, Doaba and Malwa – fed by perennial rivers and irrigation canals, earned Punjab the names 'breadbasket' and 'granary of India'. Climatically, the state experiences three seasons – summer, monsoons and winter. April, May and June are the hottest months, followed by the high humidity of the monsoons in July and August, a season eagerly awaited for the replenishment of groundwater. Winter usually sets in early November and continues through to February and is, by far, the friendliest time of the year to savour the culinary delights Punjab is famed for.

Traditional Punjabi food is characterized by freshness, purity and uncomplicated methods of preparation. Punjabi households, more often than not, display uniformity in culinary habits and any variations are mostly in terms of cooking techniques or seasonings. Wheat, millets, barley and corn remain the staple grains. Their flours are used to fashion a variety of BREADS that are consumed with all meals, among them griddle-cooked rotis and parathas, deep-fried puris and *bhaturas*, and tandoor-baked kulchas and naans. Stuffed or plain parathas and *aloo*-puris (puris with spicy POTATO curry) are the preferred breakfast in Punjabi households.

Rice is a later addition to the Punjabi diet but has managed to carve out a close second spot as a preferred grain. It is eaten boiled and in PULAO or BIRYANI form. It couples with *kadhi* (a slow cooked chickpea flour and yogurt sauce), *rajma* (a kidney bean CURRY), *aloo-wadi* (a potato and lentil dumpling curry) or curried chickpeas to become Punjabi cuisine's most relished food pairings. *Mattar* (green peas) pulao, often eaten with a grated cucumber RAITA, is an enlivening dish in itself. *Zarda,* a sweetened rice version, is a festive preparation and is relished particularly on and around the vernal festival of Basant Panchami. KHEER, a velvety rice pudding, is a perennial dessert which, in winter, is cooked in sugarcane juice instead of milk and is called *roh di* kheer.

Seasonal vegetables are an integral part of the cuisine with vast tracts of Punjab's plains devoted to their cultivation. Malerkotla, a former nawabdom, is the vegetable hub of the state which produces top-quality CUCUMBER, bitter GOURD, OKRA, cauliflower, ONION and GARLIC. A host of vegetables, singly and combined, among them *aloo gobhi* (potato and cauliflower), *gajjar mattar* (CARROTS and peas), *baingan bhartha* (roasted mashed AUBERGINE), crispy fried okra and stuffed bitter gourd, accord a Punjabi meal its crunch and colour. A sweet and sour PICKLE made from carrots, cauliflower and TURNIPS is de rigueur in winters, as is *gajrela*, an immensely awaited winter dessert prepared with carrots.

Dal is equally essential and no meal is deemed complete in its absence. Made from an assortment of lentils and PULSES, it is usually tempered with garlic, onions or CUMIN in aromatic desi ghee. One of the misconceptions about Punjabi cuisine is that it is excessively dependent on ghee, butter and cream. That, regrettably, is a myth largely perpetuated by lazy chefs in so-called MUGHLAI restaurants. The thick creamy texture of the famed *mah di* dal, for instance, does not result from a generous inclusion of fat. Rather, it is acquired by slow cooking the dish over several hours, often overnight. The dry version, *sukki dhuli mah di* dal, once a must at celebratory feasts, is unfortunately a rare presence at the table nowadays.

Rearing cattle is another long-standing agrarian tradition and dairy farming is an important industry. That this region has been home to a people with low levels of lactose intolerance since Vedic times accounts for the healthy consumption of milk, ghee, butter, curds and BUTTERMILK. PANEER (cottage cheese) is another dairy by-product that finds its way into meals in varied forms: crumbled into a *bhurji* (a la scrambled eggs), cubed into a curry with green peas, folded into mashed spinach or used as barbecued chunks to snack on. It also shows up as *CHHANA* along with *KHOYA* in many SWEETS.

The meat-eating preferences of Punjabis are dominated by chicken, goat and lamb in varied forms. A hunting ban many decades ago put an end to the presence of wild game on the table. Poultry and livestock farming became the order of the day, which is how tandoori chicken, chicken tikka, mutton curry, mutton *burra* and *keema mattar* (green peas and mince) took centre-stage. Freshwater fish is another important staple with the finest *singhara* (river catfish) and sole caught at Harike Pattan, where the rivers Beas and Sutlej merge. The close proximity to AMRISTAR led to their tandoori and, especially, fried forms becoming synonymous with the holy city. Other varieties of fish such as carp and *rohu* (a carp-like river fish) became available after the government encouraged pond farming.

That Punjab has a massive sweet tooth is an undeniable reality. The digestion-aiding *gur* (jaggery) and *shakkar* (powdered jaggery) are permanent fixtures in the kitchen and, more often than not, indicate the end of a meal. Special occasions often mandate kheer and *seviyan* (vermicelli, see *SEV* AND *SEVIYAN*), while winter ushers in the nut- and nutrient- rich *gajrela* and *panjeeri* (whole wheat flour fried in SUGAR and ghee). Other sweets include HALWAS, LADDUS, BARFIS, *gulab jamuns*, JALEBIS and *pinnis* made from ghee, wheat flour, jaggery and almonds. Punjabis also love their snacks. Crispy home-made *mathis*, both sweet and savoury, made from a batter of flour and semolina, are a comfort food and, when paired with MANGO PICKLE, a much-relished tea-time treat. Other favourites are SAMOSAS, deep-fried KACHORIS and PAKORAS (savoury fritters) filled with assorted vegetables and, especially, paneer. Over time, a spiced mashed potato filling, a distinctly European bequest, came to replace the Central Asian legacy of minced meat in the samosa, according it a vegetarian-appropriate status relished by one and all.

The interminable summer months beg refreshing beverages, of which sweet LASSI (a blend of yogurt and water), salty buttermilk, cumin-flavoured *jal jeera*, *shikanji* (lemonade) and fresh fruit juices are de rigueur. Traditionalists swear by *sattu*, a refreshing drink made from roasted and powdered barley best suited for the region's sweltering heat. *KANJI*, a fermented drink prepared with *kaali gajjar* (purple carrots), is a long-awaited winter special, as is sugarcane juice flavoured with a smidgen of ginger, lime juice and MINT leaves. The chartbuster, however, remains TEA. Drunk hot and sweet with milk, often flavoured with CARDAMOM, it counts as the one unshakeable influence that the British Raj left in its wake.

Home-made pickles, CHUTNEYS, *murabbas* (sweet preserves) and jaggery (unrefined sugar) are must-haves on a Punjabi table. Aiding metabolism and digestion, they are nutritious and flavourful sides to a meal. They require little cooking and are mainly made with vinegar, brine and mustard oil, thus preserving nutrients. Pickled lime, mango and sundry winter vegetables are universal, while chutneys and relishes can be region-specific. Majha likes them fresh and green, Doaba prefers them sweet and sour and made of mangoes, while Malwa embraces the whole gamut from CORIANDER and mint to mashed *chibud* (cocomelons). *Murabbas* have pronounced medicinal properties and are found in both dry and wet forms. These long-lasting sweet preserves are commonly, but not exhaustively, made of *AMLA* (Indian gooseberries) and APPLES and are eaten as an energizing dessert.

A common Punjabi spice mixture or masala (see SPICE BOX) is generally prepared from all or a few of the following spices: peppercorns (see PEPPER, BLACK), black cumin, CINNAMON, CLOVES, carom seeds, bay leaves, and green and black cardamoms. When used in their whole forms, they are referred to as *khadha* masalas. It's a rare household that will run out of stock.

Puneetinder Kaur Sidhu

- Sandhu, Amandeep. *Panjab: Journeys through Fault Lines*. Chennai: Westland, 2019.
- Sen, Colleen Taylor. *Feasts and Fasts: A History of Food in India*. London: Reaktion Books, 2015.
- Sidhu, Puneetinder Kaur. *Punjab: A Culinary Delight*. New Delhi: Times Group Books, 2019.

RABRI

Rabri is one of the most sophisticated and labour-intensive delicacies of India. Its main ingredient is the skin that forms on top of milk (typically buffalo milk) when it is heated. This film was traditionally removed to a separate bowl with bamboo sticks but today it is pushed to the side of the pot while the milk is stirred – a process that takes several hours. According to MRS BALBIR SINGH, after boiling the milk down to one quarter of its volume, SUGAR and *ruh kewra* (a fragrant essential oil from the flowers of the screwpine, see FLOWER WATERS) are added and the thickened milk is poured into a dish. The skin scraped from the side of the pot is spread over its top and shredded almonds and pistachios are sprinkled over it.

Rabri is said to have been invented in Mathura and from there went to VARANASI, LUCKNOW and western India where variations reflected the availability and type of local milk. In Bengal it was mentioned as early as the fourteenth century. *Rabri* is a standard accompaniment to *malpua*, JALEBI and other sweets and often is a topping for *shahi tukra*, a rich dessert of bread, milk, GHEE, SUGAR and NUTS. In 1965 *rabri* was one of the sweets banned in West Bengal during a milk shortage because of its excessive use of milk. The ban was overturned within the year by the Calcutta High Court due to lawsuits from independent sweet shops.

Colleen Sen

- Singh, Mrs Balbir. *Indian Cookery*. London: Mills & Boon Ltd, 1965.

RADISH

Radish (*Raphanus sativus*, Hindi *mooli*) is a cruciferous plant related to the TURNIP and horse radish. There are four varieties:

- *R. sativus* was developed in Europe and is now cultivated in India. It is globular and can be purple, red or white.
- *R. sativus* var. *caudatus* or the rat-tail radish. In India it is called *sungra, mungra* and *singri*. The long slender seed pods can grow to two feet or more in length and have a purply tint. They are eaten in salads, boiled, fried in GHEE, PICKLED or added to stews. Two cultivars have been developed in India: the Long Purple, which has long purple pods, and Madras, which has a mild flavour and is good raw or pickled.

- *R. sativus* var. *oleiformis*, the oilseed radish, adapted for the production of oil.
- *R. sativus* var. *longipinnatus*, also called daikon or oriental radish. It is white, conical and long in shape. This radish is the most well known and important in Indian cookery.

Radishes have been used for food in India since prehistoric times. In the later Vedic literature they are described as *mulaka*, a vegetable to be chewed to help digest a heavy meal. The *Mahabharata* notes radishes, POMEGRANATE, lemon and spices sprinkled over venison and the twelfth century *MANASOLLASA* describes *kavichandi*, a dish of fried meat and PULSES combined with radish and brinjal (AUBERGINE).

Radishes can be grated and eaten raw. They are sold in India with their leaves which are valued as a pot herb and often fried with spices. The leaves are sometimes combined with the chopped radish and cooked together with a vegetable CURRY or korma. Sliced or shredded, they can be used in salads or soups and dals. They are also cooked with diced POTATOES or pumpkin. Shredded and fried, they are a popular paratha stuffing in Kashmir and northern India. Kofta patties are made by binding shredded radish with spices and herbs with chickpea flour. *Badas* are fried dumplings made with shredded radish and different kinds of dal that are a popular snack, especially in South India where they are served with a CHUTNEY. Shredded radishes are often added to *karhis* (*kadhis*), creamy dishes made with chickpea flour and yogurt. Radishes can be made into PICKLES or added to SAMBARS. Radishes are grown in Kashmir in floating gardens of water-weeds bound with mud from the lake. Here they are called *muji* and a traditional Kashmiri spicy dish is *muj gard* (radish with FISH), an unusual combination. The Kashmiris also make a traditional radish chutney with curd (yogurt), spices and herbs such as CORIANDER, often with the addition of crushed walnuts.

Helen Saberi

- Devi, Yamuna. *The Art of Indian Vegetarian Cooking*. London: Leopard Books, 1995.
- Facciola, Stephen. *Cornucopia II: A Source Book of Edible Plants*. Vista, CA: Kampong Publications, 1998.

RAILWAY FOOD

At the beginning of the twentieth century, India had one of the largest railway networks in the world. The first freight train was built in Madras in 1837 and the first passenger train began a short run from Bombay to Thane in 1853. After India became a colony of the British crown in 1858, the development of railways became a priority for the British for both economic and military reasons. The first passenger trains were intended for the use of the British, although they quickly became popular among Indians. In the early twentieth century, long-distance trains such as the Grand Trunk Express, the Frontier Mail and the Deccan Queen had luxurious dining cars with butlers, chefs, uniformed waiters and à la carte menus. The catering was done by G.F. Kellner & Co. in the east and northwest (acquired by Spence & Co. in 1929); Spence & Co. Ltd. in the south; and Brandon in Central India. The food combined European and Indian influences, especially ANGLO-INDIAN, Bengali and South Indian. Western dishes might include thick or clear soup, fried FISH or minced cutlets, roast chicken or mutton and for lunch, a choice of CURRY and RICE or the previous night's roast. The trains carried live chickens while mutton was picked up at stations en route.

As late as 1929, the trains had separate dining cars for Indians. In trains without restaurants, first-class passengers could telegraph to order food at the next station which would be delivered on railway dishes. Important trains halted for breakfast, lunch or dinner in one of the several restaurants on the platform. Starting in 1936, the famous Frontier Mail train (now the Golden Temple Mail) between MUMBAI and AMRITSAR was the last word in luxury with showers and even a steam room. Its extensive menu included roast chicken, Madras mutton curry, chicken cutlet and the iconic railway mutton curry which eventually became an item in hotels. This milder version of a classic mutton curry was not too spicy and blended the taste of both Indian and English spices. Railway mutton curry was served with rice, bread or dinner rolls.

Many Indian passengers carried their own food, as they still do today. There already existed a tradition of packing for long journeys food that would keep for several days – dry snacks, such as parathas, chaat, *bhel* puri and *theplas*. Sharing food with ones fellow passengers was popular and some writers have noted that this was their first introduction to the food of other regions. The railways allowed vendors to sell food on railway platforms, a practice that continues today. The refreshment rooms at stations began offering food and had three separate rooms for Europeans, Hindus and Muslims. Some hotels set up food stalls near railway stations. People could buy cups of TEA from vendors at stations along the way. The Indian Tea Association, founded in 1881, saw the railways as a potentially large market and supplied tea and kettles to contractors at main railway junctions. The tea served used more milk and SUGAR than traditional English tea to meet Indian tastes.

After Independence, railway management was taken over by the state-owned Indian Railways. Dining cars continued to operate but they were expensive and only survived on a few lines. So the railways began operating pantry cars on long-distance trains offering freshly cooked food to passengers who chose to eat onboard at their seats. First-class passengers could order meals from bearers who telegraphed them down the line so that they were picked up when the train arrived. Depending on the service, it was served on chinaware or iron trays. Breakfast could be an omelette or a vegetable curry with toast, jam and tea. Lunch and dinner were often chicken or vegetable curry with rice, chapatis (see BREADS) and PICKLES. Certain trains were famous for specific dishes; for example, the Gitanjali Express between MUMBAI and KOLKATA was famous for its chicken cutlets.

Today you can still find dining cars, good linen, bars, excellent service and even spas on luxury trains such as the Deccan Odyssey which runs on different routes starting from Mumbai and DELHI. On trains like the Shatabdi Express, a series of fast passenger trains that run between major cities, and the Rajdhani Express that run between Delhi and state capitals, the food is served in sectioned plastic trays with each dish packed separately in an aluminium foil dish with a paper lid. Rotis are rolled up and foil packed and pickles are bubble packed. There are always vegetarian and non-vegetarian options, with PANEER and chicken curry being the differentiating factor. For dessert, ice-cream, yogurt and sometimes RASGULLAS are brought around in tubs. The food always has a signature spicing depending on the departure station; for example, the Rajdhani Express has Bengali-type food on its Kolkata-Delhi run and Delhi-style food on the Delhi-Kolkata route.

Breakfast is mainly bread, butter, omelette or a vegetarian cutlet with fried potatoes and peas and sometimes *poha* (flattened rice) or paratha. Tea and COFFEE are served in a package along with hot water in a flask. Hawkers at railway stations sell local specialties. Today passengers use phone apps to have food delivered from railway catering companies at the next station.

Colleen Sen and Sangeeta Khanna

- Chatterjee, Arup K. 'Banquet on Broad-gauge'. *The Hindu*, 28 October 2018.
- Dash, Madhulika. 'From Railway Mutton Curry to Bedmi-Aloo: When Railway Food Was an Affair to Remember'. *The Indian Express*, 30 October 2014.
- Mukhopadhyay, Aparajita. 'Spicy Curries and Cups of Tea: Dining along the Darjeeling Himalayan Line'. In *Food on the Move: Dining on the Legendary Railway Journeys of the World*, edited by Sharon Hudgins, 189–214. London: Reaktion Books, 2018.

RAITA

Raitas are refreshing and digestive side dishes (sometimes called salads) which accompany Indian meals to provide a cooling contrast to the rich, spicy main dishes such as BIRYANI or PULAO. They are an essential part of the thali (see COOKING AND DINING).

The variations seem endless, although the basic ingredient of a raita is yogurt with the addition of cooked (or raw) vegetables (such as AUBERGINE, CUCUMBER, TOMATO, ONION, beetroot, POTATOES and more) or fruit (such as APPLE or grapes) flavoured with spices and herbs. Often *boondi* – small globules of fried chickpea flour – are added for texture and flavour. *Kela ka* raita, made with BANANA (sometimes with fresh COCONUT), is traditionally served with *sonth* (a sweet and sour GINGER chutney).

In southern India raitas are called *pachdi* or *pachadi*. They are made with a seasonal vegetable such as marrow which is grated or boiled, then mixed with yogurt and spiced with CHILLI powder and given a distinct flavour by the hot garnish (*tadka*) of fried MUSTARD seeds and fresh CURRY LEAVES. *Tayar pachadi* is another version made with onion, tomatoes and cucumber and spiced with green chilli. In Kashmir, SAFFRON is sometimes added to Kashmiri *dahi* (raita), which lends a golden colour and lovely aroma, making it into a rather luxurious relish.

Helen Saberi

RAJASTHAN

The state of Rajasthan was formed in 1947 by the union of more than twenty princely states, some, such as Jaipur, Udaipur and Jodhpur, as large as small countries. It is the largest Indian state by area and the seventh largest by population. The Aravalli mountain range divides the state into the hilly southeastern region and the barren Thar Dessert, one of the hottest, driest regions of the world where temperatures have reached over 50°C. However, thanks to irrigation, Rajasthan has become a major producer of MILLET, rapeseed, MUSTARD, BARLEY, CORN, CUMIN, CORIANDER, FENUGREEK, soybeans and livestock.

Around 90 per cent of Rajasthan's populations are Hindus and Jains and the state has the highest proportion of vegetarians in India: around 75 per cent. ONIONS and GARLIC are not part of many Rajasthani vegetarian dishes because of the Jain influence. Commonly used spices include fenugreek seeds, FENNEL, NIGELLA and especially red CHILLIES, considered to have a cooling effect in very hot climate. At the same time, Rajasthan has some of India's most famous game dishes that were favourites of the Rajput rulers who, as Kshatriyas, ate meat.

Rajasthanis have been brilliant innovators in creating a delicious cuisine from limited ingredients, especially a shortage of fresh vegetables and water. Rajasthan is the second largest producer of milk in India, so yogurt and BUTTERMILK are often used in preparing gravies and GHEE is a common cooking medium for those who can afford it. Rajasthan is a major producer of lentils, especially chickpeas. PULSES are used in many ways: to make dals and *kadhis* (spicy CURRIES of yogurt and chickpea flour) and ground into flour to make BREADS and snacks. Both VADA and *dahi*-vadas are popular as are many of the *farsan* snacks also popular in Gujarat. A staple of Rajasthani cuisine are *gatte*, which serve as a substitute for vegetables in many dishes. A dough of chickpea flour, yogurt, chilli powder and water is shaped into cylinders or dumplings that are boiled, cut into small pieces and dried. Vegetables can also be dried in the sun to make *gatte*. *Gatte* can be cooked in various curries, for example with vegetables in a spicy yogurt sauce and eaten with roti. Jains make pulao and *KHICHRI* from *gatte*. Some people claim that *boondi*, small globules of chickpea flour added to RAITA and SWEETS throughout India, were invented here. *Raab* is a thick broth made from millet flour and buttermilk eaten as a soup.

MILLETS (sorghum and finger millet), barley and corn are ground into flour to produce some of the subcontinent's most delicious breads. A staple throughout Western India is *bhakri* (also called *dhebra*), a round flat unleavened bread, soft or hard in texture, made from coarsely ground flour and water. It was traditionally taken by farmers to their fields and eaten with CHUTNEY, CHILLIES or PICKLES. Today, WHEAT is increasingly replacing traditional grains. Cooking oil and ghee are precious commodities among poor people so breads are roasted on a heavy pan, with a little ghee added before serving. Another distinctive bread is a thick sweet *bina pani ki* roti ('bread made without water') prepared from a dough of wheat flour, oil or ghee and *boora* (an unrefined form of SUGAR). It can last for several weeks. *Dopatri* are thin soft rotis. *Missi* rotis are slightly crispy flatbreads made from chickpea flour dough mixed with green chillies and onion and traditionally cooked over an open flame. One of India's most beautiful breads is *khoba*, the dough of which is pinched to create a honeycombed design before baking.

Rajasthan's signature dish is dal *batti churma*, which is probably quite ancient. *Battis* are balls of unleavened dough that are roasted (traditionally in hot coals, today in ovens) until they are hard, then topped with ghee. *Churma* is a coarse powder made from a mixture of coarsely ground wheat flour or crushed *battis*, ghee, sugar and NUTS that is lightly sautéed. The dal can be made from one or several lentils, including *moong*, *masur*, *urad* and *toor*.

One of the ingredients that grows in the desert is *sangri* (*Capparis decidua*), the bean-like pods of the *khejri* tree that used to be a mainstay during famines because of their high protein content. They have an earthy, nutty flavour with overtones of CINNAMON and mocha. After soaking in water, they are cooked with *ker*, sour green berries, and vegetables to make *ker sangri ki sabzi*. The dish, sometimes mixed with raisins and nuts, is served with roti and is popular at weddings. *Sangri* can also be pickled, made into snacks or cooked in curries. The *Acacia senegal* tree yields *kumatiya*, small nutritious seeds, and *gunda/gond*, an edible gum (which, as gum arabic, is used as a food stabilizer). These ingredients plus pieces of dried MANGOES are stir-fried with spices and hot chillies to make the dish called *panchkuta*. Because it stores well, travellers relied on this dish during long camel journeys. *Panchkuta* is a standard dish during the Hindu festival Shitala Ashtami a week after Holi.

Beverages are made with yogurt, milk and buttermilk. Rajasthan has a wide variety of sweet dishes which, as in Gujarat, are served as part of a meal, not after, and are often based on lentils. Popular sweets include *boondi ki* laddu (see LADDU), *gondi ki* laddu made of *gunda* and *churma ki* laddu. The last sweet is made from *churma* dough that is deep-fried, coarsely ground, sieved, cooked with jaggery, melted in ghee and shaped into balls. *Ghevar*, a disc-shaped sweet made from white flour, ghee and sugar syrup, is a staple of Rajasthani festivals. *Moong* dal *ka* halwa/*sheera* made with *moong* dal paste, ghee, milk, sugar, SAFFRON and nuts is prepared at Holi, Diwali and other festivals. Another festival dish is *mohanthal* made from chickpea flour roasted in ghee, sugar, rosewater (see FLOWER WATERS), CARDAMOM and saffron and topped with chopped nuts.

Under the MUGHALS, Rajput princes attained the highest ranks as generals and as provincial governors and the emperors took Rajput princesses as their brides. This influenced the royal kitchens which started using some rare and opulent ingredients – saffron, rosewater, herbs and other costly aromatics. The royal cooks and *khansamahs* closely guarded recipes and only passed them on to succeeding generations. The princes treated their guests to glorious spreads served on gold and silver utensils with the number of courses sometimes running into the hundreds. Some of their recipes were compiled by Raja Digvijaya Singh (see SINGH, RAJA DIGVIJAYA).

Hunting, or *shikar*, was a traditional pastime of the Rajputs, especially the rulers, although since 1972 hunting deer and other animals has been banned under the Wildlife Protection Act. Deer, wild boar, rabbits, pheasants, quail and duck were popular targets. The hunting parties would be accompanied by the court's finest cooks (*khansamahs*) who could prepare dishes with just a few basic ingredients while on the move. One was *suda* – a leg of deer or mutton rubbed with spices and roasted over an open charcoal fire while basted with ghee. *Laal maas* ('red meat'), said to be created by the Mewar dynasty 800 years ago, is made by marinating every cut of meat from a deer or wild boar in a fiery sauce of red chillies, garlic paste, aromatic spices, onions and yogurt. (According to another story, it was invented during a culinary competition between royal chefs.) *Safed maas* ('white meat') has a yogurt and cream based white gravy. *Jungli maas* ('forest meat') is made with just chillies, garlic, ghee and SALT. Today these dishes are made with mutton or chicken. Wild boar is also used in hot tangy pickles. Rajasthani *sula* is a kind of KEBAB prepared by slicing thin slices of meat marinated in yogurt, lime juice, garlic and spices, threading them on skewers and cooking them over a hibachi-like grill.

Jodhpur is famous for its barbecued and roasted meat dishes that can be cooked out in the open, including roasted quails and *khud khargosh*, made by marinating a rabbit, wrapping it in bread, packing it into a jute bag and burying it in a pit topped with burning charcoal where it is slow cooked for several hours. This method was popular among soldiers in the field since the enemy could not see their location. Hunters prepared their game in the same way.

Another Rajasthani tradition is the production of strong liquors (see ALCOHOL) called *ashavs*, made from local herbs, spices and fruits and considered to have medicinal value. A distillery was set up in Jodhpur in 1924 but the liquors were banned at the time of Independence. In 2006, a law was passed by the government of the Rajasthan authorizing the production of so-called Heritage Liquors and the Rajasthan State Gangangar Sugar Mills Ltd. began producing eight spirits at its distillery in Jaipur using traditional earthen pots and copper and brass utensils. They included *kesar kasturi*, a distillation of saffron, dry fruits, herbs, nuts, seeds, more than twenty spices, milk and sugar (that is a speciality of Jodhpur), and *jagmohan*, a dry-fruit-based liquor with more than thirty spices and herbs originally brewed for the rulers of Mewar.

Production was halted in 2008 because the liquors were expensive to produce and sales were poor but was resumed in 2020 with the production of four beverages, including Royal Heritage Chandra Haas, a sweet-tasting liquor produced with eighty ingredients including spices, dry fruits and *ghee*, and Royal Jagmohan, a blend of spices, herbs, seasonal fruits, dry fruits, bark, *murabba* (sweet preserves), ghee, milk, crystal sugar and saffron.

Marwaris are a trading community that originated in the Marwar (Jodhpur) region in southwestern Rajasthan. From at least the time of Akbar, they migrated all over India establishing their businesses and today are found in KOLKATA, MUMBAI and other cities. Most are Hindus and Jains and the majority are strict vegetarians who avoid onions and garlic. The Marwar region is very dry and their cuisine is like Rajasthani vegetarian cuisine, with a reliance on lentils and local grains, an abundance of dairy products, especially ghee which is poured on finished dishes, and the intensive use of chillies. Because they traditionally were traders, their dishes had to be transportable and consumed without reheating. Favourite Marwari dishes include *panchkuta* (see above) and *panchmela* dal *sabzi*, made of five lentils (*urad*, *chana*, *moong*, *arhar* and *masur*/*masoor*) mixed with vegetables.

Colleen Taylor Sen

- Dash, Madhulika. 'Game Cuisine: A Rajput Legacy'. *The Indian Express*, 25 October 2014.
- Deedbania, Bapu. 'A Dummy's Guide to Marwari Cuisine'. *Mumbai Mirror*, 6 November 2016.
- Pathak, Prannay. 'A Shot of Rajasthan's Heady Heritage Liquors Will Prove to Be a Dip into the State's Royal Past'. *Outlook Traveller*, 26 July 2020.
- Sunder, Kalpana. 'Top Ten Foods to Try in Rajasthan'. *BBC GoodFood*, 17 June 2020. Available online: https://www.bbcgoodfood.com/howto/guide/top-10-foods-try-rajasthan (accessed 30 April 2022).

RAMA RAU, SANTHA

Santha Rama Rau (1923–2009) was a novelist, travel writer, prolific commentator on India in the United States from the 1950s to the 1970s, and author of *The Cooking of India* (1969), which laid out the stylistic template for future cookbooks written for a Western audience by being 'part autobiography, part travelogue, part social and cultural history, and part political platform' (Burton 2007).

It's hard to find a cookbook that quotes a finance minister on famines, which were painfully common in India in the first two decades after it gained independence, and almost tenders an apology for its recipes coming from the kitchens of the elite and not from the villages where 80 per cent of India lived. Educated in England and the United States, Rama Rau belonged to the privileged upper crust of British India – her father was an Indian civil servant and diplomat and her mother one of the founders of the International Planned Parenthood Federation. She completed her schooling in England and then went to Wellesley College in the United States.

That may explain her 'culinary cosmopolitanism' which expressed itself in her strong views on the West's obsession with the 'comprehensive and meaningless' CURRY. Rama Rau made herself abundantly clear in her *New York Times* review of Dharam Jit Singh's *Classic Cooking from India* (1956) – believed to be the first to be written by an Indian for an American audience. She commended the book for being 'a pioneer attempt' to persuade Americans that Indian food was 'not the gummy, pasty mess known here as curry'.

With its vivid pictures by *LIFE* magazine's acclaimed photographer Eliot Elisofon and its kaleidoscopic view of the sub-continent's kitchens, *The Cooking of India* introduced a new voice in the world of cookery that kept getting amplified in the Indian cookbooks that followed.

Sourish Bhattacharyya

- Burton, Antoinette. *Post-Colonial Careers of Shantha Rama Rau*. Durham and London: Duke University Press, 2007.
- Weber, Bruce. 'Santha Rama Rau, Who Wrote of India's Landscape and Psyche, Dies at 86'. *The New York Times*, 24 April 2009.

RAMPUR

Rampur, a Rohilla Pathan princely state established under the British colonial rule in 1774, survived the destruction of the Revolt of 1857 and became the cultural node or *markaz* of north Indian Muslim culture in the nineteenth century. The culinary influence of Awadh and MUGHAL cuisines, which had begun around the second decade of the nineteenth century, was further strengthened by the exodus of culinary masters, the *khansamahs,* from these cultural centres to Rampur. (A number of cookbook manuscripts on Awadhi and Mughal cuisines were collected or commissioned by the Nawabs since 1816 and are preserved in the Raza Library of Rampur.) A conscious effort was made by the Nawabs of Rampur to amalgamate these flavours into its Pakhtun – people from the highlands of Afghanistan-Pakistan border – tribal foodways and to textualize the nouveau 'haute' Rampur cuisine as an instrument of gastrodiplomacy. Nawab Hamid Ali Khan (r. 1894–1930) and Nawab Raza Ali Khan (r. 1930–49) sent *khansamahs* abroad to learn French and English cuisines. These new flavours settled into the culinary arc with roasts, puddings, stews, cutlets, etc. finding place on the elite tables by the twentieth century.

Rampur cuisine is a meat-heavy foodway defined by hardy, rustic flavours that still echo the Pakhtun culinary tradition. The preparations can be distinguished from Awadhi and Mughal cuisines as having a more meaty than spicy aspect, with a judicious and understated use of basic whole spices. Muneeza Shamsi, niece of Her Highness Raffat Zamani Begum, describes 'the careful melding of spices' as the hallmark of Rampur cuisine. The kormas, *qaliyas* (meat CURRY with TURMERIC and sometimes vegetables), PULAOS and KEBABS are common to most Indian Muslim cuisines. However, the Rampur cuisine has distinctive variations as well as some unique dishes created in the famed royal kitchens: the *uroos e behri,* a two-foot-long fish kebab which resembles a fish with scales; *shabdegh* (meat and TURNIP curry); *mutanjan* (sweet and savoury pulao); *dar e bahisht* (an almond and milk based sweet); *murgh dumpukht* pulao (pulao with whole chicken); and *kundan qaliya* (light meat curry with SAFFRON and turmeric). The narrative arc of the cuisine marks the complex trajectory from its princely past to the subaltern present as the aspects of the carefully curated 'haute cuisine' passed into food memories following the abolition of privy purses in 1971. The cuisine of the masses that evolved at tandem, incorporating the local flavours and some filtered down influences from upper classes, ultimately survived on the Rampur *dastarkhwan*.

Today Rampur's emblematic foods include HALWA *sohan* – a sweet made of *samnak* (wheat germ flour), milk, GHEE and SUGAR cooked for about nine hours – which has Persian and Afghan roots. Among the various styles of KEBABS, the *chapli* kebabs, descended from Afghan highland cuisine, are rustic flat meat patties. The iconic *taar* roti (meat curry and leavened BREAD) of Rampur is a one dish meal served at weddings and funerals. This continues the tribal tradition of feeding the tribe with a simple meat curry slow cooked in *deghs* (large, small-mouthed pans) over open fires. It is often accompanied by a *yakhni* pulao, a light aromatic RICE cooked in meat stock, and the peerless *gulathhi* (sweet made from rice and milk). Another speciality is the *adrak* halwa (GINGER and milk sweet) said to be created by a *hakeem* (indigenous doctor) to trick a nawab into eating ginger.

Since 2010, a blitzkrieg of food shows, magazine articles, books and social media featuring members of the royal family has generated visibility and interest around the forgotten culinary aspects of Rampur cuisine. *Khansamahs,* claiming knowledge of 'authentic' recipes and descent from the famed royal *khansamahs* of yore, team up with members of the erstwhile royal family and present Rampur food festivals and food shows. They have created dishes like *gosht ka* halwa (sweet with meat base), *neem ka* halwa (sweet using bitter leaves of the *NEEM* tree) and *lehsuni KHEER* (GARLIC and milk sweet) to excite and intrigue the media. New restaurants have sprouted in posh areas catering to the relatively recent trend of eating out and the inspiration from cooking shows has led to the inclusion of grand-sounding dishes like '*changezi* chicken', '*hariyali* kebabs', etc. into the house menus.

Tarana Khan

- Habibulla, Jahanara. *Remembrance of Days Past: Glimpses of a Princely State during the Raj*, translated by Tahira Naqvi. Oxford and New York: OUP, 2001.
- Shamsi, Muneeza. 'Across India, Pakistan and Britain: A Family's Culinary History in the Twentieth Century'. Unpublished manuscript.

RASGULLA

Rasgulla (Hindi) or *rasagolla* (Bengali) is a Bengali SWEET popular throughout South Asia and worldwide. Rasgullas are small balls made from *CHHANA* and SUGAR and served in a sugar syrup; they have a soft, spongy texture. Sometimes rosewater (see FLOWER WATERS) or CARDAMOM is added.

The origin and history of rasgulla are steeped in controversy. The traditional story was that it was invented in 1868 by Nabin Chandra Das, a sweet maker (*moira*) in the Sutanuti district of Calcutta (see KOLKATA). However, there are indications that a similar sweet may have existed earlier. A sales brochure produced by Das's descendants even states, 'It is hard to tell whether nor not cruder versions of similar sweets existed anywhere at that time.' One day, a local non-Bengali merchant tried the rasgulla in Das's shop and liked it so much he bought huge amounts. The popularity of rasgulla spread following N.C. Das's invention of a way of vacuum-packing the sweet.

In another origin story, the rasgulla first appeared in the eleventh century in the Jagannath temple at Puri in Odisha where it was offered as *prasad* to the goddess Lakshmi (see TEMPLE FOOD). Texts suggest it represented a tribute to the eyes of Lord Jaganath (an incarnation of Vishnu) which are depicted as large and slightly oblong.

A priest from the temple may have taught the villagers at Phala, who had surplus milk, how to make the confectionary. Another variation was created in the village of Salepur where a local *moira* steamed the cheese and let the balls slowly rise in the sugar syrup, which produced a spongy version. Some people believe that it was this version that N.C. Das, unable to replicate the process, imitated by adding *reetha* (soap berries, *Sapindus mukorssi*) to create the sponginess. And some Bangladeshi food historians claim rasgulla originated in Bangladesh.

In 2015, the government of West Bengal applied for GEOGRAPHICAL INDICATION status for *banglar rasogolla* (Bengali rasgulla). The application was for a specific variation that differed in 'colour, texture, taste, juice content, and method of manufacturing' from that produced in Odisha. GEOGRAPHICAL INDICATION (GI) status was granted in November 2017. In 2018, Odisha applied for its own GI status for Odisha *rasagola* which was granted in July 2019. Both states hold festivals and exhibitions celebrating their emblematic sweets.

Rasgulla is the parent of a whole 'family' of Indian sweets. In 1918 N.C. Das's son K.C. Das invented *rasmalai* – flattened *chhana* patties served in thickened sweet milk. *Khirmohan* are *chhana* patties dipped in thickened milk and sprinkled with *KHOYA*. *Chamcham* is the same item formed in an ovoid shape. Dry sweets made without the syrup include *raskadamba*, balls of *chhana* wrapped in *khoya*; *kamala bhog*, orange flavoured; and *rajbhog*, stuffed with dried fruits and NUTS.

Colleen Sen

- Dash, Madhulika. 'The Food Story: How India's Favourite Sweet Dish Rosugulla Was Born'. *The Indian Express*, 14 November 2017.
- Sinha, Anil Kishore. *Anthropology of Sweetmeats*. New Delhi: Gyan Publishing House, 2000.

RICE

Cultivated rice belongs to two major species: *Oryza sativa*, or Asian rice, and *Oryza glaberrima*, or African rice. Although there are many *Oryza sativa* varieties cultivated commercially, they belong to two major subspecies: *indica*, a long grain rice characterized by a wide adaptability that accounts for the bulk of the world's rice production, and *japonica*, a round grain rice. Modern genetics of landraces from Northeast India may indicate a third distinct origin for the so-called *aus* (*Oryza sativa*) rice varieties.

India is the second largest producer and the largest exporter of rice in the world. The top rice-growing states in India are West Bengal with around 14 per cent of total production of 122 million tonnes in 2020–1; Uttar Pradesh with just over 13 per cent; Andhra Pradesh with 12 per cent; and Punjab with 10 per cent. Rice is also grown in Tamil Nadu Karnataka, Bihar, Odisha, Chhattisgarh and Haryana. Once home to 100,000 varieties of rice, today only about 6,000 varieties are grown in India. Meanwhile, demand is escalating faster than production and at the same time there are questions about the ecological soundness of rice growing in a water-stressed country like India. Irrigated rice

FIGURE 38 RICE. Colleen Sen.

systems predominate and are characterized by high cropping densities and intensive use of agrochemicals, energy and water. These inputs are making rice farming untenable given increasing costs, energy scarcity and the uncertainties posed by climate change.

Rice is the staple food for 65 per cent of India's population. It is a major source of energy and an important source of protein. One hundred grams of raw white rice provide 361 kcal of energy and six grams of protein. Rice also contains substantial amounts of zinc and niacin. On the other hand, it is low in calcium, iron, thiamine and riboflavin and has virtually no beta-carotene (vitamin A).

One of the earliest evidences of growing of rice identified as *Oryza sativa* date back to the seventh millennium BCE in pre-Neolithic Koldihwa in Uttar Pradesh. Archaeological evidence suggests that rice was growing in the sub-continent as early as 6000 BCE and has been cultivated in the sub-continent since 2000 BCE. Thus, it is not surprising that rice is central to the culture of many communities. It is intricately woven into the country's history, culture, nutrition, literature and economy. This makes rice of pivotal importance in food security and sustainability – not just economic sustainability but environmental, cultural and social sustainability as well.

Rice, along with BARLEY (*yava*), is mentioned in the *Atharvaveda* (*c.* 1000–900 BCE) as one of the two immortal sons of heaven. However, the grains mentioned in the *Rigveda* (1750–1200 BCE) are *yava*, *tokman* (in Sanskrit, the green shoots of any grain) and *dhanya* (MILLETS). Many scholars argue that rice was not cultivated by the people who wrote the *Rigveda* because of the absence of the word *vrihi*, meaning paddy, which appears only later. By the time of the *Atharvaveda*, rice came to share the status of the most important grain, along with barley. In the *Atharvaveda* and the *Yajurveda* (1200–800 BCE), both *vrihi* and *nivara* (wild rice) find mention in the texts. The later Vedic texts use *tandula* for threshed paddy and *akshat* for unbroken rice.

Later texts give more and detailed information about rice. *Vrihi, sali* and *sastika* are mentioned as the main varieties. They mention *krsnavrihi* (black rice), *shuklavrihi* (white rice), *mahavrihi* (long rice), *nivara* (wild rice), *hayana* (annual red rice), *asuvrihi* (fast growing rice) and *masusya* (another variety of wild rice). Others are *raktasali* (red rice), *mahasali* (long grained rice), *kasthasali, kalama* and *sugandha*. *Sastika* was mentioned by Panini as the variety that took sixty days to mature. Two more varieties, *masusya* and *priyangu*, are described as having gold-like husks. By the time of the Classical period (300 BCE–75 CE), Kautilya's *Arthashastra* tells us that rice, along with millets, had replaced barley and WHEAT as the main crops. Kautilya also mentions two additional varieties of rice, *daraka* and *varaka*.

There are many references to rice-based products and dishes in the Vedic literature. The *Atharvaveda* mentions *kshiraodana*, or rice cooked in milk. *Purodasa* is a rice cake used as offering to the Gods. By the time of the *Upanishads* (*c.* 800–200 BCE), rice was an integral part of the diet and was cooked in various dishes, both savoury and sweet. The *Upanishads* mention a variety of rice preparations: *kshiraodana* (cooked rice mixed with milk), *dadhiodana* (cooked with curds), *tilaudana* (cooked with SESAME), *mamsaudana* (cooked with meat), *ghritaudana* (cooked with GHEE) and *mudgaudana* (cooked with mung beans). *Apupa* and *saskuli* are rice cakes mentioned in the *Brahmanas* (900–700 BCE) as often being used in ceremonial purposes. A MODAKA is a typical sweet ball.

Rice products used even today find mention in the *Brahmanas*. *Laja* and *prthuka* were used for sacrificial purposes. *Laja* is puffed rice which looks like a white flower and *prthuka* is flattened or beaten rice. *Parivapa* was an offering for the Gods made from parched rice fried in butter. *Prthuka* was also used in gruels made with long pepper (see PEPPER, LONG), dry GINGER and POMEGRANATE juice. These are mentioned in the *Charaka Samhita*, which names them according to their consistency.

During Buddhist times, the venerable monk Sariputra, standing on the Vulture Hills in Rajgraha, spoke to Maitreya Bodhisattva, 'Maitreya, here, today, the Lord, looking upon a stalk of rice, spoke this aphorism to the monks ...' Thus was born the *Salistamba Sutra*, the first sutra of Mahayana Buddhism. Why is this significant? The sutra is named after the paddy stock. Numerous *Jataka Tales* also mention rice in various contexts and forms. Buddhist works such as the *Majjima Nikaya* (3 BCE–2 CE) mention that rice (*sali* and *vrihi*) were the staple food in Northeast India and served in public rest-houses across the country.

A reading of the great epics, *Ramayana* and *Mahabharata*, shows that rice was the staple food for the ruling dynasties. *Odana, laja* and *saskuli* find mention in both epics. We also come across *payasa* (see KHEER), rice cooked in milk, which was given to King Dasarath by a sage to enable his three wives to bear him sons. In the *Ramayana*, a dish called *mamsabhutadana*, which translates to rice cooked with meat, was said to be the favourite food of Sita. Rice is also inbuilt onto the narration of various stories of the *Mahabharata*.

The medicinal texts of the Ayurveda physicians Charaka and Sushruta (see FOOD AND MEDICINE) give a lot of importance to rice, identifying the *sali* (ripening in winter) variety as superior to the *vrihi* variety (ripening in autumn). Charaka documents fifteen superior varieties and five inferior varieties of *sali* rice. *Sali* varieties were considered sweet in taste, cooling in potency, light in digestion and capable of imparting strength, while *vrihi* varieties were described as sweet, astringent and hot in potency. *Raktasali* is considered as the most nutritive as both food and medicine. According to Sushruta, among the *vrihi* rice the *krishnavrihi* was the most popular for consumption.

Charaka also mentions the *sastika* as the most nourishing variety and documents ten varieties. The medicinal value of *sastika*, other varieties of *sali*, and parched rice has been documented in both *Charaka Samhita* and *Sushruta Samhita* for the treatment of various ailments such as diarrhoea, vomiting, fever, haemorrhage, chest pain, wounds and burns. *Nivara*, a wild rice with a sweet astringent taste, was considered the most nutritious and was able to generate heat. It had curative properties, especially during the monsoons.

Rice gruels had an important role to play as healing and nourishing food and were cooked with clarified butter, water, milk, fruits, meat, tubers or PULSES. They were named according to the proportion of water added to the gruel and the consistency of the cooked rice. The gruel *yavagu* has been mentioned in several medical texts as a food for recovering patients, or *pathakalpana*. The basic ingredients of *yavagu* were *raktasali*, water and additives like long pepper, black pepper (see PEPPER, BLACK), rock SALT and ghee made from cow's milk. Rice-based preparations such as *vilepi*, *manda*, *anna* and *krsara* are also a part of *pathyakalapana* in Ayurveda.

Rice finds abundant mentions in tribal lore from aboriginal and indigenous tribes. Rice, paddy, cooked rice and rice beer are all woven into countless stories about the origin of the earth, the sun and the moon. There is no variation in the part that rice or millet plays in the life of a Gond, a Juang, a Gadaba or a Muria.

Most Hindu festivals celebrate the agrarian cycles of sowing and harvesting rice. The festivities of Pongal, Uttarayana, Lohri, Khichdi, Shishur, Saenkraat, Poush Sankranti and Maagh Bihu, are all celebrated on Makar Sankranti in January, the day the sun enters Capricorn. Baisakhi in Punjab, Poila Boishakh (first day of the Bengali calendar) and Rongali Bihu in Assam are celebrated as festivals that thank the powers-that-be for an abundant harvest. The festival of Onam, celebrated during August–September in Kerala, celebrates the homecoming of the legendary emperor Mahabali and the harvest of rice and rain flowers in Kerala. Around the same time it is Kaati Bihu in Assam when farmers pray for protection of their crops. Around September, Bengalis celebrate Nabanna and Odias celebrate Nuakhai, both harvest festivals associated with the harvest of new rice. Na-Khuwa Bhooj is a harvest festival celebrated in the tribal homes of rural Assam after the harvest of paddy in the months of November and December.

Rice is also an integral part of all Hindu ceremonies. Rice should be given to a child in the *annaprasana* (see RITES OF PASSAGE) ceremony as her/his first food after mother's milk. Pouring puffed rice into the fire is a significant ritual, especially in Vedic marriage ceremonies. Kalidasa, in his *Kumarasambhava*, gives a poetic and beautiful description of this ritual at the marriage ceremony of Lord Shiva and Parvati. *Nivara* (wild rice) is cooked and consumed on days of fasting as a non-cereal grain, and cakes made of it are offered to Brihaspati in *vajapeya*, a ceremonial sacrifice to fire.

Rice Varieties

Rice is predominantly categorized into three main types based on the size of the grain: long grain, medium grain and short-grain.

Long grain has long, slender kernels with low starch and when cooked, each grain is separate and rather dry. It is mostly used for cooking PULAOS and BIRYANIS and also used for making desserts like FIRNI. There are many varieties but today only a few are available commercially. **Basmati** is considered to be the best long grain rice for its taste, aroma, texture and size. The finest comes from Dehradun in the state of Uttarakhand. **Patna** is a lower-grade long grain rice grown in Bihar.

Medium grain varieties are the ones most widely available. Some of the better-known ones are hybrid varieties like **Ponni** and **Sona Masoori** which are popular in South Indian states such as Tamil Nadu, Telangana and Andhra Pradesh and in Uttar Pradesh. Ponni is named after the river Kaveri and is easily digestible. Sona Masoori is valued for its aroma, nutrients and softness. These are mostly used to make plain white rice which is eaten with side dishes such as SAMBAR, rasam, yogurt and CURRIES. Medium-grained indigenous varieties can also be highly aromatic like the **Kalizeera** from Chhattisgarh, **Kala Namak** from Uttar Pradesh, **Tulaipanji** from West Bengal and **Jeeraga Samba** from Tamil Nadu. Varieties such as the high-fibre red or black medium grain rice **Palakkad Matta** from Kerala and **Chak Hao** from Manipur are known for their robust and earthy flavour. While the Matta is used as plain steamed rice or for making DOSA, IDLIS and *APPAMS*, the Chak Hao is used for making KHEER (sweet rice porridge).

Short-grain varieties are squat and plump and can be sticky or dry when cooked, based on the starch content. One of the best known is **Gobindobhog** that is cultivated in West Bengal. It is a white, aromatic, starchy rice with a sweet buttery flavour. It is often used in preparation of kheer and savoury-sweet pulao. Other varieties include the floral **Ambe Mohar** from Maharashtra and the highly aromatic **Joha** from Assam.

Tanushree Bhowmik

- Church, Arthur Herbert. *Food Grains of India*. London: Chapman & Hall, 1886.
- Deb, Debal. *Seeds of Tradition, Seeds of Future: Folk Rice Varieties of Eastern India*. New Delhi: Navdanya/Research Foundation for Science Technology & Ecology, 2005.
- Jayashri. '9 Most Popular Types of Rice in India – A Complete Guide'. *Three Whistles Kitchen*, 3 July 2019. Available online: https://threewhistleskitchen.com/popular-indian-rice-types/ (accessed 19 May 2022).
- Singh, R. K. and U. S. Singh, eds. *A Treatise on the Scented Rices of India*. New Delhi: Kalyani Publishers, 2003.
- Sinha, A. K. and P. K. Mishra. *Rice Varieties of Bengal: Characterization and Conservation of Traditional Rice Varieties of West Bengal*. Chisnau, MD: Lambert Academic Publishing, 2017.

RIDDELL, DR ROBERT FLOWER

One of the first great catalogues of ANGLO-INDIAN cookery was written by Dr Riddell who was the superintending army surgeon at the court of the Nizam of HYDERABAD. His classic book *Indian Domestic Economy and Receipt Book* went into several editions including the seventh edition (revised) which was published in Calcutta in 1871 after the author's death. Dr Riddell featured recipes for dishes made at the Nizam's court and also gave directions for plain wholesome cookery, both Oriental and English. He went to great lengths to explain the vast differences between a number of regional cuisines, noting, for example, the differences between Muslim and Hindu cookery. He includes information connected with 'household affairs, likely to be required by families, messes and private individuals residing at the presidencies or out-stations'.

Dr Riddell also compiled a large volume on the subject of gardening and vegetable growing in India, *A Manual of Gardening for Western and Southern India*.

Helen Saberi

RITES OF PASSAGE

Annaprashana

Annaprashana (Sanskrit *anna* = cooked rice, *prāśana* = feeding) is an important Hindu ritual to celebrate the introduction of solid foods as a complementary feed and the onset of weaning. It is the seventh of the sixteen *saṃskāra*, or rites of passages, recommended in the Hindu way of life. Communities throughout India put rice on the plate for infants as their first taste of cooked food. The ritual of *annaprashana* is known by many names – *choroonu* in Kerala, *mukhe bhaat* in Bengal and *bhaatkhulai* in Garhwal. The *annaprashana* ceremony is often concluded with a large feast of traditional foods for family and friends. It is performed after the infant is six months old and before the completion of the first year. Even months (of their life) for boys and odd months for girls are considered.

RICE is slow cooked in cow's milk to a thick porridge and sweetened with SUGAR. This is known by many names – KHEER, *payesh*, *payasam*, etc. – and nuances in recipes may vary. Local varieties of rice are chosen with preference for a new harvest as such rice cooks to a very soft consistency. Cooking time, preference for textures like creaminess and caramelization of milk depend on the family's tastes.

For many infants this is the first experience of texture and often the first taste of cow's milk. Some children may have been fed a very thin gruel of rice or CORN flour as a lickable food starting at about four months.

In many communities, the *annaprashana* also includes a savoury course. KHICHRI is prepared with new rice cooked with *toor* dal and GHEE, macerated with a pinch of SALT when still warm and served. It is also the infant's first taste of salt. Khichri remains a staple weaning food together with porridge (mostly of finger MILLET, *ragi* in Tamil Nadu, Karnataka, Maharashtra and Kerala). Among the Munda tribe, khichri is prepared using indigenous rice, black gram along with chopped leafy vegetables such as *koinaar* leaves (*Bauhinia purpurea*) and AMARANTH leaves.

Ghee is considered very sacred in ceremonial preparations and food for the occasion is consecrated with it. HONEY and sugar are used as sweeteners. In recent years, Anganwadi, a nationwide rural healthcare initiative, has used the *annaprashana* ceremony as an opportunity to talk about the importance of supplementary feeding in child nutrition and as a medium to deliver knowledge and healthcare in rural areas. For poor families, organizing such a ceremony and a feast thereafter is a financial burden. The Anganwadi organizes such an event twice a month in every village and many young mothers participate in it. Using the traditional rituals as a tool to solve a multifaceted socio-cultural problem is putting the much-needed focus on nutrition in early childhood.

Widowhood

Losing one's spouse to death is hard for both men and women. In India, while much has progressed in the last century in how this period of bereavement is handled for widows and widowers, there are still pockets of tough orthodox traditions, particularly among Hindus. The most immediate signs of exclusion are in the days following the death when the surviving partner follows a strict *sattvic* diet (and perhaps the close bereaved family as well).

Food and dietary rules continue to be an important aspect beyond bereavement and, in some communities, are an important narrative in widowhood. For women, eating TURMERIC and its derivative *kumkum*, and betel leaves with areca as part of a PAAN and flowers that are all symbols of marriagehood are strictly avoided.

Orthodox castes in Bengal, Tamil Nadu and Karnataka and Namboodiris of Kerala may have a stricter dietary regimen – exclusion of alliums, DRUMSTICK, meat and FISH are most common. Bengali Brahmin widows have particularly had stringent dietary rules that shun eating of meat, lentils such as *masoor* dal, vegetables like *poi shak* (*Basella alba*) and snake GOURD, among others. Because of these stringent traditions, widows have evolved a rich tradition of vegetarian Bengali fare with a plethora of resourceful ideas and a creative attitude to cooking. In *niramish*, their distinctive simple cooking has assumed the form of a cuisine – they use leftovers and kitchen scraps, and process lentils and beans with often time-consuming methods to bring a dash of deliciousness to simple vegetarian fare. They recreate their longing for meat and fish by being imaginative in their recreation of forms and meaty textures from plant-based sources like in *niramish dimer dalna*, a mock-egg curry fashioned from cottage cheese.

While such dietary stringency may not be widely practised, there is a general expectation of simplicity and austerity. The age of the woman, caste and community are important considerations too.

The presence of widows at weddings has been a matter of much debate as they were long considered inauspicious. Reform movements, education and migration have brought about much-needed change. While society has largely progressed to include them in the festivities, their participation in many important rituals may be excluded in the absence of a spouse. Interestingly, this exclusion applies to spinsters and bachelors too, emphasizing that social customs place immense value on marriagehood.

In modern-day India, most of these restrictions have vanished with a movement towards a more pragmatic and inclusive society. Food restrictions, if any, are quite temporary, in line with many other practices.

Death

People mark the loss of a dear one with food at the moment of death, during the funeral rites that mark the day, the ensuing mourning period, the first death anniversary, and keeping the dead in living memory. The exclusion and inclusion of foods mark this period as families and communities face grief and consolation.

The moment of death is marked among Hindu communities by pouring water (collected from the river Ganges) or placing a *tulsi* (holy BASIL) leaf in the deceased's mouth. The Chettiars of Tamil Nadu pour milk and salted SESAME oil into the mouth of the deceased as they believe this prevents bloating of the body. The Badagas of the Nilgiris pour GHEE into the mouth.

Death rituals constitute the last of the *saṃskāra*, or rites of passage, in the Hindu way of life. The family re-enters the kitchen and resumes cooking only after the funeral or mourning period is over and upon completing a ritualistic purification of the space. The mourning generally lasts twelve days and is followed by a community feast on the thirteenth day. It is customary to avoid cooking meat during this period. The heirs (or father, brothers) offer balls of cooked rice called *piṇḍa* as a symbol of food for eleven days to the spirit. While the Vedas do not mention this, ritual manuals such as the *Āpastamba Sūtra*, *Baudhāyana Sūtra* or *Ghriya Sūtra* explain such practices. On death, the mortal body is lost and it is thought that the spirit regains a form by metaphysically eating a *piṇḍa* and proceeds into the afterlife. *Piṇḍa* are dressed with black sesame seeds, a drop of ghee and yogurt and served to the spirit during the ritual and eventually cast into flowing water. In Bengal, the family offers a *piṇḍa* of cooked rice and fish to the deceased's soul.

Across communities, the day of the death itself is marked with mourning and the funeral. Family, friends and community members arrive to offer condolences. The kitchen is immediately isolated and the family pauses cooking activities. An old saying goes, 'The fire in the house is not lit until the fire in the cremation pyre has gone out.' In some communities, neighbours and family bring food and host the guests who have arrived. Today, it is common to seek the help of caterers to bring food for the family and guests during this period. Food served on the day of the death is light, soothing and comforting with most families choosing a *moong* dal khichri or a light gruel of WHEAT prepared in their regional style.

Traditional foods made with little flavouring, often a mix of CUMIN and black pepper (see PEPPER, BLACK), are prepared. A SWEET must be prepared each day to be offered to the deceased soul and the family who have gathered for the mourning. It is interesting to note that some families cook with native vegetables and avoid CHILLIES and vegetables introduced to India after the Columbian exchange during this period. Oil is also avoided in many Hindu communities. Hence, there are no frying and tempering of spices in oil. On the tenth day, a meal without salt is cooked. Salt is considered the essence of life and a saltless meal symbolizes the liberation of the soul from worldly attachment. The mourning period is shorter among non-Brahmin Hindu castes and the foods may not adhere to a strict ritualistic code. Often, food preparations that the deceased was fond of are offered as food to the soul during the mourning period and in the following feast.

A feast to mark the end of the mourning period is unanimous, as all faiths advise resuming life. The feast includes foods that have been abstained from during the mourning period such as oil, turmeric, spices, meat, fried foods and sweets. Bengalis, mainly the upper castes, prepare *hobisshi* or *haabishaanyo*, a porridge of rice and native vegetables such as green BANANAS, pointed gourd (*Trichosanthes dioica*) and pumpkin cooked in a clay pot during this period. The food is usually *sattvic* (devoid of spices, ONION, GARLIC and meat) but ends with a feast that will include fish and meat on the thirteenth day for those who consume it. Among the Kashmiri Pandits, *mooli*, white RADISH, is offered on the fifth day after the death to the soul. On the tenth day, meat is cooked if the deceased consumed it. If this is not done, meat may not be consumed during the yearlong mourning period. Among the Pahadi communities of Himachal Pradesh and Uttarakhand, VADAS of black lentils are an important preparation served with *kadhi*, while nuances of abstinence from the kitchen and other mourning rites may vary.

Sikhs visit the gurdwara soon after the funeral where prayers are offered and the grieving family distribute *kharah prasad*, a HALWA made with equal portions of whole wheat, butter and sugar. On the thirteenth day, they organize a feast for the relatives and friends. Chettiars mark the second day after death with a ritual called *kal eduthu pilal*, where a special lentil pancake and boiled eggs are served. On the fifth day, a Brahmin priest is invited to complete the funerary rites by offering *piṇḍa*. Among PARSIS, the first three days of mourning are marked by abstaining from meat. *Dhansak*, a one-pot dish of lentils, vegetables and meat, is served to the guests and the bereaved hosts, becoming the first meat dish to be eaten after death. From the Avestan word *staomi*, for 'praise', *stum* is a special ritual for food offerings. In this ritual, a Zarathushtian who observes the strict rules of ritual purity cooks food for the deceased soul and the family of the departed one. *Papra* and *bakhra* are two dishes prepared as part of '*stum*'. The *stum* ritual is generally performed three times a day, at breakfast, lunch and dinner/supper. In the breakfast *stum*, TEA or milk and certain sweetmeats connected with breakfast like *ravo* (semolina custard) are offered. Lunch and supper *stum* include rice, lentils, vegetables, occasionally meat and sweet dishes.

Among the Jews in India (see BENE ISRAELIS), *shiva*, a seven-day mourning period following the death of a family member, ends with a feast to the community. On the day of the death itself, the family does not enter the kitchen until after the burial. The mourners eat a hard-boiled egg as an edible reminder of the circle of life. The extended family and community provide the first meal, *seudat havra'ah*, the meal of consolation to the bereaved. *Shiva* is also marked with keeping a vigil when two meals, often with chicken and mutton cooked in traditional spices, are served to the deceased. *Birde*, a dish of rice and sprouted field beans is served. Mourning families mark the end of *shiva* by consuming a fig, a banana and a glass of milk.

The ANGLO-INDIANS of Fort Kochi, influenced by their time as a Dutch colony, bake *breudher*, a ceremonial bread, which has earned the sobriquet 'bread of the dead'. Traditionally, *breudher* was served for the ritualistic breakfast following a Memorial Mass on the seventh day after a bereavement. The SINDHIS mark their mourning with simple foods like *khichri* and *kadhi*, avoiding onion and garlic to remain *sattvic* for the period. On the eleventh day, *tayri*, a sweet rice dish prepared with FENNEL seeds and NUTS, is cooked and shared with the family. The BOHRA Muslims mark the completion of the burial with a quiet meal of bread dipped in milk, *moong* dal khichri and *kadhi*. Dal *gosht*, a curry of lentils and mutton, is served frequently during this period among Bohra Muslims today.

The age and cause of death too affect the traditions around it. If the deceased is an older adult having lived a fulfilled life, the death is considered a moment of accomplishment of life itself and celebrated with sweets. Sikhs celebrate the liberation of this soul with halwa and puri served to all the mourners. Sindhis celebrate centenarians by distributing *boondi* or sweets on the third day.

People continue to remember the dead in different ways. The death anniversary is observed among Hindus by the surviving sons. *Piṇḍa* continues to remain an essential offering during this ritual, which is called *shraddha*. A feast is prepared at the end of the ceremony to serve the priests and guests. The meal cooked for a *shraddha* feast is unique. Turmeric, which has an important presence in all auspicious events, is completely avoided. Other communities may or may not observe such an anniversary. Hindus remember their ancestors during *pitru paksha* (*mahalaya paksha, sola shraddha*), the second fortnight of the Hindu calendar month of Bhadrapada. A *sattvic* diet or fasting is common during this period and special foods like *anarsa* are prepared. Families organize special feasts before a wedding in the family or other auspicious occasions to appease ancestors. Tamilians cook a feast for a *samaradhanai* puja in memory of the deceased, and, sometimes, a *sumangali* puja is organized in memory of young women who had an untimely death, women who died married or remained spinsters. Goan Catholics organize *bhikareanchem jevon*, a meal for beggars. These feasts are mainly regional delicacies – among Goan Catholics, meat, fish, rice and a special curry called *samarachi kodi* with dry prawns and *amsol*; among Tamils, sweets like *obbattu* or *adhirasam* are cooked for this feast. Parsis prepare *varadh-pattar* (*varadh-vara*), a special preparation made and consecrated at the time of a wedding. It is a simple sweet of flour, semolina, ghee and sugar and cooked for the ancestors as a symbolic invitation to preside at the wedding.

Local brews and fermented spirits are an essential part of funeral rites for many communities where brewing is a part of their culinary repertoire (see ALCOHOL). Cashew *feni* in Konkan, toddy in parts of Andhra Pradesh and Telangana, *apong* and other rice beers in the Northeast are a part of communities' expression of love for their departed.

Pregnancy and childbirth

Conception, pregnancy, birthing and postpartum care are steeped in traditional beliefs and practices across India. A wide variety of customs and practices across the country reflect socio-economic status, caste and religious affiliation. The role of women in India's primary healthcare system as Accredited Social Health Activist (ASHA), Auxiliary Nurse Midwife (ANM) and Anganwadi workers is crucial to maternal health care in rural areas. They ensure health and nutrition support during pregnancy and early childhood in many of the inaccessible parts of the country. Modern maternal healthcare facilities are available in urban areas although economic disparity may influence accessibility.

Pregnancy is often determined by early physiological changes in the woman's body in consultation with other women in the family before being medically confirmed. Many customs followed during this period aim at safe birthing and positive outcomes of the pregnancy. There has been a widespread belief of 'eating down' – the belief that pregnant women should eat less than before pregnancy or should not increase their diet during pregnancy mainly to limit the baby's size and avoid a difficult delivery (Brems and Berg 1989; Chatterjee 1991). Nutritional deficiency of the mother has remained one of the most critical concerns in this context.

Many foods are consumed to manage morning sickness in the first trimester. POMEGRANATE seeds, a warm tea of anise and AJOWAN, onions crushed with MINT leaves and salt, and fresh juices of GINGER and *AMLA* (Indian gooseberry) are well-known recipes.

Hindus celebrate conception and the first pregnancy with many rituals and a feast for the family. These rituals are typically organized in the seventh or ninth month of the pregnancy and are variously known as *godhbharai* (much of North India), *shaad* (Bengal), *dohale jevan* (Maharashtra), *valaikaappu* (Tamil Nadu), *seemantham* (much of South India) or *agarni* (Parsi). Playful games to divine (guess) the gender of the unborn child are played by women folk during this ceremony in many communities. The mother-to-be draws foods hidden on a plate or a bag through a game of chance; for example, rice and sweet *poli* are cooked for *dohale jevan*, and drawing rice symbolizes a male progeny while *poli* could mean a female child. Tamil Brahmins play a similar game where drawing *APPAMS* symbolizes a female child and *kozhukattai* a male one for the mother-to-be.

Parsis celebrate *agarni* in the seventh month with *agarni no lavro*, a sweet of *boondi* (fried beads of *besan*) soaked in an aromatic sugar syrup, gathered and set in tall conical moulds. Family and friends are a part of this ceremony and a feast follows. Christian communities in Tamil Nadu mark this stage of the pregnancy as *sooliazhappu*, when the mother-to-be is fed foods she likes at a festive gathering of family and friends. Among Chettiars, such a ritual is contingent on its traditional practice in the family. When it is conducted, *marundhu kudikaradhu* forms an important part of the ceremony where an elder from the family gathers special herbs from the village and they are crushed to extract a juice (the *marundhu*) which is offered to the mother-to-be.

The humoural classification of foods as 'hot' or 'cold', widely acknowledged in India, emerges as an essential food concept during pregnancy. The criteria for the classification are very regional, often without much consensus. However, women avoid foods considered 'hot' during the pregnancy for fear of inducing abortion or harming the foetus and prefer 'cold' foods in this period. There is a general perception of some foods like sesame seeds, millets, horse gram, spicy foods including higher intake of chillies and foods of animal origin like eggs, fish and meat as being 'hot'; hence, to be consumed in moderation during this period. Women fear that PAPAYA may induce abortion and a similar attitude may also be towards JACKFRUIT (Karnataka and Tamil Nadu), PINEAPPLE (parts of Tamil Nadu), banana (Andhra Pradesh, Telangana and parts of Gujarat) or castor oil.

Indigenous knowledge on beneficial foods for pregnant women abounds; nuts, ghee and fresh vegetables are advised. Milk is considered an important source of calcium and is recommended infused with SAFFRON and aromatic spices like CARDAMOM.

Craving certain foods is the most notable phenomenon universally but is a distinct, recurring theme in the Indian food narrative around pregnancy. Many women crave *achar*, Indian-style pickles, and candy of sour fruits like TAMARIND; the former is cautiously eaten in moderation. Pregnancy-induced pica, a craving for nutritionally void foods, is also noticed in many regions, eating clay being the most common, together with eating tamarind seeds, and also the ash from the *chulha*, traditional wood or biomass fuelled stoves (see COOKING AND DINING). In the weeks leading to the end of the pregnancy, there is a widespread belief that consuming cow's butter and ghee as fat will aid birthing. When back pain and labour set in, the midwife may give castor oil to accelerate uterine contractions.

In most of rural India, women's daily diet is seldom nutritionally adequate and is only worsened by dietary constraints and socio-economic conditions during pregnancy and lactation. The avoidance of many nutritious foods due to 'eating down' and notions of safe foods results in a restrictive diet that could affect the overall health and well-being during pregnancy, childbirth and infancy. These are particularly prevalent among the lower socio-economic and disadvantaged groups who have little to no access to modern medical facilities, knowledge and antenatal care.

Families celebrate the moment of childbirth with special foods. Tamil Brahmins prepare *okkarai*, a mealy sweet of Bengal gram and jaggery; Parsis prepare *tafteh*, a warm sweet soup of eggs, turmeric and seeds thickened with a roux, which is served to guests visiting the mother and child. In Gujarat, *katlu*, a LADDU of nuts, herbs and *gond*, is gifted to the young mother. In Tamil Nadu and Kerala, some communities send gifts of paddy panicles and a coin to close family members to share the arrival of a new child. Today, though some of these practices may have been discontinued, they can still be observed in temple festivals to mark the birth of Gods.

The preparation for healthy lactation begins during pregnancy. Breast-feeding is acknowledged as best for an infant's growth, but formulated infant feeds have steadily grown in the Indian market in the last few decades. In most of rural India, women health workers drive efforts to fill the gaps in knowledge and skills in postpartum care. The lack of such necessary support structures leaves women without access to accurate information. These workers also help mobilize communities to encourage much-needed privacy and time for rest and maternal bonding.

Studies have shown that postpartum mothers in the rural areas of India are not allowed a substantial meal for the first few days after birth, for reasons varying from quick recovery after childbirth, fast shrinking of the uterus to metaphysical reasons of 'ritual pollution'. Across the country, a period of confinement following childbirth, typically lasting forty days, is defined by codes of ritual, seclusion and foods dictated by family traditions, and there are vast regional differences.

Despite socio-economic vagaries, there is a rich postpartum food culture seen across the country. This food is influenced by four factors: the mother's need for a high-calorie diet to enrich her milk, digestives for the mother to cope with such a diet, the mother's recuperation and healing after pregnancy with calcium and iron-rich foods, and galactagogues to enhance lactation during the early days of breastfeeding.

Prelacteal foods are a common practice in many communities. Muslims perform *tahneek* soon after the baby is born and before the initiation of breastfeeding. A softened DATE is rubbed into the infant's upper palate by a respected member of the family in hopes that attributes of this individual will transfer to the child. HONEY may also be used. Among the Hindus, jaggery dipped in ghee is used to write the word *om* on the baby's tongue. *Ghutti*, a herbal formulation mixed with breast milk, is commonly given to the infant in North India.

Colostrum has long been considered unhealthy for the newborn and is expressed by hand and discarded, thus delaying breastfeeding initiation and leading to the loss of the nutrient-rich colostrum. The infant may be fed cow's milk, water or honey during this initial, very important period for the establishment of lactation. However, campaigns on the benefits of colostrum are helping change practices in rural areas.

Various herbs and foods are used as galactagogues that may help increase breastmilk supply, typically by increasing prolactin levels in the mother. Although the use of galactagogues remains rich in communities, it is seldom attested by the medical community. The most common ingredients seen across recipes are: *shatavari* (*Asparagus racemosus*), FENUGREEK, cumin, *gond* (tragacanth gum), *saunth* (dried ginger), garlic, NIGELLA seeds, dried dates and guar gum. Cow's milk infused with extracts of fresh turmeric roots, *saunth* and crushed garlic mixed with milk are, perhaps, the most well-known galactogogues. The knowledge of such recipes remains in the maternal kitchen, with women as key stakeholders in preserving the recipes as living traditions. They use ingredients from their pantry in an established knowledge of food as medicine. Most of the foods given during this period classify as warming foods in Ayurveda, endorsing a practice of keeping the mother's body warm and consuming warm foods to promote lactation, as is seen in many communities across the world. Ghee, jaggery and garlic are notably recurring ingredients in many of these recipes.

Nut and spice blends like *batteesa*, *panjiri*, *kevka* are prepared in bulk quantities, enough to last the first forty-five days after birth and are consumed in different ways. *Achwani* is a tea of ajowan, sweetened with jaggery and mixed with a blend of dry fruits like almond, cashew, raisins, *chironji* and *godambi* (*Semecarpus anacardium*) fried in ghee and mixed with *kamar kas* (*Butea frondosa*) and long pepper (see PEPPER, LONG). A variation of this recipe is *jirwani*, where cumin seeds are added. *Harira* is a warm tea of jaggery infused with *saunth*, cumin and turmeric with the addition of nuts like almonds and cashews.

In North India, herbal powders are prepared by women and used as part of a postpartum diet. *Battisa* and *keoka* are good examples. *Battisa* is a blend of thirty-two spices, most notably the roots of long pepper, *Mimosa pudica* and *Butea monosperma* among others.

This powder is mixed with desiccated COCONUT, roasted wheat flour, ghee and jaggery and gathered into laddus. *Keoka* is a blend of CORIANDER seeds, cumin, ajowan and *saunth*, toasted, powdered and consumed by young mothers in many communities. This blend is versatile and is added to various sweet dishes and daily food like roti, puris or porridge. *Panjiri* is a blend of nuts like almonds, cashews and many of the spices mentioned above mixed with roasted wheat flour, ghee and crystalline jaggery, achieving a coarse, granola-like texture. When prepared for postpartum use, *panjiri* notably includes *gond* and roots of long pepper. *Kudimilagu* masala is a blend of ajowan, *saunth* and other herbs. Popular with coastal communities in Tamil Nadu, it is used to season *sura meen kuzhambu* (shark curry).

Most postpartum foods use the metaphor of commonly known regional preparations enriched with these dense nutrient extracts, which makes its preparation easy in the home kitchen. Laddus are a common preparation. A base of equal parts of ghee and jaggery – with s*aunth*, powdered dry ginger, makes *sunthavda* in Maharashtra or *saunth ke* laddu elsewhere in North India; with roasted and powdered *gond* to make *gond ke* laddu. *Battisa* or *keoka* powders enrich these laddus. Women consume *paushtik* laddu, with nuts, *gond* and fenugreek seeds, during pregnancy in Maharashtra. *Lehgyam* is an electuary prepared by cooking herbs in a jaggery syrup to yield a thick, shelf-stable compound. *Thengain pookkula lehyam* is prepared from a paste of young coconut flowers in Kerala while *prasava legyam* is prepared in Tamil Nadu. Chewing betel leaves helps to reduce the stomach's bloating, is a good digestive and a source of calcium for lactating mothers. Mothers resort to pantry staples for colic pain relief in infants. ASAFOETIDA mixed with sesame oil or betel leaf coated with castor oil is warmed and placed on the baby's stomach.

Religion, disparity in access and availability, and caste and gender-based discrimination contribute to understanding the role of foods available to the mother during pregnancy. Many conceptions and cultural practices regarding healthy and harmful foods exist, and there is a high level of trust in community practices and home remedies. However, these may also pose nutritional challenges for the mother and child.

Coming of age

The onset of puberty in girls is an important occasion that is marked by various rituals and ceremonies throughout India. Tamil Brahmins make *vella puttu*, a sweet of wheat and jaggery with a mealy texture, to celebrate the start of a girl's puberty. In Karnataka, girls are fed a diet rich in finger millet and sesame to prepare their bodies for womanhood. Among coastal communities in Tamil Nadu, *alapu maavu urundai*, a sweetmeat of rice flour, *saunth* and *karupatti* (palm sugar), and *ulundhu kali,* a thick porridge of ground black lentils, rice, coconut and *karupatti* is prepared to celebrate the day. The young girl is fed a diet rich in eggs and *moringa* (drumstick) leaves for a month to help her body adjust to the new changes. The extended family may bring *ulundu soru*, a gruel of black lentils and rice cooked with fenugreek, *saunth* and coconut, and served with *kozhi kari* (chicken curry).

The Chettiars of Tamil Nadu prepare a meal of *kathirikai kootu* (AUBERGINE stew), boiled egg, *vazhakkai poriyal* (stir-fried plantain) and lentils to feed the young girl. Interestingly, this menu is repeated when the girl has her first menstrual cycle after getting married. To address the girl's need for more nutrition, *aadi koozh* (*kummayam*), a halwa, is prepared by roasting black lentils flour and jaggery. This, they believe, strengthens the pelvic muscles. A feast called *samnjadhu vadikkararadhu* may also be organized for family and relatives where many regional delicacies are served to the guests.

Parsis prepare *tafteh* to serve to guests on the occasion. As part of the ritual, a small knot of rice, which is a symbol of fertility, is tied in the corner of the girl's sari *pallav* before sprinkling it with rosewater (see FLOWER WATERS).

Entering puberty is an important ritual for boys in the three so-called 'twice-born' *varnas* of Brahmin, Kshatriya and Vaishya who observe *upanayanam,* an important event described in the Hindu *saṃskāras*, rites of passage. Also known as the sacred thread ceremony, it is typically performed for boys starting at the age of seven and traditionally marked the start of their formal education in the liturgical texts. Here, the boy is fed a meal of rice, dal, ghee and PAPAD as a symbolic last meal before the *upanayanam* ceremony is performed.

Weddings

People throughout India, as in other parts of the world, celebrate conjugal alliances with rituals, celebrations and feasting. The duration and scale of the celebration with the rituals and traditions observed are intrinsic to the communities involved in the betrothal. Most weddings are organized by two mutually agreeing parties, although many tribes acknowledge that eloping or kidnapping is a legitimate form of marriage.

Food and food articles are inseparable from the ethos of wedding celebrations. From the acceptance of proposals, engagement, pre-nuptial festivities to weddings and post-wedding customs, special foods mark the moment. Many are steeped in symbolism, others hark back to the communities' past. Traditionally, and even today in rural India, traditional food and regional delicacies are a part of the wedding menu. However, today weddings in urban India are seen as a stage to show off a plethora of exotic cuisines. Traditional food of the communities may be cooked only for the main ceremony with all the other events leading up to the wedding offering a variety of typical Indian, foreign and fusion foods.

Leaves like the betel (see PAAN), banana, MANGO, NEEM, *tulsi* (holy BASIL) and *durva* grass (*Cynodon dactylon*) are intrinsically woven into the tapestry of Indian weddings. Betel leaves are a recurring motif: a pair of betel leaves with areca nuts is exchanged between the families as a token to confirm a wedding among many Hindu communities and tribes. Hindus distribute invitations for the wedding with an arrangement of betel leaves and areca nuts together with coconut and turmeric forming an important part of the invite. The betel is associated with the Trinity – Brahma, Vishnu and Shiva; Brahma: areca nut, Vishnu: betel leaf, and Shiva: lime. A Bengali bride covers her face with a pair of betel leaves before circumambulating her husband seven times and revealing her face to her husband after this.

Eating paan (betel quid) is another expression of auspiciousness and joy. In Tamil Nadu, the bride's brother gives the ceremonial first betel to the couple to chew. This ritual is called *thamboola charvanam*. Paan is considered a sensual food that induces fertility and increases virility and hence wedding ceremonies across religions in India have incorporated it. It finds mention in the *Kamasutra* as an aphrodisiac for men and women. Offering of betel quid is also very common in Muslim wedding traditions. Christian communities may choose to do this depending on their denomination.

Turmeric is perhaps the most quintessential food article in Hindu weddings. A paste of turmeric is applied on the bride and groom as part of preparatory celebrations. Turmeric is valued for its antibacterial virtues while its deep, staining yellow colour stands for auspiciousness. A cotton thread stained in turmeric and fingers of turmeric rhizomes are used for the *thaali* or *mangalsutra*, the wedding necklace that is tied around the neck of the bride. Subsequently, gold chains with symbolic pendants are worn as the *mangalsutra* for daily use. Among many Christian communities too, turmeric is applied on the groom and bride to mark the start of the wedding festivities.

Mango leaves are strung as borders on doorways and when in season, the flowers and fruits make an appearance on the wedding feast. In South India, coconut and banana leaves figure prominently in the decorations; the coconut frond is fashioned into decorations for the *pandal* (the stage where the marriage ceremony takes place) and coconut flowers are a potent symbol of fertility. Coconuts of brass or silver are used as toys in the playful wedding ritual *nalangu*, where the bride, groom and their families are acquainted with each other. Banana flowers too are important symbols of fertility and plenty in this context.

Rice and puffed rice are used in numerous rituals to symbolize wealth and prosperity for the couple. The couple offer puffed rice to the sacrificial fire during the wedding ritual as the fire (*agni*) is personified as a witness to the wedding. The guests bless the couple with turmeric-coated grains of rice. As the bride leaves her maternal home, she throws rice over her head symbolizing her departure to a new home, leaving behind blessings and prosperity to the home that has nourished her. The young bride enters her new home by tipping over a pot filled with rice.

Fish is a very important motif most prominently seen among Bengalis and Parsis. In Bengal, the groom's family take a large *rohu* fish with them. The fish is decked up as a bride, draped in a beautiful silk saree and decorated with jewellery, vermilion, paan and some turmeric paste just as a bride. Among Parsis, fresh uncooked fish was included as part of a traditional platter called *dahi machli ni ses* along with the other symbolic items. This has now been replaced with the *mawa ni boi*, a confectionary trompe l'oeil of *boi* (*Mugil cephalus*), which caught off the coast of Gujarat and is specially enjoyed by Parsis. The decorated fish here signifies good luck and prosperity. Certain foods like bitter gourd are unanimously avoided in weddings across India. Among some Christian denominations, fish and eggs are avoided while Hindu Brahmins avoid bottle gourd, snake gourd, plantains, and rarely, ash gourd.

Special tablescapes and platters are set up to consecrate the wedding stage and these include important foods, articles of silver, flowers and fruits. In Kerala, a barrel of paddy takes centre-stage and a lush bunch of coconut flowers are arranged on it like a fountain. Tamil Brahmins set up a plate called *seeru*, where a pair of conical moulds called *paruppu thenga* is filled with a variety of sweets such as *manoharam* and *pottukadalai urundai*, typically made of fried chickpea flour soaked in jaggery syrup. In Maharashtra, platters of sweets and savouries like laddu, *chiwda*, *karanjya* and *anaarse* prepared by the bride's family are arranged for all to see. Roman Catholic and Protestant Christians exchange *thattu,* a tray of fruits, *kalakand* (crystalline sugar lumps), betel leaves and money at the time of engagement. On the day of the wedding, the bride carries *maruveedu neetu*, a platter of sweet and savoury foods, including *adhirasam* and *murukku*. In Chettinad, the bride's family arranges a grand scene of a variety of sweet and savoury preparations together with fruits in counts of 51 or 101 pieces per item.

Sugar is an important ingredient in wedding display and edibles. In Maharashtra, sugar sculptures are prepared for *rukhwat*, an elaborate display set up by the bride's family. Similarly, colourful *chivukula* (lit. birds) are made in Andhra Pradesh with sugar fondant and arranged on plates for display. In Karnataka too, elaborate *sakkare acchu*, moulded sugar figurines, are made for weddings. *Batasha*, a meringue-like sugar crisp, is distributed among Gujaratis and Parsis.

Weddings are important moments to establish the family's heritage in art and craft. In Bengal, *nakshi pitha*, intricately carved cakes of rice flour deep-fried and dipped in sugar syrup, and *goyna bori*, sun-dried cakes of black lentils fashioned like pieces of jewellery (*goyna* meaning jewellery), are artistically made for weddings. In Tamil Nadu, a soft dough of black lentils is made into spiral-shaped savoury snacks called *kai murukku,* the name borrowing from the small twists (*murukku* in Tamil) made on the dough by hand. Such *murukku* made for weddings are elaborate with some reaching up to eleven or sixteen spiral lines. Among the Muslims of Malabar (see MAPPILAS), hard to make foods like *panineer petti* (lit. rose box), an assembled sweet of layers of pancake and a filling of cashews, eggs and cardamom; and *panjara patta*, a delicate pancake made from the froth of the batter, were specially prepared for the groom. In the Marathwada region of Maharashtra, women folk hand roll wheat pastas, *valvat* or *gavhale*, in myriad shapes for the bride's trousseau.

Among Banjaras, marriage preliminaries are formally completed with '*gole khayero*' (eating jaggery) between the two families, signifying the acceptance of the engagement. The wedding is followed by a feast, called *ghot*, with meat taking centre-stage. A Tamil engagement is concluded with *paal theratti paal*, a sweet of reduced milk solids sweetened with sugar.

Food in the days leading to the wedding is usually simple, in preparation for a large feast on the wedding day. Parsis observe khichri *no divas* (lit. the day to eat khichri) on the third day before the wedding. Malabar Muslims enjoy subtle *nei choru* (ghee rice).

The Hindu wedding ceremony is done at a pre-ordained time called *muhurat* which may be chosen in the morning or in the evening depending on the community. Most communities in Tamil Nadu, Kerala and Karnataka have a morning *muhurat* followed by a lunch, while most North Indian communities have an evening *muhurat* followed by dinner. Wedding feasts are usually grandiose affairs where impressing and satisfying the guests are seen as the main purpose. A Parsi *lagan nu bhonu* starts with the sweet and spicy *lagan nu achaar*, a pickle of CARROTS, milk solids and spices; includes *patra ni machhi*, a delicacy of steamed pomfret among others; and ends with *lagan nu* custard.

In Tamil Nadu, the Hindu wedding feast, *kalyana sappadu,* is a delicious spread served on a banana leaf and eaten delicately with one's fingers. Dal and ghee are served first followed by small portions of the various side dishes. *Palpayasam,* a sweet pudding of milk reduced by caramelization and sugar, is served as a palate cleanser before the final course and is the most important sweet dish of the day. *Sadya* in Kerala is a similar spread with *palada pradhaman*, a thick jaggery sweetened porridge with tiny bits of rice pasta, being the most important sweet dish presented on the leaf. For Christians from Tamil Nadu and Kerala, *avial*, a coconut-based stew of vegetables, is an important preparation. It is a symbol of abundance and prosperity.

The end of the wedding is also marked with food for the guests to take home. Among Chettiars, *thavala vadai*, small deep-fried dumplings of Bengal gram, are served to signal the end of the ceremony and guests taking the cue, head home. Small bags with sweet and savoury delicacies, betel leaves, areca nuts and coconut are distributed to guests as they take leave. Many communities have a custom of packing food for the groom's family as they leave the bride's home. Known as *kattu sadam* or *kattu choru*, lots of food, particularly *citrannam*, rice dishes flavoured with tamarind, lime or yogurt, are prepared.

This custom stems from the time families travelled long distances and having some food for the journey back was a sign of hospitality.

The first year of marriage, too, is marked with festivals like Pongal (Sankranti) and Diwali taking a new dimension to honour the groom and the bride. The symbolism of sugar continues, and in Maharashtra the new bride wears halwa *dagine*, jewellery fashioned from sugar and sesame seeds, for her first Sankranti as a married woman, in hope for sweet times ahead.

The Indian wedding scene has seen rapid cultural change in the last three decades and assimilation of cultures and traditions from all over India and abroad is common. Today wedding feasts are incomplete without a CHINESE INDIAN or chaat (typical STREET FOOD) themed evening, providing an element of the exotic – North Indian weddings offer South Indian staples and vice versa. The urban millennials organize destination weddings where exotic foods and drinks take centre-stage.

Priya Mani

- Badhwar, Inderjit. 'For Most Indian Widows a "Normal Human Being's Life" Is Not Something Even to Be Dreamt of'. *India Today*, 15 November 1987.
- Bandyopadhyay, Mridula. 'Impact of Ritual Pollution on Lactation and Breastfeeding Practices in Rural West Bengal, India'. *International Breastfeeding Journal* 4, no. 2 (26 March 2009). doi:10.1186/1746-4358-4-2.
- Banerjee, Tupur. 'Gender in Food: Food Habits of Bengali Women'. *Sahapedia*, 5 September 2016. Available online: https://www.sahapedia.org/gender-food-food-habits-of-bengali-women (accessed 30 April 2022).
- Bhula, Pooja. 'Delicacies at a Dirge'. *DNA*, 29 October 2017.
- Brems, Susan and Alan Berg. 'Eating Down during Pregnancy: Nutrition, Obstetrics and Cultural Considerations in the Third World'. Discussion paper prepared for the UN Advisory Group on Nutrition, Population and Human Resource Division, Washington DC, 1988.
- Chatterjee, Meera. 'Towards Better Health for Indian Women: The Dimensions, Determinants and Consequences of Female Illness and Death'. Paper prepared for the World Bank Economic Sector Work on Women and Health, 1991.
- Ghosh-Jerath, Suparna, Ridhima Kapoor, Satabdi Barman, Geetanjali Singh, Archna Singh, Shauna Downs and Jessica Fanzo. 'Traditional Food Environment and Factors Affecting Indigenous Food Consumption in Munda Tribal Community of Jharkhand, India'. *Frontiers in Nutrition* 7 (1 February 2021): 600470. doi:10.3389/fnut.2020.600470.
- Gupta, Varud and Devang Singh. *Bhagwaan Ke Pakwaan: Food of the Gods*. Gurugram, Haryana: Penguin Random House India, 2019.
- Guttman, Vered. 'Food and Death: A Look at the Tasty and Tearful Tradition of Jewish Mourning'. *Haaretz*, 19 July 2018.
- Jayarajan, Sreedevi. 'The Big Fat Malabar Muslim Wedding Is All About Food and How'. *The News Minute*, 20 February 2021. Available online: https://www.thenewsminute.com/article/big-fat-malabar-muslim-wedding-all-about-food-and-how-143834 (accessed 30 April 2022).

- Karanjia, Ramiyar P. 'Marriage Customs and Ritual'. *n.d.* Available online: https://ramiyarkaranjia.com/marriage-customs-and-ritual/ (accessed 30 April 2022).
- Lal, B. Suresh. 'Tribal Marriage Systems in Andhra Pradesh: A Study on Banjaras'. *Indian Journal of Social Development* 9, no. 2 (2009): 289–95.
- Laroia, Nirupama and Deeksha Sharma. 'The Religious and Cultural Bases for Breastfeeding Practices among the Hindus'. *Breastfeeding Medicine* 1, no. 2 (2006): 94–8.
- Lipovenko, Dorothy. 'From Hard Boiled Eggs to Indian Buffets: The Foods of Indian Shivas'. *Forward*, 4 January 2011. Available online: https://forward.com/food/134412/from-hard-boiled-eggs-to-indian-buffets-the-foods/ (accessed 30 April 2022).
- Mantche, Chandra. 'A Study on the Marriage System of the Tai-Khamtis'. *International Journal for Innovative Research in Multidisciplinary Field* 6, no. 4 (2020): 114–20. doi:10.2015/IJIRMF.2455.0620/202004022.
- McKenna, Kathleen M. 'The Practice of Prelacteal Feeding to Newborns among Hindu and Muslim Families'. *Journal of Midwifery & Women's Health* 54, no. 1 (2009): 78–81.
- Noble, William A. and Louisa B. Noble. 'Badaga Funeral Customs'. *Anthropos* 60, no. 1/6 (1965): 262–72.
- Petitet, Pascale Hancart and Vellore Pragathi. 'Ethnographical Views on the "Valaikappu": A Pregnancy Rite in Tamil Nadu'. *Indian Anthropologist* 37, no. 1 (2007): 117–45.
- Razdan, Vinayak. 'Rituals in Death'. *SearchKashmir*, 13 August 2013. Available online: https://searchkashmir.org/2013/08/rituals-in-death.html (accessed 30 April 2022).
- Routray, Sailen. 'What an Oriya Widow Can Eat'. *Contributions to Indian Sociology* 42, no. 2 (May 2008): 307–10.

SAFFRON

Saffron (Hindi *kesar*), the dried orange-red thin thread-like stigma of the crocus (*Crocus sativus*), is the world's most expensive spice. Each purple crocus flower has three stigmas and it takes more than a quarter of a million stigmas to make just 500 g of saffron. The harvesting is done by hand and is very labour-intensive. Saffron is prized for the unique aroma, taste and colour it gives to dishes.

The earliest saffron was a wild species which is believed to have originated in Greece. At that time, saffron was used in perfumes and for medicinal purposes. The Persians may have been the first to cultivate saffron for use in medicines and cosmetics and for flavouring food. From here its use and cultivation spread west to the Mediterranean and east to the Indus Valley.

Kashmir may have cultivated saffron as early as 500 BCE. According to a Buddhist legend, the first Buddhist apostle to Kashmir, Madhyantika, first planted saffron there. It was well established by the third century CE when a Chinese medical writer Wan Zhen makes note of saffron being grown in Kashmir, 'where people grow it principally to offer it to the Buddha. The flower withers after a few days, and then the saffron is obtained. It is valued for its uniform yellow colour. It can be used to aromatize wine.'

The soil and climate in Kashmir provide excellent conditions for growing the crocus. The purple flowers are harvested by hand in the autumn before the sun rises. Kashmiri saffron threads are extremely long with a thick head and an exceptionally deep red colour. Pampore, a town eleven km from Srinagar, is considered by many to produce the world's finest saffron. FAO (Food and Agriculture Organization) of the UN has named Kashmir (and regions in Afghanistan and Iran) to be 'Globally Important Agricultural Heritage Systems'. Unfortunately, drought and political strife are causing problems with the Kashmiri harvest. Production has declined and growers are finding it increasingly hard to engage in their trade.

During the time of the MUGHAL emperors, saffron became an important and luxurious spice. Many Mughal dishes were of Persian origin and saffron was used to flavour rice dishes such as BIRYANIS and PULAOS and colour the grains of rice a rich gold. Made into an infusion, saffron was sprinkled over finished dishes and decorated meats and BREADS baked in the tandoor. Saffron is sometimes added to kormas and vegetable dishes. In many desserts such as KHEER, KULFI and JALEBI, saffron bestows a golden hue.

In Hinduism, saffron paste is used to anoint the statues of deities. At Indian religious festivals, whether Hindu, Jain, Muslim or Christian, desserts coloured and flavoured with saffron are offered to the celebrants. Because of saffron's cultural significance, it was adopted as one of the official colours of the Indian flag.

Helen Saberi

- Ganeshram, Ramin. *Saffron: A Global History*. London: Reaktion Books, 2020.
- Willard, Pat. *Secrets of Saffron*. London: Souvenir Press, 2001.

SAHNI, JULIE

Julie Sahni (b. 1945), formerly Deepalakshmi Ranganathan Iyer, may not have the star power of Madhur Jaffrey, but she has been responsible for promoting and popularizing the food traditions of her mother country in the United States ever since she opened her pioneering cooking school at Brooklyn Heights, New York City in 1973, and then wrote her magisterial first book, *Classic Indian Cooking*, in 1980.

A Delhi School of Architecture graduate, Sahni left India in 1968 to pursue a master's in Urban Planning at Columbia University, where she met her ex-husband Virant Sahni, a physicist. Thereafter, juggling a marriage that disintegrated, raising a son as a single mother and doing a full-time job at the New York City Planning Commission, she opened her eponymous cooking school in the same year Jaffrey's *An Invitation to Indian Cooking* arrived in bookstores across the United States (and around the world).

According to Sahni, her workplace colleagues were the ones who encouraged her to launch the school at her home. A year after she started her cooking classes, Sahni became instantly famous after an article about her by Florence Fabricant appeared in *The New York Times*. Even then, as she spent her evenings teaching Americans how to cook Indian food, in the daytime, she was heading a task force responsible for standardizing New York's sidewalk cafes.

After her first book (which, when last counted, was into its forty-second print run in as many years) in which she famously said that Indian food was the 'easiest of all international cuisines', Sahni moved on to become a full-time chef at the trendy Indian and Bangladeshi restaurant, Nirvana Penthouse, in 1983. Eventually, she transitioned to a crowded career as teacher of Indian cookery, writer of acclaimed books (including *Indian Regional Classics* and *Moghul Microwave*) and articles in newspapers and magazines, instructor in universities, guest speaker and TV presenter, and curator of culinary tours to India for the students and faculty of the Culinary Institute of America and New York University.

A bundle of indefatigable energy, Sahni is said to be working on a book that catalogues the recipes of dishes created by the Indian DIASPORA in countries as diverse as Fiji and Trinidad & Tobago.

Sourish Bhattacharyya

- Sen, Mayukh. 'An Undersung Trailblazer of Indian Cooking'. *The New Yorker*, 30 October 2021.
- Shah, Khushbu. 'Julie Sahni's Second Act'. *Food & Wine*, 2 March 2020.

SALT

In India salt (mainly sodium chloride, Hindi *namak*) comes from several sources: sea brine, lake brine, subsoil brine and rock salt deposits. Before Independence in 1947, India had to import salt but today it is the third largest salt producer in the world and even exports its surplus to Asia and the Middle East. Over three-quarters of India's salt is produced in Gujarat, especially on the Gulf of Khambhat, followed by Tamil Nadu and Rajasthan. Most salt manufacturers are small producers. In Gujarat salt has been made for at least 5,000 years in a 9,000 square mile marshland called the Rann of Kutch. Salt is produced from inland lakes and the sea by draining the water into large shallow basins and letting it evaporate – originally by the heat of the sun but today mainly by artificial means. In recent years, climate change has begun to seriously disrupt the industry.

A highly valued salt is *kala namak*, black salt from Himachal Pradesh. It is pinkish brown when powdered and has a slightly smoky aroma. *Sendha namak* is a pink salt believed to have healthy properties and is used as a substitute for table salt in some Hindi fasts. Although the name means 'rock salt', it is produced from seawater. Another pink salt called Himalayan salt is a rock salt from Pakistan. Salt assumed ritual significance in ancient India. Its use was forbidden to students and widows and black salt was forbidden at the *shraddha* ceremony (see RITES OF PASSAGE).

In the early nineteenth century, the British prohibited Indians from collecting or selling salt and imposed a heavy tax on its sale. In 1930, Mahatma GANDHI led thousands of people on a march to the Arabian coast to illegally make salt from seawater. Similar marches took place in other parts of the subcontinent and sixty thousand people were arrested, including Gandhi himself. The following year, the Gandhi-Irwin agreement allowed anyone to produce salt as long as it was not sold.

Colleen Sen

- Kurlansky, Mark. *Salt: A World History*. London: Penguin Books, 2003.

SAMBAR

Sambar is a tart, lentil-based vegetable stew cooked almost daily in just about every home and popular restaurant in India's five southern states. Prepared with *arhar* or *toovar* dal (pigeon peas), vegetables (mainly yellow pumpkin, ash GOURD, AUBERGINE, OKRA, CARROTS, French beans and DRUMSTICKS), pearl ONIONS, whole red CHILLIES, TAMARIND pulp and the spice mix called sambar powder (see SPICE BOX), this stew is either eaten with rice at lunch or dinner, or served as an accompaniment to popular 'tiffin' or breakfast dishes such as DOSA, IDLI, VADA and *utthapam*.

The recorded history of this dish is somewhat fuzzy. One theory is that it was invented in the royal kitchen of Shahuji I Bhonsle (r. 1684–1712), the second Maratha ruler of Thanjavur, which, in present-day Tamil Nadu, is noted for its heritage temples and distinctive 'Tanjore' art. It is believed that Shahuji's cook tweaked the recipe of the popular Maharashtrian sweet-and-sour lentil preparation *amti*, replacing the KOKUM (*Garcinia indica*) that lends sourness to the dish with tamarind pulp, which is more commonly available in southern India. In this story, the dish is named after the person for whom it was first made, Shahuji I's cousin, Sambhaji, who was the second *chhatrapati* (sovereign) of the Maratha Empire founded by the much-revered Shivaji Maharaj. One chink in this theory is that Shahuji I's father (and founder of the Thanjavur branch of the Maratha Empire), Vyankoji or Ekoji I Bhonsle, was Shivaji's half-brother and not very fond of the most famous Maratha. It is possible, though, that Shahuji I was building bridges with Sambhaji and named sambar after the visiting Maratha chhatrapati as a show of respect.

K.T. ACHAYA draws our attention to a preparation named *huli*, which was uncannily similar to *sambar*, made with cooked *toovar dal* and boiled vegetables. It is mentioned in the 1648 biography of a local ruler, titled *Kanthirava Narasaraja Vijaya*, written by the Kannada scholar Govinda Vaidya. The word *huli* in Kannada could mean either 'tiger' or 'sourness'.

However it originated, sambar today is an essential part of the culinary culture of India's southern states. Whether one goes to an UDUPI RESTAURANT or to a family meal, sambar is as ubiquitous as dal is in the north and the east or *amti* is in Maharashtra. The recipe varies from one region to another – the website ArchanasKitchen.com lists twenty-seven variations, from *arachuvitta* with fresh ground spices and fresh COCONUT, to ones that are unique to Coimbatore, with drumsticks only; MANGALURU, with okra; Udupi, with ivy gourd and aubergine; and Andhra Pradesh, *mukkala pulusu* with *chana* (split chickpeas) and *urad* dal (split black gram). The ingredients may vary from black-eyed peas to drumstick leaves, but what makes them a part of the sambar family is that they all are lentil-based vegetable stews.

Sourish Bhattacharyya

- Daniyal, Shoaib. 'Food Feuds in India: Not Just the Rosogolla, the Sambar Also Has Dodgy Origins'. *Scroll.in*, 21 November 2017. Available online: https://scroll.in/article/858378/food-feuds-in-india-not-just-the-rosogolla-the-sambar-also-has-dodgy-origins (accessed 1 May 2022).
- Prasad, Shruti. '27 Best Sambar Recipes That You Can Try for Your South Indian Meals'. *ArchanasKitchen.com*, 20 June 2019. Available online: https://www.archanaskitchen.com/27-best-sambar-recipes-that-you-can-try-for-your-south-indian-meals (accessed 1 May 2022).

- Shekar, Anjana. 'How Thanjavur Maratha cuisine Found Favour in the South'. *The News Minute*, 1 June 2021. Available online: https://www.thenewsminute.com/article/how-thanjavur-maratha-cuisine-found-favour-south-149888 (accessed 1 May 2022).

SAMOSA

One of the most popular Indian dishes is the samosa – a deep-fried, or sometimes baked, triangle-shaped pastry filled with minced meat or vegetables, usually POTATOES. It is a popular tea-time snack, an omnipresent STREET FOOD and a staple of every reception, especially in North America where it sometimes reaches gigantic proportions (as large as six inches in diameter.)

Its origins lie in the Middle East where it was called *sambusak* – from the Arabic *se*, three, referring to its shape, and *ambos*, a kind of bread. A thirteenth-century Baghdadi cookbook, *Kitab al-Tabikh* (*The Book of Dishes*), has recipes for versions containing

FIGURE 39 SAMOSA. Samosas and chutney served at a roadside stand. Kaushalspeed/ Wikimedia Commons.

meat flavoured with CORIANDER, CUMIN, pepper (see PEPPER, BLACK), CINNAMON, MINT and pounded almonds; HALWA; and SUGAR and almonds. It likely reached India during the time of the Delhi Sultanates, a series of Central Asian dynasties who ruled India from 1206 to 1555. The poet Amir Khusrau (1253–1315), who served at the court of one of the Delhi Sultans, wrote a famous riddle:

Samosa kyun na khaya? Joota kyun na pehna?
Talaa na tha
Translation: Why wasn't the samosa eaten? Why wasn't the shoe worn?
The samosa wasn't fried (*talaa*), the shoe didn't have a sole (also called *talaa*.)

Generally, the North Indian Muslim version tends to be smaller and filled with minced meat while the Hindu version is larger and filled with vegetables, often potatoes and peas, or sometimes *KHOYA* (dried milk solids) or *moong* dal. CHUTNEYS are a common accompaniment. In West Bengal and East India, the version called *singhara* is smaller and sometimes contains peanuts, cauliflower and raisins. The flakey square-shaped Hyderabadi *luqmi* has a meat filling. In Karnataka, ONION and keema (minced meat) samosas are popular while a Gujarati version called the *patti* samosa has a cabbage filling. Everywhere, samosa is a popular street food either served by itself with a cup of TEA or crumbled as part of a chaat, a family of savoury snacks made with fried dough and other ingredients.

Colleen Sen

- Al-Baghdadi, Muhammad Bin Al-hasan Bin Muhammad Bin Al-karim. *A Baghdad Cookery Book* [Arabic orig. *Kitāb al-Tabīkh*]. 1226, translated by Charles Perry. Totnes, Devon: Prospect Books, 2005.
- Pal, Sanchari. 'History of the Samosa, India's Favourite Street Snack'. *The Better India*, 4 January 2017. Available online: https://www.thebetterindia.com/80824/samosa-history-india/ (accessed 1 May 2022).

SANDESH

Bengalis are famous for their love of *mishti*, or SWEETS, and the apogee of the Bengali sweetmakers' art is sandesh. The word means 'news' or 'message', from the practice of sending food, particularly sweets, with a messenger as a gift. Like many Bengali sweets, sandesh is made from *CHHANA*, sometimes translated as 'curds', made by splitting milk with a souring agent. This technique was likely borrowed from the Portuguese cheesemakers who settled in Bengal in the early sixteenth century, although *chhana* was known in India much earlier.

The next step is to mix the *chhana* with sugar, stirring it gently in a large conical shaped pan in a little clarified butter over low to medium heat until the mixture thickens and becomes smooth. Small variations in the length of cooking are said to change the taste of the final product. Some afficionados believe *chhana* prepared over a wood-fuelled fire has more flavour than that made over coal. Although cow milk is considered superior to buffalo milk, some sweet makers add a certain proportion of buffalo milk to add body and texture.

In a professional establishment, flavouring, spices and colouring are added to parts of the *chhana* and distributed among the *moiras* (sweet makers). With great dexterity, they shape the individual pieces of sandesh by hand into ovals or balls or press them into pretty moulds shaped like flowers, fruits or shells. Sandesh is dry and ranges in texture from soft and spongy to very hard. Top-quality sandesh has a delicate complex flavour that must be carefully savoured.

A shop opened by Bhola Moira in 1851 seems to have been the first to sell sandesh. With the rise of an affluent middle class in the nineteenth century, sweet makers vied for their custom by developing and promoting new varieties. Other early sweet-makers include Makhlan Lal, S.K. Modak, Bhim Chandra Nag, Nabin Chandra Das and Sen Mahasay, the last three of which still operate today.

There are more than a hundred varieties of sandesh, with names that reflect their flavouring, texture, shape, size, design, ingredients and the poetic fancies – or advertising flair – of their creators. Examples are *desh gorob* (glory of the nation), *manoranjan* (heart's delight), *monohara* (captivator of the heart), *abak* (wonder), *nayantara* (star of the eye), *bagh* (tiger) and *abar khabo* (I'll have another). Some were named after famous people including Lord Irwin, Motilal Nehru and Soviet premier Bulganin. Sandesh makers have added chocolate, APPLES, ice-cream and other non-traditional flavourings, and make sandesh shaped like slices of toast, sandwiches, cakes, chops, pastries, biscuits and other Western food items.

Each season has its specialties. In the summer, sandesh is flavoured with MANGO, JACKFRUIT and other fruits of the season; and in winter, hard sandesh is flavoured with sugar made from the sap of the DATE palm (*nolen gur* sandesh).

Colleen Sen

- Banerjee, Tania. 'How a Portuguese Technique Led to a Bengali Sondesh Explosion'. *The Juggernaut*, 2 July 2021. Available online: https://www.thejuggernaut.com/sondesh-bengali-sweets (accessed 1 May 2022).
- Sen, Colleen Taylor. 'Sandesh: An Emblem of Bengaliness'. In *Milk: Beyond the Dairy, Proceedings of the Oxford Symposium on Food and Cookery 1999*, edited by Harlan Walker, 300–8. Totnes, Devon: Prospect Books, 2000.

SAPODILLA

Sapodilla is the name of the fruit and evergreen tree *Manilkara zapota* which is native to Mexico and Central America. In India it is known by a number of names, including *sapeta* or *sabeda* in eastern India, *sapota* in southern India and *chiku* in northern India. *Chiku* comes from the name for the gummy latex called chicle which was obtained from the bark of the tree and used as a base for chewing gum. Although the tree has grown since ancient times in Central America, it was brought to India only in the nineteenth century, probably by the Spanish or the Portuguese. Two routes have been suggested – over the Atlantic to Mozambique then on to Goa, or over the Pacific to the Philippines to Malaysia and on to the east coast of India. The fruit is recorded as reaching Ceylon (Sri Lanka) in 1802. Today the tree is cultivated widely in Gujarat, West Bengal, Andhra Pradesh, Maharashtra and Tamil Nadu. A number of large-fruited varieties have been developed, the most popular commonly called *pala* sapota. The towns of Gholvad and Dahanu in Maharashtra are considered to be pioneers of the *chiku* in India and in December 2016 the Gholvad Dahanu *chiku* was given a GEOGRAPHICAL INDICATION tag. Today India is probably the largest grower in the world.

The flesh of the brown-skinned oval fruit (which resembles a kiwi fruit) when fully ripe is soft and famous for its sweetness with the flavour of pears, CINNAMON and brown SUGAR. The fruit is generally peeled before eating and the two to three large black seeds inside the fruit should be discarded as they are toxic. *Chiku* is delicious just eaten on its own but is sometimes added to salads, including a sweet version of chaat, or used in making SWEETS, desserts (such as KULFI, HALWA, KHEER, ice-cream) and milkshakes. PICKLES can also be made from the fruit.

Helen Saberi

- Dinshaw, Khursheed. 'In India, the Chikoo Fruit Spreads Its Sweet Legacy'. *Whetstone*, *n.d.* Available online: https://www.whetstonemagazine.com/journal/in-india-the-chikoo-fruit-spreads-its-sweet-legacy (accessed 5 May 2022).
- Doctor, Vikram. 'Chikoos: The Afterthought Fruit in Abundance'. *The Economic Times*, 4 November 2009. Available online: https://economictimes.indiatimes.com/blogs/onmyplate/chikoos-the-afterthought-fruit-in/ (accessed 5 May 2022).
- Speciality Produce. 'Chikoo', *n.d.* Available online: https://specialtyproduce.com/produce/Chikoo_11506.php (accessed 5 May 2022).

SESAME

Sesame (*Sesamum indicum*, Hindi *til*) is the world's oldest oilseed crop and is indigenous to the subcontinent. Charred remains of sesame seeds have been found in the Harappan Civilization dating back to as early as 3500 BCE. By 2000 BCE, India was exporting sesame to Mesopotamia, and later to Greece and Rome.

Today India is the world's largest producer of sesame, although productivity is lower than in other countries because it is often grown in marginal and submarginal lands. It has been called a survivor crop because it is grown by subsistence farmers in regions with drought conditions and high heat. New varieties and technologies are being developed to improve productivity. The leading producing states are Rajasthan, Uttar Pradesh, West Bengal, Jharkhand, Andhra Pradesh and Telangana.

The sesame plant is an annual herb up to two metres tall and has capsules filled with tiny flat seeds. The exteriors may be yellow, brown, white or black in colour; all have a white interior after hulling. The seeds have a pleasant nutty flavour that is enhanced by roasting. Sesame seeds have one of the highest oil content of any seed and both seeds and oil are used extensively throughout India, especially in sweets and snacks. Ancient texts mention LADDU made from sesame seeds and jaggery, a forerunner of the modern *chikki* (a kind of NUT brittle). *Til ka* laddu is a popular sweet during festivals. In Bihar they are known as *tilkut* and are a popular winter sweet. In South India a rice dish called *ellu sadam* (*ellu* means 'sesame' in Tamil) is prepared with ground sesame seeds, *channa* dal (see PULSES), red CHILLIES and dried COCONUT. Ground sesame seeds are an ingredient in the South Indian spice mixture *milagai podi* (see SPICE BOX).

Oil made by pressing sesame seeds was so popular in ancient times that it gave its name to the modern Hindi word for oil, *tel*. Although the yield from pressing the seeds is low, it has a fairly long shelf life and is high in polyunsaturated fatty acids.

Three kinds of sesame oils are sold. Light brown sesame oil has a distinctive burnt nutty taste and is more suitable for stir frying, seasoning or as a marinade. It is not used much in Indian cuisine. Gingelly oil, also from sesame seeds, which is processed at a slightly higher temperature, has a golden colour and a lower smoke point, making it suitable for deep-frying. (The word 'gingelly', which first appeared in the sixteenth century, was probably introduced by the Portuguese as a variation of the Arabic *juljulān*, meaning sesame.) Gingelly oil is used in South and West India for making PICKLES because of its high preservative qualities and as a cooking medium. In Tamil Nadu it is an ingredient in *ullundu kali*, a black *urad* dal porridge believed to strengthen the bones because of its high iron content, and is the cooking medium for chicken curry. It is also used as an oil for massage. The dark brown sesame oil used in Chinese and Japanese cuisine is made from toasted seeds and has a much more intense flavour. It is mainly added to foods before serving.

Perhaps because of its antiquity, sesame has considerable religious significance. It is one of the nine sacred grains, or *navadhanya*, that are used in many rituals, including the naming ceremony of an infant and the initiation of a student. Sesame seed is associated with Lord Vishnu and sesame oil and seeds are part of fast days for Vaishnavs. Many Hindus offer *pindas*, balls of cooked rice with GHEE and black sesame seeds, to ancestors during funeral rites (see RITES OF PASSAGE). At the end of the mourning period, family members are given three balls of black sesame seeds, boiled rice and jaggery called *tillanna*. Three balls are also fed to crows, birds that are believed to act as messengers to the afterlife.

Colleen Sen

- Achaya, K. T. *Historical Dictionary of Indian Food*. New Delhi: OUP, 2002.

SEV AND SEVIYAN

Sev and *seviyan* are terms for noodles in India, *sevika* being the Sanskrit name for noodles. *Sevika* may derive from an unrecorded word meaning 'thread' connected to the root *siv*, which refers to sewing. *Sevika* was first mentioned in the MANASOLLASA in the twelfth century but is probably much older.

Sev is the term for crunchy, fried 'noodles' which are a popular snack food all over India. They are prepared from *besan* (chickpea) flour made into a batter, seasoned with TURMERIC, cayenne and AJOWAN before being extruded, either thick or thin, through a special press called a *sev*-maker and then deep-fried in hot oil.

Seviyan (also *seviya/semiya/sivayya/shavayi*) usually refers to the thicker and shorter form of vermicelli which has for long been made in India from hard (durum) wheat. In South India, where it is called *semiya*, it is boiled with milk and SUGAR and made into *payasam* (see KHEER). *Seviya* kheer (sometimes called kheer korma) is a creamy, raisin and nut milk pudding popular throughout North India. The PARSIS, at New Year, make a drier, rich, sweet delicacy with *seviya* which is fried brown in GHEE with the addition of NUTS, raisins, sultanas and flavoured with rosewater (see FLOWER WATERS), nutmeg (see NUTMEG AND MACE) and CARDAMOM. *Seviya upma* is savoury noodle dish with vegetables, sometimes with the addition of CHEESE.

Helen Saberi

- Devi, Yamuna. *The Art of Indian Vegetarian Cooking*. London: Leopard Books, 1995.

SHEHERWALIS

The Sheherwalis are a community of Jain merchants who migrated from the semi-arid regions of Rajasthan to conduct business in Bengal some three hundred years ago. They became the personal bankers of the Nawabs of Bengal, starting with Murshid Quli Khan (r. 1704–25), who gave his name to the city Murshidabad. Other Jain families settled in Murshidabad and neighbouring towns where they began adopting local ways of living, slowly evolving as a prosperous community distinct from the Marwaris.

The Jain Sheherwalis are vegetarians and their excellent vegetarian cuisine is a wonderful mélange of the cuisines of western and eastern India. Flavours of food rich in GHEE and bold spicy tastes that could survive in the tough climate of Rajasthan met the distinctive local flavours of Bengal and the royal cuisine of the MUGHALS. A richer Sheherwali version of Rajasthan's iconic dal-*baati-churma* is made with dry fruits and a generous helping of rosewater (see FLOWER WATERS) and SAFFRON. They modified this famous dish by using local ingredients and experimenting with different kinds of fillings for the *baati*. A variety of PICKLES and CHUTNEYS are compulsory components of any Rajasthani spread. Sheherwali cuisine is famous for its pickles, especially *kutti mirchai ka achaar* (red CHILLI pickle) made with lime juice.

Favourite preparations in Sheherwali homes include *kathail ka tarkari* (a vegetable preparation using raw JACKFRUIT), *chhaata ka tarkari* (a dish made with LOTUS pods), *mocha ka tarkari* (a BANANA flower preparation), *kathbel* chutney (WOODAPPLE paste), *muri ka* laddu (puffed RICE sweetened with jaggery), *peetha* (steamed rice dumplings stuffed with *KHOYA*), *kacche aam ka kheer* (raw MANGO pudding) and *borey ka boondiya* (a sweet made of white bean powder.) Sheherwalis adopted the use of the Bengali spice mixture *panch phoran* (see SPICE BOX) in some of their preparations. Vegetables are cut accurately to maintain an even size. Even peas are graded – the tender-most and smallest pods are used for salad, the slightly larger ones for CURRY and the biggest for KACHORIS.

Another influence was that of the Mughals when KOLKATA became a refuge for the exiled Nawabs of Awadh and the family of Tipu Sultan of Mysore. They brought their households, including their cooks and spice mixers (*masalchis*) who introduced such exotic spices as saffron, mace (see NUTMEG AND MACE), dried fruits and cooking techniques such as *dumpukht* (see COOKING AND DINING). The Sheherwalis adopted the use of *kewra jal* and rosewater in most of their SWEETS, drinks and other preparations to impart the same regal flavours.

For a Sheherwali, no summer is complete without enjoying a ripe bounty of mangoes handpicked from the orchards of Azimganj and Jiaganj. Over 100 cultivars of mangoes are grown in Murshidabad. While in season, mangoes feature in all meals, either eaten naturally or in a wide array of preparations from pickles and chutneys to drinks.

Sheherwalis eat sweets before, during and after a meal. A typical breakfast consists of a glass of milk and a portion of sweets such as *malpua*, *channabara* or *raskadam*. The fun of winter would be incomplete if not accompanied by *khaaja* (jaggery and SESAME seed sweet preparation) and *nimas* (milk froth), all outcomes of regional influences. This intense sweet tooth is inherited from the Sheherwalis' Rajasthani roots and was later influenced by the Bengalis' love for sweets. The Sheherwalis made the Portuguese technique of cheese making their own, adapting it to make *CHHANA* and basing a whole array of sweets on it.

Sandip Nowlakha

SHERBET

Sherbets (*sharbats*) are historically, and basically, cold, sweetened non-alcoholic beverages which have provided refreshment throughout the Middle East and the Indian subcontinent for centuries. The name derives from the medieval Arabic word *sharab* which meant a drink or a dose of medicine. Later, *sharab* came to mean an alcoholic beverage so when the Arabs brought Islam to Persia and Turkey and alcohol was prohibited, the Persian word *sharbat* (*şerbet* in Turkish) took on the meaning of a sweet non-alcoholic beverage. Both Persia and Turkey were renowned for their refreshing sherbets of SUGAR (or honey) and water flavoured with fruit juices, rosewater (see FLOWER WATERS), spices, seeds and NUTS and, often, cooled by crushed ICE or snow.

The natural sweet beverage of India was sugarcane juice, often spiced with GINGER. The new types of sweet drinks called *sharbat* were introduced to India during the rule of the Delhi Sultanates (1206–1526) and were traditionally made with cane juice. They were often coloured and flavoured with essences such as rose, *kewra* and herbs. IBN BATTUTA (who lived in India from 1325 to 1354) wrote that before people started to eat they were brought 'gold, silver and glass cups filled with fine sugar-water perfumed with rosewater which they call sherbet'.

Babur was known to have sent for frequent loads of ice from the Himalayas to cool his sherbet drinks. When Tahmasp, the Shah of Persia, offered hospitality to the Mughal emperor Humayun at the Persian court in 1544, he decreed: 'Upon his auspicious arrival, let him drink fine sherbets of lemon and rosewater, cooled with snow ...' He was starting a Persian tradition that was to continue for hundreds of years.

The Mughals were renowned for their lavish banquets, weddings and entertainments. Sherbets were served to guests. One notable Persian-style *sharbat* is *badam sharbat*, made from almonds, sugar and rosewater.

Sherbet drinks have beneficial cooling effects in a hot climate and are still popular in India. Syrup-based sherbets are a colourful sight at roadside stalls. As summer approaches, syrups are made and bottled. Guests are often welcomed with a refreshing sherbet – a couple of tablespoons of the syrup are poured into a tall glass, topped up with crushed ice and iced water and stirred well. Sometimes, a spoonful of *tukmuria* (BASIL seeds) is added. They swell up, become transparent and jelly-like and are said to have cooling properties. Sherbets are a popular drink when Muslims break their daily fast during the holy month of Ramadan.

In South India a version called *sarbath* is popular. One version is made of Indian sarsaparilla (*Hemidesmus indicus*) and lemon dissolved in milk or soda water. In Kerala *kulukki sarbath* is popular. *Kulukki* in Malayalam means shaken and this *sarbath*, made with water, lemon, *tukmuria* and spiced with green CHILLI, is shaken vigorously. Different flavours are produced by the addition of fruits such as PINEAPPLE or orange (see CITRUS FRUITS).

Helen Saberi

- Davidson, Alan. *The Oxford Companion to Food*. 2nd edition. Ed. Tom Jaine. Oxford: OUP, 2006.
- Westrip, Joyce. *Moghul Cooking*. London: Serif, 1997.

SHREWSBURY BISCUITS

Shrewsbury biscuits are the best-known bakery products of the military cantonment city of Pune, Maharashtra. The buttery, eggless biscuits, according to one account, were introduced by Royal Bakery & Confectioners, which has been around since 1910 and is better-known today for its milk bread sold under the brand name Milk-o-Vita. It was, however, the Kayani Bakery, launched by Hormuz and Khodayar Irani in 1955, which made Pune synonymous with the biscuits. The bakeshop also acquired a cult status and national fan following.

In 2017, the Pune Cantonment Board informed the bakeshop's owners that their licence would be revoked because it had not been renewed for eleven years. The move galvanized loyal customers, who filed a petition on Change.org against it, and egged on the local media to criticize it. In the face of such opposition, the authorities had to relent and allow Kayani Bakery to reopen after a month. The bakery, which is also famous for its *mawa* cake (see PARSIS) and orange- and GINGER-flavoured biscuits, now has competition from Khodayar, founded in 2001 by Danesh Khodayar who was a partner at Kayani till 1995.

The link with Shrewsbury is a mystery. An English county town in Shropshire, Shrewsbury is famous for a dough cake made with all-purpose flour, egg, SUGAR, butter and lemon zest. (In 1658 the recipe appeared in an English cookbook titled *The Compleat Cook*, which also adds rosewater to the list of ingredients.) A century later, a local cake maker named Pailin used to bake biscuits that also included caraway seeds, nutmeg (see NUTMEG AND MACE) and rosewater (see FLOWER WATERS). The BBC Local website reproduced Pailin's recipe for the biscuits, commenting that they tasted like Turkish delights because of the spices and rosewater.

Pune's Shrewsbury biscuits are fundamentally different because they are eggless and also have nothing to do with the English town. The second-generation owner of Royal Bakery, Russi Irani (his son Sheriar now manages the bakehouse), attributed the unique taste of the cake (and biscuits) baked in Shrewsbury to the grass that the local cows fed on. The wholesome qualities and aroma of the grass got transferred to the milk that the cows produced, and from there on, to the butter that went into the biscuits.

The same story is repeated in another report quoting Russi's nephew, Ardashir Irani, who owns and runs City Bakery. It is clearly an urban legend popular in the Irani family, for, as Russi and Ardashir have stated, the butter used for the biscuits is the locally available Amul (see DAIRY SECTOR). Be that as it may, the biscuits are perhaps the most popular bakery product in India. Russi Irani explained their unceasing popularity to the taste that Mumbai's elite acquired for them when they would descend upon Pune for the horse-racing season. The most vocal admirers of the biscuits were the Hindi film stars and trend-setters of the 1950s and the '60s, Raj and Shashi Kapoor. Later, in the late 1970s and the '80s, the international followers of the controversial godman Bhagwan Rajneesh (Osho) also became avid consumers of the biscuits. Pune may have nothing in common with Shrewsbury but it has made the English county town a household name in India.

Sourish Bhattacharyya

- BBC Local. 'Shrewsbury Biscuits', *n.d.* Available online: http://www.bbc.co.uk/shropshire/food/2002/10/shrewsbury_biscuits.shtml (accessed 1 May 2022).
- Chatterjee, Avijit. 'Baking Bread, Cakes & Biscuits Is All in Their Hands'. *The Times of India*, 31 July 2017.
- Nair, Mahesh. 'Shrewsbury: A Legend That Takes the Biscuit'. *The Indian Express*, 19 January 2021.

SHRIKHAND

Loved by some and disliked by others, *shrikhand* (*srikand*) is a popular sweet in Gujarat and Maharashtra, where it may be served as a part of a meal rather than at the end as a dessert. Puris (see BREADS) are a classic pairing. *Shrikhand* is made by straining yogurt to make *malai chakka* (hung yogurt), beating it until it is light, adding SUGAR and flavouring it with SAFFRON or CARDAMOM. The traditional method of beating the *malai chakka* is with a hand operated *puran yantra*. According to Saee Koranne-Khandekhar, the use of an electric blender adds heat to the dish which interferes with the fermentation and turns it into a syrupy mix. Sometimes seasonal fruits such as MANGO, strawberry or custard apple are added. Recipes for a dish called *sikharini* are found in ancient Jain texts as well as in medieval Indian cookbooks from West India such as the *Lokapakara* (early eleventh century CE).

Colleen Sen

- Koranne-Khandekar, Saee. *Pangat, a Feast: Food and Love from Marathi Kitchens*. Gurugram, Haryana: Hachette, 2019.

SIKKIM

Sikkim, playfully dubbed the ‘eighth brother’ of the seven ‘Northeast Sister’ states, is snuggled between Tibet, Bhutan, Nepal and the Indian state of West Bengal. It is home to Kanchenjunga, the third highest peak in the world, and a variety of flora and fauna. Close proximity to the Himalayas and sub-tropical temperatures allow Sikkim to boast of majestic views of snow-clad mountains that serve as a backdrop to Tibetan prayer flags fluttering against the winds. These prayer flags are indicative of the population make-up of the land. While a community called Lepchas are considered to be the indigenous Sikkimese, they are outnumbered by the Nepali majority, who make up more than half of the population, and Bhutias who are Tibetan migrants scattered across present-day Nepal, Bhutan and Sikkim.

Three items that bind the people of Sikkim together are a staple diet of RICE; hard or soft *chhurpi* (traditional fermented chunks of CHEESE); and hot, steaming MOMOS (steamed dumplings). Every home in Sikkim, from the outlying districts to the capital city of Gangtok, cooks these dishes, albeit with slight variations depending on individual taste. Rice is relished with meat CURRY, a simple soupy lentil dish or stir-fried seasonal vegetables.

While momo and *thukpa*, a noodle soup, are comfort foods, *chhurpi* is a frequent accompaniment to a meal that is lovingly and painstakingly churned and produced in a process that may last up to twenty days. The fermentation of food was born out of necessity during earlier times. Food was preserved to enable it to last through the long and harsh winter. Everything from spinach to BAMBOO SHOOTS (*mesu*), soya bean and RADISH, among other vegetables, was fermented. The tradition is still followed today and has given rise to many fermented food items such as *chhurpi* and beverages like the mildly alcoholic *chhaang*, made from BARLEY, MILLET or rice, and *raksi*, a distilled beverage.

Pickling food mainly for preservation is a common trait. Nearly every community has its own version of PICKLES. The most popular come from Turuk Kothi, a heritage home of a Nepali family that has been running a regal homestay for five generations. Locals, as well as visitors, lap up their signature pickles of *dalley* (fiery small CHILLIES characteristic to Sikkim) and bamboo shoots, FISH, chicken and pork.

The Nepali touch in Sikkimese cuisine is evident in the widespread consumption of dal *bhat* (lentil soup with rice) and dishes that are fried in oil and laced with spices such as CARDAMOM, CLOVE, bay leaves and CINNAMON. Pickling meats, vegetables and *dalley* (a round hot chilli) is another standard practice, believed to have been ushered in by the Nepali Pradhan community (Kshatriyas who trace their roots to Rajput dynasties). How Bhutias and Lepchas eat is starkly different in terms of spice intake. Influenced by Tibetan cooking, both prefer broth and soup-based food. They also enjoy consuming all kinds of meat including beef without restriction, unlike the Nepali population who traditionally do not eat beef in accordance with their Hindu faith.

Hoihnu Hauzel

- Indian Culture. 'The Culinary Treasures of Sikkim', *n.d.* Available online: https://indianculture.gov.in/food-and-culture/north-east/culinary-treasures-sikkim (accessed 1 May 2022).

SINDHIS

Sindhis are refugees or descendants of refugees who left Pakistan following the partition of the subcontinent in 1947. There are an estimated 3 million speakers of the Sindhi language in India, over 30 million in Pakistan and a sizeable Sindhi DIASPORA. The area was a centre of the Harappan Civilization. In 711 CE, the Arabs conquered Sindh and introduced Islam to the subcontinent. In 1843, most of Sindh became part of the Bombay Presidency and later, a province in British India. It was integrated into the province of West Pakistan from 1955 to 1970 when it was re-established as a separate province. The Sindhis who fled to India in 1947 managed to pull themselves together and set up a new livelihood in a land which was now theirs but to which they were foreign. Apart from a few meagre belongings, they brought their culture and their cuisine with them.

Many refugees found their way to Bombay (see MUMBAI) via the sea route from Karachi Port and others overland through Rajasthan and Punjab. The cuisine remained largely original. Culinary acumen remained sharp among the women of the house, especially the older generations. The flavours, therefore, remain home-like and understated, true to their original renderings. How else would you explain the popularity of the simple dal *pakwan* which is just a fried WHEAT crisp topped with dal? Across the globe, the diaspora has maintained flavours that are largely true with very little deviation. Sindhi cuisine has met the demands of home-loving Sindhis rather than the demands of a cross-section of subcontinental expectations which would have ruined the originality. Despite this, the irrepressible Sindhi living outside Pakistan survives with great ease like his favourite *palla/hilsa* (Shad) FISH which adapts to ever-changing currents and salinity.

Emblematic dishes in Sindhi cuisine include the Sindhi curry which has a lot of umami from one of its essential ingredients – DRUMSTICK (*Moringa oleifera*), now widely acclaimed as a superfood. Dried raw MANGO powder and black CARDAMOM are standout spices lending a sour and smoky touch to Sindhis' preferred flavour matrix. *Sai bhaji* is a simple mix of lentils and green vegetables, but the trick is in mashing it to the right consistency. The winter season brings on the new crop of fresh garlic chives that are essential for making a classic lamb mince with peas, called *keemo thoum*. *Teevarn*, the Sunday mutton CURRY, is a matter of pride for the man of the house who insists on being a part of it from buying the lamb meat to seeing it through the cooking process.

Festivals and the occasional visits by celebrated sons-in-law make for meals that feature the very rare and wild *dhingri* and *gucchi* MUSHROOMS. *Zereshk* (barberries) from Afghanistan and Iran also find their way into PULAOS.

At the base of most gravies that form the body of the curry is a *daag*, a catchall term for a melange of sautéed ONIONS, TOMATOES and spices, the proportions closely guarded by the matriarch of the family. Most Sindhis always have a *kadhai* (a wok-shaped pot for deep-frying) full of oil ready to be used at will. The famed *aloo tuk* demonstrates that the humble potato can be elevated to a preparation that would rival any from the top restaurants in the world. Chunks of potatoes are fried, then smashed to expose internal edges and deep-fried again to create a super crispy snack.

One of the favourites among meat eaters in India and Pakistan is the Sindhi biryani made with mutton or chicken and, very rarely, with beef or buffalo meat. It has two standout qualities. Layering with fresh green CORIANDER and MINT adds a bouquet of herbaceous notes. The second is the addition of *aloo bukhara* in the meat masala, a PLUM that is plucked before full maturity and allowed to dry. This lends a sour-sweet taste to the biryani without intruding into the other spice flavours. This is one dish that is more popular in Pakistan than in India. Yet, over time, the taste of Sindhi biryani has spilled across the border and the demand for commercial, ready-to-use Sindhi biryani masalas from Pakistan continues to grow.

Sindhis love SWEETS and may end their meals with a choice of *singar mithai,* a fudge-like sweet made with thin noodles made from chickpeas. Or a *geear* which is like an upgraded version of the famous JALEBI. Then there is the PAPAD for which Sindhis are famous. In the border communities of Sindh and Rajasthan, it makes for a practical snack to be roasted on demand as a symbol of old-world hospitality for weary travellers of arid lands. The test of a suitable bride across these regions was her ability to roast a papad well on an open fire without singeing it.

Suresh Hinduja

• Reejhsinghani, Aroona. *The Essential Sindhi Cookbook*. New Delhi: Penguin Books, 2004.

SINGH, MRS BALBIR

Mrs Balbir Singh (1912–94) (the name she always used professionally) was the author of the pioneering Indian cookbook *Indian Cookery*, sometimes hailed as the finest Indian cookbook ever written. First published in London by Mills & Boon in 1961, it has gone through dozens of editions, sold hundreds of thousands of copies worldwide and influenced generations of household cooks and celebrity chefs. Mrs Singh is often compared to the American cookbook writer and celebrity chef Julia Child who introduced generations of Americans to upscale French cuisine through her comprehensive *Mastering the Art of French Cooking* and television shows.

Born Balwant Kaur into a family of landowners in undivided Punjab in 1912, Mrs Singh graduated in 1936 from Punjab University where she met her husband Dr. Balbir Singh, a physician. After partition, they moved briefly to London where she enrolled in a domestic science class. Here she began to share recipes passed down from her mother with her classmates, many of them English women back from India. Returning to New Delhi in 1955, Mrs Singh began giving cooking lessons at Lady Irwin College and later in her home in Vasant Vihar, Delhi. The class became a rite of passage for newly married middle-class brides, and soon she was teaching forty students a class, six days a week.

Before the publication of *Indian Cookery*, there was no cookbook that gave precise and detailed instructions on how to prepare Indian dishes. Mrs Singh described her book as an 'exciting and comprehensive treasury of recipes from India, including curries, kebabs, rich dishes, breads, desserts, sauces, ice-creams, sharbats and squashes, pickles, chutneys and other preserves'. While most of the recipes are for traditional North Indian dishes, such as mutton rogan josh, tandoori chicken, *shami* KEBAB and, her most famous recipe, chicken tikka masala, there are also recipes from other regions, including Kashmir, South India and Goa. There are no shortcuts: for example, the recipe for *navrattan* PULAO requires twenty-seven ingredients and involves several dozen separate steps.

In 1967, Mrs Singh hosted India's first televised cooking show on Doordarshan, the national network. In 1994, she published her second book *Continental Cookery for Indian Homes.* She died the same year at the age of eighty-two. Her granddaughter, Pallavi Sitalni, has launched a brand of spice blends based on those in the book and is preparing an updated version of her grandmother's famous book.

Colleen Sen

- Sen, Mayukh. 'Setting the Table: K.T. Achaya's Pioneering Scholarship on Indian Food'. *Caravan Magazine*, 31 May 2018.
- Venugopal, Nikhita. 'Why Haven't You Heard of India's Julia Child?' *Taste*, 19 July 2018.

SINGH, RAJA DIGVIJAYA

Raja Digvijaya Singh (1918–90), the titular ruler of Sailana in Madhya Pradesh and late father of the present incumbent, Raja Vikram Singh, was the author of the best-selling book *Cooking Delights of the Maharajas* which shares 164 of the more than 1,000 recipes painstakingly collected by his father, Raja Sir Dileep Singh, the last officially recognized ruler of the eleven-gun-salute state that spread across 769 sq km in its heyday. The celebrated cookbook writer was also an avid gardener who continues to be remembered in Sailana for developing its famous cacti garden which houses more than 1,200 varieties from around the world.

The book, first published in 1983, went into fifteen reprints and ensured a permanent niche for Sailana in India's culinary map. A stellar collection of recipes collected from the major princely states and Sailana's own kitchen, many of them translated under Digvijaya Singh's supervision from their Sanskrit, Persian and Urdu originals, the book continues to inspire home chefs and food festivals. It has had a longer shelf life than its now-forgotten predecessor, *Cooking of the Maharajas*, which was written by the glamorous standard-bearer of the famous Holkars, Shivaji Rao Holkar (better known as Richard), and his American wife Sally, officially referred to as Shalini Devi.

Raja Sir Dileep Singh, according to a popular story, started cooking after he and his friends lost contact with their domestic staff during a royal hunt. On the days they were left on their own, with very little food to eat, Dileep Singh swore to himself that he would learn cooking so that he could be spared of such embarrassing moments in the future. That set off his quest for recipes from across the country for which he turned to fellow royals, from the Maharaja of Kashmir and Nizam of HYDERABAD to the Begum of Bhopal and Maharaja of Bhavnagar.

The original custodians of the borrowed recipes are acknowledged, although most of the recipes are old Rajput delicacies, some of them with Sailana's original tweaks. Popular among the latter are the mutton *dahi* vada (where the lentil-based VADAS of this popular Indian chaat are replaced by mutton balls soaked in yogurt, spiked with sweet and tangy CHUTNEYS and garnished with POMEGRANATE seeds), *amba kaliya* (mutton cooked with raw MANGOES, a dish dating back to Emperor Shahjahan), *maans ki kadhi* (yet another version of a popular vegetarian dish where mutton mince balls replace chickpea fritters) and keema with bitter GOURD or green CHILLIES.

The game meat dishes *khargosh ki mokal* (rabbit) and *sooar ke saanth* (wild boar meat with crackling skin and fat) also have their roots in Sailana's Rajput heritage, as do some of the desserts such as KHEER made with GARLIC or rose petals, HALWA made with mutton or eggs, and FIRNI (the quintessential rice pudding) where CORN substitutes for the RICE. The cookbook has a substantial vegetarian section (perhaps inspired by Digvijaya Singh's vegetarian wife) and almost all the inclusions are originals from the Sailana kitchen.

It is said that whenever a royal visitor would drop in at Sailana, and the tradition then was that each of them came with his personal entourage, Dileep Singh would invite the visiting royal cook to prepare a dish and gave him all the spices and herbs he asked for after keeping a record of how much they weighed before going into the kitchen. As soon as the spices were used, he would have the leftovers removed and weighed so that the quantities of the ingredients used could be calculated and added to the recipe. Following Dileep Singh's notations, his son later personally cooked each dish and tweaked the recipe (some, such as that of the mutton rogan josh, were particularly problematic) so that it appealed to contemporary taste buds. In the Sailana tradition, the recipes are passed on from father to son to safeguard them from being shared with the families of the daughters-in-law.

Sourish Bhattacharyya

- Singh, Digvijaya. *Cooking Delights of the Maharajas: Exotic Dishes from the Princely House of Sailana*. Mumbai: Vakils, Feffer and Simons, 2015.
- Sanghvi, Vir. 'From the Sailana Kitchens'. *HT Brunch*, 23 January 2011.

SOFT DRINKS

Soft drinks, as in sweetened carbonated water, came to India around the same time as they became popular in England in the 1830s. It started with soda water, which was in great demand among European residents in the sub-continent, and tonic water, laced with quinine and just right for gin, and graduated to the beloved raspberry soda of the Parsis until Coca-Cola and PepsiCo established their ubiquitous presence in the country's $8-billion (2020 estimate) non-alcoholic, ready-to-drink retail beverages market.

India already had a long tradition of thirst quenchers such as *nimbu pani* or *shikanji* (fresh lemon juice and water mixed with SUGAR and rock SALT) and *jal jeera* (lemonade spiked with ground roasted CUMIN and crushed MINT). In 1837, a British chemist named

Henry Rogers produced India's first batch of 'aerated water' from his laboratory in Mumbai. The water was purified in a plant imported from England. It was just what the European settlers and their PARSI compradors needed to escape their dependence on the dodgy, brackish well water available before Bombay (see MUMBAI) developed modern waterworks. Rogers set up a factory and was doing good business. Aerated water had carbonic acid, which seemed to stand up against bacteria, especially the one causing cholera.

The entrepreneurial Parsis sensed a business opportunity in the rising demand for aerated water – and carbonated tonic water from the late 1850s – in hotels and restaurants run by Europeans. But Rogers' lemonade had its critics. The Gujarati social reformer Karsandas Mulji complained in 1866 that for an orthodox Hindu drinking it was like 'sacrificing his religion' because it had been produced by foreign hands and it was against Hindu tradition to make profit out of selling water. The Parsis had a solution.

They took over the soda business, bought Rogers' company in 1915, and went on to invent the raspberry soda, a ruby-red syrupy sweet drink that had nothing to do with the berries (which don't even grow in India). Today, it is an integral part of Parsi wedding feast or an IRANI CAFE menu.

The best-known brand is Duke because it was picked up by PepsiCo in 1994, withdrawn from the market in 2004, and re-introduced in 2011. The Parsi cricketer Dinshawji Cooverji Pundole launched the soda in 1889, a year after he played a series of matches in England and claimed a princely haul of eighty-six wickets. To celebrate the fact, he named the soda after Duke and Sons, makers of the balls he had bowled with such devastating effect. When Coca-Cola arrived in India in 1950, Duke launched a drink named Mangola with Alphonso MANGO pulp. The brainchild of Dinshawji's son, it acquired a massive following in the Parsi community. After PepsiCo acquired Duke, Mangola was replaced by the American corporation's own brand, Slice.

In Pune (then called Poona), Ardeshir Khodadad Irani started manufacturing soda water in 1884 for the whiskies of his British patrons, who no longer had to depend on siphon machines shipped all the way from England. Irani's soda is called Ardy's today. It is run by the fourth generation of the family from the same factory at Pune where Irani launched his business. Ardy's is the staple soft drink of DORABJEE & SONS, believed to be India's oldest continually running restaurant. Available only in Pune, it comes in multiple flavours, including raspberry, GINGER, ice-cream and peach Melba, and the caffeine-free Indi Cola.

Another soda with a limited market is Palonji which is sold in the vanishing Irani cafes in Mumbai (the best-known being Boman KOHINOOR's Britannia & Co.) and in suburban railway stations. The brand was launched in 1864 and acquired by its present owner, P.V. Solanki, in 1979. It has seen a revival in the recent past, having made it to the beverage list of the trendy London restaurant, Dishoom.

In 1927, Mohsin Abdul Rahim Hajoori in Surat launched a non-alcoholic beverage named Whisky No, after inheriting his brother Abbas Abdul Rahim Hajoori's aerated drinks business. A cocktail of aerated APPLE and grape juices that tasted suspiciously like whisky, rum and cola mixed together, the drink was created to appeal to the sentiments of both orthodox Muslims and Mahatma Gandhi's followers who swore to abstain from ALCOHOL. It was also a *swadeshi* (nationalist) riposte to beverages produced by British-owned companies. (Its tagline even today is 'Apna Desh, Apna Drink' – Our Country, Our Drink.) Within years, Whisky No found receptive customers outside Surat, starting with Mumbai.

In 1960, when Gujarat achieved statehood and adopted the policy of prohibition, which is still in force, the Hajoori family opted for the name Sosyo. The drink's formulation came from Italy and the name was adapted from the word for 'social' in Italian, *sociale*. The drink and its siblings are still around, namely, the hugely popular Kashmira Masala Soda, the orange-flavoured fizzy drink On-e-ka, and Pineax, the PINEAPPLE-flavoured soda.

Even earlier, Spencer & Co., the British store that sold imported food and drinks for the European and affluent residents of Madras (CHENNAI) since 1865, had local competition. P.V.S.K. Palaniappan Nadar was only twenty-three when he opened the Kali Aerated Water Works in Virudhunagar, south of Madurai in present-day Tamil Nadu. He used German bottles for his aerated water to emphasize that he had nothing to do with the British establishment. In 1958, his four sons developed a grape-flavoured carbonated drink named Bovonto. Coca-Cola had established itself by then and Pepsi was still struggling to find a foothold (it left the market in 1962 because of sagging sales and re-entered it in 1990 with the joint-venture brand, Lehar Pepsi), but Bovonto remained a best-seller in Tamil Nadu. In 1977 the original Bovonto was split into eight companies run by different members of the family but the individual units were reunited in 1993. The second and third generations of the family realized that they would be better off benefiting from the economies of scale in a hyper-competitive market.

In Ramachandrapuram in Andhra Pradesh, Adduri Ramachandra Raju, a clerk with a civil contractor's firm, bought a discarded soda machine and launched a bottled soda water business in 1912. Raju travelled around with his wicker basket packed with soda bottles but found few takers because the local people thought the bottles had ghosts hidden in them. Their misgivings vanished after they saw the soda water being relished by the British soldiers camping there during the First World War. After establishing contact with soda makers in London, he and his younger brother launched the flavoured, coloured soda Artos in 1920. When the Second World War triggered shortages of bottles, carbon dioxide gas, sugar and flavourings in India, the Raju brothers prepared fruit concentrates with locally grown oranges, lemons from the bazaar, and used jaggery to produce liquefied refined sugar. Today, Artos' market is limited to three districts in Andhra Pradesh.

Coca-Cola, meanwhile, had made its tentative entry into India. A company executive sent in 1940 for a market recce sent back a mixed report. In 1941, Coca-Cola sent out a group of 'Technical Observers' to set up makeshift bottling plants to supply the drink to American soldiers posted in India. Well-travelled Coca-Cola Export Corporation (CCEC) executives found India to be incomprehensible but offered Coca-Cola as a solution to what was described as 'a modernity gap'. The executives plunged into the Indian market with a furniture maker as their business partner – Sardar Mohan Singh, who outfitted the homes of American military brass in India. Singh was part of India's new political and economic elite and Coca-Cola's first franchised bottling plant in India – Pure Drinks – was set up on a road leading out of Connaught Place, the toniest shopping-and-residential district of New Delhi. The bottler secured an investment from the rich and powerful Maharaja Yadavindra Singh of Patiala who was also one of the country's largest citrus (see CITRUS FRUITS) growers.

In 1950, Pure Drinks was officially inaugurated by the country's aristocratic industries minister, Harekrushna Mahtab. India's first prime minister, Jawaharlal Nehru, chose to sit in the audience but was happy to be photographed sipping Coca-Cola. It may have been a karmic connection that his Congress party paved the way for the return of Coca-Cola to India in 1992–3, years after it had been shown the door in 1977 by the socialist, George Fernandes, who became the industries minister after the Indian electorate voted in the country's first non-Congress government, the Janata Party, which was in power from 1977 to 1979.

CCEC opened its India office in 1958 and was very successful. It was, however, not without its challengers. A year before Coca-Cola inaugurated its Pure Drinks bottling plant, Jayantilal Chauhan launched Gluco-Cola in 1949. A member of the Mumbai family that produced the hugely popular Parle Gluco biscuits, Chauhan had just opened Parle Bottling because he saw an opportunity in the cola business. Parle Bottling backed up the drink with a front-page newspaper ad campaign that stoked nationalist feelings by equating the unnamed foreign competition with a bikini-clad woman – a cabaret artiste at a Paris cafe. The attributes of 'India's First Cola', the ad campaign said, were that it was 'caffeine-free'; it came in large bottles and therefore gave customers 'more for your money'; it was made with 'pure sugar'; and it was 'not habit forming' and therefore was 'ideal for children'.

Coca-Cola, which had registered its brand in India, took Parle Bottling to court for trademark infringement. Chauhan succumbed and renamed his beverage Parle Cola, but Coca-Cola was still not satisfied so Chauhan pulled out his 'cola' in 1951. Parle came back with an orange-flavoured drink in 1952 called Gold Spot, after a popular brand of peppermint named Parle Gold Star, and it soon touched a 'soft spot' in the market. Buoyed by Gold Spot's success, Jayantilal and his son Ramesh set in motion a rapid expansion plan. Their company was called Parle Bisleri, after an Italian mineral water company. It had had to contend with the political and financial clout of Coca-Cola. The declaration of the state of Emergency by Indira Gandhi in June 1975 was followed by all kinds of curbs on consumption besides a blanket curtailment of people's rights. The Chauhans scaled down but did not give up. Ironically, Ramesh Chauhan sold Parle Bisleri's lucrative soft drinks portfolio – and 70 per cent of the market share – to Coca-Cola in 1993. The price, $40 million, helped Chauhan build his Bisleri bottled water empire. Also, 80 per cent of his sixty-two bottlers wanted to switch over to Coca-Cola.

In 1977, Industries Minister George Fernandes moved to invoke the Foreign Exchange Regulation Act and The Patents Act 1970 against the Coca-Cola Export Corporation. The Reserve Bank of India gave the corporation a year to convert itself into an Indian company with 60 per cent Indian shareholding and transfer its concentrate – a trade secret till this date – to this new entity. Refusing to comply, Coca-Cola exited India within a month and IBM, Mobil, Kodak and fifty-four other multinationals followed.

North American newspapers quoted Fernandes accusing Coca-Cola of repatriating $11.5 million in profits to Atlanta up until 1974, after having made an initial investment of just $75,900. The Minister also said the government was coming out with an alternative soft drink to provide jobs to the 6,000-odd workers employed in Coca-Cola's twenty-two bottling units. Coca-Cola, as *The New York Times* reported, sold 900 million bottles in its last year in India.

With Coke's departure (Pepsi had left India in 1962), the field was wide open for a procession of Indian soft drink brands, starting with Campa-Cola produced by Pure Drinks, which had passed onto the hands of Mohan Singh's son. Its tagline was: 'The Great Indian Taste'. Pitted against it was Thumbs Up from Parle Bisleri which was added to the company's portfolio six years after the launch of Limca (a short form of *limbu ka*, 'from a lemon'), a 'cloudy' lemon drink that Ramesh Chauhan created to challenge Duke's lemonade. He also re-energized Gold Spot with a TV campaign in the early 1970s featuring rising star Rekha directed by the not-yet-celebrated Shyam Benegal.

RimZim, the masala soda, was yet another hit from Chauhan's assembly line, but Thums Up stole the thunder – the drink's tagline since 1980, 'Taste the Thunder', is embedded in India's pop culture. It sliced off a sizeable chunk of the cola market with its distinct taste – spicier and less sweet than its competition – that sat easily on the Indian palate.

The Janata Party government led by Morarji Desai from 1977 to 1979 came up with its own 'swadeshi' (nationalist) cola and asked the Central Food Technological Research Institute (CFTRI) in Mysore, Karnataka, to prepare a concentrate. A contest was held to name it and a Member of Parliament suggested 77 to commemorate the year when Indira Gandhi was ousted. The name became Double Seven. CFTRI, in the meantime, came up with a formula that tasted like Coca-Cola but was low on caffeine, as well as a concentrate for a lemon-flavoured drink whose ads showed a young woman looking ecstatic holding a glass of Double-Seven Lime and Lemon with the tagline: 'The Taste That Tingles'. The target audience, sold on Coca-Cola, did not share the government's enthusiasm for Double-Seven. Eventually Double Seven died a natural death.

In 1984, Indira Gandhi was assassinated by her bodyguards and her son Rajiv succeeded her. He was the first Indian leader to start the process of liberalizing the 'licence-permit raj' economy and, soon, there was talk of Pepsi returning to India. Chauhan, meanwhile, rolled out Citra, a clear lemon drink which was different from the 'cloudy' Limca and came in green bottles. The year 1985 also saw India's homegrown soft beverages czar create the mango drink Maaza especially for the Dubai and Kuwait markets. PepsiCo announced its intention to re-launch itself in India in 1989 after renaming its product Pepsi Era to adhere to a rule that multinationals must use hybrid brand names. Its re-entry was to be the showpiece of the Rajiv Gandhi government's new foreign direct investment policy, but it was unseated in December 1989 and the new food processing minister (also a socialist), Sharad Yadav, insisted the brand must have an Indian flavour. He suggested the name Lehar Pepsi which was uncorked in 1990.

Then PepsiCo signed a tripartite deal with Punjab Agro Industries Corporation and Voltas, a refrigeration company owned by the Tatas, one of the country's two big business conglomerates, on 6 June 1986. The idea was to gain a soft entry through the business of making POTATO chips and producing TOMATO pulp, with the raw material sourced from local farmers at remunerative prices.

The move set off a wave of angry protests across India but PepsiCo had its way and launched Lehar Pepsi in June 1990, triggering an advertising war with Thums Up, the market leader. In January 1991, faced with its worst balance of payments crisis, India took a hefty loan from the International Monetary Fund (IMF) that required an opening up of the economy.

On 24 October 1993 Coca-Cola opened its production unit in Agra, and its sponsorship of the ICC Cricket World Cup in 1997 gave it a huge image lift. PepsiCo bought out the stakes of Punjab Agro Industries and Voltas. The entry of Coca-Cola set the stage for a high-priced, high decibel advertising war between the two multinationals. But Pepsi could not dislodge Coca-Cola from its pole position and even its Tropicana brand was not able to upset the applecart of Real from Dabur, a vintage Indian Ayurvedic company that has diversified into an array of consumer products.

Today Coca-Cola commands a portfolio of fifteen brands, including Thums Up, Limca, Maaza and RimZim, which was re-launched in 2018, and the latest entrant, Vio's spiced BUTTERMILK (*chhaas*). Against them is PepsiCo's lineup of seventeen, from Pepsi, Gatorade and the energy drink Sting to Lipton iced tea, Lays potato chips and Quaker oats. The two giants may have spread their footprint across the country but Indians continue to romance the smaller, older brands – even Campa-Cola announced a major nationwide push in 2019. That adds the zing of diversity to India's crowded soft-drinks market, making it, to use a word from RimZim's tagline, more *chatpata* (spicy) for the consumer.

Sourish Bhattacharyya

- Ciafone, Amanda. *Counter-Cola: A Multinational History of the Global Corporation*. Oakland, CA: University of California Press, 2019.
- Das Gupta, Surajeet. 'How India Became Pepsi's Right Choice'. *Business Standard*, 28 March 2014.
- Menon, Smitha. 'Made in India: From Jolly Jelly to Gold Spot, Stories behind the Soft Drinks We Grew Up On'. *Conde Nast Traveller*, 25 August 2020.
- Obermeier, Kylie. 'When India Kicked Out Coca-Cola, Local Sodas Thrived'. *Atlas Obscura*, 15 February 2019. Available online: https://www.atlasobscura.com/articles/what-is-thums-up (accessed 1 May 2022).
- Patel, Dinyar. 'How Parsis Shaped India's Taste for Soft Drinks'. *BBC News*, 22 March 2020. Available online: https://www.bbc.com/news/world-asia-india-51942067 (accessed 1 May 2022).

SPICE BOX

Like all things Indian, spice mixes are marked by incredible diversity, varying markedly from one region to another, from one part of a state to another, from one home to another. British colonialists invented the fiction of the CURRY POWDER, but Indian cooking, or more accurately, the multitude of cooking styles, doesn't lend itself to a one-size-fits-all spice mix.

The best-known Indian spice mix, the garam masala (which translates as 'hot spice mix') itself is so mind-bogglingly diverse that one can get tired of collecting recipes for it. Packaged brands of this spice blend may be easily available in physical and online stores but fastidious cooks still like to keep making their own favourite version – tweaking the proportions of the constituent spices or dropping one and adding another; using whole spices (in the case of *panch phoron* or *khada* masala, for instance) as opposed to powders and pastes; and taking calls on matters such as whether or not to grate the nutmeg (see NUTMEG AND MACE) or to use green CARDAMOM with the skin on or off.

Each such judgement call can make a subtle difference to the flavour profile of the spice mix. Even the stage at which the spice mix needs to be introduced is critical to how a particular dish ends up tasting. 'If you rush this, the curry will have a raw unsavoury flavour and if the heat is turned up too high, you may end up burning your spices', advises Lathika George. 'Use your three senses – your ears to hear the sizzle, your eyes to see it happen and your nose, the most important of all, to sense the moment.' George does not list any recipe for a standard masala, for each dish in her cookbook comes with its own spice mix.

The blends owe their discreteness also to the multitude of different spices and herbs found across the country. From stone LICHEN to dried rose petals, from *triphal* (India's answer to Sichuan peppers) to *pran* (Kashmiri shallots), regional spice mixes include these lesser-known stars and stand out for their distinctive flavours. Notable among these local

FIGURE 40 SPICE BOX. Turmeric on sale in the market. Colleen Sen.

stars are the East Indian bottle masala and LUCKNOW's *lazzat-e-tam*, the latter coming with its own share of romance and mystery.

The spice mixes listed below capture some of this tantalizing variety, but the truth is, there's a unique spice mix for just about every dish that is prepared in an Indian home. Take biryani, for instance. This ubiquitous preparation comes in myriad forms not only because of the differences in the styles of preparation or the kind of rice used, or even the cuts of meat that go into it, but also because each biryani has its own spice mix, just like each fish CURRY or even something as seemingly humble as an AUBERGINE preparation.

The following is a selection of some of the popular spice mixes:

***Achari* masala**: Used primarily to flavour PICKLES, especially in northern India, it is now also a part of an entire class of *achari* mutton, chicken, PANEER and vegetable (especially POTATO) dishes where the pickle-like taste dominates. It is made by dry roasting and grinding whole red CHILLIES with CORIANDER, FENNEL, MUSTARD, CUMIN, FENUGREEK, NIGELLA and carom seeds, and mixing in TURMERIC powder, dry MANGO powder (*amchur*), ASAFOETIDA and SALT at the end of the roasting process.

It is believed that the *achari* dishes were created when families were left with pickle oil in their treasured *martaban* (the terracotta jar used primarily to store pickles) – precious oil they did not wish to discard. The flavourful oil lent itself to tangy and slightly bitter, aromatic dishes so the tradition of *achari* cooking was born. As the *martaban* gave way to packaged, mass-produced pickles, readymade *achari* masala powder started showing up in people's homes and in restaurants.

***Bafat* masala**: A must for seasoning the signature Catholic dish pork *bafat* or *dukra maas* in MANGALURU, the *bafat* (or *bafad*) masala, said to be of Indo-Portuguese origin, can also be used for the preparation of chicken or vegetable *sukka* (a dry dish with COCONUT in it) and fish curries. The masala consists of Kashmiri chillies, long red Kumta chillies, short red Madrasi chillies, coriander, cumin, black peppercorns (see PEPPER, BLACK) and dried pieces of turmeric (known locally as *haldiche kudke*) or, if these are not available, turmeric powder. When used for the pork preparation, whole CLOVES and CINNAMON are added. These ingredients are ground together into a fine powder that the Mangaloreans know as *bafad* masala.

Bhaja moshla: Not to be confused with *panch phoron* and *jhalmuri moshla*, the simple *bhaja moshla* ('dry roasted spices' in Bengali) is the key to the unique flavours of the typically Bengali *panchmishali torkari* (mixed vegetables), *ghugni* (spiced chickpea or Bengal gram curry with a mutton piece thrown in occasionally) and the best-selling street snack *phuchka* (see STREET FOOD). This masala is prepared by slowly dry roasting cumin, fennel and coriander seeds, whole cardamom, and bay leaf on a low flame (to extract the maximum flavours) and grinding them together.

Bottle masala: A speciality of the EAST INDIAN Catholic community is the aromatic bottle masala which is said to consist of from twenty-five to thirty to up to sixty spices and herbs, including allspice, black pepper, caraway seeds, cardamom, cinnamon, clove, cumin, POPPY SEEDS, SESAME, wheat and chickpeas, and the rare *dagar phool* (stone lichen), *maipatri* (mugwort), *tiraphal* (pepper leaves) and bulbs of the *nagkesar* flower (*Mesua ferrea* L.). The recipe could vary from one family to another and there's invariably a disagreement over the ingredients used (Reshampatti or Kashmiri chillies, for instance). Traditionally, the constituents of bottle masala would be dried out in the sun in the hottest, driest days before the onset of the monsoons, then roasted on a wood-fired stove (*chul*) and pounded with a tall wooden pestle in a deep wooden vat. The entire process would take three to four days and women of the Agri community used to perform the task. Coloured bottles – notably beer bottles – were used to store the masala to protect it from the sun till a new batch was made again the next year.

In *The East Indian Cookery Book*, first published in 1981 by The Bombay East Indian Association, bottle masala is listed in thirty-four recipes, including dishes that are special to the community such as duck *moile* and prawn *lonvas*. It stands out among Indian spice blends because of its subtlety.

Chaat masala: Sharp and tangy, chaat masala gets its name from the popular street snack chaat, which owes its distinctive flavour to this spice mix. It is also stirred into the Indian-style lemonade (*shikanjvi*) or sprinkled on cut fruit, green salads (especially the popular *kachumbar* – mixed diced ONION, CUCUMBER and TOMATO), dal and vegetable dishes, and raw onion rings (*lachcha pyaaz*) served at Punjabi restaurants to add zing to their taste. The use of rock salt (*kala namak*) and *amchur* (dried mango powder) set this blend apart from garam masala. It consists of cumin, coriander, fennel and carom seeds, *amchur*, rock salt, freshly ground black pepper (and/or red chilli powder), ground GINGER, dried MINT and asafoetida powder. These are dry roasted and ground together, and the powder is stored for three to four months in airtight containers.

Chettinad masala: This spice mix is central to the Chettinad cuisine of the Nattukotai Chettiars (or Nagarathars), an enterprising sea-faring mercantile community that traditionally lived in the arid belt between Ramanathapuram and Pudukottai in Tamil Nadu. The masala consists of Marathi *moggu* (dried buds of the kapok or the silk cotton tree), nutmeg and mace, rock lichen, star anise, cloves, cinnamon sticks, black peppercorns, black and green cardamom, coriander, fennel, cumin and poppy seeds, red chillies and bay leaf. These are dry roasted, allowed to cool and pounded in a mortar into a fine powder which gives character to the *kuzhambus* (thick gravies) that are responsible for Chettinad's culinary reputation.

Dhansak **masala**: The difference between this and sambar masala is subtle and is best described by Parsi caterer and food historian Kurush Dalal: '*Dhansak* masala has many more spices, but mostly the more aromatic, sweeter spices. *Sambhar* masala has the strong pickle-type spices, such as mustard seeds, chillies and also, curiously, salt.' He emphasizes that *dhansak* masala is used with several other dishes from BOMBAY DUCK cutlets to aubergine and mutton biryani, but Parsi *sambhar* masala is nearly only used in *dhansak* (see PARSIS).

Garam masala: The centrepiece of the India spice box is this blend that literally translates as 'hot spice mixture'. Despite its name, there's nothing 'hot' about it. The heat probably reflects the combined effect of many spices on revving up human metabolism. The combination keeps changing from one region of the country to the other, from one home to the next, or from one cookbook writer to another, but according to Julie SAHNI the most used spices are cumin and coriander seeds, cardamom pods, black peppercorns, broken-up cinnamon sticks, cloves and grated nutmeg. Some may even include red pepper or SAFFRON. One recipe given by Madhur JAFFREY in *BBC Food* has black cumin seeds (*Nigella sativa* L.), instead of the regular variety, and a whole (not grated) nutmeg.

The spice mix is widely available in powdered form but traditional cooks like to use freshly roasted and ground garam masala according to their personal preferences. When used whole and added to hot oil before the other ingredients, these spices go by the collective name of *khada* masala and their function is to release their essence into the cooking medium. When lightly roasted and ground into a powder, garam masala is gently sprinkled towards the end of the cooking process, thus acting as a flavour enhancer. Evocatively describing 'the magic of the garam masala', Monica Bhide writes: 'It makes such a difference in a dish: cinnamon adds sweetness, pepper adds heat, nutmeg adds complexity, coriander makes it a touch lemony and adds texture. The spices all play so well together!'

Goan masalas: Goa's signature dishes stand apart from each other because each comes with its own masala. For the rest of the world, Goa is synonymous with pork VINDALOO (*vindalho*), which is said to have descended from the Portuguese carne de *vinha d'alhos* (meat marinated in wine vinegar and garlic). What determines the flavour profile of a vindaloo, though, is the robust wet masala that shows no Portuguese influence except the use of vinegar (palm, not wine). It is made by dry roasting cumin seeds, cloves, black peppercorns, cinnamon sticks, roughly chopped ginger and garlic cloves, and dried Kashmiri and Byadagi red chillies and then grinding them together with palm vinegar (to lend the required moisture), turmeric powder, palm jaggery and a little ball of TAMARIND.

The vindaloo masala is quite similar to the *recheado* masala paste, which is stuffed into FISH such as pomfret and mackerel before they are stir-fried and served. (*Recheado* means 'stuffed' in Portuguese.) The significant presence of garlic cloves lends a distinct flavour to the masala, which is a thick paste that is freshly made. The process of preparing it starts with soaking the constituent spices in palm vinegar for a couple of hours. The ingredients include Kashmiri red chillies and garlic cloves (a good number of them), cumin, cloves, cinnamon sticks, peppercorns, fried sliced onion, cooking oil, salt and SUGAR (or palm jaggery).

Xacuti (*shagoti* in Konkani), a dish credited to the fisher-folk of Arambol, acquires its unique flavours from the complex spice mix that goes into it. The dry and chilli-hot masala is made with Kashmiri dry red chillies, turmeric, white poppy seeds, fenugreek seeds, red mustard seeds, cinnamon, clove, green and black cardamom, black peppercorn, cumin, fennel, coriander and caraway seeds, mace, whole nutmeg, bay leaves and *dagad phool* (rock lichen). Each spice is dry roasted individually and then pounded together with a pestle in a large mortar. In this day and age, an electric grinder is pressed into service, but this leads to a loss of essential oils and therefore the flavours get compromised.

Similarly, the pickle-like prawn *balchao* has its unique spice mix comprising Kashmiri and Byadagi dry red chillies, cumin seeds, turmeric powder, black peppercorns, garlic cloves, cinnamon sticks, cloves and palm vinegar. In sharp contrast to the bright red *balchao* masala, the *temperado*, which is also a filling for fish, is dull green, its colour coming from the green chillies that go into it. The ingredients, besides green chillies, are turmeric powder, garlic cloves, ginger, cumin seeds, black peppercorns, granulated white sugar (or cane jaggery) and vinegar to make it easier to grind the masala.

Another bright green masala paste goes into making chicken *cafreal*, a dish believed to have been brought by the Portuguese from Mozambique to Goa. Like all Portuguese imports, cafreal, too, got 'Goafied'. Among the ingredients of its masala paste, fresh coriander leaves are the most important. With rum as the lubricant, the leaves are ground along with roughly chopped green chillies and ginger, garlic cloves, coriander, cumin and fennel seeds, cloves, cinnamon sticks, black peppercorns, granulated white sugar and turmeric powder. The masala paste is used to marinate the chicken pieces for some time before they are fried. These fried chicken pieces are then covered with a layer each of fried onions and boiled potatoes and fried on both sides till they turn light brown.

***Goda* masala**: Maharashtra too has its share of multiple, often confusing, spice mixes. There's the ubiquitous *kanda lasun* (onion-garlic), a dry, powdered masala that you'll find appearing as a paste in the famous snack vada *pav* (see below). Then there's *goda* (pronounced 'go-da') masala, which literally means 'sweet masala' but it is sweet, to quote Amit Dassana, 'not in taste but in aroma'.

There's also a *kala* masala over which a debate rages among cookbook writers. As Kaumudi Marathé noted in *The Essential Marathi Cookbook*, 'There is still some debate if *goda* and *kala* masalas are the same. Some say they are not while others say that only Marathi Brahmins traditionally used *goda* masala. Some still refer to *goda* masala as *kala* masala.' The difference between the two, according to Dassana, is that *goda* masala does not have one of the key ingredients of *kala* masala, namely, sautéed sun-dried sliced onions, which turn flaky and can easily be ground into a masala mix.

So what are the ingredients of *goda* masala? Recipes, as usual, vary, the big debate being on the use of coconut (desiccated or dry roasted copra?). The ingredients, as listed by Dassana, are: coriander seeds, desiccated coconut flakes, sesame, cumin and caraway seeds, poppy seeds, dried red chillies (Kashmiri or Byadagi), black peppercorn, cloves, cinnamon sticks, black cardamom pods, green cardamom, bay leaf, asafoetida, star anise, stone flower, niger seeds and *nagkesar* (seeds from an evergreen tree).

These ingredients need to be roasted, one after another, on a pan with a teaspoon of oil. When the spices let off their fragrance and the chillies their fieriness, the sesame seeds change colour and the desiccated coconut turns golden brown, they must all be set aside for a little bit of cooling, only to be re-assembled for grinding in either a mortar or an electrical grinder. The masala is now ready to be used in a variety of dishes, from *amti* dal to *pudachi wadi* (stuffed chickpea fritters) and *bharleli vangi* (stuffed baby eggplant).

Gunpowder: see *podi* below.

Jhalmuri moshla: It is a spice mix that goes into a street snack that is hugely popular in West Bengal and neighbouring Bangladesh (and is even sold in London by the chef Angus Denoon from his famous Every Body Love Love Jhalmuri Express van). *Jhalmuri* ('chilli-hot puffed rice' in Bangla) is made with puffed rice (*moori/muri*), *chanachoor* (a spicy and sweet mix of fried chickpea flour noodles, lentils and peanuts), boiled Bengal gram (*kala chana*), chopped boiled potatoes, cucumber, onions and green chillies tossed together, doused with tamarind water, lemon juice and mustard oil and served in *thongas* (paper packets) made from newspapers. The uncomplicated masala for this snack is prepared with roasted cumin, coriander seeds, bay leaf, black salt, black pepper powder, *amchur* (dried green mango powder) and red pepper powder. All these ingredients are ground together to make the masala that gives *jhalmuri* its proverbial kick.

***Kanda lasun* masala**: Associated with the fiery cuisine of Kolhapur, the largest town in Maharashtra outside MUMBAI located in the state's southwestern part, the *kanda lasun* ('onion-garlic' in Marathi) masala is an elaborately produced blend of eighteen spices. It defines two of Kolhapur's signature dishes – *tambda rassa* (a copper-red, or *tambda*, soup made with mutton stock) and the town's popular version of the Maharashtrian comfort food *misal* (moth bean sprouts soup topped with *sev*, or fried chickpea flour noodles, chopped onions and coriander leaves), eaten with sliced bread and not *pav* (as in Mumbai or Pune).

In the recipe provided by Aditya Mehendala in *Rare Gems: A Non-vegetarian Gourmet Collection from Maharashtra* (2015), a part of the spices going into the *kanda lasun* masala are roasted. These are: dried Kashmiri and Byadagi red chillies (the latter could be substituted by the local Jawari/Desi variety), bay leaf, cumin, and white sesame, coriander and black cumin seeds. Then there are ingredients to be fried. These are: desiccated coconut flakes, black peppercorn, black cardamom pods, cloves, dried lichen (*dagad phool*), star anise, *nagkesar* and asafoetida. To these ingredients are added garlic cloves and onion rings (fried till they turn reddish brown), ginger and crushed sea salt, and they are all ground together to get the hot *kanda lasun* masala.

Kashmiri *ver*: Coming in the form of dried aromatic cakes, this spice mix, when sprinkled at the end of the cooking process, adds a new dimension to the flavour of a variety of dishes, from dal to mixed vegetables. 'It can be used anytime in almost any dish to add that extra punch of flavour', writes the home chef and blogger Jasleen Marwah. 'What I like about it is that you don't need much of it and it adds that warmth to a meaty dish without overpowering it.'

As in the rest of the cuisine of the Kashmir Valley, the Muslims and the Hindu Pandits have their own recipes for *ver* (pronounced as 'were'). Muslims use *pran* – the potent Kashmiri shallots – and garlic in their *ver* but Pandits do not. The basic ingredients – *pran*, dried Kashmiri chillies, fennel and cumin seeds, ginger, and garlic – are all added one by one into a traditional *langdi* (mortar) to be pounded together by a *sota* (pestle). Some recipes substitute garlic with asafoetida dissolved in water and add black cardamom pods.

To this base mix is added a finely ground masala comprising black peppercorns, cloves, cinnamon sticks, cumin seeds and some dried ginger powder (the Kashmiri *sonth*). This masala is blended with the base mix and salt. Cooking oil is then added to the blend so that it can be shaped into wheel-shaped cakes with a hole in the middle to be dried out in the sun.

Koli masala: Not to be mistaken for an ingredient that goes into FISH KOLIWADA, which is essentially a Punjabi batter-fried fish preparation from Mumbai's Sion Koliwada area, this spice mix defines the flavours of the seafood-centric cuisine of the Kolis. Originally fisherfolk, Kolis are the original inhabitants of Mumbai, their presence dating back to the time when the metropolis was just a collection of fishing villages.

The bright red Koli masala is made with a procession of ingredients: asafoetida, bay leaf, black cardamom, black cumin seeds, black peppercorn, dried Byadagi red chillies, cassia buds, cinnamon sticks, cloves, coriander, cumin, fennel, mustard and white sesame seeds, dried lichen, dried mugwort, green cardamom, grated nutmeg, star anise, *teppal* or *triphal* (the Indian cousin of Sichuan peppers), and turmeric root (*haldi ki gaanth*). These ingredients are dry roasted and ground to produce this masala, which lends character to the impressive repertoire of seafood and vegetable dishes of the Kolis.

Kundapur masala (or *taal* powder): What *bafat* masala is to the cuisine of Mangalore's Catholic community, the red chilli-dominated Kundapur masala is to the cuisine of the landed Bunts, who are famous for their *gassis* (curries) and *sukkas* (dry preparations). Kundapur (or Kundapura) is a coastal town in the temple district of Udupi, which is a two-hour drive away from the port city of Mangalore. It is famous for its chicken ghee roast and also for the *taal* powder, which consists of a heavy presence of Byadagi dried red chillies (the extensive use of coconut in Bunt cuisine balances this preponderance of chillies), coriander, cumin and fenugreek seeds, whole black peppercorns, and garlic cloves (unpeeled and dehydrated – dry roasted till they turn crisp). The red chillies are first roasted in coconut oil and set apart. The other spices then follow. Once they cool down, they are ground together with the red chillies and dehydrated garlic, and the masala is ready for use (and for storage for up to a year).

***Lazzat-e-tam* (*potli ka* masala)**: Much mystery surrounded this aromatic spice mix upon which are founded the *nafasat* (refinement) and *nazakat* (delicateness) of Lucknow's fine cuisine (also known as Awadhi cuisine), especially its biryani and the soft-as-butter mutton *galauti* KEBAB. Available only in a few old grocer's shops at Lucknow's Bawarchi Tola in the Aminabad locality, the *lazzat-e-tam* was somewhat of an enigma because its recipe was a closely guarded secret for a long time. It became known as *potli ka* masala, in fact, because cooks in the past would carry a pouch (*potli*) of it literally close to their chest and produced it only when required so that no one else in the kitchen could guess its contents. The veil of secrecy was lifted by Sangeeta Bhatnagar and R.K. Saxena in their now hard-to-find book *Dastarkhwan-e-Awadh* (*The Table of Awadh*).

The recipe calls for a multitude of ingredients such as cloves, green cardamom, nutmeg and mace, cinnamon, black peppercorns, cumin, coriander, caraway and fennel seeds, *baobeer* (barberries), allspice, dried coconut, *jarakush* (dried lemongrass), edible sandalwood powder, dried rose petals, *makhana* (lotus seeds), poppy seeds, ANISE seeds, bay leaf, white pepper, fennel leaves, *kewra* (screwpine) water and *mitha attar* (an essential oil of rose) (see FLOWER WATERS). It is believed that *paan ki jadh* (betel leaf roots) and *khus ki jadh* (vetiver roots) also go into *lazzat-e-tam*, although the quoted recipe does not include these. The dry ingredients are lightly roasted on a griddle on slow flame, allowed to cool down and then pounded or ground into a fine powder. To this powder are added *kewra* and *mitha attar* at the end, giving *lazzat-e-tam* its distinctive fragrance.

Malvani masala: Named after a coastal town in Sindhudurg, the southernmost district of Maharashtra famous for the island-fort built by the warrior-king Chhatrapati Shivaji, this spice mix provides the flavour base of the region's signature dishes, notably *kombdi vade* (chicken curry with *vade*, or fluffy fried breads, made with sorghum or a mix of rice and lentil flours, and washed down with *solkadhi*, the refreshing *KOKUM*-flavoured coconut milk drink), *paplet saar* (pomfret curry), *bangda* fry (fried mackerel rubbed with Malvani masala), *kelfulachi bhaji* (stir-fried BANANA flowers) and Malvani *kurkuri bhindi* (crispy-fried OKRA).

The masala's ingredients are dry red chillies, coriander, fennel, cumin and poppy seeds, whole black peppercorns, mace, cloves, cinnamon stick, star anise, stone lichen, nutmeg powder, turmeric powder and asafoetida. The ingredients are dry roasted and then ground into a coarse dull brown powder exuding enticing aromas.

Meet mirsang: This is the salt and chilli paste used in Mangalorean homes to marinate fish, especially when the favourite mackerel fry is being made. It helps rid the fish of its fishy smell and makes it taste good as well. Traditionally ground with a generous helping of vinegar in a mortar and pestle (*gatno*), the paste consists of red chillies (Byadagi/Kumti/Kundapur), cumin seeds, turmeric powder and salt. It also comes packaged in stores.

Panch phoron: Used extensively in West Bengal and Bangladesh, and also in Assam, the Mithila region (which straddles certain districts in Bihar, Jharkhand and Nepal), and Odisha, the name of this robust spice mix literally translates as 'five spices' in Bangla. It is called *pas puron* in Axomiya (Assamese), *pancha phutana* in Odia, *painch phoranah* in Maithili and *padkaune* masala in Nepali. From *santuala* (mixed vegetable) and *dahi baigan* (fried brinjals in curd), loved by the Odias, to the sweet and savoury CHUTNEY made with tomato and DATES, which is served before desserts towards the end of every Bengali celebratory meal, *panch phoron* drives the flavour of a variety of dishes. It also used for pickling vegetables.

Unlike most other spice mixes, *panch phoron* is not used as a powder or a paste but as a blend of five whole spices, which typically are fenugreek, nigella, cumin, black mustard and fennel seeds. They are added when the mustard oil (the region's favoured cooking medium) is hot so that their sharp yet delicate flavour can express itself well. Only after they start sizzling do the main ingredients go in. Some go slow on the fenugreek so that the bitterness of the seeds is not pronounced in the dish being prepared.

Bengalis replace mustard seeds with *radhuni*, which are often confused with celery seeds but are actually the dried fruit of the wild celery plant (*Trachyspermum roxburghianum* L.). The look and flavour of these seeds are very much like that of *ajwain* (carom seeds, see AJOWAN) – in fact, the Sanskrit root (*ajomodika*) of their Hindi name (*AJMUD*) is the same as for *ajwain*. It is critical to the taste profile of *shukto*, the slightly bitter dish made with mixed vegetables including bitter GOURD, *bori* (sun-dried lentil dumplings) and mustard paste which is served at the beginning of a traditional Bengali meal.

Parsi *sambhar* masala: Not to be confused with the masala used in the southern Indian states to add to the soupy SAMBAR, the Parsi *sambhar* masala is the key differentiator of the community's favourite dish *dhansak*, and is also used to flavour other meat and vegetable dishes. Freshly ground every morning on the 'curry stone' (masala *no patthar*) in old-fashioned households, the dull red wet masala consists of Kashmiri chilli powder, roasted mustard seeds, broken cinnamon sticks, black peppercorns, whole cloves, ground turmeric, fenugreek seeds, untoasted sesame (gingelly) oil and salt.

To this list, Niloufer Ichaporia King, drawing from Bhikoo Manekshaw's *Parsi Food and Customs* and Sarla Sanghvi's original 1959 Time and Talents Club cookbook, adds asafoetida in its natural resinous form ('This is the only use of asafoetida I know of in Parsi cooking', she writes.) and a broken-up star anise pod.

Podi: This is an umbrella term for a dry condiment, also known as gunpowder, which is popular across southern India where it is mixed with boiled rice or IDLIS (steamed rice pancakes) and GHEE to temper its pungency, or had with DOSAS. In its many manifestations – *milagai podi* in Tamil Nadu, *vangi podi* in Andhra Pradesh and chutney *pudi* in Karnataka and Kerala – the common ingredients are dry roasted and ground lentils (commonly *urad* – split black gram, *chana* – Bengal gram and *tuvar* – pigeon peas), dried red chillies (Guntur in Andhra Pradesh or Byadagi in Karnataka), cumin seeds, sesame seeds or peanuts, and coconut or untoasted sesame oil. To these may be added, depending on the region or the family, copra (dried coconut), garlic cloves, toasted CURRY LEAVES, tamarind and even jaggery.

***Salan* masala**: It is hard to imagine the famed HYDERABADI biryani without the accompanying *mirchi ka salan*, plump green chillies cooked in thin gravy. The masala is what gives the *salan* its base. It is made with dry roasted peanuts, sesame seeds and desiccated coconut flakes, fried onions and ginger-garlic paste all blended together into a coarse lump. The paste is introduced after the green chillies are fried, followed by cumin and mustard seeds (till they crackle), and curry leaves (till they turn crisp). Once the paste is stirred in, turmeric powder, garam masala and filtered tamarind water are added. At the end chillies are again added and cooked in the gravy till they start wilting a little.

South Indian sambar masala: This is the masala that lends character to the stew/soup called sambar which is made with lentils, vegetables and tamarind pulp and is eaten daily in all the southern states of India and in northern Sri Lanka. (It is slightly sweeter and is called *saaru* in the Old Mysuru region of Karnataka.) The recipe varies from one household to another.

In the temple town of Udupi, the sambar masala blends together coriander seeds and red chillies sautéed separately in coconut oil, roasted and ground cumin seeds, fenugreek seeds, *urad* dal (split black gram) and *chana* dal (Bengal gram), and curry leaves (roasted till they turn crisp); turmeric powder is added separately. Sambar is cooked in two stages. The vegetables, tamarind pulp, sambar masala, turmeric, salt and asafoetida are first boiled together until the vegetables are half-cooked. Cooked lentils are then added and the stew is taken off the fire only after the vegetables are done.

Tandoori masala: More pungent than garam masala because it has ground dried red chillies in it, this spice mix gives tandoori cuisine its distinctive flavour. Primarily mixed in yogurt to be used in marinades for meats, fish, seafood, paneer, vegetables and fruit before they are roasted in a tandoor, the masala blends dried red chillies (preferably Kashmiri because of their bright red colour), cumin and coriander seeds, whole cloves, cinnamon sticks, ginger, turmeric and mace – all toasted and ground together into a powder – apart from garlic powder and salt. Some tandoori masala recipes, interestingly, call for the addition of garam masala.

Vadouvan: This is a blend of Indian spices and French herbs that originated in Puducherry (the former French colony of Pondicherry) in southern India. Ingredients may include garlic, cumin seed, turmeric, cardamom, mustard seed, coriander, fenugreek, red pepper, onions or shallots, and thyme. Traditionally, the mixture is dried, crushed, mixed with castor oil, and rolled into balls which are dried in the sun or in an oven. It has a slightly smoky flavour. *Vadouvan* is likely a variation of the Tamil spice mixture *vadakam*. In recent years, it has become fashionable in the West as chefs such as Daniel Boulud have begun using it in their dishes.

Sourish Bhattacharyya

- Bhide, Monica. 'Garam Masala: A Taste Worth Acquiring'. *NPR*, 27 April 2011. Available online: https://www.npr.org/2011/04/27/135761263/garam-masala-a-taste-worth-acquiring (accessed 2 May 2022).

- D'Cruz, Beverly Ann. 'How Mumbai's Masalawaalis Make a Single Spice from 30 Ingredients'. *Atlas Obscura*, 20 September 2019. Available online: https://www.atlasobscura.com/articles/bottle-masala (accessed 2 May 2022).
- Jaffrey, Madhur. 'Garam Masala'. *BBC Food*, *n.d.* Available online: https://www.bbc.co.uk/food/recipes/garammasala_90213 (accessed 2 May 2022).
- Sahu, Deepika. 'The Power of Five Seeds'. *The Times of India*, 26 August 2012. Available online: https://timesofindia.indiatimes.com/The-power-of-five-seeds/articleshow/12594289.cms (accessed 2 May 2022).

STEEL, FLORA ANNIE

Flora Annie Steel was the co-author, with Grace Gardiner, of one of the most important books for women living in India in the nineteenth century, *The Complete Indian Housekeeper and Cook*, published in 1888. It was an invaluable resource and provided practical advice on all aspects of housekeeping and colonial life in India. There are chapters on such things as 'The Duties of the Mistress', 'The Storeroom', 'Hints on Breakfasts, Dinners, Luncheons etc.', (including 'Afternoon Teas'), 'The Duties of the Servants', 'Hints on Camp Life', 'Tables of Wages, Weights, etc.', 'Hints on Outfits, etc.', 'Hints on Nursing', 'Advice to the Cook', and more. There are numerous recipes for soups, FISH, sauces, high-class entrees and garnishes, savouries, vegetables and salads, game, hot puddings, cold SWEETS, pastes and pastry, baked goods, confectionery, jams, preserves, eggs, ices, sandwiches, native dishes and vegetarian cookery. The book became a bestseller and was published in many editions till 1921.

Flora Annie Steel was born Flora Annie Webster at Sudbury Priory, Harrow in 1847. She was the sixth child of George Webster. When she was just twenty, she accepted a written proposal of marriage and within months sailed out to India with her husband Henry William Steel, a member of the Indian Civil Service. She was one of many young women setting out to India in those days and most of them had no idea what they were letting themselves in for. Life in India for these young women could be very difficult, not least the heat they had to contend with but also having to take on many responsibilities including the supervision of the kitchen and getting to grips with the formalities of entertaining. However, Mrs Steel adapted well to her new life which included being constantly transferred to different stations, often miles from other Europeans. She was renowned for her energy and took on many responsibilities with the local population. She became the 'local doctor', a schools' inspectress and acted as peace maker when local disputes arose. She also became interested in Indian culture and history. Her daughter's birth gave her the opportunity to mix with the local women and learn their language and about their way of life. She encouraged the production of local handicrafts and collected and translated folk tales. In 1884 her first book, *Wide Awake Stories*, was published.

A year after the publication of *The Complete Indian Housekeeper and Cook* in 1889, Flora moved back to Scotland with her husband and daughter, where, with her life in India usually being her inspiration, she wrote numerous books including a novel *On the*

Face of the Waters (1896), which describes the Indian Mutiny. She died in 1929 shortly after completing her autobiography *The Garden of Fidelity*.

Helen Saberi

- Steel, Flora Annie. *The Garden of Fidelity: Being the Autobiography of Flora Annie Steel 1847–1929*. London: Macmillan, 1929.
- Steel, Flora Annie and Grace Gardiner. *The Complete Indian Housekeeper and Cook*. 4th edition. 1888. Reprint. London: William Heinemann, 1921.

STOKES, SATYANANDA

Samuel Evans (later Satyananda) Stokes (1882–1946) was an American Quaker missionary, theological writer and follower of Mahatma GANDHI who introduced India's most commonly grown APPLE variety, the Red Delicious, which has transformed the economy of the Himalayan state of Himachal Pradesh. Today, thanks to Stokes's legacy, the state that was never known for apples is a close second to the Kashmir Valley, which has been historically famous for its indigenous Ambri variety.

Son of a wealthy American businessman, Stokes chose a life of service to the poor and arrived in India in 1904 to work at a home for people living with leprosy at Sabathu in Himachal Pradesh's beer-producing district of Solan. His work attracted the attention of the Archbishop of Canterbury who advised him to establish the Indian chapter of the Franciscan order. Stokes, who had mastered the Pahari dialect and dressed like the people around him, toyed with the idea for two years and embraced a life of poverty. In 1912, however, he turned his back on religious practice, married a local woman named Agnes and settled down as a farmer on land in Thanedar village in the Kotgarh Valley, eighty-two km from Shimla, the summer capital of the British Raj.

Here Stokes built his stately home, Harmony Hall, in the local architectural style but he soon realized that the local farming practices and harsh winter were not conducive to economically viable agriculture. He then hit upon the idea of getting into fruit cultivation. Pursuing his idea, in 1914 Stokes went to the United States with soil samples. Here he came across the Red Delicious variety which was being propagated by the Stark Brothers Nurseries (founded 1816) which, incidentally, is still in the apple business. Stokes brought back saplings and planted them in his orchard in 1916.

The Red Delicious (and its sibling the Golden Delicious) found an instant following because it was sweeter than the Pippins variety, which was then locally available in small quantities, and was suited to the local palate. As the apple variety became famous, Stokes started distributing saplings for free to farmers, and still found time to write a book on the historicity of Christ. He also plunged into the nationalist movement, becoming the first and only American to be ever elected to the All-India Congress Committee. He was arrested and imprisoned on sedition charges in 1921, which provoked Mahatma GANDHI to editorialize on the matter in his journal, *Young India*.

All this while, the propagation of apples continued unabated and Stokes, after being freed, set up an academy at Harmony Hall to train future horticulturists. From a Christian missionary Stokes had become an 'apple missionary', and converted to Hinduism in 1932 under the influence of the teachings of Dayananda Saraswati, founder of the Arya Samaj reform movement. When Samuel Evans Stokes died as Satyananda on 14 May 1946, Himachal Pradesh (then a part of the Punjab state) was producing 15,000 boxes of apples a year. The latest figures for 2019 show that the state accounted for 37 million boxes (or

447,000 metric tons) of apples, second in volume only to the Kashmir Valley, worth Rs 45 billion. Stokes could never have dreamt of it.

Sourish Bhattacharyya

- Mulki, Mayur. 'Satyananda Stokes and the Apple State'. *LiveHistoryIndia*, 18 August 2018. Available online: https://www.livehistoryindia.com/story/religious-places-/satyananda-stokes-and-the-apple-state (accessed 1 May 2022).
- Nighoshkar, Devyani. 'An Orchard in the Hills: At Himachal's Thanedhar Estate'. *Firstpost*, 15 September 2019. Available online: https://www.firstpost.com/long-reads/an-orchard-in-the-hills-at-himachals-thanedhar-estate-lessons-in-apple-picking-and-history-7317251.html (accessed 1 May 2022).
- Roshan, Manas. 'The Swadeshi Apple'. *Mint*, 20 October 2017.
- Sharma, Asha. *An American in Gandhi's India*. Bloomington, IN: Indiana University Press, 2008.

STREET FOOD

Comprising ready-to-eat, affordable and accessible local dishes served by hawkers from push carts and vans on roadsides and beaches mainly for the benefit of the working class, office-goers, pilgrims, commuters and tourists, street food is ubiquitous across India and is rooted in the history of its cities and towns. Given the overflowing cornucopia of culinary offerings, street food draws from the geographical and cultural specificities

FIGURE 41 STREET FOOD. Plate of momos. Ritesh Man Tamrakar/Wikimedia Commons.

FIGURE 42 STREET FOOD. Students enjoying street food in New Delhi. Ashish Sen.

of a particular place, so if MUMBAI has its vada *pav*, DELHI its *chhole bhature*, KOLKATA its *phuchka* and CHENNAI its *atho man*, the list does not stop at these metropolises but extends deep into cities and towns across the country.

Cities such as AMRITSAR and Indore owe a part of their reputation to their vibrant street food culture. Each one of them has its signature dish as well as inventions such as tandoori momos; 'frankies' (paratha rolls filled primarily with fried vegetables but, now, increasingly with mutton, chicken and egg); the spicier, oilier precursors of the top-selling McDonald's product in India, McAloo Tikki Burger; Maggi instant noodles cooked in myriad ways; and even Szechwan dosa. Street food is serious business in India; according to the National Association of Street Vendors of India (NASVI), which organizes India's only recognized street food festival, it provides a living to more than 3 million families. And although street food vendors do come into conflict with municipal authorities and courts, they have developed a healthy working relationship with the Food Safety and Standards Authority of India (FSSAI), which has been working on the idea of 'safe food hubs' and bridging the trust divide between the vendors and the authorities. Also active are brands such as Dettol, which is promoting a culture of hygiene beyond hand washing in the street food sector.

Cities have their famous food streets that are both sources of sustenance for hungry souls and tourist magnets. Delhi has Chandni Chowk and Matia Mahal. Kolkata has Dharmatala (renamed Lenin Sarani) and Tiretti Bazar, which is famous for its Sunday Chinese food bazaar. There's Chowk in LUCKNOW, which is frequented by hundreds of KEBAB lovers daily. Indore is famous for its Sarafa Bazaar, which is a jewellery market by day and a street food mile by night. And then there is Mohammad Ali Road in Mumbai, Sowcarpet in Chennai, the Charminar neighbourhood in HYDERABAD, V.V. Puram in BENGALURU, Sadar Bazar in Agra (the city of the Taj Mahal), Manek Chowk or the Kankaria Lake in Ahmedabad, Ghantaghar Bazar in Jodhpur, Mauryalok Complex in Patna and the stretch around the Golden Temple in Amritsar.

In these cities, many of the street food outlets have grown into shops that now have a long history, and some, like Karim's, established in 1913 in the shadow of Jama Masjid, India's largest mosque ensconced in the historic parts of Delhi, have evolved into celebrated restaurants, albeit down-at-heel and still affordable.

At Gali Paranthewali in Delhi's Chandni Chowk, which has traditionally been the go-to destination for fried stuffed flatbreads (paratha), Pandit Gaya Prasad Shiv Charan's shop dates back to 1872. Across the street from Jama Masjid, in Matia Mahal, the Old Kheer Shop, serving only *Bade Miyan ki kheer* (rice pudding, see *KHEER*), was opened in 1880. And at Bazar Sitaram not too far away, the city's best KULFI with fresh seasonal fruit pulp, a must at summer weddings, is served at Kudemal Mahavir Prasad, whose family history goes back to 1906. As these random examples indicate, each one of these establishments is associated with a single delicacy which, for decades, has been responsible for its abiding fame.

Likewise, Lucknow has its Tunday Kababi (so named because the man who first ran this famous kebab shop did not have one arm) and Idrees, the biryani maker, at the historic Chowk, and its redoubtable chaat shops such as Shree Kalika Chaat House (Aminabad), Pandit Chaat Corner (Naka Charbagh), Chappan Bhog (Sadar) and Shukla Chaat (Hazratganj). Then there is Ram Asrey, a SWEET shop in business since 1805, which is famous for its *malai ki gilori* or *balai ki gilori* (a triangular sweetmeat, shaped like a *PAAN*, with a dollop of fresh cream stuffed with NUTS and SUGAR crystals and decorated with a silver leaf, or *VARK*). The shop is equally known for its winter delicacy, *kali gajar ka* HALWA, prepared with purple CARROTS.

On Ahmedabad's streets, the reigning delicacies come with tantalizing names such as *bakhri* pizza (loaded with Amul cheese), Gwalior dosa (oozing butter) and Surti *ghotala* omelette (originally from Surat, this 'scam' – *ghotala* – of an omelette is packed with processed cheese). A city in love with its *farsaan*, snacks, Ahmedabad has its favourites such as Induben Khakrawala, where *khakras*, crackers made with moth beans and wheat flour, come in multiple flavours and shapes, and Das Khaman, which has been in business since 1922 selling an appetizing variety of the savoury *khaman*, steamed savoury cakes prepared with freshly ground *chana* dal (gram) flour and tempered with ASAFOETIDA, MUSTARD seeds and dried red CHILLIES.

Known across India as the *chatoron ka shahar* (city of foodies), Indore is famous for its *batla KACHORI* (peas-stuffed pastries) and *khopra* patties (COCONUT-stuffed POTATO patties) of Vijay Chaat House; Johny (that's indeed the name of the shop!) Hot Dog's eggs *benjo*, which is a spicy omelette stuffed in a slit buttery bun; the *dahi* vadas (lentil balls dipped in yogurt and topped with CHUTNEYS and spices) of Joshi; the much-copied *bhutte ka kees* (grated corn cooked in milk with spices and garnished with fresh coconut shavings) and *garadu* (a deep-fried yam snack) at A-1 Garadu; and the *jalebas* (magnum *JALEBIS*) of Jai Bhole Jalebi Bhandar. Each shop or stall is associated with a particular edible attraction, making it a foodie magnet.

Examples such as these can be multiplied across the country – enough to fill an entire volume – and they show up in different entries of this book, but a survey, however brief, of Indian street food cannot be complete without a mention of Hyderabad, the IT city in the south that was named the UNESCO Creative City of Gastronomy in 2019.

The food sector employs 12 per cent of the city's population, which goes to show that eating out is taken seriously in Hyderabad. Its food street is the area around its defining landmark, the Charminar. In the shadow of this striking monument with four minarets built in 1591, shops sell local favourites such as *patti* SAMOSA (thin and crusty triangular pastries stuffed with spiced vegetables), *pathar ke gosht* (escalopes of meat cooked on hot stone) and the creamy mutton soup called *marag*, as well as the local Osmania biscuits, plum cake, coconut-stuffed sweet buns known as *dilkush* and other baked snacks served with the sweet and milky Irani *chai* at go-to destinations such as Cafe Niloufer, Karachi Bakery and Nimrah Cafe.

Also famous around Charminar are the restaurants serving biryani and *HALEEM* (a meat, WHEAT and lentil stew that comes with a GEOGRAPHICAL INDICATION tag). Notable among them are Paradise, Pista House, Shadab, Shah Ghouse and Lucky, which, despite their shabby appearance, make millions and also divide the food connoisseurs, each of whom has a particular favourite among these formidable names. Equally famous around Charminar (and beyond) are the '*bandi*s' – pushcarts (some, such as Ram Ki Bandi, have graduated to become multi-outlet restaurant chains) – that sell 'fusion' food items, including DOSAS with a cube of Amul butter melting on them at Govind's food truck, the double cheese dosa at Ram's outside Karachi Bakery in the Moazzam Jahi Market, and the egg dosa prepared at a stall on the Yousufguda Main Road. These are not dishes that diners are likely to encounter on a regular table or a fancy restaurant, but they have caught the fancy of the local populace and hence are popular among tourists too.

Street food is also evolving across India and it is evident everywhere. In Delhi, for instance, momos, or dumplings introduced by people of Nepalese and Tibetan origin, are coated with the tandoori spice mix and grilled in a charcoal-fired oven at QDs, a restaurant that is hugely popular among university students. Momos now also come with hitherto unheard-of stuffing such as BUTTER CHICKEN and even chocolate.

In Kolkata, scoops of ice-cream dipped in colas are a summertime hit at Balwant Singh Eating House. And the city's famous traditional sweet shops are also changing with the times, as is evident from Girish Chandra Dey & Nakur Chandra Nandi introducing butterscotch SANDESH and Balaram Mullick & Radharaman Mullick appealing to the young generation with its orange *roshogolla* (see RASGULLA). In Ahmedabad, the state capital of the predominantly vegetarian Gujarat, people make up for the absence of meats and fish in their diet by patronizing roadside stalls and humble shops selling a mind-boggling variety of stuffed omelettes. In Surat, the city of diamonds close to Ahmedabad, the Bhai Bhai Omelette Centre sells more than 100 types. But, the record in this department belongs to Delhi's Rahul Eggs, which has a menu spilling over with 350 varieties including the popular Tandoori Jalandhari Omelette which comes stuffed with chicken tikka and is topped with mayonnaise and tomato ketchup.

The inventiveness does not stop with momos and omelettes. The popular Amarnath chaat cart in Bengaluru, for instance, serves ice-cream *bondas* (a scoop of ice-cream coated in breadcrumbs, fried, then cut into two halves and served with either LYCHEE or strawberry jelly) and chocolate-stuffed IDLIS or dosas with flavoured jellies and ice-cream. Dosa Verito, in Hyderabad's twin city Secunderabad, serves 151 varieties of dosa, including one stuffed with macaroni and another with blueberry ice-cream. Even the samosa is being re-imagined. At the Aman Samosa Shop in Delhi, you get a Chinese samosa (stuffed with noodles), macaroni samosa (with macaroni and cheese) and also a chocolate samosa (a dessert invented by Vineet Bhatia in London and now much copied all over).

India's street food vendors are pushing the envelope of creativity, venturing into territories that the more established restaurants are loath to explore, even as they preserve traditional dishes that could have disappeared with time.

Anubhav Sapra and *Sourish Bhattacharyya*

SUGAR

Sugarcane (*Saccharum officinarum*) is a member of the bamboo family. It originated as a wild grass in New Guinea in ancient times and is the origin of all modern cultivated species. It thrives in tropical climates and can grow in a wide range of soil conditions. At some point in prehistory, the plant reached India where it was probably hybridized with a wild grass to yield thinner and sweeter canes. In ancient times sugarcane was grown throughout North India, especially Bengal. Today the leading sugar-producing states are Uttar Pradesh, Maharashtra, Karnataka and Tamil Nadu. In recent years, India has vied with Brazil for the position of the world's top sugar producer. In the 2020–1 marketing year, production is projected to reach a record 34 million metric tonnes due to bumper crops. The sugar is processed in nearly 500, mainly cooperative, sugar mills. Harvesting the cane is very labour-intensive and employs around 50 million people.

Most Indian sugar is consumed domestically, although a small amount is exported. Per capita consumption rose rapidly from 22 g/day in 2000 to 55.3 g/day in 2010 but has levelled off in recent years because of health concerns, especially the growing prevalence of diabetes. Consumers are now being encouraged to make healthier food choices, and in 2019 the FSSAI introduced a colour-coding system to indicate a product's relative fat, sugar and sodium levels.

FIGURE 43 SUGAR. Sugarcane mill driven by bullock. British Library/Wikimedia Commons.

In ancient times, the main method of sweetening in India was HONEY (which was forbidden to Jains because it destroyed the bees' homes). Sugar is not mentioned in the *Rigveda,* although the *Atharavaveda* (1000–900 BCE) refers to the chewing of sugarcane (Sanskrit *ikshu*). Early texts mention twelve varieties of cane. Around the eighth century BCE, Indians developed a technique for processing sugar. Buddhist texts refer to the crushing of the reed in a press called a *yantra* driven by oxen – a precursor to the mortar and pestle press that was used into the twentieth century. It may have been based on the press used to extract *soma* in Vedic rituals. The juice was filtered, then boiled in a large metal pot over a fire fuelled by sugar cane stalks. Stirring concentrated the sweetness of the extraction and prevented crystallization; vegetable clarifiers brought impurities to the surface which were skimmed off. The syrup, called *phanita,* was cooked down until it resembled a soft bread-like dough which was dried in the sun until it hardened. This was the product known in Hindi as *gur* (from a Sanskrit word meaning 'ball'), in English jaggery (a word derived from the Sanskrit *sarkara*, a form of sugar). *Gur* began to be used in the preparation of sweets and still is today.

The Spanish friar Sebastien Manrique, who spent 1628 to 1641 travelling across India and Arakan (now in Myanmar), noticed how the people of Bengal were adept at preparing 'in their own way' many kinds of milk-based food and sweetmeats, 'for they have a great abundance of sugar in those parts'. Manrique added: 'Entire streets could be seen wholly occupied by skilled sweetmeat makers, who proved their worth by offering wonderful sweet-scented dainties of all kinds which would stimulate the most jaded appetite to gluttony.'

Further refining produced *khanda* (the origin of the English word 'candy' via the Arabic *qandi*). In 326 BCE the Greek historian Herodotus described 'stones the colour of frankincense, sweeter than figs or honey'. After being boiled down, the sugarcane juice was rinsed in water from aquatic leaves to wash away the molasses; a layer of sugar crystals formed. After it was dissolved again and crystallized, it formed an almost white sugar called *misri* (from Egypt) or *chini* (from China). The origin of these names is uncertain: perhaps they were invented by some early marketing experts to add prestige and value to their product!

Another product was *sarkara* (from a Sanskrit word meaning word meaning pebbles or coarse sand), which denoted hard sugar crystals drained from syrup that were white in colour. Indian physicians believed that products became sweeter and cooler as their whiteness increased but also more difficult to digest. Chewing sugarcane was considered nutritionally superior to drinking the pressed juice. Sugar was also a component in beverages, both non-alcoholic and alcoholic (see ALCOHOL). The word *sarkara* became the origin of the word for 'sugar' in many Indo-European languages. Some form of sugar was exported in small quantities to Greece but, like rice, it was used mainly as medicine. At least two Chinese missions were sent to India to learn the technology of sugar refining in the seventh century CE.

By the sixth century CE, sugar cultivation and processing had reached Persia, and from there that knowledge was brought into the Mediterranean by the Arabs. Arab entrepreneurs adopted sugar refining techniques from India and built large plantations and refineries. Sugar cane was grown in southern Europe starting in the ninth century. Christopher Columbus took sugar cane to the New World on his second voyage in 1493. It flourished on the island of Hispaniola. The Dutch were responsible for creating a plantation system based on large land holdings and African slave labour. The system spread throughout the Caribbean and to Brazil. Starting in the mid-nineteenth century, following the abolition of slavery in the British Empire in 1845, millions of Indians migrated to the Caribbean, Mauritius and other parts of the world as indentured labourers to work on the sugar plantations (see DIASPORA).

Sugar is also made from the sap or nectar of several varieties of palm trees, including the palmyra, toddy and COCONUT palms. The liquid is boiled down to a thick fudge-like consistency which is used widely in South Asian cooking. *Nolen gur* is a famous Bengali winter delicacy made from the fruit of the date palm that is added to SANDESH, KHEER and other Bengali sweets.

While sugar is a common component of sweet dishes throughout the subcontinent (see SWEETS), in some regions it is added to savoury dishes. Bengalis typically add a pinch of sugar to vegetarian dishes, as do Gujaratis, who also include a lump of *gur* in their thalis (see COOKING AND DINING).

Colleen Sen

- Gopal, Lallanji. 'Sugar Making in Ancient India'. *Journal of the Economic and Social History of the Orient* 7, no. 1 (1964): 57–72.

SWEETS

In no other part of the world are sweets (Hindi *mithai*) as important as in India. Members of all communities give and consume sweets to celebrate happy events and to mark RITES OF PASSAGE such as the birth of a child or a marriage. In the Hindu classification of foods by qualities, SUGAR, milk and GHEE, the bases of many sweets, are considered *sattvic* – a

FIGURE 44 SWEETS. Sweet stall in Mathura, Uttar Pradesh. Ashish Sen.

Sanskrit term meaning pure, conducive to lucidity and calmness – and thus can be eaten by everyone, even the most orthodox vegetarians. Sweets are considered ritually pure and are offered to the gods and distributed to the devotees at Hindu temples. Sweets are sometimes eaten during fasts or are used to break a fast.

At the end of Ramadan, the month of fasting, Muslims prepare *khorma* (*khurma*), a thick pudding made of sautéed vermicelli, thickened milk, sugar, DATES and, sometimes, NUTS, raisins, rosewater (see FLOWER WATERS) and SAFFRON for breakfast. Christians celebrate Christmas with delicious fruitcakes, while Parsis enjoy dishes that reflect European, Iranian and Indian influences such as *mava malido*, an egg and semolina pudding, or *koomas*, a spiced baked cake.

Normally, Indian meals do not end with a dessert, except sometimes with a fruit or sweetened yogurt, but sweets and savoury items are part of the late afternoon meal called tea or TIFFIN. Some sweets are made at home but, today, most are purchased from professional sweet-makers, called *halwai* or *moira*, since the process of making some sweets can be extremely lengthy and labour-intensive. Originally all Indian sweets were made by hand but today some sweet-makers use machines to prepare certain basic ingredients and for some stages of preparation, including curdling, grinding, mixing and packing in vacuum tins. Some sweets are prepared only during certain seasons.

The two main ingredients in Indian sweets are sugar and milk. India is the world's second largest sugar producer after Brazil. Indians are also the world's largest consumers of sugar, consuming 60 per cent more than China's comparable population, while middle-class Indians consume more sugar per capita than Americans. After sugar, the most common ingredient in sweets is cow or buffalo milk. According to the FAO, India is the largest producer of milk in the world, producing 180 million tons in 2017–18; around half of this is used in the manufacture of traditional dairy-based sweets and products (see DAIRY SECTOR). Buffalo milk has double the fat content of cow milk and is preferred by some sweet aficionados. One way of using milk in sweets is to slowly boil it down until it thickens into a solid called *KHOYA* (also spelled *khoa*) or *mawa*, which is a common ingredient in many sweets, especially in North and West India. Another product made from milk is *CHHANA*, or curds, which is produced by bringing milk to a boil and adding a souring agent. *Chhana* is used mainly in sweets in the eastern part of India. Unlike *khoya*, *chhana* has a short shelf life and is best prepared a few hours before making the sweets.

Other ingredients include ghee, chickpeas and lentils (see PULSES), *besan* (ground chickpea flour), RICE and rice flour, WHEAT and other grains, fruits, vegetables, NUTS (especially almonds, cashews and pistachios), seeds (especially SESAME seeds), and raisins. Most costly varieties are decorated with rose petals or silver leaf (*VARK*). Ghee is the preferred cooking medium. Popular flavourings include rosewater or *kewra* (screwpine) water (see FLOWER WATERS) and spices, especially CARDAMOM. Traditional colouring agents include SAFFRON, cochineal (red) and pistachio, although today manufactured dyes are often used. Most sweets are subjected to some form of heat treatment that enables them to be preserved.

Categories of sweets include the following:

- Hard or semi-hard and dry: BARFI, HALWA, LADDU, *MODAKA*, *pedha*, SANDESH.
- Soft: halwa.
- Frozen: KULFI, ice-cream.

- In a liquid or syrup: RASGULLA, JALEBI, *gulab jamun*, *ras malai* (see RASGULLA), *LEDIKENI*.
- Crunchy: *chikki, gur papdi.*
- Puddings/custards: KHEER, *payasam*, *zarda*, FIRNI, *RABRI*.
- Crepes: *pantua*, *malpua*.
- Yogurt-based: *misthti doi*, *SHRIKHAND*.
- European: *bibinca*, fruit cake, biscuits.

Sugarcane was not known to the inhabitants of the Indus Valley/Harappan Civilization; their main sources of sweetening were HONEY, dates, palm sugar and such fruits as jujube, *JAMUN* and MANGO. The earliest sweet dish that was mentioned in Sanskrit texts around 1000 BCE is *apupa*, a round cake made of BARLEY meal or rice flour cooked in ghee over a slow fire and sweetened with honey, a precursor of the modern Bengali *malpua*. There are also references to *ksira* (milk and boiled rice), the ancestor of modern rice puddings.

Sweet dishes and snacks feature prominently in old cookbooks such as the eleventh century *Lokopakara* which has recipes for dishes found today in Karnataka and Maharashtra, such as *mandige*, a thin pancake filled with COCONUT, CARDAMOM powder, sugar and sesame seed; *savige*, a thin vermicelli used to make *laddus;* and *sikharini* – strained yogurt mixed with various spices and flavourings – a precursor of the modern *shrikhand*. In the *MANASOLLASA*, an early twelfth-century work, some sweet dishes were made by curdling hot milk to make *chhana* that was mixed with sugar, ghee and spices and formed into balls that are sautéed. The common wisdom has been that it was the Portuguese who introduced the technique of making curds to Bengal leading to the creation of sandesh, rasgulla and other famous sweets, but this may not necessarily have been the case.

During the Delhi Sultanate, a series of Muslim dynasties from Afghanistan and Central Asia who ruled North Indian over the period 1206 to 1526, several sweet dishes were introduced including *lauz*, or firni, a rice pudding with dried fruit and saffron, and many kinds of halwa.

The Portuguese who settled in Goa and Bengal starting in the late sixteenth century brought breads, cakes and pastries and trained local chefs to make them. One of their contributions was Western-style cheese, made by separating curds from milk. In Goa, the Portuguese influence can be seen in *bibinca*, a cake made by stacking layers of pancakes, and *boliho de coco*, little coconut cakes. Christmas cake, or plum pudding prepared by soaking fruits and nuts in rum or brandy for several weeks, became a holiday staple among ANGLO-INDIANS, Goans and other Christian communities.

In Ayurveda, the Indian system of medicine, dishes made from sugar were believed to have restorative powers and cooling properties (see FOOD AND MEDICINE). Even today, some sweet makers produce items containing Ayurvedic herbs. *Salan pak* is a Gujarati sweet made in the winter with over thirty ingredients including spices and a host of Ayurvedic herbs.

North India. The main ingredient in sweets made in Uttar Pradesh, Punjab, DELHI and other parts of northern India is *khoya*. It is the key ingredient in barfi and *pedha*, a round sweet flavoured with chopped nuts and cardamom and associated with the cities of VARANASI and Mathura. AGRA PETHA, a famous dish of Agra, is a cross between fudge and preserves. A traditional Punjabi winter sweet is *panjiri*, or *dabra*, which is made of whole wheat flour, dry fruits, edible gum and various spices and has a powdery texture. AMRITSAR is famous for its *kulfa,* kulfi served on a bed of firni and topped with vermicelli.

Rabri is thickened milk mixed with chopped nuts and the skin formed on the milk during cooking. Firni is a kind of custard made of rice flour or cornstarch cooked in milk with sugar, nuts, cardamom powder, and rosewater or *kewra* water. *Gulab jamun* are brown balls of *khoya* and flour that are fried and then soaked in sugar syrup. In Delhi and other cities, a popular winter sweet is *makhan malai* (also called *nimish*, meaning dew) made from boiled milk and cream exposed to the night air so that dewdrops fall on it.

In Kashmir, the most popular sweets include *akhor barfi* made from local walnuts; *firun*/firni, a custard made from ground rice, sugar, milk, saffron (which is native to Kashmir) and nuts and set in traditional earthenware pots; and *zarda*, a sweetened rice pulao prepared with nuts, saffron and aromatic spices. The last two dishes are often served during Eid-ul-Fitr and other Muslim celebrations.

West India. In some parts of western India, sweets are eaten during the meal, and a pinch of sugar may be added to vegetarian dishes. Laddus, especially *churma laddu* – deep-fried balls made from wheat flour and nuts – are popular. The Surat region of Gujarat is well known for the expertise of its sweetmakers. A famous Surati sweet is *ghari*, a puri (puffy wheat bread) filled with sweetened *khoya* and nuts. Another famous Surati sweet is *halwason* – hard squares made from broken wheat, *khoya*, nutmeg (see NUTMEG AND MACE) and nuts. *Mohanthal* is a kind of barfi made from chickpea flour, ghee, sugar, almonds, saffron and pistachios. One of the most elaborate sweets is *sukhan feni* – very fine strands of sweet, flaky dough garnished with pistachios. A traditional Maharashtrian sweet is *puran poli* (also known as *holige*), wheat pancakes filled with lentils and sugar and served with hot milk or ghee. An emblematic (and very ancient) dish of Gujarat and Maharashtra is *shrikhand*. Its unique sweet and sour taste makes it loved by some and disliked by others.

In Goa, the Portuguese influence is evident in the language and cuisine, especially the wide array of European-style cakes and pastries. *Bibinca* (*bebinca*) is a many-layered baked pudding made of egg yolks, sugar, flour, coconut milk and garnished with nuts. *Baath* is a cake made from semolina, eggs, ghee, coconuts, sugar and caraway seeds.

South India. The most emblematic South Indian sweet dish is *payasam*, a pudding of rice and milk or coconut milk, sometimes with dal, fruit, raisins and nuts. In Kerala, the king of *payasams* served at festive occasions is *ada pradaman*, made from a special pressed rice, coconut milk, jaggery, coconut milk, coconut flakes, ghee, cardamoms, cashews and raisins. In Tamil Nadu, a favourite sweet is *pal payasam* – small puris dipped in sweetened kheer and served hot or cold. The most important festival is Pongal, which is also the name of the dish served at this time: a mixture of boiled rice, dal, milk, jaggery, ghee, nuts, raisins and coconut.

The city of HYDERABAD, once home to the court of the Nizams, has a rich culinary and sweet culture influenced by Persian cuisine. Double *ka mitha* (also known as *shahi tukra*) is a bread pudding, and is probably an adaptation of English bread and butter pudding made from Western-style bread, *khoya*, saffron and spices sautéed in ghee, soaked in milk, covered with sugar syrup and baked. Vermicelli (*seviyan* in Hindi and Urdu) are very thin wheat noodles used in many dishes including *reshmi zulfein*, made with lotus seeds, and *sevia ka muzaffar*, vermicelli with fried cardamom pods, thickened milk and dried coconut. *Khubani ka meetha* is a very popular local dish made of cooked sweetened APRICOTS topped with cream.

East India. Bengalis are famous for their love of *mishti*, or sweets. Most commercial sweets are made from *chhana*; *khoya* is used as a secondary ingredient. The extensive use of *chhana* by professional sweetmakers began in the mid-nineteenth century when B.C. Nag, N.C. Das and other Calcutta sweet shop owners expanded their repertoire by inventing new varieties of sweets to serve an affluent and growing urban middle class. The most famous sweets are *rasgulla*; *rajbhog*, a giant *rasgulla*; a dark-coloured fried version called *ledikeni*; *cham-cham* (small patties dipped in thickened milk and sprinkled with grated *khoya*); *ras malai*, *khoya* and sugar balls floating in cardamom-flavoured cream; and *pantua*, made in spheres, fried to a golden brown and dropped in sugar syrup. The apogee of the Bengali sweetmakers' art is SANDESH.

Sweets generally made at home include *patishapta,* a semolina pancake filled with sugar, coconut and *khoya*; *pithe*, coconut balls or disks coated in batter, deep-fried and served in sugar syrup; and *malpua*, patties made of yogurt, flour and sugar fried until golden brown, then dipped briefly in sugar syrup. *Misthi doi* or *lal doi,* yogurt sweetened with sugar, is a standard end to a Bengali meal.

Bihar has its own iconic sweets, the most famous of which is *tilkut*, made of pounded sesame seeds, jaggery and *khoya*; *khaja*, a small fried pastry soaked in sugar syrup; and *lavanglata* (also found in Bengal and eastern Uttar Pradesh), a small fried pastry filled with *khoya* and nuts, soaked in sugar syrup and sealed with a clove.

Colleen Sen

- Banerjee, Satarupa. *Book of Indian Sweets*. New Delhi: Rupa & Co., 1994.
- Sen, Colleen Taylor. *Food Culture in India*. Westport, CT: Greenwood Press, 2004.
- Sinha, Anil Kishore. *Anthropology of Sweetmeats*. New Delhi: Gyan Publishing House, 2000.

SYRIAN CHRISTIANS

Generally known as the St. Thomas Christians, the community's origin traces back to the arrival in 52 CE of the apostle Saint Thomas. The name may have come from the liturgy of worship in the Aramaic (Syriac) language. The present-day Syrian Christians are also called Nazaranis, meaning followers of Jesus of Nazareth. Syrian Christians are spread throughout the southwest coast stretch of Kerala. They are identified by family names that showcase the family's profession, the grandparents or place of origin. The community of Syrian Christians is very close-knit and interconnected through marriage, including arranged marriages. The social life of Syrian Christians revolves around the Church and family, which are very much entwined. Marriages, christenings and other celebrations include traditional foods. In a traditional marriage feast, the first course is the *APPAM*, a fermented crepe made with RICE flour, COCONUT and toddy/yeast. It is served with FISH *moilee* and followed by other courses including duck roast, chicken or mutton fried with POTATOES.

Syrian Christian cuisine is a confluence of various cultures and traditions. Thousands of years of seafaring travel and trade between Keralites, Arab and Jewish traders are evident in the traditional cuisine influenced primarily by Church celebrations. Each family is a treasure trove of traditional food and passes down original recipes prepared especially during feasts and festivals. It is an extraordinary community shaped by food and culture.

There are many rituals associated with the birth of a child and the forty days that follow with the pregnant woman eating specially made nourishing food like *aadu* soup, made with tender mutton or baby goat. In the last month of pregnancy, the pregnant girl is brought to her home after prayers from her husband's house. A death in the larger Syrian Christian community sees all related families and acquaintances paying their respect to the bereaved family and partaking in a vegetarian feast together.

The day's food in a typical Syrian Christian home depends on the Christian religious calendar:

- Fridays are vegetarian.
- Easter Sunday is celebrated with meat dishes.
- The twenty-five days of Advent leading to Christmas and the fifty days preceding Easter require vegetarian diets.
- The plum cake or the English fruit cake is a tradition during Christmas.
- The Feast of Jonah (three days in January remembering the three days the Prophet Jonah spent inside the whale) requires a strict vegetarian diet where no fish is consumed.
- For the eight days lending to 8 September (the birthday of Mother Mary), fasting and a strictly vegetarian diet are observed.

There is also a special *appam* called *INRI appam* during the *Pesaha* homily, or Passover meal, where they remember the passing of the Angel of Death over the Jews in Egypt, the passing over of the Jews to the promised land of Israel, and the Last Supper. Syrian Christians, especially in the Pala region of Kerala, commemorate these events using the unfermented *INRI appam* and the *Pesaha pal*, a special coconut milk sweetened with jaggery and with a hint of spices like GINGER powder and CARDAMOM. Worldwide travel and modern customs have changed many of these traditions. Instead of fasting for the entire period of Lent, for example, Syrian Christian families eat an assortment of seafood and vegetarian dishes.

Coconut is a key ingredient of Syrian Christian cooking. In addition, the variety of spices available on Kerala's coast imbues traditional cuisine with enhanced flavours. Unlike the North Indian garam masala (see SPICE BOX), the Syrian Christian spice blend uses earthy spices like CINNAMON, NUTMEG AND MACE, and CLOVES as a base. This is similar to the Middle Eastern spice *baharat*. Syrian Christian cuisine uses ONIONS, shallots and GARLIC liberally.

Syrian Christian cooking technique mainly consists of five different methods:

- *Varutharachathu*, where the spices and coconut are roasted together and ground to make a gravy.
- *Varatiathu*, or *ularthiathu*, where the spices and ingredients are sautéed to get a dry roasted consistency.
- *Varathathu*, deep-fried with or without spices.
- *Piralen*, a preparation of meat or poultry with a gravy coating.
- *Mapas*, where the gravy base is made with coconut milk and aromatic spices.

Pallapam, kallappam and *vellayappam* are various forms of fermented pancakes all made from rice batter. *Puttu* is a breakfast dish made from rice flour and freshly grated coconut steamed in a tubular vessel called *puttukutti* and served with steamed ripe plantains or black chickpea (*kadala* curry).

There are many seafood delicacies, including *meen vevichathu* (a spicy red fish curry with KOKUM) and fish *moilee* (a light coconut-based stew). The meat dishes include *erachi ularthiyathu* (a dried and sautéed beef preparation with earthy spices and coconut), *aadu* stew (mutton), *kozhi mappas* (chicken stew) and duck roast. Coconut vinegar is traditionally used for all these preparations. CURRY LEAF is used in almost all dishes. Many seasonal PICKLES and seasonal preserves are common in traditional Syrian Christian homes. *Uppu manga* (salted MANGO) is preserved and pickled in a brine in earthen pots called *cheena bharani* (a reference to Chinese pottery). *Uppu manga chalichachthu* is a special and tasty condiment made with this preserve, shallots, CHILLIES and coconut oil.

This cuisine has some unique snacks like the *kuzhal appam*, a fried crispy savoury snack curled up like a tube; *acchu appam*, a deep-fried rose cookie made of rice, influenced by Jewish culture; and *churuttu*, made of fried rice flour with a delicate, crispy transparent outer case filled with rice grits – it is sweetened with *paani*, which is made from palmyra juice.

May Fridel

- Kannampilly, Vijayan. *The Essential Kerala Cookbook*. New Delhi: Penguin India, 2003.
- Therissi, John Kottukapally. *Syrian Christian Favorites*. Kottayam, Kerala: Dee Bee Info Publications, 2001.

TAMARIND

Tamarind (Hindi *imli*, from Sanskrit *amlika*) is the fruit from a large evergreen tree that grows in tropical and subtropical regions. Its name comes from the Arab *tamar-u'l Hindi*, or date of India, perhaps because of the resemblance of its pulp to a DATE. The tree is native to tropical Africa and reached India in the first millennium BCE, perhaps brought by Ethiopian traders. In India, it is grown in the drier, warmer areas of the south and central regions in orchards, private gardens and along the roadside.

Tamarind is prized for its pods that are filled with small beans surrounded by a firm but soft pulp. It has a unique flavour: sour, rich and salty with a touch of sweetness. After removal, the pulp is compressed into cakes that are a common souring agent in Indian cooking, especially in the South and the West. Tamarind is an essential ingredient in rasam (a thin spicy and sour lentil soup), SAMBAR and tamarind rice (Tamil *puliodar*, *puli* meaning sour) and in Goan hot and sour dishes such as *sorpotel* and VINDALOO. Tamarind-based CHUTNEYS accompany SAMOSAS and other snacks and are used as toppings for *bhel puri*, *golgappa* and other STREET FOODS.

Virtually every part of a tamarind tree can be used. The pulp is fairly rich in protein, carbohydrates, calcium, phosphorous, iron, vitamin C and other nutrients. The leaves, flowers and immature pods are also edible and used to make CURRIES and other dishes, especially in times of scarcity. The medicinal value of tamarind is mentioned in Sanskrit literature. The laxative properties of the pulp and the diuretic properties of the leaf sap have been confirmed by modern medical science. The seed can be powdered and made into a paste to treat external ailments. Ancient Ayurvedic texts describe after-dinner drinks made with the juice of the sour fruit as a digestive.

Tamarind is one of the forest products collected by the local tribals in Bastar, Chhattisgarh. The tree is considered sacred by some rural people. Some people believe it is unsafe to sleep under the tree at night because of the acid emissions.

Colleen Sen

- Venugopal, Nikhita. 'Tamarind: India's Quintessential Candy Flavor'. *The Juggernaut*, 6 July 2021. Available online: https://www.thejuggernaut.com/tamarind-candy (accessed 2 May 2022).

TAMIL NADU

Tamil Nadu, India's tenth largest state in area, is located at the southern tip of the Indian subcontinent. It is bordered by the states of Kerala, Karnataka, Andhra Pradesh and the union territory of Puducherry. Its diverse geography is similar to that of a large country. Tamil Nadu is divided between the flat country along the eastern coast and the hilly regions in the north and west, the Eastern Ghats to the north and the Nilgiri and Meghamalai mountains to the west. The Bay of Bengal is to the east and to the south are plains and the Indian Ocean. The rivers are mainly tributaries of the Kaveri River which waters the plains of eastern Tamil Nadu.

The summer months run from March to June and have intense heat with an average temperature of 26–38℃. The monsoon is very important for Tamil Nadu as all the rivers are rain-fed. This season continues until September when the northeast monsoon brings in even larger amounts of water from October to December. The cool climate or tropical winter runs from January to March.

Although the state is the most urbanized in India, more than half the population lives in rural areas and agriculture is the mainstay of the economy. The onset of monsoon on 15 June marks the *kharif* season when farmers grow RICE, *arhar* (pigeon peas) and DRUMSTICKS. Tamil Nadu is, by far, the largest producer of drumsticks, BANANAS and COCONUTS and the sixth largest producer of rice in India. The cool hills of the Nilgiris and Meghamalai are home to many TEA and COFFEE plantations. Other produce includes *ragi*, *jowar*, bitter GOURD, Banganapalli/Safeda MANGO and watermelon. Lentils, rice, coconut, JACKFRUIT, banana, and other native fruits and vegetables form the base of the diet of most people in Tamil Nadu.

Around 88 per cent of Tamil Nadu's population are Hindus, 6 per cent Christians and less than 6 per cent Muslims. Hinduism lies at the core of the state's culture. Tamil Nadu has tens of thousands of temples, the most famous of which are those at Mamallapura (a UNESCO World Heritage Site), Chidambaram, Kanchipuram, Thanjavur, Madurai and the Srirangam pilgrimage centre in Tiruchchirappalli.

Tamil Nadu has a long history and a rich culture. According to one theory, people migrated from the Harappan Civilization to Tamil Nadu in 1500 BCE. The Sangam Age from 300 BCE–300 CE (named after the Sangam academies of poets and scholars in Madurai) was a period of cultural and artistic refinement. Festivals such as Pongal celebrating harvest and spring came up at this time. Sangam literature indicates that festivals, feasts and meals were abundant. The five traditional landscapes of mountains, forests, fertile plains, deserts and the coastal region each had their own food cultures. In the arid region pickling and preserving methods were common, frying and sun drying were popular in the forest regions, while steaming and boiling developed in the fertile plains.

Varieties of white RICE, meat, spinach, vegetables, puffed rice, PULSES, cereals, legumes and PICKLES were dietary staples and the diet was predominantly meat-based except in the farming area where vegetables dominated. People hunted wild boar and cooked meat on an open fire. Sometimes the meat was marinated in curd before cooking. Some people ate tortoises, lizards and even rats. Crab, seafood and FISH were standard along the coast.

There are accounts of mashed AUBERGINE served with rice and BUTTERMILK. A *kozhambu*, a CURRY made of JACKFRUIT seeds, raw MANGOES and TAMARIND extract, was eaten with bamboo rice and buttermilk. Another recipe called for lentils, tamarind pulp and broad bean seeds. On Pongal (a harvest festival), women came together and made the eponymous *pongal*, a rice and lentil community dish similar to a KHICHRI.

Important dynasties ruled Tamil Nadu from the fourth to the seventeenth centuries. The first were the Pallavas (fourth to eighth centuries), followed by the Chola dynasty (ninth to thirteenth centuries). The Cholas had many ports along the Bay of Bengal and traded and settled in Thailand, Andaman and Nicobar Islands, Malaysia, Indonesia and Bali. They imported new flavours and exported indigenous Tamil vegetables and spices. The Chola kings enjoyed throwing feasts with meat, fruit and liquor. Street carts were filled with duck eggs, goat meat, roasted NUTS, COCONUT, MILLET, jaggery toffee, GUAVA, *JAMUN*, bamboo and rice crackers. One popular dish was broad country beans cooked in a tamarind gravy served with BAMBOO SHOOT curry. Some common Indian ingredients did not exist in Indian food until the Cholas traded through sea routes. During this time period the Chettiars, a community of merchants, settled in these areas and brought back spices and vegetables to Tamil Nadu, changing the cuisine.

A mighty Hindu kingdom called Vijayanagar eventually ruled over much of what is today Tamil Nadu from 1336 to 1646 CE. At its peak, its capital city was the largest or second largest (after Beijing) city in the world with an estimated population of 500,000. The Portuguese traveller Domingo Paes, who visited Viyayanagar in the early 1520s, wrote:

> This is the best provided city in the world, and is stocked with provisions such as rice, wheat, grains ... and some barley and beans, moong dal, pulses, horse gram and many other seeds which grow in this country and which are the food of the common people, and there is a large store of these and very cheap; but wheat is not so common as the other grains since no one eats except the Moors (i.e. Muslims).
>
> (Sewell 2010)

They were eventually defeated by the Nayaks who formed smaller kingdoms in Madurai and Thanjavur. In 1640, the East India Company of England opened a trading post at the fishing village of Madraspatnam (now CHENNAI) and in 1684, the British established the Madras Presidency which covered most of South India. After Indian independence in 1947, it became Madras State. Later, the state's Telugu-, Malayali- and Kannada-speaking areas went to Andhra Pradesh, Kerala and Karnataka, respectively. The remaining predominantly Tamil-speaking region was renamed Tamil Nadu in 1968. British control led to the introduction of new crops, fruits and vegetables from Africa and the Western Hemisphere such as POTATOES, TOMATOES, PINEAPPLE and cashew nuts. Eventually, they were blended into Tamil cuisine.

Cabbage, cauliflower, pomelo, tea, peach, betel leaf (see PAAN), NIGELLA, bell pepper (see CAPSICUM), new millets and, most importantly, tomato, potato and CHILLIES were introduced by the British to India after discovering these new crops in Africa, the Americas and Australia. Today chillies and tomatoes are such essential ingredients in Tamil Nadu cuisine that it is hard to believe that they were introduced only four hundred years ago.

The idea of CHUTNEY was taken by the British and incorporated into their cuisine as a form of a condiment or sauce. Arguably one of the most lasting impacts of the Madras Presidency on food is mulligatawny, a soup whose name comes from the Tamil words for pepper (*milagu*) and water (*tanni*). A standard mulligatawny soup consisted of tamarind, red chillies, GARLIC, MUSTARD seeds, GHEE, SALT, FENUGREEK seeds and peppercorns. Originally it was eaten as a soup with rice. The British added mutton or chicken, butter and flour to make it thicker and richer. Nowadays, restaurants serve the soup with lemon served on the side for sourness.

Tamil Brahmins eat only vegetarian food. They are divided into Iyers and Iyengars, but their food is largely the same [see PALGHAT IYERS]. Many Brahmins settled in Tirunelveli, North Arcot and Mylapore. Traditional Brahmin food is eaten on a banana or plantain leaf. A popular dish is *vazhaithandu poriyal* which is banana stem (which is similar to a YAM or potato) stir-fried with *urad* dal, mustard seeds, CURRY LEAVES and shredded coconut. A typical Brahmin meal is centred around *sadham* (rice) with a touch of ghee, served with a *poriyal* (any type of vegetable), a *kuzhambu* (curry) or *kootu* (stew), a pickle, *thayir sadham* (curd rice with crunchy bits of *urad* dal, mustard seeds and curry leaves), rasam (a light dal soup usually flavoured with lemon, pepper or tomato) and *pappadam*, a crispy bread made of lentils and rice (see PAPAD).

During feasts, Brahmins eat on banana leaves. In some areas such as Palghat, everyone is still served TIFFIN (breakfast), lunch, tea and dinner on a banana leaf. People eat with their hands and someone serves the food and goes around with the dishes. Every dish has a specific place on the banana leaf. Two or three fresh pickles (usually one chilli, one mango and one leaf/vegetable as long as it is not preserved) are placed in the top left corner; then four vegetables are placed on the top half of the leaf – one sweet, one bitter, one flavoured with coconut and one salty to create a balance of flavours. On the top right are placed the *pappadam*, *vadai* (see VADA), sweet *payasam* (either as rice or vermicelli *KHEER*), *pachadi* (RAITA, usually cucumber) and a *poli* (sweet roti). Rice and ghee are put on the bottom half. The first course of rice is eaten with *parrapu* (dal), then a SAMBAR or *kuzhambu*. A popular curry is *moor kuzambhu* made with either OKRA or mango (similar to the North Indian *kadhi*), followed by rasam and rice. The meal ends with *thayir sadham* (curd rice).

In the eighth century, Muslim traders came to Tamil Nadu and settled on the Bay of Bengal, bringing with them new culinary techniques and spices. The settlers intermingled with the local Tamils to create a richer, more spice-based cuisine that has not been showcased in mainstream media. A typical dish is *idiyappam* (*sevai* or string hoppers). It is usually served with *meen anam,* a coconut and fish (usually barracuda) curry with garlic, ONION, tamarind, Kashmiri chilli powder and tomato. In a Tamil Muslim biryani, North Indian spices are replaced with black pepper and curry leaf. It is a much drier biryani that is very popular during Ramanathapuram (Ramadan).

Another biryani unique to Tamil Nadu is the *dindigul* popularized by the Dindigul Thalappakatti restaurant in Dindigul, a city 420 km southwest of Chennai, which was opened in 1957. The biryani is made with mutton or chicken and *seeraga samba* rice, an aromatic local long-grain rice that received a GEOGRAPHICAL INDICATION tag. It is made with ginger, garlic, green and red chillies, onion, CORIANDER, MINT, tomato and spices, including pepper, CINNAMON, CARDAMOM, stone flower, and CLOVES.

The Arcot state, which ruled the Carnatic region between the Eastern Ghats and the Bay of Bengal from 1690 to 1855, had a great impact on the food of Tamil Nadu. The Arcot or Ambur biryani uses *seeraga samba rice* and is made with soaked red chillies ground to a thick paste and curd, unlike any other Tamil biryani. It is usually served with onion raita, a boiled egg and aubergine curry (*brinjal serva*). Other dishes include the Arcot *nawab* KEBAB made with mutton, mutton 65 and the mutton *bonda*. A variation of *gulab jamun* is *makkan peda* which is made with curd, *KHOYA*, baking soda, ghee, nuts, flour, oil, water and SUGAR.

The city of Madurai is the cultural capital of Tamil Nadu, famous for the Meenakshi temple and many other historic sites. It is also known for its small road-side food stalls (*kadais*). Most of these stalls are quite old and are family-owned, such as the Panaimarathu Kadai (Palm Tree Shop) which is eighty-two years old. Its name comes from the one palm tree outside its shop. Other names for shops include Thambi Kadai (younger brother's shop) or Bun Parotta Kadai. Madurai Paati Kadai is owned by an elderly lady who sold tiffin (breakfast items) on a tricycle; her business grew so much that now she sells food from a food shack. The state capital Chennai (formerly Madras) is famous for its STREET FOOD.

Surya Vir Vaidhyanathan

- Ammal, S. Meenakshi. *The Best of Samaithu Paar: The Classic Guide to Tamil Cuisine*. New Delhi: Penguin/Viking, 2001.
- Murugappan, Meyyammai and Visalakshi Ramaswamy. *The Chettinad Cookbook*. India: Self-published, 2014.
- Sewell, Robert. *A Forgotten Empire: Vijayanagar*. Whitefish, MT: Kessinger, 2010.

TARO

Taro (*Colocasia esculenta*, Hindi *arbi*) is the name of one of a group of tropical and semi-tropical root crops. Its centre of origin is India or Southeast Asia, and it may have been cultivated as early as 5000 BCE. The roots (actually corms, thick underground stems) are the size of a large POTATO. (Taro is sometimes called the 'potato of the tropics'.) It has a gnarly hairy exterior and a white flesh that turns brownish-purple when cooked. In parts of India it is a staple food. It is usually grown in gardens, although efforts are being made to grow it commercially. Taro is an excellent source of carbohydrate and fibre but is low in protein.

In Kerala, it is steamed and eaten as a staple, added to SAMBAR or cooked with COCONUT milk. In Bengal, taro slices are fried to make chips and used in many CURRIES, especially with FISH head or shrimp. Taro's large dark green leaves are prepared as a vegetable, but must be thoroughly cooked before eating because they contain toxic calcium oxalate crystals. (Many people also have an allergic reaction to handling them.) Taro leaves are often coated with batter and deep-fried as a snack. A famous Gujarat snack is *patra*: taro leaves are coated with a paste of chickpea flour, spices and jaggery (see SUGAR), stacked on top of each other and formed into rolls, then steamed or deep-fried. In Nagaland, fermented dried leaves are powdered, cooked as biscuits, dried and stored to be later added to meat dishes.

Colleen Sen

- Varshney, Vibha. 'Taro: In Which You Can Eat Both Shoots and Leaves'. *Down To Earth*, 1–15 October 2020.

TEA

Tea (Hindi chai) comes from the plant *Camellia sinensis* of which there are three main varieties: China (*C. sinensis* var. *sinensis*), Assam (*C. sinensis* var. *assamica*) and Cambodia (*C. sinensis* var. *cambodiensis*). India is the second largest producer of tea in the world and accounts for around 22 per cent of the world's tea production. Most of the tea grown is consumed within the country, with 20 per cent exported globally.

Tea in India was described as early as the late sixteenth century by a Dutch explorer Jan Huygen van Linschoten. He wrote that leaves from the Assam tree were used by the hill tribes in northeastern India as a vegetable and as a drink. In the early seventeenth century, Dutch merchants were the first to bring green tea from China. The British, at their trading posts at Surat and Bombay, became acquainted with tea drinking and it quickly became popular, although at that time it was considered a medicinal drink. It was drunk without milk, although SUGAR was sometimes added as well as a variety of spices.

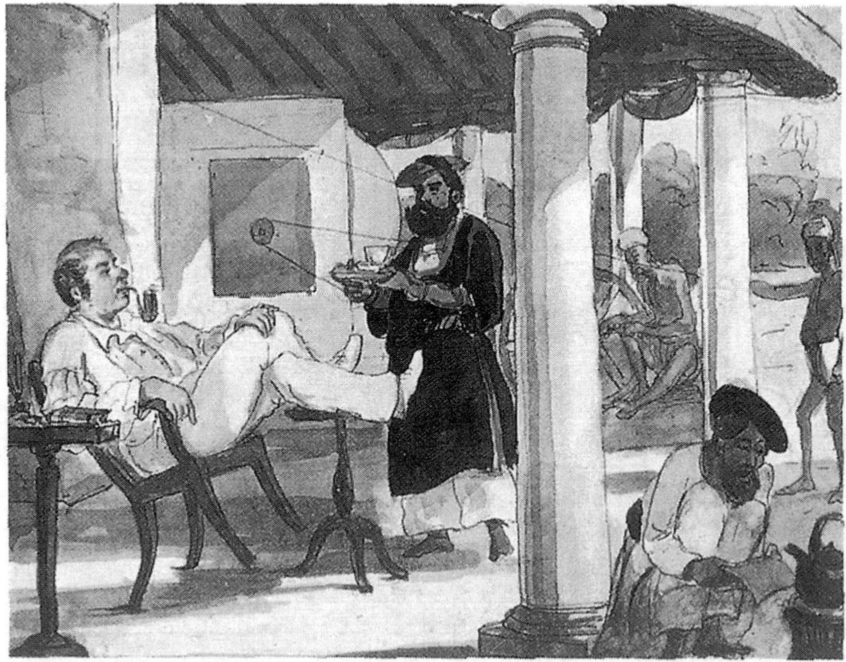

FIGURE 45 TEA. The Colonel's Morning Tea on the Veranda. Captain G. F. Atkinson, **'Curry and Rice' on Forty Plates.**

The tea was, however, expensive and, as early as 1774, the East India Company was exploring ways to break the Chinese monopoly and the possibilities of growing tea in India. The East India Company sent a few seeds to the British emissary in Bhutan to plant there. Several years later, British naturalist Sir Joseph Banks was hired to recommend crops to the East India Company that might be grown for profit and he suggested tea. However, little was done for nearly fifty years and it was not until the mid-nineteenth century that the British discovered the tea plant growing wild in northeast India. A Scottish major Robert Bruce who was working in Assam in 1823 noticed that the hill tribes were making a kind of PICKLED tea from a plant which looked similar to the Chinese *Camellia sinensis* but had broader leaves. It was the Assam variety, *C. sinensis* var. *assamica*. Robert Bruce died in 1824 but his brother Charles arranged for some of these plants to be cultivated in the botanical gardens of Calcutta. Convinced that this was tea, he informed the government in 1832.

The demand for tea in Britain in the 1830s was growing so when the East Company was stripped of its monopoly of the China trade in 1834, a Tea Committee was set up to introduce tea culture to India. There was much debate as to whether tea plants from China should be cultivated or native (Assam) plants. Some insisted that China plants were best for commercial production and that native plants would produce an inferior tea, even though the Assam tea plant would be better suited to local conditions. The China plants fared badly and many mistakes were made. However, despite these setbacks, the first black tea produced from Chinese plants was processed, several tea chests were shipped to London and auctioned at India House in 1839. The Assam Tea Company was formed in 1840 and established its own plantations in Assam.

Although both Chinese tea plants and the local Assam variety were planted, the Assam plants were found to be more successful and gradually took over. In the 1860s tea plantations were developed in other parts of India, notably Darjeeling. Tea mania struck and there was a scramble for entrepreneurs to set up tea plantations and make their fortunes. But it was not until the 1870s that the tea industry in India stabilized and finally began producing good quality tea at a profit and tea drinking by the British in India got underway.

Today India produces approximately 30 per cent of the world's black teas and 65 per cent of CTC teas. CTC refers to a method of processing black tea, named for the process 'crush, tear, curl' (sometimes 'cut, tear, curl') in which black tea leaves are run through a series of cylindrical rollers. The rollers have hundreds of sharp teeth that crush, tear and curl the leaves. This tea is the result of a growing British and Irish market and the preference from the 1950s onwards for quick-brewing tea bags.

In India there are three distinct tea-growing regions which produce teas that differ in style, taste and flavour – Assam, Darjeeling and Nilgiri.

Assam, located in the northeast corner of India on the low-lying alluvial flood plains of the Brahmaputra River Valley, is the largest black tea-producing region of the world. With a climate of heavy rainfall and hot temperatures, it is well suited for producing rich, full-bodied teas, mostly using the CTC method, which are ideal for blending and for tea bags and are recommended to be drunk with milk and sugar. Assam tea makes up approximately 50 per cent of India's total output of tea.

Darjeeling is a hill resort in the Himalayan foothills of northeast India. Altitude of 6,000 feet above sea level and the soil and sloping terrain with a cool and moist climate all combine to produce teas. They are famed for their delicate flavour likened to Muscatel and are often called the 'champagne of teas'. Darjeeling tea (grown at an elevation ranging from 600–2,000 metres above sea level in eighty-seven identified gardens and tea estates) was the first product of India to be awarded the GEOGRAPHICAL INDICATION tag in 2004.

The beautiful mountains of Nilgiri (Hindi for 'blue mountains') stretch across the states of Tamil Nadu, Karnataka and Kerala. The high elevation within the tropics results in teas with a smooth and mellow flavour. Nilgiri teas are often used for blending. Nilgiri is also known for its special 'frost teas'. Frost is usually a curse for tea bushes but the tea farmers in Nilgiri have turned this into a blessing. When there is a frost, the leaves freeze. These are picked and sent immediately for withering, resulting in a fragrant tea with spicy notes.

Other areas producing tea in India are Dooars, a tiny province to the west of Assam; Sikkim; the Terai, just south of Darjeeling; the Kangra Valley in Himachal Pradesh; and Travancore. A small amount of green tea is produced in the Kangra Valley, mainly for the Afghanistan market.

Tea drinking, at first, was strongly associated with the British in India. It was drunk in the same way as it is today in Britain, with milk and sugar (except it might be in the form of jaggery or date palm sugar). Sometimes spices and other ingredients were added such as almonds.

In British India the day began early, often before dawn, with *chota hazri* ('little breakfast'), sometimes called 'bed tea'. Servants brought an early morning pot or cup of tea with milk and sugar and perhaps some fruit or a biscuit for their employers, often administrators or army officers, who liked to work in the cool period before sunrise. For travellers on Indian trains, *chota hazri* became an established custom, as it did with those who went riding before the main breakfast which was served at about 9 or 10 o'clock.

The tradition of afternoon tea which became embedded in colonial life was brought by the many British women who travelled to India, often in search of husbands, during the nineteenth century. It was usually served after TIFFIN. In Indian cities and at hill stations, the British set up exclusive clubs centred on sports, the bar and the dining room. Afternoon tea was served accompanied by typical ANGLO-INDIAN fare such as club sandwiches, toasts grilled with toppings of GARLIC, green CHILLIES and grated cheese, spicy *PAKORAS*, SAMOSAS, and English cakes. Tea planters established clubs too, such as the Darjeeling Club and the High Range Club in Munnar.

Tea drinking was slow to be taken up by the Indian population because it was too expensive but in 1881 the Tea Association of India was set up to formulate policies for the development and growth of the tea industry. However, it wasn't until 1901 that they realized that there was potentially a large market for tea in India. They set up a marketing campaign but it was not very successful. It was not until the First World War there were some signs of success. Tea stalls were set up in factories, coal mines and cotton mills and workers were allowed tea breaks. On the Indian Railways, the Tea Association equipped small contractors with kettles and cups and packets of tea and set them to work at the major railway junctions in Punjab, the North-West Frontier and Bengal. Tea shops were set up in large towns and cities but it wasn't until the 1950s that tea became a drink for the masses. Today tea (called chai) is a normal part of everyday life and is brewed at railway stations, bazaars and offices. Sold by chaiwallahs who typically boil the tea with buffalo milk and sugar and serve it in disposable clay cups called *kullars*, this 'railway tea' is the most common in India. Masala chai has spices added and is particularly popular in Punjab, Haryana and elsewhere in northern and central India; the people in eastern India (West Bengal and Assam) generally drink their tea without spices. Tea is also drunk in the home and is often served with tiffin, especially in Tamil Nadu and Andhra Pradesh. The tradition of afternoon tea continues, especially in West Bengal where tea is accompanied by Western-style cakes and Indian savoury snacks.

There are some new trends in tea drinking:

Cutting chai which originated in MUMBAI and is basically a half portion of tea which is served in a special glass rather than a cup. People usually have at least two to three cups of tea a day, so the concept of cutting chai was to drink the equivalent of half a cup each time thus allowing you to drink more cups but at the same time moderating the amount drunk.

Chai latte is a combination of black tea and hot milk (any kind of milk, buffalo or cow). There are many versions of this tea that include other toppings and spices such as *adrak* chai (tea with milk and GINGER). The difference between chai and chai latte is that chai is usually made with a loose leaf style tea which is brewed in hot milk sweetened with HONEY or sugar. Chai latte, on the other hand, is often made with either soluble powder or a syrup imitating a chai flavour. Chai latte is much sweeter than chai tea.

Tandoori chai is made by taking iron tongs to place an earthen cup (*kullar*) in a glowing hot tandoor. When the cup is very hot, it is taken out and sweet milky chai (usually with a blend of spices) is poured in, which sizzles and froths over. This is then poured into another *kullar* and served. This process gives the tea a smoky, earthy taste with some caramelization from the sugar. Tandoori chai was invented by Amol Dilip Rajdeo who runs India's first tandoori tea corner by the name of 'Chai La! The Tandoor Tea' in Pune. It is said that he got the idea from watching his grandmother place TURMERIC milk in a corner of a bonfire for reheating.

Helen Saberi

- Battle, Will. *The World Tea Encyclopaedia*. Kibworth Beauchamp, Leicestershire: Matador Self Publishing, 2017.
- Doctor, Vikram. 'Tandoori Chai: The Tea Trend Indians Would Really Adopt'. *ET Panache*, 7 May 2019. Available online: https://economictimes.indiatimes.com/magazines/panache/tandoori-chai-the-tea-trend-indians-would-really-adopt (accessed 3 May 2022).
- Freeman, Michael and Timothy d'Offay. *The Life of Tea*. London: Mitchell Beazley, 2018.
- Saberi, Helen. *Tea: A Global History*. London: Reaktion Books, 2010.

TELANGANA

Telangana is India's youngest state, having been carved out of Andhra Pradesh on 2 June 2014. Earlier part of the erstwhile state of Hyderabad, which was merged with the Indian Union in 1948, the people of Telangana regions had been rebelling for their separate statehood since Independence. In 1956, the Hyderabad State was dissolved as part of the linguistic reorganization of states and the Telangana regions were merged with the Telugu-speaking Andhra State (part of the Madras Presidency during the British Raj) to form Andhra Pradesh. A peasant-driven movement began to advocate for separation from Andhra Pradesh starting in the early 1950s and continued until Telangana was granted statehood on 2 June 2014 under the leadership of K. Chandrashekar Rao, who had founded the Telangana Rashtra Samiti (TRS) in 2001.

While Telangana cuisine has a few dishes of global repute, such as *kacchi gosht ki* biryani, HALEEM, *paya* and *shorba*, in common with Hyderabadi or Nizami cuisine, the former is far more robust, rural and rooted-to-the-earth, and without the frills and finesse of cooking techniques which characterize the latter. Telangana also shares several common dishes with the Andhra and Rayalaseema regions, such as a popular meal combo of *ragi sankati* (finger millet cooked into a gooey mass) and *natu kodi pulusu* (chicken cooked in a spicy and tangy TAMARIND-based CURRY) or desserts like *ariselu* (cakes made of RICE flour, jaggery and SESAME), and *bobbatlu* (WHEAT flour rotis stuffed with *chana* dal-jaggery filling).

The geographical topography of Telangana is hot and semi-arid, suited to cultivation of MILLETS which are as much a staple as rice, especially in rural areas. Sorghum, or *jowar*, is made into flatbreads, or rotis, such as *jonna rotte*, while *sajja rotte* is made of pearl millet or BARLEY flour and *mokka rotte* is made of CORN flour. *Jonna rotte*, which is the most common, comes loaded with health benefits including being gluten-free, being high in iron and antioxidants, boosting immunity and helping lower blood sugar. Another popular staple is *ragi sankati* (a gooey porridge made from boiling finger millet and a bit of rice) which is often paired with *natu kodi pulusu*.

Food is enhanced by such healthy ingredients as sesame and groundnut, while seasoning is usually done with red CHILLIES, chilli powder and souring agents like tamarind and roselle leaf, known locally as *gongura*. Commercially, there are not many Telangana speciality restaurants, even in the capital city HYDERABAD, though a few do offer a smattering of Telangana specials on their Hyderabadi menus.

'Since as long as I can remember, there has been nothing like a distinct Telangana cuisine, really, as it was always associated with rustic and rural folks and was in the shadow of the more popular Andhra cuisine promoted in towns and cities by the more enterprising and affluent Andhra foodpreneurs, just like Telangana's economy', sums up entrepreneur Ravikanth Reddy, the founder of the Hyderabad-based Great Hyderabad Food and Travel Club (FAT Club).

Reddy, who hails from Adilabad, remembers a typical meal at home consisting of rice/*jonna* or *jowar* rotis (cooked on a clay *tawa* on firewood), lentils (*toor*, or pigeon pea dal) and *pesar pappu* (split *moong* dal mostly), a stir-fried vegetable curry (*koora*) such as *vankaya koora* (AUBERGINE curry), or a curry using tamarind pulp (referred to as *pulusu*) – a tangy spicy dish to mop up the dry millet breads or rice.

A dish often promoted at Telangana food festivals is *pachi pulusu*, which requires no cooking but makes for a lip-smacking side, with rice and *mudda pappu* (a thick dal preparation). *Pachi pulusu* is made by crushing tamarind and green chillies, adding water and garnishing it with finely chopped ONION, green chillies and a bit of roasted CUMIN powder. Some use a *tadka*, or seasoning, of cumin and MUSTARD seeds, CURRY LEAVES and dried red chillies. *Pachi pulusu* is often had in summer for its coolant properties.

Another popular dish at food promotions is the *ankapur kodi koora*, a country chicken curry using COCONUT flakes and groundnut, named after its place of origin, the village Ankapur in Nizamabad district.

Meat is cooked during festivals and on special occasions and chicken curry is cooked to welcome house guests. While FISH is not so commonly consumed as Telangana is land-locked, both country chicken and mutton (goat and sheep) are popular and it is not uncommon to have almost all parts of the animal cooked in some form or the other. 'Other than the hide of the animal there is very little which is left unused for consumption when a goat or ram is slaughtered', says Reddy.

Besides the more common *bheja* (brains) fry or *paya* (goat trotters) *shorba* (soup), a signature offal dish is the *talakaya koora* (goat head curry), which is considered good for bone health.

Telangana also has its own version of blood pudding, *nalla*, usually served as a starter during religious ceremonies which revolve around goat sacrifice. *Nalla* is made of fresh blood from the slaughtered animal which is collected in a brass vessel and boiled in water until it clots or coagulates like PANEER or tofu. The jelly-like mass is then cut into small squares and toss fried with onions, GINGER-GARLIC paste, red chilli powder, SALT and TURMERIC and garnished with green chillies and CORIANDER leaves.

While a Telangana breakfast in urban areas comprises the typical South Indian fare of IDLI, DOSA and *upma*, there are certain unique snacks typical to the region. One is *sarvapindi*, now increasingly coming into focus during food promotions at star hotels and standalone restaurants (especially hosted on 1 June, Telangana Formation Day) as a popular evening snack and as a breakfast dish usually carried by farmers to the fields. Made of rice flour, *chana* dal, sesame, red chilli flakes and peanuts, *sarvapindi* is enormous and circular shaped. Traditionally it used to be steamed on a heavy-bottomed brass vessel, though now it is more often deep-fried. *Sakinalu*, crisp and circular discs made of rice flour and sesame, is another snack prepared during Sankranthi or Harvest festival.

Telangana and Andhra Pradesh share common sweets like *ariselu*, *bobbatlu*, and *kajikawa* or *garijalu*, *maida* pastry sheets filled with coconut-jaggery-CARDAMOM filling. *Parda pheni*, a layered pastry made of flour and sugar, is a distinct sweet of Telangana. Another distinct and not so common Telangana dessert is *mallida laddu*, made of wheat flour, jaggery or sugar, and cardamom, which is offered to Goddess Gowri during the Bathukamma festival when women celebrate with song and dance, carrying flower-bedecked pots to the river or nearest water body.

Swati Sucharita

- Rao, Sudhakar N. *Aromas of Telangana*. Hyderabad: Culinary Academy of India, 2020.

TEMPLE FOOD

Hinduism. Offering food to the presiding deity or deities of a temple and distributing it to worshippers are a part of Hindu religious life. While food offerings are essential in Vaishnav ceremonies, Siva worshippers generally avoid contact with the God's leftovers, which are eaten by the priests. Temple foods are usually, but not always, vegetarian and do not have ONION or GARLIC or intense spicing. Originally they were only made with food produced locally as the deity was offered the first harvest and today are based on local ingredients where available. Generally, 'foreign' ingredients such as TOMATOES, CHILLIES, cauliflower, cabbage and POTATOES are absent. SWEETS are a speciality of many temples since they are easier to distribute and transport than wetter dishes.

The food is prepared in communal kitchens. In the largest temples they are staffed by hundreds of cooks and their assistants and are off limits to outsiders. Dishes are prepared using traditional cooking devices, such as *chulas* – clay ovens fuelled with wood and charcoal – and clay pots. A standard ritual is for the priest to offer food to the statue (*murti*) of the deity, then leave it in its presence for a while to satisfy their spiritual hunger and, finally, distribute it to the worshippers and pilgrims as *prasadam* in Sanskrit and

FIGURE 46 TEMPLE FOOD. *Langar* at the Gurdwara Bangla Sahib. Ji-Elle/Wikimedia Commons.

FIGURE 47 TEMPLE FOOD. *Annakuta* at a Swaminarayan temple. Colleen Sen.

prasad in Hindi (a word that also means grace). They may eat it on the spot and/or take it home to share with family and friends. Because it has been processed by the deity, it is highly valued. Historian Alka Pande describes the experience this way:

> Many devotees feel spiritually uplifted simply by offering and receiving Prasad. It can be thought of as the grace of a god … [which] energizes, invigorates and induces devotion to the lord … The consuming of Prasad is the most exalted divine intimacy, an intensely personal experience, the saliva of deity and devotee being mixed through

the sharing of food. At this spiritual level, the food, the deity, and devotee become coextensive – the essence of this experience being expressed in the saying 'You are what you eat and you eat what you are.'

India's most famous temple food comes from the town of Udupi in Karnataka, site of a famous Krishna temple, many smaller temples and eight monastic institutions. Each temple has its own form of *prasad* based on local ingredients. One of the most famous is the Udupi Sri Krishna Matha that was founded in the thirteenth century. Its speciality is DOSA served with CHUTNEY and plain POTATO filling without onions. People sit cross-legged on the floor of a large hall while young boys serve RICE, rasam (a thin South Indian dal), fried and curried vegetables, sweets including *payasam* (see KHEER), several chutneys and GHEE from giant containers onto BANANA leaves. In the last century, some of these cooks opened their own restaurants serving similar vegetarian food, see UDUPI RESTAURANTS.

The Sri Venkateswara temple in Tirupati, Andhra Pradesh, is the most visited temple in India and the world's second most visited holy place after the Vatican. Its kitchen serves an average 60,000 people each day and up to 200,000 during festivals. Its speciality is the iconic Tirupati *LADDU* – sweet balls made of lentils, sugar, NUTS and spices, including a giant version called *kalyana laddu* that weighs 500 g. The Jagannath temple in Puri, Odisha, dedicated to Lord Krishna, serves hundreds of dishes, including vegetables CURRIES, *KHICHRI*, local dals, RAITAS, and drinks made from jaggery (see SUGAR) and fruit. There are dozens of sweet dishes alone, all cooked in ghee. The gods are served ritually five times a day and visitors can eat either in a large dining hall or buy *prasad* at a market within the temple walls. The kitchens are spread over an acre where food is prepared by five hundred cooks and three hundred assistants. The food is cooked in hundreds of enormous *chulas*. Much of the food is boiled or steamed for long periods. The *prasad* is distributed to the cooks and their families, who sell it to the devotees visiting the temple. Legend has it that the food is cooked by the goddess Lakshmi.

The Ganapati temple at Kottarakara dedicated to Ganesh is famous for its *unni-appam*, fried dumplings made from rice flour, COCONUT, jaggery, ghee, dry GINGER, CARDAMOM and mashed local bananas. The temple makes 50,000 of these dumplings a day and as many as 170,000 during festivals. Unusually, these *APPAMS* are cooked in front of the deity instead of in a separate secret chamber.

The *panchmritam* at the Murugan temple in Palani, Tamil Nadu, is the first temple food to be given GEOGRAPHICAL INDICATION status. It is composed of five ingredients: banana, jaggery, cow ghee, HONEY and cardamom, with DATES and sugar candy sometimes added for flavour. The result is a brown-coloured jam-like substance that is sold in bottles. It was once made by the cooks' stomping the ingredients with their feet but today the process is automated. It is believed to have many curative properties and is so popular that it is available online. It is offered both as *prasad* and sold in stalls run by temple administrators. It is offered with milk to the deity at night and then distributed to the worshippers as prasad the next day.The presiding deity is Lord Murugan, an ancient deity going back to Vedic times.

One of the world's most spectacular food events is the Annakut, or mountain of food, held annually at a temple in Mount Govardhan near Vrindavan in Uttar Pradesh at the end of the rainy season. It commemorates an event in Krishna's childhood when he persuaded the local cowherds to make their annual offerings of harvest grains and PULSES to Mount Govardhan instead of to the god Indra. Angered, Indra punished the people by sending a violent rainstorm. Krishna lifted Mount Govardhan and sheltered the people. To commemorate this event, which is often depicted in Indian paintings, worshippers build a large mound of rice, sometimes weighing thousands of kilos, in the temple courtyard, facing the sanctum where the deity resides. They surround it with hundreds of dishes of sweets, savouries, vegetables and grains, all vegetarian and containing no onion or garlic. Pilgrims come to Govardhan to view these displays and enjoy the food, which is later distributed to devotees.

A similar food festival is organized every year by members of a community called the Vallabhites, or Pushti Marga (meaning the way of God's nourishment or grace), founded in Gujarat in the fifteenth century. They worship Krishna in his infant form, depicted with one arm upraised, a ball of butter in his hand. This sect lavishes so much attention on food that they have been called 'the undisputed gourmets of Hinduism'. At the Vallabhite temple in Jatipura, the image representing baby Krishna is fed eight times daily. The food, an amalgam of Gujarati, Rajasthani, South Indian and local cuisines, is always sweet or bland because SALT and spices are injurious to a child's sensitive palate. The Pushti Marga community holds large food festivals, the showpiece of which is a special *prasad* called the Chhappan Bhog (meaning fifty-six dishes). Fifty-six categories of vegetarian food are each prepared in five or six ways and fifty-six baskets of each dish are made. The dishes are displayed in a temporary enclosure at the side of a hill. A similar, though often scaled down, version of the festival is celebrated at Pushti Marga temples in India and abroad. Members of the Swaminarayan sect also prepare Chhappan Bhog.

Not all temple food is vegetarian. In West Bengal, Assam, Odisha, Tripura and Nepal, animal sacrifice (*bali*) is practised at many Shakti temples. These temples are dedicated to the worship of the goddess Kali, an avatar of Durga, and the belief is that eating meat stimulates her bloody vengeance against the evil buffalo demon. There are several Kali temples in Kolkata, the most famous being at Kalighat. Here a daily sacrifice of a single goat is commissioned by the Brahmin priests. Some of the meat is cooked and offered to Kali as part of her daily meal (*bhog*), which includes dal, FISH, khichri and vegetables, all cooked in ghee. Portions are also bought and consumed by worshippers as *prasad*. People can also make individual goat sacrifices to Kali for her help in solving a problem. This meat is taken home, cooked and eaten by the sacrificer's family. At Kalighat Temple, 700 or more goats may be offered in sacrifice (usually vow-related) on any of several auspicious festive days, including during Kali Puja in the fall. Tuesdays and Saturdays are especially auspicious and have an average of seventy or more goat sacrifices in one day. Immediately after the sacrifice, the priest dips his hand in the blood and smears it across the foreheads of the person who offered the sacrifice and their family. Today the goat is increasingly being replaced by vegetables such as a GOURD or an anthropomorphic dough figure.

Sikhism. Sikh temples, called gurdwaras, provide free meals to people from all communities on a daily basis, a practice known as *langar*. The food is always vegetarian, making it accessible to everyone. The Harmandir Sahib gurdwara at Amritsar, called the Golden Temple, feeds an average 50,000 people a day and double that number on festive days. There are two kitchens: one that prepares dal and the other where rotis are assembled. A meal always has vegetables and kheer, a sweet rice pudding. Gurdwaras also sell sacred offerings called *kada prasad*, a HALWA made with water, sugar, ghee and whole wheat flour.

The *langar* has its origin at Sufi shrines (*dargahs*). Sufism, known as *tasawwuf* in the Arabic-speaking world, is a form of Islamic mysticism that emphasizes introspection and spiritual closeness with God. Serving food to the needy has been a tradition among

Sufis, especially the Chishti Order, and food metaphors are common in Sufi writing. The distribution of food at these shrines is considered a tribute to the saint honoured there as well as a gift from the saint and ultimately from God. Because many people travel long distances as pilgrims, shops sell food at the markets surrounding the shrine. As the food is considered to be imbued with blessings, it is considered an honour to accept it and the food is consumed by the rich and the poor, and even devotees from other faiths. India's most famous Sufi shrine is in Ajmer, Rajasthan, which has the tomb of the thirteenth-century Sufi saint Khwaja Moinuddin Chishti. During the saint's birthday, people are served *kesaria bhat*, a dish made from broken wheat, sugar, ghee and dried fruit that is served from giant cauldrons. According to legend, the MUGHAL emperor Akbar ordered a giant cauldron built at Ajmer to celebrate a victory. Today it can serve around 15,000 people – an example emulated by his son Jahangir who built a smaller cauldron. (see also BOHRAS).

Colleen Sen

- Kumar, Rakesh. 'Massive Kitchens, Unique Tastes: India's Ancient Temple Cuisine Sits in Class of Its Own'. *CNN Travel*, 30 September 2021. Available online: https://edition.cnn.com/travel/article/india-temple-food-cmd/index.html (accessed 3 May 2022).
- Narayan, Shoba. *Food and Faith: A Pilgrims' Journey through India*. Monee, IL: Jasmine Press, 2021.
- Pande, Alka. *Mukhwas: Indian Food through the Ages*. Delhi: Cambridge University Press, 2013.
- Samanta, Suchitra. 'The "Self-Animal" and Divine Digestion: Goat Sacrifice to the Goddess Kali in Bengal'. *The Journal of Asian Studies* 53, no. 3 (August 1994): 779–803.

THANDAI

Thandai (meaning 'cooling' in Hindi), also known as *shardai*, is a cold summer beverage made with almond milk and a mixture of watermelon seeds, FENNEL seeds, rose petals, pepper (see PEPPER, BLACK), POPPY SEEDS, CARDAMOM, SAFFRON and SUGAR. It is often associated with the festivals of Maha Shivaratri and Holi. Sometimes a little amount of *bhang* (the leaves and flower heads of cannabis) is added.

Helen Saberi

TIFFIN

Tiffin, an ANGLO-INDIAN term, was used by the British during the Raj to mean a light lunch. Today the word *tiffin* is still used in parts of India where it means a light snack in the middle of the day or in the afternoon. The word *tiffin* itself is thought to be derived from 'tiffing', an eighteenth-century English slang term for sipping. An early example of the use of the word *tiffin* appeared in a guide book *Cordiner's Ceylon* in 1808: 'Many persons are in the habit of sitting down to a repast at one o'clock, which is called tiffen, and is in fact an early dinner' (*Hobson-Jobson* [1886] 1986). This repast would be a light family meal of salads, leftovers of meat from the previous day made into mince, pies or even a CURRY with fruit fools, jellies and ice-creams to follow.

The word *tiffin* has been adopted, especially in Andhra Pradesh and Tamil Nadu, for a light afternoon teatime snack with specialities such as DOSA, *uppuma* (a savoury semolina and PULSES snack), *murukku* (a fried crunchy snack made with gram and RICE flour) and, of course, the ever-popular SAMOSAS and PAKORA. In CHENNAI there are mobile carts, coffee shops, sweetshops and cafes on every street selling SWEETS and savouries with COFFEE and TEA for tiffin. MUMBAI is also noted for its South Indian tiffin snacks which are available at any time of the day or night.

A tiffin-carrier is a nest of several circular metal containers in which the courses of a meal can be carried on a journey or to the office (see *DABBAWALLAHS*).

Helen Saberi

- Saberi, Helen. *Teatimes: A World Tour*. London: Reaktion Books, 2018.
- Yule, Henry and A. C. Burnell. *Hobson-Jobson: A Glossary of Colloquial Anglo-Indian Words and Phrases, and of Kindred Terms, Etymological, Historical, Geographical and Discursive*. 1886. Reprint of the new edition, edited by William Crooke. 1903. London: Routledge & Kegan Paul, 1986.

TOMATO

Tomato (*Solanum lycopersicum*, Hindi *tamatar*) is a member of the nightshade (Solanaceae) family that also includes AUBERGINES and POTATOES. It is native to a dry zone on the coast of western South America but became fully domesticated in Mexico before the Spanish conquest and was brought to India by the Portuguese. One of the earliest references is in an 1801 cookbook which refers to the tomato as *wilayat baigan*, or foreign aubergine. (Naming a new vegetable after one that is already known was a common practice.) By 1832 William Roxburgh in his *Florica Indica* recorded it as being 'very common in India'. In 1891 George Watt noted that 'Bengalis and Burmans use it in their sour curries'.

Tomato is one of India's most important vegetable crops, consumed both raw and cooked. Farmers follow a unique mixed cropping system where marigold is sown along the tomato field borders and water channels to control insects. While tomatoes are grown throughout the country, the leading producing states are Andhra Pradesh, Tamil Nadu, Gujarat, Karnataka and Maharashtra.

Like other imports, the tomato became a substitute or replacement for an existing ingredient, in this case, TAMARIND and *KOKUM* (*Garcinia indica*), both of which impart the sourness that is integral to many Indian CURRIES. Tomatoes contain high levels of glutamic acid that increase with ripening and, together with ONIONS, they form an umami-rich flavour base for curries and other dishes. Tomatoes are stuffed with potatoes or gram flour to make *bharwan*. Both raw and ripe tomatoes are pureed and cooked to make a variety of CHUTNEYS. Jams (*murabba*) and PICKLES are popular ways to preserve tomatoes. The tomato is ubiquitous in regional dals. On account of their non-native origin, temple and ritualistic foods never use tomatoes (see TEMPLE FOOD).

Tomato's perishable nature causes a volatile market price depending on output and season. Huge post-harvest losses of tomatoes occur due to inadequate storage and processing facilities. Many local hybrid varietals like the Pusa and Arka offer high-yielding and disease-resistant tomatoes with more pulp, robustness and longer shelf life, but many fall short on the prized tartness.

Priya Mani and Colleen Sen

TRIPURA

Tripura is a former princely state and remnants of the royal past still remain in the capital city of Agartala, where the Ujjayanta Palace stands today. Bordered by Bangladesh on three sides, the indigenous Tiprasa people, who are the original inhabitants of the Twipra/ Tripura Kingdom and speak a Tibeto-Burman language, have been reduced to a minority and non-tribal Bengalis form the majority.

Agriculture has the potential to develop. Past performance has been constrained not just by the terrain but also by a lack of development of irrigation, limited use of modern inputs, and inadequate access to agricultural extension services and markets. The state has favourable climatic conditions for cultivating various fruit and horticultural crops including RICE, JACKFRUIT, PINEAPPLE, POTATO, sugarcane, CHILLI and natural rubber.

Tripura food is heavily inspired by the food culture of their neighbour Bangladesh. Most people live on FISH, rice and vegetables. Their meat requirement, which remains an important part of their diet, is met by mutton, chicken, pork and fish. *Wahan mosdeng*, a dish famous among the Tripuri people, is one delicacy prepared with pork. A small section of Muslim Bengalis prefer beef, although the red meat is scarce in this Hindu-majority state.

Rice is the major crop of the state and is cultivated on 91 per cent of the cropped area. Sticky rice is the most important item in every kitchen. One interesting method of preparation is to wash the grain, wrap it in BANANA leaves and steam it. It comes out like a cake that is then taken with a traditional dish called *chakwi*, made with BAMBOO SHOOTS and pork. *Bhangui*, another essential rice dish, is prepared with sun-dried rice boiled with GHEE, GINGER and ONION.

A key ingredient in Tripuri cuisine is *berma*, a salted and fermented fish used in a myriad of classic dishes, including the stir-fried dish *kasoi bwtwi*. Other main ingredients in this dish are French beans, chopped onions, green chillies, tofu, GARLIC, SALT, TURMERIC powder. For a vegetarian version, the *berma* is left out. Traditionally, this dish is served with a type of local leaves known as *khundrupui*.

As in the other Northeast states, the Tripuri brew their own version of rice beer, called *chuwk*. Usually it is the women who are in charge of the tedious job of brewing rice beer or *chuwk*. However, inhabitants of Tripura believe that it is the *chuwarak* that has the most potential to be an ALCOHOL of its own class. *Chuwarak* is a distilled alcohol prepared using a variety of ingredients such as *mami* rice, PINEAPPLE, JACKFRUIT, etc.

Hoihnu Hauzel

TURMERIC

Turmeric (Hindi *haldi*) is one of India's most versatile and ancient spices. It is used in a variety of ways: as a dye, a ritual and ceremonial item, a medicine, an antiseptic, and, above all else, as a flavouring. Turmeric is made from rhizomes of *Curcuma longa*, a perennial plant belonging to the Zingiberaceae (GINGER) family. It is native to South Asia or South East Asia and was first domesticated in India, where it still grows wild. Turmeric residue has been found in cooking pots excavated from the Harappan Civilization. Its long history is also indicated by its many names in Sanskrit such as *ratrimanika*, 'that which glows in the night time'; *rubergavasa*, 'that which dissolves fats'; *madhunashini*, 'that which destroys sugar' (i.e. antidiabetic); and *uvati*, 'that which provides eternal youth'. The English name is thought to come from the Latin *terra merita*, meaning 'worthy (or meritorious) earth'.

India is the world's largest producer of turmeric, accounting for three-quarters of the world's total production, as well as the world's largest exporter and consumer. The major producing states are Telangana, Maharashtra and Tamil Nadu. Turmeric requires warm temperatures and abundant annual rainfall. While around forty-five species of turmeric are grown in India, the two main types are Madras and Alleppey, from districts in Tamil Nadu and Kerala, respectively. Alleppey turmeric has a darker, richer colour; a mellower flavour; and a higher curcumin content (up to 6.5 per cent) than Madras turmeric.

The rhizomes, usually called 'fingers', look like ginger; however, scraping off the rhizomes' skin reveals a brilliant orange flesh. This rhizome is the fresh spice, which is used in PICKLES and vegetables dishes. However, the most commonly used form of turmeric is achieved when the manufacturers cut off the fingers, boil and dry them, and then grind them into a powder. Turmeric's taste has been described as peppery, pungent, earthy, warm and bitter. It is a main ingredient in most CURRY POWDERS.

From time immemorial, turmeric and other spices have played an important role in Indian, Chinese and Indonesian medicine. Starting around 500 BCE, turmeric became a revered member of the Ayurvedic pharmacopeia (see FOOD AND MEDICINE). Ayurvedic physicians prescribed boiled milk with turmeric and SUGAR for colds, and turmeric juice to help heal wounds, bruises and leech bites. A paste made from turmeric, lime and SALT was applied to sprains. Inhaling the fumes of burning turmeric provided relief from congestion. Turmeric paste was prescribed for smallpox, chicken pox, shingles, ulcers, conjunctivitis, skin blemishes and even malaria. There are more than 100 synonyms for turmeric in Ayurvedic literature, including *bhadra*, meaning 'auspicious or lucky'; *haridra*, 'dear to Lord Krishna'; *jayanti*, 'one who is victorious over diseases'; and *varavarnin*, 'giving a fair complexion'.

To this day, some Indian women apply turmeric face masks or commercial creams with turmeric to lighten and enhance their complexions. South Asians apply a paste of turmeric and water as an antiseptic to cuts and strains; take a teaspoon in warm milk or yogurt, either after a meal as an aid to digestion or to relieve the symptoms of a fever; and breathe steam infused with turmeric to relieve congestion. Today turmeric and curcumin are being studied in clinical trials for various diseases and conditions, including inflammation, cancer and depression.

Turmeric has played an important role in Indian culture and religion since the spice is considered very auspicious. Buddhist monks and Hindu *sadhus* use it to dye their robes. A turmeric paste is applied to foreheads during religious rituals and weddings. During a traditional Indian wedding ceremony, the bride and groom apply a paste of turmeric and sandalwood powder to each other's foreheads (see RITES OF PASSAGE). Turmeric powder is shaken over temples during festivals; added to the vast tureens of RICE, lentils and vegetables prepared for worshippers; and thrown over other celebrants during Holi, a popular spring festival.

Helen Saberi and Colleen Sen

- Saberi, Helen and Colleen Sen. *Turmeric: The Wonder Spice*. Evanston, IL: Agate Digital, 2014.

TURNIP

Turnip (*Brassica rapa* var. *rapa*, Hindi *shalgam*) is a hardy root vegetable long considered a modest food for the poor and used as fodder for farm animals. It is grown for its roots, which are most commonly white in colour with a purply top, and green leaves. Turnips can be grown in temperate, sub-tropical and tropical regions but a cool and moist climate is the most favourable. Major states for turnip cultivation in India are Bihar, Haryana, Himachal Pradesh, Punjab and Tamil Nadu. A number of cultivars are grown in India such as Purple Top White Globe, Punjab Safed and Pusa Kanchan.

Turnips are a seasonal vegetable but are very versatile and can be boiled, roasted, mashed, pureed and added to soups, kormas and CURRIES. Shredded or chopped, they are added to salads. They are also good PICKLED, sometimes with other winter vegetables such as cauliflower. The leaves are cooked as a green or can be added to soups.

Turnips are a popular vegetable in Kashmir where they are called *gogji*. Unpeeled turnips are sliced into thick rounds with a hole in their centre and strung up to dry for later use. A favourite dish, *rajma gogji*, is turnip cooked with red kidney beans and spices and served with RICE. Turnips are also cooked in a cream sauce (*malai shalgam*). A *burta* is made with mashed turnip mixed with spicy pureed TOMATOES.

Turnip root is a rich source of vitamin C, the leaves are rich in vitamins A, C and K, folate and calcium.

Helen Saberi

- NDTV Food. '5 Best Turnip Recipes | Popular Shalgam Recipes', 24 January 2019. Available online: https://food.ndtv.com/lists/5-best-turnip-shalgam-recipes-1635484 (accessed 2 May 2022).
- Samtani, Geeta. *A Taste of Kashmir*. London: Merehurst, 1995.
- Timesofindia.com. 'Easy Recipes to Cook Turnip and Why You Should Have This Wonder Vegetable', 7 December 2020. Available online: https://timesofindia.indiatimes.com/life-style/food-news/5-reasons-why-you-need-to-include-turnips-in-your-diet-and-some-easy-ways-to-do-so/photostory/79592704.cms (accessed 2 May 2022).

UDUPI RESTAURANTS

One of the most popular categories of eateries are Udupi (sometimes written Udipi) restaurants, originally known as Udupi hotels – a word once in common use to mean any establishment serving meals. (Their non-vegetarian counterparts are called 'military hotels'). Their origin lies in the town of Udupi in Karnataka, site of a famous Krishna temple, many smaller temples and eight monasteries (*math*) that served vegetarian food to worshippers. The temple kitchens were, and still are, staffed with Brahmin cooks. In the twentieth century, some of these cooks opened their own restaurants serving similar vegetarian food – first locally, then all over the country and eventually abroad. These restaurants are the progenitors of South Indian vegetarian restaurants around the world, even if they no longer have Udupi in their name.

The first major entrepreneur was K. Krishna Rao. After working in a monastery kitchen in Udupi, in 1925 he began managing a small vegetarian restaurant in the George Town district of Madras. Later he opened his own establishments, which he named Udupi Hotel. In 1939 Rao opened Old Woodlands Hotel in CHENNAI, and when he lost his lease, built New Woodlands Hotel. It became the flagship of restaurants in Bangalore (BENGALURU), New DELHI, MUMBAI, and other Indian cities as well as London, New York and Singapore. Rao is considered the creator of the masala dosa – a DOSA, often very large, filled with spiced POTATOES.

Another major chain is the Dasaprakash group, founded by K. Sitharama Rao in the 1920s. It expanded mainly in South India. The Dasaprakash hotel in Chennai, which opened in 1954, features statues of gods, a puja room and a wedding hall. Chains based in Bengaluru include the MAVALLI TIFFIN ROOMS group. In Mumbai, the most prominent chain is the Kamarth group, which has expanded all over South India as well as to Atlanta and Tokyo. In 1981, P. Rajagopal founded the Saravanaa Bhavan chain in Chennai, which today has ninety outlets in thirty-eight countries. At first, many Udupi hotels had separate dining rooms for Brahmins and/or barred Muslims and Dalits from entering but this practice ended in the 1950s. The practice of hiring only Brahmin cooks also came to an end, in part because fewer Brahmins wanted to enter the profession.

There were two categories of food served at these restaurants: TIFFIN, which consisted of South Indian snacks, COFFEE and TEA, and meals, including breakfast. Traditionally, meals were served on BANANA leaves, with one set menu for everyone. Today steel thalis are common (see COOKING AND DINING). Offerings include a number of South Indian vegetarian dishes, including rasam (a thin, spicy dal), IDLI, DOSA, VADA, coconut CHUTNEY and *payasam* (see *KHEER*). The traditional drink in South India is filtered coffee. In recent years, menus have expanded to include North Indian and Chinese vegetarian dishes and even non-vegetarian dishes.

Colleen Sen

- Madsen, Stig Toft and Geoffrey Gardella. 'Udupi Hotels: Entrepreneurship, Reform and Revival'. In *Curried Cultures*, edited by Krishnendu Ray and Tulsi Srinavas, 91–109. Berkeley: University of California Press, 2012.

UTTAR PRADESH

Uttar Pradesh is the fourth largest state in India and, with a population of 200 million, the most populous. The state was created in 1950 as a successor to the United Provinces, which in turn was a successor to the United Provinces of Agra and Oudh established in 1902 during the British Raj. Around 80 per cent of the population is Hindu and 19 per cent Muslim. It shares borders with Rajasthan, Haryana, Himachal Pradesh, Delhi, Uttarakhand, Bihar, Chhattisgarh, Madhya Pradesh and Jharkhand and has an international border with Nepal. Around 45 per cent of the population is vegetarian.

The Doab – the flat alluvial tract between the Ganges and Yamuna rivers – is the heartland of the ancient Hindu civilization, with settlements going back to the second millennium BCE. The events in the Indian epics the *Ramayana* and the *Mahabharata* took place in the region, and, later, Jainism and Buddhism emerged here. Parts or all of Uttar Pradesh was ruled by the Delhi Sultanate from 1206 until 1526 when it came under Mughal rule. Architecture, painting, music and dance all flourished during the Mughal period, reaching its apogee under Emperor Shah Jahān, builder of the Taj Mahal. In 1858 the British established direct rule.

The central part of the state was once part of the kingdom of Awadh ruled by the Nawabs from 1832 to 1856 CE when the last ruler was deposed by the British. The food shows the influence of Iran, Central Asia and local traditions. LUCKNOW, the state capital, is famous for its cuisine. The western region has two distinct cuisines: that of RAMPUR and of Mathura, also known as Brajbhoomi, the land of Lord Krishna. Here food is prepared in the *sattvic* manner, that is, without meat, ONIONS or GARLIC. Dairy products play an important role, including GHEE, yogurt, butter and SWEETS made from *KHOYA*. The region around Mathura is famous for its sweets such as *peda* and AGRA *PETHA*. A popular breakfast dish in this region and throughout UP is the *bedmi* roti: puris stuffed with ground *urad* dal and spices, eaten with a potato CURRY. It is also eaten as a snack throughout the day.

The heart of the eastern region is the ancient city of VARANASI. Vegetarian dishes are the order of the day here and pure ghee is a characteristic feature of dishes, including sweets and *KACHORI*-sabzi. The most popular breakfast dish and STREET FOOD are *kachoris*, a deep-fried snack made from wheat flour and filled with lentils (*badi kachori*) or POTATOES (*choti kachori*) and served with JALEBI. A famous dish is Banarsi PAAN, which is served after meals.

The southern part of the state is part of the Bundelkhand region that extends into Madhya Pradesh and is marked by barren hills and sparse vegetation. The traditional staples here were different kinds of MILLETS, cooked with spices, a little oil and ingredients from local rivers and pounds, such as LOTUS root and water chestnut. A typical dish is *anwariya*, made from pureed *AMLA* that are sautéed until they become a soft paste, then mixed with chickpea flour, water, TURMERIC and SALT, boiled and tempered with spices. The northwestern parts of Uttar Pradesh in the foothills of the Himalayas, called the Terai, are a richly forested and cultivated land.

Agriculture is the mainstay of the state's economy. Blessed with extremely fertile land and abundant forests, Uttar Pradesh has a rich agrarian tradition that is intermingled with nature worship, tribal traditions, sacred religious complexes and pockets of distinctive Muslim communities who brought their own influences. Since the late 1960s, with the introduction of high-yielding varieties of seed for WHEAT and RICE, greater availability of fertilizers and increased use of irrigation, the state has become a major producer of food grains in the country. Wheat is the staple food of the state and roti paired with vegetables and lentils is the daily fare of the common person.

Although the last three decades have seen an enormous spurt in restaurant culture in the state, traditional cuisines thrive only in homes, especially during festivals and religious rituals. For all the faults of religion in the recent past, and earlier too, it has helped preserve some of the ancient culinary traditions.

Most celebratory foods are fried and made with dairy. The cuisine of Uttar Pradesh, like others, demonstrates a clear demarcation between greater traditions and lesser traditions. Greater traditions are followed by people who have access to resources, the Brahmins and the business class and most of the urban populace while the lesser traditions are followed by tribals and poorer segments of society.

In Uttar Pradesh and other parts of North India, foods were traditionally divided into two categories: *kaccha* and *pakka. Kaccha* foods are prepared in the family kitchen by boiling or roasting – such as rice, dal, KHICHRI, some BREADS made without oil, and vegetables and served to the family. This is the basic core meal of much of India. *Pakka* foods are prepared by frying in or basting with ghee, an ingredient considered ritually pure. This includes fried breads such as paratha and many sweets. These foods can be taken out of the kitchen to eat and shared with people outside the family. *Pakka* foods are served at temples and during festivals so that everyone can eat them. (The actual categorization is a bit more complex; for example, rice cooked with ghee to make ghee rice is *pakka* while khichri that is only tempered with ghee is *kaccha*.)

Pakka khana is reserved for religious occasions for two reasons: the incorporation of ghee and milk supposedly makes the food sacred and the use of the round bottom pan called *kadhai* is also considered sacred. This concept of *pakka* and *kaccha khana* tends to broaden the divide between the haves and have-nots, between the upper and lower castes.

Another social impact on culinary practices comes from the affordability of food. In a system of cash cropping (a crop produced for its commercial value rather than for use by the grower), the main crop is meant for those who can afford it and the by-products are consumed by those who cannot. Unfair as it is, it has meant that the lesser traditions have evolved even more robustly. For instance, if rice is expensive and even its farming is not affordable to the poor, they depend on millets that are grown with minimal investments. They also forage flora and fauna that are considered weeds and pests. Spices are replaced with herbs and CHILLIES, fats are replaced with lard and MUSTARD or SESAME oil, fresh produce is replaced with foraged or sun-dried leaves and vegetables, lentils and NUTS are replaced with wild beans, and butchered meat with foraged animals and offal.

Uttar Pradesh's fourteen tribes have slightly different rituals, although the essential grammar of food remains the same. Living in forests and on the outskirts of villages and cities, their culinary traditions are largely independent of cultivated crops. Most of their requirements of food, medicine and even utensils are fulfilled by the forests and rivers, recipes are simple, food pairings are perfectly suited for human health, and they practise seasonal eating. These tribes worship at their own shrines, organize fairs and festivals religiously and some kind of sacrificial food is commonly a part of these festivals. Brewing ALCOHOL and tapping toddy for alcohol is common and its consumption is also part of some religious festivities.

Many of these lesser traditions have survived among the common people living in cities and towns because there has been a constant social upgrade, called Sanskritization, of the tribals and the lower strata of the caste system into mainstream society and religious traditions. For example, consuming foraged wild purslane and millet roti on a certain festival during the monsoons is practised by all social strata though the roots lie in tribal culture. This practice has helped preserve some of the foraged produce and heirloom vegetables.

The aristocratic cuisines have been a result of the exchange of lands and marriages. Because of their close trade links with businesses for such things as spices and silks, there was no limit to ingredients or influences. The use of spices is extremely refined and abundant in the cuisines of the royalty and the business community. All kind of nuts and dried fruits that were imported from other parts of the world became a natural part of these cuisines, making them richer in composition and flavours as well as in the way the food is served in its finery.

The popular cuisines come from the greater traditions, from densely cultivated crops and from a position of affordability. Hence we see liberal usage of fine grains, dairy, nuts, spices and SAFFRON, etc. along with game meats, FISH and poultry. A meal typically consists of one lentil preparation, one grain-based flatbread like roti, paratha or puri, sometimes a rice preparation also becomes a part of it, one or two seasonal vegetables, some condiments like CHUTNEY, PICKLES and the curd-based RAITA, a chopped salad or just a few slices of raw ONION or RADISH or even a few slices of CUCUMBER and TOMATO sprinkled with SALT and lemon juice. The grains, lentils and vegetables keep changing with seasons in every household because there is ritualistic inclusion of most seasonal foods.

Sangeeta Khanna

- Indian Culture. 'A North-Indian Thali: The Varied Tastes of Uttar Pradesh'. *n.d.* Available online: https://indianculture.gov.in/food-and-culture/north/north-indian-thali-varied-tastes-uttar-pradesh (accessed 3 May 2022).
- Khanna, Sangeeta. *Culinary Culture of Uttar Pradesh: A Food Trail*. New Delhi: Times Books, 2019.

UTTARAKHAND

Uttarakhand, India's twenty-seventh state carved out of Uttar Pradesh on 9 November 2000, is nestled in the foothills of the Himalayas, sharing its borders with Tibet to the north and Nepal to the west, and the state of Himachal Pradesh to the northwest.

A picturesque state blessed with snow-topped peaks, valleys and 'hill stations' established during the British Raj, Uttarakhand at once evokes images of the '*shikari*'-turned-conservator Jim Corbett (after whom the country's oldest national park is named), pilgrimages to the holy Char Dham (Badrinath, Kedarnath, Yamunotri and Gangotri), ritual dips and the last rites for loved ones at the Ganga in Haridwar, and mountain treks as well as river-rafting breaks for adrenaline junkies. The state, known as Dev Bhoomi (Land of the Gods) in popular lore, is famous for gifting some of India's bravest soldiers and generals, and also the most sought-after cooks, but its cuisine remained little-known till it came into its own after attaining statehood.

Despite the ubiquity of momos (dumplings) and instant noodles popularized by its Tibetan and Nepali residents, or of Punjabi and South Indian dishes that have acquired a national following, the cuisine of Uttarakhand, which has seen a revival since the formation of the state, stands apart because of its simplicity and lightness and the uniqueness of the ingredients that go into it. As a result of the rocky terrain and sub-zero temperatures in certain months, which makes agriculture difficult in many parts of the state, and also because of the remoteness of its communities, the cuisine relies primarily on ingredients that are unique to the region.

Some of these have generated much interest in social media food groups in recent years and include *bhang jeera* (seeds of the cannabis plant), stinging nettle grass (locally known as *sisunak* or *bichchu ghas*, which goes into making *kandalee ka saag*), fiddlehead fern (*lingde*), *jakhiya* (MUSTARD-like seeds of the tick weed that add a crunch and tang to a plain POTATO dish or a yogurt RAITA with CUCUMBER, TOMATO and ONION dices thrown in), *gahat* (horse gram) and *jhangora* (barnyard MILLETS, which go into making a local *KHEER*).

The state is divided into two administrative divisions – Kumaon and Garhwal – that are also culturally distinct and have their own favourite dishes. Kumaon, studded with popular tourist destinations such as Nainital, Almora, Ranikhet and Pithoragarh, brings certain distinctive food products to the Indian table, notably basmati RICE and the white and buttery GI-tagged Munsiyari *rajma*, or kidney beans. Garhwal, on the other hand, is crisscrossed by mountains, valleys and gushing rivers and is famous for its long martial tradition. It is also, literally, the spiritual soul of India being home to Haridwar and the Char Dham, but it is not agriculturally well-endowed.

The people of Uttarakhand are mainly vegetarian – this Himalayan state, in fact, has the highest percentage of upper-caste Brahmins, traditionally the priestly class, in India – and their simple fare consists of BREADS made with millet flour or red rice, lentils (principally horse gram), black soybean (known locally as *bhatt*) and leafy greens (AMARANTH, or *chaulai*, being the favourite), besides potatoes, TARO and red pumpkin, all tempered with either GHEE or MUSTARD oil. The food is not spice-rich – ASAFOETIDA (*hing*), CUMIN (*jeera*), dried red CHILLIES and the local favourite *jakhiya* seeds are the spices that are commonly used. Elaborate masalas are conspicuous by their absence in Uttarakhand's cuisine.

Typically, a traditional meal in Uttarakhand would consist of at least some of these dishes, each with a principal ingredient that is unique to the state: the calcium-rich *madua ki* roti made with finger millet flour and slathered with ghee to make it easy on the digestive system; *laal chawal* (red rice); *mooli pyaj ka thechwa* (round white mountain RADISH, pounded and crushed on a *sil-batta*, not cut, with onions); *bhang kaddu* (red pumpkin spiked with cannabis seeds); Munsiyari *rajma*; *gahat ke dubke* (thick horse gram broth with spicy dumplings); *gaderi matar* (taro and peas); *jakhiya lauki* (bottle GOURD with *jakhiya* seeds); *bhang* chutney (cannabis leaf CHUTNEY); and, lending them its distinctive flavour, *pisyoon loon* (different kinds of Himalayan rock SALT, crushed and flavoured with CORIANDER, GARLIC, GINGER, cumin and mustard).

Other local favourites, particularly in Kumaon, are *chainsoo* (ground *urad* dal, or black gram, paste flavoured with coriander); *phanoo* (a soupy combination of different dals – pigeon pea, or *arhar*; mung bean; and *urad*); *kafuli* (spinach and FENUGREEK leaves slow cooked in a gravy thickened with WHEAT or rice flour); and dal *bade* (split *urad* dal fritters). For non-vegetarians, just about every part of a goat is up for grabs – skin and offal seasoned with green chillies, fresh coriander, ginger, garlic and mustard oil (*kachmoli* or *panchola*); blood, dried and sautéed with regional spices (*loaash*); semi-dry CURRY made with innards (*bhutwa*); and of course, the popular Pahadi mutton curry cooked traditionally on wood fire in a *bhaddu* (heavy bell metal vessel with a round circular base and narrow top).

For those with a sweet tooth, the state's most popular offering is the fudge-like *bal mithai* made with caramelized *KHOYA* and quilted with SUGAR balls, followed by *jhangore ki* kheer, which comes loaded with the goodness of barnyard millets and dry fruits; *singal*, or fried spirals of semolina, BANANA, curd, milk, sugar and CARDAMOM; and *arsa*, a must for festive occasions and weddings, these are sweet dough balls prepared with ground rice and jaggery and fried in mustard oil. Uncomplicated, loaded with natural and unusual flavours, very different at times from what is encountered elsewhere in the country, the cuisine of Uttarakhand is the culinary discovery of the last two decades whose popularity shows no signs of abatement.

Sourish Bhattacharyya

- Kotnala, Tarun. 'Goat Cookery in Uttarakhand'. *Active Flavours*, 29 July 2020. Available online: http://activeflavours.com/goat-cookery-in-uttrakhand/ (accessed 2 May 2022).
- Pal, Sanchari. 'Food Secrets: On the Trail of Kumaon's Culinary Wonders'. *The Better India*, 17 June 2016. Available online: https://www.thebetterindia.com/58647/food-cuisine-kumaon-uttarakhand/ (accessed 2 May 2022).
- Pathak, Prannay. 'When Will the Vibrant Textures and Flavours of the Hills Have Their Moment?' *Outlook Traveller*, 4 September 2020.

VADAS

Vadas (also written *badas*) are fried snacks that have variously been described as fritters, croquettes, fried dumplings or even doughnuts, depending on their shape. A popular street food, especially in Western India, they are also eaten for breakfast, especially in the South. They are an ancient dish. The *Dharma Sutras* (800–300 BCE) describe vadas (called *vataka*) as ground fermented lentils (especially *urad* dal) made into various shapes and fried in GHEE. Vadas make an appearance in the twelfth century CE *MANASOLLASA*.

Vadas are usually made from legumes, notably pigeon peas, *urad* dal and *moong* dal (see PULSES). They are soaked in water, then ground into a batter that is seasoned with various spices and sometimes fermented. The mixture is then shaped and deep-fried. A well-known vada, served in South Indian restaurants, is *medu* vada, made from *urad* dal. It looks like a doughnut with a hole in the centre and is accompanied by SAMBAR and coconut CHUTNEY.

In Maharashtra, a popular street food dish is *batata* vada, deep-fried mashed POTATO dumplings quilted in chickpea batter. An inventive street food vendor, Ashok Vaidya, who operated outside the Dadar railway station in MUMBAI, served this *batata* vada wedged between two slices of *pav* (the local BREAD derived from the Portuguese 'pão') like a burger with a whole green CHILLI and a slathering of GARLIC chutney. This dish is called *vada* pav. His son, Narendra, continues the family tradition along with the son of his father's business partner, even as stalls selling vada *pav* are omnipresent today in Mumbai.

What's popular as *batata* vada in Maharashtra re-emerges in southern India as the *bonda*, which is primarily made with mashed potatoes, although in UDUPI RESTAURANTS diced French beans, CARROTS, peas and CORIANDER leaves are added. In Tamil Nadu, black gram batter replaces the chickpea flour that is popular in Karnataka, and in Kerala the base could be tapioca mash, sweet potato and ONIONS, hard-boiled egg or even minced meat. Chicken or mutton keema vadas are made by forming minced meat into patties and then deep-frying them.

Sourish Bhattacharyya and Colleen Sen

• Shankar, Kartikeya. 'Vada Pav: History of the Popular Mumbai Snack'. *Times of India*, 17 July 2021. Available online: https://timesofindia.indiatimes.com/life-style/food-news/vada-pav-history-of-the-popular-mumbai-snack/articleshow/76973714.cms (accessed 2 May 2022).

VARANASI

Varanasi (Banaras, Benares), a city in Uttar Pradesh, is one of the oldest inhabited cities in the world, whose history goes back to the first Indo-Aryan settlement in the middle Ganges Valley. The northern part of the city is on a plateau called Rajghat and archaeological evidence indicates that the ancient city of Kashi was located here 2,500 years ago. Varanasi became a centre of Aryan religion and philosophy as well as a commercial and industrial centre famous for its muslin and silk fabrics, perfumes, ivory works and sculpture.

The city's location on the left bank of the Ganges made the land richly fertile and provided water year-round. River routes were used for trade by Buddhists, MUGHALS and,

FIGURE 48 VARANASI. Morning tea. Ryan Hartman/Wikimedia Commons.

later, the British. Since ancient times, the city has been a centre of learning and the *guru-shishya* (teacher-student) tradition. Others came to the city for penance because of the religious values attached to the river. The city also had become the centre of *tantra* studies and practice.

Different trades flourished because of a well-connected transport system, including bead making, silk and brocade weaving, and SWEET making practised by the Aheers, a community of milkmen. Aheers remain influential in the city and are major landowners. Although dairy is an important business in Varanasi, organized dairy has not been able to replace the age-old small holding dairy businesses and traditional distribution system (see DAIRY SECTOR).

More people settled here after Aurangzeb's plundering of the city in 1656 when royal families from across the country came to restore and build temples and ghats and palaces. The culinary repertoire of the city still displays these regional influences which are largely confined to the areas where the communities settled almost a thousand years ago. The trading communities of the country, especially Rajasthanis, Marwaris, Agarwals and Gujaratis, set up essential businesses such as grocery and food shops. A census taken by James Prinsep in mid-1800s indicated that 70 per cent of the city population was Marathas in addition to Bengalis, Biharis, Gujaratis, Tamilians and even Nepalis. The present-day culinary culture of the city is largely defined by the *sattvic* food (prepared without meat, ONIONS or GARLIC) these communities have brought in, shaped by the local produce and climate.

Varanasi is one of the most important centres of Hindu religion. In the first millennium BCE, long before the emergence of Shiva and Vishnu as the great gods of Hinduism, the land of Kashi was inhabited by ancient deities associated with trees and pools of water who were known as *yakshas* and *yakshis*. The local people had no idols but worshipped a tree or a piece of stone for abundance in life, fertility, for health or for well-being of cattle. This *yakshadharma* or 'life cult' was the prevalent religion of the non-Aryans of ancient India. Even today, in an ancient city like Varanasi, there are numerous tree shrines and *chauras* (the shrine of a local mother goddess) where people worship for worldly abundance. The identity of some of the city's older *mohallas* (neighbourhoods) is still defined by which community settled there or by which shrine or *chaura* is in the area. Some trees and man-made stepwells have a tradition of an annual fair or festival where a certain type of food is prepared, creating a strong link between produce, season and religion.

This sense of place is so strong that certain foods and produce made at a certain place are considered sacred or special and no one tries to recreate them in a different location. However, the current wave of foodie travellers has caused a proliferation of all kinds of food in almost every area of the city. Until just two decades ago, the specialities of the old gullies (narrow lanes) remained localized to an extent that other parts of the city didn't even know about their existence. An example is a milk fat speciality called *malaiyyo*. It is available only at the end of the Thatheri Bazzar gully which is inhabited largely by the Aheers. Made only in the winter, *malaiyyo* is basically milk foam lightly flavoured with SAFFRON and sugar, topped with almonds and pistachios and served in clay bowls. Today we can find *mailaiyyo* filled with strawberry, PINEAPPLE and even blueberry filling.

Specific markets and supply chains maintain hyperlocal food systems. The markets of Dalmandi, Gola Dinanath, Chowk, Phool mandi, Dasashwamedh, Bansphatak, Thatheri and other bazaars have preserved the old foods and ingredients. Here you will find specific types of PICKLES, *murabbas* (candied fruits), *ittars* (essential oils used to make perfumes), spice blends, herbs, *thandai* (a cold drink made of milk, sugar, almonds and various spices) and ingredients for PAAN along with certain seasonal foods. It is still a delight to find grain-free *mithais* being made for certain festivals like Shivratri, Navratri, Diwali or Annakut in remote corners of the gullies, saving the tradition from the perils of mass production.

Old residents of the city still follow a specific food calendar. Minor festivals in each transitioning season call for the consumption of a certain food as a ritualistic observance of tradition. The links between households where fresh food is cooked at least three times a day and the smaller markets scattered around the city are so strong that it is the appearance of a new seasonal produce that announces a festival and a dish. For example, just before the winter harvest festival of Makara Sankranti, hawkers bring freshly pressed rice flakes, jaggery and SESAME seeds along with other ready-made treats that are a part of this festival.

Food habits in a Varanasi household are mostly vegetarian, and even the meat eaters consume liberal amounts of vegetables. (In 2019, the BJP government banned the sale and consumption of meat within a 250-metre radius of all Varanasi temples and heritage sites.) Fresh produce of every season punctuates everyday meals and grains and lentils are chosen according to the best pairing possible for the vegetables of the season. A typical Varanasi meal platter consists of one or two grains in the form of flatbreads and rice, one lentil preparation, one or two vegetables, curd-based RAITA, CHUTNEYS and PICKLES as condiments and a dessert or two. Dairy based *mithais* (sweetmeats) are served with meals, even breakfast, or as a snack.

Sangeeta Khanna

- Khanna, Sangeeta. *Culinary Culture of Uttar Pradesh: A Food Trail*. New Delhi: Times Books, 2019.
- Motichandra, Dr. *Kashi ka Itihas*. Varanasi, Uttar Pradesh: Vishwavidyalaya Prakashan, 2012.

VARK

Vark (*varak*) is pure silver (or gold) leaf used along with crushed mother-of-pearl and star ruby emulsions by the MUGHALS to decorate their elaborate court food. Today on special occasions such as weddings and religious festivals *vark* is still used to decorate SWEETS (such as carrot HALWA), NUTS, DATES, desserts, RICE dishes and KEBABS.

Vark is made by compressing silver dust between layers of thin paper or parchment. The papers are encased in a protective pouch which is hand-hammered until the dust is compressed into a piece of gossamer-thin foil which is tasteless and odourless but is visibly stunning, adding luxury to the sweet or dish. Traditionally, the silver dust was manually pounded between layers of ox gut or cow hide. It was easier to separate the *vark* from the animal tissue rather than paper but paper is used now. To place *vark* on food, the top sheet of paper is pulled off the *vark*, gently inverted, and the *vark* is placed onto the food. The bottom sheet is then gently removed.

Vark is safe to eat. In fact, since ancient times, Unani (Greek) and Ayurvedic physicians have used powdered precious metals (and jewels) in their remedies for many illnesses (see FOOD AND MEDICINE). Silver has anti-microbial properties. Gold *vark* is even more stunning but is used quite rarely now.

Helen Saberi

- Devi, Yamuna. *The Art of Indian Vegetarian Cooking*. London: Leopard Books, 1995.
- Sahni, Julie. *Classic Indian Cookery*. London: Grub Street, 1997.

VEGETARIANISM

Although people, especially outside of India, often believe that most Indians are vegetarians, a survey by the Pew Research Center (2020) found that only 39 per cent of Indian adults describe themselves as vegetarian. (The definition was left up to the respondent.) The percentage varies greatly by religion: over 90 per cent of Jains say they are vegetarians, compared with 44 per cent of Hindus, 8 per cent of Muslims and 10 per cent of Christians. Even among groups with low rates of vegetarianism, many people restrict their meat consumption on certain days or under certain circumstances. Economic factors also play a role, as meat is expensive.

Among Hindus, another 40 per cent follow various restrictions on certain occasions, as do roughly two-thirds of Muslims and Christians. FASTING is a common practice among all groups and around three-fourths of Indians fast to mark certain occasions. Hindu fasts are almost always vegetarian and may involve other restrictions. However, very few Indians are vegans since dairy products are an important source of protein for all groups.

Among Hindus, worshippers of Vishnu (Vaishnavs) are always vegetarian. While most Sikhs eat meat (but not beef or pork), members of certain sects are vegetarians, perhaps reflecting their Vaishnav pre-conversion origins.

In the states of Andhra Pradesh, Assam, Bihar, Jharkhand, Kerala, Odisha, Tamil Nadu, Telangana and West Bengal, less than 5 per cent of the population is vegetarian. The highest proportions of vegetarians are in Rajasthan (75 per cent), Punjab and Haryana (69 per cent each) and Gujarat (61 per cent). Vegetarianism tends to be more common among higher caste Hindus; lower rates can be attributed to the presence of non-Hindus as well as Scheduled Tribes and Scheduled Castes. However, geography and history also play a role. For example, the high level of meat consumption in Telangana, whose population is 85 per cent Hindu, can be attributed to the availability of livestock in the state and the strong Muslim influence in the state capital, HYDERABAD. West Bengal and Kerala have long sea coasts, so sea food plays an important part in their diets. One explanation for the consumption of meat by Kashmiri Pandits (Brahmins) is the cold climate which limits fruit and vegetable production. Meat consumption also varies by sex. The government-sponsored National Family Health Survey (2015–16) found that 80 per cent of Indian men and 70 per cent of women eat eggs, meat, FISH, or one or all of these on a regular basis.

People follow other dietary restrictions. Most Jains and many Hindus avoid eating ONIONS and GARLIC. Beef is taboo for most Hindus; in fact, according to the Pew Research Center survey, a majority of Hindus (70 per cent) say a person could not be considered a Hindu if they eat beef, compared with just under 50 per cent who say this would be true of people who do not believe in God or never offer prayers – indication of how important diet is to identity in India. (The percentage is even higher for Jains (85 per cent) and Sikhs (82 per cent).)

Although cows were the mainstay of the Vedic economy and held in high regard, there is textual evidence that they too were sacrificed. Others argue that these are mistranslations and that the ancient Indians never ate beef. Whenever it occurred, the inviolability of the cow probably occurred gradually. The *Arthashastra* (probably compiled between the third century BCE and the second century CE) refers to herds of aged, sterile and diseased cattle, implying that they were allowed to die a natural death. The *Law Code of Manu* (probably compiled between 200 BCE and 200 CE) does not specifically list beef in the list of forbidden foods or forbid the consumption of meat in general but does say that abstaining from meat (and alcohol) will bring great rewards. It also gives a long list of penances and punishments for anyone who kills a cow. Today, at least twenty-three states prohibit the slaughter of cows and the sale of beef, while the export of beef is prohibited. Many states now also disallow the serving of eggs at school lunches.

The ancient Vedic Indians were meat eaters. Their religion centred on the sacrifice of animals and consumption of their flesh. But the seeds of vegetarianism may have been sown during the Vedic period (1700–1100 BCE), since occasionally a figure made of flour was substituted for the animal victim. Milk, GHEE, yogurt and other dairy products, which became staples of Indian vegetarian diets, were also widely consumed at this time. Between the eighth and sixth centuries BCE, new attitudes and customs emerged that would become central to Indian culture, expressed in texts called the *Upanishads*. While they do not overtly advocate vegetarianism, non-injury for all living beings (*ahimsa*) tops the list of the virtues to be cultivated. Some people renounced the world by moving to forest retreats where they practised yoga and meditation and adopted stringent eating habits. Some ascetics only ate food that was wild and uncultivated (a practice that survives to this day in the Hindu fast called *palahar*). The abundance of vegetation in India clearly favoured this kind of diet; it is difficult to imagine vegetarianism emerging in a much colder climate. Some ascetics attracted followers who formed small groups that became sects and then congregations called *sangha*. While some of these sects disappeared, two survived to become major world religions: Jainism and Buddhism.

The leading exponent of Jainism was Vardhaman Mahavira (599–527 BCE) who left home and family in search of enlightenment and gained followers. A central doctrine of what came to be called Jainism is *ahimsa*, often translated as non-injury or non-violence. Jains believe everything, from rocks and plants to gods, has an eternal soul, or *jiva*, although some souls are more powerful and complex than others. Mahavira's 'pure unchanging eternal law' holds that 'all things breathing, all things existing, all things living, all things whatever, should not be slain or treated with violence'. When it comes to food, the rules of Jainism are the most stringent of any religion. Five things are absolutely forbidden: meat and meat products, fish, eggs, alcohol, and HONEY. Jain monks and nuns follow even more stringent rules, avoiding fruits and vegetables with seeds or those that grow underground, fermented foods, buds and sprouts, and others. Some Jains avoid these items during certain fasts and festivals. However, Jains, and indeed most vegetarians in India, are not vegans, although veganism appears to be increasing.

Another movement is Buddhism, which was founded by Siddhartha Gautama (563–483 BCE), later known as the Buddha ('enlightened one'). At one point, he joined the ascetics where he practised austerities and almost starved to death. He rejected this approach in favour of what he called the Middle Way – a path of moderation between the extremes of self-indulgence and self-mortification. The concept of *ahimsa* is also central to Buddhist doctrine. Early Buddhism placed no restrictions on the diets of laymen, although the food served at Buddhist monasteries was vegetarian. Outside the monasteries, where Buddhist monks begged for their food, they had to accept anything that was given to them, even meat or fish, provided it was not slain on purpose for the monk and the recipient did not see, hear or even suspect the killing of the animal. Only a few substances were absolutely forbidden to all Buddhists, including alcohol and certain meats.

Many people found the moral and ethical teachings of the new movements attractive, especially since both welcomed women and members of oppressed castes. Over time, the Brahmins co-opted the idea of vegetarianism and became vegetarians themselves. Even today, most Brahmins in India are vegetarians except in West Bengal, Kashmir and some other regions. Vegetarianism became a marker of both caste and class: people who wanted to move up the social scale adopted a vegetarian diet – a process known as Sanskritization. In more recent times, an advocate of vegetarianism on moral and health grounds was Mahatma GANDHI although he did not object to the consumption of eggs.

In the West, the 1960s saw a surge of interest in India as hippies flocked to the subcontinent, in part inspired by the example of the Beatles who went to India in 1968 to study Transcendental Meditation. All four Beatles became vegetarians at some point. Today vegetarianism and veganism are becoming more popular throughout the world for health and moral reasons. Vegetarians and even vegans are no longer regarded as eccentrics and mainstream restaurants offer a variety of vegetarian dishes.

Colleen Sen

- Bose, Adrija. 'Vegetarian India a Myth? Survey Shows over 70% Indians Eat Non-Veg, Telangana Tops List'. *HuffPost India*, 14 July 2016. Available online: https://www.huffpost.com/archive/in/entry/how-india-eats_n_10434374 (accessed 4 May 2022).

- Corichi, Manolo. 'Eight-in-Ten Indians Limit Meat in their Diets, and Four-in-Ten Consider Themselves Vegetarian'. Pew Research Center, 8 July 2021. Available online: https://www.pewresearch.org/fact-tank/2021/07/08/eight-in-ten-indians-limit-meat-in-their-diets-and-four-in-ten-consider-themselves-vegetarian/ (accessed 4 May 2022).

VINDALOO

Vindaloo (sometimes *bindaloo*) is a hot and spicy CURRY, characterized by a vinegary sharpness. The original dish came to India via the Portuguese in the early fifteenth century and colonized the region that is now Goa. The word comes from the Portuguese dish *carne de vinha d'alhos* (meat marinated in wine-vinegar and GARLIC) which was the Portuguese sailor's 'preserved' food. Pork and garlic were layered in barrels and then soaked in red wine which acted as a preservative both for the long journey by sea and the hot weather. In early recipes, only black pepper (see PEPPER, BLACK) or long pepper (see PEPPER, LONG) was used so the dish wasn't as hot as it later came to be known. The introduction of the fiery hot CHILLI pepper by the Portuguese came later. The local Goans 'Indianized' the dish and the name evolved into 'vindaloo'. Palm vinegar was substituted for the wine-vinegar and additional spices such as CINNAMON, CARDAMOM and GINGER were added. In the early days, the dish was still made with pork, partly because of the Portuguese influence but also because converted Hindus and Catholic Goans had no problems consuming pork and wine. Later the vindaloo was made with other meats such as beef or duck and large amounts of dried red chillies were added from which it acquired its legendary hotness.

The British were introduced to vindaloo in 1797 when they invaded Goa and this chilli-based 'hot' curry appealed to their taste. They even made their own version of PICKLED vindaloo, similar to the original Portuguese dish, in jars to be taken back to Britain. Vindaloo recipes in the early British India cookbooks remained fairly close to the Goan original but when it became a popular dish in the curry houses of England it unfortunately lost much of its tangy taste and the subtlety of spices was overpowered by the searingly hot chillies.

Helen Saberi

- Burnett, David and Helen Saberi. *The Road to Vindaloo: Curry Cooks & Curry Books*. Totnes, Devon: Prospect Books, 2008.
- Chapman, Pat. *The New Curry Bible*. London: Metro Publishing, 2004.
- Collingham, Lizzie. *Curry: A Biography*. London: Chatto and Windus, 2005.

WEST BENGAL

West Bengal is India's fourth largest state by population and the fourteenth largest by area. It borders Bangladesh, Nepal and Bhutan, and the states of Odisha, Jharkhand, Bihar, Sikkim and Assam. West Bengal is 75 per cent Hindu and 23 per cent Muslim, with minorities of Christians and adherents of tribal religions. Only a very small proportion of Hindu Bengalis are strict vegetarians, with fish being an important part of peoples' diet.

Bengalis take food seriously and are said to spend a larger portion of their disposable income on food than people elsewhere in India.

The state carries within itself the multiple legacies of the indigenous tribes; the extended Bengali identity that once encompassed the now sovereign nation of Bangladesh and the state of West Bengal; the settlers, the traders and the invaders; and the colonial Bengal Presidency which at its peak included Myanmar, Penang, Singapore and Malacca alongside the influences of globalization. In fact, the land has absorbed and adopted so much that defining the perimeters of its food is a challenging task. The food of West Bengal is neither homogenous nor monolithic. Even if we consider the food of the largest linguistic community in the state – the Bengalis – it still remains fragmented and multi-hued.

What gives West Bengal and its food this unique, plural identity is its geographical position within the fertile Gangetic-Brahmaputra River system and vis-à-vis the Bay of Bengal, thus connecting it to two of the world's biggest movers of goods and people – the ancient Silk Road and the colonial spice trade. The state is in the proximity of two biodiversity hotspots of the world, the Eastern Himalayan hotspot (a region with rich levels of biodiversity that is threatened by human habitation) and the Indo-Burma hotspot. It is also connected to three of India's agro-biodiversity hotspots – the Eastern Himalayan, the lower Gangetic plains and the Gangetic delta. This geographic position shaped the local, indigenous food habits while exposing it to global influences.

The most iconic saying about Bengali food habit is '*machhe bhaate Bangali*', fish and rice makes a Bengali. There is no specific reference to when the people of Bengal started eating RICE and FISH but given its riverine topography, both were probably part of the diet from the start. Domestication of rice started in the Bengal region around four thousand years ago and around 15,000 varieties of rice were grown in West Bengal until the 1940s. In the *Charyapada*, a collection of mythical poems (eighth to twelfth century CE) said to be the oldest collection of verses written in Abahatta, the linguistic ancestor of Bengali, rice is the only grain mentioned. Tarak Chandra Das (Das 1931, 1932) was convinced that fish eating in Bengal pre-dates the Vedic Aryans. It was only around the tenth and eleventh centuries that scriptural scholars started advocating the benefits of fish eating. A terracotta plaque dating back to the Sunga dynasty (second to first century BCE) found near KOLKATA depicts a mermaid and three men standing on the shore with what appears to be a big fishing net hanging over their shoulders. This establishes that fishing was one of the occupations prevalent in the region. There are also terracotta plaques of fish taken to markets in wicker baskets and being cut for cooking.

Today freshwater fish from rivers, wetlands and ponds are considered better than sea fish, except for *bhetki*, the Asian seabass. One reason is that some deepwater fish have an unpleasant taste and can cause illness unless eaten extremely fresh. A favourite frying medium is MUSTARD oil, since its pungency is believed to bring out the flavour of the fish. The iconic Bengali dish is *maacher jhol* – a fish stew made by cutting fish (often carp) into large pieces, bones and all, sautéing with spices in mustard oil, and simmering the fish in water with vegetables. Fish head, considered a delicacy, is prepared with dal, POTATOES, rice and mixed vegetable peelings. The most coveted Bengali fish is the *hilsa*, a shad-like sea fish, which is coated with TURMERIC, CHILLI powder and SALT and fried. Careful attention must be paid to removing the myriad tiny bones (see FISH).

While the upper castes ate limited varieties of meat, mainly goat, deer, turtle and lamb, the lower strata consumed a much wider variety of animal protein. Sri Harsha paints a picture of a Bengali festive meal in *Nishadhacharita* (Canto XVI), the last of five Sanskrit epic poems written in the late twelfth century CE. He describes the wedding feast of Raja Nala and Princess Damayanti consisting of vegetables, various fish, venison, goat meat, sweetmeats (*pithe*) and betel leaf and betel nut (see PAAN). Bengali lexicographer Vandyaghatiya Sarvananda mentions the use of pepper (see PEPPER, BLACK), long pepper (see PEPPER, LONG), CUMIN, CLOVES, CARDAMOM, nutmeg (see NUTMEG AND MACE), SAFFRON, ASAFOETIDA, CAMPHOR and GINGER in his *Tikasarvasva* (1159 CE). *Prakrit Paingal*, a manual on the Prakit and Apabhramsa languages written by an anonymous poet around the thirteenth century, mentions that lucky is a man whose wife serves him 'freshly cooked rice, ghee made from cow's milk, leafy greens and a curry of *mola carplets* on a banana leaf'. The *Mangalkavya*, a group of religious texts written between the thirteenth and seventeenth centuries, mentions dishes like *chorchori* (a dry dish of mixed vegetables), *ghanto* (a mixed vegetable curry), *pithe*, *shukto* (a bitter vegetable dish that begins a Bengali meal), *shaak* (leafy green vegetables), *bori* (dried lentil dumplings) and *kasundi* (a pungent mustard paste) besides vegetables, fish and meat dishes. This culinary repertoire has remained untouched by the vagaries of time over centuries in an average Bengali household, while soaking in various influences.

The other defining characteristic that has remained unchanged since the thirteenth century is the strict order of courses that Bengalis follow while eating. A meal should begin with plain rice with ghee, followed by vegetables and ended with SWEETS. This is a complete 180-degree departure from the order prescribed by texts written in the north of the subcontinent.

Bengal came under Muslim rule from the beginning of the thirteenth century and remained so for more than five hundred years. The first Muslim ruler of Bengal was Bakhtiar Khilji, a Turk. Along with him came not just Turks but considerable number of Afghans, Arabs, Uzbeks and people from Iran. Driven by the raids of Genghis Khan and other invaders, Bengal became a destination for people fleeing from the north and from East Africa. Thus the Islamic rulers of Bengal did not just bring a religion to the land but influences from different parts of the world. Ghulam Murshid, however, proposes that it was not until the two hundred and fifty years rule of the independent sultans of Bengal that the cultural links between the local population and imported influences were truly consolidated. With the weakening of the political ties with northern India, it was, not surprisingly, easy now for Bengal to develop a unique cultural identity. It appears that there was no marked difference between the culinary habits of the Hindus and the Muslims, besides religious and caste diktats around meat eating.

In 1575, Bengal was brought under the Mughal Empire. The MUGHAL nobles never took to the land and found the taste of the locals inferior. Historian Ghulam Hossein Selim noted in *Riyaz-us-Salatin* (1786) how the high and low of the land eat fish, rice, mustard oil, curds, fruits, sweets and lots of red chilli peppers and salt, and did not eat WHEAT and rotis. Goat meat and poultry cooked in ghee did not agree with them at all. It is not until the nineteenth century that one finds mention of Muslim dishes like rice pulao and *qaliya* (an aromatic mutton curry) in the Bengali cuisine through works of poets like Ishwar Gupta.

The Mughals considerably improved the infrastructure and communication of the land, making it better connected to the rest of the subcontinent and to the trade routes of Bay of Bengal. Around the same time, the vegetarian Vaishnava Bhakti movement of Bengal was established by Shri Chaitanya Mahaprabhu in the sixteenth century, slowly establishing strong links with Vrindavan (Uttar Pradesh). It was also with the Mughals that Marwari traders from Rajasthan came to establish businesses and work as money lenders. This introduced to the Bengali palate many wheat and dal dishes, sweets and savoury snacks. Vaishnav literature from Bengal mentions wheat *LADDUS* made in ghee, SESAME-based sweets, dal and other dishes. *Chandimangal*, written around the sixteenth century, mentions different kinds of dal which till now could not find a place in the diet due to the prevalence of fish. Chitrita Banerji (2005) writes that the advent of Vaishnavism in Bengal necessitated an alternate plant-based protein in the diet, introducing Bengalis to dal. Seventeenth-century French traveller François Bernier wrote that the Portuguese were buying wheat-based ship's biscuits from Bengal.

This improvement in infrastructure and trade also paved the way for European traders. The first to arrive were the Portuguese in 1518 who came in quest of SUGAR, indigo, saltpetre and cotton. They established trading posts in Chittagong, Saptagram and Hoogly. Although the Portuguese hold over Bengal lasted only till the eighteenth century, they left the largest and the most sustained imprint on food. They brought in a number of new vegetables, fruits and other items. The most noted amongst them being the chilli and potatoes, besides cabbages, cauliflower, TURNIPS, sweet potato, OKRA and fruits like PINEAPPLE, PAPAYA, custard apple, GUAVA, peanuts and cashews. It was with the Portuguese that the leavened loaf – *pauruti* – and biscuits came into the Bengali vocabulary and palate. M.X. d'Gama in 1868 opened *Maxo*, a confectionary, in Kolkata and established the sale of cakes, chocolates and plum puddings in Bengal. Arguably one of the most significant contributions of the Portuguese to Bengal's food was the introduction of CHEESE making in Bandel in Hoogly. For many believe that this curdling of milk into soft fresh cheese led to the birth of Bengal's hallmark sweet confectionery – the *rosogolla* (see RASGULLA).

Throughout the Indian subcontinent, Bengalis are famous for their love of *mishti*, or sweets. Most are made from two basic ingredients: milk products and sugar, sometimes flavoured with spices, fruit, NUTS and other ingredients. This association of Bengal with sweets is historical. In fourth century BCE, Panini wrote, '*gurasha auang desho goura*', which means 'Gour is the place of *gur*', recording the practise of sugar making in Bengal. In 1778, the first Chinese settler in Bengal, a man who the British called Tong Atchew, set up the first sugar mill in India in Achipur. Today Bengali sweets are considered the apogee of the sweetmaker's art and non-Bengali establishments call themselves 'Bengali Sweet Shops' or take the name of well-known Calcutta establishments.

In the 1700s, the British East India Company established their base in Calcutta (later renamed Kolkata) and by 1793 had complete control of the region. The two hundred years of British rule considerably changed the food of Bengal, especially aiding the city to emerge as a centre of cosmopolitan food influences. The long interaction between the local population and the British gave rise to a unique ANGLO-INDIAN culinary culture that recreated European dishes by infusing them with local spices and produce and reimagined local dishes to suit the much milder European palate. While the British introduced dishes like the roasts, stews, cutlet, patties and chops, they also naturalized and popularized many of the Portuguese imports. Relations with all the regions under the Bengal Presidency brought in Burmese and Southeast Asian influences on Bengali food, such as milder COCONUT milk-based sauces.

In the second half of the nineteenth century, Bengal was introduced to its longest-standing addiction – TEA. By mid-twentieth century, tea became the beverage of choice amongst the urban educated youth, slowly extending its reach to every section of the society. COFFEE was introduced in Bengal much earlier than tea but it never gained popularity.

The biggest contribution of the British colonization of Bengal on its food is not so much in the ingredients and dishes that they brought with them as in the role they inadvertently had in liberalizing food habits, especially among urban, upper-class Bengalis. This happened because of the introduction of Bengali youth, including women, to Western, liberal education that broke down many religious and institutionalized taboos. Consumption of many of these 'foreign' food items became a symbol of breaking caste and religious barriers. For example, by the mid-nineteenth century, eating pork or beef became a way of breaking age-old food taboos amongst the educated, urban youth in Kolkata.

This was also the time when commercial eating places and restaurants slowly started coming up. While this made European food accessible to the Bengali gentry, this period also popularized Muslim-influenced food. This happened mostly because of the Muslim *bawarchis* (cooks) who found employment in these commercial kitchens. Thus Bengalis society in the nineteenth century started becoming familiar with KEBABS, kormas, PULAOS, BIRYANIS and other kinds of Muslim food (Murshid 2018).

Bengal's culinary map has also been influenced in degrees by the Armenians, Jews, PARSIS, the French and the Chinese. Although Bengal had trade and diplomatic relations with China since ancient times, the first diaspora was established in 1781 in Calcutta. The Chinese contribution is key to the use of white refined sugar which changed the nature of Bengali desserts and to Bengal's sweet making industry. In 1788, the first sugar mill was established in Achipur by the British with indentured labourers from China.

Increased education and the Bengal Renaissance (a cultural, social, intellectual, and artistic movement in Bengal from the late eighteenth century to the early twentieth century) also had its impact on food and food writing in Bengal. The period saw the first printed documentation of Bengali cookbooks, many written by women (see DEVI, PRAGYASUNDARI AND MUKHOPADHYAY, BIPRADAS). As the authors mostly hailed from the urban, educated, upper-caste sections of Bengali society, this established the food eaten by this particular segment as the benchmark for Bengali food in the universal imagination. The Bengal famine in 1943 and the Bengal Partition in 1947 became the next milestones in reshaping the food of West Bengal. The food scarcity and horrors of the two events made the Bengali palate cling to frugality and maximizing products. The Bengali kitchen became known for its use of peels, field weeds, tubers and much more. The Partition also made the spicier, bolder palate of the Hindu migrants from East Bengal (now Bangladesh) mingle with that of the people from West Bengal, popularly called Bangals and Ghotis respectively.

Modern Bengali food further changed with influences of a globalized hyperconnected world in the twentieth and twenty-first centuries. Although the food of Bengal is continuously evolving and has absorbed various influences, it has managed to maintain a distinct identity. That identity comes from the produce, the water and the ethos that shape the cooking and eating. The average modern Bengali still eats what her ancestors were eating in the medieval period, albeit with some changes. At the same time, Bengal has nurtured within herself pockets of original forms of the influences that have shaped her food.

Tanushree Bhowmik

- Banerji, Chitrita. *Life and Food in Bengal*. Revised edition. New Delhi: Penguin, 2005.
- Boileau, Janet P. 'A Culinary History of the Portuguese Eurasians: Origin of Luso Asian Cuisine in Sixteenth and Seventeenth Centuries'. PhD thesis, School of History and Politics, University of Adelaide, Adelaide, 2010.

- Das, Tarak Chandra. 'Cultural Significance of Fish in Bengal'. *Man in India* 11 (1931): 275–303, and 12 (1932): 96–115.
- Murshid, Ghulam. *Bengali Culture Over a Thousand Years*, translated by Sarbari Sinha. New Delhi: Niyogi Books, 2018.
- Salim, Ghulam Husain. *A History of Bengal*. Translated from the Persian original by Maulavi Abdul Salam. Calcutta: Asiatic Society of Bengal, 1890.

WHEAT

The domestication of wheat (*Triticum*, Hindi *gahen*) began in the Near East around 8500 BCE, about the same time as BARLEY. Two varieties, einkorn and emmer, were carried east to the Indus Valley. They were both gradually replaced by other kinds of wheat starting in the Bronze Age, notably *T. durum* which has a large hard, low gluten grain and *T. aestivum* which has a high gluten content and thus is used for making bread. Today most wheat grown in India is *T. aestivum*. Some durum is grown, mainly in Madhya Pradesh. Wheat is an adaptable crop and can grow in many climates and soil, although it grows best in cool moist weather for most of the growing period followed by dry warm weather, such as the Pakistan-North India-Afghanistan region.

The so-called Green Revolution, which started in 1965, increased productivity of wheat and RICE by expanding irrigation and other sources of water supply, such as tube wells; increasing use of fertilization and pesticides; and the introduction of new varieties, including high-yielding dwarf varieties of Mexican wheat. The greatest effect was seen in Punjab, Haryana and western Uttar Pradesh where farms were larger and there were assured sources of water. The average yield of wheat production nearly doubled from 1969–70 to 1988–9. Large farmers (with twenty acres or more) were the first to adopt the new varieties. Today India is not only self-sufficient in wheat but exports it.

Although it was grown and used in the Harappan Civilization to make BREAD, the Rigveda makes no mention of wheat. The main grain and staple of the Indo-Aryans was barley. However, wheat is mentioned in other early Vedic texts. Archaeological evidence indicates that wheat was the staple food in Sind (2500–1700 BCE), Punjab (2500–1700 BCE) (1500–100 BCE), Uttar Pradesh (1700–600 BCE) and Maharashtra (1370–1000 BCE). A popular way of preparing both wheat and barley was as *yavaga* – a porridge made by pounding the grain with a mortar and pestle to remove the chaff and then boiling it in water or milk. In the Sutra period (800–500 BCE), the literature mentions *samyava*, a wheat flour fried in GHEE, mixed with milk and jaggery (see SUGAR) and sometimes flavoured with spices, and *abhyusa*, parched grains beaten with a pestle and also mixed with jaggery.

By the Middle Ages, wheat had begun to replace barley, especially in southern and western India. The twelfth-century *MANASOLLASA* describes many wheat-based dishes, many of them sweet. Disks of white flour were sautéed to make a bread called *mandakas*, similar to modern parathas, and *polikas*, a sweet paratha stuffed with lentils and sugar. *Phenaka*, modern *pheni*, was thin strands of dough made from durum wheat and used in sweet dishes.

Wheat dishes played an important role in the cuisine of the rulers of the Delhi Sultanate, who controlled much of northern India from 1125 to 1526. They included parathas, *naan-i-tandoori* (bread stuffed with dried fruits and baked in a tandoor), SAMOSAS, and

HALEEM. This tradition was continued under the MUGHAL dynasty. Besides many breads, they enjoyed *thuli*, cracked wheat porridge; *chikkhi*, a dish made from washed wheat flour (gluten); and *haleem*. Today bread made from wheat is the main staple of North India and Pakistan, where '*roti khaye?*' – have you eaten bread? – means 'have you eaten today?' Wheat is also prepared in other forms: cracked to make dishes such as *haleem* or cooked in ghee and mixed with sugar to make HALWA and other desserts.

Colleen Taylor Sen

WOODAPPLE

Woodapple, the fruit of a small tree *Feronia limonia* (Hindi *kaith*), is indigenous to South India and is found in most parts of the Indian subcontinent. In Ayurveda it is known as *kapipriya* and *kapittha*. The seventh-century Chinese Buddhist monk Xuan Zang mentions the *kapittha* as a fruit of India. In English, it is also called the elephant apple, and formerly had the botanical name *F. elephantum*, because elephants like to eat it and swallow it whole. It seems that monkeys like it too – the Sanskrit name *kapipriya* means 'dear to monkeys'.

The spherical apple-sized fruit has a whitish colour. It has a hard woody shell which contains a brown acidic, aromatic pulp full of tiny hard seeds. The pulp is eaten raw with SUGAR or SALT, pepper (see PEPPER, BLACK) and oil. The pulp is also used to make jellies, CHUTNEYS and SHERBET. The fruit is renowned for its many medicinal properties and is used in Unani and Ayurvedic medicine (see FOOD AND MEDICINE).

The name woodapple is also sometimes confusingly used for the *BAEL*, although the two fruits are different.

Helen Saberi

- Anupama. 'Kaith Medicinal Uses in Ayurveda'. *Bimbima*, 14 February 2016. Available online: https://www.bimbima.com/ayurveda/kaith-medicinal-uses-in-ayurveda/126/ (accessed 2 May 2022).
- Davidson, Alan. *The Oxford Companion to Food*. 2nd edition. ed. Tom Jaine. Oxford: OUP, 2006.

WYVERN

Colonel Arthur Robert Kenney-Herbert(1840–1916), widely known by his pen-name 'Wyvern', was a British Indian Army officer who served with the Madras Cavalry, but became more famous as the cookery writer with a witty conversational style for *Madras Athaeneum* and *The Daily News*, and author of *Culinary Jottings: A Treatise in Thirty Chapters on Reformed Cookery for Anglo-Indian Exiles*. It went through seven editions after it was first published by Higginbotham & Co. in Madras in 1878.

Educated at Rugby School, Kenney-Herbert came to India in 1859 at age nineteen as a cornet (the lowest-ranking commissioned officer in a cavalry) and retired in 1892 with the rank of colonel. These were the years of the high noon of the Raj. As a result, Kenney-Herbert had a career undisturbed by any military action of note. He rose to become the deputy assistant quartermaster general and military secretary to the Governor of Madras, but none of his professional achievements matched those of his career as a culinary commentator at a time when, to quote his own words, 'quantity' had 'superseded quality' on the British Indian table, and 'the molten curries and florid oriental compositions of the olden time – so fearfully and wonderfully made – have been gradually banished from our dinner tables'.

Elizabeth David, one of Wyvern's ardent followers, said of him: 'I should recommend anyone with a taste for Victorian gastronomic literature to snap him up ... His recipes are so meticulous and clear, that the absolute beginner could follow them, yet at the same time he has much to teach the experienced cook.' Kenney-Herbert stands out for his meticulous instructions (from boiling vegetables to making an omelette), his efforts to demystify the principles of French gastronomy, and his emphasis on incorporating locally grown vegetables (from snake GOURD to AUBERGINE) in European cookery.

What stands out also is Kenney-Herbert's paternalistic – some would call it racist – attitude towards Indian domestics, whom he refers to as 'Ramasamy', who possess 'admirable materials out of which to form a good cook', but must be prevented from clinging 'affectionately' to the 'ancient barbarisms of his forefathers'. What is missing is a section on desserts, which Kenney-Herbert makes up for in his later book *Sweet Dishes: A Little Treatise on Confectionery and Entremets Sucre* (1884).

After hanging up his military beret, Kenney-Herbert retired to London where he started a cookery school – Common-sense Cookery Association – on Sloane Street in 1894. He wrote another book *Vegetarian & Simple Diet* in 1894, which was laudably reviewed by the medical journal *Lancet*, followed by *Common-sense Cookery for English Households* (1905).

Sourish Bhattacharyya

- Doctor, Vikram. 'The Return of Culinary Jottings for Madras'. *ET Panache*, 3 May 2008. Available online: https://economictimes.indiatimes.com/the-leisure-lounge/the-return-of-culinary-jottings-for-madras/articleshow/3006067.cms (accessed 4 May 2022).
- Kenney-Herbert, A.R. *Culinary Jottings: A Treatise in Thirty Chapters on Reformed Cookery for Anglo-Indian Exiles*. 1885. Facsimile reprint. Totnes, Devon: Prospect Books, 1994.

YAM

Yam is the name for the edible tuber of plants belonging to the genus *Dioscorea;* however, the English word 'yam' (which comes from a West African word *niam*) is often used for other root crops, such as the TARO and sweet potato. In Hindi, yams are called *alu*, a generic name for underground tubers. The plants are vines that grow in temperate and tropical regions. The plants are very ancient, perhaps 26 million years old, and were domesticated independently in Africa, the Americas and Asia. While yams have a great diversity of colours, shapes and sizes, many are oblong with a brown bark-like or hairy skin. They need to be cooked to destroy a bitter toxic substance that can cause an itchy throat and other problems. Still, yams have many medicinal uses in Ayurveda, Unani and other traditional medical systems, including for skin and digestive diseases, and are being studied by modern researchers (see FOOD AND MEDICINE).

D. Esculenta, also called lesser yam (Hindi *kam aloo*), is grown in Kerala, Goa and parts of Maharashtra. It has a slightly sweet taste and is boiled and prepared like POTATOES or taro. *Diasocorea alata* (Hindi *ratalu*), also called water or purple yam, grows wild in forests and can be white, red or purple. It has a slightly sweet taste and can be used in sweet or savoury dishes. In Gujarat it is an ingredient in the mixed vegetable dish *undhiyu* and is fried in a batter as a snack. *Amorphophallus paeoniifolius*, or elephant foot yam (Hindi *suran, jimikhand*), is grown throughout India and belongs to the Arum family. It got its name because the plant is very big and resembles the foot of an elephant. Its beige coloured flesh has a texture like that of a sweet potato and has an earthy flavour. It is both wild and cultivated across India as a cash crop and in the past has served as a famine food because of its high carbohydrate content. In South India it is mainly steamed and served with CHUTNEY or first boiled and then sautéed with spices. In East India it is mashed and mixed with CHILLIES and ONIONS to make *bharta*, cooked as a CURRY or fried to make chips. Sometimes the green leaves and stems are used as vegetables.

Colleen Sen

- Timesofindia.com. 'Suran or Jimikand: Secret Benefits of This Vegetable and Tips to Cook It'. 17 June 2020. Available online: https://timesofindia.indiatimes.com/life-style/food-news/suran-or-jimikand-secret-benefits-of-this-vegetable-and-tips-to-cook-it/articleshow/76245383.cms (accessed 3 May 2022).

BIOGRAPHIES

Ummi Abdullah, called the 'Matriarch of Malabar Muslim Food', is the author of seven books in Malayalam and English on Mappila cuisine, including *Malabar Muslim Cookery*, *Cooking in My Dreams* and *A Kitchen Full of Recipes*. Her legacy is being continued by her granddaughter **Nazaneen Jalaludheen**.

Chitradeepa Anantharam is a journalist with twenty-three years of experience and has been working for the English-language national newspaper *The Hindu*. Her areas of interest are textiles, art, local history, regional cuisine and street food. She is the translator of *Suryavamsam*, the biography of the Tamil writer Sivasankar.

Tanushree Bhowmik is a Delhi-based development professional, food historian and food researcher. Her interests include ancient, medieval and colonial Indian food, and food for healing. Her articles have appeared in *The Hindu*, *The Scroll*, *Live Mint* and elsewhere. She and her husband co-manage *ForkTales*, a podcast to document the history of Indian food systems.

Prasun Chatterjee is a historian and independent researcher who has contributed to journals and is the author of the forthcoming book *Travel and Description in Medieval India*. He is also a senior publisher and editor who has been associated with both academic and commercial publishing.

May Abraham Fridel, who grew up in Kerala, is the founder and chief executive officer of Passion for Spices, a cooking school that teaches children and adults how to prepare healthy flavourful menus, and an advocate of a sustainable lifestyle. She is the author of *Indian Cuisine Diabetes Cookbook: Savory Spices and Bold Flavours of South Asia* published by the American Diabetic Association.

Hoihnu Hauzel is a Gurugram-based independent journalist and food writer. She is the founder of northeastodyssey.com and thenestories.com and the author of *The Essential Northeast Cookbook* (Penguin India).

Suresh Hinduja is the founder of the hugely popular social media network on food and drink gourmetindia.com. As consulting chef he has given a futuristic twist to traditional Indian cuisine called Naya Zaika. He is the author of the *Times Food Guide Bangalore* and a judge at many international culinary events.

Mehru Jaffe is a Lucknow-born journalist and author of *A Shadow of the Past: A Short Biography of Lucknow* and several other books.

Maya Kaimal is a cookbook author, the former photo editor of *Saveur* magazine, and founder of Maya Kaimal Foods, a range of Indian retail foods.

Kalyan Karmakar is an award-winning food and travel writer. Since 2007, he has written the blog 'Finely Chopped', is the author of *The Travelling Belly* and the curator of 'Times Kitchen Tales' for *The Times of India*.

Anurag Katriar is the founder of Indigo Hospitality Pvt Ltd, a company that owns and operates some of the most iconic restaurant brands in India. Originally hailing from Jharkhand, Anurag has also served as the president of National Restaurants Association of India (NRAI).

Dr Tarana Husain Khan is a writer and cultural historian who writes about Rampur cuisine, culture and oral history. She is also involved in reviving lost heirloom recipes and rice varieties and is the author of a historical novel, *The Begum and the Dastan*.

Sangeeta Khanna is a microbiologist by education, works in the realm of food and nutrition and focuses on sustainable food systems.

Megha Kohli is currently the corporate chef at Café Mez & The Wine Company in New Delhi and Mademoiselle, a boutique hotel in Goa. She has won many awards, including Times Chef of the Year 2020. Her cooking features fresh local produce and progressive versions of Indian food. Her mantra is that cooking is an emotional process and not a technical one.

Saee Koranne-Khandekar is the author of *Crumbs: Bread Stories and Recipes for the Indian Kitchen* and *Pangal, A Feast: Food and Lore from Marathi Kitchens*. Her work has appeared in several magazines, literary journals and online publications.

Priya Mani is a Copenhagen-based designer and cultural researcher working to create gastronomical experiences. Mani grew up in India and studied at the National Institute of Design. She won the IACP 2022 Award for Best Individual Instagram for *A Visual Encyclopedia of Indian Foods*.

Jyotirmay Nirjhar has a double MA in Sociology and Literary and Cultural Studies. He lives to eat, loves exploring and aims to be a student for life.

Sandip Nowlakha is the owner of the Garden Cafe, Fillers and Corner Cafe, a global consultant in the vegetarian food service sector, and a founding member and vice president of the Murshidabad Heritage Development Society.

Kamal Kant Pant is the Principal and Member Secretary of IHM, Pusa-New Delhi, and has a long career as a hotel manager and heading educational institutions in tourism and hospitality management. He has been working to research and document the traditional cuisines of Madhya Pradesh and the Himalayan states of India.

Kaveri Ponnapa is the author of *The Vanishing Kodavas*, an extensive cultural study of the Kodava people and a well-known food writer. She writes at her blog 'The Coorg Table' and her articles on food appear in leading Indian publications.

Ruth Dsouza Prabhu is an independent journalist based in Bangalore, India. Her work has been published in the *New York Times, The National, Fodor's Travel* and *Whetstone* among others. She is currently documenting the food of Mangalurean Christians.

Marryam H Reshii has been writing about food and lifestyle for the last thirty years. She is the food critic for *The Times of India*, an independent writer on cuisine and matters gastronomic, and the author of *The Flavour of Spice*.

Puneetinder Kaur Sidhu, author, travel writer, food critic and columnist, is an irrepressible itinerant, an adventurous foodie, and writes on a wide variety of subjects.

Swati Sucharita, a print media journalist, has worked at *The Times of India* across Delhi, Bengaluru, Ahmedabad and Hyderabad, where she is currently honing her skills as a content consultant. She blogs on her food experiences at eatopianchronicles.com.

Surya Vir Vaidhyanathan is an seventeen-year-old alumnus of Vasant Valley School, New Delhi. He is passionate about political science and the culinary arts and is currently a student at Georgetown University, Washington, DC, where he hopes to obtain a Bachelor of Arts in Government.

Nikhita Venugopal is a food and culture journalist based in Bengaluru, India. Her work has appeared in *The Washington Post*, *The Ringer*, *Whetstone, Eater* and more.

THE EDITORS

Born in Toronto, **Colleen Taylor Sen** is an author and culinary historian who writes about the food of the Indian Subcontinent and other subjects. Her books include *Food Culture in India*; *Curry: A Global History*; *Turmeric: The Wonder Spice*; and *A Guide to Indian Restaurant Menus* and *Feasts and Fasts: A History of Food in India*. She is coeditor of *Street Food around the World: An Encyclopedia of Food and Culture* and *The Chicago Food Encyclopedia*. Her books have been translated into Arabic, Chinese, Japanese and Korean. Her most recent work is *Ashoka and the Mauryas: The Rise and Legacy of Ancient India's Greatest Dynasty*.

Sourish Bhattacharya is a Delhi-based food writer/blogger. He is Managing Editor of the Indo-Asian News Service, and has held senior editorial positions in the popular culture and lifestyle space at *Mail Today*, *Hindustan Times* and *The Indian Express*. He has also contributed to *BBC Good Food*, *Time Out*, *India Today Spice*, *Sommelier India*, *Mumbai Mirror*, *India Today Travel Plus* and other publications. A promoter of food events, he has served as curator of conferences and awards at the India International Hospitality Expo; co-founded the global advocacy forum, Tasting India Symposium; and briefly presided over the Delhi Gourmet Club.

Helen Saberi is the author of a number of books including *Noshe Djan: Afghan Food and Cookery*, *Trifle* (co-authored with Alan Davidson), *The Road to Vindaloo*: *Curry Cooks and Curry Books* (co-authored with David Burnett), *Tea: A Global History* and *Teatimes: A World Tour*. She worked as Alan Davidson's principal assistant on *The Oxford Companion to Food* and was also a major contributor. She has written papers on the foodways of Afghanistan for the Oxford Symposium on Food and Cookery and other essays on Afghan food and culture for publications, including a chapter for the book *Afghanistan Revealed.* She lives in London, UK.

INDEX

Note: For most transliterations, a/aa, u/oo and i/ee are interchangeable spellings.

D

X

Y